Family, dependence, and the origins of the welfare state

The development of the European welfare state in the first half of this century has often been seen as a response to the rise of class politics, its institutions as a means of alleviating the insecurities and inequalities of the labor market. Yet as this study demonstrates, the social reformers and activists who shaped early welfare policies in Britain and France were often quite as concerned with gender relations and family maintenance as they were with social class. Feminists hoping to win a measure of independence for wives, doctors and social workers concerned with children's health, industrialists combating demands that all workers be paid a "family wage," and pronatalists worried about the capacity of the population to meet the demographic challenges of mass wars all sought to redistribute income and resources not simply across class lines but toward families with dependent children and the mothers occupied in caring for them. Very different distributive policies emerged from their campaigns, with important consequences for the wage system, the well-being of children, and the citizenship status of men and women.

FAMILY, DEPENDENCE, AND THE ORIGINS OF THE WELFARE STATE

BRITAIN AND FRANCE, 1914–1945

Susan Pedersen

CAMBRIDGE
UNIVERSITY PRESS

Published by the Press Syndicate of the University of Cambridge
The Pitt Building, Trumpington Street, Cambridge CB2 1RP
40 West 20th Street, New York, NY 10011-4211, USA
10 Stamford Road, Oakleigh, Melbourne 3166, Australia

First published 1993

Printed in the United States of America

Library of Congress Cataloging-in-Publication Data
Pedersen, Susan, 1959–
Family, dependence, and the origins of the welfare state : Britain
and France, 1914–1945 / Susan Pedersen.
p.   cm.
Includes bibliographical references and index.
ISBN 0-521-41989-1
1. Family services – Great Britain – History – 20th century.
2. Family services – France – History – 20th century.   3. Family
policy – Great Britain – History – 20th century.   4. Family policy –
France – History – 20th century.   5. Welfare state.   I. Title.
HV700.G7P43   1993
362.82′8′094109041 – dc20   92-47002
                                                                          CIP

A catalog record for this book is available from the British Library.

ISBN 0-521-41989-1 hardback

For Tom

CONTENTS

List of tables and figure   *page* xi

Acknowledgments   xiii

Abbreviations   xv

Introduction: On dependence and distribution   1

Part I: Programs and precedents   23

1 The family in question: State and family in prewar thought and politics   25

    Emile Zola, H. G. Wells, and the crisis of the family   26

    Dependence and the state in Britain   32

    Dénatalité and the state in France   59

    Conclusion   77

2 The impact of the Great War   79

    The wartime social contract   81

    Gender, dependence, and the labor market   89

    Gender, dependence, and welfare   107

    Policy legacies and political agendas   120

    Conclusion   130

Part II: Reworking the family wage in the twenties   135

3 Family policy as women's emancipation? The failed campaign for endowment of motherhood in Britain   138

"Separate but equal": The vision of maternalist
    feminism   140
Fantasy as social science: Seebohm Rowntree imagines
    the family   152
Labour women and the "men's movement"   160
Civil servants and the contracting state   169
Conclusion   175

4 Family policy as "socialism in our time"? The
   failed campaign for children's allowances in
   Britain   178
   The Disinherited Family and the organization of the
       Family Endowment Society   179
   Economic arguments for family allowances: Liberal and
       socialist views   185
   From inquiry to stalemate: The Joint Committee on the
       Living Wage   197
   Family policy and the trade unions   208
   Conclusion   219

5 Business strategies and the family: The
   development of family allowances in France,
   1920–1936   224
   Family allowances and ideologies of social renewal   227
   Family allowances as paternalistic control: The
       Consortium Textile de Roubaix-Tourcoing   236
   Family allowances in the service of economic
       reconstruction: The Caisse de Compensation de la
       Région Parisienne   261
   Conclusion   285

Part III: The politics of state intervention in the thirties   289

6 Engendering the British welfare state   292
   Unemployment policies and the enforcement of
       dependence   294
   A new case for children's allowances   316
   The place of family policy in the Beveridgian welfare
       state   336
   Conclusion   354

7 Distributive justice and the family: Toward a
   parental welfare state   357
   "Il faut faire naître": The creation of a pronatalist
       consensus   359

Contents ix

The progress of state intervention   372
What manner of family? Gender and dependence in
    the parental welfare state   392
Conclusion   410

Conclusion   413

Bibliography   427
Index   465

TABLES AND FIGURE

Tables

1.1 Women workers as a percentage of the
"economically active" population, by sector   *page* 37
1.2 Distribution of "economically active" men and
women, Britain   37
1.3 Labor force participation rates by age and sex, 1911   38
1.4 Distribution of "economically active" men and
women, France   71
2.1 Women as a percentage of the total work force,
1914 and 1918   90
2.2 Distribution and density of women workers by
sector, 1921   124
2.3 Labor force participation rates by age and sex,
1921   125
5.1 National growth of the *caisses de compensation*   232
5.2 Growth of the Consortium Textile de Roubaix-
Tourcoing   243
5.3 Monthly rates for Consortium family allowances   244
5.4 Weekly Consortium family allowance for families
meeting all conditions for receipt, 1923 and 1930   245
5.5 Family allowances actually received by Consortium
workers, 1923–38   247
5.6 Consortium wages and cost-of-living indices   260
5.7 Growth of the Caisse de Compensation de la
Région Parisienne   268
5.8 Monthly rates for CCRP family allowances   270
5.9 CCRP family allowances as a percentage of a full-
time monthly wage at the average hourly rate for
Metals Group firms   272

xi

5.10 Index of real wages in Metals Group firms and
      national production indices   284
6.1   Operation of the anomalies regulations, 3 October
      1931 to 29 April 1933   303
6.2   Percentage of insured workers drawing
      unemployment benefit   305
6.3   Normal wages of workers receiving benefits from
      the Unemployment Assistance Board, 1937   315
6.4   Family needs compared with unemployment
      benefits, 1935   324
6.5   Children's allowances in social programs, 1942   328
6.6   Payment of family allowances to the mother:
      public support and opposition by sex and class,
      1943   347
7.1   Expansion of the *caisses*, 1934–9   379
7.2   Family allowances as a percentage of the base
      wage, 1938 and 1939 laws   388
7.3   Family allowances as a percentage of the base
      wage, Vichy laws of 15 February and 29 March
      1941   389
7.4   Development of family allowances, 1938–58   391
7.5   Breakdown of social benefits, 1938–58   392
7.6   Income differentials between unmarried workers
      and workers with families at the base wage level,
      1939 and 1949   392
C.1   Breakdown of social insurance and family
      allowance benefits, 1960–85   414
C.2   Spending on social security schemes as a
      percentage of GDP, selected European countries,
      1960–85   416
C.3   Breakdown of contributions for social insurance
      and family allowances, 1960–85   417

Figure

5.1   Ties between employers' organizations and the
      family allowance funds   266

ACKNOWLEDGMENTS

Academic communities, like welfare states, can be redistributive and solidaristic – as I discovered in writing this book. Two years of research in London and Paris, as well as some periods of relief from teaching, were made possible by a Summer Travel Grant from the Center for European Studies, a Krupp Foundation Fellowship, a Lurcy Foundation Fellowship, a Social Science and Humanities Research Council of Canada Doctoral Fellowship, and grants from the Joint Committee on Western Europe of the American Council of Learned Societies and the Social Science Research Council, in the form of an International Doctoral Research Fellowship and a Susan O'Connor Fellowship of the Tocqueville Program, with funds provided by the French-American Foundation.

Archivists and administrators in Britain and France helped locate documents or made valuable private materials available. I thank especially M. Jean Lygrisse, a former *sous-directeur* at the French Ministry of Labor, who furnished key early documents on family allowances and kindly shared his own work with me. M. Jourdan, Mme Cherubini, and Mlle Laut of the Caisse d'Allocations Familiales de la Région Parisienne made the early records of the *caisse* available. Archivists of the Union Féminine Civique et Sociale, the Union des Industries Métallurgiques et Minières, and the Groupe des Industries Métallurgiques de la Région Parisienne tracked down some of the interwar records of these organizations – in one case to a lunchroom cupboard. The cheerful staff of the Trades Union Congress Filing Department brought me documents and the odd cup of tea during the weeks I spent reconstructing the history of the Joint Committee on the Living Wage. In addition, I, like many researchers, am grateful for the help and good humor of David Doughan of the Fawcett Library.

Many scholars and colleagues have commented on various parts of this book. I wish to express my deep gratitude to the two mentors

xiii

who supervised the dissertation on which it is based. The late Professor John Clive may have insisted that he knew "almost nothing" about the subject; certainly he regretted my decision to abandon Hannah More for Eleanor Rathbone. Nevertheless, if this work is comprehensible to the reader not versed in the intricacies of the welfare state, it is because of his insistence that even the history of social policy could be written, if not always with grace, at least with lucidity. Professor Charles Maier, whose own work has been my model for comparative history, guided this project from its first incarnation in a ten-page undergraduate paper in 1982. From his early encouragement to his final critical reading of the complete draft, he repeatedly forced me to rethink my arguments, to the real improvement of the coherence of this work. Jane Jenson, Peter Hall, John Macnicol, and Robert Moeller valiantly read the entire manuscript and saved me from many mishaps; Gisela Bock, Jane Caplan, Herrick Chapman, Anne Cova, Victoria de Grazia, Sarah Fishman, Laura Frader, Susan Grayzel, Adrian Jones, Seth Koven, Richard Kuisel, Jane Lewis, Karen Offen, Theda Skocpol, Pat Thane, and J. M. Winter also commented helpfully on particular chapters and associated papers. Deborah Cohen and Patricia Lynch, students and friends, helped to prepare the footnotes and bibliography.

Much of this book was written at Harvard's Center for European Studies, whose chairman, Stanley Hoffmann, and director, Guido Goldman, must be thanked for creating and preserving this haven of scholarly exchange and communitarian warmth in an often heartless academic world. My parents have also provided much love and support during the long years of academic apprenticeship. But my greatest debt is to my husband Tom Ertman, who has shared my travails and enthusiasms, great and small, over the years I spent writing this book. Tom read every chapter, most more than once, and all were improved by his discerning criticism. And although he bore the burden of its nurture with exemplary grace, he knew when it was time to make this child leave home. Dedications are inadequate recompense, but this one is heartfelt.

ABBREVIATIONS

AN	Archives Nationales, Paris
ASE	Amalgamated Society of Engineers
BLPES	British Library of Political and Economic Science, London
CCAF	Comité Central des Allocations Familiales
CCRP	Caisse de Compensation de la Région Parisienne
CFTC	Confédération Française des Travailleurs Chrétiens
CGT	Confédération Générale du Travail
CGTU	Confédération Générale du Travail Unitaire
CNAF	Congrès National des Allocations Familiales
CSN	Conseil Supérieur de la Natalité
CTRT	Consortium Textile de Roubaix-Tourcoing
FES	Family Endowment Society
GC	General Council of the Trades Union Congress
GIMM	Groupe des Industries Métallurgiques, Mécaniques et Connexes de la Région Parisienne
ILP	Independent Labour Party
IWM	Imperial War Museum, London
JCLW	Trades Union Congress and the Labour Party, Joint Committee on the Living Wage
NCLW	National Conference of Labour Women
NFWW	National Federation of Women Workers
NUSEC	National Union of Societies for Equal Citizenship
PRO	Public Record Office, London
SSFA	Soldiers' and Sailors' Families Association
TUC	Trades Union Congress
UAB	Unemployment Assistance Board
UFCS	Union Féminine Civique et Sociale
UIMM	Union des Industries Métallurgiques et Minières
WCG	Women's Cooperative Guild
WIC	War Cabinet Committee on Women in Industry, 1918–19

INTRODUCTION
On dependence and distribution

The laws and conditions of the production of wealth, partake of the character of physical truths. There is nothing optional, or arbitrary in them. Whatever mankind produces, must be produced in the modes, and under the conditions, imposed by the constitution of external things, and by the inherent properties of their own bodily and mental structure....

It is not so with the Distribution of Wealth. That is a matter of human institution solely. The things once there, mankind, individually or collectively, can do with them as they like.... The distribution of wealth, therefore, depends on the laws and customs of society. The rules by which it is determined, are what the opinions and feelings of the ruling portion of the community make them, and are very different in different ages and countries; and might be still more different, if mankind so chose.

John Stuart Mill, *Principles of Political Economy* (1848)

The first of my books in which her [Harriet Taylor's] share was conspicuous was the "Principles of Political Economy."... The purely scientific part of the Political Economy I did not learn from her; but it was chiefly her influence that gave to the book that general tone by which it is distinguished from all previous expositions of Political Economy that had any pretension to being scientific, and which has made it so useful in conciliating minds which those previous expositions had repelled. This tone consisted chiefly in making the proper distinction between the laws of the Production of Wealth, which are real laws of nature, dependent on the properties of objects, and the modes of its Distribution, which, subject to certain conditions, depend on human will.

John Stuart Mill, *Autobiography* (1873)

Because John Stuart Mill had the amiable habit of attributing all of his best ideas to his wife, posterity has not ceased to argue about when to take her claim to influence seriously. Yet it is significant that Mill specifically recalled Harriet Taylor's part in formulating the argument

1

– hammered home insistently in the section entitled "On Distribution" in the *Principles of Political Economy* – that while the production process was indeed ruled by immutable economic laws, the system of distribution was "a matter of human institution solely." Few today might share Mill and Taylor's optimistic belief in the utter malleability of relations of distribution, but their claim that these need not be left to the vagaries of the market became the fundamental premise of welfare liberalism. And to no group did this insight offer more than to women. If in industrial societies productive work – or, more precisely, *remunerated* work – had been disproportionately in male hands, then the contention that the distributive system need not reflect such patterns held great promise for feminists. Small wonder that Harriet Taylor found the laws of production arid compared with the charms and promises of distributive economics.

When British feminists after the First World War began to campaign for the state "endowment" of mothers and children, they took Mill and Taylor's distinction as their point of departure.[1] But it was Eleanor Rathbone, the most prominent feminist of that era, who, in her 1924 classic, *The Disinherited Family*, elaborated the real costs of the practice of leaving distribution to negotiations at the point of production, or, in other words, to the wage. Wages, she noted, took no account of varying family needs. Income was distributed to workers, and disproportionately to adult men, without reference to the number of children dependent on them or to the needs of unwaged women occupied in caring for them. The resulting poverty of families with young children as compared with childless workers could not be erased by raising wages or by any vertical redistribution. *Whatever* the wage system, *whatever* the distribution of wealth, variations in family size and structure would mean vastly different living standards for persons within the same social class.[2]

There was, Rathbone thought, a ready solution to this problem. If British policymakers would only cast their eyes toward the Continent, they would discover in the French and Belgian systems of family allowances a means of equalizing the cost of reproduction across either particular industries or society as a whole; by paying such benefits to mothers, policymakers could also begin to recognize the social value of unremunerated domestic work. Yet Rathbone's proposal that chil-

---

[1] Mary Stocks, the Oxford-educated economist, symbolically placed Mill's passage on the malleability of the distributive system at the head of her pamphlet *The Case for Family Endowment* (London: Labour Publishing Co., 1927).

[2] Eleanor Rathbone, *The Disinherited Family* (London: Edward Arnold, 1924).

dren be treated essentially as a collective charge met with a good deal of opposition in the Britain of the 1920s. Children do not arrive by accident or in response to ministerial orders, the economist Alexander Gray protested in a rebuttal published in 1927; why, then, should "the State" or "society" – words that "merely mean other people" – have to support them? Since each child "owes its existence to the action of two individuals," he pointed out, "whether or not the child is born with rights against the totality of all other fathers and mothers, it is surely true that in any ordered community a special duty rests on its own parents."[3] Children were neither an insurable risk nor a collective good: thus, their upkeep could quite properly be left to their parents.

Across the channel, Fernand Boverat – pronatalist, *ancien combattant*, and the most indefatigable of the coterie of social activists who kept the problem of French demographic decline in the public eye during the decades after the First World War – could not have disagreed more. Boverat did not share Rathbone's feminism and was not particularly concerned to give mothers a measure of economic independence, yet he agreed absolutely that the support of children could not be treated simply as a matter for private concern. The children born to any individual couple would, as adults, sustain the economic, military, and demographic strength of France, he argued: as insured workers, they would pay for the nation's ill and old; as soldiers, they would guarantee its safety; as parents, they would ensure its future. But if children were in fact a collective resource on which all members of society depended, then the self-denying citizens who raised those children had a legitimate claim on society's aid. The redistribution of income between the childless and those with children was not merely prudent or humane; it was, Boverat insisted, the most basic requirement of social justice.[4]

The problem of the nature and extent of public responsibility for family maintenance that preoccupied Rathbone, Gray, and Boverat was much debated during the first half of the twentieth century in most industrialized countries. Many of these states had come during the nineteenth century to extend and enforce the dependence of children, establishing universal schooling and prohibiting child labor. Patterns of economic development, demographic changes, and protective legislation made it difficult in some countries for mothers to

---

[3] Alexander Gray, *Family Endowment: A Critical Analysis* (London: Ernest Benn, 1927), pp. 125, 127.

[4] For a thorough discussion of the social assumptions underlying the writings of Boverat and other pronatalists, see the section entitled "Il faut faire naître" in Chapter 7.

earn as well, creating a familial cycle of poverty in which the period of greatest dependence coincided with the family's smallest capacity for self-support. Only toward the end of the century, however, did politicians and social reformers begin to question the capacity of the wage system ever to meet such needs and the adequacy of social policies premised on the absolute responsibility of parents to maintain. With liberal and market principles everywhere facing collectivist challenges, the proposal to "socialize" some portion of the cost and care of children ceased to appear entirely utopian.

And indeed, in the period between the wars, measures equalizing the burden of family maintenance were established within private industries and through state policies in many European countries. The inflationary pressures and social instability of the First World War had led to the introduction of special bonuses to workers with children and other flexible payment schemes, and many of these programs survived into peacetime; by the time the International Labour Office surveyed the situation in 1923, extensive family allowance schemes had been set up by employers' organizations or administrative fiat in France and Belgium and through collective bargaining agreements in Germany and Austria.[5] Even those countries that avoided such measures and clung to the ideal of the family's responsibility for self-support could not avoid extending state responsibilities for dependents in some areas. The elaboration of unemployment insurance in Britain after 1918, for example, was riddled with controversies over whether the state was required to pay benefits to unemployed workers on an individual or family basis and, once the latter course of action was decided on, over which family members could legitimately be considered "dependent." Whether through widows' pensions providing wives with security against loss of maintenance, children's allowances distributing the burden of reproduction among the population, or dependents' benefits paid to unemployed or incapacitated workers, by the Second World War many states had come to define particular family relations as worthy of support and to build protections for such relations into their welfare policies. The legacies of their choices remain with us today, evident not only in the vastly dissimilar provisions for children throughout the industrialized world,[6] but also in the anomalies and gender biases that riddle many

[5] International Labour Office [ILO], *Family Allowances: The Remuneration of Labour According to Need*, Studies and Reports, Series D (Wages and Hours), no. 13 (Geneva: ILO, 1924).

[6] Comparative studies note that provisions for dependent children tend to be both less

welfare states, the consequence of normative visions of family life that were embedded within them at their making.

Dilemmas about the appropriate treatment of familial dependence dogged interwar policymakers, yet the Anglo-American scholarship on the emergence of the welfare state has paid little attention to this history. Influenced by the social democratic theories of T. H. Marshall in particular, scholars have tended to view the welfare state as the outcome of the effort to "abate" the inequalities of class and to extend the definition of citizenship – in Marshall's words, "a status bestowed on those who are full members of the community"[7] – to encompass social as well as civil and political rights. An economic order founded on competition inevitably generated inequalities and insecurities among the citizenry, Marshall explained in his famous lectures at Cambridge in 1949, and only universal social entitlements could combat these negative effects, extending contact across class lines and minimizing insecurity by equalizing incomes and sharing risks.

Yet however democratic his intent, Marshall's formulation actually narrowed the definitions both of the role of the welfare state and of the nature of the citizen. First, by arguing that the class divisions generated in the labor market were the *only* real source of inequality between citizens, Marshall overlooked the ways in which other social relations – and especially family relations – also produced inequalities and insecurities, as well as the myriad ways in which the institutions of the welfare state either redressed or compounded these problems. Second, while he insisted that social citizenship was open to all, his

adequate and more variable across countries than are provisions for the elderly, since most industrialized countries now presume it unreasonable to expect adult children to maintain their aged parents and find it far easier to force people to distribute the cost of their own old age across their working life than to force them to support other people's children. For such comparisons, see the recent volume of essays on policies toward childhood and old age edited by John L. Palmer, Timothy Smeeding, and Barbara Boyle Torrey, *The Vulnerable* (Washington, D.C.: Urban Institute Press, 1988), and especially the essays by Michael O'Higgins, "The Allocation of Public Resources to Children and the Elderly in OECD Countries," pp. 201–28, and by Timothy Smeeding, Barbara Boyle Torrey, and Martin Rein, "Patterns of Income and Poverty: The Economic Status of Children and the Elderly in Eight Countries," pp. 89–119. Yet as Sheila Kamerman and Alfred J. Kahn argue in their contribution to the same volume, even relatively modest family policies remain very important means of support for families with low incomes or single parents; see Kamerman and Kahn, "Social Policy and Children in the United States and Europe," in ibid., pp. 351–80.
[7] T. H. Marshall, *Class, Citizenship and Social Development: Essays by T. H. Marshall* (Garden City, N.Y.: Doubleday, 1964), p. 84.

further clarification that such rights were compensation for the "universal" obligations of military service and wage earning narrowed this expansive vision substantially;[8] women, who were rarely soldiers and often not wage earners, were by definition placed outside the pale of citizenship. Both arguments helped to shift attention away from the issues of dependence that had been a central concern of interwar policymakers – and indeed of Sir William Beveridge, one of the architects of the social security system that Marshall thought he was describing. As his famous 1942 report shows, Beveridge considered varying family burdens, quite as much as interruptions of wages, to be a primary cause of poverty; like Rathbone, Boverat, and others, he categorized the population as much by sex and marital status as by labor market position and proposed to tie entitlements to such functionally defined social and familial roles. Unlike these theorists of family-based redistribution, however, Beveridge ordered the sexes hierarchically, treating men as representatives of "the family" as a whole and women as autonomous citizens primarily in the absence of men. Yet Beveridge was convinced enough of the desirability of a family form based on male "breadwinning" and female dependence to leave this unequal treatment naked for all to see, covered only with the rhetorical fig leaf of his claim to be treating such couples as a "team."[9] Marshall, by contrast, developed a theory of "social citizenship" that claimed to be universal but was constructed in such a way as to be applicable only to men. Women were not defined by Marshall as "dependent"; they disappeared from the picture entirely – and with their going, the manifold ways in which the welfare state addressed family and dependency relations vanished as well.

Despite these limitations, Marshall's writings formed the basis for the "social interpretation" that dominated scholarship on the welfare state in the sixties and seventies and that deepened the tendency to trace political developments to the bedrock of class. The assumptions that inequality originated in the social relations of production, and that the primary task of the welfare state was thus to provide greater security to workers, were scarcely called into question. Even those policies most transparently aimed at relieving dependence and paid *without* reference to employment status – such as children's allowances

---

[8] Interestingly, Marshall himself recognized that women had been "protected" in the nineteenth century precisely because they were not citizens, but he was unable to see how his own definitions of citizenship and social rights extended that exclusion into the twentieth century; ibid., pp. 81, 117.

[9] *Social Insurance and Allied Services: A Report by Sir William Beveridge*, PP 1942–3, VI, Cmd. 6404.

or widows' pensions – appear in some studies from the seventies as transfer payments providing "income maintenance for typical phases of nonemployment in the life cycle."[10] Although a trenchant critique of the "social interpretation" did develop in the eighties, it focused less on the failure to consider problems of dependence than on the degree to which state actors and state structures, rather than working-class movements, were the principal architects of policy.[11] And if Peter Baldwin has moved the defense of the social interpretation to a higher plane by demonstrating that middle-class groups can also have an "interest" in solidarity and provide a "class base" for its extension, his intervention has, if anything, furthered the tendency to see class as the *only* relevant social division and the only possible basis for a politics of "interest." In an account rendered plausible by a focus on pensions and other policies that do aggregate individuals largely by occupational group and class – to the exclusion of messier unemployment, maternity, and family policies, which constitute groups by sex and family position as well – the welfare state is re-created as transparently "about" class, even if it is now the middle rather than the working class that is seen to have forced its elaboration.[12]

Although partisans of the social interpretation have paid little attention to relations between the state and the family, more interest has been shown in such questions by a group of scholars skeptical of

---

[10] Peter Flora and Arnold J. Heidenheimer, "The Historical Core and Changing Boundaries of the Welfare State," in Flora and Heidenheimer, eds., *The Development of Welfare States in Europe and America* (New Brunswick, N.J.: Transaction Books, 1981), p. 25.

[11] For a review of the "social interpretation," see Michael Shalev, "The Social Democratic Model and Beyond: Two 'Generations' of Comparative Research on the Welfare State," *Comparative Social Research*, 6 (1983). The writings of Theda Skocpol and her collaborators have been especially important in exposing the shortcomings of the "working-class strength" or "logic of industrialism" explanations of the rise of the welfare state and in reviving interest in the ways in which state structures helped determine outcomes. See especially Theda Skocpol's introduction "Bringing the State Back In: Strategies of Analysis in Current Research," in Peter Evans, Dietrich Rueschemeyer, and Theda Skocpol, eds., *Bringing the State Back In* (Cambridge University Press, 1985), pp. 3–37; Ann Shola Orloff and Theda Skocpol, "Why Not Equal Protection? Explaining the Politics of Public Social Spending in Britain, 1900–1911, and the United States, 1880s–1920," *American Sociological Review*, 49: 6 (Dec. 1984), pp. 726–50. Furthermore, while this work did not initially integrate gender into the analysis, Skocpol has more recently begun to explore the political and structural conditions that enabled women to influence social policy formation in the United States; see her study of the development of the U.S. welfare state, *Protecting Soldiers and Mothers: Political Origins of Social Policy in the United States* (Cambridge, Mass.: Harvard University Press, 1992).

[12] Peter Baldwin, *The Politics of Social Solidarity: Class Bases of the European Welfare State, 1875–1975* (Cambridge University Press, 1990).

the wider relevance of the British experience and critical of the analytical distinction, central to Marshall's ideas, between the public and cooperative world of welfare and the private and competitive world of the market. As Gøsta Esping-Andersen, Martin Rein, Lee Rainwater, and others have noted, many institutions of social solidarity developed out of mutualist, corporate, or industrial initiatives, exist at the intersection of labor and social policy, and are difficult to see as either public or private. To capture the ways in which such institutions develop and diverge, they argue, one must examine not "the welfare state" in isolation, but rather the entire universe of distributive mechanisms that provide the framework through which individuals seek economic and social security within any given country.[13] And in focusing on distribution more broadly, these scholars have come, once again, to consider the questions of familial dependence and distribution that absorbed policymakers in the twenties and thirties. Indeed, in *The Three Worlds of Welfare Capitalism*, Esping-Andersen attempts to develop a model for analyzing the emergence and divergence of welfare regimes that considers the family, as well as the labor market and the welfare state, as one of the three central arenas of distribution. Drawing on conceptions and typologies developed by Richard Titmuss some twenty years earlier, Esping-Andersen states that any satisfactory analysis and typology of welfare regimes must take into account relations between all three realms.[14]

Yet Esping-Andersen's own attempt to integrate the family into his analysis remains, at best, halfhearted. Whereas Titmuss insisted that "the risks and situations of dependency" were a central and unavoid-

---

[13] Gøsta Esping-Andersen, "The Comparison of Policy Regimes: An Introduction," esp. pp. 3–12, and Martin Rein and Lee Rainwater, "From Welfare State to Welfare Society," esp. p. 143, both in Martin Rein, Gøsta Esping-Andersen, and Lee Rainwater, eds., *The Rise and Fall of Policy Regimes* (Armonk, N.Y.: Sharpe, 1987).

[14] Titmuss's typology distinguished among "residual" welfare states that intervene only when the market or the family break down, welfare states geared toward industrial achievement in which policies were often linked to economic performance and were not redistributive, and states that provided universal services outside the market. He argued that all three types could be understood only in terms of their relation to the "work ethic" and the family; *Social Policy: An Introduction* (London: Allen & Unwin, 1974), pp. 30–2. Esping-Andersen offers a new elaboration of Titmuss's typology in *The Three Worlds of Welfare Capitalism* (Princeton, N.J.: Princeton University Press, 1990), in which the United States is taken as illustrative of a "residual" welfare regime, Germany of a "corporatist" regime, and Sweden of a social democratic or universalist regime. A similar typology appears in textbook form in Arnold J. Heidenheimer, Hugh Heclo and Carolyn Teich Adams, *Comparative Public Policy: The Politics of Social Choice in America, Europe, and Japan*, 3d ed. (New York: St. Martin's, 1990), pp. 218–66.

able focus of social policy for *all* types of welfare state,[15] Esping-Andersen brings in "the family" only when it is an obvious focus of policy – for example, when discussing states that explicitly delegate functions to the family as a "subsidiary" institution. He continues to characterize welfare regimes primarily according to the relationship between the labor market and welfare institutions and to explore individual rather than familial strategies for achieving security, judging his "welfare regimes" primarily in terms of "the degree of market-independence" they allow to "an *average worker*."[16] This focus not only (once again) excludes women except when present in the labor force – as Mary Langan and Ilona Ostner protest, "Women appear almost by accident and then vanish again"[17] – but also obscures the many ways in which both the wage system and the welfare state link payments and entitlement to gender and presumed family role.

A third school of revisionist scholarship on the welfare state has placed these questions of gender and dependence at the center of its analysis. The feminist scholarship on the welfare state, now in its

---

[15] Titmuss, *Social Policy*, p. 87.

[16] Esping-Andersen, *Three Worlds*, p. 50; my emphasis. This is, of course, Esping-Andersen's definition of "decommodification," the term he uses to compare the degree to which welfare regimes structure their entitlements so as to allow citizens to leave the labor market to pursue other activities necessary to their lives without subjecting them to humiliating conditions or tests; see pp. 21–3, 35–54. Yet the concept of decommodification is problematic, since, as Mary Langan and Ilona Ostner have pointed out, it overlooks the fact that the household is also a sphere of labor, especially for women, and that men's and women's entry into and exit from the labor market cannot be understood except in relation to such labor. Thus, while women's domestic labor may make men's entry possible, their own entry may be dependent on state policies that collectivize some portion of that work. Similarly, states with high indexes for decommodification may provide men with more flexibility and leisure, but women may experience such policies differently since, when decommodified, they often return to another sphere of labor. See Mary Langan and Ilona Ostner, "Gender and Welfare," in Graham Room, ed., *Towards a European Welfare State?* (Bristol: School for Advanced Urban Studies, 1991), pp. 30–1. More problematically, since "decommodification" can be measured only among groups that are already in the labor force (or "commodified"), Esping-Andersen has effectively adopted an analysis that categorizes whole policy regimes according to their policies toward wage earners alone. By doing so, he not only excludes many citizens – and especially many women – from his analysis, he also comes up with conclusions that conceal as much as they reveal. He shows, for example, that the Swedish welfare state offers women workers a greater chance for decommodification than German policies do, but we cannot actually conclude from this that Swedish women are less rigidly tied into the labor market than are German women, since many German women with young children are outside of the labor market (and hence outside of Esping-Andersen's analysis) entirely.

[17] Langan and Ostner, "Gender and Welfare," p. 130.

second decade, has questioned the universalist rhetoric employed both by policymakers and by many scholars, pointing out that ostensibly "universal" welfare states are often deeply structured along gender lines, distributing rights-based entitlements to men both for themselves and for their wives and children and providing lesser, means-tested assistance to women only in the absence of men. More important, such critics have shown that these gendered institutions do not simply reflect the sexual divisions of the labor market but may in fact reinforce these divisions; indeed, being based on normative rather than actual patterns of familial dependence and maintenance, welfare institutions can place heavy additional burdens on women (and sometimes men) whose actual labor market or familial situation is not in keeping with normative roles.[18]

Exceptionally important and fruitful as this work has been, it too has some limitations. First, like the partisans of the social interpretation, feminist critics have tended to take the British case as paradigmatic. The very richness of feminist scholarship on Britain has proved something of a barrier to comparative analysis,[19] leading at times to a worrying conflation between the British case and that of "the welfare state" in general.[20] When contrasts are made, they are

[18] Carole Pateman has brilliantly analyzed the implications of the male breadwinner welfare state for women's equal citizenship in "The Patriarchal Welfare State," in Amy Gutman, ed., *Democracy and the Welfare State* (Princeton, N.J.: Princeton University Press, 1988), pp. 231–60. On Titmuss, Marshall, and the difficulties of positing "social citizenship" for women, see also Gillian Pascall, *Social Policy: A Feminist Analysis* (London: Tavistock, 1986), pp. 6–15; Hilary Rose, "Rereading Titmuss: The Sexual Division of Welfare," *Journal of Social Policy*, 10: 4 (Oct. 1981), pp. 477–502.

[19] Early important works elaborating how the welfare state in Britain has assumed a family with a male breadwinner and dependent wife include Elizabeth Wilson, *Women and the Welfare State* (London: Tavistock, 1977); Mary McIntosh, "The State and the Oppression of Women," in Annette Kuhn and AnnMarie Wolpe, eds., *Feminism and Materialism* (London: Routledge, 1978), pp. 254–89; Mary McIntosh, "The Welfare State and the Needs of the Dependent Family," in Sandra Burman, ed., *Fit Work for Women* (London: Croom Helm, 1979), pp. 153–72; Hilary Land, "The Family Wage," *Feminist Review*, 6 (1980), pp. 55–78; Jane Lewis, "Dealing with Dependency: State Practices and Social Realities," in *Women's Welfare, Women's Rights* (London: Croom Helm, 1983), pp. 17–37; and Jennifer Dale and Peggy Foster, *Feminists and State Welfare* (London: Routledge, 1986).

[20] Both Pateman and Joan Acker to some extent treat a family-wage or male-breadwinner model as universal: see Pateman, "The Patriarchal Welfare State," and Acker, "Class, Gender and the Relations of Distribution," *Signs*, 13: 3 (Spring 1988), pp. 473–97. Linda Gordon's useful review of recent scholarship on the welfare state also relies very heavily on the British and U.S. experiences, both of which strongly exhibit a male-breadwinner logic; see Gordon, "The New Feminist Scholarship on the Welfare State," in Linda Gordon, ed., *Women, the State, and Welfare* (Madison: University of Wisconsin Press,

often to Sweden, whose elaborate network of maternal and infant services has often drawn praise from scholars exploring conditions under which married women are able to take up waged work.[21] Although a few scholars have begun the difficult task of integrating gender fully into a comparative analysis of the emergence and variations of the welfare state, such work is still in its infancy.[22] Second, the focus on "gender" has occasionally obscured the fact that many social policies are concerned less with men or women than with children; gender relations are not always the central concern. Indeed, the decision to address and define men and women not in terms of their presumed relationship to each other, but rather through other

1990), pp. 9–35. In an important article, Jane Jenson did criticize the cultural specificity of the work of Mary McIntosh and others; as she noted, French policies did not presume that men could support entire families and treated women as *both* workers and mothers. See Jenson, "Gender and Reproduction: Or, Babies and the State," *Studies in Political Economy*, 20 (Summer 1986), pp. 9–46.

[21] See especially Mary Ruggie, *The State and Working Women: A Comparative Study of Britain and Sweden* (Princeton, N.J.: Princeton University Press, 1984).

[22] The criticisms of Esping-Andersen's typology developed in Langan and Ostner, "Gender and Welfare," and in Ilona Ostner and Jane Lewis, "Notes towards the Gendering of European Welfare Regimes" (typescript), constitute one important beginning. Both of these articles attempt to differentiate welfare regimes by comparing the treatment of men and women; the latter attempts to develop a typology of welfare states based on whether the male breadwinner ideal is weakly or strongly endorsed. There are, I believe, two weaknesses with this work thus far. First, while both articles rightly point out that the domestic sphere is often an arena of labor for women, the implication that such labor exists in any functional and discoverable relationship to the gendered structure of the labor market and the welfare state is questionable. As we shall see in the case of Britain, income maintenance programs that compensate men for their wives do so on the grounds of wives' presumed *dependence* and not their domestic *labor* – hence, the state's relative lack of interest in whether or not the wife actually *does* the housework and its continued deafness to the argument that the unmarried deserve equal benefits since they would be required to pay for domestic service in the market. Second, by differentiating between states in terms of the degree to which they endorse or undercut male breadwinner ideals, such work may search for policies that are relatively unimportant while overlooking the central logic of a given state.

A second line of approach has been suggested by Seth Koven and Sonya Michel, who have attempted to specify the conditions under which women are able to influence the formation of policy. Yet Koven and Michel focus too narrowly on the "state," both as the architect of policy and as their main explanatory factor, thus overlooking the degree to which policies may be developed directly by social groups with a capacity to circumvent the state. Second, they restrict their focus to maternity and infant policies and thus are not able to explain the degree to which *gender* itself became a fundamental structuring principle of different welfare states. See Michel and Koven, "Womanly Duties: Maternalist Politics and the Origins of Welfare States in France, Germany, Great Britain and the United States, 1880–1920," *American Historical Review*, 95: 4 (Oct. 1990), pp. 1076–1108.

social relations or identities, may make the later construction of more explicitly "gendered" policies difficult.

The main currents of scholarship on the welfare state have thus largely neglected the historical evolution of policies toward the family and dependence, even though these policies were central to the shaping of the institutions of the welfare state. Proponents of the social interpretation have focused too closely on class to recognize the existence of either policies or interest groups defined along generational or gender lines, while recent work on distributive systems or welfare regimes continues to treat the family as a "subsidiary" institution, rather than as a changing set of relationships that interact in crucial ways with many labor and social policies. And if feminist scholars have been able to uncover some of these interactions, they have not provided any real explanation for differences across national lines. What we need, then, is to study the comparative evolution of the institutions of the welfare state in relation not only to the structure of the labor market in any given country, but also to the patterns of family life, whether actual or ideal, that they assumed and attempted to reinforce. Neither historical developments nor later divergences can be understood in the absence of such an analysis.

This book studies the emergence of state policies toward family dependence in Britain and France in the period between 1914 and 1945, in an attempt to understand why these welfare states developed along such different lines. Britain and France provide a particularly good comparison, since the two differ markedly in the realm of social policy, and their divergence has been closely related to their treatment of familial dependence. As the feminist critics contended and this study demonstrates, the British welfare state developed along deeply gendered lines. Both labor and social policies were premised on a normative vision of the family in which men were presumed to be the principal family breadwinners, and dependence was considered the normal destiny of wives. This book details the key moments during the interwar period at which this vision became more than a pious hope and was embedded in actual policies. Married men came during these years to be insured against loss of wages both for themselves and their presumably dependent families, with provisions for wives and children incorporated into military pay during the First World War and into unemployment insurance shortly thereafter. Married women's entitlements, by contrast, gradually came to be based more on their husbands' presence and insurance record than on their own waged or unwaged work. Wives married to insured men thus found themselves protected against widowhood after 1925, whether or not they had in fact been "dependent," while in 1931 their own independent access to unemployment benefit was severely circumscribed on the assumption that they could be "kept" by their husbands. By the Second World War, a particular ideal of the appropriate relations between state, family, and labor market – a "male breadwinner" logic of family maintenance – had come to structure many programs, and the Beveridge Report made this ideal more explicit, basing entitlements for whole families on the labor market position of the husband and father, while proposing that employed married women be allowed to "opt out" of social insurance entirely.

Policies redistributing income toward women and children were deeply at odds with this logic, and groups important in the policymaking process in Britain proved themselves far more hostile to such proposals in the interwar period than were their counterparts on the Continent. Enthusiasm was pronounced only among some feminist and socialist organizations and among a few social investigators and economists convinced by Rathbone's case. Although sympathy did develop during the depression for measures that would lift poor families out of poverty, a substantial scheme of family allowances was not introduced until 1945, after Beveridge had made it one of the "assumptions" of his plan. Even so, allowances were paid at a low level and for many years excluded the first child: while they were an important resource for particularly poor or large families, they by no means "socialized" the cost of children among the population. Nor have either British scholars or the British public ever really accepted the principle of redistribution along family lines: scholars continue to examine family policies for their impact on the vertical relations of class, while public debate has tended to dwell less on the possibility of a systematic redistribution toward dependent children than on the need to direct assistance toward the poor.[23] Yet the focus on class

---

[23] Thus, even John Macnicol's classic study of the movement for family allowances tends to view allowances as a less adequate and inegalitarian alternative to wages, rather than as a form of redistribution addressing quite different inequalities; see Macnicol, *The Movement for Family Allowances, 1918–1945: A Study in Social Policy Development* (London: Heinemann, 1980). John Baker compares the British tendency to define distributive questions in terms of class with the French tendency to define them in terms of equality across families; see John Baker, "Comparing National Priorities: Family and Population Policy in Britain and France," *Journal of Social Policy*, 15: 4 (Oct. 1986), pp. 421–42. These national preferences are also clear from the fact that French family policy is defined and protected by powerful ministries and semipublic institutions, while this advocacy role in Britain is performed – as best it can be – largely by the voluntary lobbying organization Child Poverty Action Group. On their campaigns, see Michael McCarthy,

has not actually translated into effective policies toward poor families. Although British spending on family benefits has increased steadily over the past twenty-five years, families with young children continue to live at levels not only below those of childless couples, but also below those of the other main vulnerable group, the elderly.[24] British distributional policies, one scholar concludes, remain "insufficiently geared to questions of horizontal distribution – that is, to achieving equity between family types."[25]

France provides an excellent counterexample, but for very different reasons. As Douglas Ashford has pointed out (and done much to remedy), the French welfare state has been understudied and much misunderstood.[26] The incoherent and anarchic structure of French welfare institutions presents a discouraging prospect for the tidy-minded researcher, and such institutions seem even more puzzling when it is revealed that they do not redistribute income across class lines at all.[27] Historical studies, noting that comprehensive social insurance was set up in France only in 1945 – and unemployment insurance in 1958 – have tended to dismiss France as a "late developer,"[28] while sociologists and political scientists, struck by its heavy

---

Campaigning for the Poor: C.P.A.G. and the Politics of Welfare (London: Croom Helm, 1986)

[24] Using Family Expenditure Survey data for 1971, 1976, and 1982, Michael O'Higgins found that in both 1976 and 1982 families with preschool-age children were living at a standard of economic welfare less than half that of childless young couples and *below* that of retired persons, whether single or married; see O'Higgins, "Inequality, Social Policy and Income Distribution in the United Kingdom," in Jean-Pierre Jallade, ed., *The Crisis of Redistribution in European Welfare States* (Stoke-on-Trent: Trentham, 1988), p. 62.

[25] Ibid., p. 67.

[26] Douglas Ashford's comparative study of France and Britain recognizes the interdependence of wage and welfare policy and places the key elaboration of divergent systems in the interwar years; see Ashford, *The Emergence of the Welfare States* (Oxford: Basil Blackwell, 1986). Ashford also highlights the inapplicability of Anglo-American models to French developments and provides a more nuanced historical explanation for the variability and complexity of French programs in "Advantages of Complexity: Social Insurance in France," in John S. Ambler, ed., *The French Welfare State: Surviving Social and Ideological Change* (New York: New York University Press, 1991), pp. 32–57.

[27] The "nonredistributive" character of French social policy is well established. David Cameron summarizes research showing that while British, Swedish, and Norwegian social policies are strongly redistributive between social classes, French transfer payments in 1970 were almost evenly distributed among households across social classes – indeed, they were, if anything, mildly regressive; see Cameron, "Continuity and Change in French Social Policy: The Welfare State under Gaullism, Liberalism, and Socialism," in Ambler, ed., *The French Welfare State*, p. 86.

[28] France appears as a somewhat exceptional case in a number of historical accounts. Peter

reliance on semiprivate and occupational funds, have characterized it as a rather peculiar variant of a "corporatist" or "Bismarckian" welfare state exemplified by Germany.[29] Only during the past decade, when Anglo-American scholars began to notice that France had weathered the welfare crises of the seventies and eighties surprisingly well, and that French spending on social welfare had surpassed German and British and was beginning to approach Scandinavian levels, has a literature emerged that studies the French welfare state for what it did accomplish, rather than for its supposed shortcomings.[30] Yet while such recent literature has recognized the comparative importance and success of French family policy,[31] the very fact that such

Flora and Jens Alber, for example, in attributing welfare state development largely to economic development and political modernization, admit that their model does not work well for France, which introduced insurance programs very late, at a high level of socioeconomic development and political mobilization. Flora and Alber attribute this "exceptionalism" to political instability but do not show how private developments acted as an alternative to state policies. See Flora and Alber, "Modernization, Democratization, and the Development of Welfare States in Western Europe," in Flora and Heidenheimer, eds., *The Development of Welfare States*, pp. 37–80. Britain and Germany, on the other hand, appear in the Flora and Heidenheimer volume as paradigmatic cases, while Sweden and Britain are considered paradigmatic by Hugh Heclo, *Modern Social Politics in Britain and Sweden: From Relief to Income Maintenance* (New Haven, Conn.: Yale University Press, 1974).

[29] Both Gøsta Esping-Andersen, *Three Worlds*, and Jean-Pierre Jallade, "The Redistributive Efficiency of European Welfare States: Basic Issues," in Jallade, ed., *The Crisis of Redistribution*, pp. 14–19, treat France this way. Unfortunately, the first published results of the Luxembourg Income Study (LIS), which could have demonstrated the great differences from Germany in the area of family policy, included data on Sweden, Germany, and Britain but not France; see Timothy M. Smeeding, Michael O'Higgins, and Lee Rainwater, eds., *Poverty, Inequality and Income Distribution in Comparative Perspective: The Luxembourg Income Study (LIS)* (New York: Harvester Wheatsheaf, 1990), and Smeeding, Torrey, and Rein, "Patterns of Income and Poverty."

[30] In 1986, social spending, including pensions and other forms of insurance, family allowances, medical care, and income maintenance programs, measured 31.3% of GDP in Sweden, 29.8% in Norway, 28.6% in France and in The Netherlands, 26.4% in Belgium, 26.3% in Denmark, 25.4% in Austria, 23.4% in West Germany and Luxembourg, 23.2% in Ireland, 22.8% in Finland, and merely 20.4% in the United Kingdom, just ahead of Greece at 19.5%. See ILO, *The Cost of Social Security: Thirteenth International Inquiry* (Geneva: ILO, 1992), pp. 83–4. Furthermore, as David Cameron and John Ambler point out, the growth of the French welfare state accelerated during the period of rightist dominance – thus confounding scholars who would see welfare states as an outgrowth of social democracy – and continued in the eighties, a decade in which many welfare states moved into deficit and crisis; see Cameron, "Continuity and Change," in Ambler, ed., *The French Welfare State*, pp. 83–4, and John S. Ambler, "Ideas, Interests and the French Welfare State," in ibid., pp. 23–8.

[31] The important recent volume edited by Ambler includes a chapter on family policy; Rémi Lenoir, "Family Policy in France since 1938," in Ambler, ed., *The French Welfare*

policy has long been recognized and studied in France as an academic subject in its own right has discouraged integrated analysis.[32] Family policies are included in studies of "the welfare state," but either as exceptional additions to the usual institutions of social welfare – a peculiarly French consequence of Catholicism or pronatalism – or as further evidence of the French welfare state's "nonredistributive" character.[33] The institutions of family policy are recognized, but the principles underlying such policy are not.

Yet as this book argues, the particular choices made in France to address the problem of dependence have shaped its welfare state in important ways. Many of the most unusual and persistent features of French policy – the identification of "families" rather than individuals as the bearers of social entitlements, the tendency to define distributive justice in terms of income equalization between families rather than across social classes, and the continued reliance on employers' contributions for the majority of social security funding – are, as we shall see, in large part the legacy of policies developed to share the burden of dependent children in the period between the wars. Despite the

State, pp. 144–86. The central importance of family policy in France and its relative independence from other forms of policy is also stressed by Colin Birks, "Social Welfare Provision in France," in Roslyn Ford and Mono Chakrabarti, eds., *Welfare Abroad: An Introduction to Welfare Provision in Seven Countries* (Edinburgh: Scottish Academic Press, 1987), pp. 66–98.

[32] Thus, the best accounts of French family policy have tended to treat its development within the context of a broader "familist" movement or of population policy, rather than of social security, and to be published by the Union National des Caisses d'Allocations Familiales (UNCAF) or the Institut National des Etudes Démographiques (INED); see especially Robert Talmy, *Histoire du mouvement familial en France, 1896–1939*, 2 vols. (Paris: UNCAF, 1962); Dominique Ceccaldi, *Histoire des prestations familiales en France* (Paris: UNCAF, 1957); Jean-Claude Chesnais, "La politique de la population française depuis 1914," in Jacques Dupâquier, ed., *Histoire de la population française*, vol. 4 (Paris: INED/Presses Universitaires de France, 1988), pp. 181–231. The work of Henri Hatzfeld, now twenty years old, remains exceptional in its integration of the development of family allowances into a broader account of the development of social security; Hatzfeld, *Du paupérisme à la sécurité sociale, 1850–1940* (Paris: Armand Colin, 1971).

[33] Thus, while Jean-Pierre Jallade does consider family policies in his study of the redistributive impact of the French welfare state, he does so only in the conventional terms of class analysis. He therefore concludes that they "conflict with redistributive objectives" and are "unfair to the poor" because they do not redistribute *between* social classes – thereby denying that policies equalizing income between the childless and those with children can also be a form of redistribution, especially given the very substantial poverty levels of families with young children: Jallade, "Redistribution in the Welfare State: An Assessment of the French Performance," in Jallade, ed., *The Crisis of Redistribution*, pp. 237–8.

fact that social insurance in France lagged twenty years behind Britain and forty years behind Germany, in the area of policies distributing the burdens of children's dependence France was undoubtedly a pioneer. Quite substantial allowances for dependent children were granted to civil servants by the state and to many industrial workers by private business consortia during and immediately after the First World War. In 1932, the state extended these benefits by requiring all employers in industry and commerce to affiliate to one of the private, business-controlled funds (*caisses de compensation*) that had been set up to equalize the cost of such benefits across firms in particular sectors or regions. Family allowances were extended to agricultural workers and small farmers in the years immediately before the Second World War, and their value raised very substantially across the board. Neither the Vichy years nor the advent of the Fourth Republic decisively altered the character of French family policy, and by 1949 almost 40% of social security spending went to family benefits. Although France gradually developed solidaristic programs aimed at socializing the risks of unemployment, invalidity, old age, and illness, and relative spending on family policies declined, French family benefits remain among the most generous and "redistributive" in Europe, equalizing income across family types and guaranteeing decent living standards to families with dependent children regardless of parental occupation, marital status, or class.

France thus made far more extensive and explicit provision for dependent children in the interwar period than did Britain. Yet it did not do so in the way Eleanor Rathbone would have hoped, by defining mothering as worthy of remuneration and transferring income explicitly from men to women. To the contrary, while the French have paid more attention to the unequal burden of dependent children, they have made less of an effort to grant social rights to individuals for their presumed fulfillment of particular family responsibilities, whether "mothering" or "breadwinning." If we can characterize the evolution of British social policy as the articulation of a male breadwinner logic of welfare, French policies came to rest on a very different logic, which I will term "parental." Parental policies do not assume that women are necessarily dependent, nor that men always have "families to keep"; rather, they presume the dependence of children alone and hence redistribute income primarily across family types and not along gender lines. Put simply, while male-breadwinner policies compensate men for dependent women and children during legitimate interruptions of earnings, states with parental policies compensate adults for dependent children irrespective of earnings or need.[34] By focusing policy on children – essentially, by assimilating children to other "risks" to be shared – the French have been able to adjust family income to family needs while remaining relatively agnostic about the respective occupations and roles of women and men.

Why did France and Britain develop along these very different lines? The policy-making arena was crowded in both countries with those claiming to represent a wide array of interests, putting forward very different visions of distributive justice – visions that were often quite as concerned with gender and generation as with class – and attempting to build coalitions and to interest state actors in their cases. Yet if we were to look to such political ideas and campaigns alone, the final shape of policy would appear unexpected and virtually incomprehensible. As we shall see, it was in Britain that the most forthright claims were made for greater state control of the distributive system and for an increased share of the national wealth for children, yet it was in France that such aims were partially achieved. An adequate history of the evolution of family policies must therefore move beyond the intentions of reformers, laying bare those economic, ideological, or political structures that sustained and transformed certain initiatives, while condemning others to failure.

Certainly the structure of the labor market itself provided one important framework for policy. The very different labor market structures of the two countries – and especially very different rates of labor-force participation by married women – did help to make particular policies imaginable. Yet it would be misleading to argue that policies simply reflected patterns of dependence produced by the labor market. Such a view is inadequate, first because these labor market structures were themselves in part political creations; as we shall see, the weak position of married women workers in Britain was in part the consequence of state policies that marginalized such workers after the First World War and during the Slump. Furthermore, states need not have seen gendered labor markets as patterns to be reinforced: rather, as wartime experiences showed, in circumstances of national crisis policymakers could view them instead as barriers to be overcome.

---

[34] It is not argued here that France had no policies aimed at encouraging a male-breadwinner family model – indeed, in the postwar period, French policymakers made a great effort to encourage women to stay home by building up additional allowances for single-earner families or those with unwaged mothers. Yet such efforts were hindered by the prior development of family allowance policies that operated along very different lines and have been increasingly abandoned. For such efforts, see Chapter 7.

Similarly, the presence of women in the labor market, rather than in the home, could contribute to the introduction of policies benefiting unwaged mothers. Thus, it was France – where married women were far more likely to be employed – rather than Britain that gradually instituted a small benefit for unwaged mothers, precisely because pronatalists were able to convince the government that mothers would have to be paid to break with the "normal" pattern of wage earning. The labor market, while important, influenced policy in complex and not always predictable ways.

This book argues that we can best understand why policies toward dependence developed so differently in these two welfare states if we examine how proposals to base social entitlements on family status or gender role were articulated and received within two realms – the open realm of public and political debate and the more restricted realm of political or economic consultation. I distinguish between these realms because groups able to articulate interests rhetorically were not necessarily able to aggregate and mobilize them as a political force, and it is the disjunctures and incompatibilities between rhetorical and institutional power that can help us understand divergent outcomes. Of course, political debates were themselves important: as we shall see, very different conceptions of the appropriate relations between the state and the family, as well as very different redistributive programs, emerged in these two countries before the First World War. Changing patterns of industrial relations and political mediation were also critical: very different groups had the power to force, circumvent, or block state action in the two countries and hence to translate programs into policies.

Nevertheless, it was the interaction between programs and institutions and between rhetoric and political capacity that decisively shaped the character of social policy. In brief, while debates in France succeeded in defining the aim of family policy in ways that coincided with the interests of those able to influence outcomes, the debate in Britain was captured by those with little influence over policy-making. In Britain, then, policies toward families with dependent children were shaped largely by those groups – notably civil servants and trade unionists – seeking to protect wages and wage negotiations from "political" and state interference and resistant to the redistributive agendas articulated by feminists and socialists. In France, by contrast, the success with which social Catholics and pronatalists defined aid to families with dependent children as a patriotic measure proved a useful cover for employers eager to distribute allowances in lieu of wages.

Relations between redistributive agendas and institutional forces thus go some distance toward explaining particular policy outcomes. Yet it is striking that the country in which a feminist vision of welfare was most clearly articulated developed along the most sexually inegalitarian lines. Feminists like Rathbone saw family policy as a step toward women's economic independence; by recognizing "the value to the community of the function of motherhood, properly discharged," the state could equalize income and power not only between the childless and those with children, but also between men and women.[35] Their campaigns certainly established the claim that mothers be regarded as an important political interest, but simultaneously made powerful male organizations and institutions more conscious of their members' identities and claims as husbands and fathers. In France, by contrast, the very weakness of feminism and of organized men enabled employers and politicians to channel income to "the family," without inquiring too closely into the distribution of that income within the family itself. But while such measures sometimes diverted significant economic resources to mothers, the fact that they were never publicly associated with women's rights meant that they could easily be rescinded or deformed. The articulation of gender interests and antagonisms thus had a disproportionate if contradictory influence over the shape of policy and will be paid special attention in this account.

In focusing on arguments over the treatment of dependence, not only does this study seek to demonstrate the centrality of such questions to the early elaboration of the welfare state, it also argues for a more complex definition of "interest" and a more sophisticated view of the process through which such interests are articulated and represented. Interests are often seen in narrow, individual, and purely material terms. Yet as this study shows, the interests served by particular policies were often very complex. This was particularly true of dependency policies, which, after all, addressed relations among individuals rather than personal risks and thus often pitted the loyalties of particular family members against one another – or, alternatively, forced individuals to choose between rival identities themselves. To understand how coalitions and alliances could develop around such policies, then, we need to accept that people can have more than a single interest and do not understand their interests only in material terms. Max Weber is a better guide than Marx: rather than refine our definition of "interest" to reflect more perfectly the model of rational economic calculation, we need to recognize, as We-

---

[35] Rathbone, *Disinherited Family*, p. 295.

ber did, the degree to which political choices may reflect conceptions of honor as well as material advantage. Furthermore, although Hugh Heclo has warned against giving too much weight to "generational politics," arguing that class-based politics "easily overshadow age-defined cleavages,"[36] this book will show that, under certain conditions, interests defined on generational, gender, or familial lines could indeed make themselves felt – whether through organizations (such as the pronatalist lobbies) determined to represent the interests of the child or through groups usually seen as the pure representatives of "class" (such as trade unions) but sometimes equally devoted to the privileges of their members as men. This book thus avoids identifying key groups – whether trade unions, employers' organizations, feminists, or civil servants – from the outset as the bearers of transparent class interests, uncovering instead the more complex identities and loyalties that motivated their actions.

The three parts of the book compare the evolution of British and French approaches toward familial dependence from early developments in the period before 1918, through the campaigns and private initiatives of the twenties, to the emergence of national policies during the depression and the Second World War. In Part I, Chapter 1 traces the construction of a policy framework through the competing visions of social reformers during the prewar period, while Chapter 2 outlines the implications for family policy of new patterns of industrial and political mediation developed to answer the military and manpower needs of the First World War.

The emerging character of wage and welfare systems in the two countries was by no means clear to contemporaries, however. Part II examines a series of campaigns in the twenties aimed at using dependency policy to transform economic relations at the workplace and in the family. The failure of British feminists' and socialists' attempts to use welfare benefits to redistribute income along sex and class lines, discussed in Chapters 3 and 4, contrasts sharply with the success with which French employers used allowances for children to control labor and restrain wages, as revealed in Chapter 5. In Part III, Chapters 6 and 7 explain how government responses to the unemployment and population crises of the thirties and to the Second World War transformed these private initiatives, leading to the partial realization of the alternative models of the male breadwinner and parental welfare states.

---

[36] Hugh Heclo, "Generational Politics," in Palmer et al., eds., *The Vulnerable*, p. 384.

Part I

PROGRAMS AND PRECEDENTS

The family, founded on marriage, hierarchically constituted under paternal authority, has as its end the transmission, support, development and perpetuation of human life. It thus holds certain inalienable rights, anterior and superior to all positive law....

    Art. 6.: The family has the right to live by its labor. All forms of production that harm the vitality of the father, mother or child, or that disturb family life, should be proscribed. A wage sufficient to support a family should be assured by the appropriate organizations, under the protection of the profession and the law.

> [Eugène Duthoit], "Déclaration des droits
> de la famille" (1920)

The State will pay for children born legitimately in the marriage it will sanction. A woman with healthy and successful offspring will draw a wage for each one of them from the State, so long as they go on well. It will be her wage....

    That is the gist of the Socialist attitude towards marriage; the repudiation of private ownership of women and children, and the payment of mothers.

> H. G. Wells, *Socialism and the Family* (1906)

And is the position of paid domestic servant the ideal of the women in the emancipation movement?

> *Freewoman* (29 Feb. 1912)

H. G. Wells was – at this stage– a Fabian socialist with a penchant for rationalized public affairs and unruly private ones. The editors of the *Freewoman* were libertarians devoted to the cause of women's economic and sexual emancipation. Eugène Duthoit was a Catholic law professor determined to bring the moral teachings of Leo XIII to the University of Lille and his home region of the Nord. Yet as the foregoing brief excerpts make clear, all had a stake in the early-twentieth-century debate over the nature and future of the family.

    They were not alone. By the end of the century, census reports, social investigations, and concerns about military preparedness had made the poverty (or, in France, the paucity) of children a question of "high politics." Yet many thought these economic and demographic troubles were linked to a wider crisis in family relations and roles and argued that the state must intervene not only to protect children but to sanction or reform particular domestic relations and parental behaviors. Some of these ideas were considered radical: Wells, for example, thought comprehensive state entitlements should be introduced to emancipate mothers from dependence on men (a proposal that repelled the stalwart individualists at the *Freewoman*). Others were considered conservative: Eugène Duthoit thought that only by extending the rights of fathers over their families could the nation revitalize its population and protect children from the demoralizing effects of cultural decadence. Chapter 1 examines these and other visions of family renewal in detail, uncovering in particular the extent to which the health and well-being of the rising generation was imagined to be dependent on the recognition or remuneration of particular gender roles.

But talk is cheap, and comprehensive family policies often extremely expensive. While governments in both countries did extend medical and educational services for children and strengthened legal protections against overwork or parental abuse in the decades before the First World War, in neither country were they able to contemplate massive increases in public spending or comprehensive redistributive policies. It was the First World War that, by disrupting patterns of familial dependence and maintenance and eroding normal constraints on public spending, forced governments to develop new and expansive policies mitigating the economic burden to parents of dependent children. They did so in consultation with interests and groups granted new authority by the war, however, and, as Chapter 2 shows, in ways that their early advocates had not anticipated.

1

THE FAMILY IN QUESTION
State and family in prewar thought and politics

When British and French social reformers and politicians discussed measures to aid families in the period between the wars, they often had the same policy in mind: cash allowances for dependent children. Yet the associations evoked by this policy could not have been more different. A measure identified in France with a right-wing reaction against liberal individualism, perceived as a prophylactic against the degenerate practices of birth control and (sometimes) of married women's work, was supported in Britain by socialists and feminists who saw it as a means of ameliorating the poverty of families with dependent children while at the same time providing unwaged mothers with a measure of financial independence. Encumbered by divergent social agendas, such proposals would provoke very different responses in the two countries.

What campaigners for family allowances were burdened or blessed with in the interwar period was the legacy of a debate that had been at its height some twenty-five years earlier: the fin-de-siècle debate over the structure of the family, the appropriate roles and responsibilities of women and men, and the limits of state intervention in the realm of the "private." Bourgeois society had had an answer to all of these questions, of course, but these answers were increasingly under attack by the end of the century – from imperialists and pro-natalists worried that couples would not provide enough soldiers for future wars if left to their own devices quite as much as from feminists or socialists no longer willing to consider the health and well-being of mothers and children an entirely private matter. This was not a debate about social policy, but when proposals to aid families with dependent children on a systematic basis first emerged in either country, they did so marked with the anxieties and ideals of the groups that first gave them voice. It is in this period, then, and with this debate that our story properly begins.

25

We can begin to grasp the nature of the fin-de-siècle debate about the family by turning briefly to two fictional works, H. G. Wells's *Marriage* and Emile Zola's *Fécondité*. The works are chosen advisedly: both men were avowed partisans of some political movements that dominated the discussion over family policy in the prewar period. Zola was a member of the pronatalist Alliance Nationale pour l'Accroissement de la Population Française from its founding in 1896; H. G. Wells had already written pamphlets for the Independent Labour Party and the Fabian Society recommending vastly extended public provision for mothers and children.[1] Part literature, part tract, both novels accurately forecast the terms on which battles over family policy would be fought during the next fifty years. If we want to understand the very different visions of social renewal that came to be attached to arguments for state intervention into the realm of the family, we can begin by looking briefly at *Marriage* and *Fécondité*.

Emile Zola, H. G. Wells, and the crisis of the family

Zola published *Fécondité* in 1899; its English translation, *Fruitfulness*, appeared one year later.[2] It is unabashedly the story of a loving couple, Mathieu and Marianne Froment, who find both private happiness and worldly success through their cohesive and abundant family. Marianne has a child every two years until she has produced an even dozen; Mathieu, initially a factory manager, leaves business for farming and energetically expands his efforts and holdings to keep pace with his multiplying offspring. The rather prosaic story of their success gains dramatic interest when contrasted to the fate of four other families, each of which represents a form of "degeneracy" threatening French society and each of which succumbs to the more vigorous Froments. The Beauchènes, initially Mathieu's employers, watch their factory fall gradually into the hands of one of his sons, after the untimely death of their own, much-pampered *fils unique*. The financial empire of the Seguins, from whom Mathieu initially rents his humble cottage, is ruined through extravagance and dissipation, until its remnants are absorbed by the expanding holdings of another of Mathieu's

---

[1] For Zola's affiliation, see David Baguley, *Fécondité d'Emile Zola* (Toronto: University of Toronto Press, 1973), p. 42. Wells's writings for the Independent Labour Party are discussed later.

[2] Emile Zola, *Fécondité* (Paris: Charpentier, 1899); trans. Ernest Alfred Vizetelly, *Fruitfulness* (London: Chatto & Windus, 1900). All quotations are from the English translation (page references are given in parentheses), but readers should be aware that the sexually explicit passages in the French original were removed from the English translation.

sons. Mathieu's peasant neighbors, who refuse to cultivate their land and groom their worthless only son for a Parisian career, see both their land and their much-neglected daughter claimed by yet a third of Mathieu's sons. Even the humble accountant Morange loses both wife and daughter at the hands of the abortionist, victims of their own ambitious desire to restrict their births to conform to their means. The novel closes on a note of both dynastic and imperial conquest. The now-legion clan of the Froments convenes to celebrate Mathieu and Marianne's seventieth wedding anniversary and are startled by the messianic arrival of a handsome stranger – who is, it transpires, their colonist grandson – bearing tales of new lands awaiting cultivation and peopling. Having redeemed the land of their fathers and the businesses of their enervated compatriots, the Froments turn to "France abroad" for new fields of endeavor.

Our second couple, Godwin and Marjorie Trafford, are no less successful, but they lack the bucolic setting and the instinctual marital harmony of the Froments. Wells published *Marriage* in 1912, as one in a series of semiautobiographical novels through which he worked out his own ideas on the appropriate roles for men and women in society.[3] The first third of *Marriage* presents the conventional story of a young girl, pretty, intelligent and "Oxbridge"-educated, who falls in love with and marries a dashing and brilliant scientist. The real drama of the novel begins some time later, however, when the two, "disillusioned, stripped of the last shred of excitement" (p. 193), face the fact that they are linked for life in a relationship that has not made either completely happy. Marjorie is full of goodwill but extravagant: she spends Trafford's salary and much of his meager capital in furnishing their home. Her husband Trafford, deeply committed to his research, soon comes to realize that he will have to give it up to support Marjorie and their children. He feels cheated, though – his intelligence traduced to maintain a glittering domestic facade. Increasingly unhappy, he decides to go away – far away – for a time, "to think," and, on his mother's urging, insists that Marjorie go with him. In a rather extreme precursor to the modern vacation-to-save-our-marriage, Trafford and Marjorie spend six snowbound months in a log cabin in Newfoundland, fighting off wolves, having unreadable exchanges about sexual relations in the course of human "evolution," and rediscovering, it seems, the "natural" and elemental attraction between man and "mate." They leave Newfoundland un-

---

[3] H. G. Wells, *Marriage* (1912; rpt. London: Hogarth, 1986); page references are given in parentheses.

transformed but recommitted to the endless process of negotiation and compromise intrinsic to modern marriage.

These two novels could not be more different, yet each presents a coherent exposé of a crisis of the family in contemporary society. Both novels set up their couple as paradigmatic, locked in problems and situations emblematic of their time. The discussions and solutions outlined in both novels are almost uncannily reflective of a broader public debate and are thus useful texts with which to begin a comparison of French and British opinion on the subject of the relationship between state and family. We can compare the novels on three crucial points: their view of the nature and location of the crisis of the family, the extent to which they perceive this crisis as an economic one, and their proposed solutions.

Why is the family in crisis in fin-de-siècle France? It is in crisis, Zola answers, because it is literally dying. *Dénatalité*, the voluntary restriction of births, is ruining both familial cohesion and national greatness. Zola's splenetic outbursts against wet-nursing and abortion, cabarets and artistic decadence, venal peasants and irresponsible aristocrats, child-denying women and a sex-denying church provide a well-stocked gallery of villains responsible for this tragedy. "Civilization" is making the family sick: driven by greed, surrounded by a depraved culture and life-hating ideology, misled by the false science of Malthus, men and women are deserting the organic rhythms of the earth, forgetting natural sexual hierarchies and roles, and refusing to reproduce. The crisis of the family is not the result of any incompatibility between the sexes, however. Safe on their farm, effectively quarantined from the infection of Parisian decadence, Mathieu and Marianne live in perfect harmony, "without a quarrel, without ever a deed of unfaithfulness" (p. 396).

In *Marriage*, by contrast, conflict is inherent to the relations of love and dependence within the family itself. Zola's idealized patriarchy has long since vanished, but its defeat has left relations between husbands and wives tenuous, liminal, and newly problematic. Trafford and Marjorie argue constantly and find in neither nature nor politics reliable guides to life. "Nature," in Newfoundland, is not a bountiful mother; indeed, it is in fighting its destructiveness that Trafford and Marjorie prove the hegemony of culture and intelligence. In Wells, the line between a vicious public sphere and a consoling private one has vanished; rather, conflicting claims of men and women to independence and work, family life and love must be fought out concurrently in politics and in the home. The crisis of the family in Zola's work is caused by a conflict between an idyllic family and a diseased society; in Wells's it is only one aspect of a broader societal conflict between women and men.

How central are economics to this struggle? The problems facing the Froments stem primarily from false values; the economic hardships of raising children do not trouble Mathieu and Marianne. True, the couple is hard-pressed at the opening of the novel, when Mathieu's earnings are small, but Marianne is a frugal housewife, and Mathieu turns courageously to scientific farming. Although Mathieu is, for Zola, unquestionably the *chef de famille*, the model of a male bread-winner surrounded by a dependent family is not appropriate. Marianne nurses and cares for the children herself, raises chickens, and keeps the accounts, while the children themselves soon contribute to the family coffers. In this rural family economy, the problem of "dependence" disappears. "Others only had to do as he had done," Mathieu thinks, "create the necessary subsistence each time that a child was born to them" (p. 302) – as if there were nothing more to it than that.

Money lies at the heart of the conflict between Marjorie and Trafford, by contrast, and calculation marks relations between husband and wife far more than those between parents and children. The economic dependence of the couple's four children, who absorb "the services of two nurses, a Swiss nursery governess, and two housemaids" (p. 265), appears entirely unproblematic; it is Marjorie's dependence that is the key to their marital conflict. Untrained in serious work, too trivial-minded to earn her own living, Marjorie marries Trafford, in her own words, "out of love, and remains clinging parasitically to him out of necessity" (p. 220). She *is* dependent, in a way that Marianne is not: although possessed of her own creative impulses and material desires, she can satisfy these only with Trafford's support. Yet Trafford cannot "keep" Marjorie without giving up his scientific work, and when he does so he resents her for it:

> He felt that he had given something for her that she had had no right to exact, that he had gone beyond the free mutualities of honest love and paid a price for her; he had deflected the whole course of his life for her and he was entitled to repayments. (p. 267)

However softened by love, the economic dependence of wives threatens to destroy the character and abilities of both sexes.

What is to be done? Although it contains no explicit program, *Marriage* is, in fact, a far more radical tract than *Fécondité*. While the latter presents a model for personal action, the former sketches out a problem that is endemic, inaccessible to personal solutions, and ripe for state action. Zola did recommend a few policies to combat *dénatalité*, especially a law requiring women to breast-feed their infants, but for the most part he was content to present an idealized vision of marital and sexual harmony that calls for emulation, not political action. The vision he presents is sexually inegalitarian, organic, and heavily romanticized. Marianne is explicitly likened to a fruitful field; Matthieu is explicitly described as the "sower." Mathieu sees their lives as an example to others and hopes "that manners and customs, and the idea of morality and the idea of beauty might be changed" (p. 303) so as to make Mathieu's "divine improvidence" vindicated: "He had placed his trust in the future, and now the whole harvest was garnered" (p. 387). Do likewise, implies Zola, and all this will be yours as well.

Wells doesn't exactly renounce a desire to influence the reader's personal conduct. The man who made *Ann Veronica* into the illicit model for the Girton undergraduate couldn't quite pass up the temptation to tell women what to do.[4] Yet the old feminist solution of education and work doesn't seem to have occurred to him, and he attributed female incapacity less to ignorance and neglect (Marjorie's "silly upbringing") than to inherent biological and intellectual inequalities between the sexes (Marjorie's "silly self," p. 215). Yet Wells did – in Marjorie's voice – imagine a solution to the problem of economic dependence. "Suppose," daydreams Marjorie,

> the community kept all its women, suppose all property in homes and furnishings and children vested in them! That was Marjorie's version of that idea of the Endowment of Womanhood which has been creeping into contemporary thought during the last two decades. Then every woman would be a Princess to the man she loved. (p. 220)

Women were fundamentally different from men, Wells thought. Marjorie's mind, as Trafford saw it, "followed a different process from his, because while he went upon the lines of constructive truth, her guide was a more immediate and instinctive sense of beauty" (p. 228). Given immutable sexual difference, Wells implied, why burden the labor market with less able women? Why not allow women to do the work at which they excelled, without the stigma of economic dependence?

Both *Fécondité* and *Marriage* were published to mixed reviews. Pon-

---

[4] On the influence of *Ann Veronica* on Cambridge undergraduates, see Dora Russell, *The Tamarisk Tree*, vol. 1, *My Quest for Liberty and Love* (London: Virago, 1977), pp. 40–1.

derous, humorless, and repetitive, *Fécondité* struck some literary critics
as a monumental artistic folly. Politically minded critics also had complaints: Catholics resented Zola's portrait of the church as a proponent
of an anemic celibacy, while socialists objected that his idealized Froments were selfishly ignorant of broader social problems. Not everyone could retreat to a farm; furthermore, the expanding financial
and economic empire of Mathieu's sons was built on the labor of many
whose plight the novel scarcely addressed. Yet even Zola's critics paid
tribute to the patriotism and social conscience that motivated him: the
status of *dénatalité* as a pressing public problem was not contested.[5]

Wells also faced his share of criticism, especially from feminists
ungrateful for his proposal to "endow" them with all property. "The
cheek of it!" the young Rebecca West exploded in the *Freewoman*:

> The mind reels at the thought of the community being taxed to allow
> Marjorie, who could steal her lover's money and barter the brightness
> of his soul for brass-footed workboxes, to perpetuate her cow-like
> kind. I can see myself as the one rebel in this humourless State going
> forth night after night to break the windows of the barracks of
> Yoshiwara where Marjorie was kept in fat ease, and going to prison
> months after months until...
>
> But "*all* women!" "Suppose the community kept *all* its women..."
> Heavens, I shall be inside too! I object to living under the same roof
> as Marjorie.[6]

But if the proposal to endow motherhood raised some eyebrows,
Wells's determination to write the history of a marriage that endured,
a sharp break from his earlier plots, in Victoria Glendinning's words,
"for once, brought Wells the approval of the moral majority."[7]

And however transient their literary reputations, both novels were
extraordinarily prescient. Both not only captured the contemporary
discomfort over the status of the family, but also accurately forecast
the terms of the debate over family policy from the prewar period
into the twenties and thirties. Both novels implied that the crisis of
the family was societywide and required a vast effort at moral and
possibly political reform, but the perceived nature of the crisis and
the espoused solution differed. As Wells understood, the crisis of the
family was perceived from the beginning as a crisis of gender relations

---

[5] Baguley, *Fécondité d'Emile Zola*, pp. 148–67, 180.
[6] Rebecca West, Review of *Marriage, Freewoman*, 19 Sept. 1912; rpt. in Jane Marcus, ed.,
The Young Rebecca: Writings of Rebecca West, 1911–1917 (New York: Viking, 1982), pp.
68–9.
[7] Victoria Glendinning, Introduction to Wells, *Marriage*, n.p.

in Britain, while in France it was specifically a crisis of cultural anxiety and *dénatalité*. Debate in the former case centered on the appropriate scope of intervention toward wives and mothers as well as children, while the French debate focused less on individual family members than on that endangered "social cell," the unitary, procreative family itself. The willingness to address gender relations directly and to call on the state to mitigate problems of female dependence identified family policy from the outset as a socialist or feminist crusade in Britain, while the French concern to "protect" the patriarchal family from the contamination of civilization and the reluctance to turn to state intervention linked French family policy to cultural and political conservatism. The broader public debate and political initiatives around family policy in the two countries, to which we will now turn, raised issues of far greater complexity than those addressed in these novels. As we shall see, however, the questions of dependence and *dénatalité* emphasized by Wells and Zola remained at the heart of the controversy.

Dependence and the state in Britain

Wells wrote *Marriage* within and against a culture in which the responsibility of men to maintain their wives was assumed, whether men viewed that obligation as a burden or as a mark of status and women saw their right to maintenance as a privilege or a sign of servitude. Men's responsibility to maintain lay at the heart of the Victorian social settlement, accepted throughout the propertied classes and through much of the propertyless as well as the sign of respectability and virtue. By the end of the century, however, new doubts were being expressed, both by women who found their status as dependents humiliating and by social reformers who began to question the capacity of the market to generate family wages: with the fin-de-siècle challenge to liberal and market principles came the demand that some portion of the support of dependent women and children, hitherto borne by individual wage earners, become the collective charge of society as a whole. But should such entitlements be given directly to women, as feminists urged, or channeled through their husbands' hands? Although the prewar Liberal government did pass a number of measures of importance to family policy, they seemed divided on this question, and the course of future policy developments remained unclear.

Upheld in their day as "natural," the familial practices and ideals of the nineteenth century have come to be seen in retrospect as deeply entwined with concomitant changes in relations of production and authority. The gendered segregation of spheres was woven into the culture of the propertied classes, so Leonore Davidoff and Catherine Hall tell us, as strategies of accumulation concentrated capital in male hands and removed businesses from the home and as the evangelical revival and the dual reactions against political radicalism and "aristocratic manners" during the decades following the French wars increasingly identified domesticity with social stability and morality.[8] Yet the "unprecedentedly acute sexual divisions of the nineteenth century" extended far beyond the propertied classes.[9] Historians disagree as to the locus, timing, and causes of the marginalization of working women: some focus on the decline of a domestic system of manufacture dependent on the labor of women and children;[10] others on the confluence of demographic pressures and the destruction of "customary" trade practices that drove men to seek to exclude women from apprenticeships and skilled work.[11] Maxine Berg also reminds us that

---

[8] Leonore Davidoff and Catherine Hall, *Family Fortunes: Men and Women of the English Middle Class, 1780–1850* (Chicago: University of Chicago Press, 1987); Catherine Hall, "The Early Formation of Victorian Domestic Ideology," in Sandra Burman, ed., *Fit Work for Women* (London: Croom Helm, 1979), pp. 15–32.

[9] The phrase is Keith Snell's, *Annals of the Labouring Poor: Social Change and Agrarian England, 1660–1900* (Cambridge University Press, 1985), p. 272.

[10] For a sophisticated version of this view, see David Levine, *Reproducing Families: The Political Economy of English Population History* (Cambridge University Press, 1987). Of course, as Maxine Berg usefully reminds us, "domestic" systems of manufacture did not necessarily expand women's skills or status. Berg's article provides a useful summary of much of the debate over the effects of the economic changes of the eighteenth and early nineteenth centuries on the gendered structures of the labor market; see Berg, "Women's Work, Mechanisation and the Early Phases of Industrialisation in England," in Patrick Joyce, ed., *The Historical Meanings of Work* (Cambridge University Press, 1987), pp. 64–98.

[11] Snell attributes women's exclusion from many trades and the development of an impassable barrier between men's and women's work to the combined pressures of high fertility, the increasing capitalization of the trades, and men's attempts to protect their own labor market position in a period of glut; Snell, *Annals*, pp. 270–319. John Rule argues, however, that eighteenth-century male artisans often saw "skill" almost as an exclusively male form of property and routinely sought to exclude women; Rule, "The Property of Skill in the Period of Manufacture," in Joyce, ed., *The Historical Meanings of Work*, pp. 99–118. Certainly gender was at the heart of the struggle to prevent the degradation of the skilled trades in the early nineteenth century; see, e.g., Barbara Taylor, *Eve and the New Jerusalem* (New York: Pantheon, 1983), pp. 83–117; Sally Alexander, "Women's Work in Nineteenth-Century London: A Study of the Years 1820–50," in Juliet Mitchell and Ann Oakley, eds., *The Rights and Wrongs of Women* (Harmondsworth: Penguin, 1976), esp. pp. 80–3. The exclusion of women did become a cardinal rule of many trade unions by the second half of the nineteenth century, but this has occasionally led feminist historians to argue as if such organization was the only cause of women's

relations of production and the experiences of workers varied enormously from trade to trade, while Neil McKendrick gives a new twist to the optimist's interpretation by pointing out that factory work at least gave women and children a measure of economic independence.[12] By the early years of Victoria's reign, however, there is little doubt that women's work – and especially married women's work – was highly contested, deplored as a threat to social harmony, and seen as a menace to the ameliorative hopes of organized men.

Groups made particularly vulnerable by the demographic and economic transformations of the fifty years surrounding the French wars looked to political reform to address their grievances, believing the hardships they faced to be the result of corrupt politics quite as much as unregulated growth and convinced that the "laws" of political economy could easily be subjected to human will. Working women took part in these radical political movements, albeit often from a somewhat different standpoint, arguing that they as well as men had the right to live by their labor and to help reshape the polity along "cooperative" rather than "competitive" lines.[13] Yet the state withstood these chal-

marginalization. For a summary of that debate, see Wally Seccombe, "Patriarchy Stabilized: The Construction of the Male Breadwinner Wage Norm in Nineteenth-Century Britain," *Social History*, 11: 1 (Jan. 1986), pp. 53–76.

[12] Berg, "Women's Work"; Neil McKendrick, "Home Demand and Economic Growth: A New View of the Role of Women and Children in the Industrial Revolution," in McKendrick, ed., *Historical Perspectives: Studies in English Thought and Society* (Europa, 1974), pp. 152–210.

[13] Ruth Smith and Deborah Valenze argue that working women in the early-nineteenth-century cottage economy perceived their identity as constituted through mutual and interdependent relations (both communal and familial) and strove to maintain those relations, rather than to extend their rights as individuals. Their perception that wage earning and domestic work were equally part of their roles as mother, wife, daughter, or sister was irreconcilable with liberal theory, which presumed a strict separation of the market and the home and could define these women only as "dependents." Smith and Valenze argue that, by midcentury, working-class men had come to accept the liberal view, and certainly many historians concur that the egalitarian politics of the Owenite and Chartist periods, itself linked to artisanal and familial relations of production, had given way by midcentury to a more defensive masculine politics located less in political movements than in a union culture premised on the exclusion of women. Working-class women's own theories of selfhood and obligation remained much the same, Smith and Valenze argue, but their actions were restricted to a smaller sphere. See Smith and Valenze, "Mutuality and Marginality: Liberal Moral Theory and Working-Class Women in Nineteenth-Century England," *Signs*, 13: 2 (1988), pp. 277–98; and, on the decline of egalitarian radicalism, Dorothy Thompson, "Women and Nineteenth-Century Radical Politics: A Lost Dimension," in Mitchell and Oakley, eds., *The Rights and Wrongs of Women*, pp. 112–38; Taylor, *Eve and the New Jerusalem*; Catherine Hall, "The Tale of Samuel and Jemima: Gender and Working-Class Culture in Early

lenges through retrenchment rather than reform: convinced that the market would sort out the self-reliant from the shirkers, it absolved itself of the responsibility to aid the able-bodied with the reform of the poor law in 1834, and with the repeal of the Corn Laws Parliament implied that the state would no longer shelter the landed interest from such character-building competition either. Responsibility for the sick or dependent was to be borne in the first instance by the other family members – an obligation that extended in law across three generations, and that the state made little attempt to mitigate.[14] By the Victorian period, the prevailing opinion was that the state should do no more than, as Pat Thane puts it, "provid[e] a framework within which individuals could become self-supporting actors within the natural order."[15] When social reformers did convince Parliament to intervene, it was less to interfere with the market than to protect those deemed too "dependent" to withstand its rigors. Certainly conceptions of the appropriate roles of the sexes underlay such determinations: unlike in France, where early factory legislation applied only to children, from the 1840s British legislators and moralists considered women as well to be in need of special protection and began to restrict the hours of work of both groups.[16]

Out of economic development and political retrenchment was born

Nineteenth-Century England," in Tony Bennett et al., eds., *Popular Culture and Social Relations* (Milton Keynes: Open University Press, 1986), pp. 73–92.

[14] From 1601, the obligation to maintain extended across three generations, parents being obliged to support children, husbands their wives (and, from 1882, wives with independent property their destitute husbands), adults their aged parents, and grandparents their grandchildren; in 1834, unmarried mothers were accorded the responsibility to maintain their children. In practice, however, the enforcement of such obligations was rather uneven. See M. A. Crowther, "Family Responsibility and State Responsibility in Britain before the Welfare State," *Historical Journal*, 25: 1 (1982), pp. 131–45.

[15] Pat Thane, "Government and Society in England and Wales, 1750–1914," in F. M. L. Thompson, ed., *The Cambridge Social History of Britain, 1750–1950*, vol. 3 (Cambridge University Press, 1990), p. 18. Note also José Harris's statement that the aim of the Victorian state was "to provide a framework of rules and guidelines designed to enable society very largely to run itself"; Harris, "Society and the State in Twentieth-Century Britain," in ibid., p. 67.

[16] Child labor legislation in France is discussed later. For British legislation, see U. R. Q. Henriques, *Before the Welfare State: Social Administration in Early Industrial Britain* (London: Longman, 1979), pp. 66–116; and, comparatively, Gary Cross, *A Quest for Time: The Reduction of Work in Britain and France, 1840–1940* (Berkeley and Los Angeles: University of California Press, 1989). For discussions of how the gender ideals of reformers shaped labor legislation, see Jane Humphries, "Protective Legislation, the Capitalist State, and Working Class Men: The Case of the 1842 Mines Regulation Act," *Feminist Review*, 7 (Spring 1981), pp. 1–33; Robert Gray, "The Languages of Factory Reform in Britain, c. 1830–1860," in Joyce, ed., *The Historical Meanings of Work*, pp. 143–179.

what we might term the mid-Victorian sexual settlement, a paradigm for social stability focused around the figure of the respectable breadwinning male and sustained equally by an economy that began in the 1850s to provide enough jobs at "family" wages to make this ideal a reality for at least a substantial minority of working-class men and by reforms of the suffrage that admitted to citizenship those men who fulfilled the requirement of respectable householder status. David Levine characterizes the period from about 1875 to 1939 as "the breadwinner economy," in which not only labor markets but patterns of acculturation and identity became sharply segregated along gender lines.[17] Work was at the heart of male experience: the workshop provided for the socialization of boys, for the definition of the boundaries of respectability and skill, and for political mobilization. If after 1848 the "laws" of political economy were increasingly viewed as inescapable, working men in the second half of the nineteenth century responded by building up trade unions that accepted the market framework while at the same time attempting to win wages and conditions conducive to "manly independence." And what was the chief characteristic of the "independent" worker? It was not only the pursuit of a form of work that – unlike such "female" pursuits as domestic service – was free of the taint of personal subordination; more crucial, as Keith McClelland puts it, "was the belief that those who were independent and in possession of their 'manhood' were those able to maintain *dependents*."[18] Working men became independent agents and citizens by virtue of their support of women and children.

There is every evidence that working women defended their position as vigorously as they could, the history of many trades containing accounts of bitter "border disputes" between women and men.[19] From the census figures, however, it does seem clear that the sex segregation of the formal labor force and the exclusion of married women became a good deal more pronounced between 1860 and 1914. Women constituted about 30% of those designated by the census as "economically active" throughout the second half of the nineteenth century in Britain, as Table 1.1 shows, but they were proportionally underrepresented in all sectors except domestic service, an occupation that was itself considered a mark of dependent status and, not sur-

---

[17] Levine, *Reproducing Families*, pp. 179–80.
[18] Keith McClelland, "Time to Work, Time to Live: Some Aspects of Work and the Reformation of Class in Britain, 1850–1880," in Joyce, ed., *The Historical Meanings of Work*, p. 206.
[19] See especially the excellent essays collected in Angela John, ed., *Unequal Opportunities: Women's Employment in England, 1800–1918* (Oxford: Basil Blackwell, 1986).

Table 1.1. *Women workers as a percentage of the "economically active" population, by sector*

Date[a]	Agriculture/ fishing		Industry/ transport		Commerce/ banking		Services[b]		All sectors	
	Br.	Fr.	Br.	Fr.	Br.	Fr.	Br.	Fr.	Br.	Fr.
1861/1866	8	30	26	28	1	33	60	40	31	31
1881/1886	7	33	24	30	3	36	55	41	30	34
1901/1906	6	38	22	33	11	40	56	43	29	37
1911	7	38	22	33	18	41	56	41	30	37

[a] British figures are for the first date cited in each case; French figures are for the second.

[b] Services include domestic, professional, civil, and military services, thus incorporating for France a standing army of as many as 500,000 men. Workers whose occupation is listed as "other" in British records (including homeworkers and the self-employed) have been incorporated into this category.

Source: Figures are calculated from government statistics given in B. R. Mitchell, *European Historical Statistics* (1975; rev. ed., New York: Facts on File, 1981).

Table 1.2. *Distribution of "economically active" men and women, Britain*

Date	Agriculture/fishing		Industry/transport		Services/trade	
	Men	Women	Men	Women	Men	Women
1861	25	5	58	45	17	50
1881	18	3	60	44	23	53
1901	12	2	66	45	22	53
1911	12	2	67	46	22	52

Note: Figures are percentages of all employed men or all employed women.
Source: See Table 1.1.

prisingly, appropriate preparation for marriage.[20] Their distribution did not mirror the distribution of male workers, as in France; rather, as Table 1.2 shows, whereas two-thirds of all male workers were concentrated in industry and transport by 1911, more than one-half of all women workers were in the service sector. Marked by their concentration into dependent work, women workers were also marked by their youth: young people of both sexes remained absolutely central

[20] Leonore Davidoff, "Mastered for Life: Servant and Wife in Victorian and Edwardian England," *Journal of Social History*, 8: 4 (Summer 1974), pp. 406–28. But for some idea of how such norms could be challenged, see Liz Stanley, ed., *The Diaries of Hannah Cullwick, Victorian Maidservant* (New Brunswick, N.J.: Rutgers University Press, 1974).

Table 1.3. *Labor force participation rates by age and sex, 1911*

	Men		Women	
Age	England/Wales	France	England/Wales	France
14–15	74	—	48	—
16–17	92	81[a]	69	57[a]
18–19	96	—	74	—
20–24	97	95	62	58
25–34	99	95	34	53
35–44	98	95	24	52
45–54	97	94	23	52
55–64	90	87	20	46
65–74	64	n.a.	14	n.a.

[a] Ages 15–19.
Sources: Maurice Garden, "L'évolution de la population active," in Jacques Dupâquier, ed., *Histoire de la population française*, vol. 3, *De 1789 à 1914* (Paris: Presses Universitaires de France, 1988), p. 256; Census of England and Wales, 1931, *General Report* (London: HMSO, 1950), p. 163.

to the labor market, their wages – especially those of daughters – often given directly to their mothers. As Table 1.3 shows, while labor force participation rates declined only gradually with age in France, participation rates for British women fell sharply around the age of 25. It was *married* women in particular who moved out of the formal labor market in Britain during the course of the nineteenth century: in 1851, 25% of married women were still officially classified as "occupied"; by 1901, that figure had fallen to 10%, and fully 77% of all women wage earners were single.[21] If married women did maintain a position as skilled workers in some regions and particular trades, they clung to such work in the face of a labor market skewed against them and a dominant discourse of the deleterious effects of their work on the sobriety of their husbands, the health of their children, and their own morality.[22]

[21] For figures on married women and a careful exposition of the classifications and methods used in the census, see Catherine Hakim, "Census Reports as Documentary Evidence: The Census Commentaries, 1801–1951," *Sociological Review*, 28: 3 (Aug. 1980), pp. 551–80.

[22] A good account of the Victorian panic over married women's work in the textile trades, including proposals for their legal exclusion, is provided by Margaret Hewitt, *Wives and Mothers in Victorian Industry* (1958; rpt. Westport, Conn.: Greenwood, 1975). A survey of women's work in Birmingham undertaken by Edward Cadbury, M. Cécile Matheson, and George Shann immediately before the war still found that the husbands of working

The census figures are, of course, problematic guides to women's work experience, not only because they overlook a good deal of casual, seasonal, or occasional earning by women, but also because the very categories used by the census assumed a clear distinction between "occupied" wage earners and "unoccupied" housewives, whereas, as historians have shown, many working-class women moved in and out of the labor market, seeing both their housework and their wage earning less as "individual" occupations than as temporary strategies dictated by family needs.[23] The role of household manager and mother, and not primarily that of wage earner, lay at the heart of many – if by no means all – working-class women's lives. Mothers were the nexus of the complex system of negotiations and obligations by which working-class families survived: when it came to ensuring the family's well-being, Florence Bell concluded in her 1907 study of ironworkers' families in Middlesborough (where there was almost no work available for women): "The husband's steadiness and capacity to earn are not more important than the wife's administration of the earnings."[24] Wives not only bore the responsibility for managing on whatever their husbands gave them, they also upheld the family's status in the eyes of the community and trained up children to contribute to the family's support.[25]

There was little need for state intervention in this picture, at least in theory. Social initiatives were in any case left largely to the localities, whose responsibility to finance relief deepened their preference for limited intervention. What the localities relied on, of course, was the

women were more likely to be "unsteady and drunken" and their children sickly and irregular in their school attendance than the husbands and children of unwaged housewives; see Cadbury et al., *Women's Work and Wages: A Phase of Life in an Industrial City* (London: T. Fisher Unwin, 1909), esp. pp. 210–30.

[23] For work by women that tended to escape the census, see especially Leonore Davidoff, "The Separation of Home and Work? Landladies and Lodgers in Nineteenth- and Twentieth-Century England," in Berman, ed., *Fit Work for Women*, pp. 64–97. Both Diana Gittins and Elizabeth Roberts offer sensitive accounts of working–class women's perceptions of their roles as housewives and their use of wage earning as another strategy for family survival. See Gittins, "Marital Status, Work and Kinship, 1850–1930," in Jane Lewis, ed., *Labour and Love: Women's Experience of Home and Family, 1850–1940* (Oxford: Basil Blackwell, 1986), pp. 223–48; Roberts, *A Woman's Place: An Oral History of Working-Class Women, 1890–1940* (Oxford: Basil Blackwell, 1984), pp. 110–68.

[24] Lady Bell, *At the Works: A Study of a Manufacturing Town* (1907; rpt. London: Virago, 1985), p. 182.

[25] Ellen Ross, "'Fierce Questions and Taunts': Married Life in Working-Class London," *Feminist Studies*, 8: 3 (Fall 1982), pp. 575–602; see also idem, "Labour and Love: Rediscovering London's Working-Class Mothers, 1870–1918," in Lewis, ed., *Labour and Love*, pp. 73–96.

proliferating network of voluntary and philanthropic services – off-shoots of the religious and moralizing imperatives everywhere present in Victorian society – which by the 1890s had come to "employ" some one-half million unpaid women.[26] Yet the principles underlying both poor relief and philanthropy remained, at least ideally, those of 1834: when confronted by poverty, both Poor Law Guardians and philanthropic visitors saw their first task as that of restoring the family's capacity (or, they often felt, the will) for self-support – a responsibility that they ascribed, in the case of dependent children, in the first instance to the father but extended in his absence or incapacity to the mother or even the grandparents as well.[27] When intervention was justified, it was to enforce the family's own obligations to its more vulnerable members. John Stuart Mill, for example, had always admitted that the state was obliged to protect children. "Parental power is as susceptible of abuse as any other power, and is, as a matter of fact, constantly abused," he wrote in the *Principles of Political Economy*. "Whatever it can be clearly seen that parents ought to do or forbear for the interests of their children, the law is warranted, if it is able, in compelling to be done or forborne, and is generally bound to do so."[28] There was a large gulf, however, between the claim that the state could legitimately intervene to enforce parental responsibilities and the argument that the state should displace parents to fulfill those responsibilities itself, and this was a line that few argued should be crossed during the Victorian period.

We have seen how the gendered separation of spheres and the freedom of the family from state intervention came to be seen as the

[26] Louisa Hubbard gave this estimate of the number of women working "continuously and semi-professionally" as philanthropic volunteers in an essay published in 1893, quoted in Frank Prochaska, "Philanthropy," in F. M. L. Thompson, ed., *The Cambridge Social History of Britain*, vol. 3 (Cambridge University Press, 1990), p. 385; Prochaska calls philanthropy "the taproot of female emancipation in the nineteenth century" (p. 386). See also his *Women and Philanthropy in 19th Century England* (Oxford University Press, 1980).

[27] Some of the Victorian Boards of Guardians recognized the difficulties that fatherless families would have maintaining themselves, but in the 1870s, under pressure from the Local Government Board, local authorities limited such women's access to outdoor relief as well. See Gareth Stedman Jones, *Outcast London*, 2d ed. (New York: Pantheon, 1984), p. 275; Pat Thane, "Women and the Poor Law in Victorian and Edwardian England," *History Workshop Journal*, 6 (Autumn 1978), pp. 38–9; Michael Rose, *The Relief of Poverty, 1834–1914* (London: Macmillan, 1972), p. 40; and, on the rationalization of charity, Charles Loch Mowat, *The Charity Organisation Society, 1869–1913* (London: Methuen, 1961).

[28] John Stuart Mill, *Principles of Political Economy* (1848; rpt. Harmondsworth: Penguin, 1985), p. 323.

guarantor of both bourgeois virtue and a stable working class. By the end of the century, however, this sexual settlement had come into question, in part because of the rise of the feminist movement, but also as part of the growing crisis of liberal values at the end of the century. The spreading revolt against domesticity among middle-class women during the last third of the century was driven in part by the claim of single women to callings and careers outside the domestic sphere,[29] and in part by the moralizing impulse at the heart of "separate spheres" ideology itself, but by the end of the century it had also become a revolt against the very gender ideals at the heart of the Victorian settlement. In the 1880s and 1890s, feminists developed a powerful critique of marriage as, essentially, "legalized prostitution." They argued that women, denied the right to earn their living, were reduced to contracting their person for support, while men, bound by no such constraints, took advantage of a double standard of sexual morality.[30]

For twenty-five years, these arguments formed the theoretical basis for feminist campaigns for work, the vote, and a single standard of sexual morality. In her 1909 book *Marriage as a Trade*, the actress, playwright, and suffragette Cicely Hamilton argued that the artificial limitation of women to the "trade" of marriage had stunted their character and prevented their intellectual growth.[31] Suffragist Ada Nield Chew similarly argued that the claim that women were maintained by their husbands in return for housework was belied by the fact that those who worked hardest were in fact paid the least and merely disguised the bald truth that the wife "is 'kept' for the sexual satisfaction of her husband, and earns her living by selling her sex, just as does her outcast sister of the streets."[32] A contract exchanging maintenance for exclusive sexual access was an immoral one, argued Dora Marsden's ultraegalitarian paper, the *Freewoman*, but if women wished to free themselves from sexual slavery, they must also abjure

---

[29] See, in particular, Martha Vicinus, *Independent Women: Work and Community for Single Women, 1850–1920* (London: Virago, 1985).

[30] On the feminist critique of marriage, see Susan Kingsley Kent, *Sex and Suffrage in Britain, 1860–1914* (Princeton, N.J.: Princeton University Press, 1987), pp. 80–113; Lucy Bland, "Marriage Laid Bare: Middle-Class Women and Marital Sex, 1880s-1914," in Lewis, ed., *Labour and Love*, pp. 122–46; Judith R. Walkowitz, "Male Vice and Feminist Virtue: Feminism and the Politics of Prostitution in Nineteenth-Century Britain," *History Workshop Journal*, 13 (Spring 1982), pp. 79–93.

[31] Cicely Hamilton, *Marriage as a Trade* (1909; rpt. London: Women's Press, 1981).

[32] Ada Nield Chew, "The Economic Freedom of Women," *Freewoman*, 2: 35 (13 July 1912), p. 167.

their parasitic claim to maintenance.[33] Only work – or, as Olive Schreiner put it, the claim of "all labour for our province" – would restore women's bodily integrity and make equal relations between the sexes possible.[34]

Motherhood posed something of a problem for feminists, especially when eugenicists began attacking the celibate woman as a particularly egregious form of shirker. As early as 1889 the left-leaning "sex radical" and self-proclaimed "feminist" Grant Allen insisted that women's emancipation "must not be of the sort that interferes in any way with this prime natural necessity...that most women must become the mothers of at least four children, or else the race must cease to exist," and twenty years later worried eugenicists were still arguing that the "best women" must be willing to accept "the necessary and wholesome restrictions and responsibilities of normal marriage and motherhood."[35] Middle-class women who had always claimed that their emancipation would serve broader social ends were particularly susceptible to such rhetoric and usually retorted that women did and would continue to desire children, provided that their maternity was "voluntary" and not forced on them by their "inability to earn [their] bread by any other trade but marriage."[36] Mabel Atkinson and Wilma Meikle both assured nervous eugenicists that the feminists of the immediate prewar period were not the "embittered...cranks" or "pathetic" "superfluous women" of the Victorian period, but rather healthy – and above all *married* – women who would be able to combine careers with motherhood.[37] They planned not to trade marriage

[33] "The Immorality of the Marriage Contract," *Freewoman*, 11: 31 (20 June, 1912), pp. 81–3.

[34] Olive Schreiner, *Woman and Labour* (1911; rpt. London: Virago, 1978), p. 195.

[35] Grant Allen, "Plain Words on the Woman Question," *Fortnightly Review*, 46: 274 (Oct. 1889), pp. 450–1; the second quotation is from W. C. D. Whetham and Catherine Whetham, *The Family and the Nation* (London: Longmans, Green, 1909), p. 199. On the difficult confrontation of feminism and eugenics, see Judith R. Walkowitz, "Science, Feminism and Romance: The Men and Women's Club, 1885–1889," *History Workshop Journal*, 21 (Spring 1986), pp. 37–59; Jeffrey Weeks, *Sex, Politics and Society* (London: Longman, 1981), pp. 122–40; Richard Allen Soloway, "Feminism, Fertility and Eugenics in Victorian and Edwardian England," in Seymour Drescher et al., eds., *Political Symbolism in Modern Europe* (London: Transaction Books, 1982), pp. 121–45.

[36] Hamilton, *Marriage*, p. 148; Ethel Snowden, *The Feminist Movement* (London: Collins [1913]), pp. 15, 189; Helena Swanwick, *The Future of the Women's Movement* (London: G. Bell & Sons, 1913), p. 22.

[37] Wilma Meikle, *Towards a Sane Feminism* (London: Grant Richards, 1916), p. 88; Mabel Atkinson, "The Feminist Movement and Eugenics," *Sociological Review*, 3: 1 (Jan. 1910), p. 51; see also Beatrice Webb, "Personal Rights and the Woman's Movement. II. The Falling Birth-Rate," *New Statesman*, 3: 66 (11 July 1914), pp. 428–30.

for a career, as an earlier generation had been forced to do, but to reconcile economic equality and personal autonomy with marriage itself. The feminist revolt against "parasitism" thus made the economic condition of wives and mothers central to all debates over the condition of the family at the end of the century. But was the feminist panacea of freedom through work relevant to working-class mothers? Clementina Black of the Women's Industrial Council, who edited a survey of married women's work before the war, insisted that skilled and well-paid married women did indeed value the personal independence gained by their work while also being conspicuously successful wives and mothers,[38] but as other investigators pointed out, most married women could command only unskilled jobs, usually had trouble finding those, and were, in any case, already "fully occupied" with their work in the home.[39] As the Fabian Mabel Atkinson noted, the revulsion from parasitism felt by a propertied woman sheltered by servants and maids from hard physical labor might seem rather remote to the working-class housewife, who felt that she had rather too much work to do and entirely too little help.[40] B. L. Hutchins, also a Fabian and the author of several books on women in industry, likewise pointed out that the "individualistic" ideals of modern feminism overlooked the fact that many women did wish to marry and to raise children, and that these goals were often hard to reconcile with wage earning. The problem was not that many mothers were "parasitic," but that their work had no value in a market economy. As she pointed out:

> The central difficulty of the woman's question seems to be the fact
> that, however hard a woman may work at unpaid service in her

[38] Clementina Black, ed., *Married Women's Work* (London: G. Bell & Sons, 1915), pp. 1–15. For some evidence that weaving couples had more egalitarian marriages than couples in which the wife had been a domestic servant before marriage, see Diana Gittins, *Fair Sex: Family Size and Structure in Britain, 1900–1939* (New York: St. Martin's, 1982), pp. 95–107; for a similar argument for teachers, see Dina M. Copelman, "'A New Comradeship between Men and Women': Family, Marriage and London's Women Teachers, 1870–1914," in Lewis, ed., *Labour and Love*, pp. 175–93.

[39] When Eleanor Rathbone surveyed forty families of casual workers in Liverpool around the turn of the century, she also found that while sixteen of the wives did bring some money into the house and even those with young children wanted to take on more work, the almost complete lack of demand for their unskilled services meant that only six of the total number earned more than a "trifling" sum; see Rathbone, *How the Casual Labourer Lives* (Liverpool: Northern Publishing Co., 1909), p. xiv.

[40] [Mabel Atkinson], *The Economic Foundations of the Women's Movement*, Fabian Tract no. 175 (London: Fabian Society, June 1914), p. 15.

home, if she has no money of her own she is formally dependent on another for support, although she may create use values equal to her maintenance many times over, and her position thus cannot be economically distinguished from that of the purely parasitic woman who lives only to spend what is given to her.[41]

The problem Hutchins outlined was not only debated by the intellectuals and reformers of the Fabian Women's Group; it also came to absorb working women's organizations before the war. The very phrase "working women" – which I use here deliberately – is significant, since this was the phrase used by those organizations of working-class housewives, usually unwaged, that developed within and alongside the labor movement around the end of the century. As we have seen, the effective marginalization of married women in the labor market did mean that working-class women's identity turned heavily on their role as homemakers. They continued to see this role as a form of "work," however, and thus objected less to the sexual and domestic division of labor, as such, than to the fact that what they did do was often overlooked and inadequately rewarded. Far from seeing themselves as "parasites," the egalitarian members of the Women's Cooperative Guild stated at their 1910 congress that "the wife contributes by her work in the family equally with the husband," and that therefore "some form of economic independence should be legally assured to [her]."[42] The rise of feminism within a working-class culture already convinced of the centrality of women's domestic work to family welfare thus gave strength to a new demand: women would be mothers but must be granted a measure of economic independence.

It was from this position that state intervention came up for discussion. In the period immediately before the war, politically active women conducted a lively debate among themselves over whether endowment, wage earning, or the legal enforcement of a wife's right to maintenance would best ensure the economic independence of the working-class housewife. Many social workers and feminists supported the proposal to give married women a legal claim to some portion of their husbands' pay. This solution found favor with the settlement worker Anna Martin, who in a series of influential articles in the *Nineteenth Century and After* wrote that working-class women's primary complaint was their inability to enforce their theoretical right

[41] B. L. Hutchins, *Conflicting Ideals: Two Sides of the Woman's Question* (London: T. Murby, 1913), p. 53.
[42] Women's Cooperative Guild, *28th Annual Report* (1911), p. 27.

to maintenance.[43] Some socialist women active in the Fabian Women's Group and the Independent Labour Party, by contrast, tended to support endowment for mothers when children were small, and waged work at other times.[44] Finally, a few feminists, socialists, and sex radicals envisaged complete state support for mothers, a plan that would have entirely decoupled motherhood and economic dependence.[45] H. G. Wells – through the media of several socialist pamphlets, the novels *Ann Veronica* (1909), *The New Machiavelli* (1911), and *Marriage* (1912), and a controversy in the *Freewoman* in 1912 – was probably the most notorious advocate, although his claim that endowment would replace "the irresponsible man-ruled family" with "the matriarchal family [and] the citizenship and freedom of women" probably did little to win over respectable opinion to the cause.[46] And

---

[43] Anna Martin, "The Mother and Social Reform," *Nineteenth Century and After*, I, 73: 435 (May 1913), pp. 1060–79; II, 73: 436 (June 1913), pp. 1235–55. Clementina Black also supported this proposal, as did Lady Laura McLaren, who tried to have it adopted by the Women's Liberal Federation. See Black, ed., *Married Women's Work*, p. 14; Laura McLaren, *The Woman's Charter of Rights and Liberties* (London: John Sewell, 1909). The real difficulties experienced by women in enforcing their claim to maintenance *without* taking the drastic step of leaving their husbands are explored in Iris Minor, "Working Class Women and Matrimonial Law Reform, 1890–1914," in David E. Martin and David Rubinstein, eds., *Ideology and the Labour Movement* (London: Croom Helm, 1979), pp. 103–24; and for the development of the law on separation and maintenance, see Morris Finer and O. R. MacGregor, "The History of the Obligation to Maintain," app. 5 of the *Report of the Commission on One-Parent Families, PP* 1974, XVI, pp. 104–8.

[44] This point of view is found in Atkinson, *Economic Foundations*, pp. 19–22, and Maud Pember Reeves and Mrs. C. M. Wilson, "A Policy for Women Workers," *New Statesman*, special supplement entitled "Women in Industry," 2: 46 (21 Feb. 1914), pp. xii–xiv.

[45] This idea was not always defended in particularly feminist terms. Ethel Snowden, for example, seemed to be thinking more of the interests of "children" or "society" than of the self-determination of women when she wrote that however useful a year or so of maternity benefit would be, "it would be better still if women could be kept at home altogether until their children themselves are working for money"; Snowden, *The Feminist Movement*, p. 217. The Fabian Society as a whole did exhibit a good deal of interest in schemes of "motherhood endowment" but often tended to envisage these in terms of extended social services for mothers and (especially) for children, rather than in terms of cash benefits to increase mothers' independence. For Fabian attitudes, see Henry Harben, *The Endowment of Motherhood* (London: Fabian Society, Mar. 1910); Sidney Webb and Beatrice Webb, "What Is Socialism? XIV. Protection for the Child," *New Statesman*, 1: 14 (12 July 1913), pp. 430–2; "Pensions for Mothers," *New Statesman*, 1: 13 (5 July 1913), pp. 394–5.

[46] The quotation is from H. G. Wells, *The New Machiavelli* (London: John Lane, 1911), p. 411. Wells also presented his position in *Socialism and the Family* (London: A. C. Fifield, 1906), *New Worlds for Old* (1908; rpt. New York: Macmillan, 1919), and "Mr. Wells to the Attack: Freewomen and Endowment," *Freewoman*, 1: 15

such ideas remained controversial among feminists: Wells's proposal to use endowment to encourage the propagation of the "fit" and to entrust its administration to medical experts and civil servants was rebuffed by "freewomen" unwilling to consign women to a primarily domestic role, however rewarded, or to entrust the supervision and payment of these mothers to a state that, after all, was still force-feeding suffragettes. State insurance could reasonably be used to cover women's absence from work during confinements, argued the *Freewoman*, but in no case should women be paid simply to stay at home and breed.[47] As Ada Nield Chew retorted, "Women *cannot* live individual lives and develop on individual lines whilst nearly all are forced to follow one occupation, and are dependent for a livelihood either on men or on State endowment."[48] Women's independence, honor, and social development depended on their participation in waged work; housework and child care should be professionalized, not endowed.

I have dwelt at some length on the arguments over marriage and motherhood within prewar feminism and socialism not because these groups articulated dominant views, but rather because their shared concern to reconcile women's claims to personal rights and economic independence with the health and well-being of children led them to envisage an unprecedented degree of state intervention in the family and because their concerns would remain central to the policy agenda (if not its outcomes) for half a century. Out of these fin-de-siècle debates emerged a tentative coalition of egalitarian socialists and left-leaning feminists, heavily concentrated in the Fabian Society, the National Union of Women's Suffrage Societies, the Women's Cooperative Guild, and the Independent Labour Party, which would be the main bearer of family policy ideas and campaigns in the interwar period. Whatever their future quarrels, all of these groups agreed that if the state were to address the problems of familial dependence, the needs of unwaged wives would have to be considered as well. Yet as we shall see, the fact that child policy was from the outset hostage

(29 Feb. 1912). For another sex-radical program, see Dr. M. D. Eder, *The Endowment of Motherhood* (London: New Age Press, 1908).

47 "Women Endowed," *Freewoman*, 1: 17 (14 Mar. 1912).

48 Ada Nield Chew, "Mother Interest and Child Training," *Freewoman*, 1: 16 (7 Mar. 1912); see also her rejection of both the endowment of motherhood and the proposal to give working-class women a legal claim on their husbands' pay as attempts by middle-class women to foist on poorer women "the ideal of the domestic-tabby-cat-woman," which they had themselves discarded, in "The Problem of the Married Working Women," *Common Cause*, 5: 255 (27 Feb. 1914), pp. 909–10.

to the intent to emancipate wives would cause grave difficulties in the future.

If women had provided the only critique of the Victorian sexual settlement, fin-de-siècle politicians might have been tempted to avoid the question, but by the end of the century there were other cracks in the male breadwinner model of family maintenance as well. As many historians have noted, the Boer War, German economic rivalry, and the nagging fear that Britain was losing its imperial hegemony led a coterie of intellectuals and politicians across party lines to fear that laissez-faire might not have been the best spur to either economic efficiency or "race betterment" and fostered a new concern about the health and well-being of children.[49] Social surveys, coming into their own in the same period, had an equally disquieting effect. Men like Charles Booth and Seebohm Rowntree, themselves raised on the assumptions of political economy and in the methods of the Charity Organisation Society, were distressed to find that a very substantial proportion of those below even the most stringent "poverty line" were there not because of "degeneracy" or some moral failing, but rather simply because wages were too low to meet their and their family's needs. Worse, Rowntree's specification of a familial "poverty cycle" showed that poverty was worst during the years in which a couple had several young and dependent children – or, in other words, that young children suffered disproportionately the effects of poverty.[50] Revelations of the extent of unemployment, underemployment, and casual labor made Victorian complacency about the market's capacity for self-regulation and the family's responsibility for self-reliance seem equally dated.

The entry of such questions into the realm of political debate was, in the first instance, part of the broader politicization of social policy in the period between 1884 and 1914. As José Harris has shown, a number of factors, especially worsening crises of local taxation and

---

[49] On the connections between ideas of national efficiency and social reform, see G. D. Searle, *The Quest for National Efficiency* (Oxford: Basil Blackwell, 1971); Bernard Semmel, *Imperialism and Social Reform* (Cambridge, Mass.: Harvard University Press, 1960); and, for maternal and infant policies in particular, Anna Davin, "Imperialism and Motherhood," *History Workshop Journal*, 5 (Spring 1978), pp. 9–65; Jane Lewis, *The Politics of Motherhood* (London: Croom Helm, 1980); Deborah Dwork, *War Is Good for Babies and Other Young Children* (London: Tavistock, 1987).

[50] Booth found in 1887 that more than 30% of the East London population had an income inadequate to maintain them; Rowntree's study of York in 1889 found 28% of the population in the same condition. Booth's and Rowntree's findings are summarized in Michael Rose, *The Relief of Poverty, 1834–1914* (London: Macmillan, 1972), pp. 15–17, 27–30.

national finance, made social policy a question of "high politics" and convinced politicians to shift its cost very largely onto the national state.[51] To say this is not to discount, of course, the continued purchase of nineteenth-century ideals and practices. Virtually all political actors admitted that the family remained the principal source of support and care for dependent members and insisted that the state neither could nor should replace such functions: indeed, as late as the thirties, the policies of the National Government – including the despised "means test" – were aimed at enforcing that obligation to maintain.[52] What many began to question, however, was the presumption that state intervention *inevitably* "demoralized" families – that families were weak and perverted wherever they relied on state aid, as Helen Bosanquet of the Charity Organisation Society put it in 1906.[53] But if the COS continued to cling to the "principles of 1834," the Liberal landslide of 1906 gave the edge to those politicians and reformers who were convinced that the relief of poverty and the "uplift" of working-class family life would require some measure of state intervention.

There was little agreement, however, on the proper form of such intervention or on the principles on which it should be based. Should the government concentrate on reworking the labor market in order better to enable men to support their families, limiting direct assistance to women and children to cases in which the man was unable to work? Or should the needs of children be addressed directly, through universal services and benefits that would assist (or, critics charged, replace) parents in their struggle to maintain? Or, finally, should assistance to families be channeled primarily toward mothers, who had, feminists tended to argue, the greatest responsibility for children but often the least recognition and the smallest resources? These approaches were not seen to be incompatible in the prewar period, and we can find some evidence of all three approaches in the social legislation of the 1906–14 period. In the long run, policymakers would have to choose between rival approaches, but they would do so under conditions which they could not yet imagine.

Given the centrality of male breadwinner ideals to the mid-Victorian settlement, it is unsurprising that many of the politicians and reformers associated with the "new liberalism" sought to address the prob-

---

[51] José Harris, "The Transition to High Politics in English Social Policy, 1880–1914," in Michael Bentley and John Stevenson, eds., *High and Low Politics in Modern Britain* (Oxford University Press, 1983), pp. 58–79.
[52] Crowther, "Family Responsibility," p. 135.
[53] Helen Bosanquet, *The Family* (London: Macmillan, 1906), pp. 339–40, 313.

lems of poor families not by rejecting such ideals but rather by placing them on a new and more stable foundation. "New Liberals" remained committed to ideals of individual effort and free competition: where they differed from their Victorian predecessors was in their acknowledgment of the degree to which an unregulated economy and political indifference could pervert and constrain such efforts. Thus, although they envisaged an unprecedented degree of positive state action, such action was intended to enable rather than to replace individual effort. The philosopher L. T. Hobhouse expressed this viewpoint well when he explained in 1911 that while the state should not actually "feed, house or clothe" its citizens, it should "take care that the economic conditions are such that the normal man who is not defective in mind or body or will can by useful labour feed, house, and clothe himself *and his family*."[54]

The great welfare reforms introduced by the last Liberal government can be seen as an attempt to fulfill these principles of state action. The story of the establishment of the labor exchanges (1909) and of national insurance (1911) has been told many times;[55] what is significant for our story is that these reforms did set in motion a process whereby a man's role as family breadwinner – and hence the practice of providing for children through the male wage – would be guaranteed through "honorable" social entitlements and not coerced by threats of punitive action alone. William Beveridge, Sidney Webb and Beatrice Webb, Winston Churchill, and other progressive reformers hoped to rationalize the functioning of the labor market and "decasualize" the work force: exchanges would enable workers to find employment more readily, while insurance would tide workers over brief spells of unemployment in those trades especially vulnerable to such fluctuations.[56]

These policies were directed largely at working men; indeed, efforts to "rationalize" the labor market or to tie entitlements to labor market status could not but marginalize women, whose relation to work was

---

[54] L. T. Hobhouse, *Liberalism* (1911; rpt. Westport, Conn.: Greenwood, 1980), p. 83; my emphasis. On "new liberalism" generally, see Michael Freeden, *The New Liberalism* (Oxford University Press, 1978).

[55] See especially José Harris, *Unemployment and Politics: A Study in English Social Policy, 1886–1914* (Oxford University Press, 1972); Bentley Gilbert, *The Evolution of National Insurance in Great Britain* (London: Michael Joseph, 1966); J. R. Hay, *The Origins of the Liberal Welfare Reforms, 1906–1914* (London: Macmillan, 1975).

[56] On this point, see especially Noelle Whiteside, "Welfare Insurance and Casual Labour: A Study of Administrative Intervention in Industrial Employment, 1906–26," *Economic History Review*, 2d ser., 32: 4 (Nov. 1979), pp. 507–22.

often more casual. By July 1914, some 2.3 million workers were insured against unemployment; 63% of this group was skilled, and it included almost no women.[57] Health insurance, being work related, also disproportionately benefited men; while some 700,000 women workers were covered by 1914, they – unlike their husbands – lost the benefit of contributions when they married. If they continued in work, they had to establish eligibility over again; if they left employment, their only health coverage became the maternity benefit for which they were eligible if married to an insured man.[58] Yet even if the insurance system benefited men more than women, it is important to remember that it was not intended at this stage to provide maintenance for an entire family or to replace the putative "family wage." Insurance benefits were paid only for limited periods of time, were strictly related to the numbers of contributions, were paid at levels well below subsistence, and did not include allowances for dependent family members.

Furthermore, while the "new liberal" labor reforms may have assumed that wage earning was normally an affair of men, the 1906 government did not ignore wage-earning women entirely, nor did they accede to John Burns's call for legislative restrictions on married women's work. One Liberal reform, the Trade Boards Act of 1909, attempted to spread the benefits of "decasualization" to women by regulating the wages of homeworkers directly. Action in this area was urged by an alliance of social reformers, labor leaders, and feminists distressed at the low pay and evil conditions suffered by women homeworkers, yet the debate they sparked also brought out the ambivalence felt by many labor leaders when confronted by married women's work. Ramsay MacDonald and Margaret MacDonald, for example, preferred government registration of homeworkers' premises to minimum wage legislation in the hopes such supervision would force the work into factories and equally force married women – "who really ought not to be in industrial work at all" – out of the labor market.[59]

The "new liberal" insurance policies broke with the Victorian legacy by recognizing that poverty could result from such unpredictable risks

[57] Pat Thane, *The Foundations of the Welfare State* (London: Longman, 1982), pp. 94–6.

[58] The treatment of women workers as a separate class was roundly criticized by feminists. See, e.g., "Problems of the Day: State Insurance," *Englishwoman*, 11: 1 (July 1911), pp. 13–19.

[59] Ellen F. Mappen, "Strategies for Change: Social Feminist Approaches to the Problem of Women's Work," in John, ed., *Unequal Opportunities*, p. 249; see also Duncan Bythell, *The Sweated Trades: Outwork in Nineteenth Century Britain* (New York: St. Martin's, 1978), pp. 244–5.

as ill health and unemployment rather than from vice, but the moral vision underlying these measures – a vision of a polity constructed around the figure of the responsible, breadwinning, male citizen – was based on a revision rather than a rejection of the Victorian heritage. It may have been the relative conservatism of the Liberals' social ideals that to some extent reconciled working people toward their plans, since, as Henry Pelling, Pat Thane, and James Cronin remind us, working people and their organizations were often and understandably skeptical of proposals for state intervention in social and family life. Ideals of "independence" and self-help had rooted themselves firmly in working-class culture and sustained working-class institutions. Many thus believed that unions and friendly societies could best insure workers against the risks of unemployment or ill health; almost all agreed that wage increases were a more reliable basis for family welfare than social policy innovations.[60] Thus, while the Trades Union Congress and the fledgling Labour Party did come to favor both old-age pensions and the unemployment provisions of the Liberals' insurance plans, their main political concerns remained the defense of unions' legal immunities and hence their freedom of operation, the struggle for "fair wages" – usually seen as a male wage capable of supporting a family – for workers in state and local government or on government contracts, and the expansion of public works programs to meet periods of unemployment.[61]

Measures aimed at rationalizing the labor market and forcing workers to insure themselves against periods of unemployment were not undertaken as family policies, but by targeting working men and strengthening their capacity to maintain, they can be seen as representing one approach to the problems of family dependence. A second possible approach can be detected in changing policies toward children, and especially in the gradual acceptance of the view that state aid to children need not destroy work incentives or "pauperize" families. Of course, the most important innovations in state policy toward children in the years before the war were hardly economic. Nevertheless, through the introduction of compulsory medical examination and with the establishment of a probationary and juvenile court system

[60] Henry Pelling, "The Working Class and the Origins of the Welfare State," in *Popular Politics and Society in Late Victorian Britain* (1968; 2d ed. London: Macmillan, 1979), pp. 1–18; Pat Thane, "The Working Class and State 'Welfare' in Britain, 1880–1914," *Historical Journal*, 27: 4 (1984), pp. 877–900; James E. Cronin, *The Politics of State Expansion: War, State and Society in Twentieth-Century Britain* (London: Routledge, 1991), pp. 37–44.

[61] Harris, *Unemployment and Politics*, pp. 235–44.

through the Children's Act of 1908 the state effectively accepted that its responsibility to children did justify a more serious curtailment of parental authority than hitherto admitted.[62] Yet while such reforms did recognize children as wards of the community and made parents liable for neglect, they did not really speak to the problem of child poverty or to the lack of fit between wages and family needs. Regulatory reforms or even policies aimed at increasing working-class access to such previously middle-class preserves as education and medical care were no alternative to universal wage or welfare benefits. As Eleanor Rathbone wrote years later:

> There is no real analogy between services such as education and medical inspection of schools and the provision of food and clothing. Before education and medical inspection were supplied free, the working class did not supply them out of wages; broadly speaking, they went without.[63]

Increased supervision of children could not solve the fundamental problem that male wages were not always adequate to meet family needs.

Social reformers and philanthropic visitors were well aware of this problem of course, but the proposal to aid children without reference to the father's work was always a controversial one. Concern for child health did drive both the Conservatives under Balfour and the Liberals after 1906 to mitigate the harshness of the treatment of fatherless children under the Poor Law: aid to children, they concluded, did not necessarily "pauperize" parents, nor should widows with young children be denied outdoor relief or be forced into wage earning if some help would enable them to care for their children in their own homes.[64] Yet many continued to feel that while the government could indeed tighten laws requiring parents to maintain and could ease treatment of fatherless children, any wider care or feeding of children would merely lessen parental responsibility and "demoralize" the population. Some of the charitable and social workers gathered at the

---

[62] George K. Behlmer, *Child Abuse and Moral Reform in England, 1870–1908* (Stanford, Calif.: Stanford University Press, 1982), p. 193; Maurice Bruce, *The Coming of the Welfare State*, 4th ed. (London: B. T. Batsford, 1968), pp. 225–6.

[63] Eleanor Rathbone, *The Disinherited Family* (London: Edward Arnold, 1924), p. 303.

[64] Thane, "Women and the Poor Law," pp. 44–6; idem, *Foundations*, pp. 79–80; Derek Fraser, *Evolution of the British Welfare State*, 2d ed. (London: Macmillan, 1984), p. 149. By 1914, of 235,000 children receiving poor relief, only 68,000 were in workhouses, while a full 108,000 were children of widows and deserted wives cared for in their own homes. Finer and MacGregor, "The History of the Obligation to Maintain," p. 121.

1905 conference of the National Union of Women Workers insisted that it was far more important to inculcate a sense of responsibility in working-class parents than to take the care of children out of their hands. Opposing the settlement worker Honnor Morten's call for state feeding of schoolchildren, one argued that "it is not *lack of food* from which the children suffer, but wrong food, bad housing and ventilation, want of personal cleanliness, irregularity of habits, insufficient sleep, and lastly, lack of self-control." "Ignorance on the part of mothers," she concluded, "is often at the bottom of the evil."[65]

By 1905, however, such opinions had become almost impossible to sustain. Collective feeding of schoolchildren had been a goal of many left-leaning organizations and local councillors from the 1880s, and after the evidence on "physical deterioration" thrown up by social investigation, government medical officers, and the Boer War, advocates turned for support to those not always motivated by "progressive" sentiments.[66] In 1904, T. J. Macnamara, a Liberal M.P., countered the charge that state provision of school meals and inspection amounted to "rank socialism" by saying that such measures were, "in reality, first-class imperialism": a healthy population would preserve Britain's world position against its European competitors.[67] Nor were socialists loath to seize on demographic or military fears to win support for their pleas for a "collectivization" of the costs of reproduction; Sidney Webb, for example, used statistics on the deliberate restriction of births to argue in favor of medical care, milk, and meals for mothers and babies.[68]

In 1906, the Liberal government responded to these voluntary precedents and pressures by inaugurating a measure of some importance for the history of family policy. The Education (Provision of Meals) Act of 1906 gave local authorities the power to provide meals to schoolchildren either free or at minimal cost, without requiring an investigation of dependence or an attempt to recover the cost from the parents. Historians have commonly seen the school meals act as

---

[65] Margaret Horn, "The Feeding of School Children," in National Union of Women Workers, *Conference* (1905), p. 165.

[66] On pressures leading up to the School Meals Act and controversy between progressives and the Charity Organisation Society, see Ellen Ross, "Hungry Children: Housewives and London Charity, 1870–1918," in Peter Mandler, ed., *The Uses of Charity* (Philadelphia: University of Pennsylvania Press, 1990), esp. pp. 175–86.

[67] T. J. Macnamara, "Physical Condition of Working-Class Children," *Nineteenth Century and After*, 56: 330 (Aug. 1904), p. 311.

[68] Sidney Webb, *The Decline of the Birth Rate*, Fabian Tract no. 131 (London: Fabian Society, Mar. 1907).

the first step in the construction of a welfare state built around the conception of universal entitlement. In Bentley Gilbert's words, "For the first time the State used its power on behalf of a particular segment of the population who were selected on the sole criterion that they were poor, who had rendered the State no service, who were afflicted by no contagious disease except the disease of poverty, and who finally were to suffer no penalty or disenfranchisement on account of the aid they received."[69] From our perspective, however, school meals were important less because they were granted without punitive tests than because they made the child's right to aid paramount, more important even than the father's responsibility to maintain. The introduction of school meals could thus be seen as a precedent for the disaggregation of family income and for further independent benefits for children.

The bill's advocates and authors, as well as the M.P.s who debated the measure in the spring of 1906, were well aware of the principles at stake. When the Liberal M.P. W. T. Wilson opened the debate on the second reading, he countered the expected objection that it was the parents' responsibility to feed their children by stating that low wages and "force of circumstances" in many cases rendered this impossible and state intervention necessary.[70] Yet Conservative and "old Liberal" members did dwell on the fear that state aid would undermine parental and especially paternal responsibility: as one Conservative member protested, it "took away the distinction between the parents who did their duty and those who did not."[71] Labour members equally predictably responded with evidence of wage rates well below the level necessary to maintain a single man, much less a family: if children were hungry, they argued, it was because a poorly ordered economic system left such wages uncorrected, and not because men were guilty of neglect. The bill passed easily, sustained by enthusiasm for the new government, even if some of the arguments made in its favor implied that in a "properly ordered" world decent wages would render such aid unnecessary.[72] With the introduction of a child tax allowance for lower-income taxpayers three years later, however, Liberals also recognized the claim of middle-income citizens to some relief for dependents – an innovation that campaigners for family allow-

---

[69] Gilbert, *The Evolution of National Insurance*, p. 116; see also Thane, *Foundations*, p. 75.

[70] 152 *H.C. Deb.*, 4th ser., 2 Mar. 1906, cols. 1390–1.

[71] Henry Craik, speaking during the second reading, ibid., col. 1403.

[72] For these debates, see ibid. cols. 1390–1448; 166 *H.C. Deb.*, 4th ser., 7 Dec. 1906, cols. 1315–466; also Freeden's *The New Liberalism*, pp. 224–9.

ances between the wars saw as a further precedent for cash allowances for those below the level of tax.

The philosophical differences between those who supported some measure of aid to hard-pressed families and those who believed in a "collectivization" of the costs of reproduction could be papered over in the case of children, but they became more intractable whenever a third proposal came up: the proposal to address the poverty of dependent women and children by providing benefits to mothers directly. As we have seen, the presence of highly organized feminist movements in Britain meant that proposals to aid "the family" inevitably led to claims that such aid be directed particularly toward mothers: the claims of women, both as citizens and as (in the language of their advocates) "working mothers," were from the outset part of the debate. Certainly many women's groups believed that improvements in the health and well-being of children could only be achieved if the state improved both the status and resources of the working-class housewife. The Fabian Women's Group, the Women's Cooperative Guild and the Women's Labour League all mounted campaigns before the war aimed at winning extended services and benefits for mothers directly, and while the Guild concentrated primarily on extending maternity services, the Fabian Women's Group tested the merits of paying cash benefits for children directly to mothers – a study later written up under the (now famous) title of *Round About a Pound a Week*.[73] Such benefits not only would begin to establish a set of rights and entitlements for mothers as citizens, but would also give unwaged housewives a measure of independence from their husbands.

Voluntary organizations, local authorities, and eventually the Local Government Board itself did begin to build up maternity services in the years before the war, but proposals to assist mothers through cash benefits – calling into question as they did the principle of the obligation to maintain and the status of the family as a haven of nonmarket mutuality in a world wracked by economic competition – remained

---

[73] Maud Pember Reeves, *Round About a Pound a Week* (1913; rpt. London: Virago, 1979). For women's campaigns around maternal and infant health, see Sally Alexander, Introduction to ibid.; Sheila Ferguson, "Labour Women and the Social Services," in Lucy Middleton, ed., *Women and the Labour Movement* (London: Croom Helm, 1977), pp. 38–56; Caroline Rowan, " 'Mothers, Vote Labour!' The State, the Labour Movement and Working-Class Mothers, 1900–1918," in Rosalind Brunt and Caroline Rowan, eds., *Feminism, Culture and Politics* (London: Lawrence & Wishart, 1982), pp. 59–84; Caroline Rowan, "Women in the Labour Party, 1906–1920," *Feminist Review*, 12 (1982), pp. 74–91; Jean Gaffin and David Thoms, *Caring and Sharing: The Centenary History of the Cooperative Women's Guild* (Manchester: Co-operative Union, Ltd., 1983).

highly controversial both for Liberals and within the working-class movement. On one occasion in 1913, however, Parliament did debate a proposal to give a cash benefit to working-class mothers. The question at hand was simply whether Parliament should amend the National Insurance Act of 1911 in such a way as to make the maternity benefit, for which insured women and the wives of insured men were eligible, payable in both cases to the woman herself. The sum at stake was small but significant – thirty shillings, or about a week's pay for a male manual worker – and a number of women's organizations, most notably the thirty-thousand-strong Women's Cooperative Guild, had been pressing the government to make the benefit payable by right to the wife.[74] The principles involved were difficult ones, however, and divided the House on somewhat unpredictable lines. In the end, the benefit was made payable to the wife through the support of many Conservatives and over the objections of much of the Labour Party.

Given the fact that men's citizenship status and respectability were both defined in terms of their responsibility to maintain, small wonder that the attempt to grant independent entitlements to women was perceived by some M.P.s as an attack on working men. And indeed, although those arguing for payment to women did reiterate their belief that the benefit would *generally* be safe in men's hands, the discussion did quickly degenerate into a quarrel over whether "the working classes" (meaning working-class men) were indeed "kind to their wives and families."[75] George Roberts (for Labour) and Charles Masterman (for the Liberals) agreed that the implication that working-class husbands could not be trusted with thirty shillings might cause, in Masterman's words, "a very great resentment among the working-class population."[76] If some few men would spend the money unwisely, the same might be true of some women, and as Roberts put it, "It would be a positive disaster for the State to set up irritating conditions between a man and his wife."[77] After all, Mr. Glyn-Jones (for Labour) pointed out, not only did the husband have a legal obligation to maintain, but even the contractual relationship on which insurance was based operated between the approved society administering benefit and the *husband*; to pay to the wife would thus break with the fun-

---

[74] Gaffin and Thoms, *Caring and Sharing*, pp. 69–71; Women's Cooperative Guild, *Annual Report*, 31 (1914), p. 23.
[75] 56 *H.C. Deb.*, 5th ser., 25 July 1913, col. 3118.
[76] Ibid., col. 3101.
[77] Ibid., col. 3102.

damental principle both of law and of insurance.[78] Just because there were "a few bad husbands," Roberts protested, there was no reason to pass "panic legislation against all husbands." The bill, he said, "legislates against a whole sex in the community," implying that "working-class husbands cannot be trusted to do the right thing towards their wives" and setting up "almost a position of war between the sexes."[79]

Supporters of payment to the wife tried to respond by stressing the wife's own claims. It was inappropriate to raise the specter of the woman wasting the money, since, Frederick Booth of the Liberals explained, "if she misspent it, after all she is misspending her own money; but if the man misspends it, he is misspending his wife's money, and that is all the difference in the world."[80] And Roberts's argument that the payment of a *woman's* benefit to the *woman* was "sex legislation," while the payment of the *woman's* benefit to the *man* was merely part of the natural order of things did not go unchallenged, even from within his own party. Philip Snowden, the future Labour chancellor, rather oddly accused Roberts of "belong[ing] to the Mosaic period" and "plac[ing] the man's wife in the same category as the man's ox and the man's ass."[81] John Ward, a trade unionist sitting as a Liberal, likewise objected to the implication that the wife was simply a "dependent"; rather, she was by her own work in the house "really earning part of the wages that the man actually receives."[82] The Liberal Cecil Beck concluded that men "whose pride of manhood is outraged by the fact that 30 [shillings] is conveyed directly to their wives . . . do not deserve the encouragement of this House."[83] Nor did they get it. After 1913, a man could collect the maternity benefit only if he had a signed authorization from his wife.

The thirty shillings handed out to the expectant wives of insured working men might seem a meager precedent for the "endowment of motherhood." Yet the debate in the House prefigures with almost eerie precision the later debates over family allowances or other benefits for mothers. Later supporters of entitlements for mothers would insist these need not be seen as an attack on working men; opponents would retort that since respectable men did maintain families, all social entitlements for these families should rightfully be channeled through men's hands. What is interesting, however, is that at this stage these

---

[78] Ibid., cols. 3105, 3161.
[79] Ibid., 6 Aug. 1913, cols. 1498–1504.
[80] Ibid., 25 July 1913, col. 3110.
[81] Ibid., 6 Aug. 1913, cols. 1532–3.
[82] Ibid., col. 1506.
[83] Ibid., col. 1507.

latter arguments were not so hegemonic as to convince the House that a *maternity* benefit should be paid to the husband.

In the end, the active debate over the allowable limits of state intervention in family life, and the emergence of an unsteady coalition of reformers at the interstices of the feminist and labor movements committed to increasing the entitlements of dependent mothers and children, did not push family policy development down a single track in the prewar period. Rather, a many-sided debate was matched by multiple and often-conflicting policies backed by shifting coalitions. No clear line of development in policy or political action is discernible. While Liberals and Labour could agree on the need to regulate the economy, and there was considerable support across political lines for improved social services for children, measures that threatened to undo men's breadwinner status by granting entitlements to unwaged mothers were far more controversial. In 1914, it was still unclear whether family policy would be restricted by the state's endorsement of the ideal of the male family wage (as suggested by "new liberal" insurance policies) or would proceed toward comprehensive entitlements for mothers and children (as suggested by school meals and maternity benefit).

Ultimately, as we shall see, the ability of campaigners and politicians to translate their visions of family life into policies would depend on the shape and structure of the British polity and the relative weight of various elites, institutions, and parties within it. In 1914, however, the relative power of the groups concerned with the problems of family maintenance was in flux. The Charity Organisation Society and other voluntary organizations were increasingly under attack, but many trade unions and working-class organizations remained wedded to the ideal of a male family wage, suspicious of state intervention, and consequently skeptical of any proposal to grant entitlements to women and children. Yet while trade unions were consulted by the Liberals before the introduction of labor exchanges, they were by no means an "estate of the realm" with power to determine policy.[84] On the other hand, feminist and working women's organizations, often viewed as largely peripheral, were able to capture the ear of the Liberal government on issues of concern to women and the family. The Treasury, for example, invited and incorporated suggestions concerning maternity benefit from the Women's Cooperative Guild when constructing the 1911 Insurance Act; similarly, the Women's Industrial Council exerted real influence in the realm of labor policy, especially

[84] Harris, *Unemployment and Politics*, p. 354; Gilbert, *Evolution*, p. 254.

over the Trade Boards Act.[85] Many people believed that women's suffrage, if and when granted, would further consolidate women's influence over family and social policy.

But who, in the end, determines policy: the voters, Parliament, or some less accessible coalition of interests? The war did hasten women's enfranchisement, but as we shall see in Chapter 2, it also decisively altered the institutional balance of power in Britain. When feminists and socialists stated their claim to independent benefits for women and children in the 1920s, they found that the enfranchisement of women gave them little ability to affect policy. Ironically, it was in France, where women remained voteless in the interwar period but where trade union power was similarly restricted, that a comprehensive family policy developed.

Dénatalité and the state in France

From the bleak portrait of bourgeois life given in *Fécondité*, one might conclude that "respectable" opinion and political leaders in *fin-de-siècle* France were entirely and willfully ignorant of the pressing problem of *dénatalité*. Despite the pleasure many demographic alarmists took in portraying themselves as an embattled minority, fighting the good fight against liberal individualism, nothing could be farther from the truth. The crisis of the birthrate was recognized and deplored across the political spectrum, with even many feminists and socialists rivaling Catholics and nationalists in their professions of loyalty to the cause of demographic renewal. What was at stake was not whether *dénatalité* would be recognized as a pressing national problem, but rather who would successfully define and capture the issue and thus shape the policies through which it would be combated. A coalition of right-wing pronatalists did succeed in this arena and was able not only to marginalize feminists, neo-Malthusians, and others contesting their views, but also to construct a coherent program for demographic revival. Yet their achievements were limited in the prewar period, in part because their own attitudes to state intervention were, at this stage, ambivalent. As in Britain, the growing rhetorical consensus did not immediately translate into a coherent social policy. Rather, a wide range of varying public and private initiatives in family policy coexisted. No comprehensive policy emerged until the interwar period.

---

[85] Gaffin and Thoms, *Caring and Sharing*, pp. 69–71. A good case for the influence of the "social feminists" of the Women's Industrial Council and the Women's Labour League is made in Mappen, "Strategies for Change."

Confronted by the figures on French population decline, even skeptical feminists had to admit that the prevailing sense of alarm over
the birthrate was understandable. After many centuries as the most
powerful and populous European nation, France was the first to
experience a decisive fall in the birthrate. By the latter half of the
nineteenth century, statistics revealed a clear trend of relative demographic decline – a trend rendered all the more alarming in light
of France's defeat in the Franco–Prussian war and of German unification. Between 1871 and 1911, the population of France grew by
a mere 8.6%, from 36.1 to 39.2 million, while the German population
grew by almost 60% to reach some 65 million, and the population of
Great Britain by 53.6% to reach over 40 million. By the early twentieth
century, the French population contained a high proportion of old
people, was less dense than its European neighbors, and was heavily
dependent on immigration. Between 1908 and 1913, there were a
mere 114 births per year for every 1,000 French married women
between the ages of 15 and 49, compared with 196 German births
and 171 English births; deaths actually exceeded births during seven
of the years between 1890 and 1914. Colin Dyer has estimated that
when the death rate is taken into account, the French population was
growing at the imperceptible rate of 0.06% per year, compared with
a German rate of 1.18% and an English one of 1.03%.[86]

A dirgelike lament about the dangers of depopulation ran through
public discourse throughout the Third Republic. During the twenty
years before the war, however, the most insistent and influential voice
on the problem of *dénatalité* was that of the Alliance Nationale pour
l'Accroissement de la Population Française, which was founded in
May 1896 under the direction of Jacques Bertillon, Emile Javal,
Charles Richet, Auguste Honnorat, and Emile Cheysson. These men,
all well known in conservative social reform circles, were, respectively,
a statistician, two doctors, a civil servant, and a noted social scientist.[87]
Their prominence and professions accurately reflect both the *bien-
pensant* respectability and the claims to scientific method typical of the
program and actions of the Alliance Nationale. Under its aegis gath-

---

[86] On population, see Colin Dyer, *Population and Society in Twentieth-Century France* (New
York: Holmes & Meier, 1978), pp. 5–28; Philip E. Ogden and Marie Monique Huss,
"Demography and Pronatalism in France in the Nineteenth and Twentieth Centuries,"
Journal of Historical Geography, 8: 3 (1982), pp. 283–92; Wesley Camp, *Marriage and the
Family in France since the Revolution* (New York: Bookman Associates, 1961).

[87] For an account of the Alliance Nationale's founding and founders, see Robert Talmy,
Histoire du mouvement familial en France (1896–1939), 1 (Paris: UNCAF, 1962), pp. 66–
74.

ered a group of men convinced not only that the declining birthrate would soon imperil France's world position, but also that many of the institutions of the Third Republic were themselves exacerbating the problem. *Dénatalité*, the Alliance Nationale argued, resulted from the growing hegemony of a liberal and individualistic political and economic order that disproportionately rewarded the childless; it could therefore be attenuated only if these liberal institutions – the tax system, the civil service, the military, perhaps the wage system itself – were reworked to favor the prolific *père de famille*. The Alliance Nationale's initial program was limited to winning tax relief for fathers of large families, but it soon branched out to propose that the period of military service be shortened for fathers of families, that all government positions be reserved for members of large families, that the inheritance laws be altered to allow a father to divide his property unequally among children – since, it was argued, the Napoleonic Code's insistence on equal inheritance induced peasants to limit their families – and finally, that the state institute a system of family allowances for large families.[88]

The conservative patriots grouped in the Alliance Nationale frequently deplored the "individualist" doctrines of economic liberalism to which, to their minds, France had too long been subjected, but in adopting such views they situated themselves within and not against the dominant traditions of French political economy. Despite – or perhaps because of – their nation's revolutionary tradition, mid-nineteenth-century French political economists had viewed the thoroughgoing economic transformation of Britain less with admiration than with apprehension. The June Days of 1848 and the censuses of 1856 and 1866 – which provided evidence of France's disproportionately low rate of population growth – quickly convinced them that untrammeled urbanization and industrialization could carry violence, degeneracy, depopulation, and national decline in their train.[89] Thus, while British politicians and political economists had come by the mid-

---

[88] On the program of the Alliance Nationale, see, in addition to Talmy, Joseph J. Spengler, *France Faces Depopulation* (Durham, N.C.: Duke University Press, 1938), pp. 235–8; Alain Becchia, "Les milieux parlementaires et la dépopulation de 1900 à 1914," *Communications*, 44 (1986), pp. 223–30.

[89] The attempt to distinguish French "social" economy from classical political economy of the Manchester school pervades Jérôme-Adolphe Blanqui's *History of Political Economy in Europe* (1842; trans. New York: Putnam's, 1880); for the impact of 1848 and the censuses on political economists, see especially Yves Charbit, *Du Malthusianisme au populationnisme: Les économistes français et la population, 1840–1870* (Paris: Presses Universitaires de France, 1981), esp. pp. 21–66.

Victorian period to accept industrial transformation and to see in the laws of the market a new basis for social stability, French political economists still hoped to "manage" economic change through policies that Gérard Noiriel has termed "neoliberal": the preservation of small businesses, the location of large businesses in rural rather than urban areas, hiring strategies that would allow families to combine peasant agriculture with wage labor, and paternalistic management of family firms.[90] Both British liberals and French "neoliberals" believed "social peace" depended on the stability of the family, but while the British sought to construct social policies that would transform emasculated proletarians into prudential male breadwinners, French "neoliberals" still hoped to preserve a family model based on the interdependent and self-supporting families of peasant agriculture and cottage industry and, by so doing, limit the growth of working-class radicalism and render Malthusian checks unnecessary.

The Alliance Nationale replicated the ambivalent relationship of mid-nineteenth-century political economists to economic and social liberalism and their nostalgic idealization of familial interdependence, but they also relied on the ideas of the man who did the most to develop sociological studies of the family from the 1830s to the 1880s, the mining engineer and social thinker Frédéric Le Play. Like many of his contemporaries, Le Play worried that the transition from a peasant to an industrialized economy would destroy the fabric of French society; like many anti-Republican and conservative thinkers, he blamed the revolution for weakening or destroying social hierarchies and corporatist institutions able to knit unequal members of society together.[91] Unlike many who shared his political views, however, Le Play did contend that France's social problems must be analyzed through empirical research; he himself spent several decades studying work, community, and family organization in mining and other towns. Le Play used this research to construct a typology differentiating between families based on their respective authority over children and ability to maintain the integrity of property; he also began to advocate reforms – especially the restoration of testamentary liberty for fathers over the disposal of property – which, he thought, would restore familial cohesion and reward mutual effort. Le Play's

---

[90] Gérard Noiriel, *Workers in French Society in the 19th and 20th Centuries* (1986; trans. New York: Berg, 1990), pp. 66–71.

[91] On the right and corporatism, see J. S. McClelland, ed., *The French Right: De Maistre to Maurras* (London: Jonathan Cape, 1970); Matthew Elbow, *French Corporative Theory, 1789–1948* (New York: Columbia University Press, 1953).

political and social ideas continued to be promulgated after his death in 1882 by followers organized into groups that went by the title of Réforme Sociale. From these groups the Alliance Nationale drew not only recruits but also much of their style of argument and their platform, including their tendency to insist that demographic renewal was inseparable from the restoration of Le Play's ideal "stem family."[92] Le Play's insistence on the preservation of "authority" in economic as well as domestic relations also won him the endorsement of industrialists, including the textile magnate Eugène Mathon, whom we shall meet again as the main architect of family allowances in the Nord.

Although most prominent pronatalists were conservatives loyal to the republic, and although they stressed the material as well as moral causes of the decline in the birthrate, they usually refrained from attacking the church, which they clearly saw as an ally in the fight for population increase. Angus McLaren has pointed out that in the second half of the nineteenth century, the Catholic church moved away from its earlier tolerance of celibacy or sexual restraint within marriage toward an open endorsement of virtually unlimited childbearing.[93] The church also became increasingly concerned with the impact on family life of a developing capitalist economy. In the papal encyclical *Rerum Novarum,* issued in 1891, Leo XIII exhorted Catholic employers to take seriously their responsibility for both the moral guidance and the material well-being of their employees: a "just wage," he insisted, must be adequate for a virtuous and hard-working man to support his wife and family respectably.[94] To "social Catholics" influenced by his teachings, the declining birthrate appeared as the consequence of an abdication of paternal authority in both the factory and the home.[95]

---

[92] On Le Play, see Catherine Bodard Silver, Introduction to *Frédéric Le Play: On Family, Work and Social Change* (Chicago: University of Chicago Press, 1982); Talmy, *Histoire du mouvement familial,* 1, pp. 41–8; Sanford Elwitt, *The Third Republic Defended* (Baton Rouge: Louisiana State University Press, 1986), esp. pp. 16–26. Charbit argues that the political economists grouped around the *Journal des Economistes* became less influential on demographic questions after 1870, and the leading role on such issues devolved onto the Le Playist Réforme Sociale groups and, after 1896, onto the Alliance Nationale; Charbit, *Du Malthusianisme au populationnisme,* p. 223.

[93] Angus McLaren, *Sexuality and Social Order* (New York: Holmes & Meier, 1982), pp. 31–43.

[94] "Rerum Novarum," in Claudia Carlen, comp., *The Papal Encyclicals, 1878–1903* (Wilmington, N.C.: McGrath Publishing, 1981), pp. 241–61.

[95] For a typical example of the social Catholic position on the population question, see Maurice Deslandres, "Le problème de la population," *Semaine Sociale,* 7 (1910), pp. 159–202; on the development of social Catholicism in general and the rapprochement between

By identifying the struggle against *dénatalité* with a drive to revive corporatist structures and limit both the pace of economic change and the power of the centralized state, pronatalists thus constructed a rhetoric likely to appeal to both Catholic and conservative reformers. The implicit targets of such formulations were not only the growing socialist movement but also the Radicals and Radical Socialists, ostensibly disinterested in the problem of depopulation and supposedly willing to use centralized state power to destroy any institution rivaling the state for the loyalty of the individual citizen. At least in the realm of social policy, this opposition was largely fictive, however, for in spite of the history of anticlerical legislation and the Dreyfus affair, Radicals adhered to a "solidarist" doctrine that was both anticollectivist and anti-individualist. While they permitted state mediation between rival economic and political forces, solidarists also looked to voluntary associations to bring about much of the work of social and moral reform.[96] The nationalist revival immediately before the First World War further consolidated bourgeois opinion, while once again highlighting the long-term military threat posed by a low birthrate.[97]

Sanford Elwitt has argued that by the turn of the century the affiliations and divisions that historians have laboriously identified in Third Republic politics had largely worn away: on crucial issues of bourgeois defense, social reform, and "social peace," Catholics cooperated with secular Republicans, conservative paternalists with Radical solidarists.[98] It is clear that the population panic of the end of the

church and state, see François Lebrun, *Histoire des Catholiques en France* (Toulouse: Privat, 1980), chap. 6; Harry Paul, *The Second Ralliement: The Rapprochement between Church and State in France in the Twentieth Century* (Washington, D.C.: Catholic University of America Press, 1967).

[96] On solidarism, see J. E. S. Hayward, "Solidarity: The Social History of an Idea in Nineteenth-Century France," *International Review of Social History*, 4: 2 (1959), pp. 261–84; idem, "The Official Social Philosophy of the French Third Republic: Léon Bourgeois and Solidarism," *International Review of Social History*, 6 (1961), pp. 19–48; Elwitt, *The Third Republic Defended*, pp. 170–216. There is perhaps no better indicator of the growing hegemony of corporatist thought even in staunchly republican circles than the appearance in 1902 of Emile Durkheim's preface to the second edition of *The Division of Labor in Society*, in which he put aside individualist or statist solutions to argue in favor of a revival of corporate institutions as a means of mediating class and labor conflicts; see Durkheim, "Preface to the Second Edition," in *The Division of Labor* (1893; 2d ed. 1902; rpt. New York: Free Press, 1984), pp. xxxi–lix.

[97] On the nationalist revival in the immediate prewar period, see Eugen Weber, *The Nationalist Revival in France, 1905–1914* (Berkeley and Los Angeles: University of California Press, 1959); William Buthman, *The Rise of Integral Nationalism in France* (New York: Columbia University Press, 1939).

[98] Elwitt, *The Third Republic Defended*, esp. pp. 289–91.

century was one important stimulus to this *ralliement*. All shades of "respectable" opinion, all solid patriots with the good of France at heart, buried their confessional and political animosities to urge more births from ambivalent women and a recalcitrant working class. Membership and participation in the social Catholic Semaines Sociales conferences, the Réforme Sociale groups, the Alliance Nationale, the Chamber of Deputies' profamily lobby, and after the war, the yearly conferences on the birthrate and of the Family Allowances Funds united conservative social reformers across traditional confessional and political lines. Francis Ronsin, the historian of the one (peripheral) anarchist birth-control movement that did oppose the pronatalist consensus, has pointed out that the supposedly "liberal" republic tolerated propaganda by fascists, racists, and royalists, but not birth-controllers – perhaps the best example of how pronatalist fervor came to be seen as the basic test of patriotism.[99]

There were those, however, who if they did not contest the status of *dénatalité* as a grave social problem, did challenge the right of the Alliance Nationale to define both its causes and its cure. The growing French feminist movement in particular staked its claim to be consulted on public policies affecting mothers, in the process defining an ideal of complementarity, of "equality in difference," both more strategic and more to their liking than what they perceived to be the "individualist" doctrines of their British counterparts. The ideal of the *mère au foyer* had always been quite as essential to bourgeois republicanism as it had to Victorianism, and in both countries feminism grew by appropriating a rhetoric of women's superior morality and "motherly" values deeply embedded in bourgeois culture.[100] Yet while many British feminists had come by the turn of the century to question the centrality of marriage and motherhood to women's lives and could draw on liberal ideas to demand equal access to "men's sphere" of

---

[99] Francis Ronsin, *La grève des ventres: Propagande néo-malthusienne et baisse de la natalité française (19ᵉ–20ᵉ siècles)* (Paris: Aubier Montaigne, 1980), p. 149.

[100] Bonnie G. Smith traces the construction of bourgeois domesticity in *Ladies of the Leisure Class: The Bourgeoises of Northern France in the Nineteenth Century* (Princeton, N.J.: Princeton University Press, 1981). On "republican motherhood" and the ideal of the *femme au foyer*, see Joan Landes, *Women and the Public Sphere in the Age of the French Revolution* (Ithaca, N.Y.: Cornell University Press, 1988), pp. 169–73; Yvonne Knibiehler and Catherine Fouquet, *L'histoire des mères du moyen-âge à nos jours* (Paris: Montalba, 1977), pp. 176–209; James F. McMillan, *Housewife or Harlot: The Place of Women in French Society, 1870–1940* (New York: St. Martin's, 1981), pp. 9–16, 29–37; and, for the inculcation of these values in schoolgirls, Linda L. Clark, *Schooling the Daughters of Marianne: Textbooks and the Socialization of Girls in Modern French Primary Schools* (Albany: State University of New York Press, 1984).

work and politics, French feminists continued to see women's special responsibility for children both as the fulfillment of feminine values and as the key to a wider "moralization" of society. Certainly their tenuous political position and class loyalties shaped these preferences: unwilling to jeopardize a republic perceived as inherently unstable, and themselves deeply enmeshed in philanthropic and moral reform movements dedicated to bringing the bourgeois virtues to the working class, they looked to motherhood as one of the few female activities accorded any degree of honor by the republic and the most solid basis for their claim to political rights.

When confronted with the figures on declining births, then, French feminists did not make light of the seriousness of the problem – although they did object to pronatalists' contention that the road to demographic renewal lay in tightening family ties through a reaffirmation of paternal authority. To the contrary, they argued, it was precisely because "male egoism" had reigned unchecked that the country was now menaced by alcoholism, prostitution, maternal ill health, and as a corollary, *dénatalité*. If it was indeed essential to society that women embrace motherhood – and they did not dispute this claim – then motherhood must be recognized as a "social" and not a private function, and the rights of mothers be extended. At its most radical – for example, in the writings of Nelly Roussel – such "maternalist" rhetoric was used to demand that motherhood be endowed by the state or to justify a "birth strike" (*la grève des ventres*) until the rights of mothers were recognized. For the most part, however, feminists were loath to raise the specter of birth control and preferred to combat pronatalist rhetoric by insisting that inadequate public support rather than any lack of enthusiasm on the part of women lay behind the declining birthrate.[101]

In theory the feminist movement could have looked for support from socialists, who also offered a somewhat different understanding

---

[101] On the ideas of the feminist movement with regard to motherhood, see Steven C. Hause with Anne R. Kenney, *Women's Suffrage and Social Politics in the French Third Republic* (Princeton, N.J.: Princeton University Press, 1984), pp. 14–27; Anne Cova, "French Feminism and Maternity: Theories and Policies, 1890–1918," in Gisela Bock and Pat Thane, eds., *Maternity and Gender Policies: Women and the Rise of the European Welfare States, 1880s-1950s* (London: Routledge, 1991), pp. 119–37; Karen Offen, "Depopulation, Nationalism and Feminism in Fin-de-siècle France," *American Historical Review*, 89: 8 (June 1984), pp. 648–76; Laurence Klejman and Florence Rochefort, *L'égalité en marche: Le féminisme sous la Troisième République* (Paris: Presses de la Fondation Nationale des Sciences Politiques, 1989), esp. pp. 303–5, 326–37; McMillan, *Housewife or Harlot*, pp. 76–96.

of the causes and cures for *dénatalité*. Both Jules Guesde and Paul Lafargue, for example, attempted to use the bourgeois preoccupation with the birthrate to castigate capitalism as the scourge of family life and to demand public support for women as mothers.[102] Yet as Charles Sowerwine's work on this area shows, attempts at alliance by bourgeois feminist groups and socialist women repeatedly failed, doomed by feminists' hostility to all doctrines of class struggle and by the socialist movement's concern to protect its own women's organizations from the bourgeois taint.[103] The exceptionally low rates of childbearing among French women provide some clue as to working women's own opinions, but only a few libertarian crusaders led by Paul Robin forthrightly defended birth control as an agent of economic betterment and sexual emancipation. For the most part, the debate over *dénatalité* divided those who believed in increasing the rights of mothers from those who eschewed a language of rights altogether.

In the realm of rhetoric at least, there is no question which side won. Feminists and socialists – precisely those groups that constructed the first case for family endowment in Britain – found themselves placed increasingly on the defensive. The first and second Extra-Parliamentary Commissions on Depopulation, established in 1901 and 1912, were dominated by the members of the Alliance Nationale and endorsed much of its program. Although the legislative results of the commissions were minimal, they did help to consolidate the right-wing pronatalist lobby in the Chamber which reemerged after the First World War.[104] Unlike Britain, then, where family policy was problematic primarily because it was linked to feminist aims to increase wives' independence and power, pronatalists' success in linking family

[102] The affection of Pierre-Joseph Proudhon for the ideal of the "femme au foyer" is well known; on Jules Guesde and Paul Lafargue, see Léon Gani, "Jules Guesde, Paul Lafargue et les problèmes de population," *Population*, 34 (1979), pp. 1023–43. In a regional study of socialist politics in the Nord, Patricia Hilden concludes that in the late 1890s the Socialist Party gradually abandoned its earlier attempt to organize women as workers and began to adopt a "separate spheres" approach; see Hilden, *Working Women and Socialist Politics in France, 1880–1914: A Regional Study* (Oxford University Press, 1986), esp. pp. 131–5.

[103] Charles Sowerwine, *Sisters or Citizens? Women and Socialism in France since 1876* (Cambridge University Press, 1982); also Marilyn Boxer, "Socialism Faces Feminism: The Failure of Synthesis in France, 1879–1914," in Boxer and Jean H. Quataert, eds., *Socialist Women: European Socialist Feminism in the Nineteenth and Early Twentieth Centuries* (New York: Elsevier, 1978), pp. 75–111.

[104] On the commissions, see Becchia, "Les milieux parlementaires"; Offen, "Dépopulation."

policy to a nationalist and patriarchal social vision left it relatively uncontroversial in a nation with a weak feminist movement and an exclusively male electorate throughout the interwar period.

Nevertheless, if the conservative monopoly of the pronatalist issue effectively severed the link between family policy and women's independence, it raised new dilemmas about the terms on which a profoundly antisocialist coalition could advocate state intervention. Corporatists, Catholics, and the social scientists associated with Le Play were all historically hostile to state intervention, and as the socialist movement gained strength, even the Radical Party jettisoned its commitment to state-financed social reform.[105] The link between pronatalism and fiscal conservatism left the members of the prewar semipublic Depopulation Commissions in a paradoxical situation, demanding on the one hand less state intervention and on the other a wide range of economic inducements to childbearing, all of which would require tax increases.[106] But if the gradual monopoly of family policy by the right limited state solutions, it encouraged other, private initiatives of real significance for the future of family policy.

When we leave the realm of political discourse about the family to examine actual policy developments, we find a rather confusing landscape. The prewar period saw the development of a variety of different initiatives, often based on differing principles that were not, in the long run, compatible. Some of these measures were labor policies intended to control the wages and conditions of work, while others were more properly assistance measures; some addressed women, and others men. Nevertheless, all were primarily aimed at ensuring the health, well-being, and proliferation of children. We can identify four main threads to prewar family policy.

First, as in England, the state accepted responsibility for overseeing children's welfare, both by limiting their employment and by extending oversight over abused or abandoned children. Social Catholics and ostensibly liberal economists had collaborated to pass legislation restricting children's employment during the July monarchy;[107] the

---

[105] Judith F. Stone, "The Radicals and the Interventionist State: Attitudes, Ambiguities and Transformations, 1880–1910," *French History*, 2: 2 (June 1988), pp. 173–86.

[106] Becchia, "Les milieux parlementaires," p. 219.

[107] The early development of child labor legislation in France is extensively treated by Katherine A. Lynch, *Family, Class and Ideology in Early Industrial France: Social Policy and the Working Class Family, 1825–1848* (Madison: University of Wisconsin Press, 1988); see also Colin Heywood, *Childhood in Nineteenth-Century France: Work, Health and Education among the 'Classes Populaires'* (Cambridge University Press, 1988), esp. pp. 217–

Third Republic finally rendered such legislation effective with the introduction of a factory inspectorate in 1874, comprehensive education laws in the early 1880s, and further statutes in 1892 and 1900 limiting young workers' hours and forbidding the employment of children under age 13.[108] Public outcry against both infant mortality rates and *dénatalité* also drove legislators to enact a series of measures aimed at protecting newborn, abandoned, or abused children, as well as the children of poor and single mothers. In 1874, after a medical outcry against the high rates of infant mortality among children nursed commercially, the government passed a law requiring that all such children be registered; the wet-nursing business declined soon afterward.[109] In 1889, the state claimed the power to make neglected or abused children wards of the state, and in 1898 administration was eased by a law giving a judge the power to confer guardianship on the public authority for children (the Assistance Publique) or on a third party.[110] Fears about the birthrate also convinced some localities to move away from their earlier criteria of the mother's morality and respectability when granting poor relief and to focus simply on the health and well-being of the children. In theory, under the 1905 law on poor relief, able-bodied indigents were expected to work regardless of sex; however, fear that women would abandon children led public officials to extend aid to able-bodied single mothers after the birth of the child, a development that parallels the return to outrelief for widows with young children in England. In contrast to older practices, officials treated the needs of the child as paramount and grew increasingly unwilling to take children away or to cut off aid for cohabitation or "immorality."[111] Through these measures, the state

---

36; Lee Shai Weissbach, *Child Labor Reform in Nineteenth-Century France: Assuring the Future Harvest* (Baton Rouge: Louisiana State University Press, 1989); and, comparatively, Cross, *A Quest for Time*.

[108] Heywood, *Childhood*, pp. 264–7, 314–15.

[109] On the 1874 Loi Roussel and the decline of the wet-nursing business, see George D. Sussman, *Selling Mothers' Milk: The Wet-Nursing Business in France, 1715–1914* (Urbana: University of Illinois Press, 1982), pp. 101–29, 161–85.

[110] On legislation for children, see especially Rachel Fuchs, *Abandoned Children: Foundlings and Child Welfare in Nineteenth-Century France* (Albany: State University of New York Press, 1984), pp. 49–61; Catherine Rollet-Echalier, *La politique à l'égard de la petite enfance sous la IIIe République* (Paris: Presses Universitaires de France, 1990), pp. 131–53.

[111] Rachel Fuchs notes that this loosening of conditions meant that a full 15% of newborns in the Seine area received public aid at the end of the century: Fuchs, "Morality and Poverty: Public Welfare for Mothers in Paris, 1870–1900," *French History*, 2: 3 (Sept.

limited parents' power to abuse or exploit children and enforced their responsibility for proper care, while also increasing the capacity of poor single mothers to provide such care.

Second, the state regulated the position of working women, attempting to channel women's wage earning into areas compatible with motherhood and, when pressed, providing entitlements for working mothers. It is in this area in particular, that French policy stands in sharp contrast to British, reflecting both the very different patterns of industrialization in the two countries and the tendency of politicians and moralists to worry less about women's wage earning than about the ostensibly demoralizing effects of urbanization and factory work. Despite the centrality of the ideal of the *femme au foyer* to both bourgeois and Proudhonian thought in France, women – including married women – continued to play a central role in the labor market throughout the nineteenth and early twentieth centuries. Women officially constituted 30% of the French labor force in 1866; by 1911, this figure had risen to almost 37%, compared with 29.6% in Britain. In part, this was because France, as a less industrialized country, had a smaller population employed in occupations strictly separate from the home. Fully two-fifths of the economically active population (and two-fifths of working women) were in the agricultural sector on the eve of the First World War, compared to a mere tenth of all workers and 5% of working women in Britain. But as we saw in Table 1.1, women were also more strongly represented in industry and commerce in France than in Britain: one-third of the work force in industry and transport and two-fifths of the work force in commerce was female in France in 1911 (compared with less than a quarter and less than one-fifth respectively in Britain). As Table 1.4 shows, the broad distribution of working women in France was not sharply dissimilar from the distribution of working men. Once again, the persistence of homework and artisanal and small-scale production helped to preserve women's place in the economy: even in 1906, some 60% of France's 11 million blue-collar workers worked at home or in firms with less than ten employees.[112] Yet some factory owners, and notably

1988), pp. 288–311. A helpful survey of poor relief institutions is provided by John H. Weiss, "Origins of the French Welfare State: Poor Relief in the Third Republic, 1871–1914," *French Historical Studies*, 13: 1 (Spring 1983), pp. 47–78.

[112] Michèle Perrot, "On the Formation of the French Working Class," in Ira Katznelson and Aristide R. Zolberg, eds., *Working-Class Formation: Nineteenth-Century Patterns in Western Europe and the United States* (Princeton, N.J.: Princeton University Press, 1986), p. 72. On the structure of the labor force in the nineteenth century – and especially on the preservation of the artisanal economy, the propensity of families to combine ag-

Table 1.4. *Distribution of "economically active" men and women, France*

Date	Agriculture/fishing Men	Women	Industry/transport Men	Women	Services/trade Men	Women
1866	51	48	31	27	18	26
1886	47	46	29	24	23	30
1906	42	43	35	30	22	27
1911	40	42	38	33	21	24

Note: Figures are percentages of all employed women or all employed men.
Source: See Table 1.1.

those in textiles, also continued the practice of hiring workers in family groups up to the turn of the century.[113]

These divergent patterns of industrialization and employment underscore one point crucial to our study: the male breadwinner wage norm was far less well established in France than in Britain. Not only were women more likely to be in the formal labor market in France, but they were likely to remain there after marriage. As we saw in Table 1.1, while formal labor force participation rates plummeted for women in Britain around the age of marriage, those for French women declined only slightly and gradually by age. Married women, taken as a group, were fully *five times* as likely to be in the labor force in France as in Britain in 1911: some 48.8% of French married women were categorized as "occupied," compared with only 9.6% of British married women.[114] In 1912, according to Patricia Hilden, some 65% of households in the textile towns of Roubaix and Tourcoing were wholly or partially dependent on the wages of the wife or mother.[115]

The uneven nature of industrialization in France and the continued importance of women's work were reflected in rather different policies for working women in France. Whereas British policymakers assumed that mothers with small children would only in exceptional circumstances be in the labor market, the French accepted that large numbers of married women would be "economically active." True, nineteenth-

ricultural work with industrial earning, and the importance of women's work – see Alain Cottereau, "The Distinctiveness of Working-Class Cultures in France, 1848–1900," in ibid., pp. 111–54; Noiriel, *Workers in French Society*, pp. 3–32.

[113] William Reddy, *The Rise of Market Culture: The Textile Trade and French Society, 1750–1900* (Cambridge University Press, 1984), p. 163.

[114] Labor force participation rates for married women can be found in T. Deldycke, H. Gelders, and J.-M. Limbor, *La population active et sa structure* (Brussels: Editions de l'Institut de Sociologie de l'Université Libre de Bruxelles, 1968), pp. 169, 185.

[115] Hilden, *Working Women*, p. 36.

century liberal economists, social Catholics, and Proudhonian socialists had all inveighed against married women's wage earning in terms very similar to those employed by social reformers in Britain; what particularly bothered them, however, was not whether a woman brought money into the household, but rather whether she earned these wages, as Jules Simon put it, "under the domination of a foreman, among companions of doubtful morality, in constant contact with men, and apart from her husband and children."[116] French politicians thus concentrated less on forcing women out of the labor market than on preserving forms of work they considered compatible with childbearing and, when pressed, on introducing measures that they felt would help women reconcile their roles as workers and mothers.

Legislators had, by the end of the century, recognized that married women often needed to work precisely in order to support their families. Although wives owed obedience to their husbands under the Civil Code, republican politicians did mitigate husbands' authority through a series of laws in the 1890s and early 1900s that gave women some limited rights to contract for themselves and to dispose freely of their own earnings.[117] Furthermore, whereas British protective legislation had from the 1840s assimilated women to children, the French Senate in the 1880s still resisted proposals to treat women as minors. Only in 1892 did legislators ban women as well as children from night work and limit the hours of both, and even then they were driven less by a concern to lighten women's burdens than by their fear that wives' prolonged absence from home contributed to the "degeneracy" of working men; they thus applied the legislation to factories but not to agriculture, commerce, and "family workshops."[118] In consequence, as both Marilyn Boxer and Mary Lynn Stewart have shown, the law had the effect of crowding women into poorly paid and exploited homework industries, an outcome that would not (whatever legislators thought) have benefited children, since infant mortality rates were

---

[116] Jules Simon, *L'ouvrière* (Paris: Hachette, 1862), p. v; Joan Scott, "'L'ouvrière! Mot impie, sordide . . .': Women Workers in the Discourse of French Political Economy, 1840–1860," in *Gender and the Politics of History* (New York: Columbia University Press, 1988), esp. p. 146.

[117] For this legislation, see Yvonne Netter, *Le travail de la femme mariée* (Paris: Presses Universitaires de France, 1923), and Esther Kanipe, "The Family, Private Property and the State in France, 1870–1914," Ph.D. diss., University of Wisconsin, 1976. Kanipe attributes legislative solicitude toward women workers very largely to politicians' hope that women would moderate men's radicalism.

[118] Cross, *A Quest for Time*, pp. 47–8.

actually higher among the children of housewives and domestic workers than among those of factory workers at the end of the century.[119] Concern for children could operate in working women's favor, however. Whereas left-wing Republicans were unable to win legislative support for maternity leaves in the 1890s, pronatalists' evidence that such leaves would limit infant mortality led to the passage in 1913 of a law making state-funded leaves mandatory for all wage-earning women, including domestic workers.[120]

Although inspired by the demographic crisis, the preceding measures hardly answered the pronatalists' case. Laws protecting children without increasing parental resources would hardly encourage births, while measures aimed at poor, single mothers or women workers – although welcomed by feminists – scarcely met pronatalists' demands for a restoration of paternal authority and for aid to large families as a matter of right. In the twenty years before the war, however, the legislative coalition organized by the Alliance Nationale did introduce a series of amendments and propositions aimed both at discriminating in favor of fathers of large families in military and government service and at lightening their economic burdens. By establishing the precedent that family situation as well as individual need must be taken into account in assessing a citizen's political obligations, these measures paved the way for later family policies, even if pronatalists could not win need-blind family allowances for all large families until after the First World War.

The Alliance Nationale's first success was in winning tax relief – proportional to the number of children – in inheritance and housing taxes. They had more trouble convincing politicians of the need for cash benefits, since policymakers – as in Britain – resisted aiding poor families if the father was present. Yet large families would be difficult for even the most assiduous and devoted breadwinner to support, argued the Alliance Nationale, and in 1913, after a campaign of more than ten years, the Chamber finally passed a measure granting allowances for dependent children beginning with the fourth to all needy

---

[119] The argument that protective legislation marginalized women workers is convincingly made by Marilyn Boxer, "Protective Legislation and Home Industry: The Marginalization of Women Workers in Late Nineteenth- Early Twentieth-Century France," *Journal of Social History*, 20: 1 (Fall 1986), pp. 45–65, and by Mary Lynn Stewart, *Women, Work, and the French State: Labour Protection and Social Patriarchy, 1879–1919* (Kingston, Ontario: McGill-Queen's University Press, 1989). For infant mortality rates, see Rollet-Echalier, *La politique à l'égard de la petite enfance*, p. 487.

[120] Mary Lynn McDougall, "Protecting Infants: The French Campaign for Maternity Leaves, 1890s-1913," *French Historical Studies*, 13: 1 (Spring 1983), pp. 79–105.

heads of families. The allowance was small, and the applicant was required to prove need, but this law marked a decisive break with the principle – still governing poor relief in England – that the obligation of the father to maintain overrode the child's claim to assistance. Implicit in British assistance was the message that parents should not have more children than they could support. The French policy implied, by contrast, that the production of children was a meritorious act even by those who could not support them. It did not, however, imply that it was an act requiring recompense regardless of the family's need: pure entitlements for large families had to wait until the interwar period.[121]

Interwar supporters of family allowances hoped to compensate for the dependency of children by redistributing income from the childless to those with children, as a matter of right and without reference to need. From this point of view, the 1913 law on assistance to large families was a modest beginning indeed. Yet the Finance Ministry was too allergic to social spending, and indeed the legislature itself too hostile to state intervention, to introduce more comprehensive state-financed measures before the war. Family-based assistance need not be initiated by the state alone, however. Some innovations of real significance for the development of French family policy were introduced within private firms or by the state as employer, not benefactor.

In England, the health and insurance services developed by voluntary or mutual associations were by the end of the century being taken over by the local or national state. In France, by contrast, antistatist and illiberal currents influencing pronatalist thought interacted with a powerful tradition of business paternalism to provide a basis for industrially based, private measures of family assistance. The state, in its role as employer, did to some extent give the lead. The Ministry of the Navy had granted child benefits to sailors with long service as early as 1860, and in the fifteen years before the First World War many other ministries introduced such benefits for their employees. From 1908, teachers began to be paid annual benefits for children below the age of 16, and in 1909 allowances were introduced for civil servants under the central direction of the Treasury. Until

---

[121] On the early parliamentary initiatives of the Alliance Nationale, see Talmy, *Histoire du mouvement familial*, 1, pp. 74–98, and for the background to the 1913 law, pp. 107–13, 159–61. The (unsuccessful) campaign to lighten military service requirements for fathers of large families is also discussed by John C. Hunter, "The Problem of the French Birth Rate on the Eve of World War I," *French Historical Studies*, 2: 4 (Fall 1962), pp. 490–503.

1917, however, such innovations were fragmentary and the levels of benefit quite low.[122] More widely noted at the time were the innovations of those few Catholic employers who took to heart the injunction of Leo XIII to pay workers with children a family wage. A few Catholic employers had already attempted to transform their works into total "moral communities," the most famous of such experiments being that of the cotton manufacturer Jacques Harmel and his son Léon, who in the 1870s and 1880s not only built schools and cottages and provided social benefits and medical care for their work force, but also encouraged the development of social and mutual associations run on relatively democratic lines. Léon Harmel believed that the paternalistic initiatives of capitalist employers were not enough to create true "social peace" and, in collaboration with Count Albert de Mun, urged Catholic employers to make ever greater efforts to reconcile economic development with the teachings of the church. In 1891, then, Harmel responded to *Rerum Novarum* by establishing a fund to pay allowances for children, administered – quite exceptionally – by the workers themselves.[123]

Other employers committed to a tradition of paternalistic management – including the Bon Marché – followed suit.[124] Some of these certainly acted from less elevated motives than had the Harmels, being aware that allowances could help firms tighten their control over the work force and limit wage demands. In 1890, for example, one of the great railway companies, the Compagnie du Chemin de Fer du Nord introduced a special family benefit for employees with at least three dependent children. The company insisted that the measure was purely benevolent but soon found allowances a useful means by which to adapt wages to both regional and periodic variations in the

[122] On the introduction of allowances in the civil service and other areas before 1920, see Jacques Hochard, "Les origines françaises des allocations familiales avant 1920," in *Actes du 108e Congrès National des Sociétés Savantes (1983): Colloque sur l'histoire de la sécurité sociale* (Paris: Association pour l'Etude de l'Histoire de la Sécurité Sociale, 1984), pp. 101–13.

[123] On Harmel, see Henri Rollet, *L'action sociale des catholiques en France (1871–1901)* (Paris: Boivin, 1947), pp. 222–67; Parker Thomas Moon, *The Labor Problem and the Social Catholic Movement in France* (New York: Macmillan, 1921), pp. 113–20; Talmy, *Histoire du mouvement familial*, 1, p. 91.

[124] Early paternalistic initiatives in the field of family policy are discussed in Jean Pinte, *Les allocations familiales* (Paris: Sirey, 1935), pp. 69–73. On the Bon Marché, see Michael Miller, *The Bon Marché: Bourgeois Culture and the Department Store, 1869–1920* (Princeton, N.J.: Princeton University Press, 1981), pp. 149, 233; and for the paternalistic initiatives of the 1880s more generally, see Noiriel, *Workers in French Society*, pp. 78–84.

cost of living and to the varying needs of their employees. In 1911, ostensibly in view of the rising cost of living, the company thoroughly recast the program, extending benefits to families with any dependent children, rather than merely to large families. This decision raised the proportion of the work force benefiting from allowances from under 7% to almost 40%: a measure originally intended to assist those with extraordinary burdens became one aimed at directing cost-of-living increases primarily to families with dependent children. In other words, in an inflationary period, allowances redistributed some portion of the total wage bill from childless workers to those with children.[125] The Alliance Nationale made every effort to encourage such private initiatives, but in the period before the war they were undertaken only by particularly devout employers, the state administration, or those sheltered from competitive pressures, such as the railroad companies. The proliferation of allowances had to wait until the war, when – as we see in the next chapter – the peculiar conditions of government control and rampant inflation encouraged their rapid extension.

Leaders of the Alliance Nationale consistently denounced the government and the legislature for disinterest and inaction on questions of the family. Historians of the period have repeated these charges. "There is," Jean-Marie Mayeur writes, "a huge literature deploring the depopulation of the country; it forms an interesting contrast to the indifference of the authorities and of Parliament."[126] Our survey

---

[125] The survey of CCFN policy is drawn from the records of the Compagnie du Chemin de Fer du Nord, held in the Archives Nationales: AN 48 AQ 3393, loose documents, and files "Secours de famille – Ordres de Service," "Comité du 27 oct. 1911," and "Allocation pour cherté des vivres," and 48 AQ 3392, file "Indemnités pour charges de famille." The other major railroad companies (*grands réseaux*) also began paying family allowances in the prewar period. See, e.g., Paul Dépret, *Etude sur l'oeuvre sociale de la Compagnie des Chemins de Fer de l'Est* (Verdun: H. Fremont et Fils, 1936), pp. 149–63; Armand Moreau, *L'oeuvre sociale du P.L.M.* (Paris: Imprimerie du Montparnasse et de Persan Beaumont, 1927), pp. 150–6.

[126] Jean-Marie Mayeur and Madeleine Reberioux, *The Third Republic from Its Origins to the Great War, 1871–1914* (Cambridge University Press, 1984), p. 43. Robert Talmy similarly begins his two-volume study of the familist movement with the claim that the family was ignored and ridiculed in nineteenth-century political life; Talmy, *Histoire du mouvement familial*, 1, p. 19. Alfred Sauvy, demographer and statistician, likewise emphasized both the dire state of the French population in the interwar period and the relative tardiness of policy in this area; Sauvy, *Histoire économique de la France entre les deux guerres*, 3 vols. (Paris: Economica, 1984). The laxity of the government in the sphere of population policy was accepted as historical fact even by Alain Becchia, although his own work clearly points to the pervasiveness of pronatalist sentiment in government; Becchia, "Les milieux parlementaires," p. 201. It is only in comparison

thus far leads us to quite a different conclusion. Concern over the birthrate was pervasive in official circles, and many of the Alliance Nationale's supporters were in government or, worse, were the very *fonctionnaires* so vilified by their own propaganda. The prewar period saw the emergence of a clear public discourse and political coalition around pronatalism; in the 1913 law on assistance to large families, this coalition won an important precedent for state aid to the "normal" male-headed family. Other important initiatives took place within the "private" sphere of industry not because governments were unconcerned about the birthrate but because the parliamentary right's own ambivalence toward state intervention and taxation limited the kind of demands pronatalists could make. Despite growing consensus across the confessional and party divide, therefore, policy initiatives developed along a number of independent tracks. Only the further economic and population pressures of the next forty years would bring them together.

Conclusion

Why do children matter? The early debate over their poverty or, in France, dearth, suggests that they "matter" politically largely as future soldiers. Interest in assistance to children in both France and Britain arose during a period of heightening international competition and tensions. In an era of mass war, no country could look on a declining birthrate or widespread ill health among children with equanimity.

In both countries, however, far more than military preparedness was at stake. Ideologies and agendas clashed as questions over the state's responsibilities for children became embedded in wider debates over the allowable limits of state intervention and the appropriate relationship between the sexes. In Britain, concern over children quickly became intertwined with feminist claims for economic independence and socialist visions of an expanded state. This rhetorical link between family policy and the transformative politics of feminists and socialists meant that entitlements for children were seen from the beginning as endangering the male family wage and thus the very constitution of the family. In France, by contrast, a weak feminist movement was unable to wrest the issue away from the pronatalist right, who identified assistance to the "normal" male-headed family as part of a wider program of social and moral reconstruction. British

with other countries that the French government's real obsession with the population question stands out.

campaigners hoped to use state policy to equalize the very domestic hierarchies French campaigners aimed to protect.

Demands for aid to the family were thus linked from the outset to the attempt to reward particular gendered identities and roles, yet prewar policies in both countries did not consistently endorse any one view. While we can see school meals or maternity benefit in Britain as a precedent for later universal entitlements for mothers and children, the social insurance measures developed in the same period drew on a different, wage-centered logic. Similarly, in France, policies aimed at helping women reconcile maternity with wage earning coexisted with allowances for large families paid to men. Which of these precedents would prove decisive, and whether in the long run family policies would address male breadwinners, mothers, or simply children, was by 1914 still unclear. After all, while the prewar debate had articulated claims on behalf of each of these identities, neither political parties nor organized interest groups directly represented such interests, nor was it evident that effective political coalitions could be based on gender and familial identities and roles. The needs of war, however, would endow particular economic groups – especially employers' associations in France and trade unions in Britain – with new powers. These interests were not centrally concerned with children, but they were concerned to protect or to disaggregate the male "family wage." It was their preferences that would shape the policies of the postwar period.

2

THE IMPACT OF THE GREAT WAR

The total wars of the twentieth century have often been seen as the cradle of the welfare state, but only recently have historians begun to trace the ways in which wartime policies presumed or reinforced particular models of gender relations and family life.[1] That wartime policies would be centrally concerned with the family should come as no surprise, since the enlistment and conscription of able-bodied men could not but dislocate relations between parents and children, husbands and wives. Mobilization figures for Britain and France are direct indicators of the scale of social disruption. Five and one-quarter million men served in the British Army between 1914 and 1918, or almost 50% of all men in the United Kingdom aged between 15 and 49 in 1911. French figures are even more startling: almost 8 million Frenchmen were mobilized, a full 79% of men aged between 15 and 49 in 1911.[2] The gaps these men left were economic as well as emotional: mobilization in France brought industry to a virtual standstill, while in both countries the loss of wages created much private distress.

The war governments in both countries thus faced similar problems. How could they find enough men for the trenches and at the same

---

[1] For a review of some of the older literature on the effects of total war on social policy, see Arthur Marwick, *War and Social Change in the Twentieth Century* (London: Macmillan, 1974); also Richard Titmuss, *Problems of Social Policy* (London: HMSO, 1950). Two recent collections trace some of the effects of war on gender relations in the belligerent countries: Richard Wall and Jay Winter, eds., *The Upheaval of War: Family Work and Welfare in Europe, 1914–1918* (Cambridge University Press, 1988); Margaret Higonnet et al., *Behind the Lines: Gender and the Two World Wars* (New Haven, Conn.: Yale University Press, 1987).

[2] Figures on population and mobilization are drawn from B. R. Mitchell, *European Historical Statistics* (1975; 2d rev. ed., New York: Facts on File, 1981), pp. 46, 62–3; J. M. Winter, *The Great War and the British People* (Cambridge, Mass.: Harvard University Press, 1986), p. 28; Colin Dyer, *Population and Society in Twentieth-Century France* (New York: Holmes & Meier, 1978), p. 40.

time expand munitions production and keep up civilian morale and living standards? At first glance, the solutions devised to these problems look similar. Both countries brought essential industries and services under state control and "diluted" a skilled labor force with less skilled workers, including many women. Both also instituted broad public assistance programs for the wives and dependents of mobilized men. These wartime innovations reconfigured family structures while challenging accepted ideals of domesticity and family life; new arrangements of work and welfare temporarily altered relations of dependence and maintenance between the sexes. But how permanent were such changes? How did this massive dislocation in both the labor market and the family affect the future of social policy?

We can examine wartime labor and welfare policies in both countries for some answers to these questions. As we have seen, the prewar period saw the introduction of a variety of policies concerned with dependent families, but in neither country did a unified, coherent system develop. It was the war that imposed order on diversity and that privileged a particular logic of welfare in each state. The task of unearthing this "logic" can be a difficult one, however, since wartime experiences were often contradictory or deceptive. The introduction of large benefits to soldiers' wives, for example, could be seen either as a precedent for family allowances or as state recognition of soldiers' rights to a family wage; similarly, the high wages paid to women substitute workers could appear as a challenge to the unequal position of women workers or merely reflect the desire to preserve men's higher rates of pay for returning soldiers.

Confusing as wartime innovations certainly were, this chapter argues that they did help to fix the parameters for postwar social policy in both countries. In Britain, despite large transfers of income to women, wartime labor and social policies were designed to protect men's labor market position after the war. Women continued to be viewed as purely temporary workers, while the state adopted new responsibilities for guaranteeing men's breadwinner status by providing for their dependents during legitimate interruptions of earnings. In France, by contrast, industrialists and ministers attempted to cope with wartime inflation without harming working-class living standards by extending allowances for dependent children to large numbers of workers. Such programs effectively redistributed income from childless workers to those with children, thus serving as an important early example of "parental" social policy. In brief, the war furthered the defense in Britain, and the disaggregation in France, of the male family wage.

These divergent outcomes can be described, but they must also be explained. Why were particular policies pursued, and why did they have the consequences they did? To answer this we must look not merely at the content of policy, but also at the political context in which it operated. The war created new needs, but it also altered the political climate and relations through which those needs were defined and met. As we shall see, changing patterns of political mediation and, in particular, the degree of incorporation of trade unions and employers' associations helped to determine the nature and duration of wartime policies.

The wartime social contract

When France entered the war in August 1914, it was to face a enemy who was already the object of a good deal of revanchist ill will. The memory of the Franco-Prussian war still rankled; the loss of Alsace and Lorraine was by no means accepted as final. Nor were such sentiments confined to the propertied classes. Popular and working-class opinion, the murder of Jaurès notwithstanding, rallied swiftly to the war; a rhetoric of proletarian solidarity gave way to an older Jacobin evocation of "the nation in arms."[3] This initial response and the prior existence of universal military service (extended to three years in 1913) made conscription both inevitable and relatively uncontroversial. However unprepared for mass warfare in other respects, the French government did find itself in 1914 with virtually unlimited powers over the disposition of the bodies and abilities of its male citizens.

No such powers were available to Asquith, nor would he have wanted them. Britain's long reliance on a policy of naval superiority and the Liberal Party's traditional opposition to state coercion made conscription impossible in 1914. Lord Kitchener, it is true, explained to the Cabinet on 7 August that the war would be fought on land by armies of an unprecedented size, but only Churchill supported conscription in Cabinet discussions that month.[4] Not until voluntary recruiting had been exhausted, various schemes of "registration" tried and found wanting, and the Liberal government diluted through

---

[3] Recent revisionist accounts of popular and working-class responses to the war, notably those by Jean-Jacques Becker and John Horne, stress the degree to which the popular classes and even organized labor rallied to the war and to which civilian morale held. Becker, *The Great War and the French People* (1983; New York: St. Martin's, 1986); Horne, *Labour at War: France and Britain, 1914–1918* (Oxford University Press, 1991).

[4] R. J. Q. Adams and Philip P. Poirier, *The Conscription Controversy in Great Britain, 1900–1918* (London: Macmillan, 1987), pp. 55, 65.

coalition did the Cabinet and Parliament agree to compel men to fight. With the Military Service Acts of January and May of 1916, first unmarried men and then all men between the ages of 18 and 41 became liable for military service.[5]

It would be hard to exaggerate the importance of these early decisions about military service. Not only did they leave the French and British governments with very different levels of coercive power, they also exaggerated what was already the most profound difference between the two countries: the relative status and effectiveness of their labor movements. French workers in 1914 were far less well organized than their British counterparts: only some 355,000 workers belonged to unions affiliated to the Confédération Générale du Travail (CGT) in 1913, compared with well over 2 million British workers in unions affiliated to the Trades Union Congress, not to mention another million or more organized outside the TUC. Different patterns of mobilization merely widened this discrepancy. Already fragile French trade unions were decimated by call-ups. Numbers affiliated to the CGT fell to a mere 50,000 in 1915; not until 1917 did the confederation recover its prewar strength and embark on three years of unprecedented growth. The number of British trade unionists, by contrast, held fairly steady during 1914 and 1915 and grew rapidly from 1916 until 1920, by which date more than 6 million were in unions affiliated to the TUC. Most crucially, while conscription threw shop-level organization into disarray in France, many British unions – and especially the important "craft" unions in the engineering sector – retained some control of the organization of labor on the shop floor.[6]

The preservation of working-class organization in Britain meant that the labor movement was, from the beginning, aware of its strength and able to set some conditions for its cooperation in the prosecution of the war. True, both the Labour Party and the Parti Socialiste had rallied to the war, their collaboration formalized in Britain by the inclusion of Arthur Henderson in Asquith's coalition cabinet formed in May 1915 and in France by the appointment of Albert Thomas as under secretary for munitions that same month. Yet only in Britain was such collaboration made contingent on effective power sharing and concessions. The War Emergency Workers'

---

[5] The course of decision making over recruitment and conscription is covered thoroughly by Adams and Poirier, and by Keith Grieves, *The Politics of Manpower, 1914–1918* (Manchester: Manchester University Press, 1988).

[6] Comparative figures are given by Horne, *Labour at War*, p. 398; see also Henry Pelling, *A History of British Trade Unionism* (London: Macmillan, 1963).

National Committee (WEWNC), Labour's wartime "kitchen cabinet" of party, trade union, and cooperative society delegates, was able to provide a degree of coordination and was accorded a degree of influence never achieved by its French counterpart, the Comité d'Action, important as the latter was in formalizing cooperation between the party, the trade unions, and the consumer cooperatives.[7]

These two factors – the vastly different degree of power over its male citizenry at the disposal of the government, and the relative strength of labor organizations – determined the shape of the wartime social contract and influenced the labor and social policies that were its secondary outcomes. The primary intent of the wartime contract in both countries was, of course, simply the provision and delivery of men and munitions, but the nature of that contract was decisively shaped by governments' calculations over how, and in collaboration with which institutions, these goals could be achieved. In Britain, the strength of labor organizations meant that the recruitment of men and the production of munitions required ongoing negotiations between the government and the unions, while in France conscription and the weakness of labor enabled the government more or less to order men to the factory or the trenches and then delegate to the army or to industrialists the responsibility for using them to greatest effect.

When Lloyd George came to realize the need for massive increases in war production, he turned not only to businessmen to staff his new Ministry of Munitions, but also to trade unionists to deliver the workers and shop-floor changes necessary to make such production possible. The Treasury Agreement of March 1915, a further agreement between the 174,000-member Amalgamated Society of Engineers (ASE) and the government soon thereafter, and the Munitions Acts of July 1915 and January 1916 established the framework for that collaboration: trade unionists agreed to abrogate customary trade practices in exchange for guarantees that such changes would be for the period of the war only and that the pay and position of unionized workers would not be damaged. Existing demarcations between jobs as well as restrictions concerning the class of worker employed on such jobs were relaxed for the period of the war, allowing the introduction of semiskilled and female labor on work previously done only

---

[7] On the WEWNC, see especially Royden Harrison, "The War Emergency Workers' National Committee, 1914–1920," in Asa Briggs and John Saville, eds., *Essays in Labour History, 1886–1923*, vol. 2 (London: Macmillan, 1971), pp. 211–59. John Horne compares the work of the WEWNC and the Comité d'Action in *Labour at War* but, to my mind, rather overestimates the capacities of the French labor movement.

by members of the skilled unions. Strikes and lockouts were made illegal, and all conflicts were to be settled through compulsory arbitration. A system of "leaving certificates" was introduced, effectively limiting a worker's power to change jobs without the consent of his or her employer. Finally, a network of munitions tribunals was set up to hear complaints concerning the operation of the act. The act of July 1915 gave the newly founded Ministry of Munitions power to control any private establishment essential to war production: all the provisions of the act applied to such firms, and profits were limited to 20% above prewar levels. By 1918, almost 5 million workpeople were employed in firms operating under the Munitions Acts.[8]

Comprehensive as such controls may seem, they did not result in the subjugation of the independent worker to the servile state, as ASE shop stewards and later some historians were wont to argue.[9] Rather, while ministerial controls certainly constrained workers' mobility, they also opened up working conditions to scrutiny and oversight, involving union officials and shop stewards in the regulation of production at every level. Both Lloyd George and Christopher Addison discovered that whatever their theoretical powers as minister of munitions, in practice "the actual arrangements for the introduction of diluted labour had to be made separately in each workshop, by agreement with the skilled workers there."[10] Furthermore, as Gerry Rubin has shown, although the Munitions Acts were intended to limit the mobility of workers, the tribunals established to adjudicate complaints could also be used by trade unionists as a forum in which to expose employers' evasions of ministry regulations. Unequal as the contract-

[8] There are many studies of the wartime regulation of labor. Two good contemporary accounts, from widely different perspectives, were written by Humbert Wolfe, controller of the Labour Regulation Department at the Ministry of Munitions during the war, and by G. D. H. Cole, wartime director of the Research Department of the Amalgamated Society of Engineers, for the Carnegie Endowment for International Peace: Wolfe, *Labour Supply and Regulation* (Oxford University Press, 1923); Cole, *Trade Unionism and Munitions* (Oxford University Press, 1923). For an excellent and nuanced recent study, see Gerry R. Rubin, *War, Law, and Labour: The Munitions Acts, State Regulation, and the Unions, 1915–1921* (Oxford University Press, 1987); the figures for the numbers of workers covered by the acts are from Rubin, p. 17. It is important to remember that the Munitions Acts were applied far beyond engineering; less than half of all workers regulated by the acts were in the metals sector.

[9] See especially William Gallacher, *Revolt on the Clyde* (New York: International Publishers, 1937); James Hinton, *The First Shop Stewards' Movement* (London: Allen & Unwin, 1973).

[10] David Lloyd George, *War Memoirs, 1917* (Boston: Little, Brown, 1934), p. 179; also, Imperial War Museum [IWM], Man Power Distribution Board Papers, evidence of Dr. Addison, 17 Oct. 1916.

ing partners might be, a type of "industrial corporatism" was established in Britain for the period of the war.[11]

Nor was collaboration confined to industrial mobilization. In the absence of conscription, recruitment of soldiers could also become a matter for union negotiation and concern. Initially, the government's concern was to prevent enlistment among skilled workers, since high rates of volunteering – near or over 20% in coal mining, engineering, and the manufacture of explosives – had already led employers and civil servants to fear for the productive capacities of crucial war industries.[12] Within a year of the outbreak of war, the Admiralty and War Office began to allow employers to issue badges to workers deemed essential to war production, a practice later taken over directly by the Ministry of Munitions, which, by October 1915, had designated some 1.5 million men as employed on essential work and hence exempt from recruiting. When the government finally conceded the necessity of conscription, it had to contend with this prior system of exemptions, as well as with the reluctance of the Ministry of Munitions to relinquish any of its workers. The skilled trade unions, moreover, had agreed to the "dilution" of labor only to increase production, not to enable the government to call up skilled men; the passage of the Military Service Acts did not, to their mind, abrogate this prior agreement. The threat that unionized munition workers could be "debadged" and sent to the front led to a serious strike at Sheffield in November of 1916, and in its wake, conscription became subject to the same kinds of negotiation involved in the deployment of labor. A "Trade Card Scheme" was then introduced, whereby the task of exempting men on essential work from military service was delegated to the skilled trade unions themselves – to the disgust of semiskilled men, who were without such protection. The "Trade Card Scheme" did not survive continued pressure from the army for more men, but its abolition and the simultaneous introduction of a bill to extend dilution to work not covered by the Munitions Acts provoked in the spring of 1917 the most significant engineering strike of the war. The government, in response, halted plans to extend dilution, abolished the hated "leaving certificates," and maintained the position of skilled men by exempting all workers in a "Schedule of Protected Occupa-

---

[11] Rubin, *War, Law, and Labour.*

[12] Adams and Poirier, *The Conscription Controversy*, pp. 90–1. As J. M. Winter shows, however, rates of enlistment were highest (over 40% during the first eighteen months) among professional and white-collar workers; see Winter, *The Great War and the British People*, p. 34.

tions." In early 1918, the ASE refused to participate in further negotiations aimed at revising this schedule in order to release more men for the army, on the grounds that no skilled man should be recruited while dilutees remained in industry. Not until after the final German offensive of March 1918 was the government able to call up a "clean cut" of young workers in protected occupations without serious unrest.[13]

The deployment of men, then, whether for the factories or the front, was constrained in Britain by an ongoing series of negotiations with the trade unions, conducted both nationally and at the level of the individual firm. This process contrasts sharply with the measures used to ensure the adequate provision of men and munitions in France. The fact that all men of military age were liable for service made negotiation almost irrelevant. True, the government soon discovered that conscription without regard to previous occupation could cripple war production. Rather than exempting such men from military service, however, the government returned skilled workers to the factory without discharging them from the army: they remained under military discipline and were liable to be transferred to other areas or sent back to the front for absenteeism, activism, or insubordination. Such a strategy left the deployment of labor in the hands of the state, while simultaneously providing a docile work force for the war factories: mobilized workers constituted almost a third of the 1.6 million workers under the supervision of the Ministry of Munitions in August of 1917. Yet despite restrictions on their liberties, mobilized workers were resented as shirkers (*embusqués*) by other sectors of the populace, especially peasants and servicemen's wives, whose sons or husbands had not been able to avoid the trenches.[14]

The weakness of labor also meant that the French "contract" gave pride of place to employers. As John Godfrey's careful book on the subject makes clear, negotiations over war production initially took

[13] The complex course of government policy in the area of the recruitment of skilled men is covered by Wolfe, *Labour Supply*, and by Grieves, *The Politics of Manpower*. On the May 1917 strikes and the limitation of dilution, see Commission of Enquiry into Industrial Unrest, *Summary of the Reports of the Commission*, PP 1917–18, XV, Cd. 8696; IWM, Man Power Distribution Board Papers, "Memo from Arthur Henderson to the MPDB," 16 Nov. 1917.

[14] On mobilized workers, see William Oualid and Charles Picquenard, *Salaires et tarifs, conventions collectives et grèves: La politique du Ministère du Travail* (Paris: Presses Universitaires de France, 1928) pp. 34–5, 49, 61, 216; Gerd Hardach, "La mobilisation industrielle en 1914–1918: Production, planification et idéologie," in Patrick Fridenson, ed., *1914–1918: L'autre front* (Paris: Editions Ouvrières, 1977), pp. 86, 97–9. On resentments against such workers, see Becker, *The Great War*, pp. 135, 143.

place between the bureaucracy, the employers, and the legislature, with trade unionists effectively excluded until quite late in the war.[15] To some extent, the state simply delegated the task of organizing war production to employers: while the latter were forced to accept state-supervised coordination of purchasing and fixed prices, both the importation and allocation of raw materials made scarce in France by German occupation of the North and the task of allocating workers returned from the front in 1914 were turned over directly to the powerful iron and steel confederation, the Comité des Forges.[16] Laws on hours and night work were disregarded with the consent and encouragement of the Ministry of Labor's own factory inspectorate, and – unlike in Britain – the profits of firms contracting with the government were never controlled. Even the socialist Albert Thomas relied on high profits while minister of munitions as an incentive to increased production. Only gradually would Thomas and other ministry officials realize the cost of these arrangements, both for workers' well-being and for their own authority, and begin to intervene in the organization and treatment of labor in individual war factories. When strikes broke out in the Paris engineering sector in the winter of 1916–17 the ministry began to set wages directly, and wage fixing and compulsory arbitration were gradually extended through the munitions sector.[17]

The war thus strengthened both organization among employers and the ties between the latter and the government. Indeed, wartime needs led the government to encourage businessmen to consolidate their associations and to create new ones, especially in the engineering trades. Louis Loucheur, the minister of munitions who replaced Albert Thomas in September 1917, and Etienne Clémentel, the minister of commerce, were both modernizing technocrats with visions of a postwar economic revival built on the systematic concentration of industry, collective bargaining among powerful associations of labor

---

[15] John F. Godfrey, *Capitalism at War: Industrial Policy and Bureaucracy in France, 1914–1918* (Leamington Spa: Berg, 1987). John Horne shows in *Labour at War* that the CGT also collaborated with the government, but its role was largely advisory.

[16] Godfrey, *Capitalism at War*, pp. 49–50, 211–38; Henry Donald Peiter, "Men of Good Will: French Businessmen and the First World War," Ph.D. diss., University of Michigan, 1973, pp. 79–80; Oualid and Picquenard, *Salaires et tarifs*, p. 49; Gerd Hardach, *The First World War, 1914–1918* (Berkeley and Los Angeles: University of California Press, 1977), pp. 86–91.

[17] Peiter, "Men of Good Will," p. 86; Hardach, "La mobilisation industrielle," pp. 97–9; Becker, *The Great War*, pp. 205–12; Arthur Fontaine, *French Industry during the War* (New Haven, Conn.: Yale University Press, 1926), p. 43.

and capital, and the application of modern management techniques. In July 1919, partly in response to their pressure, businessmen formed the Confédération Générale de la Production Française (CGPF), which, although dominated by heavy industry, became the umbrella employers' association during the interwar years.[18]

In Britain and France, then, an identical need to ensure adequate supplies of munitions and men led ministers to inaugurate quite different social contracts. The continuous contract operating between government and labor in Britain had no parallel in France, where ministers and civil servants found their attempt to safeguard workers' conditions limited by their prior delegation of authority to employers. The reworking of the labor market and of family maintenance in both countries, to which we shall now turn, cannot be understood except in light of these different patterns. It is worth recalling, however, that although these wartime arrangements had an important impact on gender relations in both countries, in neither were women's organizations important partners in the wartime contract. Feminists, especially in Britain, found themselves deeply divided over the war, and in 1915 an influential group of women left the National Union of Women's Suffrage Societies to devote themselves to pacifist activities. Yet even those who loyally suspended their agitation for the vote and rallied to the war effort often discovered that the government had little enthusiasm for their services.[19] Feminists could not convincingly claim to represent "women" as a collectivity, nor were women workers well enough organized for the leaders of the women's unions to be included in the initial negotiations that established the framework for the wartime use of women's labor in Britain, although such labor leaders did serve on important government committees later in the

---

[18] On Loucheur and Clémentel, see Godfrey, *Capitalism at War*; Richard Kuisel, *Capitalism and the State in Modern France* (Cambridge University Press, 1981), pp. 37–50; Stephen Douglas Carls, "Louis Loucheur: A French Technocrat in Government, 1916–1920," Ph.D. diss., University of Minnesota, 1982, pp. 183–4; Martin Fine, "Towards Corporatism: the Movement for Capital–Labor Collaboration in France, 1914–1936," Ph.D. diss., University of Wisconsin, 1971, pp. 56–9.

[19] Much work has been done on the crisis of feminism during the war. Johanna Alberti summarizes the wartime divisions in the National Union in *Beyond Suffrage: Feminists in War and Peace, 1914–28* (London: Macmillan, 1989), pp. 38–70. Laurence Klejman and Florence Rochefort's recent history of French feminism stresses the movement's wartime loyalty and patriotism, as do Steven C. Hause and Anne R. Kenney: Klejman and Rochefort, *L'égalité en marche: Le féminisme sous la Troisième République* (Paris: Presses de la Fondation Nationale des Sciences Politiques, 1989), pp. 189–98; Steven C. Hause with Anne R. Kenney, *Women's Suffrage and Social Politics in the French Third Republic* (Princeton, N.J.: Princeton University Press, 1984), pp. 191–7.

war. Although many wartime social services and much of industry came to rely on the work of women, such developments were gradual and took place within a network of arrangements that women had little part in making.

Gender, dependence, and the labor market

If the war opened up an opportunity for new departures in the area of family policy, it was in part because it threatened to change the structure of the labor market beyond all recognition. Family policies, of course, do not mirror *actual* patterns of familial maintenance and dependence created by the labor market; rather, they reflect idealized abstractions of such patterns. Yet if ideal and reality diverge too radically – if, for example, a vast number of women enter the work force despite assumptions of their "dependent" status – wage and welfare policies based on the "ideal" of dependence will become increasingly dysfunctional. The question is, simply, whether this happened during the war. Was the dislocation of the labor market systematic or long lasting enough to influence decisively the future shape of family policy? Especially in Britain, where the sex segregation of labor and the male-breadwinner norm was strongest, did the widespread introduction of women into "men's work" force policymakers to abandon the assumption that work was normally a male preserve, and male workers responsible for maintaining dependent wives and children?

Certainly, the short-term changes in the labor market were substantial. In both countries, women's employment expanded both absolutely and in proportion to men's. In Britain, the numbers of women considered gainfully employed grew from slightly under 6 million in July 1914 to 7,311,000 in July 1918, or from 31 to 37% of all women and girls over age 10. In France, where well over 5 million men entered the army within the first ten months of the war, women moved quickly to replace men in the spheres of agriculture and commerce. Studies by the French Ministry of Labor show that women's industrial employment declined by as much as 50% during the first traumatic year of the war; by 1916, however, even industrial employment had risen to 20% above prewar levels. Perhaps even more significant was the extent to which, in both countries, the war "feminized" the labor force as a whole, with women moving into sectors previously closed to them. The careful inquiries conducted during the war by the British Association in Britain, and the estimates offered by Jean-Louis Robert for France, summarized in Table 2.1, show that by 1918 the sex composition of the labor force in both countries had changed dra-

Table 2.1. *Women as a percentage of the total work force, 1914 and 1918*

Sector	Britain 1914	Britain 1918	France 1914	France 1918[a]
Agriculture and fishing	9	14	38	—
Industry and transport	23	34	35	40
Trade and finance	27	53	41	55
Services (nondomestic)	34	46	27	—
Total	24	37	38	46

[a] French figures for 1918 are estimates by Jean-Louis Robert.
Sources: British Association for the Advancement of Science, *British Labour: Replacement and Conciliation, 1914–21* (London: Pitman & Sons, 1921), p. 2; Jean-Louis Robert, "Women and Work in France during the First World War," in Richard Wall and Jay Winter, eds., *The Upheaval of War: Family, Work and Welfare in Europe, 1914–1918* (Cambridge University Press, 1988), p. 262.

matically, with women comprising 34% of the industrial work force in Britain and 40% in France, and over 50% of all workers in trade and finance in both countries.[20]

Many of these women were absorbed into the burgeoning munitions sector. By the Armistice, almost 1 million women had moved into the metal and chemical industries or were directly employed in the government arsenals in Britain; they comprised 29% of the 3.3 million workers in these sectors. Women also made up 25% of the 1.7 million workers employed in the war factories in France by September 1918; of these workers, another 29% were reservists, 10% foreigners, 2%

[20] The British authorities kept far better records than did the French of the effects of the war on the sex composition of the labor force; see especially War Cabinet Committee on Women in Industry, *Report, PP* 1919, XXXI, Cmd. 135, esp. pp. 80–1; British Association for the Advancement of Science, *British Labour: Replacement and Conciliation, 1914–21* (London: Pitman & Sons, 1921); Irene Andrews and Margaret Hobbs, *Economic Effects of the World War upon Women and Children in Great Britain* (1918; rev. ed. New York: Oxford University Press, 1921); Gail Braybon, *Women Workers and the First World War* (London: Croom Helm, 1981). Jean-Louis Robert derives plausible estimates of the scale of French changes from the rather contradictory *enquêtes* of the French Ministry of Labor in "Women and Work in France during the First World War," in Wall and Winter, eds., *The Upheaval of War*, pp. 251–66; see also William Oualid, "The Effect of the War upon Labour in France," in Charles Gide, ed., *Effects of the War upon French Economic Life* (Oxford University Press, 1923), esp. pp. 156–8. The only recent general account of women's work in France is Françoise Thébaud's rather unsatisfactory *La femme au temps de la guerre de 14* (Paris: Stock, 1986).

prisoners of war, and 34% civilian men.[21] The traditional and often
ill-paid women's trades stagnated or declined in the face of these new
opportunities. In Britain, domestic servants deserted in droves. Overall numbers of women in service fell from 1,658,000 to 1,258,000 in
the course of the war, to the distress of middle-class mistresses and
their daughters, who, like Vera Brittain, could find themselves recalled from more rewarding work as nurses to care for ailing parents
or understaffed households.[22]

Women workers in both countries also experienced improved – if
not equal – conditions and pay as a result of the war. Such improvements were by no means immediate, especially in France, where
regulatory machinery was slow to develop. In time, however, full
employment, the decline of the low-paid sectors, the spread of unionization and of labor militancy, and the extension of statutory wage
regulations all combined to "level up" wages substantially. Women's
earnings, especially in war industries, improved absolutely but also
relatively, as wage differentials both between skilled and unskilled
and between men and women narrowed.[23] And in Britain, where
custom, prejudice, and even organization had reduced married wom-
en's labor force participation rates to around 10% before the war,
married women reentered the work force in considerable numbers.
Although there are no reliable general figures for the expansion of
married women's work, investigations done within particular factories
commented on the unusually high numbers of married women employed, as high as 40–60% in some war factories.[24] Married women's

---

[21] British Association, *British Labour*, p. 2; Ministère du Travail, *Tarifs de salaires et conventions collectives pendant la guerre (1914–1918)*, vol. 4 (Paris: Imprimerie Nationale,
1923), p. vi.

[22] Figures on domestic service are given in the War Cabinet Committee on Women in
Industry, *Report*, p. 80; Vera Brittain, *Testament of Youth* (1933; rpt. New York: Seaview
Books, 1980), pp. 421–2.

[23] This point has been made repeatedly, especially for Britain. For the narrowing of sex
and skill differentials in Britain, see Arthur L. Bowley, *Prices and Wages in the United
Kingdom, 1914–1920* (Oxford University Press, 1921), esp. chaps. 6 and 7; Bernard
Waites, *A Class Society at War: England, 1914–18* (Leamington Spa: Berg, 1987), pp. 130–
148. For France (and comparatively), see Laura Lee Downs, "Women in Industry, 1914–
1939: The Employers' Perspective. A Comparative Study of the French and British
Metals Industry," Ph.D. diss., Columbia University, 1987, esp. pp. 81, 85. It is worth
noting, however, that women's wages in the older "women's trades" often did not even
keep pace with inflation.

[24] British Association, *British Labour*, p. 30; Imperial War Museum, War Cabinet Committee on Women in Industry, Verbatim Minutes of Evidence (henceforth cited as IWM,
WIC Minutes), Bean evidence, 28 Oct. 1918.

exclusion from waged work, key to the argument for the "family wage," appeared to be breaking down.

In this process, many women also appear to have shed their old reputation for docility and in some cases to have developed increasingly militant attitudes. Women war workers, for example, initiated the 1917 strike wave in the Paris region. Unionization among women also grew, especially in Britain, where the number of women belonging to trade unions mushroomed from under one-half million in 1914 to one and one-quarter million by 1918 – a figure more than twice that of the *entire* membership, women and men, of the French CGT in that same year.[25] Middle-class feminists, Fabians, and social reformers in Britain, watching this experiment, could not believe that changes on this scale could be rolled back and prophesied that women's economic gains would carry over into peacetime.[26]

Yet the war experience had, if anything, the opposite effect; by and large, it confirmed prewar patterns. In Britain, the war deepened the definition of wage earning as merely a temporary expedient for women, while in France women retained their position as a segregated but "normal" class of workers. Such an outcome seems almost counterintuitive, for it was in Britain that the government established the most comprehensive training schemes for women, that women's war work received greater attention, and that an entire network of regulations and institutions evolved to supervise and "protect" these workers. To explain why such expansion, high pay, and unionization did not in the end transform "women" into "workers" in Britain, while wage earning remained a legitimate role for French women even after marriage, we must place these women's experiences within the context of the social contract previously described. Women's place was determined, in large part, by the nature of the agreements arrived at between employers, trade unionists, and the government, as we shall see by looking briefly at the two cases.

The first and most obvious explanation for the limited impact of the war on women's workplace position in Britain is that the very agreements regulating the expansion of women's work stipulated that any changes were to be for the period of the war only. The landmark Treasury Agreement of 1915 and the subsidiary agreements that followed committed trade unions active in the munitions trades to relax demarcation restrictions, admit less skilled and female labor, and ac-

[25] British Association, *British Labour*, p. 86.
[26] See, e.g., B. L. Hutchins, *Women in Industry after the War* (London: Athenaeum, 1919), p. 5.

cept compulsory arbitration, in exchange for government pledges that such changes would last for the war only and would not be used to cheapen production and lower "the rate for the job." Those areas in which a government-sponsored expansion of women's employment was greatest were thus often also the areas in which regulation was most intense and the postwar exclusion of women most firmly insisted upon.

A brief examination of the successful introduction of women into the munitions and engineering trades can expose some of the reasons for this apparent paradox.[27] The introduction of women threatened skilled men's status because it posed an immediate question: how could women, a group considered almost by definition unskilled, be able to perform tasks hitherto the preserve of fully skilled men? There were really only three possible answers to this conundrum: either they were able to do so because of a simplification of the labor process; or the work had not been particularly "skilled" in the first place; or the women had themselves acquired "skill."

The Amalgamated Society of Engineers tended to prefer the first answer and employers the second, but the truth was somewhat more complicated. Even before 1914, skilled status had been socially as well as technically defined: membership in a skilled trade union and work-shop solidarity were as important determinants of skilled status as was technical ability – especially when, as was the case in the decade before the war, the simplification of the labor process and the decay of the apprenticeship system had eroded the technical requirements of many jobs and the versatility of many skilled engineers.[28] Some work done by skilled men could thus be performed by women with little or no training; other processes could be broken down to enable less skilled workers to take them over – the practice known as "dilution." More problematically, however, when women did acquire and use a wider

---

[27] The following discussion of women's work in engineering is based heavily on an earlier research project: Susan Pedersen, "Explaining the Persistence of Gender Hierarchy at Work: The Dilution of Labor in British Munitions Industries, 1914–1918," B.A. thesis, Harvard-Radcliffe, 1982. See also Marion Kozak, "Women Munition Workers during the First World War with Special Reference to Engineering," Ph.D. diss., Hull University, 1976; Barbara Drake, *Women in the Engineering Trades* (London: Allen & Unwin, 1917). By far the most valuable archival records are the WIC Minutes, cited in note 24.

[28] G. D. H. Cole, director of the Research Department of the ASE during the war, drew attention to the explosive combination of the prewar degradation of the apprenticeship system and the ASE's continued ability to prevent employment of unskilled and non-union labor. See IWM, WIC Minutes, Cole evidence, 30 Oct. 1918, p. R24; Cole, *Trade Unionism*, pp. 41–3, 46.

range of skills – whether through the ministry training courses given to some tens of thousands of women, through the specialized courses established by feminist organizations eager to show what women could do, or simply by learning on the job in what proved to be a long and exhausting war – their prior definition as "unskilled" proved almost impossible to break down.[29] Sex, in other words, was a category that preceded and overrode categorization by skill. While ASE members could do technically simple work without losing their claim to skill, neither training nor performance were likely to win such status for women. Employers, government officials, and trade unionists throughout the war regarded the phrase "skilled woman" almost as an oxymoron, dividing workers into "skilled men," "semiskilled men," "unskilled men," and "women."[30] While substituted women were to be paid "men's rates" if doing "men's work" – according to ministry regulations – it was men's prior performance of the work rather than its technical content or the ability of the women now performing it that justified such pay.

This was a potentially explosive situation. The fact that women learned to do skilled men's work but were themselves only rarely considered skilled workers gave government managers and contractors a real incentive to regrade work. Certainly some employers altered processes in order to lower their technical difficulty, but trade unionists also complained that managers commonly made superficial changes simply to pay the women wages they considered appropriate to women – usually about half an average man's wage.[31] Thus, while

[29] Although women were not supposed to set their own machines and grind their own tools, supervisors admitted to the War Cabinet Committee on Women in Industry that such practices were common; numerous records also exist of women taking over wide areas of work that, before the war, would have been the province of skilled men. See, e.g., IWM, WIC Minutes, Evidence of Miss Lowery, Welfare Superviser, Foster, Blackett, and Wilson, Hepburn-on-Tyne, 5 Nov. 1918, p. T46, and the IWM Oral Histories of the First World War, Interviews with Isabella Clarke, Bessie Davies, and George Ginns. On ministry training, see IWM, WIC Minutes, Evidence of James Currie, Director of Training of Munition Workers, Labour Supply Department, 3 Oct. 1918, p. J79; also L. K. Yates, *The Women's Part: A Record of Munitions Work* (New York: George H. Doran, 1918).

[30] See, e.g., "Dilution, Its Urgency, Principles and Practice," *Dilution of Labour Bulletin*, 2 (Nov. 1916), pp. 21–3.

[31] The evidence given by employers and managers confirms that women's wages were kept from equalling men's through a variety of strategies, including reclassifying work, changing processes, or simply cutting piecework rates. See IWM, WIC Minutes, C. F. Chance evidence, 16 Nov. 1918; Mason evidence, 16 Nov. 1918; Gilmore evidence, 19 Oct. 1918; Smith evidence, 28 Oct. 1918; Bean evidence, 28 Oct. 1918; Carlin evidence,

197,000 of 225,000 women employed in government establishments and 195,000 of 594,000 women employed in the metal industries in July 1918 were said to be "directly replacing men," fewer than 5% of all women munitions workers in 1918 were paid at skilled men's rates.[32] The effect of such regrading was to destroy any semblance of a rational relationship between the technical content of many processes and "the rate for the job": by 1918, when Beatrice Webb toured a war factory while serving on the War Cabinet Committee on Women in Industry, she remarked that "the piecework rates had no relation at all to the character of the effort expended." Simple operations that could not be broken down could be more highly paid than difficult but "regraded" ones, exposing the degree to which gender and organizational status underlay pay differentials.[33]

"Dilution" thus not only challenged the monopoly of particular types of work by skilled men, it also threatened to expose the degree to which "skill" was socially, rather than technically, defined. It is important to remember, however, that skilled workers were "diluted" with both women and less skilled men – and to understand why craftsmen responded to the two groups quite differently. Less skilled men were a threat because their employment could lead to the permanent regrading of some engineering work as "semiskilled," especially if these men were organized by a general union – such as the Workers' Union – willing to countenance the downgrading of work in order to preserve their members' position after the war. The ASE thus adopted a two-pronged strategy toward male dilutees, limiting their introduction and the scope of their work when possible, and – against their official policy of excluding all dilutees – organizing them when necessary.[34] The ASE and other craft unions were involved in skirmishes both with the government and with unions representing the semiskilled over the allowable limits of dilution throughout the war; they succeeded in halting the process on work outside the scope of the

15 Oct. 1918; Macarthur evidence, 4 Oct. 1918; also War Cabinet Committee on Women in Industry, *Report*, pp. 122–3; Cole, *Trade Unionism*, p. 165.
[32] War Cabinet Committee on Women in Industry, *Report*, p. 81; IWM, WIC Minutes, Mrs. Blanco White evidence, 1 Oct. 1918.
[33] IWM, WIC Minutes, Bean evidence, 28 Oct. 1918, p. D31.
[34] The ASE claimed that they did not allow dilutees into their organization (IWM, WIC Minutes, ASE evidence, 30 Oct. 1918, p. R96), but other observers noted that men who acquired real skills were sometimes admitted, much as the ASE had come to accept five years of employment on skilled work as an equivalent for apprenticeship before the war; see Currie evidence, 3 Oct. 1918, p. J81.

Munitions Acts, as well as ensuring that dilutees were conscripted before skilled men.[35]

Women may have been a greater threat in the abstract, since their very presence ran against the traditions and culture of engineering trade unionism, and their admission to the ASE would have involved a virtually unimaginable repudiation of these norms. Furthermore, as the war experience showed, if women were admitted as a separate class of worker, work turned over to them quickly tended to become "women's work" (regardless of its content) and to move outside the sphere and pay scales of men entirely. Yet women were also identifiable by sex alone and thus constituted a threat only if the government reneged on its promise to enforce their blanket dismissal at the end of the war. The fact that, as one industrial investigator put it, "the sex line of demarcation is clearly defined, unlike that between classes of men," could thus lead craftsmen to prefer dilution by women, believing that they would be able to enforce their exclusion at the end of the war.[36] ASE strategy toward women, then, was simple: they proposed to rely on government agreements and union strength to ensure the dismissal of women dilutees at the end of the war. When asked by the War Cabinet Committee on Women in Industry whether or not women could be allowed onto repetition jobs in engineering during the postwar period, ASE representatives said such speculation was out of place: "You must recognise that we have got very specific pledges from the government and also from the employers, that the women will not be engaged in industry after the war." Any employer who tried to keep them, they warned, would see his men simply walk out.[37]

Although the introduction of women into engineering and other trades covered by the Munitions Acts was the most striking change in women's economic position, and hence has absorbed a good deal of scholarly attention, substitution and dilution were practiced widely in other trades as well. These experiments were equally important, for while many women workers would inevitably leave munitions

[35] Duncan Tanner, following recent historiographic trends, stresses the degree to which craft unions resisted and resented the competition of the less skilled. See Tanner, *Political Change and the Labour Party, 1900–1918* (Cambridge University Press, 1990), pp. 363–5.

[36] Herbert R. Highton, "Report on the Engineering Industry in Clyde District, August 1916," in Drake, *Women in the Engineering Trades*, p. 132. G. D. H. Cole also stated that skilled trade unionists preferred women dilutees, since they felt they would be easy to exclude after the war; Cole, *Trade Unionism*, p. 219.

[37] IWM, WIC Minutes, ASE evidence, 30 Oct. 1918, pp. R70, R73, R96.

when the industry contracted at the end of the war, changes made in other sectors could easily have lasted into peacetime. Yet the introduction of women proceeded (and receded) along very similar lines in other industrial sectors. As in munitions and engineering, women were introduced only with the (often grudging) consent of the unions. Between 1915 and 1917, agreements were drawn up under Home Office supervision between employers and unions in textiles, clothing, bootmaking, china, food, printing, and other trades. As a rule, such agreements stipulated that women were to be introduced on "men's work" only if enough men could not be found, that they were to be paid at men's rates, that such changes must be made in consultation with local union officials, and that they were to last only for the period of the war.[38]

A set of agreements between employers, unions, and the government and the enforcement of these agreements on the shop floor thus provided for the limitation (and in some cases the exclusion) of women workers from new spheres of industrial work after the war. Yet something else sustained these agreements, especially as the war dragged on and the capacities of women became more apparent. When pressed to explain the unequal treatment of women, policymakers fell back on the rhetoric of separate spheres, reiterating that wage earning was incompatible with marriage for women, and that public policy should aim less at bettering women's working conditions than, as the government's Health of Munitions Workers Committee put it, at preserving "the womanhood of the country" for "the privilege first of creating and maintaining a wholesome family life, and secondly, of developing the higher influences of social life – both matters of primary and vital importance to the future of the nation."[39] Since, as the Board of Trade's Departmental Committee on Engineering after the War put it, "marriage has always been, and we trust will always be, a reason for the discontinuance of factory work by women,"[40] government officials, managers, and employers alike tended to agree that entry into the skilled trades and indeed equal pay would be wasted on women: only the "abnormal," one employer argued, would prefer the workshop to the home;[41] normally, another added, women did not "expect to be paid exactly the same as a man who has responsibilities and a family to

[38] Andrews and Hobbs, *Economic Effects of the World War*, pp. 61–2.
[39] Ministry of Munitions, Health of Munitions Workers Committee, *Final Report, PP* 1918, XII, Cd. 9065, p. 20.
[40] Board of Trade, Departmental Committee Appointed to Consider the Position of the Engineering Trades after the War, *Report, PP* 1918, XIII, Cd. 9073, p. 16.
[41] "Women's Wages and Apprenticeship," *Engineer*, 120 (1 Oct. 1915), p. 319.

keep."[42] Even in the case of young unmarried women, the national interest should override personal desires. As one manager put it, "Considerations of national health should be given great weight in judging what is fit work for actual or prospective mothers."[43]

The degree to which women workers' status as "women" served to underscore their abnormality as workers is especially clear from the reports of the Health of Munitions Workers Committee, which was established in September of 1915 and was much influenced by Seebohm Rowntree, the businessman and philanthropist who later directed the Welfare Department of the Ministry of Munitions and whom we shall encounter again as the most important "scientific" defender of the male-breadwinner wage norm. It is revealing in itself that welfare workers were appointed to supervise conditions for women and young boys but not for men; sex and age rather than industrial position elicited special management and care.[44] And while the welfare movement did result in improved conditions for women war workers – including the introduction of shorter shifts, factory canteens, protective clothing, and other amenities – the Health of Munitions Workers Committee often justified its concern on the grounds that these women were "potential" mothers, usually while overlooking the needs of "actual" working mothers. Despite the expansion of married women's work, the committee was ambivalent about nurseries, and its skepticism was shared by most medical officers of health, who, when surveyed in 1917, usually expressed themselves opposed to providing services, at least once the war was over, that would "make it easier for the mother and child to be parted" or "afford an argument for married women to take up work outside their homes."[45] Rather than embark on the slippery slope of helping women to combine waged work with motherhood, policymakers sought to ensure that war work would not damage women's capacity for their future reproductive role.[46]

[42] IWM, WIC Minutes, Melville Smith evidence, 28 Oct. 1918, p. D70.

[43] Ibid., Gilmore evidence, 19 Oct. 1918, p. L20.

[44] By the end of the war, there were 1,000 women's welfare supervisors, 275 supervisors concerned with "boys' welfare," but none concerned with men. Henry A. Mess, *Factory Legislation and Its Administration, 1891–1924* (London: P. S. King & Son, 1926), p. 129.

[45] Health of Munitions Workers Committee, *Final Report*, p. 28; British Library of Political and Economic Science (BLPES), Papers of the Women's Employment Committee of the Ministry of Reconstruction, 2/90, "Draft Report on Day Nurseries" (23 July 1917). Quotations are from responses to the draft report sent by Dr. J. Buchan, M.O.H. for Bradford, and Dr. Thomas Evans, M.O.H. for Swansea, appended to the report, pp. 6, 17.

[46] Rather surprisingly, it was usually the women hired as welfare supervisors who themselves came to question the official obsession with protecting "potential mothers." "We

What is particularly striking is the degree to which not only the trade union movement but also the unions representing industrial women fell into line with this point of view. Although they had not been consulted about the initial agreements governing women's employment, the National Federation of Women Workers (NFWW), which did come to be accepted as the legitimate representative of women workers' interests, loyally supported the majority trade union position.[47] Only some leaders of the general labor unions, which organized many dilutees during the war and whose members were already resentful of the privileged position of craft unionists in regard to pay and conscription, argued that women had any right to stay in the engineering and other diluted trades. If in the past women had undercut men's wage rates, some of the Workers' Union officers argued, this was the fault of the "conceit" of the craft unionists themselves, who were trying to keep up inequalities in job demarcations and pay for which the technical justification had disappeared.[48] The NFWW, by contrast, fought for the support of male trade unionists by carefully dissociating themselves from such arguments: indeed, in June 1915 the union came to an agreement with the ASE, promising that in exchange for help in recruiting women munition workers, it would support their exclusion from engineering at the end of the war.[49] Yet the NFWW always denied that it was sacrificing its members' interests to those of the men in the trade, arguing that the defense of men's rates, even at the cost of women's exclusion, served the interests of the working class as a whole. "There can be no sex war,"

---

are too much inclined to focus our view on this maternal function," Dr. Elizabeth Butler, the medical officer of one shell-filling factory, told the War Cabinet Committee. "I do not think we have any reason to believe that this physiological function is the thing which is selected by every kind of unsuitable condition as its victim." All the welfare workers and doctors stated that good food and high wages were the best solution to the problems of women's health, whether maternity related or not. IWM, WIC Minutes, Deacon, Butler, and Cullis evidence, 23–24 Oct. and 4 Nov. 1918.

[47] On the NFWW, see Barbara Drake, *Women in Trade Unions* (London: Allen & Unwin, 1920); also Mary Agnes Hamilton, *Mary Macarthur* (New York: Thomas Seltzer, 1926).

[48] Deborah Thom, "Women Munition Workers at Woolwich Arsenal in the 1914–1918 War," M.A. thesis, University of Warwick, 1974, p. 53; Richard Hyman, *The Workers' Union* (Oxford University Press, 1971), p. 112. Despite ASE discouragement, the Workers' Union grew to almost 400,000 by the end of 1918, including between 60,000 and 80,000 women. Women's membership in general unions as a whole grew from 24,000 to over 200,000 at the time of the Armistice, only part of the wider explosion of unionization among women. British Association, *British Labour*, p. 86.

[49] On the ASE–NFWW pact, see Thom, "Women Munition Workers," pp. 89–91; Cole, *Trade Unionism*, pp. 203–4; Hyman, *The Workers' Union*, pp. 119–20. The NFWW grew from slightly over 10,000 to about 60,000 members over the course of the war.

Mary Macarthur, the NFWW's brilliant leader, told the 1917 TUC, "because the interests of men and women as wage earners are identical."[50]

Such arguments raised the status of the women's leaders within the trade union movement, but they also locked them into a particular trap. Unable to demand equal access to men's jobs, the women trade union leaders were forced to rely on arguments linking women's wartime struggles not to their current interests as *workers* but to their presumed postwar roles as dependent wives and daughters. Indeed, if we pay attention to the rhetoric of trade union leaders, we can see how a vision of a gender-stratified society, based on separate familial roles for men and women, underlay much wartime trade union strategy. In 1918, Mary Macarthur admitted that she was "sufficiently old-fashioned" to believe in an ideal world in which "a woman would not be driven from home and children by economic necessity";[51] such an ideal would be realized, however, only if women gave up any claim to jobs in the "men's trades" in order to defend the postwar male family wage. Throughout the war, NFWW leaders exhorted women workers to demand equal pay, less for reasons of justice due to women, than in order to safeguard the postwar position of men. For example, in March 1916, the NFWW's *Woman Worker* reminded "girls" of their "duty" to receive equal pay, or "all their cleverness and their intelligence go to helping the employer and bringing down the wages of their husbands, fathers and brothers."[52] Similarly, and somewhat against her will, Macarthur was forced to admit the link between the exclusion of women and the male family wage when cross-examined in 1918 by the War Cabinet Committee on Women in Industry on the intent of the equal pay provisions of the Treasury Agreement:

Q: Was [the agreement] to protect [skilled men] from competition by women?
A: It was to protect them from the unfair competition of women which would lower their standard of payment.
Q: Prevent them from competition by women at lower rates.
A: Yes.
Q: In other words to exclude woman labour except at the men's rates.
A: Except at the men's rates.
Q: So that after the war they could exclude women.
A: That is part of another pledge.

---

[50] TUC, *Report*, 49 (1917), pp. 257–8.
[51] Mary Macarthur, "The Women Trade Unionists' Point of View," in Marion Phillips, ed., *Women and the Labour Party* (London: Headley Brothers, 1918), p. 19.
[52] *Woman Worker*, Mar. 1916.

Q: Does it occur to you that it was intended to protect the men under post-war conditions from the competition of women?
A: It was to protect the man and his wife and his children.
Q: To protect the man as wage earner.
A: Yes.[53]

Exclusionary strategies and a commitment to the male family wage ensured that "loyal" unions would help roll back women's gains at the end of the war.

The pervasive identification of women as "meantime" workers, eager to return to their families at the onset of peace, thus survived both the government-sponsored expansion of their employment and massive unionization. Indeed, their very presence in industry continued to be seen as justifiably up for debate, a fact that Beatrice Webb angrily protested in her minority report for the Committee on Women in Industry. "To concentrate the whole attention of the readers of the Report upon the employment of women ... without any corresponding survey of the employment of men," she objected,

> is to assume, perhaps inadvertently, that industry is normally a function of the male, and that women, like non-adults, are only to be permitted to work for wages at special hours, at special rates of wages, under special supervision and subject to special restrictions by the legislature. I cannot accept this assumption.[54]

Women, she insisted, were not "a class apart, with smaller needs, less capacity and a lower level of intelligence," and must be granted access to work on precisely the same terms as men.[55] Yet their unequal status in industry had, as she recognized, complex and partially noneconomic causes, being determined not only by trade union and occupational practices but also by custom and by the simple belief that men deserved more than women – or by what she termed "the principle of the vested interest of the male."[56] Such causes were unlikely to go away, and the war if anything codified them. Webb's analogy between the labor market position of women and that of "non-adults" was an accurate one, however much she deplored it.

When we look across the channel, we confront some familiar aspects of labor mobilization and management. Substitution and dilution proceeded along somewhat similar lines, and as in Britain, a rhetoric of the exceptional employment of married women masked what was

[53] IWM, WIC Minutes, Macarthur evidence, 4 Oct. 1918, p. K84; my emphasis.
[54] War Cabinet Committee on Women in Industry, *Report*, p. 257.
[55] Ibid., p. 254.
[56] Ibid., p. 279.

largely a sectoral shift. Although most women war workers had worked before the war as well, their work was often described as an extraordinary measure, a patriotic response by women who would naturally prefer a home-centered role. Marcel Frois, a public health expert who worked within the French Ministry of Munitions, typically described women's work as both unnatural and an extension of women's propensity for self-sacrifice; the war, he bemoaned, had "deprived [women] of the warmth and quiet of their family life," forcing them to take up "a thousand tasks for which neither their delicate hands nor their frail constitutions were intended."[57] As in Britain, a perception of the "extraordinary" nature of women's wartime employment led both the government and private organizations to call for a wide range of paternalistic controls, with the French Ministry of Munitions even borrowing from the British the idea of welfare work as a means of entering into "the personal life of women often uprooted from their homes," and providing them with moral guidance and a "familial atmosphere."[58]

Nevertheless, a closer look at the French experience reveals one fundamental difference: attitudes about women's work in France were less successfully translated into laws and agreements explicitly defining its nature, scope, and duration. Unlike in Britain, where the government actively encouraged the employment of women, state activism in France developed only after large numbers of women had been absorbed into the munitions factories, arousing the concern of a reviving union movement, or making their presence felt through strikes. The Ministry of Munitions did not set up a special committee on women's work until April 1916, and only in 1917 did the ministries of Munitions and Labor take over the task of setting wages and working out agreements throughout industry.[59]

Once again, the weakness of the French unions and the different wartime relationship between business and the government help to explain this divergence. While British craft unions were able to take advantage of their indispensability and their control of the shop floor to force the government to regulate the conditions of women's employment and to guarantee its postwar elimination, French unions had to take a rather different tack. Certainly, they also feared any

---

[57] Marcel Frois, *La santé et le travail des femmes pendant la guerre* (Paris: Presses Universitaires de France, 1926), p. 1.
[58] Ibid., pp. 138–9.
[59] Roger Picard, *Le mouvement syndical durant la guerre* (Paris: Presses Universitaires de France, 1927), p. 74.

expansion of women's work, especially when they discovered the extent to which employers were taking advantage of the war to break down skilled processes and reduce rates. Yet lacking any government pledge to "restore" prewar practices, and usually (but not always) unable to enforce such restoration on the shop floor, they insisted, as the CGT had already done before the war, that women be organized on the same terms (and in the same unions) as men.[60] Not even "collaboration" with the government could be an alternative to organization, since, as Alphonse Merrheim of the Metalworkers' Federation charged, it was not clear that Minister of Munitions Albert Thomas had the authority to countermand the decisions of the Comité des Forges.[61]

This is not to deny that many French working men shared the belief that women's place was in the home. Indeed, one historian has argued that the war, with its glorification of masculinity and dislocation of family life, actually strengthened the attachment of trade union leaders to the ideal of separate roles for men and women.[62] Merrheim could not resist calling periodically for the exclusion of women workers, and Léon Jouhaux, the CGT's general secretary, did not abstain from pronatalist rhetoric about the dangers posed by women's work to the future of the French population. Both, however, also continued to support the organization of women.[63] The nuances of union attitudes are well captured in a resolution passed at the conference of the Metalworkers' Federation in July 1918. The resolution began by expressing a level of bitterness toward women's work that the ASE would have been hard pressed to match. The systematic employment of women was, they stated, "in absolute opposition to the creation and existence of the family home," and they agreed that *en principe* a man should be able to support his family on his wage alone. Households with two wages would force down the price of labor generally, they feared, leaving families with many children or on a single wage in indigence. Nevertheless, they concluded, women should be organized into trade unions and on the same terms as men.[64]

By 1918 the Metalworkers' Federation was growing rapidly; by

---

[60] Ibid., p. 99.

[61] Horne, *Labour at War*, pp. 97–113, 69–76.

[62] Jean-Louis Robert, "La C.G.T. et la famille ouvrière, 1914–1918: Première approche," *Le Mouvement Social*, 116 (July–Sept. 1981), pp. 47–66.

[63] Horne, *Labour at War*, pp. 105–6.

[64] AN, F7 13771, File: "Congrès des Métaux, 10 July 1918"; see also Françoise Thébaud, *La femme au temps de la guerre de 14*, pp. 187–8; Robert, "La C.G.T. et la famille ouvrière, 1914–1918," pp. 58–9.

1921, it would have some 200,000 members.[65] Yet the initial weakness of the trade unions, their adoption of increasingly "proletarian" rather than craft-based ideals during the war, and the presence of conscription and of mobilized workers in factories from the outset meant that the expansion of women's employment had already taken place largely along lines dictated by employers. Some employers thus took advantage of the extraordinary circumstances of the war to retool their factories and introduce women on repetition work; they did so without the British requirement that such women be fired at the end of the war. Citroën, Renault, Panhard, and other manufacturers, who had introduced women extensively on inspection and assembly-line work during the war, would be in the forefront of the automobile industry's "takeoff" in the twenties.

Women war workers were not then employed on all work nor paid equally. Rather, they were used more or less as British trade unionists had feared and resisted across the channel – as a distinct and subordinate but nevertheless "normal" section of the labor force. While Thomas had promised that women or foreigners were to be paid "equally" when employed on identical work to that done by French men, in the case of women the ministry allowed deductions from wages if some part of the work, such as the setting-up, was not done by the woman worker, and in any case employers were equally quick to alter labor processes in order to create "new" work that could then be paid at women's rates. When collective bargaining agreements and government arbitrations arrived in force after the strike waves of 1916–17, they simply recognized this separate and unequal status. In the wage rates established by the ministries of Munitions and Labor during 1917 and 1918, women in engineering are often listed as women only under the category of laborers (*femmes manoeuvres*); basic wage rates for such women averaged around two-thirds those set for male laborers. Women do not seem to have been considered skilled workers (*ouvriers professionnels*) except to some extent in Paris, since this category was often restricted to those in the trade before the outbreak of war. And outside of the sphere of munitions, men and women were often paid quite unequally in *identical* categories, with base rates for women running two-thirds to three-quarters those of men in the same line of work. Nevertheless, however unequal such agreements were, they were missing the one central component of

---

[65] Membership figures are from AN F7 13771, File: "Ministère de l'Intérieur. Direction de la Sureté Générale," "Organisation Syndicale des Ouvriers Métallurgistes Français" (dec. 1930).

wartime contracts in Britain: neither the arbitrations nor the collective bargaining agreements ratified by the Ministry of Labor during the war stipulated the postwar exclusion of any group of workers, although the use of foreign workers was occasionally limited to a fixed percentage of the work force.[66]

This recognition of women as a distinct but legitimate sector of the work force meant that French welfare measures also had rather different concerns. Whereas the British Health of Munitions Workers Committee exhibited a good deal of concern for "potential" mothers in industry but had, by and large, deplored the presence of actual mothers, French policy aimed at helping women reconcile motherhood with wage earning. In December 1916, when the Women's Work Committee met to discuss a series of medical reports on women's work, their recommendations were concerned entirely with pregnant or nursing women. For the former, they advised easier work, shorter hours, a ban on night work and overtime, and strict enforcement of maternity leave, all without loss of pay; for the latter, they called for the provision of nursing rooms in factories, paid breaks for women to nurse, and the provision of day-care facilities.[67] In 1917 and 1918, the committee issued a series of circulars insisting on these and other health and safety provisions; labor inspectors were also told to ensure that pregnant women neither were denied work nor had their pay cut.[68] In August 1917, a legislature fearful (as always) of the impact of war on births required firms employing over one hundred women to provide special rooms where nursing mothers could breast-feed their infants at regular intervals.[69] Perhaps more surprising, when the labor market contracted again at the end of the war, French officials, in diametrical opposition to their British counterparts, instructed employers to let single women go before married women. Such women would have been fired first in Britain, on the assumption that they had husbands to keep them; in France, officials presumed that married women workers had family responsibilities and hence had some claim to work.[70]

French social policy would remain concerned with the problems of reconciling motherhood with women's wage earning, a focus that

[66] Ministère du Travail, *Tarifs de salaires et conventions collectives pendant la guerre (1914–1918)*, 4 vols. (Paris: Imprimerie Nationale, 1921–3).
[67] "La Protection de la maternité dans les usines de guerre," *Bulletin du Ministère du Travail*, 24: 1–3 (Jan.–Mar. 1917), pp. 71–3.
[68] Frois, *La Santé*, pp. 126–7.
[69] Ibid., pp. 119–37.
[70] Oualid, "The Effect of the War upon Labour in France," p. 188.

would differentiate it sharply from British choices. At this stage, however, this focus remained largely rhetorical, for the state apparatus concerned with women's "special needs" was much smaller and its power limited. "Welfare work," for example, never became a state service, but was left to benevolent organizations like the YWCA. Similarly, the August 1917 law requiring the introduction of nursing rooms was widely ignored; by October, there were only thirty-six such rooms and thirty-eight nurseries.[71] The recommendations of the Women's Work Committee notwithstanding, when the Ministry of Labor conducted an investigation of hours worked by women in war factories in April 1918 – by which date many British factories had converted to a three-shift system of eight hours each – they found that the vast majority of women were working between ten and eleven hours per day.[72] Women war workers, then, may have been far less efficiently "protected" in France than in Britain, but alternatively their categorization as abnormal or temporary workers did not receive the same institutional sanction.

In sum, then, the experience of women during the war seems somewhat paradoxical and held unexpected implications for postwar labor relations. Women war workers in Britain learned new skills, participated in a massive union drive, and saw their working conditions and pay improve dramatically – but on the singular condition that they be expelled from their jobs at the end of the war. French war workers, by contrast, seemed to have faced harsher wartime conditions but fewer long-term constraints. The war in France did not alter women's position as economically vulnerable, less organized workers. It did not change the opinion of many officials, medical experts, pronatalists, and trade unionists that women's employment was undesirable or break down the ideal of the *mère au foyer*. Nevertheless, unlike in Britain, the war did not inaugurate a set of arrangements and agreements through which women's employment was defined as temporary and abnormal. During the war, the French state ceded authority over women workers to those who wanted to exploit them, the British state to those who wished to exclude them. As we shall see, these new relations between business, the state, and the unions had long-term

---

[71] Aimée Moutet, "Patrons de progrès ou patrons de combat?" *Recherches*, 32–3 (Sept. 1978), p. 470.

[72] "Enquête sur la durée du travail des femmes dans les établissements travaillant pour la défense nationale," *Bulletin du Ministère du Travail*, 26: 9–10 (Sept.–Oct. 1919), pp. 383–94.

implications for the structure of the labor market after the war, as well as for the shape of interwar social policy.

Gender, dependence, and welfare

The expansion of employment and the "leveling up" of pay contributed in time to the improvement of the standard of living of women and children, but such improvements could scarcely have been anticipated in August 1914. The immediate impact of the war was, on the contrary, to dislocate both the labor market and family life, as the "women's trades" contracted and men enlisted. Living standards of soldiers' and sailors' families were maintained in the first instance not through the labor market but through philanthropic intervention and state support. In both countries, governments quickly introduced universal systems of separation allowances for the families of recruits and conscripts, programs that did much to protect working-class living standards and maintain morale during the next four years. Comparable in many respects, these programs nevertheless left quite different legacies. While allowances in France were distributed to all immediate family members who could prove dependence, allowances in Britain were granted by right to soldiers' wives, without tests of dependence or need, an innovation that would serve both as a precedent for the incorporation of provisions for wives and children into the payments granted unemployed men in peacetime and as a spur to the feminist campaign for a broader "endowment of motherhood," discussed in the next chapter.[73] In France, such social supports for the families of soldiers were complemented by family policies for workers as well, as employers and administrators responded to wartime inflation by introducing benefits for dependent children into the wage system itself. While French policies concentrated on children, then, British innovations were centrally concerned with wives. These developments, in conjunction with the different patterns of employment for women and men in the two countries, would have important consequences for the two nations' family policies in the postwar period.

There was a Victorian analog to the system of military separation

---

[73] For a more extensive treatment of separation allowances in Britain, from which the following discussion is drawn, see Susan Pedersen, "Gender, Welfare and Citizenship in Britain during the Great War," *American Historical Review*, 95: 4 (Oct. 1990), pp. 983–1006.

allowances set up during the war in Britain, but it was a modest precedent indeed for a program that, by the Armistice, was costing the Treasury over £100 million per year. In the Victorian period, only wives of that very small proportion of men given official permission to marry were counted as "on the strength" of the regiment and granted allowances when their husbands were sent overseas; the wives and children of the many men who married without permission continued to rely on whatever rations their husband could pass on, the market for female casual labor, or poor relief.[74] The hardships experienced by military families "off the strength" sparked attacks on the army's marriage restrictions even before the war: critics argued both that soldiers shared other men's right to marry and maintain a wife, and that marriage would lessen use of prostitutes and hence rates of venereal disease among the ranks.[75] When the war broke out, M.P.s turned to the precedent of allowances and this well-worn rhetoric of a man's legitimate right to maintain a wife to argue for comprehensive and adequate allowances for the wives and children of all enlisted men.

Once again, the fact that Britain did not introduce conscription until 1916 aided their argument. Men had to be induced to volunteer, recruiting officers and politicians pointed out, yet respectable workers would not do so unless their wives and children were cared for. The growing influence of the labor movement also stiffened the government's resolve to deal fairly with the men. In contrast to the ambivalence that marked the movement's treatment of women workers, both the TUC and the War Emergency Workers' National Committee mobilized quickly on behalf of soldiers and their wives, informing women of their rights, answering copious correspondence, and pressuring the government for higher rates and greater public control. They were aided in their efforts by a bipartisan group of M.P.s convinced that generosity to soldiers was both just and prudent. Separation allowances were every soldier's right, their defenders argued: hence, they must be available to all, adequate in amount, and directly administered by an impartial state.[76]

---

[74] Myra Trustram, *Women of the Regiment: Marriage and the Victorian Army* (Cambridge University Press, 1984).

[75] Army, *Report of an Enquiry of Mrs. Tennant Regarding the Conditions of Marriage off the Strength,* PP 1914, LI, Cd. 7441; and see the parliamentary discussion of the report, 59 *H.C. Deb.*, 5th ser., 12 Mar. 1914, esp. cols. 1518–20.

[76] The labor movement's vigilant oversight of the size and administration of allowances can be traced through the Executive Committee minutes of the WEWNC, available at the London School of Economics. Parliamentary questions were asked immediately after

The Asquith government conceded all three points, creating in the process a precedent of real importance for family policy. Asquith announced on 10 August that separation allowances would be paid to the wives of all recruits, effectively making them a universal benefit.[77] The number of wives due benefit jumped from eleven hundred to one-half million within a few months and continued to rise steadily; by the Armistice, 1.5 million wives and several million children were receiving allowances.[78] Equally importantly, the government conceded that allowances must be at least minimally adequate for subsistence needs and repeatedly raised rates. Recruiting needs, pressure from the War Emergency Workers' National Committee and Parliament, fears of unrest among conscripted soldiers, rampant inflation, and the wartime erosion of "Treasury control" brought about increases at the outbreak of the war, in 1915, in 1917, and twice in 1918.[79] Although the resulting payments were by no means extravagant, they were for the time quite generous: at thirty-one shillings per week in 1917, the allowance for a woman with four children would have amounted to only half the wage of many a skilled male worker, but it would have surpassed the wage of an agricultural laborer.[80] Furthermore, as entitlements and not "relief," allowances were paid without any test of means. While a wife dependent on the allowance alone would indeed live at the very margin of real poverty,

---

the outbreak of the war, and a full discussion in November made the case for generous provision; see especially the debates of 12 Nov. 1914 (68 *H.C. Deb.*, 5th ser., esp. cols. 46–79, 152–66) and 18 Nov. 1914 (68 *H.C. Deb.*, 5th ser., cols. 444–526); also letters to the *Times* on 7, 8, and 10 Sept. 1914.

[77] 65 *H.C. Deb.*, 5th ser., 10 Aug. 1914, col. 2261.

[78] For numbers of army wives receiving allowances, see Public Record Office (PRO), WO, 33/761 and 33/932, War Office, *Reports on the Account of Army Expenditure*, 1914–1920; a compilation is given in Pedersen, "Gender, Welfare and Citizenship," p. 985.

[79] The War Office authorized a modest increase on prewar rates soon after the war and then waited for the Commons' Select Committee on Naval and Military Services (Pensions and Grants) to decide fundamental questions of administration and amount. For the Select Committee's decisions, see *Special Report, Second Special Report, Proceedings, Minutes, and Appendices*, PP 1914–16, IV. For Cabinet consideration of the later increases, see the minutes and memoranda of the Cabinet's Soldiers' and Sailors' Pay Committee, PRO, Cab. 27/21; decisions can be found in PRO, Cab. 23/1, War Cabinet 31, 10 Jan. 1917, pp. 95–9; Cab. 23/7, War Cabinet 449, 19 July 1918, pp. 35–6; Cab. 23/8, War Cabinet 486, 15 Oct. 1918, pp. 28–9; and War Cabinet 498, 6 Nov. 1918, p. 64. For precise figures on rates, see PRO, WO 32/9316, "History of Separation Allowance"; a summary table and a fuller discussion of parliamentary debates is given in Pedersen, "Gender, Welfare and Citizenship," esp. p. 990.

[80] For figures comparing wage rates with allowances, see Pedersen, "Gender, Welfare and Citizenship," p. 1001.

casual earnings or adolescents' wages could raise living standards substantially, and indeed a parliamentary investigation found that few service families lived on allowances alone.[81]

Finally, allowances came to be state administered, although the process of wresting control out of the hands of the voluntary sector bedeviled politicians for the first two years of the war. The War Office had relied on the services of a prestigious voluntary organization, the Soldiers' and Sailors' Families Association (SSFA), to administer philanthropically funded allowances during the Boer War and happily turned to them to cope with the disarray caused by Asquith's decision on universal eligibility. The SSFA quickly established local chapters throughout Britain, enrolled volunteer social workers (fifty thousand by 1915), and began processing claims.[82] Competent and above all cheap, the SSFA's administration answered the needs of the War Office; it was, however, incompatible with the rhetoric of soldiers' rights used by many politicians. Much of the Commons deplored the vesting of administrative powers in a private "charity," particularly one staffed largely by middle-class women, who often did not disguise their intent to use their position to "rescue" their working-class charges from "lower ideals."[83] Allowances were made payable through the Post Office rather than in person early in the war, and in 1915 the Commons Select Committee on Pensions and Grants agreed to take their administration out of SSFA hands entirely – to the disgust of the suffragist and social reformer Eleanor Rathbone, who had helped to organize administration of allowances in her home town of Liverpool and who now chastised "a considerable section of the House of Commons, and especially . . . the Labour Party" for their "doctrinaire dislike [of] any form of volunteer effort" and their unrealistic

---

[81] In June 1918, when the Working Classes Cost of Living Committee collected budgets from 231 service families, there were 90 wage earners for every 100 such families, and the average service family of 5.24 individuals spent thirty-two shillings nine pence on food alone – more than the entire five-person separation allowance of thirty-one shillings. Service families had less money per person than other families, but not dramatically less. Working Classes Cost of Living Committee, 1918, *Report, PP* 1918, VII, Cd. 8980.

[82] Numbers of branches and of volunteer workers are given in SSFA, *Annual Report, 1914–1915*, pp. 14, 2002.

[83] The phrase was used during a discussion of whether the SSFA should countenance payments to unmarried women living as wives (as was War Office policy); SSFA, "General Meeting . . . " in *Annual Report, 1914–1915*, p. 1885. Some sense of the SSFA's sense of mission can be derived from Helen Anstey, "The Home-Side in War-Time," *Contemporary Review*, 108 (Aug. 1915), pp. 237–43; Charlotte Barrington, "Soldiers' and Sailors' Families," *Nineteenth Century and After*, 78: 463 (Sept. 1915), pp. 582–99.

ideas about the superior capacities of state bodies.[84] Yet the older
practice of partnership between the state and the voluntary sector, a
partnership in which women social workers had an important place
and a real stake, could not survive amid the calls for public and
democratic control of all such services. In 1916 and 1917, the administration of allowances was entrusted first to an appointed Statutory
Committee and later to the new Ministry of Pensions headed by
George Barnes, one of two Labour ministers in the wartime coalition.[85]

By 1917, separation allowances had become a universal subsistence-
level entitlement, paid to soldiers' wives as a matter of right, funded
directly by the Treasury and administered under parliamentary scrutiny by subcommittees of the Ministry of Pensions. In pressing for
this system, Labour and Liberal spokesmen as well as servicemen's
advocates across party lines had employed a language of rights and
citizenship that proved particularly potent during a war that relied,
in the last instance, on popular consent. Spokesmen for soldiers understandably insisted that separation allowances must be entirely free
of the prurient investigation and moralistic sermonizing that had often
marked both charitable aid and poor relief before the war, and pressures for parliamentary oversight were notably strengthened when
M.P.s discovered in 1914 that the War Office and the SSFA made
receipt conditional on "sobriety and good conduct" and intended to
use police surveillance to keep wives in line.[86] Such practices, they had
objected, were entirely inappropriate when administering a benefit
deemed a citizen's right.[87]

[84] Eleanor Rathbone, "Pensions and Allowances," *Common Cause*, 6: 302 (22 Jan. 1915),
p. 664. For the decision of the Select Committee, see their *Report*, cited in note 79.
[85] Parliamentary debate on the passage of the bill establishing the statutory committee is
in 72 *H.C. Deb.*, 5th ser., 29 June 1915, cols. 1832–93; SSFA protests are in *Annual
Report, 1914–15*, pp. 2002–4. Discussions and memos on the establishment of the Ministry of Pensions are in PRO, PIN 4/111; Cab. 37/155, nos. 29 and 30; and Cab. 37/
159, no. 10; for the history of the short-lived Statutory Committee, see War Pensions
Etc. Statutory Committee, *Report for the Year 1916*, PP 1917–1918, XVII, Cd. 8750.
[86] PRO, HO 158/16: War Office, "Cessation of Army Separation Allowances and Allot-
ments of Pay to the Unworthy," no. 192, 9 Sept. 1914; and Home Office to Chief
Constables, no. 191, 20 Oct. 1914.
[87] For characteristic objections to charitable administration and "surveillance," see esp. 68
H.C. Deb., 5th ser., 12 Nov. 1914, esp. cols. 50–2, 56–67; "The Soldier's Wife," *Nation*,
16: 7 (14 Nov. 1914), pp. 189–90; "The Revolt of the Soldier's Wife," *Nation*, 16: 11
(12 Dec. 1914), pp. 326–7; "Soldiers' and Sailors' Wives," *Times*, 9 Dec. 1914, p. 10;
"The Soldier's Wife: Protest against Police Inspection," *Times*, 11 Dec. 1914, p. 5.
Graham Wootton also discusses the controversy over "voluntaryism" in his study of
ex-servicemen's associations; Wootton, *The Politics of Influence: British Ex-servicemen*,

Yet the language of citizenship and rights held its own dangers, especially for women. The argument that the allowance be treated not as a charitable "dole" but as "a national obligation for services rendered" merely underscored the point that the payment was not the wife's at all, but belonged to the man "rendering services."[88] In an extreme defense of this view, one Liberal M.P. insisted that the allowance was "an amount paid by the State as part of the wage of the soldier ... and he has no right to be debarred from the receipt of it because the police may think that his wife is not conducting herself in a fit and proper manner."[89] But if such a formulation established the soldier's "right," it merely begged the question of why and when a woman would be allowed to draw *his* allowance. Her receipt, in other words, turned entirely on her status as a "wife," and whatever politicians said, investigations aimed at determining whether the woman was indeed a legitimate "wife" flowed logically from their own definition of benefits as the husband's right. The allowance was intended to replace the maintenance a man owed his wife by law, the Ministry of Pensions argued; hence, "there is no obligation on the State to continue this payment if the husband would no longer be under a duty to maintain her if he were now in civil life."[90] In other words, the wife was due an allowance so long as she fulfilled those obligations placed on her by the marriage contract – obligations the SSFA had tended to view rather conventionally as good conduct and care of children, but which the Ministry of Pensions viewed more legalistically as chastity. Since infidelity (by the wife) was grounds for divorce, the ministry pointed out, allowances should indeed be cut off in such cases, "the woman's repentance and present good character notwithstanding," unless the man asked that it be continued.[91] In all, various governmental authorities investigated at least fifty thousand cases of misconduct (some 2% of recipients) and cut off allowances in more than sixteen thousand of them – not a high figure, but enough to act as a deterrent to other women.[92]

Cabinet Decisions and Cultural Change (1917–57) (Cambridge, Mass.: Harvard University Press, 1963), pp. 16–37, 81–6.

[88] The phrase is from Rowland Kenney, "Soldiers' Dependents," *English Review*, 19 (Dec. 1914), p. 116.

[89] 68 *H.C. Deb.*, 5th ser., 12 Nov. 1914, col. 160.

[90] Ministry of Pensions, *First Annual Report of the Minister of Pensions to 31st March 1918*, *PP* 1919, XXVII, Cmd. 14, p. 69.

[91] Ibid.

[92] Statistics on forfeiture of allowances are not available for July–Aug. 1917, but the text estimate is based on figures for all other periods given in PRO, PIN 15/3304, War Office

It is important to understand the logic underlying separation allowances, for it came to pervade British social policy. Certainly the state did grant a new, generous, and "rights-based" entitlement, but it did so by categorizing women not in terms of their labor whether waged or unwaged, but in terms of their marital status and in relation to particular deserving classes of men. As revealed by both rhetoric and administrative regulations, the state viewed its obligation to aid wives as a contract made with the soldier (not the wife); in exchange for certain citizenship functions (defending the country), the man's status not only as an independent citizen but also as the "breadwinner" for his family would be preserved. This breadwinner status, moreover, was an assumption of and not a condition for benefit: even a soldier who had not been his family's breadwinner before the war was entitled to benefit. Social policy, in other words, was constructed to follow not social reality, in all its variety, but the ideal construct of the male breadwinner and dependent wife. The wife's place in this arrangement was entirely secondary: although she received the allowance, her entitlement derived from her relationship to her husband and not from any service to the wider polity. Insofar as the state concerned itself with wives, it was only to insist that they fulfill their obligations to their absent husbands.

Separation allowances thus "placed" and defined women only as dependents of men, mediating their relationship to the state and to social benefits through the marriage contract. Yet because benefits had to be paid directly to women (the men being at the front), allowances had other consequences, and ones quite at odds with their administrative logic. Allowances may have been paid in recognition of a man's right to have his dependents maintained when undertaking "service to the state," but for the vast majority of wives receiving the money at the Post Office, the allowance felt like wages, money for their own work as housewives and mothers. Furthermore, precisely because allowances were paid directly to them and did not vary according to the vicissitudes of the labor market or the husband's health, some women found allowances a far more dependable source of support than their husbands' precarious wage. An investigation conducted by the Liverpool Women's Industrial Council during the war found that the health and care of children improved among women receiving separation allowances, a finding by and large sustained by

to Women's Advisory Committee, 13 Dec. 1915; Annual Reports of the Minister of Pensions, First through Fourth (*PP* 1919, XXVIII Cmd. 14; *PP* 1920, XXII; *PP* 1921, XX); War Pensions Etc. Statutory Committee, *Report, PP* 1917–18, XVII, Cd. 8750.

historical research.[93] During the course of the war, the government paid out more than £400 million directly to women and children, a transfer of income inconceivable by prewar (and indeed postwar) standards and one that could not but dramatically alter the economic position of wives.

But how permanent could such changes be, and how could the advantages of the allowance system be preserved? Just as factory inspectors and women welfare workers found that decent pay and better working conditions had made an enormous difference to women's own sense of self-worth, Eleanor Rathbone and other workers for the SSFA found that regular benefits did a great deal for the well-being and self-respect of previously unwaged wives. An argument in favor of the preservation of allowances in peacetime thus developed among feminists and social workers, especially those whose influence had been lessened by the coming of state control. Social reformers like Rathbone admitted that such benefits should be part of a state service, but they objected to their own exclusion from administration and to the view that the allowance was the right of the man and not the wife. By paying the income directly to the woman and by making its size proportional to the number of children rather than the quality of the husband's service, Rathbone argued, the government, whatever its initial intentions, had effectively transferred the entitlement to the woman herself and established "a system of State endowment of maternity." If the allowance were recognized not as "part of the soldier's wages" but as "a statutory payment to a woman in respect of her functions as wife and mother," it could survive the return of the soldier and be continued in peacetime.[94]

By 1918, separation allowances had kept substantial numbers of working-class families from severe hardship over many years. The provision of allowances to all wives owed a good deal to a rhetoric of a man's right to maintain, already well established before the war.

---

[93] Emma Mahler, "The Social Effects of Separation Allowances: An Experiment in the Endowment of Motherhood," *Englishwoman*, 36: 108 (Dec. 1917), pp. 191–9. On the effects of the war on civilian health and income generally, see Melanie Tebbutt, *Making Ends Meet: Pawnbroking and Working-Class Credit* (Leicester: Leicester University Press, 1983), pp. 138–40; J. M. Winter, "The Impact of the First World War on Civilian Health in Britain," *Economic History Review*, 2d ser., 30: 3 (Aug. 1977), pp. 487–503; Richard Wall, "English and German Families and the First World War, 1914–1918," in Wall and Winter, eds., *The Upheaval of War*, pp. 43–106.

[94] Eleanor Rathbone, "Separation Allowances: An Experiment in the State Endowment of Maternity," I, *Common Cause*, 7: 359 (25 Feb. 1916), pp. 611–12, and II, *Common Cause*, 7: 362 (17 Mar. 1916), pp. 648–9.

Rhetoric, however, could not alone determine outcomes: only the need to ensure adequate recruits and, later, morale enabled Labour and Liberal politicians and advocates of enlisted men to override the Treasury's objections and force the state to sustain unthinkable levels of public spending on women and children. By insisting that allowances were a right, regardless of need, M.P.s established a system that enabled wives of soldiers to participate in the broader brief period of female prosperity during the war and feminists to develop a new ideal of direct public support for women's "service" of motherhood. Yet allowances were awarded not as payment for motherhood, but – if anything – as some meager recompense for the unthinkable level of coercion to which the state was subjecting its male citizenry. As we shall see, it was the presumption of women's dependence, not of a mother's entitlement, that allowances implanted in the heart of social policy.

The outbreak of war was no less disruptive of family life in France than in England, and in some ways more so, given France's general mobilization. Authorities faced the same problem of providing for families whose breadwinner had been called up, and they came up with a similar solution. A law of 5 August 1914 established a separation allowance of 1.25 francs per day (and 0.5 francs per child), a rate that would have given a wife with two children an income approximately equal to half the prewar wage of a pitworker or one-third that of a joiner in full work, proportions (although not money rates) roughly comparable to separation allowances in Britain. Certainly, cash allowances of this size would have been a windfall to the wives of agricultural workers. As Jean-Jacques Becker has noted, allowances first brought a cash economy into some rural areas and, as in Britain, roused the ire of many who felt wives were profligate and spent the money unwisely. Nevertheless, allowances were of crucial importance in maintaining civilian morale and easing the plight of families during what proved to be a long and harsh war.[95]

French policy thus seems to have paralleled British developments and would lead us to search for similar implications for the future of family policy. On closer inspection, however, we find two crucial differences between the British and French systems, differences that limited the resonance of separation allowances as a model for future welfare policy in France. First, unlike in Britain, French allowances were not pure entitlements: they were need-based and not granted simply as a right. While children under age 13 were considered dependent in all cases, adult claimants had to prove to local tribunals

[95] Becker, *The Great War*, pp. 17–21.

both that they were needy and that they had been dependent on the soldier before mobilization to qualify for an allowance. Second, also unlike in Britain, while claims from the wife were given priority over claims from a soldier's parents, both were treated according to the same system. In keeping with the French propensity to seek to maintain the family as a unit of mutual support, any family member to whom the obligation to maintain was applied in the Civil Code (father, mother, wife, or child) could, if both needy and actually dependent, claim the allowance.[96] These conditions meant that the French system of separation allowances, however generously administered, never escaped the rhetorical boundaries of need-based assistance to become a rights-based entitlement. Neither soldiers nor wives received aid by virtue of military service or marital status alone.

Only in the case of children was dependence assumed and the state's responsibility to maintain accepted. In France, however, rights-based entitlements for the support of children were granted not only to soldiers but progressively to workers as well. The payment of allowances for dependent children by some state services and large employers before the war acted as a powerful model for employers and officials eager to maintain living standards during a period of rampant inflation without granting permanent all-round wage increases. They turned to cost-of-living bonuses, children's allowances, and other flexible payment systems, the cost of which could be passed along to consumers in controlled or monopolistic sectors. Although motivated by war conditions, this process created an important precedent for family policy, as the sporadic payments to large families of the prewar period were replaced by regular benefits for all dependent children in some industries. Rather inadvertently, then, wartime conditions – in particular, inflation and extended government control – forced a hothouse development within the wage system of rights-based benefits aimed at compensating workers for dependent children.

Family benefits had been paid to some state employees even before the war, as we have seen in Chapter 1. Arrangements were quite unequal, however, with some ministries paying benefits for all dependent children and others only for children beyond the third. Frustration over inequalities and wartime inflation convinced the government to regularize these payments, and benefits for *all* dependent children were extended to government employees below a par-

---

[96] On the organization of French allowances, see André Lebreton, *La famille et les lois sur les allocations de guerre* (Saint-Brieuc: Imprimerie de René Prud'homme, 1921).

ticular wage level in 1917 and to *all* government employees in 1919.[97] Even more significant, however, was the government's role in extending child benefits to the state-regulated sector of mining and railroads. Family allowances had scarcely existed in mining before the war, but in December 1917, when the Ministry of Munitions negotiated a contract between the employers' and miners' syndicates, it extended allowances to all employees at rates determined by local commissions. Similarly, while all of the main railway companies had set up children's allowance systems between 1890 and 1916, rates were not made uniform until November 1916, when they became part of a new contract negotiated between the railroads and the state.[98] By late 1921, Charles Picquenard, the indefatigable permanent director of the Ministry of Labor, estimated that about 840,000 state and local employees and a further 630,000 railroad and mining workers were entitled to family allowances if they had any dependent children.[99]

Children's allowances even spread beyond the sheltered sector as the ministries of Labor and Munitions took over the task of arbitrating claims and setting wages for workers in the war factories and to some extent more broadly. Torn between workers' pressures to maintain living standards and employers' insistence on the need to define all awards as temporary and due to the "extraordinary" conditions of the war, ministry officials expanded the use of cost-of-living bonuses (which figured in arbitration awards from 1917) and also gradually turned to children's allowances.[100] Fifty-two of the wage settlements either established by the ministries of Labor and Munitions or agreed

---

[97] On the development of government allowances, see Georges Bonvoisin and Gustave Maignan, *Allocations familiales et caisses de compensation* (Paris: Sirey, 1930), pp. 3–4; Jean Pinte, *Les allocations familiales* (Paris: Sirey, 1935), pp. 55–7; Dominique Ceccaldi, *Histoire des prestations familiales en France* (Paris: UNCAF, 1957), pp. 14–15; Robert Talmy, *Histoire du mouvement familial en France, 1896–1939*, 1 (Paris: UNCAF, 1962), pp. 161–3.

[98] Pinte, *Les allocations familiales*, pp. 64–7; Bonvoisin and Maignan, *Allocations familiales*, pp. 5–9.

[99] Conseil Supérieur du Travail, *Compte rendu*, 25ᵉ sess., 17 Nov. 1921, p. 43.

[100] Cost-of-living bonuses were based on both the sex and the prior earnings of the worker. The bonus for a low-paid man was higher than that for a well-paid man, and that for a low-paid woman higher than that for a well-paid woman, but such equalization did not operate across sex lines: the low-paid man's bonus was 50% higher than the low-paid woman's bonus, despite his higher initial wage. Such awards thus leveled up the earnings of low-paid workers – or, more precisely, they left better-paid workers to bear the costs of wartime inflation – without eradicating the wage gap between men and women.

by contract between employers and employed late in the war included provisions for the payment of family allowances. Thirty-nine of these agreements were in the engineering industry and eleven in the chemical industry.[101]

The widespread introduction of children's allowances was an effective answer to pressures for wage increases during wartime inflation, but it was also an important stage in the development of family policy. By granting children's allowances to workers in full work, the sheltered industries and the state itself effectively admitted that an average adult wage could not adequately support children, and that they had no intention of paying regular wages capable of doing so. Thus, while British separation allowances carried the didactic message that male workers had the right either to wages capable of maintaining dependent children *and* wives or to state support in the absence of wages, family allowances proclaimed that children deserved and needed state support even if their parents were employed. Family policy was not restricted to measures aimed at unfortunates outside the labor force but was integrated into the wage system itself.

On the subject of dependent wives, however, French family policy was both less rigid and less coherent. French policymakers – unlike their British counterparts – could not simply write off married women's wage earning as exceptional or introduce policies premised on the assumption that such women were invariably dependent. While they commonly deplored married women's wage earning on pronatalist grounds, their propensity to define the family rather than the individual worker as the basic unit of economic and civic life made them reluctant to take over decisions many felt were properly left to husbands and wives. Since French men had the right under the Civil Code to veto their wives' employment, lack of regulation in this area could scarcely be seen as an attack on the rights of men. In any case, when introducing measures aimed at mitigating familial dependence, the government did not concern itself overmuch with relations of dependence between the sexes. Family allowances, as the most important early welfare measure, were concerned exclusively with children.

In their administration, however, children's allowances reflected a legal and cultural framework that considered male authority unchallenged, almost ordained. Allowances for government employees were paid by preference to the *chef de famille* (legally, the father) and were

---

[101] Ministère du Travail, *Tarifs de salaires*, vol. 4, p. 76.

granted to the mother only if the father did not work for the government and thus had no claim to such allowances. The preference in favor of the father was even stronger within the railroad companies, who refused to pay allowances to any woman worker except a widow and resisted pressures from the Ministry of Public Works throughout the interwar period to extend allowances to women employees whose husbands worked for outside firms and were not entitled to allowances.[102] Nevertheless, employment rather than paternity entitled a worker to allowances, and as we shall see, women came increasingly to share the benefits of allowances in the interwar period.

In sum, when we compare the welfare innovations of the war in France and Britain, we find a confirmation and an extension of the assumptions driving wartime employment policies. The major entitlement program introduced in wartime Britain provided need-blind allowances for soldiers' wives, although the logic behind such payment was the assumption, ambiguous for women, that the male breadwinner model was a normal and ideal one, and that men thus had a right to have their wives maintained – regardless of need – during state service or legitimate interruptions of earning. In France, by contrast, separation allowances were aimed at maintaining the living standard of the soldiers' needy relatives, and only benefits for *children* were granted as a matter of right. Rather than compensating men for women on the assumption of dependence, French policies compensated parents for children – logically enough, since children were barred from work by child labor laws and universal schooling and thus were necessarily dependent, while wives were not.

As with labor policy, we can look to differences in the power of labor and varying employer–government relations to explain these divergent social policy outcomes. Politicians in Britain across the political spectrum had often argued for men's rights to maintain wives, but a system encoding this ideal could result only from the indispensability – and political power – of labor in wartime. Men were no less indispensable in France, but their spokesmen were weaker, and conscription rendered their subjection to the state more complete. The fortuitous conjuncture of inflation and state control thus allowed the government to extend allowances in the sheltered sector without having to take account of union feeling about a system in part aimed at avoiding all-round wage rises.

---

[102] See the correspondence on this subject in Archives Nationales (AN) 48 AQ 3392, File "Indemnités pour charges de famille."

Policy legacies and political agendas

We have seen how wartime arrangements for the mobilization of workers and for the maintenance of working-class living standards, influenced as they were by the contrasting shape of the British wartime contract and the *union sacrée*, assumed quite different patterns of family life. The labor and social policies adopted by the French and British governments to manage the transition to peacetime confirmed and extended these divergent patterns of policy development. In Britain, the government directed its efforts at restoring men's position as wage earners and heads of families, first by fulfilling its pledge to "restore" the prewar structure of the labor market and second by extending social supports for men as heads of families. In France, by contrast, while the state made less of an effort to shape the labor market, it did intervene to provide independent supports for children. Such policies, unlike those in Britain, began to disaggregate family income and the family wage.

In both Britain and France, the postwar contraction of women's work was due in part simply to the fact that the expansion had been largely in sectors – like munitions – that would inevitably decline at the end of the war. Especially in Britain, however, "market forces" were further complicated by government policy, as committees concerned with postwar reconstruction deliberated over the allowable scope of women's work after the war and the government prepared to impose legislation fulfilling its pledges to the unions. A number of important committees, including the Women's Employment Committee of the Ministry of Reconstruction, the Committee on Women in Industry appointed by the War Cabinet, and the Treasury's Committee on Recruitment to the Civil Service after the War, were asked to consider whether women should have access to work on the same terms as men or whether women workers should be restricted to particular spheres. Probably the most generous and surprising proposals emerged not from these specific committees, however, but rather from the all-male Ministry of Reconstruction Committee on the Machinery of Government, which was chaired by Lord Haldane and included such efficiency-minded fellow travelers as Robert Morant and Sidney Webb. Given a wide brief to suggest means of improving the operation of government, the Haldane Committee rather astonishingly expressed their conviction

> that the absence of any substantial recourse to the services of women in the administrative staffs of Departments, and still more in their

Intelligence branches ... has in the past deprived the public service of a vast store of knowledge, experience and fresh ideas, some of which would, for particular purposes, have been far more valuable and relevant than those of even the ablest of men in the Civil Service.[103]

They recommended that examinations, permanent appointments and the administrative ranks of the civil service should henceforth be open to women on the same terms as men, with efficiency rather than sex becoming the sole test of qualification.

Lord Gladstone's Committee on Recruitment to the Civil Service did not agree. Large numbers of women had taken over administrative and clerical positions during the war, and many hoped to stay. Yet while the Gladstone committee did recommend extending the employment of women, they thought this should occur along "special" lines, and that the higher administrative grades should remain closed to women.[104] No group of employers or male workers exhibited greater hostility to equal opportunities for women than did the civil service, and this hostility was given free rein. As Meta Zimmeck has shown, while women had come to make up 56% of civil servants during the war, in the twenties the Treasury employed a range of stratagems designed to confine women to the lower administrative grades, including downgrading of posts, the limiting of recruitment to ex-servicemen, the barring of women from examinations, and most importantly, the reestablishment of the marriage bar.[105]

The proposals for the future scope of women's employment in industry that emerged from the Women's Employment Committee of the Ministry of Reconstruction and the War Cabinet Committee on Women in Industry were in theory more liberal, but in both cases the committees undercut their support for increased opportunities for women by insisting that the state must recognize that the interests of "home and family" came first. The Women's Employment Committee, for example, claimed that discrimination against women workers was unjustifiable *except* when necessary to "preserv[e] women's powers unimpaired for those primary activities which are connected with the family and the home." Such a brief gave almost unlimited scope for special restrictions, and the committee went on to hope that

---

[103] Ministry of Reconstruction, Committee on the Machinery of Government, *Report, PP* 1918, XII, Cd. 9230, p. 14.
[104] Committee on Recruitment to the Civil Service after the War, *Final Report, PP* 1919, . XI, Cmd. 164, pp. 6–14.
[105] Meta Zimmeck, "Strategies and Stratagems for the Employment of Women in the British Civil Service, 1919–1939," *Historical Journal*, 27: 4 (1984), pp. 901–24.

the "excessive" wartime employment of married women would now cease, and that "every inducement, direct and indirect, will be given to keep mothers in the home."[106] In any case, equal access for women was prohibited by Lloyd George's pledge to restore "prewar practices" in industry at the end of the war – a pledge fulfilled through the Restoration of Prewar Practices Act made binding in industry through October 1920. Employers anxious to convert to civilian production or fearful of labor unrest dismissed their women workers without this encouragement, but the Restoration Act was also applied "very widely and rigidly."[107] To the consternation of feminists, the act was used simply to fire women and hire men: women were even unceremoniously tossed out of work that had developed under their own hands, such as welding, airplane work, and optical glass making.[108] Women workers remember these dismissals as entirely unannounced: "As far as I can remember they threw us out on the slag heap," one woman employed at Woolwich Arsenal recalled.[109]

Once praised as selfless contributors to the nation's defense, women war workers suddenly found themselves stigmatized as war profiteers, especially when they declined to return home quietly. The war had offered women a unique experience of decent conditions and pay, and the Ministry of Labour discovered to its intense irritation that women showed a "marked disinclination" to take up work as domestic servants, who were in short supply.[110] Throughout 1919 and 1920, however, simple necessity and stringent administration of the "out of work" donation designed to ease the transition to peacetime (discussed later) did eventually force women back into the women's trades. The Trade Boards Act of 1909 was then extended to ensure a minimum wage in some of these industries – if at different rates for men and women – and by 1920 covered some 3 million working people.[111] The reestablishment of sex demarcations in the labor market can be traced through the reports of Adelaide M. Anderson, the chief lady inspector

---

[106] Ministry of Reconstruction, Women's Employment Committee, *Report, PP* 1918, XIV, Cd. 9239, pp. 7, 51.

[107] British Association, *British Labour*, p. 29.

[108] Clementina Black, "The Women's Reward," *Women's Industrial News*, 83 (Apr. 1919), pp. 13–16; see also Ray Strachey, "Changes in Employment," in Strachey, ed., *Our Freedom and Its Results* (London: Hogarth, 1936), pp. 129–30.

[109] Imperial War Museum (IWM), Oral Histories, Interview with Caroline Rennles.

[110] Ministry of Labour, Department of Civil Demobilization and Resettlement, *Weekly Report*, no. 1 (week ending 4 Jan. 1919), p. 12; "We Want Work," *Woman Worker*, Feb. 1919, p. 4.

[111] Gertrude Tuckwell, "The Story of the Trade Boards Act," *Contemporary Review*, 120 (Nov. 1921), p. 604; Andrews and Hobbs, *Economic Effects of the World War*, p. 217.

of factories, who drew attention to the steady decline in opportunities for women between 1918 and 1920.[112] By 1921, the good effects of the war on women's employment had entirely disappeared, and under the shadow of mass unemployment, public opinion swung violently against wage-earning women. "Unless one turns back to the very numerous documents, official and unofficial, relating to women's industrial war work," Anderson wrote almost despairingly in 1922, "it is not easy . . . to recall the full measure of pride expressed by the nation in what women did for it in time of need."[113]

In France, by contrast, the government paid little attention to the course of women's employment at the end of the war and left it largely to the "higgling of the market." Louis Loucheur, then minister of munitions, established a one-month indemnity for women who gave up work at state arsenals and urged private employers to do likewise; most, however, simply fired their female workers after the Armistice. As Laura Downs's work on this period makes clear, women in France as well as in Britain were disproportionally hard hit by this drastic and unplanned demobilization. Unlike in Britain, however, employers did rehire women when they desired to do so, and some far-sighted businessmen (like André Citroën) retooled their factories for postwar production and then reinstated women on highly rationalized assembly-line work.[114]

By the time the wartime experience had settled out, women in France had largely reestablished their prewar economic position. Although there was a shift of women workers out of their wartime jobs, rates of women's employment remained comparatively high. Fifty-three percent of the total female population age 15 and over were classified as "occupied" in 1921, whereas only 34% of the equivalent British population were so classified.[115] Women made up almost 40% of the working population in France in 1921, in comparison with slightly over 29% in Britain. Women's share of the labor market was higher in all sectors as well, with the exception of the service sector, that overcrowded and underpaid home of British women workers. Figures for the distribution by sector of both women workers and the total working population are given in Table 2.2.

---

[112] Home Office, *Annual Report of the Chief Inspector of Factories for the Year 1919*, PP 1920, XVI, Cmd. 941; *For the Year 1920*, PP 1921, XII, Cmd. 1403.

[113] A. M. Anderson, *Women in the Factory* (London: John Murray, 1922), p. 224.

[114] Laura Lee Downs, "Women in Industry," pp. 269–75.

[115] Figures for France are calculated from those of A. Sauvy, *Histoire économique de la France*, pp. 288, 294; those for Britain are from Guy Routh, *Occupation and Pay in Great Britain, 1906–1960* (Cambridge University Press, 1965), p. 44.

Table 2.2. *Distribution and density of women workers by sector, 1921*

| | Distribution of working population (%) | | | | Female proportion (%) | |
| | Britain | | France | | | |
Sector	All	Women	All	Women	Br.	Fr.
Agriculture and fishing	7	2	41	46	8	44
Industry and transport	56	41	35	27	21	31
(manufacturing only)	(36)	(38)	(25)	(24)	(31)	(37)
Commerce and banking	13	15	8	9	34	43
Services[a]	24	42	15	18	52	47
Total	100	100	99	100	29	40

[a] Services include domestic, professional, civil, and military services. Workers whose occupation is given as "other" in British records have been incorporated into this category.
Source: B. R. Mitchell, *European Historical Statistics* (1975; rev. ed., New York: Facts on File, 1981).

These differences can be seen more clearly, however, when women's labor force participation rates in 1921 are broken down by age, as they are in Table 2.3. Rates of participation were far higher for men of working age than for women in both countries, but while the pattern of participation across the life cycle was much the same for men in France and Britain, patterns for women were very different in the two countries. In both, women tended to be employed when young, and indeed participation rates for young women were higher in Britain than in France. After the age of marriage, however, rates diverged dramatically. The rate of women's participation in the work force declined only 13% between the cohorts aged 20–24 and 25–34 in France, while in Britain it declined by almost one-half. More than one-half of all women of childbearing age were officially employed in France in 1921, and their rate of labor force participation between the ages of 45 and 64 was more than two and one-half times that of their British counterparts. Whereas more than 90% of married women over the age of 25, and more than 85% of married women under age 25, were classed as "unoccupied" in Britain in 1921, an astonishing 49.6% of married women remained in the official labor market in France, a participation rate *higher* than that of widows and only 14 percentage points lower than that for single women.[116] These

[116] Participation rates for married women in particular are given for England in *Census of England and Wales, 1931, General Report* (London: HMSO, 1950), and for France in T. Deldycke, H. Gelders, and J.-M. Limbor, *The Working Population and Its Structure*

Table 2.3. *Labor force participation rates by age and sex, 1921*

Age	Men		Women	
	England/Wales	France	England/Wales	France
14–15	65	—	45	—
16–17	91	85[a]	71	60[a]
18–19	96	—	76	—
20–24	97	94	62	61
25–34	98	96	33	53
35–44	98	97	23	54
45–54	97	96	21	54
55–64	92	89	19	49
65–74	69	n.a.	12	n.a.

[a] Ages 15–19.
Sources: Alfred Sauvy, *Histoire économique de la France entre les deux guerres,* vol. 3 (Paris: Economica, 1984), pp. 288, 294; Census of England and Wales, 1931, *General Report* (London: HMSO, 1950), p. 163.

divergent patterns of work held throughout the interwar period, reinforcing dissimilar social policy tracks.

Labor-market policy formed one part of the state's reconstruction of the male breadwinner norm in Britain; social policy formed the other part. The women demobilized in 1918 and 1919 would, of course, have had their position as workers decisively strengthened had they been incorporated into unemployment insurance on the same terms as men, yet here as well the state preferred policies that largely disqualified women from benefit as workers while distributing "family" benefits to men. The war had offered the government the chance to incorporate much of the working population into the insurance system during a period of full employment and hence to build up the solvency of the Unemployment Fund, and unemployment insurance was in fact extended to most trades connected with munitions – and hence to large numbers of women – through the National Insurance (Munition Workers) Act of 1916. To William Beveridge's great disgust, however, many unions resisted inclusion in the scheme and were allowed to opt out under an amending act in 1917.[117] This compromise left the insurance system in shambles and

(Brussels: Editions de l'Institut de Sociologie de l'Université Libre de Bruxelles, 1968), p. 169.

[117] Dr. Noelle Whiteside, relying on PRO figures, states that a mere 200,000 workers were included in the scheme by January 1918; Sir William Beveridge gave the figure ultimately

the government with no clear policy for the maintenance of the unemployed during the inevitable postwar labor dislocation.

It was here that the precedent and logic of separation allowances came into play. The government had long planned to ease the impact of demobilization by introducing an unemployment benefit for soldiers and sailors; in essence, it planned to continue to pay separation allowances to these men for themselves *and their families* in peacetime. When confronted by the prospect of serious unemployment and increased labor unrest at the end of the war, the government simply suspended the partially implemented contributory insurance law and established an "out-of-work" donation for civilian workers modeled on the soldiers' and sailors' scheme. Women war workers were eligible for the out-of-work donation and were, in its initial months of operation, the majority of claimants, but stringent enforcement of the rule that benefit could be denied if the claimant refused to accept "suitable employment" succeeded in reducing the number of women receiving benefit from one-half million to 120,000 within three months: women's doles were cut off, for example, if they turned down laundry work or domestic service, even if they had no prior experience in such work and were offered wages far below the level of the dole.[118] By November 1919, when the scheme was finally ended for all but servicemen, only one-fifth of the 137,000 civilians still receiving benefits were women.[119]

If many women found it difficult to qualify for benefits as "workers" – as self-supporting individuals experienced in a particular trade and hence reluctant to take on a new type of work at less than subsistence pay – some at least must have reappeared on the rolls in the more acceptable role of dependents. They did so because, once again drawing on the precedent of separation allowances, the out-of-work donation incorporated a new feature into unemployment policy: that of dependents' benefits. Unemployed male war workers, whose claims were not disallowed at anything approaching women's rates, could

---

included as 1.1 million. See Whiteside, "Welfare Legislation and the Unions during the First World War," *Historical Journal*, 23: 4 (1980), pp. 862; Beveridge, "Unemployment Insurance in the War and After," in Sir Norman Hill et al., eds., *War and Insurance* (London: Humphrey Milford, 1927), p. 233.

[118] Andrews and Hobbs, *Economic Effects of the World War*, pp. 10–11, 211–12. The process of forcing women back into these ill-paid and much-detested lines of work can be traced through the *Weekly Reports* of the Department of Civil Demobilization and Resettlement of the Ministry of Labour, nos. 1–33 (4 Jan. 1919–6 Sept. 1919).

[119] Andrews and Hobbs, *Economic Effects of the World War*, p. 211.

thus find themselves transformed into "breadwinners" and their wives into "dependents" through the agency of social policy, whatever their earlier patterns of earning. Dependents' benefits were sharply criticized by a parliamentary Committee of Inquiry into the operation of the donation, which recommended they be abolished as soon as possible and in no case incorporated into the unemployment insurance system.[120]

Yet when the donation was phased out and the insurance system expanded through the Unemployment Insurance Act of 1920 – after which it included over 11 million workers and most occupations outside agriculture and domestic service – demands that benefits include provision for dependent spouses and children proved impossible to resist. The government, faced with unprecedented levels of unemployment and fearful of labor unrest, had in any case abrogated strict insurance principles by allowing payments to large numbers of workers who had not amassed sufficient contributions to qualify for benefit or who had exhausted their "entitled" payments. Bewildered by levels of unemployment that stubbornly refused to fall and politically unwilling to throw large numbers of unemployed workers on the Poor Law, the Coalition government turned to the insurance fund to support much of the population considered legitimately seeking work, a task for which it neither was suited nor had been intended. Once the principle of subsistence maintenance had been conceded, benefits for dependents could not but follow. Under strong trade union pressure, and through the passage of the Unemployed Workers' Dependents (Temporary Provision) Act of 1921, a fund to pay such benefits was established on a "temporary" basis; in 1922, this temporary fund was quietly and permanently incorporated into the general insurance fund.[121] In practice, the government's acceptance of its responsibility to support the dependents of the male citizen, established for the case

---

[120] Committee of Inquiry into the Scheme of Out-of-Work Donation, *Final Report, PP* 1919, XXX, Cmd. 305, p. 9. On the out-of-work donation, see the Whiteside and Beveridge articles listed in note 117; Bentley B. Gilbert, *British Social Policy, 1914–39* (London: B. T. Batsford, 1970), pp. 54–61; Paul Johnson, *Land Fit for Heroes: The Planning of British Reconstruction, 1916–1919* (Chicago: University of Chicago Press, 1968), pp. 332–4.

[121] The complicated history of the out-of-work donation and the incorporation of dependents' benefits into insurance is discussed in the articles by Whiteside and Beveridge, note 117; Gilbert, *British Social Policy*, pp. 61–86; Pat Thane, *The Foundations of the Welfare State* (London: Longman, 1982), pp. 148–73; W. R. Garside, *British Unemployment, 1919–39* (Cambridge University Press, 1990), pp. 34–43.

of the citizen-soldier through separation allowances, was extended to the case of the citizen-worker through the incorporation of dependents' benefits into insurance in the postwar period.

The French avoided some of these dilemmas by relieving unemployment only at a local level, but not even the admittedly more limited social entitlements that grew out of the war presumed women's dependence. French assistance policies continued to focus on children rather than on wives, a trend only heightened by the alarm raised by the shocking losses of the war. One and one-third million Frenchmen died during the war, or an astounding 133 of every 1,000 men between the ages of 15 and 49 (compared with 63 out of every 1,000 Britons, or 723,000 in all) – a catastrophe that would skew the population figures for generations and that made policymakers even more concerned to encourage fatherhood among those who survived.[122] The children's allowances introduced or extended in the sheltered sectors of mining and railroads during the war were continued in peacetime, and in the early twenties the legislature and the government accepted the principle that large families – so essential for demographic renewal – had a claim on the state independent of need. The state had an obligation to aid "the family," Paul Bureau argued – "to bring about a just equalizing of public costs between those who contribute to the preservation of the life of the group and those who refuse to fulfill the most important of social services, that of paternity." The mere presence of children constituted an entitlement: "Exemptions from taxes or other costs, and direct allowances, are not State charity but simple reimbursement."[123] Parliament agreed. Although politicians spent an entire decade arguing over social insurance, a measure granting state-funded children's allowances to all families with more than three dependent children went from proposal to enactment in a mere three years. Unlike the allowances introduced in 1913, the allowances established by the new 1923 law were not based on need, demonstrating a commitment to some redistribution of income to families with children as a matter of right.[124]

---

[122] For military losses, see Winter, *Great War*, p. 75. Although Germany lost almost as many men as France and Britain together, the rate of loss was actually slightly smaller than France's, at 125 per 1,000 men, a result not only of Germany's larger population but also of its more advantageous age structure.

[123] Congrès National de la Natalité, *Compte rendu*, 4 (1922), p. 28.

[124] For an account of the campaign for the "encouragement national aux familles nombreuses" allowances, see Robert Talmy, *Histoire du mouvement familial*, 2, pp. 21–5, and *Revue de l'Alliance Nationale*, 122 (Sept. 1922), pp. 257–62, and 128 (Mar. 1923), pp. 104–5. The relevant minutes of the Chamber's Commission d'Assurance et de Prévoy-

While British labor and welfare policy tended to assume that men were wage earners and women dependent wives, French policy concentrated on redistributing income to families with children, and politicians spent rather less time discussing the respective roles of women and men. Yet the fact that the French social policies did not institutionalize the ideal of separate spheres for women and men should not be taken to mean that French policymakers were concerned to safeguard women's work rights or to weaken the identification of women as primarily mothers; still less can it be read as evidence of women's ability to influence policy. Quite the contrary: as in Britain, there was a strong ideal – almost a cult – in France of the *mère au foyer,* and the immutable naturalness of separate spheres was equally accepted by the Catholic and integralist right and the republican left. Rather, wage and welfare policies ignored the situation of wives because "wives" scarcely existed in French political rhetoric as independent beings requiring consideration; voteless and bereft of civil status, they could hardly state their own case. The French feminist movement had always been both weaker and more susceptible to maternalist and pronatalist pleas than its British counterpart, and it was further thrown on the defensive by the war.[125] The relative lack of interest exhibited by politicians in the status of wives was a consequence of women's political weakness, not their strength.

The indifference of politicians to the claims of women crossed the political and confessional divide: on this subject many of the usual political antagonisms vanished. Even the supposedly "individualist" Radical Party insisted that "the family" was the basic social cell. Later Prime Minister Edouard Herriot, for example, claimed in 1919 that "a nation is not a collection of individuals placed beside each other; it is a group of interlocking families. The organic cell is not the individual, but the family."[126] In politicians' minds, however, the family was almost inevitably represented by the father. Although the Chamber's Social Insurance Commission in 1921 proposed paying the projected large-family allowances to the mother, since she usually cared for the home and the children, they gave in to protests from deputies

ance Sociales (Assemblée Nationale Archives, Box A 13, Minutes for 28 May, 9 July and 17 Dec. 1920, and 14 Mar. 1921) show evidence of pronatalist influence over policymakers; the December session was attended by four members of the Conseil Supérieur de la Natalité, including Fernand Boverat.

[125] Hause with Kenney, *Women's Suffrage,* pp. 202–6.

[126] Edouard Herriot, *Créer,* 1 (1919; rpt. Paris: Payot, 1925), pp. 124–5; see also Serge Berstein, *Histoire du Parti Radical* (Paris: Presses de la Fondation Nationale des Sciences Politiques, 1980), pp. 327–8.

who felt – in the minister of health's words – that such a provision would be "a hatchet blow against the constitution of the family."[127] Those experienced in social legislation might have had doubts about the practicality of paying family benefits to men, but when confronted by irate deputies (and an exclusively male electorate) they prudently decided to equate families with fathers. When politicians decided to honor mothers it was usually with words or objects rather than cash, as in May 1920, when the state distributed its first medals to mothers of large families as part of the new annual Fête des Mères. As we shall see, however, industrialists felt no such deference to their male employees, and pronatalists also moderated their devotion to patriarchal values in an effort to bring benefits directly to children.

Conclusion

Immediate postwar developments thus confirmed the logic of family policy that emerged during the war in the two countries. In Britain, both the labor market and the social welfare system developed along male breadwinner lines, disproportionately distributing income to men on the assumption that they were (or would soon be) supporting dependent wives. In France, both wages and welfare policies became more "parental," as they were amended to compensate parents for dependent children, but not men for women. I have argued that these outcomes were heavily influenced by changing structures of industrial and political mediation brought about by the war. Specifically, the war integrated labor into decision-making structures in Britain, while in France it forced some amount of industrial rationalization and initiated an unprecedented degree of government–business collaboration. In the war period, and in the long run, policies had to be shaped to accommodate the economic and political interests of these powerful and institutionalized forces.

The war thus brought about two developments – a particular logic of welfare and new institutional structures – of long-term importance for the development of family policy. The war had a third impact, however, and one not necessarily consistent with administrative and institutional changes. In both countries, the war enhanced the appeal and power of particular ideologies and political groups and enabled these groups to capture the issue of family policy in the interwar

---

[127] See the objections by Delachénal, Leredu, and Isaac in *JO Débats (Chambre)*, 10 and 22 Mar. 1921, pp. 1185, 1192–3, 1362. For the commission's initial decision to pay to the mother, see Assemblée Nationale Archives, Box A 13, Minutes for 11 June 1920.

period. The war, as an object lesson in both demographic suicide and family policy innovations, greatly strengthened the hand of the French pronatalist and conservative groups discussed in the preceding chapter. Innocent of wider radical visions and unencumbered by feminist agendas, family issues in postwar France emerged as the property of nationalists and pronatalists seeking to reestablish French glory.

Pronatalist ideas gained hold in the early twenties, particularly among Catholics, within business groups, and in the Chamber of Deputies. The first annual conference on the birthrate was held in 1919 under the auspices of the Chambers of Commerce; the government established the consultative Conseil Supérieur de la Natalité (CSN) in 1920; and both the Alliance Nationale pour l'Accroissement de la Population Française and the Chamber's pronatalist lobby regrouped and began developing comprehensive platforms soon after the war. Leagues and associations devoted to representing fathers of Catholic families, large families, or those winners of the hyperpotency sweepstakes, the very largest families, also sprung up in the fertile soil of *revanchiste* provincial France. In December 1920, representatives of these familial and pronatalist movements gathered together to approve a "Declaration of the Rights of the Family" drawn up by Eugène Duthoit, a follower of Le Play, one of the leading lights of the social Catholic movement and professor of law at the Catholic University of Lille. The declaration laid out a comprehensive list of the "rights" of the family – to reproduction, education, a wage sufficient for support, the protection of property, tax relief, extra votes for fathers, protection from moral depravity – which were, they insisted, "anterior and superior to all positive law."[128]

Bourgeois feminists might still try to convince pronatalists that the best way to revive the birthrate would be to improve the status of mothers,[129] and more outspoken Communist women might rail against policies aimed at "forcibly restricting woman to the role of breeding animal,"[130] but pronatalism, by 1921, was accepted by virtually all right-thinking, bourgeois Frenchmen – whether Radicals or Catholics – as an essential component of French patriotism. The Bloc National government elected in November 1919 had reacted to a libertarian campaign in favor of birth control with laws criminalizing

---

[128] For the postwar rise of the "familist" movement, see Talmy, *Histoire du mouvement familial*, 1, pp. 206–38.

[129] A. B., "La lutte contre la dépopulation est l'affaire des femmes," *La Française*, 15: 525 (15 May 1920).

[130] Marthe Bigot, "Le Congrès de la Natalité," *L'Ouvrière*, 1: 30 (30 Sept. 1922).

the diffusion of birth control propaganda and making it easier to prosecute abortionists,[131] and doctors lent their support in tracts proclaiming both the healthfulness and duty of repeated childbearing.[132] Yet the question remained whether this new pronatalist fervor could galvanize reluctant industrialists or a tight-fisted Finance Ministry into creating a comprehensive family policy. Put simply, could costly programs like family allowances be shaped into policies consonant with the economic interests of businesses in the competitive, rather than the sheltered, sector?

In Britain as in France, the war strengthened a particular conception of the family and gave rise to new campaigns determined to incorporate that vision into state policy itself. In Britain, however, while the war strengthened the identification of women as wives and mothers, it also left at least a portion of the female population enfranchised. Some feminists, then, hoped to take advantage of both the new maternalist focus and women's political rights to win new entitlements for women as mothers. If women belonged in the home, the home itself must become an arena in which women's economic independence was safeguarded, not traduced. Eleanor Rathbone for one believed that the war had made working-class wives and mothers so "divinely discontented" with their prewar status that they would become a political force to reckon with in peacetime. "We feminists," she promised, "will then find our opportunity."[133]

Unlike in France, then, family policy in Britain was put forward as a feminist demand, aimed at increasing women's independence and power within the family itself. As in France, however, the success of family policy campaigns depended not simply on the comprehensibility of their vision or the worthiness of their goals, but rather on the degree to which advocates could construct new coalitions or mo-

---

[131] Joseph J. Spengler, *France Faces Depopulation* (Durham, N.C.: Duke University Press, 1938), pp. 240–2. The "neo-Malthusian" movement in France is covered by Francis Ronsin's excellent *La grève de ventres* (Paris: Aubier Montaigne, 1980); see also Angus McLaren, *Sexuality and Social Order* (New York: Holmes & Meier, 1983), pp. 93–121, 169–83.

[132] For a thorough discussion of the ideas of the pronatalist movement, see Chapter 7. Three good examples of pronatalist propaganda in the postwar period (the first two by doctors) are Dr. J. A. Doléris and Jean Bouscatel, *Néo-malthusianisme, maternité et féminisme, éducation sexuelle* (Paris: Masson, 1918); Dr. Cattier, *Des bébés, s'il vous plaît* (Paris: Plon, 1923); E. Angot, *Féminisme et natalité* (Paris: Emile-Paul Frères, [1923]). Typically, propagandists sought less to attack feminism directly than to claim that women's primary civic responsibility, from which their rights flowed, was, in Doléris and Bouscatel's words, "enfanter, encore enfanter, toujours plus enfanter" (p. 22).

[133] Rathbone, "Separation Allowances," part 2, p. 648.

bilize those interests granted new power by the war. And here the outlook for success seemed rather mixed. Rathbone may have hoped to marshal a new, cross-class "social" feminism aimed at improving the lot of mothers, but working-class women's organizations showed a marked preference for alliance with – or even absorption into – their brother organizations of the labor movement. In the aftermath of the war, the National Federation of Women Workers merged with the National Union of General Workers, the Women's Trade Union League surrendered its autonomy in return for guaranteed women's seats on the TUC General Council, and branches of the Women's Labour League became the Women's Sections of the Labour Party. With these mergers, the Labour Party could claim to be more truly representative of working-class women than even the most sympathetic independent feminist organization. Yet while Labour certainly hoped to improve the living standards of working-class families, many continued to feel this goal would be best achieved not through special "maternalist" benefits but through the struggle for a male family wage. Labourism and feminism were poised for a number of bitter quarrels in the postwar era.

Part II
REWORKING THE FAMILY WAGE IN THE TWENTIES

Broadly speaking, what worries me [about your report] is that some of the main facts on which we base our case, and on which we have accumulated masses of evidence, are either ignored altogether or misleadingly presented. . . . There is no reference whatever to our main economic contention, viz. that on no conceivable system of redistribution of wealth as between classes is a decent standard of life for families economically possible without Family Allowances.

> Eleanor Rathbone, for the Family Endowment Society, to Walter Milne-Bailey, Research Officer of the Trades Union Congress (26 July 1928)

I must say I am rather tired of Miss Rathbone. She appears to think that it is everyone's duty to write a report on Family Allowances on the lines that she dictates, and I am certainly not going to pay any attention to bullying of this kind.

> Walter Milne-Bailey to Margaret Bondfield (27 Aug. 1928)

With the electoral victories of the Coalition government in December 1918 and the Bloc National in November of 1919, Conservatives dominated the legislatures of both countries. Yet the new political interests mobilized by the war stubbornly refused to go away. In Britain, organized labor, women's groups, and those social policy "experts" intoxicated by their brief tenure in the ministries of Munitions and Reconstruction all insisted on their right to help shape the postwar settlement. Even in France, pronatalists, Catholics, and some far-sighted employers saw the postwar period as a time of extraordinary opportunity, a unique moment at which a fundamental restructuring of the liberal economy itself was perhaps possible.

The structure of the distributive system – the principles according to which the national pie was divided – became a key arena of political contestation. While trade unions sought to preserve their new status,

135

employers hoped to use the postwar dislocation to repudiate contracts acceded to in moments of weakness. And as the erstwhile "partners" in the wartime social contract fought over the wage, the argument that distributive justice could not be achieved through wages alone grew in strength. Whether on feminist, socialist, or pronatalist grounds, many women and men argued in the 1920s that only through direct cash allowances could a decent standard of living for families with young children be secured.

How successful were their campaigns? The chapters in Part II examine three attempts to introduce allowances for children and, in one case, for mothers. British campaigns, discussed in Chapters 3 and 4, failed. An unsuccessful effort by feminists to win support in the early twenties for the "endowment of motherhood" gave way later in the decade to an equally unsuccessful attempt by British socialists to inspire the Labour Party to introduce children's allowances as part of a comprehensive attack on working-class poverty. By contrast, and as Chapter 5 shows, French employers successfully introduced comprehensive systems of children's allowances for their employees, thus creating, however inadvertently, the foundations for a national family policy.

This pattern of achievement is instructive and cannot be explained with reference to state capacity alone. French politicians and civil servants, casting fearful glances eastward toward their populous and often belligerent neighbor, were broadly sympathetic to measures aimed at lessening the economic burden of parenthood. Yet the French state emerged from the war saddled with debts, a decimated population, and a weak franc; it had no spare resources to devote to families. Similarly, overt state hostility had relatively little to do with the demolition of family policy initiatives in Britain. Certainly the Treasury would have balked if asked to find a £100 million each year with which to "endow motherhood," but only once did such a plan even reach its offices. Feminist and socialist campaigns succumbed to opposition within the left itself, and especially within the trade union movement.

We find, then, that the fate of family allowance campaigns in the twenties rested in large part on the attitudes and actions of employers' organizations and trade unions – precisely those social partners arguing over the disposition of the wage. In a sense, their concerns were entirely logical, for although some British campaigners tried to argue that allowances could come as a pure increase to wages, in the long run, as Eleanor Rathbone recognized, "there is no source out of which family allowances could be paid that could not conceivably be paid in the way of increased wages."[1] Small wonder, then, that French employers sought, through family allowances, to force a disaggregation of the wage, and that British trade unionists mobilized to resist such proposals.

Yet economic interests and institutional capacities alone cannot explain the different tracks along which family policy developed in France and Britain. Family policy was useful or dangerous not only by virtue of its impact on the wage, but also because of other connotations imposed on it through several decades of policy debate. Thus, employers in France found family allowances particularly attractive because pronatalists had already identified them as crucial tools in the task of national reconstruction – a rhetorical construction that enabled employers to disguise their economic interest as public benevolence. Similarly, British trade unionists could have reservations about family allowances while being willing to support other mandatory taxes on wages because allowances had already been identified as a means of redistributing income as much within as toward the working class, and particularly from men to women. The explicit articulation of a feminist agenda in Britain, far from garnering support, helped condemn these policy initiatives to failure.

[1] TUC, File 117.32, Minutes of evidence of the Joint Committee on the Living Wage, 26 Jan. 1928, p. 16.

3

FAMILY POLICY AS WOMEN'S EMANCIPATION?
The failed campaign for endowment of motherhood in Britain

The feminist movement that emerged after the First World War was not the movement that had preceded it. Although women had, on the face of it, gained much from the war – votes and work opportunities especially – the organizations that had led the prewar suffrage campaigns were in disarray. The constitutionalist National Union of Women's Suffrage Societies had split over support for the war, and its dissident pacifist wing had gone off to form the Women's International League for Peace and Freedom; the Women's Social and Political Union had vanished entirely. Furthermore, even those feminists committed to using their new political power to further feminist aims had trouble agreeing about what those aims were. While some believed that feminists should concentrate primarily on removing those remaining legal inequalities and on gaining access to other hitherto male spheres, others felt that feminists should focus on those problems faced by housebound mothers. These women, who came to call themselves "new feminists," argued that neither formal legal equality nor open access to "men's jobs" could adequately meet the needs of working-class mothers. Only state intervention could do so; welfare programs could circumvent the labor market to provide independent support for mothers and children and free them from a humiliating dependence on men.

The rival programs and ideals of "new" and "equalitarian" feminists, as well as the implications of these divisions for postwar feminism, have absorbed much scholarly attention. The tone of much of this work is often harshly critical of new feminists, who are often seen as betraying the cause of equality to accept a restricted and biologically defined "place."[1] Yet the implication of this work – that feminists

---

[1] Susan Kingsley Kent, "The Politics of Sexual Difference: World War I and the Demise of British Feminism," *Journal of British Studies*, 27: 3 (July 1988), pp. 232–53; Kent is

138

would have accomplished more had they adhered to a strictly "egalitarian" program in the postwar period – is certainly open to question. If we examine feminist campaigns not for their adherence to some predefined orthodoxy, but rather within the political context of the time, the overwhelming constraints on all feminist activity become more apparent.

This chapter follows the campaign led by new feminists for universal state benefits for mothers with small children in the postwar period. Impressed by the effects of separation allowances, new feminists hoped to fashion comparable state policies to compensate all mothers for their domestic labors within the home, thereby ending the economic dependence of unwaged wives on their husbands. Similar proposals emerged within the women's organizations of the labor movement, although Labour women tended to argue from the standpoint of child health rather than wifely independence. Coming as they did on the heels of a costly war and the enfranchisement of a majority of adult women, such proposals received a far more favorable hearing than they would otherwise have done, prompting politicians in all parties and even Treasury officials to grapple with the problem of the civil and economic status of mothers. Nevertheless, insofar as the feminists' campaign achieved any practical results, it contributed only to the introduction of contributory pensions for widows in 1925, a measure that presumed that wives needed benefits not as independent citizens – still less as "state mothers" – but as the bereaved dependents of working men. Although the introduction of widows' pensions, like that of separation allowances, was accompanied by a rhetoric lauding mothers' unpaid work, the policy itself – again like separation allowances – fit far more comfortably within the ideal of the family wage as espoused by organized men.

In searching to explain the failure of the feminist initiative in the years following the war, it is important to distinguish between political

equally critical of "new feminism" in "Gender Reconstruction after the First World War," in Harold L. Smith, ed., *British Feminism in the Twentieth Century* (Amherst: University of Massachusetts Press, 1990), pp. 66–83. Mary Stocks, who was a strong partisan of new feminism, defends it ably in *Eleanor Rathbone: A Biography* (London: Gollancz, 1949); see also Hilary Land, "Eleanor Rathbone and the Economy of the Family," in Smith, ed., *British Feminism*, pp. 104–23. Johanna Alberti provides a lucid and sympathetic survey of both sides of these arguments in *Beyond Suffrage: Feminists in War and Peace, 1914–1928* (London: Macmillan, 1989); see also Harold Smith, "British Feminism in the 1920s" in his edited volume, *British Feminism*, pp. 47–65. Brian Harrison, by contrast, downplays these divisions, stressing the democratic, reformist, and pragmatic concerns of many interwar feminists in *Prudent Revolutionaries: Portraits of British Feminists between the Wars* (Oxford University Press, 1987).

rhetoric and campaigns on the one hand and political capacity on the other. Feminists did compete effectively in the first arena, and their campaign was successful in defining family policy as a "women's issue," a means of shifting resources from men to women. The elegance of their ideas was unaccompanied by real political influence, however, for feminists found themselves unable either to sustain the independent organizations of the suffrage period or to use any of the older political parties as springboards for their own ideas. Their capacity to influence the shape of policy depended on their ability to gain allies within parties organized on quite different lines, and here, as we shall see, they largely failed.

We can trace the supersession of "endowment" by widows' pensions through interactions in three spheres: social investigation, Labour politics, and the civil service. Debates in each area played a role in shaping the final result: "scientific" sociologists used questionable statistics to redefine male maintenance as the "normal" family situation and thus the only reasonable basis for welfare policy; Labour politicians reinterpreted feminist demands to correspond with trade union ideals of the male family wage; and an autonomous civil service drafted legislation to conform to its own conception of the limits of state action. While in retrospect it appears as if the feminist campaign never had any real chance of success, its history remains central to our story, for the very processes through which it was defeated reveal the emerging character of the British welfare state. But before examining the subversion of the endowment campaign by these more powerful forces, let us look at its emergence as a feminist solution to the economic and political marginality of married women.

"Separate but equal": The vision of maternalist feminism

H. G. Wells and other socialists or sexual rebels had supported the "endowment of motherhood" for a dozen years before the First World War, but it was only after the war had sufficiently unsettled the relationship between men, women, and the state that some British feminists began to campaign for endowment. By far the most important convert, and the author of the argument by which state aid to mothers was made compatible with a long-standing feminist concern for women's economic independence, was Eleanor Rathbone, the wealthy and Oxford-educated daughter of a prominent Liverpool family, whom we have already encountered in the administrative ranks of the Soldiers' and Sailors' Families Association (SSFA) during the war. Rathbone had followed in her father's footsteps and devoted herself to voluntary social work after her return from Somerville in 1896. Grad-ually, however, she became critical of the lack of professionalism and "haphazard" methods of the voluntary relief agencies; together with Elizabeth Macadam, a Scottish social worker who became her lifelong companion, she helped to establish a more rigorous training program for social workers at Liverpool University. Her leadership role within a range of women's organizations – including the Victoria Women's Settlement (where Macadam was warden) and the local branch of the National Union of Women's Suffrage Societies – also provided her with a basis from which to enter local government. In 1909 she became the first woman elected to the Liverpool City Council, a position she held until 1935. During the war, her work with the SSFA and her outspoken feminism made her a force in national politics, and in 1919 she succeeded Millicent Fawcett as president of the National Union of Women's Suffrage Societies, now renamed the National Union of Societies for Equal Citizenship (NUSEC). From that position, she be-came the principal spokeswoman for new feminism throughout the twenties.[2]

Even before the war, Rathbone's social work and social investiga-tions had led her to concentrate on the problems – both practical and theoretical – posed by mothers' dependence. Years of work as a home visitor had convinced her that women caring for young children were already "fully occupied," and she came to question both a wage system and social policies that ignored such work. In 1913, in a study of the conditions of widows in receipt of poor relief in Liverpool, she was sharply critical of a Poor Law that stigmatized women solely because they had had the misfortune to lose their husbands – an event quite out of their control – but paid little attention to the competence with which they pursued their own "work," the care of their children. Surely, she said, it would be both just and prudent to provide hon-orable maintenance – pensions administered apart from the Poor Law – to widows who were raising their children properly:

> The widow who is doing her duty by her young children, tending
> them, washing, sewing and cooking for them, is not a pensioner

[2] The standard biography of Rathbone remains Mary Stocks, *Eleanor Rathbone*; see also Su-zie Fleming, "Eleanor Rathbone: Spokeswoman for a Movement," Introduction to the new edition of Rathbone, *The Disinherited Family* (1924; new ed., London: Falling Wall, 1986) pp. 9–120; Margaret Simey, *Eleanor Rathbone, 1872–1946: A Centenary Tribute* (Liv-erpool: University of Liverpool Press, 1974); Susan Pedersen, "Eleanor Rathbone (1872–1946): The Victorian Family Under the Daughter's Eye," in Pedersen and Peter Mandler, eds., *After the Victorians: Private Conscience and Public Duty in Modern Britain* (London: Rout-ledge, forthcoming), and the chapter on Rathbone in Harrison, *Prudent Revolutionaries*.

upon the bounty of the state, but is earning the money she draws from it by services just as valuable to the community as those of a dock-labourer, a plumber or a soldier, perhaps even not much less valuable than those of the Relieving Officer or Poor Law Guardian who now browbeats or patronises her.[3]

Yet it was one thing to call for pensions for widowed mothers – a demand for which there was some sympathy – and quite another to argue that all mothers should be put on the national payroll, a position rarely supported before 1914 by persons of Rathbone's social position or with her impeccable credentials in voluntary social work. Yet Rathbone had begun to move toward this revolutionary proposal, albeit from the standpoint of the interests of women in the work force, rather than the home. In *The Problem of Women's Wages*, published in 1912 but written about a dozen years earlier, Rathbone had come to the conclusion that the dependence of mothers, unjust in itself, also made women's equality at work impossible. The feminist principle of equal pay ignored what she took to be two unavoidable truths: that wages would tend to reflect the average subsistence needs of any given class of worker, and that married women would continue to withdraw from the work force on marriage in order to devote themselves to home and children. So long as these wives and children were supported largely out of the wages of adult men, men's and women's wages would inevitably tend to diverge. "The difference between the wages of men and women," she concluded, "is due to the different consequences which marriage has for the two sexes."[4]

This is where Rathbone had, even before the war, made her boldest intellectual leap. "It may be said," she wrote, "that if my argument proves anything, it proves that the lowness of woman's wages, being based on fundamental and unalterable circumstances of sex, must itself, in this best of possible worlds, be inevitable and right." "But," she continued, "the circumstances of sex are not unalterable, though the fact of sex is. The arrangement by which the cost of rearing fresh generations is thrown as a rule upon the male parent, is not the only possible, nor even the only existing one."[5] Indeed, this "arrangement" had formidable disadvantages: it was wasteful, since many men had no dependents while some women did; it exacerbated labor compe-

---

[3] Eleanor F. Rathbone, *Report on the Condition of Widows under the Poor Law in Liverpool* (Liverpool: Lee & Nightingale, 1913), p. 32.

[4] Eleanor Rathbone, *The Problem of Women's Wages* (Liverpool: Northern Publishing Co., 1912), p. 21.

[5] Ibid.

tition between men and women paid at different rates for similar work; and – as Rathbone had herself documented in her studies of the families of dockers, seamen and casual laborers – it caused great hardship to the mothers and children who had no guarantee that their particular "provider's" wages would be adequate or, for that matter, spent on them.[6] Most crucially, it left women's own contribution to society unappreciated and their persons subject to men. "Like priest and parsons, mothers have to live," she wrote in the suffrage weekly *Common Cause* in 1912, "but in their case economic and social forces have worked out a solution satisfactory alike to masculine sentiment and to masculine love of power, in the system which makes society's payment of maternity, not to the mother herself, but to every adult male worker as a hypothetical husband."[7]

In her prewar social surveys and writings, then, Eleanor Rathbone had come to the conclusion that the economic dependence of mothers lay at the heart of the unequal status of *all* women, whether married or unmarried, whether wage earners or housewives. But what was to be done? In *The Problem of Women's Wages*, she said bluntly that the wage system was a human institution and could be altered better to meet human needs – by, for example, endowing motherhood. Yet she clearly realized that such proposals were utopian in 1912 and, along with other feminists, supported the stricter enforcement of maintenance laws or legislation giving wives the legal claim to a portion of their husbands' pay.[8] By 1917, however, with enfranchisement on the horizon, women workers clamoring to preserve their wartime gains, and 1.5 million women already receiving the separation allowances that resembled an endowment of motherhood, she became more optimistic. The war also provided her with some unexpected allies. Those feminists who had seen the war as the ultimate expression of masculine values shared her belief that women did have needs or rights that could not be answered by a strict egalitarianism. Women like Kathleen Courtney and Maude Royden, both of whom were active in the Women's International League for Peace and Freedom, were attracted to the proposal to endow motherhood and thus to compensate women for the humane and caring work that they already did.

---

[6] Eleanor F. Rathbone, *How the Casual Labourer Lives: Report of the Liverpool Joint Research Committee on the Domestic Condition and Expenditure of the Families of Certain Liverpool Labourers* (Liverpool: Northern Publishing Co., 1909); E. Mahler and E. F. Rathbone, *Payment of Seamen: the Present System* (Liverpool: C. Tinling, 1911).
[7] Eleanor Rathbone, "The Economic Position of Married Women," *Common Cause*, 3: 143 (4 Jan. 1912), p. 675.
[8] Ibid.

The founding statement of this new or maternalist feminism came in September 1917, with the appearance of a volume entitled *The Making of Women: Oxford Essays in Feminism*. The book took its tone from an essay by Maude Royden entitled "Modern Love," which criticized the tendency of feminists to try to reduce motherhood to "a mere episode" in a woman's life. "I hesitate to differ from many of my fellow-feminists on this point," Royden (herself childless) wrote, but "I am persuaded that the average woman, when she surmounts the ridiculous conventions of the richer, and the grim necessities of the poorer class, finds in motherhood – and prefers to find in it – her chief work, her most absorbing interest, as long as her children are quite young."[9] The task of feminism, then, should be not only to win for women the rights and opportunities previously monopolized by men, but also to give mothers the economic and civic recognition they deserved.

It was Rathbone's contribution to the volume, an essay entitled "The Remuneration of Women's Services" (which had first appeared in the *Economic Journal* earlier that year), that attempted to reconcile this maternalist feminism with the older goal of equality in the public sphere. Essentially recapitulating the analysis she had developed before the war, she once again argued that women's unequal status as workers stemmed from the arrangement whereby the responsibility to maintain mothers and children was borne primarily by the father, and that only a measure of endowment would lighten that responsibility and make equal pay both just and possible. In this essay, however, she made it clear that she considered the injustice done to women workers to be minor compared to that done to mothers, whose work was never recognized as work, and who had no guarantee that they would receive their fair share of a wage that was based, after all, on the presumption of their existence. She asked, "Can anyone who thinks about it seriously defend the system which makes the remuneration of all the services connected with that most important supply [of children] dependent upon and subsidiary to the remuneration of a quite different and irrelevant set of services, those of the industrial workers?"[10]

The Making of Women, and Rathbone's essay in particular, proved influential, and a second edition was published within three months.

---

[9] A. Maude Royden, "Modern Love," in Victor Gollancz, ed., *The Making of Women: Oxford Essays in Feminism* (1917; 2d ed., London: Allen & Unwin, 1918), pp. 51–2.

[10] Eleanor Rathbone, "The Remuneration of Women's Services," *Economic Journal*, 27: 105 (Mar. 1917), p. 65.

Victor Gollancz, who edited the book, admitted in his preface to the new edition that the volume had been criticized for making the case for endowment of motherhood without including any definite scheme, but he assured his readers that such a scheme was now in preparation.[11] Three of the contributors to *The Making of Women* – Rathbone, Royden, and Elinor Burns – were joined by four other supporters – Kathleen Courtney, H. N. Brailsford, the socialist journalist, Mary Stocks, an economist and fellow member of the NUWSS, and Elinor Burns's husband, Emile Burns – to form the Family Endowment Committee for that purpose. In their 1918 pamphlet, *Equal Pay and the Family*, they proposed to endow all women with children below school age, and those children, for a total annual cost of £139 million. The committee followed Rathbone's analysis in identifying endowment both as the only real solution to the problem of equal pay for men and women and as a pressing public health measure. What is particularly striking about the Family Endowment Committee's proposal, however, especially in view of supporters' later decision to campaign for children's allowances alone, was its uncompromising identification of mothers as *workers*: women were entitled to support because of their care of children (and not, as with separation allowances, as wives) and were clearly expected to return to work when the youngest child reached school age, since the woman's allowance would then be discontinued.[12]

The adoption of endowment by Rathbone and her allies won them a hearing in the peculiar conditions of the war, but it also distanced them from their prewar arguments and concerns. Many prewar feminists had been strict egalitarians, concerned to open up "men's sphere" of work and politics to women. The endowment advocates, by contrast, were attempting to recast a widely accepted domestic ideology of separate spheres in a feminist direction. Its proponents largely accepted the division of the world's work along sex lines and agreed that women would be primarily concerned with domestic work and child care. They implicitly criticized both feminist skepticism of inherent sexual difference and the prewar focus on extending women's waged work. Maude Royden wrote:

> Our object will not be to enable mothers to earn their living, but to ensure that, *since they have earned it*, they should get it. . . . The one really fundamental difference between men and women is (again) a

[11] Gollancz, ed., *The Making of Women*, p. 5.
[12] Family Endowment Committee, *Equal Pay and the Family* (London: Headley Brothers, 1918).

"difference," it is certainly not an inferiority. For women to try to reduce it to a trifle when it is really so great a thing is an acceptance of masculine standards too dishonouring and too artificial to endure.[13]

The problem, for Royden, was not that motherhood was women's main job, but that this most important of all work was left to be arbitrarily and randomly supported by men.

The endowment proposal thus involved a radical rethinking both of the economic basis of the family and of the relationship of the state to the citizen. Like Catholics and pronatalists in France, British feminists argued that the practice of setting wages through the "higgling of the market" or through collective bargaining ignored the interests of families; unlike these more conservative French groups, however, feminists were not content to identify "the family" per se as the object of redistributive policies, insisting that the state also had an interest in the division of labor and resources within that family. New feminists were trying to safeguard women's sphere, while breaking its links to economic dependence and political marginality. The economic support of women should bypass the husband entirely and operate directly between the woman and the state, based on her own contribution as citizen – motherhood. "Motherhood is a service which entitles a woman to economic independence," wrote Royden.[14] Drawing on the resonant cultural equation of motherhood with military service, she argued:

> The State wants children, and to give them is a service both dangerous and honourable. Like the soldier, the mother takes a risk and gives a devotion for which no money can pay; but, like the soldier, she should not, therefore, be made "economically dependent."[15]

The state's relationship to women's sphere of reproduction and domestic service should be as direct and rewarding as to men's sphere of war and work. In this vision, the state was redefined as an entity organized not only for war and the taking of life, but also for the

---

[13] A. Maude Royden, "The Women's Movement of the Future," in Gollancz, ed., *The Making of Women*, p. 139.

[14] A. Maude Royden, "State Endowment of Motherhood," *Common Cause*, 9: 445 (19 Oct. 1917), p. 327.

[15] A. Maude Royden, "Mothers' Pensions," *Common Cause*, 9: 429 (29 June 1917), p. 147. For a compelling analysis of the cultural meaning of the mother–soldier analogy, see Nancy Huston, "The Matrix of War: Mothers and Heroes," in Susan Rubin Suleiman, ed., *The Female Body in Western Culture* (Cambridge, Mass.: Harvard University Press, 1986), pp. 119–36.

giving of it, and the citizen as either the male soldier/producer or the female reproducer. Although the distinction between the male and female spheres remained, their identification as respectively public and private disappeared.

The proposal to endow motherhood found supporters within the feminist movement but also critics: meetings of feminist societies and the columns of feminist papers resounded with arguments over endowment, and later over family allowances, from the last years of the war to the midtwenties. Women whose feminism was founded on the principles of nineteenth-century liberalism objected both to the implication that men need bear little responsibility for the children they begot and to the replacement of wages won through individual effort by state benefits granted as entitlements.[16] "It is an old-fashioned and safe rule in State aid," one reviewer of Rathbone's argument wrote in the *Englishwoman*, "to begin by providing for a man or woman what they cannot get for themselves, because such gifts do not destroy the sense of responsibility or discourage effort."[17] Millicent Fawcett, who was as firmly committed to the tenets of political economy as she was to feminism, was especially distressed by the direction she perceived the National Union to be taking after she stepped down as president. Fawcett had never accepted Rathbone's argument that equal pay was impossible without endowment, retorting that wages were based in the first instance on supply and demand and had been kept artificially low for women by trade union rules,[18] and she feared that the cure would prove worse than the disease. Family endowment, she claimed in 1922, was much like the Speenhamland system of poor relief introduced during the Napoleonic Wars, a system that, she contended, had severed the link between parental wage earning and family well-being, raised illegitimacy rates, depressed wages, and inaugurated a degree of "economic and moral ruin" only ended by the New Poor Law of 1834.[19]

---

[16] A. Lamont, "The Endowment of Motherhood: A Counter-Plea," *Common Cause*, 9: 449 (16 Nov. 1917), p. 383; also Letters, *Common Cause*, 9: 450 (23 Nov. 1917), p. 398.

[17] "Problems of the Day: The Family Wage," *Englishwoman*, 36: 108 (Dec. 1917), p. 189.

[18] Millicent G. Fawcett, "Equal Pay for Equal Work," *Economic Journal*, 28: 109 (Mar. 1918), pp. 1–6.

[19] Millicent G. Fawcett, Letter, *Woman's Leader*, 14: 34 (22 Sept. 1922), p. 271. The Charity Organisation Society obviously shared Fawcett's point of view. One of their publications argued that wages were a far better means of support than a state dole, which was merely "only out-relief under another name." Endowment would lower wages and turn people into state dependents, which would be contrary to the principles of English liberty. The aim of reducing "dependence" was misguided, and the pamphlet argued that "the ideal family life necessarily involves dependence, the dependence of the husband

Mrs. Fawcett was the most prominent feminist critic speaking from a heritage of nineteenth-century political economy, but endowment was also criticized by women who objected less to state aid than to maternalism itself. Women had not spent half a century fighting for economic and political liberty, some feminists claimed, to return to hearth and home, however rewarded. In language reminiscent of Cicely Hamilton's *Marriage as a Trade*, Helen Fraser reminded readers of the *Woman's Leader* that the feminist revolt against domesticity had been a revolt against personal and sexual submission as well as against economic dependence. Any scheme of endowment assumed "the sex-slavery of women," she charged. Women already suffered from "excessive child-bearing," she objected, and "to be asked to pursue policies and advocate schemes that will inevitably add to that evil is to do something that to some of us who have fought for the full freedom of women is intolerable."[20] Ada Nield Chew, who had so eloquently argued against H. G. Wells in the early *Freewoman* controversy over endowment, found her objections undiminished. How would transferring the support of married women and children from one particular man to all men end the real subjection of women, she asked?

> Personally, if I must be kept by men at all, I would prefer to delegate that privilege to the one man I know than to a crowd of inoffensive male creatures, on whom I, as an able-bodied adult, even though of feminine sex, have no claim whatever and desire to make none. People talk of the "State" as though it were some impersonal powerful sort of God, on whom we have all a boundless claim – or at any rate, those of us who are women with a child or two to be kept. The State is merely ourselves, and the money to keep us has to be worked for by somebody, and if men are to be the only workers we shall be dependent of them just as we have always been. Instead of one man being our master because he keeps us, we shall be allowing the mass of men to be our masters because they keep us. Merely plural instead of singular. Advantages there would be to individual women who own one tyrant as a master and to whom the change to Tyrant State would no doubt come as a blessed relief, but is the individual gain to individual woman to weigh in the balance against the freedom of a sex?

and wife upon each other, and of the children upon their parents, and that such a dependence, voluntarily accepted, produces the most highly valued of human relationships." Edith Neville, *Family Life, Considered in Connection with the Proposals for the National Endowment of Motherhood* ([London?]: Charity Organisation Society, Mar. 1919).

20 Helen Fraser, "Family Endowment," *Woman's Leader*, 14: 32 (8 Sept. 1922), pp. 252–3.

Far from ending women's dependence, then, endowment of motherhood would merely replace private patriarchy with the patriarchal state and, by essentially forcing every woman on marriage "to adopt, willy nilly, pot and pan washing and child-rearing as her work," would further reduce women's already meager sphere of freedom. "Why seek to shackle poor women to domestic work for ever?" she asked. "Why not leave them a choice, at least; and encourage them to seek real instead of mock independence?" For women as well as men, waged work not endowment was the road to freedom – economic, political, and personal.[21]

Quarrels of this nature were played out within the feminist successors to the great prewar suffrage organizations, possibly contributing to the fragmentation and decline that was their fate in the interwar period. The annual council of NUSEC resolved in 1919 "to work for the endowment of maternity and childhood by the State" but stipulated that no definite scheme could be adopted until discussed again by the council, and by 1920 could agree only to appoint a committee to discuss the question. The council did pass a resolution supporting family endowment in 1922, but the vote was challenged and declared invalid the following year.[22] The Women's Freedom League went through a similar series of flip-flops on the question, rejecting a resolution in favor of endowment of motherhood in 1919 – with some members feeling that there was "no difference at all between women being dependent upon their husbands and being dependent on the State"[23] – but narrowly passing a comparable resolution in 1922. During the latter debate, Dr. Knight truthfully warned the conference that the issue had led to "a great deal of dissension and trouble" within other women's societies and concluded that it would be "rather a pity" to subject the league to such divisions.[24] Certainly the NUSEC continued to be plagued by the issue. Not until 1925 did the annual council of the NUSEC commit itself (by a margin of 111 to 42) "to include work for the general principle of Family Allowances in [NUSEC's] general programme,"[25] a decision that drove Mrs. Fawcett to resign from the board of the *Woman's Leader*.[26]

[21] Ada Nield Chew, "Family Endowment: Another View," *Woman's Leader*, 14: 33 (15 Sept. 1922), pp. 261–2.
[22] National Union of Societies for Equal Citizenship [NUSEC], *Annual Report for the Year 1918*, p. 22; *Annual Report for the Year 1919*, p. 19; *Annual Report for the Year 1921*, p. 57; *Annual Report for the Year 1923*, pp. 61–2.
[23] Women's Freedom League, *Annual Conference Report*, 12 (1919), p. 78.
[24] Women's Freedom League, *Report*, 15 (1922), pp. 94–6.
[25] NUSEC, *Annual Report for the Year 1924–5*, p. 63; Stocks, *Eleanor Rathbone*, pp. 116–18.
[26] Millicent Fawcett, letter, *Woman's Leader*, 17: 11 (10 Apr. 1925), p. 84; Ray Strachey *Millicent Garrett Fawcett* (London: J. Murray, 1931), p. 335.

By the midtwenties, then, family endowment had aroused a good deal of dissension as well as enthusiasm within the feminist movement, demonstrating that, once the glue of the suffrage agitation had dissolved, philosophical and political differences among women could be as profound as those between women and men. In 1918, however, when the Family Endowment Committee published its first proposal, both feminist sympathy and public interest ran high. To begin with, the devastating losses of the war had, as Rathbone's fellow suffragist Maude Royden noted, taught the country "the value of babies."[27] Both voluntary and local government services to children had expanded dramatically during the war, and Labour and women's organizations – especially the much-respected Women's Cooperative Guild – pressed for improved cash maternity benefits and the establishment of medical services for all mothers and infants.[28] In 1918, the Maternal and Infant Welfare Act was passed requiring the establishment of a committee concerned with such questions by each local authority and enabling (but not requiring) that committee to develop such services as infant welfare centers, salaried midwives, and health visitors.[29] The Women's Cooperative Guild attempted, often successfully, to secure representation for its members on these committees – by 1921 there were 275 guildswomen on 186 maternity committees[30] – but also continued to press its view that economic supports for mothers were quite as necessary as services to children. By 1919, even the *Times* had come round to this point of view. In a leader article discussing the decline in the birthrate, the paper attributed the failure to prevent infant mortality "to the fact that most of the schemes of infant welfare

---

[27] A. Maude Royden, *National Endowment of Motherhood* (London: Women's International League, 1919), p. 1.

[28] The guild's thinking on maternal and infant welfare found expression in a pamphlet entitled *The National Care of Maternity*, written by Margaret Bondfield and published by the guild in 1914. The guild's proposals for a single public health authority, extended pregnancy benefit, and universal medical and maternal services administered at a local level received much attention both before and during the war. In 1917, the guild took a deputation to Lord Rhondda, then president of the Local Government Board, to press its case. See "Motherhood Grants," *Times*, 2 May 1917.

[29] On the war and the 1918 act, see Jane Lewis, *The Politics of Motherhood: Child and Maternal Welfare in England, 1900–1939* (London: Croom Helm, 1980), pp. 32–6. Deborah Dwork and Anna Davin, albeit from quite different perspectives, also agree that the war fueled official concern for child health: Dwork, *War Is Good for Babies and Other Young Children* (London: Tavistock, 1987); Davin, "Imperialism and Motherhood," *History Workshop Journal*, 5 (Spring 1978), pp. 9–65.

[30] Women's Cooperative Guild [WCG], *Annual Report*, 38 (1921), p. 10.

which are being formulated leave out of account, or minimize the importance of, the economic status of the mother."[31]

Supporters of endowment also profited from public interest in pensions for widows or deserted wives with young children, a proposal that critics of the Poor Law – including, as we have seen, Eleanor Rathbone – had come to favor even before the war. Experiments in the United States with such "mothers' pensions" were well known, and a visit by Judge Henry Neil of Chicago in 1917 sparked further interest: in 1918, the Local Government Board issued a report on U.S. schemes.[32] Such mothers' pensions were by no means advocated only by women's organizations. The State Children's Association, of which Henrietta Barnett was secretary, also hoped that a scheme of mothers' pensions would enable poor children to be cared for in their own homes rather than in institutions. The measure was supported by 120 local councils and by 200 candidates during the 1918 election.[33]

There was, of course, a world of difference between a proposal to grant pensions to unsupported mothers and one to grant pensions to all mothers, but in 1918 even the latter could seem imaginable. Separation allowances, which many thought had raised the status and confidence of married women, were still being drawn by some one and one-half million wives in early 1918, leading one Ministry of Reconstruction memorandum to predict that the "growing demand for a change in the economic position of women ... is likely to be pressed as a result of women's suffrage."[34] Politicians also awaited the effects of women's enfranchisement with some nervousness, and were inclined to listen to proposals that, at other times, would have seemed impossibly extravagant. When the Family Endowment Committee published its proposal, then, it was invited to give evidence to both the War Cabinet Committee on Women in Industry (WIC) and the National Birth Rate Commission. To both bodies the Family Endowment Committee laid out its proposal to endow mothers from confinement until the youngest child reached the age of 5, at rates of the separation allowances given to soldiers' and sailors' wives – although, as Maude Royden stressed, it proposed that "no money should be

---

[31] "Births and Deaths," *Times*, 25 Mar. 1917.

[32] "Mothers' Pensions," *Times*, 17 May 1917; "Pensions for Mothers: An American Scheme," *Times*, 2 July 1917; "Mothers' Pensions. System at Work in America," *Times*, 28 Dec. 1918.

[33] "Mothers' Pensions," *Times*, 15 Jan. 1919.

[34] PRO, PIN 15/405, Ministry of Reconstruction, "Endowment of Widows and Deserted Wives" [Feb. 1918?].

paid to the wife as a wife, but as a mother."[35] The committee admitted that such endowment would cost a massive £144 million per year, or about £250 million per year if the allowance for the children (but not the mother) were continued until the last child left school, but insisted that even the latter figure was not an impossible one "in the light of the war."[36] It can be taken as a sign of the unusual character of the period that the *Times* published quite sympathetic accounts of their evidence.[37]

What happened to this campaign? It had, in all probability, no real chance of success, especially when women's enfranchisement proved to have little impact on the party system and the economic downturn of the early twenties made budgetary stringency a priority. Yet the scrutiny given to women's demands did feed into a quite different policy-making process, resulting in the passage by the Conservative government in 1925 of legislation incorporating pensions for widows into the insurance system. But widows' pensions, unlike endowment, presumed that only women who had lost their husbands needed state aid, and that married women were sheltered by the male family wage; further, as NUSEC objected, the link between pensions and insurance made men's contribution to industry rather than the needs of women and children the main qualification for payment.[38] How, then, did a campaign to pay *all* mothers for their care of children feed into the introduction of pensions for widows as one of the rights of insured male breadwinners? To trace this process of transformation, we must turn to the reception of feminist demands by social investigators, the labor movement, and the civil service.

Fantasy as social science: Seebohm Rowntree imagines the family

Eleanor Rathbone's analysis had bound the causes of endowment and equal pay almost inextricably together, and it was this marriage that

---

[35] National Council of Public Morals, National Birth Rate Commission, *Problems of Population and Parenthood* (London: Chapman & Hall, 1920), p. 20. See also Mary Stocks's evidence to the commission, in ibid., pp. 235–42.

[36] The £144-million figure was proposed in evidence to the War Cabinet Committee on Women in Industry; Imperial War Museum, Verbatim Minutes of Evidence of the War Cabinet Committee on Women in Industry (henceforth, IWM, WIC Minutes), Family Endowment Committee evidence, 14 Oct. 1918. The larger figure was proposed and defended by Royden in evidence to the National Birth Rate Commission, *Problem of Population and Parenthood*, pp. 21, 32.

[37] "Saving the Children: Endowment of Motherhood," *Times*, 25 Feb. 1919; "Endowment for Mothers," *Times*, 19 June 1918.

[38] Fawcett Library, Box 341, NUSEC Executive Committee Minutes, 8 May 1924, p. 4.

came under scrutiny by social scientists and official committees at the end of the war. Wage regulation coupled with redistributive policies – or equal pay supplemented by endowment – was, Rathbone and other supporters of endowment argued, a just and rational alternative to the practice of paying higher wages to men on the grounds that they had "families to keep." Not only did such unequal pay benefit men who had no such burdens, they charged; it also ignored the fact that underpaid women as well as men often supported dependents. The argument for endowment thus quickly became part of a bitter debate over the relative burdens and claims of male and female workers – a war of numbers, in which rival investigators sought to demonstrate the irrationality or defensibility of the male family wage.

The Fabian Women's Group issued a first salvo in July 1915 with the publication of *Wage-Earning Women and Their Dependents*, a self-proclaimed "objective" study, based on prewar data, of the responsibility of women workers for maintaining others. It found that more than 50% of waged women had total or partial responsibility for dependents, a startling conclusion given the fact that women's supposed lack of dependents was the most common justification for their low pay. By far the weakest aspect of the Fabian investigation was its reliance on a questionnaire that received only a 10% response; however, when the group checked their conclusions by using more complete data provided by statistician Arthur Bowley, they arrived at almost identical results.

The group's method of defining maintenance was quite simple: if including both the woman and her income in the calculation made the per capita family income greater than it would be if both of these were excluded – or, in other words, if she brought in more money than the amount needed to maintain her at the same level as all other family members – she was defined as at least partially supporting others. In justifying their method, the authors stated:

> It would obviously have been more satisfactory if the actual amount contributed to the household expenses by each money-earning member of the family could have been obtained, but in the absence of all such information we considered that by pooling the family wages and comparing the women's contribution with the spending amount per head, a very accurate estimate of the part played by the woman as breadwinner in the family of which she formed a part would be obtained. We believe that if any error occurs it is on the side of under-estimating rather than over-estimating the amount of support contributed by the woman. It is the general practice of the working-man to allow a regular sum each week to his wife for the family expenses and to keep the remainder of his wages for his own personal

use. The amount retained depends to a large extent on the size of the family. In some cases where his wages are very low a man gives all he earns to his wife, but in such cases it is safe to assume that the female wage-earners (if any) in the family do likewise. In a large number of cases the proportion of the wages kept by the male is larger than that kept by the female workers.[39]

The Fabian investigation, by showing that many women as well as men supported families, made a strong case for equal pay. Yet it was the actual wartime blurring of the boundaries between men's and women's work that made the question of the relationship between men's and women's wages so pressing. When the War Cabinet's Committee on Women in Industry (WIC) began its hearings on the appropriate future scope and pay of women in industry in 1918, its members found the twin demands of equal pay and endowment confronting them at every turn. A number of welfare workers, and the indomitable egalitarians of the Workers' Union, insisted that many women workers did indeed support others while many men did not; as W. T. Kelly of the Workers' Union put it, "We cannot agree that we should assume that generally the woman has less responsibility than the man."[40] From this position, the Workers' Union urged – as did the Women's Industrial Council and the Fabian Women's Group – that wages be determined without reference to sex and the family become "a responsibility which has to be borne socially by the state."[41] Unlike the Family Endowment Society, representatives of the Fabian Women's Group and the Women's Industrial Council preferred social benefits for children alone to the endowment of motherhood, believing that such a policy would safeguard the needs of children while avoiding divisive arguments about married women's right to pursue waged work.[42] Wages for both men and women should, in any case, at all times be adequate to support at least two persons. A working woman had just as much need of domestic service as did a working man, Barbara Drake of the Fabian Society told the committee, "and I maintain that a working woman living independently ought to be

[39] Ellen Smith, *Wage-Earning Women and Their Dependents* (London: Fabian Society, 1915), p. 17.
[40] IWM, WIC Minutes, Workers' Union evidence, 15 Oct. 1918, p. J31; and evidence of Mrs. Davies, Welfare Supervisor, National Projectile Factory, Templeborough, 6 Nov. 1918, pp. Y52–3.
[41] IWM, WIC Minutes, James Beard (Workers' Union) evidence, 15 Oct. 1918, p. J18.
[42] Ibid., Barbara Drake (Fabian Women's Group and Women's Industrial Council) evidence, 18 Oct. 1918; Clementina Black (Women's Industrial Council) evidence, 5 Oct. 1918.

able to maintain someone in the position of a wife who would look after her in the same way as a woman looks after her husband."[43]

Barbara Drake's views coincided exactly with those of her aunt, Beatrice Webb, who had not enjoyed her stint as the only Labour representative on the Committee on Women in Industry, and who now prepared her minority report. While dismissing the argument that wages were now – or could ever be – set with reference to family needs, Webb did accept that some provision for domestic service (or, in other words, for a wife) should be included in standard rates for all workers, whether married or unmarried, male or female. Yet if she did not envisage a separate income for the "wife," she admitted that no system of wages could adequately meet the needs of "each individual baby." "The nation cannot be satisfied, any more than the children can, with a family or household 'average' of rations for the rising generation," she wrote, and there was "no practical way of ensuring anything like adequate provision for all the children that are born, or all that the community would wish to have born, except by some much more considerable national endowment."[44] Some form of universal provision should be investigated, and, as a first step, a system of children's allowances immediately introduced in the civil service.

The committee's majority, which included Justice Atkin, an expert in commercial law, Matthew Nathan, then secretary of the Ministry of Pensions, Lynden Macassey, an industrial lawyer and one of the architects of the wartime dilution of labor, and Janet Campbell, a medical officer attached to the Ministry of Education, also reviewed the evidence but came to quite a different conclusion. Its promoters were "probably right" to consider endowment "a corollary to the absolute avoidance of sex distinction in connection with wages," their report admitted, but they were not prepared to accept either part of the equation. Rather than endorse the principle of equal pay, they preferred to recommend that the state should intervene to set a minimum wage for women "sufficient to provide for the maintenance of a single woman"; similarly, they professed themselves unable to recommend state support for dependents "as an alternative to the principle of providing for the maintenance of children in the subsistence wage of men."[45] Whether or not men's higher wages actually resulted

---

[43] Ibid., Drake evidence, 18 Oct. 1918, p. M11.
[44] War Cabinet Committee on Women in Industry [WIC], *Report, PP* 1919, XXXI, Cmd. 135, pp. 305–7.
[45] Ibid., pp. 178–9.

from their responsibility for dependent families, they argued, the fact remained that dependent families were supported from these wages. In a fine example of selective quotation, they used Rathbone's article in *The Making of Women* to defend their claim that families were normally supported by men, while omitting her analysis of the detrimental consequences of this practice.[46]

To the case for equal pay and the endowment of motherhood (or of children), the majority of the Committee on Women in Industry answered with a conventional defense of the male family wage. In making this argument, they drew especially on the testimony of Seebohm Rowntree, the industrialist, philanthropist, and foremost interwar "poverty expert." In 1918, Rowntree had argued in both Liberal policy manifestos and his book, *The Human Needs of Labour*, for different minimum wages for men and women. Men, he claimed, must be paid a wage capable of supporting a family of five, with children's allowances for each child beyond the third. Women's wages, by contrast, need not include any provision for dependents, although they did need to cover the cost of reasonable clothing, since "a girl's chance of making a suitable match depends largely upon her ability to dress attractively."[47] Rowntree not only defended his position to the Committee on Women in Industry, he provided the committee with a basis from which to reject the claim that women workers also often bore responsibility for dependents. The committee's *Report* cited the Fabian Women's Group's investigation into the responsibility of women workers for dependents, but added that, according to Rowntree, "who has analysed them and gives good reason for his opinion," the group's results should not be considered "even approximately" accurate. Rowntree's own investigations, they added, showed that the great majority of women bore no real responsibility for dependents.[48]

Given the deference Rowntree's opinions were accorded within policy-making circles, it is worth asking how he arrived at his conclusions. To discover this, we can turn from his statements in *The Human Needs of Labour* to the more elaborate study of women's wages he published with Frank Stuart in 1921, entitled *The Responsibility of Women Workers for Dependents*. Based on a house-to-house investigation of over thir-

---

[46] Ibid., pp. 176–7.
[47] B. Seebohm Rowntree, "Conditions of Industry," in *Liberal Policy in the Task of Political and Social Reconstruction* (London: Liberal Publication Department [1918]), p. 77; B. Seebohm Rowntree, *The Human Needs of Labour* (London: T. Nelson & Sons, 1918); see also, Asa Briggs, *Social Thought and Social Action: A Study of the Work of Seebohm Rowntree, 1871–1954* (London: Longmans, Green, 1961), pp. 151–5.
[48] WIC, *Report*, p. 177.

teen thousand women workers, Rowntree and Stuart's study refuted claims that women workers had high burdens of dependence and argued that minimum wage rates be set at a "family" level for men and an "individual" level for women.[49] In stark contrast to the Fabian Women's Group, Rowntree found that only 12.06% of women workers were wholly or partially supporting others. How did he arrive at this figure?

Rowntree and Stuart began by making an estimate of a "living wage," varying it with the size of the family. If the husband or father's wage met that figure, all dependent household members were presumed to be dependent *on him*; only if his wage was below this hypothetical poverty line were other family members' earnings investigated. Thus, unlike the Fabian women who treated income as collective family property regardless of who contributed it, the Rowntree and Stuart method began by distinguishing money earned by the sex of the earner. A certain type of money – that earned by men – was assumed a priori to be collective family property and investigated to determine whether it was adequate; "female" pounds, shillings, and pence were considered from the outset to be irrelevant to total family welfare unless male wages were disproportionately low. Obviously, this method made it impossible for any working woman living in a family *not* in very dire poverty to be considered as contributing to the support of her family, regardless of the size or importance of her wage. For example, even if a male and a female earner were contributing equal amounts of money – indeed, to take the most ludicrous case, *even if the woman were contributing more* – the female earner would be identified as "without dependents" so long as the male wage outstripped Rowntree and Stuart's poverty line. In their own words: "We do not ourselves think that because a family is better off on account of the earnings of a woman worker, she must be regarded as maintaining others besides herself."[50] What, then, did their investigation actually measure? Only the proportion of working-class households in which the male earner received an income in excess of a certain figure arbitrarily established by the investigators themselves.

By investigating only the adequacy of male wages, Rowntree and Stuart read the varied economic strategies of working-class families only as successful or unsuccessful cases of male maintenance. They thus ignored precisely what the Fabians recognized: that working-

---

[49] B. Seebohm Rowntree and Frank Stuart, *The Responsibility of Women Workers for Dependents* (Oxford University Press, 1921).
[50] Ibid., p. 29.

class families survived by pooling income, all earners' wages being used to support both earning and nonearning members of the family. Women's wages were not exempt from this general rule: indeed, women's earnings were even more likely than men's to be contributed wholly to family expenses, since many married women sought waged work only when driven to it by family needs, and daughters were given less authority than sons over the disposition of their earnings.[51] By simply ignoring such cultural patterns, Rowntree and Stuart reproduced a model of working-class life in which the vast majority of families were respectably maintained by their men. Rather than providing "facts" on dependency and maintenance, Rowntree's investigations yielded much more: a representation of the working-class family economy that renormalized the male breadwinner paradigm, now elevated to the level of social-scientific "truth" and accepted as the only reasonable basis for policy making. Having "found" that only 12 percent of women workers bore responsibility for dependents (i.e., lived in families in which male wages were below the amount needed to keep the family above his poverty line), Rowntree's study unabashedly concluded that "if minimum wages are to be based on normal conditions (and no other method appears practicable), the minimum wage for a woman should merely be the sum which is sufficient for her own maintenance, in health and comfort, with a margin for contingencies and recreation."[52] Men's wages, on the other hand, should be adequate for a family of five.

Yet Rowntree did, in a manner of speaking, endorse mothers' pensions, and here we can realize the complexity of this debate. Rowntree admitted that his proposal would still leave in need those women workers who did, even according to his criteria, have families to support; he therefore called for pensions for widows and women whose husbands were incapacitated to meet their case. Pensions for mothers supporting children became, for him, not a precedent for a wider endowment, but rather a necessary corollary to the male family wage. The policy problem shifted from the payment of all mothers to the support of the husbandless; the state's sphere narrowed to replacing the absent father, not to supplanting the present one.

Rowntree's study recapitulated perfectly "official" thinking on the

---

[51] For a comparison of treatment of working–class girls' and working–class boys' wages, see, e.g., Lynn Jamieson, "Limited Resources and Limiting Conventions: Working-Class Mothers and Daughters in Urban Scotland, c. 1890–1925," in Jane Lewis, ed., *Labour and Love* (Oxford: Basil Blackwell, 1986), pp. 49–69; and, on women's earning generally, Elizabeth Roberts, *A Woman's Place* (Oxford: Basil Blackwell, 1984).

[52] Rowntree and Stuart, *The Responsibility of Women Workers*, p. 36.

question of dependence, for it was precisely along these lines that mothers' pensions won support after the war. All three of the important committees that reviewed the endowment case – the War Cabinet Committee on Women in Industry, the Women's Employment Committee of the Ministry of Reconstruction, and the National Birth Rate Commission – while declining to endorse endowment, either explicitly called for or said they would look with sympathy on proposals to provide pensions to those widows or wives of incapacitated men who were raising young children.[53] This was a cheaper policy, certainly, than the scheme advocated by the Family Endowment Committee, but one that left untouched – indeed codified – the two conditions that the feminists had explicitly challenged: unequal pay and the channeling of women's livelihood through men's hands. It also completely elided the problem of the distribution of income within the family itself. The Committee on Women in Industry, for example, like Rowntree, argued that the fact that married working women *actually* devoted their wages to the maintenance of children was no reason not to set women's wages at an "individual" rather than a family level, since presumably there was a man's wage coming in to meet such dependency needs.[54] Policymakers, in other words, endorsed the principle that male wages should be adequate to support families; they did not inquire into whether families were so supported.

If we turn briefly to some investigations of actual family budgets and consumption, it becomes clear why social reformers and feminists were so concerned to put some supplemental income into the hands of working-class housewives themselves. In 1913 and 1915, the Fabian Women's Group and the Women's Cooperative Guild had published highly acclaimed accounts of working-class "mothering," *Round About a Pound a Week* and *Maternity*.[55] Both showed clearly that although men did usually turn over most of their wage to their wives, and that

---

[53] WIC, *Report*, p. 179; Ministry of Reconstruction, Women's Employment Committee, *Report*, PP 1918, XIV, Cd. 9239, pp. 55–6, 58; National Council of Public Morals, National Birth Rate Commission, *Problems of Population and Parenthood*, pp. liv–lix.

[54] WIC, *Report*, p. 177.

[55] Maud Pember Reeves, *Round About a Pound a Week* (1913; rpt. London: Virago, 1979); Margaret Llewelyn Davies, ed., *Maternity: Letters from Working Women* (1915; rpt. New York: Norton, 1978). A good deal has been written on working-class consumption; for an early influential article, see Laura Oren, "The Welfare of Women in Labouring Families: England, 1860–1950," in Mary Hartman and Lois Banner, eds., *Clio's Consciousness Raised* (New York: Harper & Row, 1974), pp. 226–44. For an analysis of the meaning of differential consumption, see Christine Delphy, "Sharing the Same Table: Consumption and the Family," in her *Close to Home: A Materialist Analysis of Women's Oppression* (London: Hutchinson, 1984), pp. 40–56.

budgetary decisions in working-class families were overwhelmingly made by wives, a disproportionate amount of family income was spent on maintaining the breadwinner; women and children consistently had a lower standard of food and comfort. In one budget discussed by Maud Pember Reeves of the Fabian Women's Group, rent and general expenses absorbed almost 40% of the man's wage; another 35% went to his own workday dinners and personal expenses; general food shared by all came to about 20%, and a mere 5% was devoted to the workday dinners of the mother and two children. Discussing this unequal distribution of food, Reeves commented:

> The sad part of these menus is that, though on paper it looks very selfish of Mr. Q, in practice his share of the half-loaf, even though accompanied by an egg, does not seem a very satisfactory or over-luxurious breakfast for a working man. His daily dinner at 6 1/2d. cannot be an oppressive meal, whilst his tea cannot be much more satisfying than his breakfast. And yet, in order to feed him as well as this, his wife has to make about a third of the amount do for herself.[56]

The Fabians stressed that the problem was neither the selfishness of the man nor the mismanagement of the housewife; incomes were simply too small, and given scarcity, women routinely stinted themselves to provide for their husbands and children. Endowment advocates felt that only by disaggregating the family as an economic unit – by paying all wage earners standard rates regardless of sex and entrusting mothers with additional benefits for children – would these consumption patterns begin to change and the welfare of hitherto dependent women and children be ensured. The government committees of 1918 and 1919 rejected this alternative, preferring to defend the ideal of the male family wage supplemented by pensions for unsupported mothers. It was this more restricted view of mothers' pensions that the Labour Party came to support in the early twenties, despite the occasional disaffection of the women in its ranks.

Labour women and the "men's movement"

Most early endowment advocates, with the exception of Rathbone herself, were left-leaning; they looked to the labor movement for support and to some extent received it. Labour had been the only party firmly committed to universal suffrage in the prewar period

---

[56] Reeves, *Round About a Pound a Week*, p. 124.

and could thus lay special claim to the support of newly enfranchised women; they were also the most outspoken supporters of state activism in the provision of housing and social services – both areas of particular interest to women. In the 1918 "women's manifesto," *Women and the Labour Party*, the secretary of the Women's Cooperative Guild, Margaret Llewelyn Davies, even supported the endowment of motherhood, claiming that "so impressive are the arguments in its favour that a concentrated effort should be made to secure it without delay."[57] With the nonparty women's organizations deeply divided and, in any case, almost without electoral influence, the fate of proposals to endow mothers rested with the women's organizations of the labor movement.

The working-class women's organizations affiliated to the labor movement, most notably the Women's Cooperative Guild and the Labour Party's Women's Sections, did exhibit strong interest after the war both in pensions for widows and unsupported wives with children, as well as in a more general endowment of mothers. The guild's proposals were the more radical. An organization made up primarily of housewives, and noted for its feminism and independence of thought, the guild had insisted that housewives were workers entitled to economic independence even before the war, and it passed resolutions in favor of economic supports for working mothers at its congresses in 1918, 1919 and 1920.[58] While the Guild welcomed the growing interest in pensions for widows and unsupported mothers, it urged that their needs "be considered in conjunction with the equal needs of other mothers and children."[59] It looked forward to some "larger reconstructive reform...which might take the form of Universal Endowment of Motherhood."[60]

Interest in both mothers' pensions and the universal endowment of motherhood was also expressed by participants at the first National Conference of Labour Women in 1921, with more resolutions sent in by local sections on these than on any other subjects.[61] Nevertheless, in tracing the fate of endowment within the labor movement, we find

---

[57] M. L. Davies, "The Claims of Mothers and Children," in M. Phillips, ed., *Women and the Labour Party* (London: Headley Brothers, 1918).

[58] For the guild's resolution supporting universal economic supports for mothers at the 1918, 1919, and 1920 congresses, see WCG, *Report*, 36 (1919), p. 31; 37 (1920), p. 28; 38 (1921), p. 21.

[59] Ibid., 37 (1920), p. 28.

[60] Ibid., 36 (1919), p. 31.

[61] Labour Party Archives, NCLW, *First Agenda* (27–8 Apr. 1921); "Labour Women's Conference. Report..." *Labour Woman* (1 June 1921), pp. 95–6.

that it follows a similar trajectory to that described in the preceding section: the feminist demand for universal endowment was submerged in a prior consensus to win cash benefits only for those mothers without husbands. Through the mediation of the women labor leaders themselves, the demands of the Labour women's organizations were scaled down to mesh with the traditional family policy of the Trades Union Congress (TUC), which pursued somewhat different policy objectives under the mothers' pensions banner in the early 1920s.

The TUC began calling for pensions for "widows and fatherless children" early in the war, but by 1918 this demand had metamorphosed into one for pensions for mothers along the lines of those available in the United States.[62] In that form it appeared as a hardy perennial at the conferences of both the TUC and the Labour Party.[63] Both the TUC and the party also acted on their commitment with some energy, even when out of office. The party drafted a mothers' pensions bill – which would have endowed those widows, separated or deserted wives, or wives of ill or incapacitated men who had children below school age or still in school, at well above the rate of war pensions – and introduced it to Parliament in 1920 and 1921 (although it was, as a money bill, promptly thrown out).[64] Trade union M.P.s also introduced popular resolutions in favor of mothers' pensions in the Commons in 1919 and 1923;[65] they followed these up with several deputations to the government in the early 1920s. Their perseverance paid off – on the eve of the General Election in December 1923, all parties had a paper commitment to some form of provision for widows.[66]

When the women's organizations allied to the labor movement began to express interest in both mothers' pensions and the endowment of motherhood, then, the party could at least meet them halfway. The first demand was already on the Labour Party platform, and in 1921 the Joint Research and Information Department of the party and the

[62] Trades Union Congress [TUC], *Report*, 47 (1915), pp. 64–5; 48 (1916), pp. 73–4; 49 (1917), pp. 63–8; 50 (1918), p. 61.

[63] TUC, *Report*, 51 (1919) pp. 321–3; 53 (1921), pp. 61–4; 54 (1922), pp. 70–4; 56 (1924), pp. 381–3; Labour Party, *Report*, 21 (1921), p. 210; 22 (1922), p. 235.

[64] *Women's Pensions. A Bill to provide Pensions for Women with Children* [bill, printed 13 Feb. 1920]; 125 *H.C. Deb.*, 5th ser., 13 Feb. 1920, col. 388; 142, 2 June 1921, col. 1250; 9 June 1921, col. 2221.

[65] 114 *H.C. Deb.*, 5th ser., 8 Apr. 1919, cols. 1957–98; 161, 6 Mar. 1923, cols. 378–430.

[66] For a record of TUC activities, see TUC, *Report*, 55 (1923), p. 100; 56 (1924), pp. 111, 115.

TUC set up an Advisory Committee on Motherhood and Child Endowment – which included Hugh Dalton, Barbara Drake, and Susan Lawrence, among others – to investigate the more controversial policy of universal endowment. Yet the committee's report, published a year later, rejected universal endowment, while subtly suggesting that this demand was only a different name for existing Labour policy. It admitted that endowment had usually been defined as direct cash benefits to mothers but stated that endowments need not be paid in cash; education, maternity services, health care, and public provision of milk and meals could all be seen as endowments. The committee urged "that the efforts of the Labour Party should be directed first to securing these universal services" and that cash benefits be granted to a mother only when the father was absent or dead, as envisaged in the party's mothers' pensions bill.[67]

The committee's report made for a rather stormy session at the second National Conference of Labour Women in 1922. The report had recommended improved health and education services for mothers and children, always a central concern of Labour women; but it also made clear its preference for the direct provision of *goods* (clothing, boots, and food) to cash allowances, despite the labor movement's long antipathy to "in-kind" provision or "truck" payments. Mary Stocks, one of the authors of *Equal Pay and the Family*, moved the amendment:

> That in the opinion of this Conference the principle of payment in kind, as set forth in the Report, fails to provide a satisfactory basis for the service of motherhood. This Conference looks forward to such readjustment of the economic structure as shall secure to the mothers of dependent children the direct control of a money income proportionate to their family obligation, and calls upon the Labour Party to shape its policy on these lines.[68]

She was supported by Ellen Wilkinson, Barbara Ayrton Gould, and a number of working women speakers who objected that "the dishing out of things in kind"[69] implied a reluctance to trust women with managing money. Yet the report was overwhelmingly accepted, in part because of the intervention of Marion Phillips, chief woman organizer of the Labour Party, who implied that passing the amend-

---

[67] Labour Party and the TUC, Advisory Committee of the Joint Research and Information Department, *Motherhood and Child Endowment: First Interim Report* (London: TUC [1922]), p. 15.
[68] Ibid., pp. 19–20.
[69] Ibid., p. 21.

ment would require that the committee reject the social services out-lined, whereas accepting the report would leave the committee free to consider other options – including cash endowment.

The report and a record of the discussion were sent to the Women's Sections for study during the next year. There was much favorable response but also criticism that in-kind provisions resembled relief, and Marion Phillips continued to receive resolutions insisting that mothers' pensions were to be paid "irrespective of the husband's earn-ings."[70] Nevertheless, the Advisory Committee's brief second report issued a year later reiterated its support for extended health and maternity services, supplemented by pensions for the husbandless – although the representatives of the Women's Cooperative Guild on the committee found themelves unable to stomach the proposals to provide goods in kind and dissented from those portions of the re-port.[71] Once again, this report was adopted "by a very large majority" at the 1923 National Conference of Labour Women, although, once again, the criticism was made that it "did not go far enough." "They wanted payments in money and not in kind – pauper relief!" Mrs. Johnson of the Independent Labour Party (ILP) objected. Mrs. Clay-ton of Bradford agreed, saying that "what was wanted was endowment of mothers – as mothers, whether they had husbands or not."[72]

This point of view could not be accepted by the Labour Party's committee, for the simple reason that the party had already defined pensions much as Rowntree had – as complementary, and not an alternative, to the male family wage. "The Labour Party," the com-mittee noted in its interim report, "has accepted as the ordinary method of providing for a family that the father shall be responsible for securing the income. Where for any reason the income fails, other means of making it up find their place in Labour's programme."[73] As Marion Phillips told the Conference of Labour Women, endowment was "not a women's question only": its possible effects on trade unions and wage negotiations had also to be considered, and the committee's examination of Continental experiments with cash benefits had not made them optimistic on this score.[74] "Complete endowment," the committee concluded, "is dependent upon the establishment of a new system of society based on socialist principles and not possible in any

[70] Labour Party Archives, National Conference of Labour Women [NCLW], *Final Agenda* (8–9 May 1923).

[71] "The Labour Women's Parliament," *Labour Woman* (1 June 1923), pp. 92–4.

[72] Ibid., p. 94.

[73] *Motherhood and Child Endowment*, p. 8.

[74] Ibid., p. 18.

effective form in a capitalist society."[75] Thus, it disappeared from the realm of practical politics altogether.

Some of the Women's Sections may not have liked this response, but the Conference of Labour Women accepted it: unlike the later controversy over children's allowances (discussed in the next chapter), which was fought out within the party and the TUC themselves, arguments over the "endowment of motherhood" were contained within the women's organizations. This was the case in part because the awkward constitutional status of the women's conference made it difficult for conflicts within the Women's Sections to make their way to the Labour Party Conference floor. Decisions arrived at at the Conference of Labour Women had no official status in the party, and proposals to give increased powers to the women's conference had been firmly defeated at the 1921 Labour Party Conference.[76] Furthermore, although the party did reserve four seats for women on its Executive, these women were elected at the party conference – where the women's votes were swamped by the men's – and not at the women's conference; the "chief woman organizer," who had broad responsibilities for coordinating the work of the Women's Sections, was likewise appointed by the party and not by the Women's Sections. The intimidating Marion Phillips, who held this position until her death in 1932, was a particularly able officer but also tried to ensure that Labour women concentrated on issues compatible with the broader concerns of the party. Her efforts aroused some uncharitable comments: Dora Russell, who found herself combating Phillips's efforts to prevent resolutions on birth control from reaching the floor of the Party Conference, charged that women like Phillips saw themselves "more in the light of officials of the Party than representatives of the women";[77] their task was "not so much to support the demands of the women, as to keep them in order from the point of view of the male politicians."[78]

Yet Labour women were by no means simply manipulated, either

[75] "The Labour Women's Parliament," p. 93.

[76] See, Labour Party Archives, NCLW, *First Agenda* (1921); Labour Party, *Report*, 21 (1921), pp. 154–7.

[77] Labour Party Archives, NCLW, *Report*, 1929, p. 37. At the height of the birth control campaign, forty-four Women's Sections sent resolutions to the 1926 Women's Conference (which was canceled) calling on the party to support the policy decided by the NCLW, while twenty signed ones in favor of having the women representatives to the Labour Executive elected directly by the NCLW. No other issue had this level of support.

[78] Dora Russell, *The Tamarisk Tree*, vol. 1, *My Quest for Liberty and Love* (1975; rpt. London: Virago, 1977), p. 172.

by their leadership or by the men's movement, although some feminists within the party saw things in these terms. A second reason why questions like the endowment of motherhood did not place the Women's Sections on a collision course with the party is that while Labour women and middle-class feminists both defined housework as a form of "work" deserving public recognition, Labour women rarely expressed the opinion – omnipresent in feminist rhetoric – that working-class husbands *preferred* to keep their wives in dependence. Thus, when Mary Stocks charged that the Labour Party's committee had rejected endowment because men "did not like their wives to have direct control over the money," Mrs. Harrison Bell, for the Labour Executive, responded quite angrily. The "fundamental difference" between Mrs. Stocks and "old-fashioned people" like herself, she retorted, was that while Stocks regarded children as "the property of the mother," she thought that "nature had decided that children should have two parents and she thought they would be wise to act on that." The fact that men had the responsibility to support their families was something she viewed positively, and she did not think any policies should be introduced that would weaken their sense of responsibility.[79] Much of the animosity underlying this exchange was due to class, exposing the limits of alliance and understanding between middle-class feminists quick to identify working-class men as domestic despots and Labour women who had trouble seeing meddlesome local officials as welcome liberators from the men they lived with in daily life. If these were the alternatives, one woman told the 1922 conference, then she would speak up "for the woman who preferred her husband's wage to state help and state supervision": "The State was not going to find them anything without watching them, and she did not want to be watched. In her district the woman ran the house, and the husband kept his tongue still or it was the worse for him."[80] While sometimes admitting that they did not get the recognition they deserved for their crucial role in a domestic partnership, Labour women usually did insist that family life *was* a partnership: when feminists began to define "maternalist" policies as a means of displacing men, Labour women began to express objections.[81]

---

[79] *Motherhood and Child Endowment*, pp. 20–1.

[80] Ibid., p. 24. This was a position shared by many of the nonsocialist and religious women of the Mothers' Union, who, according to their secretary Mary Clay, thought mothers' pensions "at best but a poor substitute for adequate wages." National Birth Rate Commission, *Problems of Population and Parenthood*, p. 397.

[81] See especially Pat Thane's sympathetic and insightful analysis of Labour women's views

Labour women could thus accept a compromise that committed the party to develop some universal services for mothers while introducing cash endowment for those unsupported by men. This compromise held certain conflicts in abeyance, however; when we compare the rhetoric of the trade union M.P.s in the Commons with that of the Women's Sections activists, the difference in their understanding of "pensions" becomes clear. Labour women continued to see widowed mothers' pensions as part of a long-overdue public recognition of the national and even economic value of the mother's work, and their support for the measure constantly threatened to overflow – as it did a few years later – into demands for universal cash benefits for *all* mothers or *all* children. Trade unionists also sometimes assimilated motherhood to work, but far less consistently; they were more likely to think of husbandless mothers as "these helpless people" (in Arthur Hayday's words)[82] or to recast the issue as one of male workers' rights. Not the value of motherhood but the protection of the male family wage – the core value of working-class masculinity – lay at the heart of their politics. From their perspective, generous pensions for unhusbanded wives were entirely compatible with a prohibition on *any* cash benefits for a married woman during her husband's lifetime, since in the latter case the woman would be protected by her husband's wage. Because these positions were seen as two sides of the same coin, it should come as no surprise that the trade unionists who were the staunchest supporters of widows' pensions – Arthur Hayday and Charles Dukes of the National Union of General and Municipal Workers, Rhys Davies of the Distributive and Allied Workers, H. H. Elvin of the National Union of Clerks, and even Ernest Bevin of the Transport and General Workers' Union – were also the chief opponents of universal children's allowances a few years later.

When Rhys Davies introduced Labour's mothers' pensions resolution in 1923, then, he used a rhetoric quite at odds with that employed by Labour women. Rather than stressing the woman's right to payment for her work, Davies argued that *male workers* had quite as much right to be assured of pensions for their widows and children as did soldiers: "We shall not be satisfied on these benches until the man is

---

"Visions of Gender in the Making of the British Welfare State: The Case of Women in the British Labour Party and Social Policy, 1906–1945," in Gisela Bock and Pat Thane, eds., *Maternity and Gender Policies: Women and the Rise of the European Welfare States, 1880s–1950s* (London: Routledge, 1991), pp. 93–118.

[82] TUC, *Report*, 51 (1919), p. 322.

dealt with as generously by the State in his capacity as a worker as he is when he dons khaki or wears a naval uniform."[83] In other words, given that a man fulfilled his responsibility of maintaining his family through his work, he was owed the security of knowing that maintenance would be continued in case of accident or death. According to this logic, the pension was not the woman's right at all:

> The demand for pensions for mothers . . . springs not from the belief that a woman should be endowed because she is a mother, but rather when and because she is the trustee of her dead husband's family.[84]

Rhetoric like this went some distance toward transforming mothers' pensions into a policy aimed at men rather than women, but it was the civil service that completed this transformation. Labour took office in 1924 with an electoral pledge to make "generous provision" for widowed mothers, but – to the chagrin of many in the party – Philip Snowden, the new chancellor of the exchequer, declined to provide for the measure in the first-year budget and only agreed to include it in his plans for the following year in the face of cross-party parliamentary pressure and some internal lobbying.[85] The government fell before acting on this promise, however; it was Neville Chamberlain, the new Conservative minister of health, who brought in the Widows', Orphans', and Old Age Pensions Act shortly after taking office in 1925. In contrast to Labour's promised plans, the Conservative measure provided benefits not to unsupported mothers but to the widows of insured men, whether or not they had children, and was funded not through taxation but through contributions from those men.[86] By linking pensions to the man's insurance status rather than to the woman's sole responsibility for children, the Conservative bill finalized the divorce between widows' pensions and women's rights. It did so on the advice of those permanent officials who had already convinced Snowden that Labour's plans were not feasible, and it is to their deliberations that we must now turn.

---

[83] 161 *H.C. Deb.*, 5th ser., 6 Mar. 1923, col. 382.

[84] Rhys J. Davies, *Widowed Mothers' Pensions* (London: TUC and Labour Party, 1923), p. 6.

[85] For the election manifesto, see Labour Party, *Report*, 24 (1924), pp. 192–3; for pressure from the TUC and the party, 169 *H.C. Deb.*, 5th ser., 20 Feb. 1924, cols. 1884–1925; for pressure from the Conservatives and Liberals, 172 *H.C. Deb.*, 5th ser., 10 April 1924, cols. 623–5; for Snowden's response, 174 *H.C. Deb.*, 27 May 1924, col. 359; and the record of Marion Phillips's lobbying on the measure in PRO, T172/1371.

[86] On Labour opposition to the Tory bill, see especially the debate over the second reading in 184 *H.C. Deb.*, 18–19 May 1925, cols. 73–193, 267–390, and Labour Party, *Report*, 25 (1925), pp. 95–6.

Civil servants and the contracting state

From the outbursts of Labour rhetoric in the Commons on the introduction of the Conservatives' contributory scheme in 1925, one would imagine that both parties had worked out distinct, irreconcilable, and full-blown pensions schemes for unhusbanded mothers. In fact, the distinction between Labour and the Tories was largely illusory, not merely because – as the Tories claimed and Labour hotly denied – the Labour policy of state-funded pensions was a paper commitment unlikely to get past the parsimonious eye of Philip Snowden,[87] but more signally because decision making about social policy in the early twenties was shaped less by Parliament or the government than by a coterie of permanent officials. Both the contributory nature of the final pensions bill and the decision to include provision for widows without dependent children were largely the work of permanent officials, and especially of the government actuary, Sir Alfred Watson. Watson played a crucial role in transforming the radical demand for endowment into the placid widows' pensions bill.

In 1917, with the wartime bureaucracy bloated to include a number of Labour and Fabian leaders, the demand for the endowment of motherhood had worked its way into the government itself. Most of the activity took place in the Ministry of Reconstruction, where, under Christopher Addison's benign eye, liberal or socialist civil servants – notably Arthur Greenwood, Mona Wilson, and Mrs. Vaughan Nash – began to work out a mothers' pensions bill. Although the group felt that comprehensive endowment was far beyond their mandate, they did insist that any more limited scheme be compatible with a later universal measure.[88] In early 1918, the group drafted a bill to grant

---

[87] The issue that was most bitterly disputed during the second reading of the Conservative legislation was whether or not the Labour Party had in fact intended to introduce a noncontributory scheme. Labour had insisted in its manifesto for the November 1924 election that it had a measure ready for introduction in the next session of Parliament, and speakers insisted that the scheme was noncontributory, but Conservative M.P.s countered that such claims were (in Nancy Astor's words) "absolutely dishonest," and that Labour had also planned to use contributory financing – if, indeed, they had worked out a scheme at all. For the 1924 election statement, see Labour Party, *Report*, 24 (1924), p. 196; for Conservative charges about Labour's plans, see especially the speeches by Chamberlain, Worthington-Evans, and Astor: 184 *H.C. Deb.*, 5th ser., 18 May 1925, cols. 84–7; 19 May 1925, cols. 267–77, 302–8. There is no record in the PRO that any work was done on a noncontributory scheme during the 1924 Labour government.

[88] See the Reconstruction Memo by Miss Clapham, 14 Nov. 1917, sent to Greenwood, now held in TUC File HV 699 "Mothers' Pensions"; also PRO, PIN 15/405, "Endowment of Widows and Deserted Wives," typescript, n.d. 6 pages [early 1918]. For a

pensions to unsupported, widowed, and unmarried mothers at the relatively generous war pensions rate.[89] The proposal received a sympathetic reading from Sir Matthew Nathan at the Ministry of Pensions, and in April the Ministry of Reconstruction asked the Treasury for an actuarial investigation of its cost.[90]

At this point, the reconstruction proposal came up against the hostility of other politicians and permanent officials. A memo of 18 June 1918 sent to Stanley Baldwin (then under secretary of the Treasury) protested:

> One would have thought that the mounting War Pensions bill would have been enough to deter them [the Ministry of Reconstruction] from adding more millions of non-effective expense and I am not sure how far we ought to let them incur expense and waste valuable time on utopian schemes which have only the remotest connexion with "reconstruction."[91]

Baldwin and Chancellor Bonar Law agreed that there was no "practical utility" in asking the busy government actuary to investigate "a nebulous scheme... obviously outside the limits of financial possibility," and in fact, no action was taken until October, when Addison himself wrote a note to Bonar Law complaining about Treasury foot-dragging and pointing out that allowing an actuarial investigation did not commit the government to the bill.[92] On 17 January 1919, the actuary finally reported, although the replacement of Addison by Sir Auckland Geddes had already made the proposal a dead letter.

Watson's report on the proposal was nevertheless significant, although less for his assessment of its high cost (£51 million) than for his substantive criticisms. Predictably, he was skeptical of the morality of granting benefits to unmarried mothers, but his main criticisms

discussion of the place of these proposals within the development of social policies toward single mothers, see Morris Finer and O. R. McGregor, *The History of the Obligation to Maintain*, app. 5 to the *Report of the Committee on One-Parent Families*, vol. 2, PP 1974, XVI, Cmd. 5629, pp. 128–35.

[89] A draft of the Ministry of Reconstruction's proposal can be found in TUC Library File HV 699 "Mothers' Pensions," "Agenda for Office Conference. Proposed Heads of a Draft Bill for the Endowment of Widows...," typescript (19 Apr. 1918). The version finally considered by the actuary is in PRO, ACT 1/66, "Proposed Scheme for Endowment of Widows, Deserted Wives and Others Maintaining Children... " (2 Sept. 1918).

[90] PRO, PIN 15/405, Matthew Nathan to Nash, 11 Feb. 1918; PRO, T1/12225/44161, H. Eustace Davies, Ministry of Reconstruction, to Treasury, 29 Apr. 1918.

[91] PRO, T1/12225/44161, Upcott memo, 18 June 1918.

[92] Ibid., Reconstruction to Treasury, 2 Sept. 1918, with comments by Leith-Ross and Stanley Baldwin; Addison to Bonar Law, 21 Oct. 1918; Bonar Law to Addison, 24 Oct. 1918.

questioned the very idea of giving an unsupported mother a pension only so long as the woman was "working" – that is, mothering. He was convinced that the plan to terminate the allowance when the child reached adulthood was impractical, asking:

> Is it conceivable that after a woman has received a government grant in the vigorous years of early life to induce her (in effect) to refuse to work for wages, that grant can be withdrawn when the woman is between 40 and 50 years of age and must, in general, have become unemployable?[93]

The cost of the scheme was also much too great, particularly in view of the fact that the woman's benefits would unquestionably have to be continued until replaced by the old-age pension. Watson advised Addison, now president of the Local Government Board, that the scheme as submitted "really will not do": benefits would have to be much more "moderate" and recovered largely through insurance contributions. On his own authority, he began investigating possible contribution rates that "would not leave too large a balance of cost to be borne by the Exchequer."[94]

The memos that Watson then wrote for the Coalition ministers responding to Labour's mothers' pensions resolution in 1919 established the basic outlines of Chamberlain's 1925 bill. Watson did not dispute that pensions were a legitimate public charge; adequate personal insurance was, he claimed, far beyond the reach of a working man, and "public opinion" would no longer tolerate leaving some 350,000 widows with dependent children to "submit to the stigma of being branded as paupers."[95] Benefits, however, must be much lower than the pensions already granted to war widows, funded by husbands'

[93] PRO, ACT 1/66, "Mothers' Pensions: Report of the Government Actuary" (17 Jan. 1919), sec. 16.

[94] PRO, ACT 1/66, Watson to Addison, 22 Jan. 1919.

[95] PRO, ACT 1/66, "Widows' and Orphans' Pensions, Memorandum by the Government Actuary" (draft, about Apr. 1919), sec. 1. At the time of the 1911 census, there were some 1.2 million widows under age 70 (old-age pension age) in the United Kingdom. About 900,000 were the widows of insured men; about 10% under 40, 20% age 40–50, 30% age 50–60, and 40% age 60 and over. Of widows of the insured class, about one-third were themselves employed, while some 350,000 had a total of 600,000 dependent children. There were about 430,000 widows of all social grades with children under age 16, and about 800,000 such children. Only 35,000 of the able-bodied widows and 95,000 of the children received poor relief, at about five shillings per widow and one to one and a half shillings per child per week. Watson commented that these statistics "probably conceal a mass of poverty, e.g. widows who keep their homes together, somehow, with the help of children or/and lodgers, or/and go out to more or less casual 'charring.' " PRO, ACT 1/66 [Sir Alfred Watson], "Widows' Pensions" (7 Apr. 1919).

insurance contributions, and cover *all* widows, with or without dependent children, since these usually older women "must, in general, be unemployable."[96] Watson also did a little quiet lobbying, writing to a senior Treasury official in December 1920 that in view of the public interest in widows' pensions, the government should examine the possibility of incorporating provision into the insurance system.[97] His memos on the Labour Party's resolutions on mothers' pensions in 1923 and 1924 reiterated these same points: pensions must be continued after the widow's children grew up, and state financing would be prohibitively expensive.[98] He seemed to convince Snowden, who circulated to the Cabinet Watson's memo estimating the cost of mothers' pensions at £37 million per year – after which the Cabinet agreed that Snowden, while supporting the measure in principle, "should use guarded language as to the immediate intentions of the Government."[99]

Civil servants' control over policy-making was not only exercised through these memos and briefs; it was also institutionalized within the state apparatus. In 1923, the Conservative government of Stanley Baldwin entrusted a committee of high-ranking civil servants, chaired by Sir John Anderson and including Watson, with the task of investigating ways of rationalizing and extending the insurance system. The committee continued to meet during the Labour government – Snowden was informed of its existence in February but told that this information was "confidential"[100] – and in July 1924 issued a second report on contributory pensions. The Labour government fell before acting on the report, but in April 1925 Conservative Minister of Health Neville Chamberlain told the Cabinet that a slightly revised version was an acceptable basis for Conservative legislation.[101] That same year, the Widows', Orphans' and Old Age (Contributory Pensions) Act became law.

---

[96] PRO, ACT 1/66 [Sir Alfred Watson], "Widows' Pensions" (7 Apr. 1919).

[97] Ibid., Watson to Hurst, 15 Dec. 1920.

[98] Ibid., Watson's notes and memos on mothers' pensions, dated 23 Feb. and 6 Mar. 1923, and 15 Feb. 1924.

[99] PRO, Cab. 24/165, C.P. 115(24) "Mothers' Pensions" (16 Feb. 1924); Cab 23/47, Cabinet 14 (24), 18 Feb. 1924, p. 156.

[100] PRO T172 T172/1371, "Mothers' Pensions," Treasury memo for the Chancellor of the Exchequer (17 Feb. 1924).

[101] PRO, Cab. 27/276, C.P. 204(25), Committee on Insurance and other Social Services, "Second Interim Report: Contributory Pensions" (8 July 1924), contained within Chamberlain's memo, "Improved Old Age Pensions and Pensions for Widowed Mothers. Memorandum by the Minister of Health" (18 Apr. 1925). For an account of the work

Certainly the influence of permanent officials on policy-making was due in part to the apparent reasonableness, moderation, and cheapness of their plans: virtually everyone from Chamberlain to Snowden could line up behind Watson's scheme. Nevertheless, the changes due in large part to his intervention – the insistence on contributory financing and the extension of benefits to women without children – did complete the metamorphosis of widows' pensions from a step toward payment for motherhood to a necessary component of a welfare system constructed around a man's right to maintain. First, the decision to finance pensions through insurance linked them both administratively and ideologically to the working man. Since eligibility turned on the man's insurance status and not the woman's need, the system would exclude those women whom men had been least willing or able to maintain – deserted and separated wives, wives of invalid men, and unmarried mothers. The earlier Ministry of Reconstruction proposals had intended to give honorable maintenance to precisely such women, so long as they were raising children. In Mrs. Nash's 1919 scheme, benefit was to be granted to any mother who could prove she was not then dependent on a man; she did not have to prove that a man had, at some point, been willing to maintain her.[102] The Fabians and feminists who had drafted the Ministry of Reconstruction proposals wanted to use the state to limit a mother's absolute economic dependence by guaranteeing her support should her husband – whether deliberately or by misfortune – not fulfill his responsibilities.[103] Watson and the officials who sat on the Anderson committee merely stated that the inclusion of such women in a contributory system was "wholly inappropriate and impracticable" and implicitly justified their exclusion by stating that the responsibilities of the husband and father to maintain should not be undermined.[104]

Second, Watson's expansion of the scheme to include all widows of insured men, with or without children, dealt a final blow to the identification of pensions with payment for motherhood. The early memos on mothers' pensions drafted by (in Watson's words) "that remarkable assemblage, the late Ministry of Reconstruction"[105] had stressed the

of the Anderson committee and the passage of the 1925 bill, see Bentley B. Gilbert, *British Social Policy, 1914–1939* (London: B. T. Batsford, 1970), pp. 242–51.

[102] PRO, RECO 1/751, Ministry of Reconstruction, Women's Advisory Committee, "Memorandum by Mrs. Vaughan Nash on Pensions for Mothers" (9 Dec. 1918).

[103] PRO, PIN 15/405, "Endowment of Widows and Deserted Wives."

[104] PRO, Cab. 27/276, C.P. 204(25), Committee on Insurance and Other Social Services, "Second Interim Report: Contributory Pensions" (8 July 1924), p. 11.

[105] PRO, ACT 1/66, Watson to Sidney Turner, 28 Mar. 1923.

overriding importance of maintaining unbroken homes for children and insisted on the dignity and legitimacy of the mother's claim:

> These pensions should be regarded as granted to normal indepen
> dent persons, already or soon to be, full voting citizens, having full
> legal authority over their children under 21, and pensioned because
> their welfare is of national importance.[106]

This conception of the legitimate claim of the unsupported mother survived in muted form in the Labour debate. By planning to restrict pensions to women with dependent children, Labour in effect ad mitted that it was the mother's work that impeded her wage earning not her marital status. Watson disagreed; despite his parsimony he was willing to argue that marriage per se disqualified women from wage earning, even though this would triple the number of widows due benefit – from about 350,000 to about 900,000 women. Any residual identification of pensions with payment for motherhood thus disappeared.

Civil servants like Watson were not contesting the social value of motherhood; they simply denied motherhood was in any way the financial concern of the government. Watson's decisions on pensions seem to have been the result, quite simply, of, on the one hand, his tendency to regard Treasury reserves much as he would his own bank account and, on the other, a basic and probably unquestioned belief in the unnaturalness of women earning their own living. At no point did officials display any evidence that they were convinced by – or had even heard of – arguments claiming that greater efficiency, social control, and state power would derive from extended control over reproduction. Feminists, when claiming considerable public funds for women, were willing to countenance at least some degree of state surveillance of the mother's "product";[107] they believed, perhaps na ively, that women's new votes in a democratic society could easily avert misuse of such power. There is no evidence that civil servants shared

---

[106] PRO, RECO 1/751, "Memorandum by Mrs. Vaughan Nash...," p. 2.

[107] Rathbone justified state supervision of wives receiving allowances in her article "Pen sions and Allowances," *Common Cause*, 6: 302 (22 Jan. 1915), pp. 663–4. An even more repellent statement, evidence of the continued purchase of sexual purity and eugenic discourses, was given by Mrs. McKenna after reading Mrs. Vaughan Nash's proposal: "I welcome the inclusion of unmarried mothers, but there is one type of unmarried mother to whom, in no circumstances, should pension be payable. I mean the mentally deficient woman, not sufficiently feeble-minded to be placed under control, who drift from one workhouse to another, burdening the community with a succession of feebler minded children. It would be better for her to be exterminated than endowed." PRO PIN 15/405 [Mrs. McKenna] to Matthew Nathan, 25 Feb. 1918.

either their interest in placing the hand of the state "on the tiller of maternity" – the phrase is Rathbone's[108] – or their illusions about democratic control over policy-making. The enfranchisement of women notwithstanding, civil servants appear to have regarded social policy in both its formulation and scope as the preserve of men. Their conception of female citizenship was almost nonexistent; the claim that women were somehow "bearing children for the state" would have struck them as absurd if not downright obscene. Wives were the responsibility of their husbands; only in his absence would the state intervene.

Conclusion

Enthusiasm for proposals to make motherhood a state service was, understandably, both restricted and short-lived, and in retrospect it is easy to argue that the endowment campaign never had any real chance of success. The liminal moment of the immediate postwar period soon passed, followed by a defensive reaction in social thought and politics. This chapter has traced the reassertion of the male-breadwinner norm within three areas – social inquiry, Labour politics, and civil servants' policy-making. In all three areas, mothers' pensions were not so much opposed as redefined and scaled down: a campaign to grant economic independence to *all* mothers fed into a policy out-come that, in effect, recognized the vulnerability of a married woman to the loss of her husband, but not to any hardship in his presence, and the husband's responsibility to contribute to the support of his wife even after his death. Social policy, like the labor market, came to reflect the assumption that in normal circumstances women's live-lihood would be filtered through the hands of men.

The final widows' pensions bill could thus be supported as a measure entirely in keeping with conventional assumptions about husbands' responsibilities and wifely dependence. As Chamberlain's own speech presenting the bill made clear, by 1925 the question of whether the woman had children or not was considered entirely irrelevant; the question was one of the rights of the working man. As Chamberlain told the House:

> You ought to consider in this matter not merely the woman, you should consider in the first place the man. It is the man who is going to make the contribution, it is the man who is effecting the insurance; and surely the first thing a man thinks about is that you should make

---

[108] Rathbone, *Disinherited Family*, p. 324.

provision for his widow. He may have no children, he may never have any children, all the children may have died. Surely the first thing he wants to know is that something will be there for her when he is no longer there to look after her.[109]

Ellen Wilkinson was perhaps the only politician to notice the rhetorical distance that mothers' pensions had traveled since 1918 and to challenge Chamberlain's definition of the measure as a right of the insured and respectable man. Her perceptive comments deserve to be quoted at length.

> The curious thing is that in the whole course of this discussion no one has asked what this money is being paid for. We have had, for example, the statement of the Minister of Health [Neville Chamberlain], what might be described as an *argumentum ad hominem* apparently on the principle that before you give any money to women you must convince the men that it is really being given to them. But this money is being paid to the widows for a very definite service. That is, so that she can bring up her children adequately for the State....
>
> I wish hon. Members would get it into their heads that a non-contributory scheme would not be a dispensing of charity, but a very definite payment for services that the widow had rendered to the State, and that it should enable the woman to bring up the children properly. It is only because woman's work has been so badly paid, or so very largely underpaid or unpaid, that this proposition seems to be a novel idea to some hon. Members.[110]

Wilkinson's speech reiterated the "new feminist" vision: citizen mothers, as workers for the state, should be granted direct maintenance; other women should take their place in the waged work force. In both cases women's economic independence would be assured.

Yet however much new feminists like Wilkinson preferred to see widows' pensions as payment for motherhood, their claim was belied by the conditions of receipt, which identified pensions clearly as a concession granted to working men in recognition of their role as family breadwinners. Furthermore, as Conservative ministers and civil servants realized full well, while mothers were easily deployed rhetorically, they were almost impossible to aggregate and represent politically. As the debates within feminist and Labour women's groups showed, many women were repelled by the functionalism of new feminism; certainly new feminists never succeeded in constituting

---

[109]   184 *H.C. Deb.*, 5th ser., 18 May 1925, col. 89.
[110]   Ibid., cols. 182–3.

mothers as a recognized "interest" or political force. Indeed, it is possible to conclude that feminists' insistence that family policies could emancipate mothers merely confirmed other actors' dislike for such policies while identifying women ever more tightly with hearth and home. Certainly the Fabian women who had supported endowments for children even before the war believed the new feminist campaign for endowment of motherhood to be misguided. It would be difficult and clumsy to endow mothers at all, Maud Pember Reeves told the National Birth Rate Commission; rather, any pension should follow the child, whose good it was designed to protect.[111] When she presented this view to the Women's Advisory Committee of the Ministry of Reconstruction, however, she was rebuked by Miss Harris of the Women's Cooperative Guild, who said that the essential aim was to raise the status of motherhood.[112] Not until the midtwenties would feminists rethink their strategy and make a second attempt to convert the Labour Party to the more moderate proposal of children's allowances.

[111] National Birth Rate Commission, *Problems of Population and Parenthood*, pp. 301–2.
[112] PRO, RECO 1/751, Ministry of Reconstruction, Women's Advisory Committee, Minutes of the tenth meeting, 6 Jan. 1919. Maude Royden also denounced the proposal to endow children and treat mothers as mere "administrators"; Royden, "State Endowment of Motherhood," *Common Cause*, 9: 445 (19 Oct. 1917), p. 327.

4

FAMILY POLICY AS "SOCIALISM IN OUR TIME"?
The failed campaign for children's allowances in Britain

The campaign for the endowment of motherhood had been the product of the peculiar circumstances of the end of the war, when enthusiasm for "reconstruction" was at its height and feminists were optimistic about the capacity of newly enfranchised women to claim a share for themselves of the national wealth. Yet no unified women's movement arose in the twenties, and as economic conditions worsened and the debt-laden Treasury sought to restrict government spending, even the most idealistic of feminists came to realize that the plan to enlist the state in the cause of married women's economic independence was impossibly utopian. Yet the movement for family endowment did not subside with the economic downturn of the twenties, although its focus shifted. Trimming their sails to meet chillier economic winds, advocates argued that a revision of the wage system in the interests of dependent children would not only be socially just, but could also help to combat some of the economic problems that plagued Britain in the twenties.

The argument that family policies could serve wider economic ends could be made from a variety of perspectives. In France, for example, industrialists in the highly organized sectors of textiles, mining, and engineering turned to family allowances after the war as part of a larger strategy of wage restraint and rationalization; employer-funded children's allowances would, they hoped, both lessen unions' pressure for a male family wage and tie workers more tightly to their firms. In Britain, however, while a few economists and Liberals were intrigued by Rathbone's contention that such industrially based schemes could ease the effects of government deregulation in the troubled mining industry, employers' organizations displayed little interest in such experiments. Enthusiasm for children's allowances developed in Britain on the left rather than the right, and among socialists rather than industrialists. It was the Independent Labour

178

Party (ILP) that placed redistributive family policies at the heart of their program for economic recovery. Family allowances, socialists argued, could safeguard the well-being of children while stimulating a much-needed sectoral shift away from the export trades and toward domestic consumption.

Supporters of family endowment within the ILP addressed themselves less to policymakers than to their comrades within the labor movement, in the hope of convincing the Labour Party to place children's allowances on its 1929 election manifesto. They did not succeed; they did, however, convince the party and the Trades Union Congress to conduct jointly the most comprehensive inquiry into family allowances undertaken in the interwar period. Yet far from uniting the movement, this inquiry divided trade unionists among themselves and convinced most of the General Council of the Trades Union Congress of the dangers not only of "political" interference in the realm of collective bargaining, but also of collaboration with the ILP. The Labour Party had been the main hope of supporters of family endowment in the interwar period, but the veto of the General Council led the party to abandon the issue until the Second World War. This chapter explores the failure of the campaign for family allowances in the twenties, examining in particular the debate over redistributive social policies within the labor movement and the reasons for the eventual decision by the TUC to resist them.

The Disinherited Family *and the organization of the Family Endowment Society*

In March 1924, as the campaign for mothers' pensions languished under Philip Snowden's benign neglect, Eleanor Rathbone published *The Disinherited Family*, the key statement of the family endowment case and the basis of Rathbone's reputation as an independent economic thinker. *The Disinherited Family* had two aims: to provide a systematic critique of the practice of providing for dependent families through male wages and to outline alternative systems of direct provision through family endowment. Rathbone's discussion ranged widely, but the central argument of the book was economic; indeed, she advised the busy reader to turn directly to the book's second chapter, a detailed examination of the theory of the living wage.[1] A uniform living wage, adequate to meet the needs of an "average" five-person family was, she noted, the central demand both of humani-

---

[1] Eleanor Rathbone, *The Disinherited Family* (London: Edward Arnold, 1924), p. xii.

tarian social reformers such as Rowntree and of Labour and trade union leaders: how well would it meet human needs?

Not at all well, Rathbone argued, marshaling national income, wage, and population statistics to support her case. At any one time a mere 8.8% of adult male wage earners had three dependent children, 9.9% had more than three, 13% had two, 16.6% had one, and over 50% had no dependent children at all. On the other hand, a majority of children were born into families with three or more. The uniform male family wage would thus provide for a good number of non-existent families, while leaving 62% of all children in poverty at some point in their lives. And even were the uniform male family wage desirable, actual wages necessarily fell far short of this five-person ideal, since even a drastic vertical redistribution of total British national income could not bring all wages up to this standard. The theory of the uniform family wage was, she concluded, "sloppy and ill-thought out," being both unachievable and incapable in any case of meeting actual needs.[2]

Rathbone's economic discussion built up a powerful logical case for family endowment – or, in other words, for the provision of subsistence maintenance for dependent children by direct allowances rather than by wages paid to men. In the second section of the book she canvassed various methods, drawing on European and Australian initiatives. While agreeing that a national, state-financed system would be the ideal, she argued for the immediate introduction of family allowances financed through industrial pools in the mining industry and for a state system in the teaching profession.

The campaign for the endowment of motherhood had addressed the problem of married women's economic dependence directly and claimed for mothers a sizable share of the national income. "Family endowment," by contrast, aimed at redistributing income between childless families and those with children: feminist concerns no longer occupied center stage. In *The Disinherited Family*, Rathbone was willing to dispense with direct endowment of mothers, arguing that their legitimate claim could be met by making basic wages adequate for two and strengthening the wife's claim on her husband's pay. Yet the improvement of married women's domestic status arguably remained the underlying aim: payment to the mother was insisted on, and Rathbone discussed at length not merely the distribution of income between families, but economic relations between husbands and wives. Rathbone's years of social work had ingrained a genuine sensitivity

[2] Ibid., pp. 14–38, 136.

to the needs and problems of careworn working-class mothers, but she had never developed much sympathy toward the claims of "the dingy human male."[3] She drew on working-class budgets to claim that men often monopolized the so-called family wage, and attributed the opposition to family endowment to men's desire to retain absolute power over their wives and children – a trait she notoriously labeled "the Turk complex."

By discussing the distribution of national income as a general social problem, *The Disinherited Family* catapulted family policy out of the vague realm of "women's questions" into a broader economic and political debate. It became clear that reformers were calling into question not only the scope of government intervention but also the dominance of wages within the distributive system. Although left-wing endowment advocates often claimed that family endowment could come as a pure increase to wages, Rathbone frankly admitted that any substantial system would probably involve some measure of horizontal redistribution, with real or potential wages of childless men and women used to fund allowances for those with children.[4] Family policy thus emerged as a question of economic and social policy in its largest sense or, in the words of Alexander Gray, professor of political economy at the University of Aberdeen and one of Rathbone's most vituperative critics, as "the greatest revolution in the social history of our country."[5]

The reaction of economists and politicians to this proposed revolution was mixed, but the book could not be ignored. William Beveridge professed himself converted to family allowances after reviewing the book; Hugh Dalton, then at the London School of Economics, called it "one of the outstanding contributions to economic literature since the war"; and even Gray admitted that it was "indubitably one of the most virile [*sic*] books of recent years."[6] Yet even

---

[3] Ibid., p. 50. The *New Statesman* thought in 1923 that no one "save a few ultra-feminists" regarded family allowances primarily as a measure "for protecting wives against drunken or close-fisted husbands," but after a brief membership in Rathbone's Family Endowment Society, Barbara Drake concluded that the FES thought just that. "Those advocates of Family Endowment who would only be satisfied with a scheme of actual [cash] allowances are influenced by their desire to secure, not so much the greatest benefit for the child as an independent income for the mother." "Incomes for Children," *New Statesman*, 20: 517 (10 Mar. 1923), pp. 651–2; Barbara Drake, quoted in Alexander Gray, *Family Endowment: A Critical Analysis* (London: Ernest Benn, 1927), p. 122.

[4] Rathbone, *Disinherited Family*, pp. 263–7.

[5] Gray, *Family Endowment*, p. 129.

[6] Sir William Beveridge, *Power and Influence* (London: Hodder & Stoughton, 1953), p. 221;

some who found Rathbone's figures on child poverty unanswerable were distinctly uncomfortable with her conclusion that the children should then be supported through a redistribution of wages or by the state.

The creation of children was an act of choice, critics protested, not a service exacted by the state or a meritorious duty. Parenthood, the Cambridge economist Dennis Robertson rather mildly pointed out, may be a useful occupation, but it is also "an agreeable hobby," for which married men could legitimately expect to pay some economic price.[7] Since children were a choice, some economists also questioned whether they fell within the category of "insurable risks," pointing out that it was contrary to the principles of insurance to insure against something – unlike unemployment, sickness, or death – which was deliberately incurred.[8] "People have children to please themselves, not to advantage the State," the irascible Alexander Gray argued, "and it is a wholly unnatural view to regard the question of begetting and giving birth to children as an obligation which is undertaken by parents on behalf of the community, and for which they must therefore be indemnified by the State."[9] At some points, he complained, advocates of family endowment tended to talk as if "children come through nobody's fault (or merit), that they fall, like rain, on the just and the unjust," while "at other times one appears to get a glimpse of the women of the country striving to give birth to children in fulfilment of contracts accepted by the Minister of Population." But neither view, Gray countered, was correct. Rather, people had children to please themselves, and by doing so assumed toward those children an "obvious and very real duty."[10] Indeed, those who had children without being able to support them should hardly have their irresponsibility rewarded by state pensions. It was all very well to argue about society's obligation to meet "needs," he protested, but "is the need of unlimited sexual intercourse one of the needs of the individual

Hugh Dalton, "To Each According to His Need: Grants for Children," *New Leader*, 13: 6 (15 Jan. 1926), p. 9; Gray, *Family Endowment*, p. 36.

[7] Dennis H. Robertson, "Family Endowment," in *Economic Fragments* (London: P. S. King & Son, 1931), p. 150.

[8] D. H. Macgregor, "Family Allowances," *Economic Journal*, 36: 141 (Mar. 1926), pp. 7–8; Gray, *Family Endowment*, pp. 59–71. The proposal to fund children's allowances through social insurance was put forward in Joseph L. Cohen, *Family Income Insurance: A Scheme of Family Endowment by the Method of Insurance* (London: P. S. King & Son, 1926); Sir William Beveridge, "The Case for Family Allowances," in *Six Aspects of Family Allowances* (London: FES, 1927).

[9] Gray, *Family Endowment*, p. 107.

[10] Ibid., p. 125.

which society is bound to satisfy?"[11] Quite simply, parents should not have children they could not afford.

Family allowance advocates did not answer the charge that bearing children was a choice, except to point out that if workers were to adjust their family size to their wages, most working-class families could have only one, or at most two, children.[12] They did nevertheless insist that the interest of the community in children's well-being meant that it could not tolerate their suffering merely in order to punish parental irresponsibility. The family was "something more than an innocent male hobby"; it was "an aggregation of human beings, each one an end in himself or herself, each one a vital determinant of the future of the race, with an inherent right to participate in the life of the body, the mind and the spirit."[13] Skirting the question of birth control, they charged that no critic had been able to answer their main argument that the wage system did not provide for the variable needs of families and could not – without family allowances – be made to do so. Mary Stocks put the choice starkly:

> *Either* we must devise some machinery for the expansion of the family income during the peak period of the family's dependence, *or* we must frankly admit the position that the persistent destitution of a large proportion of the nation's children is a necessary feature of its economic system – since its pains and penalties, deplorable as they may be, are outweighed on balance by the social and economic dangers of any conceivable form of Family Endowment.[14]

The controversy sparked by the publication of *The Disinherited Family* gave the family endowment movement, hitherto languishing on the fringes of organized feminism, a new lease on life. In 1924, the old wartime Family Endowment Committee resurfaced as the new, all-party Family Endowment Society (FES), under the chairmanship of Kathleen Courtney, Rathbone's colleague from the suffrage days and one of the coauthors of the 1918 report *Equal Pay and the Family*. The society continued to be dominated by those educated middle-class women who had been active in feminist and reforming causes both before and after the war – women like Labour supporters Barbara Ayrton Gould and Mary Stocks and Liberals Dorothea Layton and Margery Corbett Ashby – but it also expanded to include clergymen,

[11] Ibid., p. 35.
[12] Mary Danvers Stocks, *The Case for Family Endowment* (London: Labour Publishing Co., 1927), p. 87.
[13] Ibid., p. 19.
[14] Ibid., p. 85.

medical experts, the occasional industrialist, and a disproportionate cross section of those intellectuals and professors who presided over the remnants of the Liberal Party – including Gilbert Murray, Ramsay Muir, E. D. Simon, John Murray, and William Beveridge.

The FES was pledged to secure "a more adequate method ... of making provision for families" but did not endorse any specific scheme.[15] Rather, the group concentrated on "impartial research" and advocacy, making the case in Parliament, the press, and public meetings for the reworking of both the wage and welfare systems to take account of the dependency needs of children, but leaving individual members free to support whatever particular scheme they wished.[16] By seeking support from across the political spectrum and defining the issue very largely in humanitarian terms, the society's leadership clearly sought – like the nineteenth-century reformers they saw as their forerunners – to create a national consensus on what they took to be a great moral issue. Such catholicity had its costs, however. When party politics revived after 1922, nonparty pressure groups found their effectiveness limited; not until coalition politics returned during the Second World War was the FES able to put together an effective parliamentary alliance.

Individual members of the FES were thus left to argue the merits of family endowment within whatever political party they supported, but once arguments moved into party realms, they could no longer be made to follow the analysis offered by Rathbone, Stocks, and those at the center of the movement. Rather, family policies were recast to fit the party platform and especially to mesh with its economic views. Since endowment would require either a thorough recasting of the wage or insurance system, or a massive increase in tax, supporters were understandably pressed to explain how such measures could be introduced in the economic conditions of the twenties. Yet supporters in both the Liberal and Labour parties retorted that endowment was not merely affordable, but could actually help to solve some of Britain's economic troubles. A measure that was viewed in France as a means of restraining wages came to be seen in Britain as a tool with

---

[15] FES, *Annual Report* (1925), p. 4.
[16] The FES published a considerable quantity of pamphlet literature and two journals, *Monthly Notes*, which appeared sporadically from 1927 to 1931, and the *Family Endowment Chronicle*, which appeared from 1931 to 1937. A collection of the pamphlet literature and the Society's *Annual Reports* for 1925 to 1930 can be found at the London School of Economics, R. Coll. Misc. 9. Articles debating the merits of family endowment regularly appeared in the *Economic Journal* and more sporadically in *Economica*, *Sociological Review*, *Eugenics Review*, and the political weeklies and monthlies.

which to strengthen home demand and help bring about "socialism in our time."

Economic arguments for family allowances: Liberal and socialist views

How could family endowment help solve the problems of the flagging British economy? The French industrialists who turned to allowances to restrain wages in the inflationary aftermath of the war could have given an answer to this question, but their counterparts across the channel neither asked them nor observed their innovations. Yet Eleanor Rathbone, who followed French developments closely, did recognize that allowances could potentially hold great appeal for British industrialists and was not averse to trying to interest them in the scheme. As early as June 1921, as the postwar boom fizzled out with industrial conflict undiminished, she wrote to John Forbes Watson of the Confederation of Employers' Organizations, requesting an interview to discuss the "practicability, either sectionally or nationally," of family endowment. She enclosed with her letter a brief pamphlet, entitled *Wages Plus Family Allowances: A Practical Way of Reducing Costs of Production without Lowering the Standard of Life of the Workers*, which she had printed privately in 1921. Like her later works, this pamphlet contended that the lack of fit between wages and family needs was the major cause of poverty; here, however, she explicitly justified not merely children's allowances but also wage reductions for childless men. While wages themselves could not be based on marital status, they could, she suggested, be set at a level adequate to maintain a couple; children could be provided for through employer-funded allowances.[17] It seems that Watson neither answered Rathbone's letter nor granted her an interview; except for a few isolated individuals, employers exhibited little interest in family allowances until the investigations of Management Research Groups in the late thirties.

Rathbone first approached Forbes Watson at an inopportune moment: after the industrial regulation of the war, the reconstruction schemes of the Lloyd George Coalition, and continued costly extensions of the "dole," most industrialists wanted to hear less rather than more about state intervention or social policy. By the midtwenties,

---

[17] Modern Records Center, University of Warwick Library, CBI Predecessor Archive, MSS 200 B/3/2/C262, Eleanor Rathbone to J. Forbes Watson, 20 June 1921; E. F. Rathbone, *Wages Plus Family Allowances: A Practical Way of Reducing Costs of Production without Lowering the Standard of Life of the Workers* (printed for private circulation, [1921]).

however, with unemployment still hovering around 10% and the trade deficit showing few signs of recovery, some economic "experts" – if few actual industrialists – began to question whether the usual Treasury panaceas of deflation, balanced budgets, and a return to the gold standard could possibly restore British industry to its prewar health. Of the old export trades, none was more troubled than coal, which had been taken under government control during the war and was kept in the black in its aftermath only by state subsidy. Scheduled to return to private control in 1925, the industry was given a temporary stay of execution – in the form of continued subsidies – while a Royal Commission investigated its troubles and suggested solutions. Little compromise seemed possible however between mine owners determined to lower wages and raise hours and a union convinced that private control was itself at fault and pledged to resist any worsening of conditions.[18]

The coal crisis of the midtwenties provided Rathbone with a second and more fruitful opportunity to argue the case for the introduction of family allowance schemes within industry and along French lines. In *The Disinherited Family*, Rathbone had argued that the coal industry – being organized on both sides, highly specialized, and unlikely to be able to pay a male family wage anytime soon – could be used as a test case of endowment, before the advent of a national system.[19] Her convert William Beveridge was a member of the Royal Commission and arranged for Rathbone and Lord Balfour of Burleigh to present evidence for the FES in December 1925. The controversy over whether wages in the mining industry were too high or too low did not concern the FES, Balfour stated; they merely wished to point out that *whatever* the remuneration of labor, "the most efficient division of that slice can only be obtained by the application of the principle of family allowances."[20] Rathbone pointed out that current mining wages left 4.6% of households and 20% of children below Rowntree's bare minimum "poverty line"; worse, 32.9% of households with fully 66.5% of children were below his more generous "human needs" standard. Family allowances, even if financed out of a redistribution of current wage rates, could solve this dilemma. If five shillings ten pence were taken out of every miner's weekly wage and redistributed

---

[18] On the problems of the coal industry and the Royal Commission, see Barry Supple, *The History of the British Coal Industry*, vol. 4, *1913–1946: The Political Economy of Decline* (Oxford University Press, 1987), esp. pp. 226–36.

[19] Rathbone, *Disinherited Family*, pp. 279–81.

[20] Royal Commission on the Coal Industry (1925), *Minutes of Evidence* (London: HMSO, 1926), p. 873.

in children's allowances, the wage of the lowest-paid worker would fall from forty-one to thirty-five shillings, but the income of all households with children would be well above the poverty line.[21] Rathbone's evidence convinced the Royal Commission, which recommended in its report of March 1926 that "irrespective of the level of wages," a system of children's allowances should be introduced.[22] The commission's principal conclusions pleased no one, however – the owners being unlikely to accept nationalization of mining royalties and forcible amalgamations, or miners a cut in wages – and the conflict moved as inexorably toward the General Strike as if the Royal Commission had never been appointed.

Even though little came of it, consideration of industrially financed allowances by the Royal Commission did worry a labor movement concerned to maintain wages in a period of high unemployment and weak trade. Socialists and trade unionists in France had objected to the introduction of family allowances but had not been powerful enough to block industrialists' schemes; in Britain, however, they could make their opposition felt from the outset. When the commission endorsed allowances and wage reductions together, the *Labour Woman* felt called on to warn its readership – hitherto supportive of "maternalist" social policies – that "Family Allowances under the present capitalist régime are simply a way of reducing wages."[23] The idea of family endowment was sound, the *New Statesman* admitted, but there were "weighty objections to its use as a means of dealing with our present industrial troubles," given its likely use to lower wages or to control workers.[24] Eleanor Rathbone might retort that even a family-based redistribution of the wage bill within a given industrial work force could make those workers better off, but as the *New Statesman* had already pointed out, the implication that one of the main goals was "to eliminate the 'useless expenditure' of the wage-earners who have no children dependent on them" merely evoked the "obvious retort . . . that there is far more useless expenditure in other classes."[25] Although the FES took its case directly to miners with speaking tours in Yorkshire, Derbyshire, and South Wales in 1926 and 1927 and insisted that they found a "keen interest and sympathetic attitude"

---

[21] Ibid., pp. 862–7.
[22] Royal Commission on the Coal Industry, *Report, PP* 1926, XIV, Cmd. 2600, p. 164.
[23] "Bothwell, the Coal Commission, and Family Allowances," *Labour Woman* (1 Apr. 1926), p. 55.
[24] "Family Endowment," *New Statesman*, 27: 678 (24 Apr. 1926), pp. 37–8.
[25] Ibid., and Eleanor Rathbone, "Family Endowments" [letter], *New Statesman*, 27: 679 (1 May 1926), pp. 78–9.

even to an industrially funded scheme, the Miners' Federation of Great Britain could scarcely tolerate further inroads into wages after the cuts following the 1926 dispute. In 1928 the federation resolved to support family allowances only if they were funded nationally and not through industry.[26]

The proposal to incorporate allowances for children directly into the wage system within particular industries did receive some attention in the twenties, but primarily from intellectuals and "experts" and not – as in France – from employers' organizations. Nor did it generate much interest within any political party, much less any government. Only some Liberals appeared to grasp the argument that industrially based allowance schemes could help restore competitiveness in the flagging export trades, but even they were ambivalent and were, in any case, politically increasingly marginal. The economists, politicians, and experts collected by Lloyd George to conduct an "industrial inquiry" and help devise an expansionist policy for the Liberal Party in the run-up to the 1929 election cautiously endorsed industrially based children's allowance schemes in the uncompetitive low-wage industries in their 1928 report, *Britain's Industrial Future*.[27] Family allowances were merely one of a shopping list of measures considered by the Liberal Industrial Inquiry, however, and never played a role comparable to that of public works or central control of investment in Liberal plans. Nor did the content of Liberal proposals in the end matter very much, since the electorate in 1929 seemed to agree that the Lloyd George program was only another election-year "stunt" and ended the party's hopes for an interwar revival.[28]

By the late twenties, then, there seemed little likelihood that British industries would follow Continental practice and move to adapt their wage systems to reflect varying patterns of family dependence. Yet children's allowances did very nearly become a crucial issue in the 1929 election. If industrialists showed little interest in allowance schemes and Liberals were too divided and marginal to exercise a

---

[26] Miners' Federation of Great Britain, *Annual Conference Report* (1928), pp. 37–42. For the FES campaign in the mining areas, see the British Library of Political and Economic Science (BLPES), FES Papers, R. Coll. Misc. 9, 33–40; FES, *Report*, 1926 and 1927; Trades Union Congress [TUC] File 117.32, Joint Committee on the Living Wage [JCLW], Evidence of Mrs. Freeth of the Family Endowment Society, 26 Jan. 1928.

[27] Liberal Industrial Inquiry, *Britain's Industrial Future* (London: Ernest Benn, 1928), pp. 190–2; see also Paul Western, *Family Allowances: A Policy for Liberals* (Liverpool: Lee & Nightingale, Mar. 1929).

[28] Philip Williamson, *National Crisis and National Government: British Politics, the Economy and Empire, 1926–1932* (Cambridge University Press, 1992), pp. 22–34, 46, 53.

dominant influence over economic policy, the party that did win a plurality of seats in 1929 did consider placing children's allowances on its electoral platform. It was the Labour Party and the trade union movement that debated the merits of family endowment in the late twenties, largely in response to the ILP's championship of family-based redistribution as a step toward "socialism in our time." The Labour Party did not in the end share the ILP's enthusiasm, but their long and fratricidal examination did shift the terms of debate, underscoring the unacceptability of industrially based schemes in Britain and defining family endowment less as a means of redistributing income from the childless to those with children than as a means of providing some measure of support for the disadvantaged children of the working class.

The "socialism in our time" (or "living wage") campaign of the ILP grew out of the conjunction of two factors – a revival within the party itself and the conviction on the part of much of its leadership that only consistent pressure from socialists could force the Labour Party to adopt a frankly socialist program before the next general election. The ILP had always been the home of socialist conviction, and while most Labour Party leaders remained nominal members, in the twenties the organization came to be dominated by radical intellectuals, activists, and younger M.P.s disaffected by MacDonaldite gradualism. Under the leadership of Clifford Allen, administration of the ILP was centralized, finances were put on a stable footing, and the party entered a period of unprecedented growth and creativity.[29] In a brilliant move, the radical journalist Henry Noel Brailsford was appointed editor of the ILP's *New Leader* in 1922. Over the next four years, Brailsford turned the paper into one of the best – and the largest – of the political weeklies, easily rivalling the *New Statesman* and the *Nation* in literary and intellectual quality. Brailsford found space in the *New Leader* for articles by his feminist friends and used the paper to criticize the Labour Party's gradualism and to outline the development of the ILP's own interventionist ideas.[30]

The ILP had been frankly disappointed by the cautious behaviour of the 1924 Labour government and hoped to pressure the party into

---

[29] On the ILP in the 1920s, see Robert E. Dowse, *Left in the Centre* (London: Longmans, Green, 1966); the living wage campaign is discussed by Fenner Brockway in *Socialism over Sixty Years* (London: Allen & Unwin, 1946), pp. 225–31, and idem, *Inside the Left* (London: Allen & Unwin, 1942), pp. 144–9.

[30] On Brailsford's involvement with the *New Leader* and the "living wage" campaign, see F. M. Leventhal, *The Last Dissenter: H.N. Brailsford and His World* (Oxford University Press, 1985), pp. 172–203.

constructing a more adequate socialist program. The task of a socialist party, Clifford Allen told the 1925 conference of the ILP, was to attempt to implement socialist legislation when in office, whether or not it had a parliamentary majority. Being constitutionalist, the party must of course resign if defeated in Parliament, but Allen believed that bold initiatives would "kindle" the imagination of the country, creating wide support for a united economic policy and paving the way for electoral victory and majority rule.[31] And of all the responsibilities facing a Labour government, surely none was more serious than that of securing a living wage for the working people of the country. Allen and Brailsford had urged a scientific inquiry into wages even during the 1924 government,[32] and in 1925 the ILP called on the labor movement to begin working out a program before Labour again took office.[33] Without waiting for official response, the party also appointed its own Living Wage Commission, made up of J. A. Hobson, Brailsford, wartime civil servant Frank Wise, and Transport and General Workers' Union Research Officer Arthur Creech Jones.[34] The commission reported to the ILP's National Administrative Council in April 1926, but many of its ideas – including its support for children's allowances – appeared in articles and in the council's own draft program, published in the *New Leader* at the beginning of the year.[35] By September, when the commission's final report, *The Living Wage*,[36] was published, its arguments were already familiar to most in the labor movement.

Along with the Liberal Industrial Inquiry, *The Living Wage* offered one of the few sophisticated analyses of Britain's economic problems in the 1920s. Whereas the Liberals concentrated on industrial policy

[31] Independent Labor Party [ILP], *Report*, 1925, pp. 84–94.
[32] See, e.g., Clifford Allen's presidential address to the 1924 conference, "Putting Socialism into Practice," ILP, *Report*, 1924, pp. 89–99.
[33] ILP, *Report*, 1925, pp. 116–20.
[34] ILP Archives, National Administrative Council Minutes, 22–3 May and 1–2 Aug. 1925, 13–14 Feb. 1926.
[35] Brailsford, et al., "An Interim Report of the Living Wage Policy of the ILP," Submitted to the National Administrative Council of the ILP [NAC], 1 Apr. 1926 (ILP Archives, Harvester Microforms, 1926/6); NAC Minutes, 1 Apr. 1926; NAC Draft Manifesto, "Socialism in Our Day," *New Leader*, 13: 14 (1 Jan. 1926). In an article explicating the draft manifesto, Brailsford concluded that "the more I reflect on this problem, the more does this detail [children's allowances] force its way into the centre of the scheme" (H. N. Brailsford, "Socialism in Our Generation: The Living Wage as Lever," *New Leader*, 13: 14 [1 Jan. 1926], p. 9).
[36] H. N. Brailsford, John A. Hobson, A. Creech Jones, and E. F. Wise, *The Living Wage* (London: ILP, 1926).

to stem the rot, the ILP placed state intervention in the distributive system at the center of its analysis. *The Living Wage* rejected from the outset some industrialists' argument that only wage cuts could restore the competitiveness of the flagging export trades and the health of the economy. Drawing on Hobson's theory of underconsumption, *The Living Wage* argued that current inequalities of wealth weakened home demand; an *increase* in working-class purchasing power therefore not only was socially just but also would stimulate domestic production and shift resources away from the fruitless attempt to recapture foreign markets.[37] Some thought should be given, however, to the manner in which working-class incomes were raised. Sectional wage increases would merely be dissipated in higher prices, while a substantial general increase was simply unaffordable. Marshaling statistics on national income, the ILP's commission pointed out that to double the average wage of the bottom 10 million of Britain's 12.5 million wage earners to a hypothetical "living" figure of four pounds per week would absorb half the total figure going to rent, profit, interest and salaries and would hopelessly disrupt the economy. Living wages, it concluded, "must be drawn from higher production, that is to say, from an expansion of the total national income."[38] Redistributive policies should have their rightful place in Labour's economic plans but could only be part of a larger strategy of industrial expansion. In their minds, this strategy had three interrelated main components – credit control, tax-funded social policies, and industrial rationalization.

First, any expansionist economic policy required the control and management of credit. In order to prevent increased wages from being dissipated in increased prices, production must be stimulated through the expansion of credit and the lowering of the bank rate; continued management of credit would require nationalizing the Bank of England. The struggle to raise living standards through union action and industrial reorganization could then proceed, but a Labour government could not leave working-class families unprotected during this lengthy process. An immediate, noninflationary redistributive measure was therefore necessary, both to safeguard working-class living standards and to "prime the pump" of industrial recovery.

The commission decided that children's allowances, to be financed through income and supertaxes, were the ideal measure. The case for family endowment was already familiar to the ILP: Brailsford had

[37] Ibid., p. 54.
[38] Ibid., p. 32.

worked with Rathbone and Mary Stocks on the first wartime endowment committee; Rathbone had also argued the case to the 1924 ILP summer school.[39] The ILP commission accepted her argument that children's allowances were necessary to the living wage because the burden of dependency varied both between workers and over any given worker's life and concluded that they were thus a basic measure of socialist justice. An allowance of five shillings per week (about 10–15% of an average male wage) for every child under school-leaving age in the population subject to insurance would cost £125 million yearly – a large sum, admitted *The Living Wage*, but not an impossible one for "a determined Chancellor at the head of a party which was firmly resolved to take the first big step in equalizing incomes."[40] Being a redistribution of existing income rather than the creation of new, children's allowances would be noninflationary. More important, they would provide a needed catalyst toward economic growth in the depressed mass consumption industries of agriculture, textiles, and mining: "Imagine, for example, the effect on dairy farming of an addition of 5/- a week for each child to the income of every working-class family."[41] Such expansion would, in turn, absorb some of the unemployed and improve workers' bargaining position.

Having provided financial stability and a minimal level of working-class well-being, the party could then concentrate on its central task: that of reorganizing industry so as to guarantee all workers a living wage. The commission recommended a series of reforms toward this end: the regulation of the cost of raw materials through mass importation by government monopolies; the organization of capital investment through the establishment of a national industrial bank; and nationalization of industries vital to the economic infrastructure – coal, power, and the railroads. With stable investment, cheaper raw materials, and regulated transport – and, most critically, with an expanded home market acting as a pressure toward production – faltering industries could expand production and raise wages. The commission left the responsibility of securing such wages to the trade unions, since "in the last resort it is on the organised refusal of men to work for less than a living wage that our hope of securing it lies."[42]

[39] Sidney B. M. Potter, "The ILP Summer School," *New Leader*, 8: 8 (22 Aug. 1924), pp. 3–4.
[40] Brailsford et al., *The Living Wage*, p. 24.
[41] Ibid., p. 41.
[42] Ibid., p. 7.

Only industries impervious to either the new market pressures or trade union action would be turned over to an industrial commission for reorganization.

The Living Wage offered a creative strategy for industrial reconstruction; in the words of two students of economic policy, it was "the only serious blueprint of the transition to socialism" put forward during the interwar years.[43] By grafting Labour's traditional commitment to income redistribution onto a broader strategy of economic expansion, the ILP's commission moved beyond a fastidious disinclination to "manage capitalism" to accept that the sharing of wealth could only be based on its continued creation. The capacity to imagine medium-term measures by which to control finance and safeguard the economic infrastructure distinguished the authors of *The Living Wage* from romantic socialists like MacDonald, for whom "socialism" was more a matter of the heart than of the head, and remained, in any case, reassuringly in the future. Most important, the strategy was a total one: far from being a mere laundry list of disparate commitments, the policies advocated formed "a single complex, a logical whole."[44]

The authors of *The Living Wage* admitted that their program would require not only simultaneous action in finance and industry, but also much closer cooperation between the political and industrial wings of the movement. It was this assumption that aroused the least discussion but that was in fact most problematic, since it challenged the traditional conceptions of the prerogatives of both the Parliamentary Labour Party and the TUC. Not only was the trade union movement to accept interference by Parliament in industrial matters, but the party was to abandon its attempt to prove itself "fit to govern" to its parliamentary colleagues and behave instead as the political arm of the socialist movement in the country. Furthermore, both unions and party would have to accept a measure of central direction and coordination, presumably from the authors of *The Living Wage*. Could the much maligned "intellectuals" of the movement convince its leadership of the need for actions and policies so antithetical to its traditions?

The ILP launched its campaign for "Socialism in Our Time" at its April 1926 conference, where a composite resolution supporting the proposals later elaborated in *The Living Wage* passed easily. Yet from the outset there were signs of trouble. A few speakers disputed

---

[43] Alan Booth and Melvyn Pack, *Employment, Capital and Economic Policy: Great Britain, 1918–1939* (Oxford: Basil Blackwell, 1985), p. 189.

[44] Brailsford et al., *The Living Wage*, p. 53.

whether the party would ever be able to win union support for the establishment of any money figure for a living wage,[45] and Ramsay MacDonald, who detested Brailsford, had already lambasted the proposals in the March issue of *Socialist Review*.[46] Undeterred by criticism, the ILP brought their proposals to the 1926 Labour Party Conference at Margate. Although the Labour Executive convinced the ILP to refrain from forcing a vote on their actual proposals, the conference did accept an ILP resolution in favor of a joint Labour Party and TUC inquiry into wages, industrial organization, and the socialization of key services – all canvassed in *The Living Wage* – with a view to creating a unified economic policy for the next Labour government. An ILP resolution on state-funded children's allowances, taken separately, was also referred to the Executive for investigation in view of its possible effects on trade union organization and wages.[47] In sum, while response to the ILP proposals by the political movement was warm, it was clear that the Labour Party would only act after consultation with the TUC.

Trade union consent was, however, a formidable goal, not only because the TUC was itself divided about the merits of political action, but also because the trade union leadership reacted with hostility to the skepticism about union capacity which infused all the ILP's proposals. Arthur Creech Jones, in an unpublished ILP memorandum, had argued frankly that trade unions concentrated too much on sectional interests and not enough on industrial policy. If true wage gains were to be achieved for all, the unions must be willing to accept much more central direction within the movement and to agree to increase production in exchange for effective participation in management.[48] Trade union leaders were understandably wary of this kind of analysis; soon after the ILP's conference, Ernest Bevin – ironically, Creech Jones's own boss at the Transport and General Workers' Union – wrote to Brailsford warning him that "I stand four-square against political interference with wages."[49] And when the General Council met in March 1927 to decide whether they should accede to the party's

---

[45] ILP, *Report*, 1926, pp. 76–87.

[46] On MacDonald's opposition, see David Marquand, *Ramsey MacDonald* (London: Jonathan Cape, 1977), pp. 452–7; Brockway, *Socialism over Sixty Years*, pp. 229–31.

[47] Labour Party, *Report*, 26 (1926), pp. 259–61, 274–5.

[48] A. Creech Jones, "Industrial Policy and the Living Wage," app. to Brailsford et al., "An Interim Report," pp. 18–29.

[49] Quoted in Leventhal, *The Last Dissenter*, p. 193. On Bevin's opposition to the "socialism in our time" campaign, see Alan Bullock, *The Life and Times of Ernest Bevin*, vol. 1, *Trade Union Leader, 1881–1940* (London: Heinemann, 1960), pp. 389–91.

request for consultation on *The Living Wage*, both Bevin and Walter Citrine, the TUC's able general secretary, were opposed. "I am against bringing the Political Labour Party into [wage questions]," Bevin stated:

> If we once get this wage problem into the hands of our own politicians and have the Tory Party dealing with it, when they are in office, wages will be the subject of political conflict. I prefer to keep quite clear of the political movement; . . . the problem must be dealt with by the unions themselves.

Bevin was equally wary of family allowance proposals; while Margaret Bondfield strongly supported investigation, he argued that the unions would, if consulted, be "generally opposed to cutting up wages at all." At the end of the meeting, and at the urging of Arthur Pugh among others, the General Council did agree – by eleven to six – to consult with "the political movement," but the division augured ill for the future of such consultation.[50]

With the agreement of the General Council to participate in a joint inquiry, the leading role in the campaign for children's allowances shifted to the newly created Joint Committee on the Living Wage (JCLW). However, during the next few years, the ILP remained an effective gadfly, canvassing its proposals across the country through meetings and articles. Children's allowances, as the one concrete policy recommended for immediate introduction, worked their way into the center of its propaganda.[51] In this process, and with an eye to distinguishing itself from "capitalist" advocates of endowment, the ILP both clarified its own position and decisively shifted the policy debate.

The ILP modified Rathbone's ideas on family endowment in two crucial respects. First, from being a question of national interest, children's allowances had become inextricable from class politics: class-based redistribution took precedence over child-based or gender-based claims. The poverty of children was due not only to the inability of the wage system to take account of families, the ILP argued, but

[50] TUC Archives, File 117.2, General Council (GC) Minutes, 22 Mar. 1927.

[51] Supporters of the living wage campaign kept up a stream of articles and pamphlets. See especially, Minnie Pallister, "The Justice of Family Allowances," *Socialist Review*, new ser., no. 5 (June 1926), pp. 38–43; A. Creech Jones, "A Family Income – A Trade Union View," *Socialist Review*, new ser., no. 7 (Aug. 1926), pp. 27–31; Fred Jowett, *Socialism in Our Time* (London: ILP, 1926); Dorothy Jewson, *Socialists and the Family* (London: ILP, 1926); ILP, *What Women of the ILP Stand For* (London: ILP, 1929); ILP, *The Case for Children's Allowances* (London: ILP, 1930).

also to the fact that the share of income going to the working class was too small altogether. Whereas in 1925 at least some left-wing advocates of children's allowances had been willing to consider redistribution from workers without children to those with children through industrial schemes, by 1927 all agreed that only a national system, financed through direct taxation of the rich, would be suitable.[52] Further, just as redistribution between families of all classes faded into the background, so too did the redistribution between women and men. The ILP did, in fact, insist on payment to the mother and was strongly committed to increasing mothers' independence and benefits, but only at the expense of "capitalists," not of working men.

Second, as reconceived by the ILP, children's allowances became integrated into a broader program of economic reconstruction. This gave coherence and purpose to the ILP campaign, but by attempting to use allowances to increase working-class income dramatically without having any (working-class) losers, the party's commitment to any less comprehensive family policy was left unclear. In the ILP vision, the boost given to the economy would wipe out any possible negative effects on employment or wages, while credit control would prevent inflation from reducing the real wages of those without allowances. This promise of large benefits at no cost meant that the central premise of family endowment – that income must be redistributed along family lines, *whatever* the distribution between classes – could be entirely avoided. In fact, this may have been the condition for Labour consent: the discussion at Margate had made the ILP realize that acceptance of children's allowances as a "progressive" policy would be forthcoming only if trade unions could be convinced that they were part of a larger living wage strategy or, at the very least, were unlikely to lower wages. From 1926 to 1929, the ILP kept up a steady stream of propaganda, all valiantly asserting that allowances would have no negative effects on wages. The job of assessing the validity of their claim passed to the Joint Committee on the Living Wage.

---

[52] For example, while Ernest Hunter was willing to consider even the payment of family allowances through industrial pools as "socialist" in 1925 ("A Socialist Wage Policy: Family Needs versus Flat Rates," *New Leader*, 10: 5 [30 Jan. 1925], pp. 3–4), by 1928]) he thought only a universal, state-funded scheme merited such a distinction (Hunter, *Wages and Families* [London: ILP, 1928]). With the exception of Mary Stocks – who was, in any case, more active in feminist organizations than in the Labour Party – Labour women refused to contemplate any horizontal redistribution, arguing steadily for the funding of allowances through vertical redistribution, as in Dorothy Jewson, "Liberal Women and Children's Allowances: Who Shall Pay?" *New Leader*, 14: 24 (8 Apr. 1927), p. 2.

From inquiry to stalemate: The Joint Committee on the Living Wage

In September 1927, Walter Milne-Bailey, research officer of the TUC, advised Hugh Dalton that the newly appointed Joint Committee on the Living Wage – of which he had been named secretary – should operate like a Royal Commission, taking evidence from impartial "experts" as well as from Labour supporters.[53] His hopes could not have been more amply fulfilled: like a Royal Commission, the committee interviewed numerous experts, accumulated masses of evidence, and then – long after the moment for action had passed – issued reports that utterly disregarded its own inquiry and merely reaffirmed the opinions originally held by its members. In one sense, then, the Joint Committee accomplished nothing of importance for the history of family policy; in another sense, however, its inquiry was crucial, for it crystallized the hostility of the TUC to this type of distributive policy, effectively preventing the Labour Party from acting on its own interest in children's allowances for a dozen years.

The Joint Committee on the Living Wage, made up of seven Labour Party representatives and seven TUC representatives, began meeting in November 1927 under the chairmanship of Margaret Bondfield. In recognition of the importance of their task, both organizations named high-level representatives: the TUC's representatives were all members of the General Council and included General Secretary Walter Citrine, while the Labour Party's appointees included Party Chairman Arthur Henderson and such important figures as George Lansbury, Herbert Morrison, Ellen Wilkinson, and Oswald Mosley.[54] The committee's formidable task was to determine the economic conditions necessary to generate "living wages," to examine immediate policies to improve wages, and to look at the prospects for socialization in various industries.[55] After their first four meetings, however, all devoted to interviewing the members of the

---

[53] Minutes, memos, and correspondence of the JCLW are found in the TUC Archives, Transport House, Files 117 and 118. File 117.11, Milne-Bailey to Dalton, 26 Sept. 1927.

[54] The committee's seven TUC representatives were Bondfield, Citrine, John Beard of the Workers' Union, H. H. Elvin of the National Union of Clerks, John Hill of the Boilermakers, R. T. Jones of the Quarrymen, and Ben Turner of the Textile Workers. The seven Labour Party representatives were Henderson, Lansbury, Mosley, Morrison, Wilkinson, F. O. Roberts, and George Lathan. Mrs. Jennie Adamson replaced George Lansbury in early 1928.

[55] TUC File 117.2, [W. Milne-Bailey], "Suggestions as to Scope and Procedure" (16 Nov. 1927).

ILP's Living Wage Commission, the committee members threw up their hands in disgust and restricted their inquiry to family allowances.[56]

In their interim report, they attributed this decision to the urgency of the family allowance investigation,[57] but unquestionably it was also due to the growing friction between the trade unionists on the committee and the "intellectuals" of the ILP. Even Labour members found irritating the ILP's insistence that with sustained effort the party could get much of the "living wage" program through during its first year in office. Arthur Henderson demurred:

> I am concerned that we should not go and make ourselves look ridiculous by committing ourselves to a scheme involving £125 million in addition to other schemes to which we are committed and to create the impression that we are doing it all in the first six months.[58]

More crucially, even if the political will was there, some of the committee felt that the ILP had taken the consent of the TUC for granted. Cross-examining ILP commission member E. F. Wise, Margaret Bondfield remarked that the TUC had asked for unions' opinions on family allowances once before and had received a disappointing response. "You have assumed all through," she warned Wise, "that we have the complete backing of the Trade Union movement."[59]

In fact, they had not, as the memoranda drafted by Milne-Bailey ostensibly explicating (but in reality criticizing) the ILP's program made amply clear. "The scheme advanced by the ILP is essentially a political scheme," Milne-Bailey began. "The industrial movement is from the outset and without argument relegated to a position of comparative impotence." While the ILP left the responsibility for securing living wages from reorganized industries to the trade unions, this "is merely a sop ... to cover up the belief obviously held that ... the Trade Union movement is practically powerless." Such a belief was, he said, entirely wrong; in fact, "it is mainly by industry itself that the correct line of advance should be determined, since the political side can know very little in detail about the real needs and problems of industry."[60] Having rejected the ILP's claims about the

---

[56] TUC File 117, JCLW Minutes of Meetings, 15 Dec. 1927.
[57] TUC and Labour Party, JCLW, *Interim Report on Family Allowances and Child Welfare* (London: TUC and Labour Party, June 1928), p. 4.
[58] TUC File 117.32, JCLW evidence, 15 Dec. 1927, p. 9.
[59] Ibid., p. 15.
[60] TUC File 117.2, [W. Milne-Bailey], "The ILP Living Wage Scheme" (6 Dec. 1927), p. 1.

importance of political action, the memorandum went on to demolish the specific proposals put forward in *The Living Wage*. The ILP's exposition of the underconsumptionist argument was dismissed as both confused and a policy "preached by the entire movement for a considerable time";[61] credit expansion was considered necessarily inflationary and likely to lower real wages; the high-wage policy would make British products susceptible to undercutting by foreign competitors. Yet the main charge leveled against the ILP was, in fact, that it took its socialism seriously: "Many of the political measures suggested by the ILP are merely orthodox Socialist proposals, which all of us accept. They are unfortunately, as every political realist in the Socialist movement recognises, remote objectives."[62] Within a month, the committee's consideration of the ILP's proposals was over.

All except for children's allowances, for which sympathy on the committee ran high. Yet having isolated allowances from the rest of the ILP's program, the committee found itself confronted with a new difficulty. By severing the link between children's allowances and expansionist economics, the committee could no longer avoid the question of whether allowances were desirable regardless of their effects on wages. Like the ILP, the committee skirted this question, but in a zero-sum economy, could allowances be introduced without any effect on the wages of childless men? Although the committee listened patiently to the population and health arguments of its "expert witnesses," all but the most naive understood that the committee's recommendations would depend entirely on its answer to this question.

Yet the committee's witnesses gave no uniform answer. Rather, much as one would expect, supporters of allowances, including Hugh Dalton, argued that wages were determined by the power of the trade unions, did not tend toward subsistence, and hence would not be influenced by allowances, while opponents like Alexander Gray and D. H. Macgregor claimed that even a national system funded through taxation would lower wages indirectly by reducing the amount of savings available for investment and hence limiting economic growth. Only Eleanor Rathbone for the FES and Mary Stocks representing the National Union of Societies for Equal Citizenship argued that family endowment was worthwhile *regardless* of its effects on wages. The real question, they insisted, was whether even a fixed amount of money could do more good distributed as allowances *or* as wages.

[61] Ibid., p. 4.
[62] Ibid., p. 2.

When Walter Citrine asked Rathbone directly whether wages would not certainly fall if the responsibility of rearing future generations were passed on to another source, she responded frankly:

> If you mean wages paid to the wage-earner for his work, – if you have a system of family allowances – there is no doubt that sooner or later it may react on wages. There is no source you can name out of which family allowances could be paid that could not conceivably be paid in the way of increased wages. . . . There are two questions, (1) whether it decreases or increases the total share of the workers in industry, and (2) their total well-being. Wages are merely counters. If you distribute the workers' share in allowances and wages . . . even if you do not increase the total share you enormously increase the total well-being.[63]

Mary Stocks agreed. Take, she said, the worst possible case – that of a powerful group of employers who introduced allowances and funded them entirely out of the wage bill. Such a scheme would reduce standard rates but would redistribute the amount saved to those who needed it most. "Even a scheme of that sort would increase the welfare of the workers."[64] Most systems of endowment, Rathbone implied, would involve some measure of both vertical and horizontal redistribution, increasing both aggregate working-class income and the share of such income going to families with children.

The committee, however, showed itself both unwilling to contemplate any measure that could conceivably react on wages and virtually unable to comprehend that even if allowances were funded in part out of wages, working-class income as a whole would not fall. When Joseph Cohen of the FES argued in favor of developing a family allowance scheme through the insurance system, H. H. Elvin of the National Union of Clerks protested that workers would "have to go without absolute necessities of life" to pay the insurance contribution – overlooking the point that the wives of all married men with children would get far more back than their husbands contributed.[65] Whether because the money would be paid to women rather than men, or because they could not conceive of children as a national charge, trade unionists who had come to accept an insurance system

---

[63] TUC File 117.32, JCLW evidence, 26 Jan. 1928, p. 18.

[64] Ibid., 16 Feb. 1928, p. 9. Both Rathbone and Stocks personally opposed industrial schemes. See Stocks's comments in ibid., p. 17; also Rathbone's comment "I would regret to see the system develop as it has in France," TUC File 117.32, JCLW evidence, 26 Jan. 1928, p. 9.

[65] TUC File 117.32, JCLW evidence, 23 Feb. 1928, p. 11.

funded in part by a levy on wages were unwilling to countenance similar levies for family allowances, even if the total payments to working-class families would thereby be increased. Uncomfortable with Rathbone's argument that "wages are merely counters," Milne-Bailey began casting about for an alternative policy more acceptable to the unions. The labor movement, he argued, was already committed to policies that would cost a considerable amount of money; wouldn't it be wiser to complete existing social services rather than start new ones? The committee could recommend in favor of further developing the social services, while adding a cash benefit for the first two years of a child's life, a compromise that would reflect Labour's traditional commitment to expanding the social services, while going some distance toward meeting the family allowance advocates' case.[66] The committee's interim report, which was printed for confidential use in June 1928 and circulated publicly in October, thus presented the labor movement with a choice *between* allowances for children and a string of social services, including a complete National Health Service, nursery schools, and improved maternity benefits.

This "social services" proposal may have been cobbled together only to undercut support for cash allowances, but in the interim report Milne-Bailey tried to present it as a credible alternative. In doing so, he relied heavily on the testimony of Labour women witnesses, notably Marion Phillips and Eleanor Barton of the Standing Joint Committee of Industrial Women's Organisations. The policy of the SJC, Phillips claimed, was established by the National Conference of Labour Women; since the conference had resolved in no uncertain terms in favor of cash allowances paid to the mother the year before, it may be assumed that Phillips argued this case forcefully.[67] In fact, she did not; in evidence she supported extended maternity benefit rather than cash allowances and was willing to agree with Elvin that Continental experiments "prove the importance of the development of social services rather than a direct money payment."[68] Eleanor Barton of the Women's Cooperative Guild disagreed: the guild had repeatedly resolved in favor of family endowment and was not concerned that such measures would react on wages.[69] Barton was willing to limit benefit

---

[66] TUC File 118.1, [W. Milne-Bailey], "The Case for and against Family Allowances" (1 Feb. 1928).

[67] National Conference of Labour Women, *Annual Report*, 1927, pp. 42–3.

[68] TUC File 117.32, JCLW evidence, 15 Mar. 1928, pp. 10–11.

[69] In addition to its interest in the endowment of motherhood (discussed in Chapter 3), the guild passed resolutions urging consideration of a noncontributory scheme of family

to children under age 2 only if this was a first step toward wider cash endowment, and she was strongly opposed to payment in kind. When Phillips said that she personally preferred to spend money on nurseries rather than giving it to mothers, Barton retorted:

> I hope it will not go forth that this Committee thinks that the money would be better spent by any authority than the women could spend it. Our people feel very strongly on this point and the evidence during the war was overwhelmingly in favor of the women having the money in the home.[70]

Nevertheless, when Milne-Bailey drafted the interim report, he used the testimony of Barton and Phillips to argue that there was "not a great deal of interest in Family Endowment in the country" and that, in any case, "Labour women generally" preferred an extended maternity benefit to cover the first two years of the child's life and the development of social services to a "trifling" cash allowance for all children.[71] Ellen Wilkinson was so displeased with Milne-Bailey's draft that she threatened to submit a minority report in favor of family allowances on her own,[72] and even Marion Phillips felt she had been misrepresented. Extended maternity benefit was advocated as a precedent not a substitute for family allowances, she claimed; whereas "anybody reading the summary would suppose that the industrial women were on the whole against Family Allowances."[73] Yet Milne-Bailey did not significantly alter his summary of "industrial women's views."[74] As in the case of the campaign for the endowment of motherhood, the opinions of the representatives of Labour women were distorted to lend credence to the claim that the Labour Party's anxieties about cash benefits to married women were widely shared by working-class wives. What was the purpose of all this misrepresentation? Buried on page 22 of the interim report was perhaps its only significant statement; a true avowal of the case against cash allowances:

---

allowances at its 1925 and 1926 congresses. See Women's Cooperative Guild [WCG], *Annual Report*, 43 (1926), p. 18; 44 (1927), p. 17.

[70] TUC File 117.32, JCLW evidence, 15 Mar. 1928, p. 8.

[71] TUC File 117.41, JCLW, "Interim Report on Family Allowances and Child Welfare" (draft), galley 12, para. 52.

[72] TUC File 117.11, Wilkinson to Bondfield, 21 May 1928.

[73] TUC File 117.13, Phillips to Milne-Bailey, 24 July 1928, and Phillips to Milne-Bailey, 13 July 1928.

[74] Milne-Bailey changed the phrase "Labour women generally" to "very many Labour women" when describing the group's supposed preference for a substantial baby benefit to a "trifling" allowance but left the rest of the summary unchanged; see JCLW, *Interim Report*, p. 30.

The economic aspect of Family Endowment which is of most concern to Trade Unionists is its possible effect on the level of wages. *It goes without saying that if the proposals would obviously result in a general lowering of the wage level, they would be strenuously opposed by the working class movement. Nor would the case be at all different if it was felt that Family Allowances would act as a check on an upward movement in wages.*[75]

The message was clear: family allowances were acceptable only if they had no effect on wages whatsoever.

The impression given by the interim report was that the committee was about to resolve in favor of Milne-Bailey's "compromise solution," but Milne-Bailey had underestimated the support for cash allowances in Labour circles and, indeed, on the Joint Committee itself. When the committee reconvened in the late spring of 1928 to decide on recommendations, supporters of cash allowances found themselves in the majority and were far from willing to compromise on a nebulous program of social services. By a vote of eight to three they resolved that "the guiding principle shall be that of family allowances by cash payment from birth to the present school leaving age," although Citrine and Elvin were able to secure a promise that no steps would be taken by the committee before the General Council of the TUC and the Labour Executive had a chance to consider the matter.[76] The committee adjourned with Labour members confident of union agreement. At the Labour Party Conference in Birmingham in late September 1928, Arthur Henderson revealed that the majority of the committee had resolved in favor of cash allowances and that the party was waiting only for TUC consent to place the policy on the forthcoming election manifesto.[77]

Henderson's admission made the division of opinion plain for all to see and put the ball squarely in the TUC's court. Yet the General Council was still divided on allowances and strongly resented the party's lobbying. During the summer, Citrine asked all unions to decide whether they supported allowances or social services,[78] but the almost even division of opinion – nineteen unions with 1,146,774 members for allowances, thirty-three unions with 980,786 members for services – hardly solved the General Council's dilemma. Results did take so long to collect, however, as to end any hope that the party could include the issue in the election manifesto. In April 1929, almost

[75] Ibid., p. 22, my emphasis.
[76] TUC File 117, JCLW Minutes of Meetings, 19 June 1928.
[77] Labour Party, *Report*, 28 (1928), pp. 167–8.
[78] TUC File 117.14, Citrine to all affiliated unions, 17 July 1928.

two years after its formation, the Joint Committee could only conclude that while a majority of its members had accepted the principle of cash allowances, "it regrets that it is not in a position to make any definite recommendation on the matter owing to the inability of the General Council of the Trades Union Congress to express an opinion on behalf of the Trade Union movement."[79] Having so resolved, it adjourned until after the General Election.

The Labour Party, the ILP and the FES all continued to press the issue, however. The election brought most of the committee's Labour Party representatives into the government, but the party appointed new members who reflected previous opinion exactly.[80] Within a few months, the reconstituted committee had reviewed the case and rediscovered its eight-to-three split in favor of cash allowances; this time, however, it decided to issue a report.[81] In early February, a majority of the committee adopted a brief report in favor of cash allowances of five shillings for the first child and three shillings for each subsequent child from birth to school-leaving age, paid to the mother and financed out of national taxation. Cash payments, they contended, would be the most effective means of improving the health of children: "No public authority can, in our view, make money go as far in the provision of food, clothing and healthy surroundings, as can the mothers who have learned economy in the hard school of experience." The only serious objection to allowances, they claimed, was that they might react on wages.

> We have given this objection the weight it deserves, coming as it does from responsible leaders of the Trade Union Movement, but we are convinced that these fears are groundless. We agree with those other Trade Union leaders who have told us that they are very firm in their view that a system of Family Allowances would not hamper the Unions at all in their negotiations. Indeed, we believe that during industrial conflicts the Unions will be very considerably helped by

---

[79] TUC File 117, JCLW minutes, 10 Apr. 1929.

[80] Seven members of the JCLW joined the government in 1929: Bondfield became minister of labor, Henderson foreign secretary, Lansbury first commissioner of works, Roberts minister of pensions, Morrison minister of transport, Mosley chancellor of the Duchy of Lancaster, and Wilkinson the parliamentary private secretary to Susan Lawrence. The party appointed six new representatives – Ethel Bentham, Barbara Ayrton Gould, Mrs. Joseph Jones, W. H. Hutchinson of the Amalgamated Engineering Union, Harry Snell (who, however, never attended and signed no report), and Fred Jowett (who was appointed to replace Arthur Henderson in January 1930). On the TUC side, Margaret Bondfield and Ben Turner were replaced by Anne Loughlin of the Tailors and Garment Workers and F. Wolstencroft of the Woodworkers.

[81] TUC File 117, JCLW minutes, 23 Jan. 1930.

the existence of such a scheme, since the workers' children will be removed from the "firing line" and a great factor of weakness will thus be removed.[82]

Five members representing the party and four representing the TUC signed the report.[83] Two TUC representatives and one trade unionist sitting as a party representative submitted a minority report in favor of Milne-Bailey's "compromise suggestion" of social services and a cash baby benefit.[84] The minority report's authors claimed they were neither opposed to cash benefits as such nor believed that mothers would spend money unwisely, but merely felt that a necessarily limited amount of money could do more good if expended to create collective services rather than frittered away in small amounts.[85] In its initial form, the minority report rather duplicitously asserted that its conclusions were not based on wage considerations, but in the end this diplomatic sidestep had to be amended, since W. H. Hutchinson of the Amalgamated Engineering Union wrote to Milne-Bailey that he was completely convinced cash payments would react on wages and would only sign the report if this were frankly avowed.[86]

The reports were not immediately published, but even the *Times* knew that the trade union movement and not the party was the source of the hesitation.[87] On 26 February 1930, with the party still waiting for a decision, the General Council considered not only the two official reports but also a third report, never published, by Citrine himself.[88] Citrine had declined to sign the minority report, feeling that it had treated the question of the effects of family allowances on wages "rather too briefly for my liking," and had drafted his own brief report.[89] Employers would "undoubtedly" cite both allowances and social services in wage negotiations, he stated. Of the two policies, however, allowances were the more dangerous, especially since social services were not really at issue:

[82] TUC File 117, JCLW minutes, 5 Feb. 1930; "Majority Report," in TUC and Labour Party, *Family Allowances* (London, 1930).

[83] The majority report was signed by John Beard, John Hill, R. T. Jones, and Anne Loughlin (for the TUC), and Jennie Adamson, Ethel Bentham, Barbara Ayrton Gould, Mrs. Joseph Jones, and Fred Jowett (for the Labour Party).

[84] The minority report was signed by H. H. Elvin of the National Union of Clerks and F. Wolstencroft of the Woodworkers (for the TUC) and W. H. Hutchinson of the Amalgamated Engineering Union (for the Labour Party).

[85] "Minority Report," in TUC and Labour Party, *Family Allowances* (London, 1930).

[86] TUC File 117.11, Hutchinson to Milne-Bailey, 8 Feb. 1930.

[87] "Family Allowances: Labour Differences Still Unreconciled," *Times*, 25 Feb. 1930.

[88] TUC Archives, GC minutes, 26 Feb. 1930.

[89] TUC File 118.1, [Walter Citrine], "Family Allowances" (draft) (14 Feb. 1930).

An increase in social services is the normal development of Labour policy, and presumably will be continued as opportunity offers, irrespective of the Report of this Committee. However, that question does not seem to me to be a real issue. The real question is whether the Movement should declare in favour of Family Allowances by cash payments. I hesitate to answer this in the affirmative because I do not believe anybody can authoritatively forecast what the effects will be on the wages system and wages negotiations.[90]

Citrine's opposition hardened opinion on each side, and the General Council decided to consult its Economic Committee – "the doyen of the General Council's committees" – which included Bevin and Arthur Pugh.[91] Milne-Bailey also sent all three reports to several trusted economists – C. M. Lloyd, G. D. H. Cole, R. H. Tawney, P. Sargant Florence, and John Maynard Keynes – to ask for their opinion.

The economists seem to have understood the General Council's real concern and went straight to the point. Employers would undoubtedly cite allowances in wage negotiations, said Tawney, but their argument that tax-funded social expenditure would decrease the fund available for wages was quite unsound. Sargant Florence agreed: the threat of allowances to wages was not based in economics but in psychology, since allowances could presumably destroy workers' will to hold out for a family wage. This was a risk the unions should face, however, argued C. M. Lloyd, "unless they can offer a really good prospect (which they clearly cannot at present) of raising wages substantially by purely industrial action." Allowances, both he and Cole felt, were also the only means of ensuring adequate nurture for children. On the issue of cash versus services, however, the economists were less sure. None seemed to realize that the Labour Party was already committed to further developing social services and that it was the question of cash allowances that was really up for discussion. All but Cole felt services would be more useful, economical, practical, and less likely to react on wages.[92]

When the TUC leadership met again to consider this new evidence, they still could not agree. A special session of the joint executives of the TUC and Labour Party in April 1930 merely worsened the situation, as discussion degenerated into an acrimonious exchange with rival trade union leaders citing various Continental examples in sup-

[90] TUC File 118.1, W. M. Citrine, "Report on Family Allowances" (22 Feb. 1930).
[91] Ross M. Martin, *TUC: The Growth of a Pressure Group, 1868–1976* (Oxford University Press, 1980), p. 222.
[92] TUC File 118.1, Notes by Tawney, Lloyd, Sargant Florence, Keynes, and Cole on family allowances, dated between 5 and 24 Mar. 1930.

port of their argument. The two Executives could only decide to consider the two reports independently. In late May the General Council finally voted sixteen to eight in favor of the minority report, a decision ratified – over substantial dissent – by that summer's Congress.[93] The disappointed Labour Party Conference that October could only endorse its Executive's proposal to appeal to the General Council for further investigation, but Citrine would have none of it.[94] The General Council, he wrote to Henderson, would not agree to reopen the question of family allowances.[95] Henderson, reporting to the Labour Executive, felt the issue was still not closed: allowances would be a "vital political issue" in the future.[96] In fact, however, the General Council's moratorium on further discussion held until the middle of the Second World War.

The conversion of many Labour leaders to family allowances cannot be taken to mean that if the TUC had responded promptly and positively, the policy would have been forthcoming. Even the Joint Committee's June 1928 majority resolution in favor of allowances included the proviso that the principle was to be "applied as circumstances permit"; and "circumstances," in the form of a hung Parliament, an unenthusiastic Parliamentary leadership, and the worsening budget deficit, were hardly conducive to the introduction of a policy requiring a major financial commitment and tainted with the brush of the ILP.[97] As Hugh Dalton recalled, "Snowden hated the idea like hell": if he had been unwilling to commit some £40 million to widowed mothers' pensions in 1924, it was even less likely that he could have found £125 million for children's allowances in 1929.[98] Nevertheless, the inability of allowance advocates even to get their policy on the Labour Party program left their cause without effective political backing until the Second World War. With the virtual evaporation of the Liberals after 1929, the Labour Party was the only real hope for supporters of family allowances, yet in the end the ambivalence of the trade union movement overcame the genuine support for the policy within the Party. Why did trade unionists reject allowances,

[93] TUC File 117, JCLW minutes, 12 Mar. 1930; File 118.1, "History of Case," n.d.; TUC Archives, GC minutes, 28 May 1930; TUC, *Report*, 62 (1930), pp. 218–21, 381–409.

[94] Labour Party, *Report*, 30 (1930), pp. 51–2, 169–70, 174–9, 212–13.

[95] TUC File 118.1, Citrine to Henderson, 19 Dec. 1930.

[96] Labour Party Archives, National Executive Committee minutes, 29 Aug. 1930, 28–9 Jan. 1931.

[97] TUC File 117, JCLW minutes, 19 June 1928.

[98] Hugh Dalton, *Call Back Yesterday: Memoirs, 1887–1931* (London: Frederick Muller, 1953), p. 181.

and what were the implications of this decision for the future of family policy?

Family policy and the trade unions

It is important to recognize at the outset that the trade union movement only ratified a settlement arrived at by the General Council. The movement itself at no point spoke with a single voice. When the General Council surveyed union opinion in 1929, they found that unions supporting allowances had a slightly greater total membership than those opposed, but the survey was not very meaningful: since few unions had a position on the record, the answers given to the survey often represented no more than the sentiment of a general secretary.[99] The fact that the Amalgamated Engineering Union recorded an opinion against allowances didn't prevent it from printing an article in its monthy journal urging members to support the principle;[100] similarly, while Bevin committed the 300,000 members of the Transport and General Workers' Union to social services, the TGWU had actually submitted a resolution in favor of allowances to the 1927 National Conference of Labour Women.[101] When the issue did reach the floor at union conferences, sharp debates often ensued – as the officers of both the National Union of Boot and Shoe Operatives and the National Union of Distributive and Allied Workers discovered when faced with resolutions protesting their decision to commit the union to the social services option.[102] The trade union movement as a whole, then, was less opposed to the idea of cash allowances than divided, and this division was reflected within almost all sectors and at all levels of organization.

Since the ultimate veto of the General Council had a disproportionate influence on the future of family policy, however, the reasons for disagreement deserve some scrutiny. The disappointed leaders of the FES offered one explanation for the movement's ultimate recal-

---

[99] TUC File 117.14, "Replies to Questionnaire on Family Allowances," 25 Mar. 1929.

[100] J. Marcus, "Trade Unionists and Family Allowances," *A.E.U. Monthly Journal*, no. 104 (Mar. 1929), p. 58. One year later, they printed a more negative assessment: "Family Allowances in Practice: How Other Countries Apply the Principle," *A.E.U. Monthly Journal*, no. 122 (Sept. 1930), p. 57.

[101] Labour Party Archives, NCLW, *Agenda* (1927), p. 9.

[102] National Union of Boot and Shoe Operatives, *Official Report of the 39th General Conference* (Leicester: Cooperative Printing Society, 1930); for the National Union of Distributive and Allied Workers (NUDAW), see the report of the Annual Delegate Meeting, 1 Apr. 1929, *New Dawn*, 9: 9 (27 Apr. 1929), pp. 204–6.

citrance. The TUC's decision, Mary Stocks wrote, "suggests uncomfortable reflections concerning the attitude of the trade union movement to the interests of its working mothers."[103] Having looked to children's allowances to foster married women's economic independence, they read rejection of the measure as another victory for what Rathbone called the "Turk complex." The debate over family endowment appeared, in their view, as a struggle between those committed to the preservation of male domestic authority and women striving to articulate a citizenship status for housewives and mothers.

One can certainly find both opponents and supporters who saw the issue in these terms. Ellen Wilkinson also thought the question one of women's rights, warning the 1929 Labour Party conference that they could not treat the "emancipated voting women of 1929 and 1930" as "secluded women" had been treated "in the days when most of these wage systems came into being": new women insisted that they be treated as partners in the home, and children as more than "pawns in the fight between capitalists and labour."[104] Anne Loughlin of the Tailors and Garment Workers similarly told the TUC conference in 1930 that the problem of married women's status deserved greater consideration. After marriage, many wives were "tied to that particular man, whether they like it or not, for the sake of the children." Although a few shillings a week would not make such wives economically independent, it would give them at least a small degree of autonomy, "and, after all, they are human beings before they are mothers or wives."[105]

And if some women in the labor movement did share the feminist convictions of Rathbone and Stocks, some men in the movement objected to the measure precisely because it had these overtones. Family allowances, Rhys Davies of the National Union of Distributive and Allied Workers claimed, were devised by the "ardent feminist" who "distrusts the father to do his duty to his wife and children."

> She has no faith that he will hand over his wages to his wife. She sometimes stands for the principle of State payment of wages to the wife for acting as mother and housekeeper; and she is the more fierce on that point if she has never been married herself. If she were frank with us she would say that the husband must go out to work; he should have a modicum at the end of a week for his tobacco,

[103] [Mary Stocks], "Women and Children Last," *Family Endowment Society Monthly Notes*, 7: 70 (Sept. 1930), p. 19.

[104] Labour Party, *Report*, 29 (1929), p. 162.

[105] TUC, *Report*, 62 (1930), p. 401.

the employer to hand over the balance of his wages to the State, leaving the Civil Servant to dole it out to the wife and children – a sort of Truck system more objectionable than anything we have ever experienced before.[106]

"Mr. Davies has the male complex badly developed," mocked Ernest Hunter in the *New Leader*,[107] but Davies's objections continued. At the 1930 Labour Conference, he told Dorothy Jewson that since he was himself married and a father, he had a "qualification that [she] did not possess...and consequently he could speak with some little authority."[108] Wives, he implied, were adequately represented by their husbands in the counsels of the labor movement; similarly, the well-being of families could safely be left to men.

The arguments between Davies and Labour feminists like Wilkinson, Loughlin, and Jewson lend some credence to Stocks's interpretation, but in fact none of these figures were especially representative. There is little evidence that most trade unionists shared either Davies's worry or Loughlin's hope that cash allowances would make wives more independent. To the contrary, most men and women in the labor movement on both sides of the issue accepted that while the roles of husband and wife might be different, both would put their children's interests before their own. In evidence to the Joint Committee, only the middle-class feminist organizations and Mrs. Barton of the Women's Cooperative Guild placed much emphasis on the individual economic status of the mother. Mrs. Dooley, a miner's wife and Labour councillor in Yorkshire, doubted whether working-class women were as concerned with economic independence as they were simply with family welfare. "Knowing women as I do," she told the committee,

> I do not think they would concern themselves with that [economic independence] nearly as much as with the problem of the welfare of the children.... In the industrial areas, the women never have anything of their own, but given the right sort of married man and woman, the man doesn't have any more than the woman. She has no more right for money for herself than he has for himself. If she does her work indoors, he does it outdoors.[109]

---

[106] Rhys Davies, "Family Allowances – Good or Bad," *New Leader*, 15: 106 (2 Nov. 1928), p. 8.

[107] E. E. Hunter, "Tory or Communist? Rhys Davies and Family Allowances," *New Leader*, 15: 107 (9 Nov. 1928), p. 5.

[108] Labour Party, *Report*, 30 (1930), pp. 176–7.

[109] TUC File 117.32, Evidence of Mrs. Dooley, 1 Mar. 1928, p. 26.

Not individual rights, but the collective well-being of the family was the principal concern of both parents, Mrs. Dooley implied. The test of measures like family allowances should not be their impact on the authority of either parent vis-à-vis the other, but rather whether they would help both the father and the mother fulfill their different but equally important responsibilities toward their children and so benefit the family as a whole.

Many trade unionists thought they would. Ben Turner of the Textile Workers, one of the pioneers of the prewar period and by this point in his late sixties, believed allowances would allow married women to leave work and "stop at home and be decent housewives." They were thus "the best policy whereby we can save the father's manhood and the mother's womanhood," these identities being, to his mind, inextricable from the roles of breadwinner and mother.[110] Some trade unionists also shared the opinion of many women in the Labour Party that mothers would make better use of money than would local authorities or collective services. John Hill of the Boilermakers, one of the TUC's representatives to the Joint Committee, thus explained to his union that he signed the majority report because "I would trust a mother to feed her children before anyone else in the world."[111] Ted Williams of the Miners' Federation was even willing to argue that "the mother in the home, who works in the home as hard as anyone works in the workshop or the mine . . . is entitled to some kind of remuneration."[112] Yet if few publicly doubted the devotion of mothers, some were uncomfortable with the implication that children were more the mother's responsibility than the father's. Men had responsibilities too, one member of the National Council of the Boot and Shoe Workers objected, and should not be given an excuse to treat those responsibilities lightly or reduce their housekeeping allowances.[113] Some men could oppose allowances, then, not from the "selfishness" that Rathbone was wont to attribute to them, but rather precisely because they took their responsibilities toward their families very seriously, viewing any reliance on state aid as an admission of defeat in the central test of their character both as workers and as fathers.

Relatively little attention was thus paid in Labour and trade union

[110] *Report of the First Annual Women's Trade Union Conference* (London: TUC, 1926), pp. 28–9.
[111] "General Secretary's Remarks," *United Society of Boilermakers and Iron and Steel Shipbuilders Monthly Report*, no. 697 (Aug. 1930), p. 12.
[112] TUC, *Report*, 62 (1930), pp. 404–5.
[113] National Union of Boot and Shoe Operatives, *Official Report* (1930), p. 93.

discussions to the impact of allowances on married women's economic independence: most assumed that mothers were normally unwaged but in charge of household spending and would use any increment on their children. Rather more concern was expressed about the impact of allowances on wage earners themselves – as fathers or mothers, certainly, but also as workers and trade unionists. While unwaged housewives (or "working mothers," as the National Conference of Labour Women called them) clearly supported cash allowances, women and men embedded in labor markets and industrial organizations with complex practices surrounding wage bargaining and, indeed, entry into particular jobs often found their views shaped by their industrial position quite as much as their gender – although the two could certainly be related. The Association of Women Clerks and Secretaries – led by Dorothy Evans, formerly a suffragist and member of the militant Women's Freedom League – thus did support allowances, but scarcely because its members expected to receive them. Rather, the single, professional women in the Women Clerks hoped that state support of dependent children would strengthen employed women's claims for equal pay in a "trade" marked by a marriage bar and separate sex-based pay scales and promotion ladders.[114]

Some married women trade unionists, on the other hand, could actually oppose allowances – against what one might think their interest – out of a fear that such benefits could be used to push them back into their homes with their newly endowed children. Thus, at the 1930 General Conference of the National Union of Boot and Shoe Operatives, the issue of allowances divided members on rather unusual lines. Mrs. Bell-Richards, head of the Leicester Women's Branch, strongly opposed the measure: 63% of her branch were married women, she said, and employers would certainly take into account allowances paid directly to these women workers, making her task of preserving standard rates far more difficult. Some of her male colleagues, on the other hand, hostile to women's employment in a declining trade and constantly menaced by the undercutting of men's wages, were willing to consider almost any measure – whether equal pay, allowances, or statutory regulations restricting women's access to "men's work" – that would force women out and "so see the disappearance of Mrs. Richards and her friends from the industry and from the Conference."[115]

---

[114] TUC File 117.14, Evans to Citrine, 19 Dec. 1928; also, "Family Endowment in Australia," *Woman Clerk*, 2: 4 (Oct. 1927), pp. 198–9.

[115] National Union of Boot and Shoe Operatives, *Official Report* (1930), p. 104.

Mrs. Richards opposed allowances because she perceived them to be in conflict with her constituents' interests as trade unionists. Hers was a minority view among women trade unionists, but she was not alone. During a debate over family allowances at the 1931 conference of the National Union of Distributive and Allied Workers (a union whose M.P.s included both Rhys Davies and Ellen Wilkinson), Davies found an unexpected female ally. Mrs. Bamber, one of NUDAW's national organizers, did not share Mrs. Richards's enthusiasm for married women's work, but she did interpret male trade unionists' support for allowances as the virtual abandonment of both their family duties and their belief in collective action. As both a trade unionist *and a wife and mother*, she reacted with anger to the argument that it was somehow more equitable and progressive for women to be supported through state services than through wages brought up to a decent standard by trade union action. When Wilkinson likened children's allowances to other "rights-based" benefits such as unemployment insurance, she told the conference:

> If you men want to force your women and children to the inquisition that goes on with regard to the Unemployment Insurance Benefit, I think it is time you ceased being trade unionists and handed your work over to Parliament. There is no back door out of the present system only by strong industrial organisation [*sic*]. The People who are supporting Family Allowances are supporting them because they believe it is easier than fighting for their rights from a trade union point of view.... When I was bringing up my family I advised my husband to fight for a decent standard of living to bring up his family and support his wife as he ought to do. That has always been considered the duty, and I am surprised that our men are prepared to hand over what is supposed to be their duty, which is the bringing up of their family.[116]

Mrs. Bamber's comments are illuminating and deserve some attention. While many supporters of allowances claimed they were a "socialist" measure, Mrs. Bamber claimed that they challenged the fundamental premises of *trade unionism*, quite a different thing. One of those premises was indeed that men had the duty to support their families, but in Mrs. Bamber's interpretation, this role as breadwinner by no means entitled him to family dominance; indeed, in her statement she made herself the author and instigator of her husband's role – "I advised my husband" – while simultaneously crediting herself with the accomplishment of "bringing up my family." Family allow-

---

[116] *New Dawn*, 11: 10 (9 May 1931), p. 241.

ances were problematic to Mrs. Bamber not only because they smacked of male irresponsibility – to her mind antithetical to trade unionism – but also because they contravened two other central premises of trade unionism: that earned wages were more honorable than state "doles," and that collective bargaining through self-governing industrial bodies was preferable to any gains handed down to workers from Parliament.

This, then, was the fundamental question for trade unionists: whether family allowances would in any way undermine the principles and power of trade unionism. Mrs. Bamber had one answer to that question and other trade unionists different ones, but all accepted that the question was important. If measures like family allowances were seen to cripple union action, they would surely be rejected. Would they, for example, be cited by employers during wage negotiations as a reason to lower wages? Some trade unionists thought this inevitable. Wages did reflect subsistence needs, A. A. Purcell of the Iron and Steel Trades Confederation insisted, and the only check to the operation of this "iron law" was the fact that they necessarily had to be high enough to support an average family – a check that would be removed by family allowances.[117] Peter Doig, of the Engineering and Shipbuilding Draughtsmen, similarly told Citrine that while the union favored family allowances as an abstract principle, they felt the Speenhamland experiment a century earlier had decisively proved such benefits did lower wages.[118] Other trade unionists opposed the payment of allowances through the insurance system or industrial pools on the grounds that employers would pass on costs to consumers – and therefore to workers – through higher prices. Advocates countered that a tax-based system would have no repercussions on either current or potential wages; they cited the Minority [Labour] Report of the Colwyn Committee on National Debt and Taxation, which argued that tax revenues, unlike direct charges to industry, could not be passed on in higher prices.[119]

In attempting to resolve this issue, both sides made free with supposed "evidence" from experiments on the Continent and in New South Wales. Such evidence was easily manipulated however, leading Walter Citrine to conclude that "the experience of Continental countries is of little value as a guide to what we should do in this country"

---

[117] A. A. Purcell, *The Demand for "Family Allowances"* (Manchester: Manchester and Salford Trades Council, 17 Sept. 1930).
[118] TUC File 117.14, Doig to Citrine, 26 July 1928.
[119] Committee on National Debt and Taxation, *Report*, PP 1927, XI, Cmd. 2800.

and that the union movement should "consider the question in the light of our conditions alone." As Citrine noted, trade unionists had no real ability to predict how allowances would affect wages.[120] This simple fact was enough to turn both Citrine and Ernest Bevin against the proposal. The whole question of allowances, Bevin told the 1929 Labour Party Conference, was "part and parcel of a very intricate and involved wage system, which has not grown up in a day, and which, if we begin to tamper in it slightly, might bring the whole edifice down about our ears."[121] And even if allowances did not complicate collective bargaining, what would their effects be on union recruitment and industrial action?

This was a still more difficult question for supporters of allowances. If children's allowances were seen to be inimical to industrial organization or action, trade unionists would certainly oppose them. The ILP understood this and always tried to argue that allowances would complement trade union action, for example by removing children at least from the line of fire during industrial disputes. Trade unionists worried, however, that such measures could lull workers into a false sense of complacency and into the misguided belief that working-class income could be adequately protected through political action. Trade unionists were indeed concerned about the welfare of children, T. E. Naylor of the London Society of Compositors told the 1929 Labour Party Conference, but he questioned whether the movement could best assist children through allowances *or* "by preserving the powerful position that the Trade Unions hold to-day when they have to negotiate on wages"[122]: the rhetorical opposition implied that he thought the two strategies incompatible. More than one trade union leader interpreted support for family allowances as the admission that trade unionism was "played out" and worried that unions would be likely to lose members if they made such an admission of defeat. Some trade unionists admitted this weakness frankly. "I think we must admit that we have failed in the past in the securing of adequate maintenance for our wives and children," Mr. Frazer of the Boot and Shoe Operatives told his union's general conference. "We have got to look more and more to the political side in conjunction with the industrial side to obtain for ourselves and our dependents an adequate standard of life."[123]

---

[120] TUC File 118, Citrine, "Report on Family Allowances," 22 Feb. 1930, p. 1.
[121] Labour Party, *Report*, 29 (1929), p. 161.
[122] Ibid., p. 166.
[123] National Union of Boot and Shoe Operatives, *Official Report* (1930), p. 91.

The ILP tried to encourage this view. As the ILP's P. J. Dollan put it, "Trade Unionism has everything to gain by the assistance of the State in the regulation of wages and the redistribution of the family income."[124] Yet many trade unionists were uncomfortable with such statements, for obvious and quite compelling reasons. British trade unionism was founded on the assumption that workers could best protect their interests through free collective bargaining and had agreed to state regulation only during national crises, as in the First World War. Mistrust of the "servile state" ran deep. James Beard of the Workers' Union might insist that "the state is only ourselves, after all,"[125] but most trade unionists would have disagreed, seeing at least the national state more as the preserve of conservative forces ever resistant to democratic influences. "We are not going to receive manna from heaven or from Parliament," one unionist told the NUDAW conference in 1931; "We have to get it from our own organisation."[126]

To begin with, trade unionists had real doubts that even progressive legislation could be preserved. Trade unionists who had watched their rights extend and contract as Labour and Conservative governments succeeded each other understandably felt that gains won through the political sphere were unsafe at best. The ILP might attribute the "outstanding omission" – children's allowances – in Labour's election program to a "dangerous conception" of trade unions' exclusive right to deal with wages,[127] but unionists who knew they would have the task of defending wage rates whether Labour was in office or not were reluctant to support legislation they felt could complicate their activities after their political allies had left the scene. Indeed, precisely because the trade unions would have to preserve the power of the labor movement in the country if Labour fell from office, many felt it important not to lessen its autonomy or delegate its functions. Maintaining the strength of the trade unions was more important than keeping Labour in office, John Bromley of the Locomotive Engineers and Firemen held, since the former was the very condition of the latter's existence. Supposing, he asked, "we succeed in keeping for some time a Labour Government but allow the standard of organisation of British Trade Unionism to decay, I prophesy that our Labour Party, without the driving force and help of the Trade Unions behind it, would be a very weak and ineffective instrument."[128]

[124] Labour Party, *Report*, 29 (1929), p. 165.
[125] TUC File 117.32, MacGregor evidence, 7 Mar. 1928, p. 17.
[126] *New Dawn*, 11: 10 (9 May 1931), p. 241.
[127] E. E. Hunter, "The Children's Charter," *New Leader*, 15: 93 (3 Aug. 1928), p. 7.
[128] Labour Party, *Report*, 29 (1929), p. 166.

And even if Labour could be kept in office, some trade unionists certainly had reservations about the party itself and resented being asked to put their industrial weight behind proposals they had had little part in shaping and often found impractical. Some found the very idea that they should be asked to spend time discussing proposals costing over £100 million and with little chance of parliamentary support rather absurd. When surveyed by Citrine in 1929, Charles Kean of the Wall Paper Workers' Union objected to being "constantly pestered with the apparently unattainable," while the National Union of Enginemen, Firemen, Mechanics, and Electrical Workers dryly responded that it felt that the commitments laid out in *Labour and the Nation* were enough to keep the Labour Party busy.[129] Proposals like family allowances were "sometimes promoted by those who have never had experience inside a Trade Union office with all its involved complications," Ernest Bevin pointed out, and he objected both in private and in public when unions were asked to express a view without being given time to debate the issue at their own conferences. "I would warn this Labour Party that that is not a good method of dealing with Trade Union Executives," he told the 1929 party conference.[130] There may have been little love lost between the ILP and the MacDonaldites controlling the Parliamentary Party, but to the trade union movement both could seem equally high-handed. When Labour did take office and proved scarcely more willing to consult with the General Council than the previous Conservative government had been, the council's reluctance to entrust any of their core functions to "the political movement" understandably deepened.

Nor did the ILP's association with the FES endear their cause to trade unionists; efforts by both groups to force the TUC's hand were, if anything, counterproductive. By 1928, having been subjected to a long critique of the perceived bias of the interim report, Milne-Bailey professed himself already "rather tired of Miss Rathbone,"[131] and the society's continued attempts to influence the outcome of the Labour-TUC inquiry by deluging the committee with FES publications, holding public meetings, and circulating letters to the Labour Party and TUC executives left trade unionists, in Arthur Pugh's words, "inclined to resent this attempt to force the hands of trade unions."[132] The society's tendency to adapt its propaganda to its audience, and still

---

[129] TUC File 117.14, Kean to Citrine, 9 Aug. 1928; Hall to Citrine, 12 Feb. 1929.
[130] Labour Party, *Report*, 29 (1929), p. 161; TUC File 117.14, Bevin to Citrine, 30 July 1928.
[131] TUC File 117.13, Rathbone to Milne-Bailey, 26 July 1928; TUC File 117.11, Milne-Bailey to Bondfield, 27 Aug. 1928.
[132] TUC File 118, Pugh to Firth, 11 June 1930.

more their efforts to exploit divisions within the labor movement, also aroused suspicion among the thirty-six members of the Trade Union Group in the Commons, who, although fairly evenly divided on the issue of allowances, were virtually united in their condemnation of the "sharp practice" of the FES.[133] When the ILP adopted such tactics, Pugh predicted that such an "attempt to jockey the trade unions into following the ILP policy on the Family Allowances question . . . will have a contrary effect to what its sponsors imagine."[134]

He was correct. By 1930, resentment of ILP lobbying, suspicion that the Labour Party might be unable to stand by its earlier election commitments, and the growing belief that trade unionists would have to look to their own organizations for salvation had hardened the opposition of a majority of the General Council to the ILP proposals. When Ben Turner spoke movingly in support of a motion by the Miners' Federation at the 1930 congress calling on the General Council to reconsider its vote in favor of the social services option, C. T. Cramp of the National Union of Railwaymen, speaking for the General Council, baldly told him "to confine his nice fatherly speeches that we all like to hear to those gatherings of dear philanthropic ladies and gentlemen of the family endowment society and people of that kind, not all of whom are in the Labour Movement" and concentrate instead on trade union interests.[135] Supporters of allowances had not been able to say very much about their effects on trade unionism, he said, but that, more than anything else, should be the congress's concern. Indeed, Cramp said, he opposed allowances partly because "as a Trade Unionist I object to doing anything at all which is going to benefit the non-unionist."[136] If people wanted to protect their wages and their families, they would have to do so through the trade union movement. The ILP's version of socialism did not interest him:

> If we are merely to have the Socialism handed down in packets to us by somebody else outside our own ranks, if there is not an organised expression of opinion and an organised method of production by men and women organised and associated together, you may get something called Socialism, but it will be a state of society not much better than that which we have at the present time. The Socialism of the superior person I do not want.[137]

---

[133] TUC File 118.1, Memorandum by E. P. Harries, 17 July 1930.
[134] TUC File 118, Pugh to Firth, 16 June 1930.
[135] TUC, *Report*, 62 (1930), p. 407.
[136] Ibid.
[137] Ibid., p. 409.

This may have been a defensive and economistic view of working-class politics, but by 1930 the TUC was in a defensive and economistic mood. The Miners' Federation motion was defeated, and when confronted with an ILP-led revolt at the Labour Party Conference one month later, even the federation closed ranks. The Miners' Federation did indeed support family allowances and intended to do its best to convince its TUC colleagues, John Griffiths of the federation told the conference, but his union nevertheless felt it would be "fatal to the Movement" for the party to come to its own decision in defiance of that expressed by the TUC.[138] "There were people in the Labour Movement who were on the verge of being anti–Trade Unionists," charged Arthur Hayday, at this point chairman of the General Council. If local Labour parties wanted to help the labor movement, they should stop "encouraging non-Unionists" with proposals like children's allowances and instead "become recruiting centres for the Trade Unions," which would then win improved wages for workers.[139] His own position as an MP and his seventeen children notwithstanding, Hayday remained unconvinced of the value of either political action or children's allowances, and his views were not unrepresentative of those of a good part of the General Council. Even though the party accepted that they could not go ahead without the General Council, the long controversy over the ILP's program deepened the mistrust felt between rival wings of the movement. Nor would the worsening depression, MacDonald's defection, and the rout of the 1931 election be likely to increase the TUC's willingness to trust the Labour Party with the task of defending working-class incomes, much less with bringing about "socialism in our time."

Conclusion

At some point in virtually every debate on family endowment held at the Labour Party Conference or the TUC, a woman speaker would challenge not merely the TUC's reservations about allowances but the congress's right to decide the matter altogether. The 300,000 women represented by the National Conference of Labour Women who "gave loyal service to the Movement" had already decided in favor of allowances, Mrs. Johnson of the Norwich Labour Party told the 1927 party conference; the measure did not concern the TUC and should

---

[138] Labour Party, *Report*, 30 (1930), p. 177.
[139] Ibid., p. 178.

be put directly on the party's platform.[140] Mrs. Pease of the Cambridgeshire Labour Party similarly reminded the 1929 conference that married women "belong to one of the largest trades in the world" and were "a large part of the electorate": surely their views deserved some consideration.[141] In 1930, Dorothy Evans of the Women Clerks took this point of view straight to the General Council, pointing out to the TUC conference that working mothers had already pronounced in favor of allowances at numerous conventions. Why then, she asked, was the TUC so unwilling to support them?[142]

Given that family allowances would not be accepted by the Labour Party unless endorsed by the TUC, Evans's frustration was understandable. On another level, however, it was absurd. While it was perfectly reasonable for unwaged wives to insist that Labour Party policy affecting the family should meet their needs as well as those of their husbands, it was hard to see why the TUC should take this as its mandate. Measures like family allowances could increase the well-being of the working class as a whole; they could even increase the income of unionists' families. Unlike wages, however, they were not subject to union negotiation and, unlike unemployment benefits, would not be paid to men. Even if they improved conditions, they would do so in ways that would marginalize trade unions as institutions and trade unionists as recipients. The treatment of Labour women's claims by the TUC revealed only that the TUC faithfully represented the interests of its constituents: (largely male) trade unionists. This was a shock only to those who, taking the movement's expansive rhetoric at face value, persisted in seeing it as the vanguard of a unified working class. Certainly Milne-Bailey never suffered from this delusion. "The Labour interest represented by Trade Unionism," he wrote in his 1934 study, *Trade Unions and the State*, "is not the class interest of the 'dispossessed,' the 'proletariat,' the 'victims of capitalism,' " but was rather "a vocational interest, a functional interest."[143] Labour women suffered less from explicit TUC hostility than from a structure of Labour policy-making in which their gains had to come from an institution to which they were marginal.

In the end, then, the controversy over the "living wage" program exposed less the "male prejudice" that the FES was wont to see in

---

[140] Labour Party, *Report*, 27 (1927), p. 218.

[141] Ibid., 29 (1929), p. 167.

[142] TUC, *Report*, 62 (1930), p. 397.

[143] W. Milne-Bailey, *Trade Unions and the State* (London: Allen & Unwin, 1934), p. 91.

the labor movement than the structural contradiction that lay at its heart. The Labour Party attempted to be both the party of the working class and the parliamentary arm of the trade union movement; occasionally, however, those two roles came into conflict. The ILP wanted the party to consider the former role paramount: when the General Council rejected the majority report, the *New Leader* was pleased to call on the party to go ahead without them. "It is the business of the Labour Movement to put into effect policies which will benefit the greatest number, and, however important sectional interests may be, they cannot be allowed to have overriding control."[144] As the fate of the ILP program demonstrated, however, the General Council was no mere "sectional interest." Rather, with over half of the Labour Executive elected directly by the unions, with the unions' block vote constraining all policy decisions, and local Labour parties often simply local trades councils in their "political" guise, the party was unlikely to flout the wishes of the TUC. The campaign for allowances merely made explicit in policy what was implicit in structure: while the movement could house a broad spectrum of views and enthusiasms, when the TUC considered its interests at stake, its view tended to prevail.

After the 1931 debacle, the labor movement resolved the conflict between its "intellectuals" and trade unionists, but only by accelerating the disaffiliation of the ILP from the party and increasing the General Council's explicit control over Labour policy-making. At a joint meeting of the Labour Party Executive and the General Council in November 1931, Walter Citrine attributed the 1931 catastrophe in part to the reluctance of the government to meet with the General Council and stated baldly that the council "did not seek in any shape or form to say what the Party was to do, but they did ask that the primary purpose of the creation of the Party should not be forgotten. It was created by the Trade Union Movement to do those things in Parliament which the Trade Union Movement found ineffectively performed by the two-party system."[145] The General Council, led by Bevin and Citrine, reasserted its control through increased union representation on Labour's National Joint Council, at whose meetings all policy was henceforth discussed. After 1931, the internal organization of the labor movement began to reflect more accurately the

---

[144] Political correspondent, "Trade Unions and Children's Allowances," *New Leader*, 18: 191 (20 June 1930), p. 6.
[145] TUC Archives, GC minutes, 10 Nov. 1931.

sea change undergone by the British political system since 1914, in which economic interests gained at least a consultative role over areas of policy-making in which they were implicated.[146]

The campaign for family allowances, in its socialist incarnation, was an attempt to convert the Labour Party to a far more explicit program of redistribution and economic control than the party had ever proposed. We can only speculate at how far the family allowances proposal would have gone had it been actually adopted by the party conference; most likely, the electoral weakness of the Labour Party, the conservatism of MacDonald and Snowden, and the pressure of financial orthodoxy would have been enough to preclude such radical measures. The point, however, is that the campaign never progressed that far: it was killed by opposition within the labor movement itself. The failure of the Joint Committee's investigation ended any hope for the development of a national family policy by a "progressive" alliance of feminists, socialists, and trade unionists in the interwar period, although – as Jane Mark-Lawson, Mike Savage, and Alan Warde have shown – Labour women were sometimes able to pressure local parties to reject economistic policies in the thirties and hasten the development of the maternal and child services so important to housebound women.[147] After the "no" vote of the General Council, the embargo on comprehensive family policy held until the Second World War, and even then, Citrine was confident that the Labour Party would withhold official support until the unions consented.[148]

The overwhelming concern exhibited by British trade unionists to protect the integrity of the male wage shaped not only the ultimate structure of the welfare state, but also the distributive system more broadly. In Britain the lethargy of employers and the opposition of the TUC ensured that family allowances would not be introduced even in the most compelling cases – as, for example, in the coal in-

---

[146] Keith Middlemas, *Politics in Industrial Society* (London: André Deutsch, 1979), esp. pp. 321–2; Martin, *TUC*, pp. 228–33.

[147] Mark-Lawson, Savage, and Warde argue that working-class women in particular benefited from the expansion of social services in the interwar period, but that only some local Labour Party branches made such services (rather than men's work and wages) their priority – the best predictor of the party's local enthusiasm for services being the strength of women within the party and the degree to which women were integrated into the labor force on the same terms as men. See Jane Mark-Lawson, Mike Savage, and Alan Warde, "Gender and Local Politics: Struggles Over Welfare Policies, 1918–1939," in Linda Murgatroyd et al., eds., *Localities, Class and Gender* (London: Pion, 1985), pp. 195–215.

[148] TUC File 118.2, Citrine to Dukes, 1 July 1940.

dustry – despite the sympathy of many economists, "experts," and politicians. This did not mean, however, that no family policy would develop in Britain, just that such policy was, in the terms of Sheila Kamerman and A. J. Kahn, "implicit and reluctant," always subordinated to the protection of the male family wage.[149] In France, by contrast, determined and self-interested employers overcame union opposition and government incapacity to introduce family policies that to some extent disaggregated the family wage. It is to their initiatives that we now turn.

---

[149] Sheila B. Kamerman and Alfred J. Kahn, *Family Policy: Government and Families in Fourteen Countries* (New York: Columbia University Press, 1978).

5

BUSINESS STRATEGIES AND THE FAMILY

The development of family allowances
in France, 1920–1936

Between 1929 and 1931, while British feminists and socialists watched their redistributive visions vanish under the cold light of economic depression and fiscal retrenchment, French politicians and civil servants introduced a set of legislative measures that would provide a successful framework for French family policy for decades to come. Their plans reflected not a decisive increase in state capacities, nor a willingness by the state to assume new and heavy financial burdens. Rather, policymakers acted largely to preserve and extend measures that had developed within private industry and that had gone some distance in the twenties toward the goal – increasingly seen as desirable by broad sections of public opinion – of better adjusting family resources to family needs.

The success of French private initiatives thus stands in stark contrast to British failures – and requires explanation. What drove French industrialists to establish welfare funds (*caisses de compensation*) and to pay out substantial benefits to workers with young children? Contemporary French scholars, writing in scores of unimaginative and virtually indistinguishable tomes, tended to see employers' initiatives as part of a broader public commitment – motivated by patriotism, religious sentiment, and a desire for social peace – to restore the French family.[1] Some recent scholars have echoed their formulations, so that

[1] The best guide to the literature on family allowances is Nadine Nada, *Bibliographie sur les prestations familiales, 1911–1965* (Paris: UNCAF, 1966). There are far too many individual studies to mention all of them; the best interwar studies are Jean Pinte, *Les allocations familiales* (Paris: Sirey, 1935); Georges Bonvoisin and Gustave Maignan, *Allocations familiales et caisses de compensation* (Paris: Sirey, 1930); Yves Helleu, *Les caisses de compensation d'allocations familiales depuis la loi du 11 mars 1932* (Paris: Librairie Technique et Économique, 1937); and Pierre Mazas, *Le fondement de l'obligation aux allocations familiales* (Paris: Sirey, 1936). Le Comité Central des Allocations Familiales itself gen-

France's pioneering role in the area of family policy appears merely as the inevitable outcome of prevailing cultural and religious preoccupations.[2]

But this happy scenario leaves puzzling issues unresolved. Why were costly children's allowances so attractive to private industry – and to particular sectors within private industry – at a time when French industrialists were concerned to rebuild, modernize, and streamline production after the ravages of war? There would appear to be a substantial economic disincentive to commit a significant amount of money – some 2 to 6 percent of the wage bill – to programs that, employers insisted, were entirely benevolent. The demographic fears that made state intervention imaginable and the wartime inflation that pushed the government to introduce child allowances within the sheltered sector cannot explain the extension of family policy within private industry.

It was the ability of big business to use family allowances in the service of a broader vision of economic reconstruction and rationalization that was most central to the spread of family allowances during

erated a good deal of information, including guides for recipients, manuals for *caisse* administrators, and a monthly bulletin.

[2] For a discussion of family policy within an alarmist demographic framework, see Joseph J. Spengler, *France Faces Depopulation* (Durham, N.C.: Duke University Press, 1938). Robert Talmy treats the growth of the *caisse* system within the context of the social Catholic movement in his exhaustive study *Histoire du mouvement familial en France, 1896–1939*, 2 vols. (Paris: UNCAF, 1962); Antoine Prost also stresses the influence of social Catholicism in "Catholic Conservatives, Population, and the Family in Twentieth-Century France," in Michael S. Teitelbaum and Jay M. Winter, eds., *Population and Resources in Western Intellectual Traditions* (Cambridge University Press, 1988), pp. 147–64. The best account of the development of family allowances within the context of the history of social security in France, and one that pays adequate attention to the pivotal role of industrialists is Henri Hatzfeld, *Du paupérisme à la sécurité sociale, 1850–1940* (Paris: Armand Colin, 1971). The Caisse Nationale d'Allocations Familiales has published several useful studies, most notably Jacques Hochard, *Aspects économiques des prestations familiales* (Paris: UNCAF, 1961), and Dominique Ceccaldi, *Histoire des prestations familiales en France* (Paris: UNCAF, 1957); their *Bulletin* is also helpful. Several monographs on individual *caisses* have been published under the auspices of the Comité d'Histoire de la Sécurité Sociale, which also has published relevant historical articles in its *Bulletin de Liaison*. The published acts of the Congrès National des Sociétés Savantes' yearly colloquium on the history of social security often contain useful articles on family policy. The relationship between family policy and the status of women, almost entirely ignored in the contemporary literature, has been given some treatment in Yvonne Knibielher and Catherine Fouquet, *Histoire des mères du moyen-âge à nos jours* (Paris: Montalba, 1977), and Françoise Thébaud, *Quand nos grand-mères donnaient la vie: La maternité en France dans l'entre-deux-guerres* (Lyon: Presses Universitaires de Lyon, 1986).

the interwar period. Not that employers who set up the *caisses de compensation* eschewed nationalist arguments; certainly they shared the demographic alarmism of their contemporaries and their class. As the family allowance movement spread, however, employers turned to the potent rhetorics of social Catholicism and pronatalism to justify rather than explain their central motivations. The extension of family allowances depended less on the conversion of big business to the "just wage," than the transformation of the *caisse* system to suit the economic interests of businessmen who were quite unconcerned with the social theories of Leo XIII.

From the beginning, the *caisses de compensation* were directly linked to the employers' organizations within a particular trade. A *caisse* often shared office space with a regional employers' syndicate; their staffs often overlapped. As we shall see, their leaders and principal propagandists – men like Eugène Mathon in textiles and Pierre Richmonde in engineering – also tended to direct purchasing combines and organize wage-setting strategies within their sectors. Recent historians have often made light of the organizational capacities of French businessmen before the shock treatment of the Popular Front,[3] but in the area of social policy employers demonstrated a striking capacity for combination and self-advancement. Yet even within the serried ranks of the Comité Central des Allocations Familiales, differences existed as to the precise economic aim to be sought from family allowances. Different industries attempted to use family allowances to achieve different ends.

Close study of the development of the *caisse* system in particular industries can reveal the connection between business strategies and family policy. After briefly examining the growth of the *caisse* system in the period before state control, this chapter presents detailed studies of two of the most important family allowance funds, the Consortium Textile de Roubaix-Tourcoing and the Caisse de Compensation de la Région Parisienne (CCRP). Both cases confirm the central place of family allowances within the business strategies of the highly organized employers who set up the *caisses*. Together, they also reveal that the specific uses of allowances varied with the technical needs and structure of labor relations within the given industries. While the textile employers of Roubaix-Tourcoing attempted to use allowances to recruit and stabilize the labor force, the engineering and automobile employers in the Paris region saw allowances as a means of restraining wages during the boom years of the twenties. In the short run, both strategies were highly successful. In the long run, however, the Parisian conception of allowances as a means of disaggregating a wage bill that otherwise had to allow for dependents' needs proved far more susceptible to broader extension than the combative and illiberal policies of the textile employers.

Family allowances and ideologies of social renewal

Although family allowances ultimately spread because they were compatible with employers' interests, those industrialists, reformers, and philanthropists who developed the earliest programs were often social Catholics and were impelled both by religious convictions and by a genuine humanitarian sentiment. The man usually credited with conceiving of the first *caisse de compensation*, Emile Romanet, was both a devout Catholic and an enthusiastic advocate of industrial cooperation. Social Catholics like Romanet drew on the earlier experiments of Léon Harmel: like Harmel, they saw family allowances as only one part of a broader attempt to make capitalism conform to Christian teachings. They held that paying a family wage was a religious duty for the *patron*, not a voluntary charitable gesture. The ties between an employer and his workers were like those between a father and his children, Romanet wrote; employers "must interest themselves in their workers and love them, just as a father loves and cares for the children that God has given him."[4] Similar ties of *paternité* bound the worker to his family and gave the worker a just claim to the family wage. Work was not a commodity to be bought and sold, but a human act requiring for its just recompense a sum enabling the worker to fulfill all his duties as a full human being: personal, familial, and social.[5]

In 1916, Romanet was the managing director of the Grenoble engineering firm of Régis Joya, which had already invested heavily in social work organized in accordance with Catholic doctrine. That year, when confronted with workers' complaints that they could not make ends meet on their wages, Romanet conducted a study of workers'

---

[4] Emile Romanet, *Le salaire familial* (Grenoble: Aubert, 1918); copy in Archives Nationales (AN) 39 AS 387.
[5] Emile Romanet, *La répartition équitable des bénéfices* (Grenoble: Les Alpes Industrielles, 1920), p. 6; copy in AN 39 AS 387.

budgets. Those with two or more children were in real need, he concluded, and in October he convinced Joya to begin paying family allowances. One month later, the local metal syndicate agreed that allowances on the same scale would be paid by all member firms. The cost of allowances weighed unequally on firms, however, with those employing many fathers of families bearing most of the cost. As a result, in May 1918 the Grenoble metal syndicate itself agreed to set up a fund to take over the payment of allowances, taxing all participating employers at about 5% of their wage bill. The disincentive to hiring fathers of families was removed, and the first equalization fund – *caisse de compensation* – created.[6]

The heavily paternalistic Grenoble *caisse* paid allowances to the father and for a brief period included an allowance for unwaged wives in the hopes of encouraging women to remain in the home.[7] Catholic sentiments also influenced other pioneers. Louis Deschamps, a textile manufacturer prominent in the social Catholic circles of the Semaines Sociales, founded the Caisse Patronale de Sursalaire Familial among his fellow textile employers in Rouen in 1919. Like Romanet, he saw this "family wage" as only one part of a wider social Catholic campaign to revive corporatist organization, to defend workers' rights to representation and organization, and to introduce profit sharing.[8]

The Grenoble and Rouen experiments received wide publicity, but other industrialists, while paying fulsome tribute to the humanitarian impulses of Romanet and Deschamps, had little interest in their broader Catholic agenda. They were more sympathetic to the demographic concerns that swept French ruling circles during the immediate postwar period. French businessmen, organized in the Chambers of Commerce, were important in establishing the yearly conferences aimed at coordinating efforts to increase the birthrate. Pronatalist businessmen looked to family allowances as a hopeful first step and called on employers to set up more family allowance funds.[9]

[6] Romanet, *Le salaire familial*; Etablissements Régis Joya, *Souvenir de la fête du 11 janvier 1920* (Grenoble, 1920), copy in AN 39 AS 387; and the preamble to the Bokanowski bill, cited later in text. On Romanet, see Paul Dreyfus, *Emile Romanet, père des allocations familiales* (Paris: Arthaud, 1965), esp. pp. 45–60, 67, 78–9.

[7] Henri Lapuyade, *Le sursalaire familial* (Toulouse: J. Fournier, 1921), pp. 107–8.

[8] See speeches by Deschamps in Congrès National de la Natalité, *Compte rendu*, 2 (1920), pp. 182–200; "Le sursalaire familial à Rouen," in Semaine Sociale de France, *Compte rendu*, 11 (1919), pp. 163–8; and "Le point de vue du patronat vis-à-vis des révendications du travail," in Semaine Sociale de France, *Compte rendu* 12 (1920), pp. 85–112. See also Emile Romanet, *Organisation des entreprises au point du vue social* (Mulhouse: Bader, 1921), copy in AN 39 AS 387.

[9] Talmy, *Histoire du mouvement familial*, 1, pp. 206–11.

The *caisses* did in fact spread rapidly in 1920 and 1921: the Ministry of Labor reported some twenty in existence within private industry by 1 July 1920, and a further fifteen by the end of August.[10] That autumn, the second Birthrate Conference called on the *caisses* to establish a confederation, which could then encourage employers to affiliate, collect documentation, and, crucially, fight state control.[11] In December, industrialists employing some 2 million workers met in Roubaix under the presidency of Auguste Isaac, head of the association of fathers of large families and minister of commerce in the Bloc National, and established the Comité Central des Allocations Familiales, under the leadership of textile manufacturer Eugène Mathon.[12]

The limits to their pronatalist fervor, however, are revealed by their reception to the earliest plans for state control of the allowance system, which were formulated not by socialists but rather by pronatalist deputies in the Chamber itself. Early in 1920, Maurice Bokanowski, a "left Republican" (read, centrist) and later minister of commerce, submitted a bill calling on the government to require all employers – whether in industry, commerce, agriculture, or domestic service – to enroll in a fund paying monthly allowances to mothers for each child, with additional allowances for pregnancy, birth, and nursing. The generous allowances envisaged were to be funded by the employers, who were also to retain administrative control.[13] Yet the employers who had initiated the *caisses* mobilized in strength to defeat the Bokanowski proposition. A long list of employers' and familist organizations and conferences – including the Assembly of Presidents of Chambers of Commerce, the Union des Intérêts Economiques, the Birthrate Conference, and the newly formed Congrès National des Allocations Familiales – rejected compulsory enrollment of firms. The meddling of civil servants, they charged, would increase costs, destroy the flexibility of the *caisse* system, and in the words of Auguste Isaac, "bury practical solutions in a heap of forms and red tape, which will in the end disgust everyone."[14] Even social Catholics convinced that

[10] "Les allocations pour charges de famille," *Bulletin du Ministère du Travail*, 27: 3–4 (Mar.–Apr. 1920), p. 116; 27: 5–7 (May–July, 1920), p. 221.

[11] Congrès National de la Natalité, *Compte rendu*, 2 (1920), pp. 227–8.

[12] Talmy, *Histoire du mouvement familial*, 2, p. 132.

[13] *Journal Officiel* [*JO*], *Documents (Chambre)*, 1920, ann. 386, p. 561.

[14] Auguste Isaac, "Discours," Congrès National des Allocations Familiales [CNAF], *Compte rendu*, 1 (1921), p. 14. For a discussion of the movement against state intervention, see Aymé Bernard, "Les caisses de compensation et l'intervention de l'état," Congrès National de la Natalité, *Compte rendu*, 3 (1921), pp. 120–8; Aymé Bernard, "Rapport sur l'autonomie des caisses et l'intervention législative," CNAF, *Compte rendu*, 1 (1921),

the family wage was a social duty and not charity revocable at will were reluctant to bring in the state. Louis Deschamps claimed that he would be tempted to support the bill "if I didn't know how dearly the State makes us pay for its intervention. Beware, Gentlemen, the Welfare State; and beware of its bureaucrats. Don't you think we already support a large enough number?"[15]

Despite this opposition, the Chamber's Social Insurance Commission was sympathetic to the Bokanowski proposition and authorized its reporter, Victor Jean, to draft a law covering all state and local government, large industry, and commerce.[16] They recognized, however, that such sweeping legislation would require the consent of both the ministries and the employers concerned. Charles Picquenard, the permanent official who formulated much of the policy of the Ministry of Labor during the entire interwar period, thus submitted the question to the Conseil Supérieur du Travail, which represented both employers and workers, in the hopes of getting its members to speak with a single voice. They did so, but not as the enthusiastic deputies might have hoped. Of the employers, only those public works contractors who already paid allowances – and who found their higher labor costs a disadvantage when bidding for government work – supported state intervention. Trade union delegates, while fearing that the cost of allowances would, in the end, fall on workers, nevertheless viewed allowances as a peripheral question detracting attention from the more central issue of social insurance legislation. Unions were to discover in time that family allowances could be both a crucial support for working-class families and an effective employer strategy for controlling labor and would come to argue for a national system free of employers' control. At this 1921 meeting, however, employer and union delegates agreed that discussion of legal obligation should be adjourned until social insurance had been discussed, effectively postponing action for ten years.[17]

The sharp opposition to state control expressed by the employers' representatives and the lethargy of the representatives of the unions convinced the Ministry of Labor to halt the legislative process. Despite

pp. 68–75. Individual resolutions can be found in the congress reports of the CNAF for 1921–4 and at the second and third Congrès National de la Natalité.

[15] Congrès National de la Natalité, *Compte rendu*, 2 (1920), p. 191.

[16] Assemblée Nationale Archives (Versailles), Box A 13, Procès verbaux de la Commission d'Assurance et de Prévoyance Sociales, 4 Mar. and 29 Apr. 1921.

[17] Conseil Supérieur du Travail, 25ᵉ sess. (Nov. 1921), *I. Compte rendu*, pp. 19–50; *II. Rapport sur les allocations familiales*, pp. 63–71.

the continued interest of the Chamber's Social Insurance Commission in a more extensive law, the state intervened only to require that all public works contractors pay allowances to their employees.[18] The continued hostility of employers, the opposition of the Ministry of Finance even to proposals that would cost the state nothing, and the absorption of the Chamber in the ten-year battle over social insurance shifted family allowances to the sidelines. Except in the restricted sphere of pronatalist benefits for large families, discussed in Chapter 2, the state gave employers a free rein over family policy throughout the twenties.

Left to their own devices, employers did expand the network of the funds. By 1932, when the government passed a law – discussed in Chapter 7 – making affiliation to a family allowance fund mandatory, there were 255 such funds, organized either on regional or industrial bases, covering almost 2 million workers and paying out almost Fr 400 million per year (Table 5.1). Beyond the defensive fear of state intervention, what can account for such a sustained effort on the part of French industry? Precisely what employers did with allowances will be discussed in the next two sections, but what they did not do is also significant, particularly in view of their heavily moralistic rhetoric. They did not use allowances to try to build a new economic harmony based on shared faith, nor did they tailor them to purely pronatalist ends.

Fissures between social Catholic doctrine and the interests of the large employers' organizations who led the family allowance movement were apparent as early as 1921, when the first annual conference of the funds attempted to clarify its philosophy on family allowances. Social Catholics agreed with employers that payment of allowances should rest with the "profession" and not the state, but not primarily because they wished to spare employers the nuisance of meddling bureaucrats. Rather, Catholics hoped to use institutions like family allowances to moderate economic liberalism by strengthening moral obligations across class lines. Employers, however, would have none of it. The seemingly arcane debate at conferences and within the ubiquitous law theses over whether the allowance should be called a wage supplement (*sursalaire*) or an allowance (*allocation*) was an ar-

---

[18] Assemblée Nationale Archives, Box A 13, Procès verbaux de la Commission d'Assurance et de Prévoyance Sociales, 15 and 30 June, and 6 July 1922. For the 1922 law, see *JO Documents (Chambre)*, 1922, ann. 4635, p. 1271, and ann. 4745, p. 1455; *JO Documents (Sénat)*, 1922, ann. 709.

Table 5.1. *National growth of the caisses de compensation*

Year	Number of *caisses*	Companies affiliated	Workers covered (thousands)	Families benefiting (thousands)	Allowances paid (million francs)
1920	6	230	50	11	4
1921	52	4,000	525	—	—
1922	75	5,200	665	153	70
1923	120	7,600	880	—	92
1924	130	—	950	—	—
1925	160	10,000	1,150	266	142
1926	184	—	1,220	—	168
1927	210	16,200	1,420	—	230
1928	218	20,000	1,500	300	260
1929	229	25,000	1,740	—	292
1930	232	32,000	1,820	480	342
1931	230	—	1,850	—	—
1932	255	30,000	1,850	460	380

Note: Statistics for 1920–30 are usually given as of January 1; those for 1932 as of December 31.
Sources: Georges Bonvoisin, *The French Institution of Family Allowances* (Paris: Centre d'Informations Documentaires, n.d.), p. 4; Dominique Ceccaldi, *Histoire des prestations familiales en France* (Paris: UNCAF, 1957), pp. 21, 51; CNAF, *Comptes rendus*; William Oualid and Charles Picquenard, *Salaires et tarifs, conventions collectives et grèves: La politique du Ministère du Travail* (Paris: Presses Universitaires de France, 1928), p. 484; M. R. Clark, "Organized Labour and the Family Allowance System in France," *Journal of Political Economy*, 39:4 (1931), p. 528.

gument in code over whether the allowance was a new, Christian, wage form, henceforth required of all Christian employers, or merely a voluntary charitable gesture.

Employers opted for the latter. At the first annual conference of the funds they resolved that the expression *sursalaire* be avoided, and the funds' Comité Central held firmly throughout the period to the view that the allowance was a free gift, utterly distinct from wages – and therefore subject neither to collective bargaining negotiations nor to regulations.[19] Louis Deschamps's impassioned defense of the Catholic doctrine of the "just wage" (and the term *sursalaire*) at the 1925 conference of the funds fell on deaf ears:

> We aren't benevolent employers, who bestow a bounty we could just as well not bestow; we are just employers who acknowledge in the

[19] CNAF, *Compte rendu*, 1 (1921), p. 98.

worker with children, he who has more troubles and cares than the others, a moral right – I don't say a legal right, but a moral right which is nevertheless a right – to see his added work and expenses compensated by additional resources.[20]

By the midtwenties, Catholics realized family allowances were an institution they supported but could not control, and they began to moderate their opposition to state intervention.[21]

Employers paid slightly more attention to pronatalist sentiment, particularly in view of the strength of the pronatalist group in the Chamber, but here as well they used rhetoric to muster support for policies that had primarily other ends. Few family allowance programs were set up in the first instance to increase the birthrate, but employers usually shared a vague fear of national and demographic decline and welcomed the support of the 25,000-strong Alliance Nationale.[22] Furthermore, a few industrialists were avid "repopulators," most notably the Michelin brothers, who bankrolled the Alliance Nationale during the twenties.[23] The Michelins had instituted very generous benefits for families of three children or more in 1916, and by 1925 they were convinced that their policy had had a significant effect on the birthrate in the towns in which their firms were located. They passed on their results to the Conseil Supérieur de la Natalité (CSN) and in 1926 published a pamphlet showing a birthrate anywhere from 50% to 250% higher in families of Michelin workers than among the general population of the town. They warned that if the single-child family remained the norm, the population of France would be halved in thirty years: "that means: half the fields fallow, half the factories shut; our splendid colonies, capable of feeding many populations like that of France, abandoned to foreigners." Employers could avert these dire consequences by affiliating with a family allowance fund.[24]

---

[20] Ibid., 5 (1925), p. 16.

[21] For an early Catholic argument for state intervention, see Etienne Martin Saint-Léon, "Le problème des allocations familiales," in *Semaine Sociale de France, Compte rendu,* 17 (1925), pp. 453–71.

[22] Membership figures are from *Revue de l'Alliance Nationale* [hereafter *Revue*], no. 145 (Aug. 1924), p. 246.

[23] Ibid., no. 149 (Dec. 1924), p. 355.

[24] André Michelin, *Une expérience concluante: La natalité dans les usines Michelin* (Paris: Alliance Nationale, [1926]), p. 12, copy in the Archives of the Ministry of Labor, SAN 7548, File: "Documentation sur les oeuvres sociales de Michelin et Cie, 1923–37"; see also Michelin, *Une expérience de natalité* (Clermont-Ferrand: Michelin, 1926), in Ministry of Labor, SAN 7734, File: "Encouragement à la natalité en France, 1928–1943." The Michelin claims were discussed in M. Vieuille, "Rapport sur l'efficacité de l'aide à la famille," in Conseil Supérieur de la Natalité [CSN], *Rapports et voeux,* 1925, no. 4, 7ᵉ sess. (June 1925), pp. 40–1.

The Alliance Nationale distributed the Michelin tract widely, claiming that its statistics conclusively proved that households receiving family allowances had more children.[25] This was unquestionably true, but were the allowances inducing people to have more children, or did families with children simply gravitate to firms paying allowances? Two government health inspectors argued that the Michelin study was statistically suspect: the "Michelin" and "non-Michelin" groups in the firm's factory towns were far from comparable, since Michelin employees were overwhelmingly working class and of childbearing age. Scrutinizing the figures, they pointed out that Michelin's high birthrate coexisted with a low number of children per family, indicating a high proportion of young couples but no tendency toward *familles nombreuses*.[26] The Michelins, however, continued to defend their study and to urge extension of the family allowance funds as a cure for underpopulation. "There is a cure for *denatalité*," they argued, "a simple and effective cure: the family allowance."[27]

The Comité Central, while more moderate in its claims, fed these hopes. It conducted a continuing investigation in the twenties of the birthrate among affiliated firms and pointed out that it was far higher than that of comparable age groups within the general population.[28] Georges Bonvoisin, Director of the Comité Central, presented these results at the yearly Birthrate Conferences and in articles, and the Alliance Nationale at least was certainly convinced of his claims.[29] Employers, however, were wary of excessive pronatalist enthusiasm, fearing it would feed demands for state control. In time, their fears were borne out: pronatalist groups did eventually call for state action to raise and extend allowances. In the early twenties, however, many pronatalists shared a dim view of the "red tape" of *étatisme* and lauded the "patriotism and self-sacrifice" of the employers, which, they claimed, "contrast[ed] singularly with the attitude of the

---

[25] "Les industriels et la natalité: L'action de MM. Michelin et ses résultats," *Revue*, no. 163 (Feb. 1926), pp. 33–42; Fernand Boverat, "Nos gouvernants et les caisses de compensation," *Revue*, no. 166 (May 1926), pp. 137–9.

[26] Dr. G. Dequidt and Dr. G. Forestier, "Une expérience de natalité: L'efficacité des allocations familiales sur la natalité est-elle demontrée?" *Le Mouvement Sanitaire* (31 July 1926), pp. 485–503, in Ministry of Labor, SAN 7547, File: "Aide et encouragement . . . , 1930–45."

[27] Michelin et Cie, "Une expérience de natalité," *Prosperité*, 1: 4 (Jan.–Mar. 1929), p. 3.

[28] See the yearly reports by Col. Guillermin comparing the birthrate among families receiving allowances with that of the general population in the CNAF *Comptes rendus*.

[29] See, e.g., G. Bonvoisin, "La politique des allocations exerce-t-elle une influence sur le taux de la natalité?" *Revue Médico-Sociale*, 6: 6 (1938), pp. 502–7.

Government, which does nothing serious to ensure the future of the country."[30] The Alliance Nationale provided the funds with much free propaganda, but the funds, while grateful, never delivered themselves over to pronatalist aims. In 1936, Pierre Richemond, president of the Caisse de Compensation de la Région Parisienne (CCRP), the largest fund, admitted bluntly, "To tell the truth, while congratulating ourselves on the pronatalist effects of family allowances, the equalization funds never operated on that basis."[31]

If social Catholicism and pronatalism were at best secondary considerations and at worst useful rhetorical blinds, what was the primary purpose of the *caisse* system? A close look at the links between the development of these family benefits and the industrial strategies and labor relations within particular economic sectors can suggest some answers. It was no accident that even those employers with the most activist agendas – social Catholics like Romanet or pronatalists like the Michelin brothers – were concentrated either in the most advanced sectors of the economy, like metals and engineering, or in the hard-pressed but highly organized textile sector. Industrialists in these sectors were attracted to family allowances in the hope that such flexible payment systems, in some cases coupled with Fordist management techniques, could revive French competitiveness in the postwar era.

On a few notable occasions, these leading employers made their strategy explicit. In 1922, Georges Bonvoisin explained to the second Congrès National how allowances could reconcile the seemingly contradictory needs of cost containment and aid to large families. It was evident to all, he asserted, that the crisis in industry – and especially in the export trades – was due to France's relatively high production costs; hence, the overwhelming need was to reduce what was in most industries the major production cost, the wage bill. Yet, Bonvoisin added, industrialists were also aware that they had an interest in the stability, health, and morality of the labor force, and hence in paying their workers decently. Family policy could reconcile these two seemingly antithetical interests. Workers with children did need more than single males, he admitted, but such workers were a minority, and paying all workers a family wage would be excessive and merely force up prices. A better alternative was to use family allowances to dis-

[30] "Le progrès des allocations familiales," *Revue*, no. 128 (Mar. 1923), pp. 91.
[31] Archives of the Caisse de Compensation de la Région Parisienne [CCRP], now at the Caisse d'Allocations Familiales de la Région Parisienne (rue Viala), Commission de Gestion, Procès verbal, 22 July 1936.

aggregate wages: to pay "a wage corresponding to the needs of a single person, but supplemented with allowances for fathers of families."[32]

And family allowances offered employers other benefits. They could, according to Bonvoisin, make attendance more regular, weaken unions, and break strikes. The fear of losing allowances had successfully prevented family men from joining a political strike, he reported in 1923, while in another case housewives unwilling to do without allowances were forcing their husbands back to work without the traditional "St. Monday" holiday.[33] Judging from the claims of the Comité Central, family allowances could solve businessmen's most serious economic problems. How (and how well) did they do so, and what were the consequences for the development of French family policy? Let us look more closely at their operation in specific industrial sectors.

Family allowances as paternalistic control: The Consortium Textile de Roubaix-Tourcoing

If French businessmen looked to family allowances for economic rather than ideological reasons, what exactly did they hope to gain? It is, in fact, difficult to disentangle their motives, even within the realm of economic self-interest, for the aims of rationalization, wage restraint, and labor control were often mixed. In particular cases, however, particular strategies predominated. One of the most distinctive – and extreme – uses of family allowances was that conceived by the highly organized textile industry in the towns of Roubaix and Tourcoing.

The Consortium Textile de Roubaix-Tourcoing provides a particularly good case for study not because its wage and benefit policies were typical of most *caisses*, but because they served as a model for the rest of the family allowance movement. The Consortium's family allowance system was the showpiece of the Comité Central in the early twenties: it paid the highest rates, included the vast majority of textile firms in the region, and was efficiently – if autocratically – administered. The Consortium, although only one of seventy-five French *caisses* in 1922, included 10% of all workers eligible for family allowances and paid out 20% of all allowances paid through the *caisses*. The Consortium was headed by the powerful woollen manufacturer Eugène Mathon, who, not coincidentally, was also the head of the Comité

[32] CNAF, *Compte rendu*, 2 (1922), p. 71.
[33] Ibid., 3 (1923), p. 144.

Central, and who exercised a decisive influence on the policies of both. Furthermore, the Consortium became the self-conscious spokesman of the *patronat du droit divin*, propagandizing in favor of a modernized form of paternalistic control and against the new state-endorsed commitment to collective bargaining.[34]

Family allowances were the central tool of the Consortium's strategy and were envisaged as achieving a number of ends. They could, obviously, act as an alternative to – and thus a brake on – wages, but this was not their only function. In addition, the Consortium tried to use family allowances to construct a highly illiberal labor control policy and to break the backs of the unions. Quite simply, employers set allowances at a high level and then made their receipt conditional on uninterrupted presence in the factory, thus undermining the right to strike and, consequently, union power. For most of the twenties, when the Consortium maintained employer unity and avoided all discussion with the unions, this strategy seemed successful. In the end, however, the Consortium seriously underestimated the intensity with which workers would resist its assault on labor mobility and union rights. The Catholic hierarchy also came to find the Consortium's labor policies incompatible with social Catholic doctrine, while government ministers grew uncomfortable with its abrogation of the state-supported rights of formally free labor. Locked in an increasingly bitter struggle, the Consortium ultimately sacrificed the chance to use family allowances as a means of wage restraint to a grandiose vision of total employer hegemony.

Roubaix and Tourcoing are bleak manufacturing cities near the

---

[34] Three general studies of the Consortium were done during the interwar years. By far the best is Robert Bruyneel, *L'industrie textile de Roubaix-Tourcoing devant la crise économique et la législation sociale*, Thesis, University of Paris, Faculty of Law (Paris: Bossuet, 1932). Some useful information on the immediate postwar wage negotiations can be found in Benoit Trylnik, *Le Consortium de l'Industrie Textile de Roubaix-Tourcoing*, Thesis, University of Lille (Lille: Marquant, 1926). For a study of labor relations written from the Consortium's viewpoint, see J. Delvoye, *Patrons et ouvriers – Les meneurs et la question des salaires dans l'industrie textile: Enquête faite à Roubaix-Tourcoing du 11 nov. 1918 au 31 dec. 1927* (Paris: Dunod, 1928). The relations between the Consortium, the Catholic hierarchy, and the Christian trade unions are extensively treated in Robert Talmy, *Le syndicalisme chrétien en France, 1871–1930* (Paris: Bloud et Gay, 1965), pp. 133–235; Michel Launay, *La C.F.T.C.: Origines et développement, 1919–1940* (Paris: Publications de la Sorbonne, 1986), esp. pp. 109–205; and in many of the papers given in a colloquium held in December 1990 entitled "Cent ans de Catholicisme social dans la région du Nord," published as a special double issue of the *Revue du Nord*, 73, nos. 290–1 (Apr.–Sept. 1991). For the Consortium's attitude toward social insurance and the 1930 general strike, see Hatzfeld, *Du paupérisme*; also Dominique Simon, "Les origines des assurances sociales au début des années, 1930," Thesis, University of Paris I, 1983.

Belgian border, avoided by tourists and noted only for their dominance of the French textile industry over two centuries and their
unwilling accommodation of the German army of occupation in two
world wars. In the course of the nineteenth century, the two towns
grew from villages of several thousand each into an urban conglomerate of over 200,000 people. On the eve of the First World War, the
Department of the Nord was producing two-thirds of all woollen
textiles and one-third of all cotton and recovered its dominance soon
after 1918.[35] By 1930, the Roubaix-Tourcoing area grouped over a
third of a million people, including 127,000 textile workers.

The textile industry in the Nord was organized at midcentury into
many medium-size family firms, personally managed and often closely
linked by ties of blood and marriage. The textile work force was
similarly "familial," with whole families often working for a particular
firm.[36] With the rise of a Guesdist workers' movement, the refinement
of authoritarian management techniques, and the growing physical
and ideological distance between the firm and the bourgeois home,
however, millowners' demands for deference came under increasing
attack. William Reddy reminds us that issues of cultural autonomy
and social control as well as wages underlay the strikes that swept the
Nord in 1880, 1890, and 1903. Until the First World War, however,
workers' resistance met with little success, as employers refused all
negotiation and waited for time and necessity to drive their workers
back.[37]

[35] Albert Aftalion, *L'industrie textile en France pendant la guerre*, Carnegie Endowment for
International Peace (Paris: Presses Universitaires de France, [1924?]), pp. 7–8.

[36] Much work has been done on the high rates of women's and children's work in these
towns and the tendency of millowners to employ whole families. See especially William
Reddy, *The Rise of Market Culture* (Cambridge University Press, 1984), esp. chap. 6;
Leslie Page Moch and Louise A. Tilly, "Joining the Urban World: Occupation, Family
and Migration in Three French Cities," *Comparative Studies in Society and History*, 27: 1
(Jan. 1985), pp. 52–4; Patricia Hilden, *Working Women and Socialist Politics in France,
1880–1914: A Regional Study* (Oxford University Press, 1986).

[37] Reddy, *Rise of Market Culture*, chap. 10. Robert Talmy argues in *Syndicalisme chrétien*
that as a rule the employers of the Nord were strong Catholics; Bonnie Smith, on the
other hand, has argued that the men of the Nord by and large were supporters of the
republic, held liberal sympathies, and were strongly anticlerical. Neither of these arguments accords entirely well with the history of the employers' policies toward their
workers, which were a mixture of strongly illiberal paternalism and a moralizing, rather
than religious, sentiment; see, Smith, *Ladies of the Leisure Class* (Princeton, N.J.: Princeton University Press, 1981), pp. 18–33. On politics in the Nord, see David Gordon,
"Liberalism and Socialism in the Nord: Eugène Motte and Republican Politics in Roubaix," *French History*, 3: 3 (1989), pp. 312–43; Hilden, *Working Women and Socialist Politics*

The *union sacrée* of the First World War, with its new government recognition of union rights, directly threatened this authoritarian heritage. In the aftermath of the war, faced with an increasingly militant union movement, the government negotiated regional agreements between employers and the unions affiliated to the Confédération Générale du Travail (CGT). The June 1919 agreement between the textile manufacturers of Roubaix-Tourcoing and the CGT's textile unions committed both parties to respect the eight-hour day, allowed piecework wages, and pledged workers to a drive to regain prewar production levels in exchange for better wages and working conditions. Most important, however, the agreement endorsed collective bargaining and arbitration, expressly stating that all differences were to be resolved by a commission with equal numbers of employer and worker representatives. Welcomed by the CGT, the agreement was read by industrialists as an unacceptable diminution of employer prerogatives. The textile employers of Roubaix-Tourcoing returned to the Nord at the end of the war with substantial sums in war indemnities and the determination to remake their industrial world in the tradition of late-nineteenth-century paternalism, if with better organization.[38] Especially influential in formulating these plans was Eugène Mathon.

Eugène Mathon presided, during the twenties, not only over the Consortium and the Comité Central des Allocations Familiales, but also over national and local employer syndicates. Although a Catholic, he did not join explicitly confessional organizations, preferring to lend his considerable influence and financial support to early fascist and corporatist organizations.[39] Mathon's ideas of social and industrial organization were already in place during the war years, when he argued against working with the Christian trade unions, claiming this could only lead "to collective contracts, compulsory arbitration, worker participation, and the continual intervention of the state."[40]

in France; and Bruno Duriez and Didier Cornuel, "La naissance de la politique urbaine: Le cas de Roubaix," *Annales de la Recherche Urbaine*, 4 (1979) pp. 22–84.

[38] On industrial policy after the war, see Richard Kuisel, *Capitalism and the State in Modern France* (Cambridge University Press, 1984), chap. 2. On the Roubaix-Tourcoing agreement, see Trylnik, *Le Consortium*, pp. 56–9; Talmy, *Syndicalisme chrétien*, p. 145. Indemnity figures were published in *Le Peuple*, 15 Oct. 1921.

[39] Mathon's ideas and life, including his role in the Consortium, are covered extensively in Henry-Louis Dubly, *Vers un ordre économique et social: Eugène Mathon, 1860–1935* (Paris, 1946). His fascist sympathies and his financial support for Georges Valois are discussed in Robert Soucy, *French Fascism: The First Wave, 1924–1933* (New Haven, Conn.: Yale University Press, 1986), and in Zeev Sternhell, *Ni droite ni gauche: L'idéologie fasciste en France* (Paris: Seuil, 1983).

[40] Quoted in Talmy, *Syndicalisme chrétien*, p. 142.

His antipathy to collective organization extended only to trade unions, however, and in the early twenties he began developing a plan for industrial decision making centered around an unusual degree of cooperation among businessmen.

Mathon proposed parallel structures for industrial governance: on the one hand, an "economic" corporation made up of employers alone and charged with formulating all sales, management, and production policy; on the other, a "social" corporation of both workers and employers, the council of which would be composed of both elected worker (not union) representatives and employers. The latter council would decide all questions of wages, hours, and conditions of work and would settle all strikes without recourse either to collective bargaining or to outside arbitration. If, in the case of a labor conflict, the council judged the workers to be in the wrong, it would sustain the employers and refuse to rehire the workers responsible for the strike. If the employers were judged responsible, it would support the workers. All state intervention, except in the case of a general strike, was prohibited.[41]

Mathon's ideas were couched in a language of paternalism but differed in key respects from older visions of workplace harmony constructed around employer benevolence and worker deference. While Catholic paternalists like Léon Harmel or Albert de Mun had stressed the importance of personal cross-class contact and moralization, Mathon envisioned the centralization of all management and a minimum of contact between the individual employer and the workers at the plant. A range of corporatist theorists put forward proposals during the interwar years; few, however, rejected all autonomous worker organization and weighted the scales so heavily in favor of the employers.[42] Few also had Mathon's opportunity to put their theories to the test. The Consortium Textile de Roubaix-Tourcoing, largely his creation, mirrored the structure outlined in his writings. The Consortium coordinated all industrial and labor policy, was unremittingly hostile to union organization and government intervention, centralized all wage policy, and in the case of strikes, made up the lost profits of the affected plants. Its strategy was not purely defensive, however: the Consortium also introduced one of the most comprehensive sys-

[41] The development of Mathon's corporatist ideas is laid out by Dubly, pp. 225–46, and by Talmy, *Syndicalisme chrétien*, pp. 152–5; see also Eugène Mathon, *Le producteur, la corporation, l'état* (Paris: André Tournon, 1935).

[42] For a comparison of Mathon and other corporatists' ideas, see Matthew Elbow, *French Corporative Theory, 1789–1948* (New York: Columbia University Press, 1953), pp. 122–67.

tems of family allowances in France, finding such benefit programs a potent tool for both employer solidarity and labor control.

Interest in family allowances among the textile employers was initially spurred by social Catholic sentiment, and in 1918 a number of members of the Association Catholique des Patrons du Nord, some prewar supporters of company trade unionism, and Mathon met to form "Familia," the Consortium's predecessor. Conceived as a confessional organization, Familia's express purpose was to support means of minimizing workers' risks, and "to contribute to moralization and social peace through the Union of Capital and Labor."[43] In June 1918, Mathon hired Désiré Ley, an ex-worker, anticlerical, and former liaison between the populace and the German army of occupation, as Familia's director. Before the group set up a family allowance system, they centralized all labor policy, with Ley informing all workers' organizations in July 1919 – immediately after the historic postwar collective contract – that all complaints and requests for negotiations were to be addressed exclusively to him. In August 1919, Familia assessed all participating employers at 2% of their wage bill and began paying family allowances of one franc per child per day, beginning with the second, to male heads of households. As workers flocked to participating firms, employers joined Familia, and in April 1920, with a hundred firms, the group became the Consortium Textile de Roubaix-Tourcoing, now organized on nonconfessional lines.[44]

The Consortium quickly repudiated the June 1919 agreement, according to which wages were to be indexed to inflation.[45] In 1920, when the local commission on the cost of living reported rising inflation – and hence grounds for wage increases – the Consortium divided the amount due into two parts, granting only one-half and using the remaining money to fund its family allowance program.[46] As the respected trade unionist Georges Buisson told the 1923 Confédération Générale du Travail (CGT), the ostensibly "generous" al-

---

[43] Pinte, *Les allocations familiales*, p. 82.

[44] Delvoye, *Patrons et ouvriers*, p. 40; Talmy, *Histoire du mouvement familial*, 2, p. 125.

[45] The task of determining the cost of living was entrusted by a government decree of 19 Feb. 1920 to regional commissions. The Consortium, however, contested the accuracy of the commission for the Nord and refused to accept its cost-of-living coefficients. Its own "price surveillance service" arrived at considerably lower figures. Bruyneel, *L'industrie textile*, pp. 52–61.

[46] Trylnik, *Le Consortium*, pp. 17, 62, 66; "La grève du textile à Roubaix-Tourcoing," Confédération Française des Travailleurs Chrétiens [CFTC], *Circulaire*, 21 (30 Sept. 1921), p. 112; Confédération Générale du Travail Unitaire [CGTU], Congrès, *Compte rendu* (1925), p. 145.

lowance was only "a way of swindling our comrade textile workers of Roubaix out of a certain number of thousands of francs."[47] Within a year, the Consortium grouped three hundred firms and over 60,000 workers, or the majority of the textile industry in the area. By 1930, that figure had risen to 100,000, or almost 80% of the textile workers and 60% of all employed workers in Roubaix-Tourcoing. The dramatic growth of the Consortium is shown in Table 5.2.

Although the Consortium experimented with other benefits, its family allowance program was its principal raison d'être. In both its own institutional structure and in the organization of its policies, the Consortium was able to link its aims of benevolence and labor control. First, although the Consortium claimed that its only purpose was to administer allowances, it established a parallel organization, the Commission Intersyndicale de l'Industrie Textile de Roubaix-Tourcoing, made up of precisely the same members and also directed by Ley. In a break with the personal management of the past, the Commission took over the job of studying changes in the cost of living and set all wages. Trade unionists, who developed a demonology of Ley during the twenties, marveled at this former worker's hold over the *patronat*. Henri Lefebvre of the Tourcoing CGT told one investigator in the early 1930s:

> He has subjugated the majority of the industrialists of the region, and I don't understand how they let themselves be dominated in such a fashion. His agents and collaborators check their bookkeeping when investigating their factories. The prewar employers would never have tolerated such meddling in their affairs.[48]

Ley also kept a paid staff of former workers who were used as factory spies, pinpointing troublemakers and assessing unrest.[49] Although Ley clung to the fiction that the Consortium and the Commission were entirely separate organizations, local labor inspectors, trade unionists, and even Consortium employers confused the two, since they were, in fact, one and the same.

The first test of this two-headed organization came in the fall of 1921, when Consortium firms agreed to a uniform wage cut. Neither public opinion, the resulting ten-week general strike, nor appeals from public figures from the mayors to the prime minister convinced the Consortium to talk to the unions. The 1921 strike signaled a complete

---

[47] Confédération Générale du Travail [CGT], Congrès, *Compte rendu* (1923), p. 121.
[48] Bruyneel, *L'industrie textile*, p. 199.
[49] Trylnik, *Le Consortium*, p. 48; Delvoye, *Patrons et ouvriers*, pp. 41–3.

Table 5.2. *Growth of the Consortium Textile de Roubaix-Tourcoing*

Year	Firms	Workers covered	Workers benefiting	Children covered	Family allowances paid In francs (thousands)	As % of wage bill
1920	312	68,000	11,000		7,073	3–6.5
1921			13,000		10,260	7.0
1922			24,000	20,687	14,923	5.5
1923			37,510	45,500	15,805	5.3
1924			39,000		17,764	5.3
1925			46,748	55,924	19,666	5.2
1926					24,822	5.0
1927					27,782	5.4
1928			Households		30,084	5.8
1929	500		53,000		32,460	5.4
1930		102,000	58,715	99,162	30,138	5.4
1931						
1932	223	75,000	22,000	39,750		ca. 3.0
	— Law of 11 March 1932 made affiliation obligatory —					
1933	338	109,910	20,077	35,034	9,267	2.6
1934	426	110,723	19,174	33,372	9,004	2.2
1935	434	110,264	17,511	30,593	8,548	2.1
1936	481	111,500	18,244	30,367	9,341	2.1
1937	433	111,500	17,777	30,359	13,359	2.2
1938	436	69,398	18,276	30,819	21,274	3.5
1939	444	58,505	16,535	28,367	28,926	4.4

Sources: Statistics on the Consortium for Tables 5.2–5.6 are compiled from the following documents: "Toujours à propos des allocations familiales," *La Voix Sociale*, 3:50 (1 June 1924); "L'oeuvre sociale du Consortium de l'Industrie Textile en 1925," Conseil Supérieur de la Natalité, *Communications*, 1927, no. 2, 10th session (January 1927); AN F22 1553, "L'effort social du Consortium de l'Industrie Textile en 1930" and "Le service des allocations familiales en 1938"; *Bulletin de la Statistique Générale de la France*, 16:1 (Oct. 1926), p. 14; 20:2 (Apr.–June 1931), p. 324; Benoit Trylnik, *Le Consortium de l'Industrie Textile de Roubaix-Tourcoing* (Lille: Marquant, 1926); Robert Bruyneel, *L'industrie textile de Roubaix-Tourcoing devant da crise économique et la législation sociale* (Paris: Bossuet, 1932); International Labour Office, *Family Allowances*, Studies and Reports, Series D, no. 13 (Geneva: Albert Kundig, 1924). Comprehensive statistics for the Consortium for the period after state control are in AN F22 1512.

Table 5.3. *Monthly rates for Consortium family allowances (FA)*

Children in family	1920	1930	1932	1933[a]	1938[b] FA only	with MA
1	50	60	25	25	35	50
2	125	150	87	60	100	137
3	200	240	250	110	200	262
4	275	360	375	190	375	467
5	350	450	500	270	550	675
6	425	540	625	350	725	875
7	500	630	750	430	900	1,075
8	575	720	875	510	1,075	1,275
Each addnl.	75	90	125	80	175	200

[a] As of 1 March, the date by which enrollment in a *caisse* became compulsory for all firms.
[b] Rates for 1938 were set by the Ministry of Labor, and include an unwaged mother's allowance (MA).
Sources: See Tables 5.1 and 5.2, supplemented by Robert Talmy, *Histoire du mouvement familial en France, 1896–1939*, vol. 2 (Paris: UNCAF, 1962), pp. 125, 135.

rejection by the Consortium of collective bargaining and of arbitration as a means of settling disputes. Employers maintained utter unity; indeed when certain employers seemed inclined to give in to the urgings of the Ministry of Labor, Ley and Mathon intervened to prevent any dissension in the employers' ranks. The strike also demonstrated the usefulness of family allowances to the Consortium, since industrialists justified their wage cut by pointing out that family allowances gave workers a much higher standard of living than the one they had had in the prewar period.[50]

The parallel structure of the Consortium and the Commission linked strikebreaking and benevolence on an institutional level. The Consortium also carefully manipulated the family allowance system in the interests of wage restraint. The allowances paid by the Consortium were among the highest in France (see Table 5.3 for rates); birth bonuses, equivalent to more than a weekly wage, were also paid.[51]

[50] On the 1921 strike, see the reports by the prefect to the minister of the interior, 1921, AN F7 13912.
[51] The *prime de naissance* was Fr 100 if both parents worked, Fr 200 if the mother did not work. Birth bonuses, included in the statistics for allowances, absorbed Fr 7,101,025 between 1921 and 1930 (when they were suppressed due to overlap with new social insurance provisions). This amounted to some 3.7% of the Consortium's total expenditure of Fr 230,876,443 on family benefits in the 1919–30 period.

Table 5.4. *Weekly Consortium family allowance (FA) for families meeting all conditions for receipt, 1923 and 1930*

Children in family	1923		1930	
	In francs	As % of wage[a]	In francs	As % of wage[a]
1	12	11.6	14.4	9.1
2	30	28.9	36.0	22.8
3	48	46.3	57.6	36.5
4	72	69.4	86.4	54.7
5	90	86.8	108.0	68.4
6	108	104.2	129.6	82.1
7	126	121.5	151.2	95.7
8	144	138.9	172.8	109.4

[a] Percentage of the average Consortium wage for a full week's work. This figure was arrived at by multiplying the Consortium's wage bill per working hour by 48 hours; the resulting figures were 103.68 francs per week in 1923 and 157.92 francs per week in 1930.
Source: See Table 5.2.

As Table 5.4 shows, from 1920 to 1932, workers with two dependent children (under age 13) could increase the family income through allowances by about 25% of an average wage, while those with six dependent children would essentially receive a second full adult wage.

Yet allowances were *not* wages and, as "benevolent" donations theoretically unconnected to a worker's output, they could be manipulated by employers to guard against labor unrest. In 1922, strict rules were laid down governing the operation of the Consortium's fund. Workers had to have worked one month in the factory to qualify for allowances and three months for the birth bonuses. Allowances were paid on the 30th of each month in proportion to the time worked but were suppressed for the entire month if the worker had left the factory at any time without prior permission, whether for personal reasons or collective grievances. Most important, the system was altered so that any worker – not only fathers, nor even parents – living in a household with dependent children could claim allowances, an important change given the fact that one-half of the Consortium's labor force during the period were women and young people.[52] Yet this change was instituted not to benefit women and working adolescents, but to pull them into the Consortium's factories. The administrative

[52] In 1930, of the 105,310 workers employed in textiles in Roubaix and vicinity and in Tourcoing, 49% were adult men, 38% adult women, and 13% adolescents of both sexes.

regulations deserve explication. The allowance for all children under age 13 was divided by the number of adults over 13. If the latter all worked in a Consortium plant, the family received 100% of the small children's allowances; but should one or more work elsewhere, the family quota was reduced proportionally. In a concession to Catholic sentiment, only the mother was, if unwaged, held out of the count. A family with two children was entitled, say, to 120 francs per month. But if it also included three adults over the age of 13 and only one worked at a Consortium firm, the family would receive only 40 francs.[53]

Family allowances thus served to make a portion of the worker's wage dependent not upon work performance, but simply on the continued and reliable presence of *all* adult or adolescent members of his or her family within the Consortium's factories. These rules increased the number of workers receiving some portion of a family allowance from 24,000 to over 37,000; about one-half of Consortium workers now had a direct economic incentive for their regular attendance. The 1922 rules were designed to tie workers to their jobs, minimize labor mobility, prevent any possible repetition of the 1921 strike, and ensure a steady supply of workers for Consortium firms. They did so: a Consortium employer reported to the annual conference of the *caisses* in 1923 that the requirement of a qualification period for allowances had reduced such job changes by 70%, and that the suppression of allowances led workers to do everything possible to negotiate before resorting to walkouts.[54] Despite these stringent conditions, benefits on this scale were not bypassed lightly, and workers did what they could to qualify. The number of employees benefiting climbed steadily: by 1930, workers in 58,000 families were receiving some allowance from the Consortium for some 99,000 children.

Although the number of benefiting employees grew, the cost of the allowances to the employers remained stable throughout the twenties, at about 5.5% of the total wage bill. Costs were contained because although benefits were high for families with many children, more than one-half of benefiting families had only one dependent child. Furthermore, the stringent conditions governing receipt meant that families rarely received the full rate, whether because of missed work,

---

[53] The new regulations are discussed thoroughly in A. Glorieux, "Répartition des charges," CNAF, *Compte rendu*, 3 (1923), pp. 97–109. See also Trylnik, *Le Consortium*, pp. 21–3.

[54] Glorieux, "Répartition," p. 104.

Table 5.5. *Family allowances (FA) actually received by Consortium workers, 1923–38*

	1923	1925	1930	1938
Total wage bill (thousand francs)	295,847	375,256	559,991	615,238
Total FA paid (thousand francs)	15,805	19,666	30,138	21,274
Households benefiting	26,660	33,226	58,715	18,276
Average annual FA/household	593	592	513[a]	1,164
As a % of an average wage			10.9	13.1
Hours of work equivalent	274	235	156	
Children benefiting	45,400	55,924	99,162	30,819
Average annual FA/child	347	352	304[a]	690
Full rate first child	600	600	720	420–600
Full rate second child	900	900	1,080	780–1,280
Total allowances due if all households received full rates (thousand francs)	33,414	41,063	87,467	26,066[b]
Proportion of allowances lost through stringent regulation (%)	53	52	66[a]	18

[a] Actual amounts received were particularly low in 1930 owing to the general strike in the fall of that year, which would have cost most workers at least two months' allowance.

[b] This figure was arrived at by estimating the average benefit for families receiving the unwaged mother's allowance at 720 francs/year, the rate for a mother in a family with two dependent children.

Sources: See Table 5.2. The wage bill for 1938 is given by Henri-Louis Dubly, *Vers un ordre économique et social: Eugène Mathon, 1860–1935* (Paris, 1946), p. 169.

short time, or simply because all adult members did not work at Consortium firms. In 1923, for example, some 37,510 workers in 26,660 families were receiving allowances for 45,550 dependent children from the Consortium. Those families contained another 35,790 members over the age of 13, however – only 16,366 of which were mothers exempt from the requirement that all adults work at Consortium firms. The fact that the remaining 18,424 family members over the age of 13 did not work at Consortium firms thus cost these families in aggregate about a third of their allowances.[55] Table 5.5 calculates the savings to the employers of these stringent regulations

[55] Detailed statistics on the family structure of Consortium recipients for 1923 were found in "Toujours à propos des allocations familiales," *La Voix Sociale*, 3: 50 (1 June 1924), p. 4.

by comparing allowances actually paid with the figures due had full allowances been paid for all dependent children. As we can see, had all families received the full rate in 1923, the cost to the Consortium would have been over Fr 33 million; in fact, the Consortium paid slightly under Fr 16 million. Although a majority of benefiting children lived in families with two children or more and the full allowance for two children was 1,500 francs per year, the average benefit paid per family was less than half that amount. For workers, this was still a large figure: slightly over a month's average full wage, or the equivalent of some 274 hours of work. Yet Consortium costs were easily recovered in the increased stability of the work force: as one Consortium apologist rather ingenuously admitted, workers' benefits need entail no extra employer expense.[56]

The Consortium's mix of employer organization, labor control, and family policy was quite effective. The Consortium survived from 1921 to 1928 without another general regional strike, and those local grievances that did develop were dealt with very harshly by Ley, who personally conducted all strike negotiations. In his confidential circulars, which were – as he intended – routinely leaked to the press, Ley continued to blame all labor unrest on union organizers, who, he claimed, were outside agitators, entirely unrepresentative of the textile workers. Nevertheless, the transparency of the links – both institutional and strategic – between labor control and family policy led to the steady growth of both worker resentment and Catholic and government criticism of the Consortium, contributing significantly to growing union awareness of the dangers of the family allowance system and to calls for state control.

One might expect that the Consortium's family allowance policies would have received a warm welcome in Roubaix-Tourcoing: the area was noted for both its high birthrate and its religiosity. Important familist organizations were founded in the Nord, and the area boasted many adherents to the social Catholic doctrines of the Semaines Sociales and the Jeunesse Ouvrière Chrétienne. Furthermore, Catholicism remained an important force among the working class as well as the bourgeoisie, seemingly a propitious environment for the realization of class harmony founded on shared faith.[57] Yet the Consortium not only neglected to exploit familist and Catholic sentiment

---

[56] Delvoye, *Patrons et ouvriers*, p. 68.

[57] On the Catholic church in the Nord, see Yves-Marie Hilaire, "Les ouvriers de la région du Nord devant l'église catholique," *Le Mouvement Social*, 57 (Oct.–Dec. 1966), pp. 181–201; Launay *La C.F.T.C.*; and Talmy, *Syndicalisme chrétien*.

to undermine working-class unity, it also launched a direct attack on the Catholic trade unions, forcing much of the church hierarchy into opposition. Consortium policy also forced the socialist and communist unions to define their position on family policy, but it was less their positions than the growing disaffection of Catholics and government ministers that limited the success of the Consortium's strategy.

The earliest and most virulent of the Consortium's critics were the socialist and communist trade unionists, who gradually woke up to the fact that the *caisses*, with their registration system and antistrike provisions, could make labor organization much more difficult. In December 1922, Georges Buisson, the influential secretary of the Fédération des Employés, conducted a study of allowances and reported one year later to the CGT congress. Drawing evidence overwhelmingly from Roubaix-Tourcoing, Buisson pointed out that Consortium employers themselves admitted that the allowances had been invaluable in making a general wage reduction possible; allowances were a new tool with which to control and terrorize workers. Nevertheless, he argued, family allowances were of incalculable benefit to large families, and the system had to be changed rather than abolished. Following Buisson's address, the CGT adopted a resolution that warned workers about employers' use of allowances to dominate workers and to attack trade union rights and reiterated its support for state measures of social security and collective bargaining. This resolution encapsulated CGT doctrine concerning family allowances and was reaffirmed unchanged in 1929.[58]

From 1923 to the law on family allowances in 1932, Buisson continued to denounce employer administration of the *caisse* system, with particular reference to Désiré Ley, who undoubtedly made Buisson's task easier with his explicit claims to employer hegemony. "What is behind all this employer benevolence?" Buisson asked.

> I am going to turn for an answer to M. Ley, the damned soul of the Textile Consortium, one of the grand masters of the Family Allowances Committee. The allowance, M. Ley tells employers, is a prudent measure. Not only will it lead to a reduction in the wage bill, but it will be instrumental in dividing the working-class movement and preventing the revolution.

[58] Georges Buisson, "Le sursalaire familial," in CGT, Congrès, *Compte rendu* (1923), pp. 119–25; CGT, (1929), pp. 239–40. For CGT attitudes toward allowances, see the series of articles written by Eugène Morel for *Le Peuple*: "Le syndicalisme doit déterminer sa position à l'égard du sursalaire familial," 17 Dec. 1922; "Le sursalaire familial," 24 Dec. 1922; "L'opinion de J. Lapierre, secrétaire adjoint de la CGT, sur les allocations familiales," 29 Dec. 1922.

Naturally, it's always charity. And also, there's the organization of child welfare; the whole record-keeping system, the penetration into the family. They want to follow the worker step by step! Control is greater than ever before; under the guise of justice and charity, an arrogant and authoritarian *patronat* presses on with its struggle against the trade unions and against the working class itself.[59]

The attitude of the communist unions toward family allowances will be discussed in greater detail in connection with labor relations in the Parisian metalworking trades, their greatest stronghold. Like the CGT, however, the communist confederation learned of the dangers posed by family policies to union organizing when confronted by the strategies of the Consortium; like the CGT, they agreed that administration of the funds must be taken out of employers' hands. Yet the communists in Roubaix-Tourcoing – like the socialists – initially found themselves outflanked. In 1922, soon after the Consortium had instituted its new rules penalizing any unexcused absence from work with total forfeiture of one month's allowance, the communist unions called a twenty-four-hour strike in sympathy with striking workers in Havre. Many sympathetic workers came out, but when they discovered that their solidaristic act had cost them that month's family allowance they left the union in disgust: the Tourcoing textile union lost 2,500 adherents in a short period. By 1925, the leaders of the communist textile unions frankly admitted that Consortium workers getting family allowances would not join limited or sympathetic strikes and that the unions should have firmly opposed the 1922 rules from the beginning. Worse, the substantial benefits offered by the Consortium and other employers' confederations were hurting organization itself, especially among women.[60] The real problem, one activist from the Nord told the communist Confédération Générale du Travail Unitaire (CGTU) National Committee in 1926, was that the workers thought much like the Consortium about family allowances, finding them to be very good things indeed.[61] The success of Consortium policy was reflected in declining unionization rates: although the CGT claimed, before its split, some 20,000 adherents in Roubaix, 12,000 in Tourcoing, and a further 7,200 in Halluin and Lannoy, by 1930 a reliable

---

[59] Georges Buisson, "La participation aux bénéfices – les allocations familiales," in *Pour l'éducation ouvrière* (1924), pp. 26–7.

[60] CGTU, Congrès, *Compte rendu* (1925), pp. 143–5, 517–48; also CGTU, Congrès, *Compte rendu* (1927), pp. 608–9.

[61] "Comité Confédéral National," *La Vie Syndicale*, 21 (Jan.–Mar. 1926), pp. 41–3.

observer estimated total CGT strength in the Roubaix-Tourcoing area at about 16,000, with the CGTU membership much lower.[62]

Both the CGT and the CGTU opposed the growing fragmentation of payment systems. Their gradual support for state- or worker-controlled family allowance funds was a strategic decision, not one based on familist convictions. The social Catholic trade unions, affiliated to the Confédération Française de Travailleurs Chrétiens (CFTC), however, thought differently. Drawing on the doctrines of Leo XIII, they supported family wages for male heads of households, condemned married women's work, and in general appear as natural allies of the *caisse* movement. They were also a significant force in the Nord, with about four thousand members in Roubaix-Tourcoing in 1930 and, due to the support of a good portion of the local Catholic hierarchy, an influence disproportionate to their size.[63]

The Catholic trade unions directed little criticism at the Consortium's family policy. They did feel, however, that the benefits of allowances should be extended to all workers by law. Despite the fact that the CFTC called for neither state administration nor worker control, but rather merely the legal obligation of all employers to adhere to existing *caisses*, and despite the fact that other Catholic leaders had made the same demand, Mathon denounced the CFTC to the Vatican as "Marxist" for desiring to substitute state regulation for private initiative. He wrote:

> Obviously, if family allowances become a legal obligation, they lose thereby their nature as agents of sympathetic benevolence between employers and workers, to become a pure tax exactable by force. This would abolish at a stroke a natural tool of understanding and social peace.[64]

Yet other prominent Catholics were less certain that the Consortium's family allowance system was consistent with Catholic doctrine. Some found the Consortium's system simply not patriarchal enough: from 1922, the Consortium paid to the worker regardless of sex or age, while Catholics insisted that the father alone, as head of house-

---

[62] Figures are given in CGT, *Congrès* (1921), delegate lists, and Bruyneel, *L'industrie textile*, p. 70.

[63] Bruyneel, *L'industrie textile*, p. 70.

[64] Quoted in Talmy, *Histoire du mouvement familial*, 2, p. 136. Summaries of Mathon's letters to Sbaretti are in Talmy, *Syndicalisme chrétien*, pp. 166–70. The following account of the conflict between the Consortium and the Catholic trade unions relies heavily on Talmy's work.

hold, was the appropriate recipient of such aid. "We don't live in a patriarchal society anymore," responded one Consortium employer; however much one deplored the disaggregation of the family, it was unjust to deny allowances to the women and children working for Consortium firms on the grounds that paternity alone gave rights to aid.[65] Rhetoric aside, the Consortium's family allowance system bore little resemblance to the family wage of Catholic ideals, personally bestowed on the deserving *père de famille* by the devout employer. Worried by Mathon's diatribes, the social Catholic law professor Eugène Duthoit wrote to the Vatican in 1927 that the system of family allowances epitomized "a kind of anonymous bureaucratized paternalism," aimed at forcing all family members over age 13 into Consortium firms.[66]

Religious leaders devoted to cross-class harmony found even more problematic the fact that the Consortium refused to work with the Christian trade unions and attacked them as agents of "bolshevik" subversion. The Catholic unions protested in vain that they opposed socialist doctrines of class struggle, negotiated independently, and were "resolute partisans of class harmony and social peace."[67] In 1923, in an earlier letter to the Vatican, Mathon had complained of the antiemployer tone of the Catholic Confederation's propaganda and of the partisan and misplaced support of local priests for the Christian trade unions. Between 1924 and 1928, the Consortium broke off all relations with the Christian unions. Duthoit, however, pointed out that although the Consortium claimed to be a Catholic organization, it was organized on strictly nonconfessional lines and tied to secular mutualist funds. Duthoit's criticisms were echoed by much of the local clergy. Shocked by Ley's incessant attacks on the Christian trade unionists ("agitators, men without faith, arrogant, incompetent, demagogic...."),[68] the aptly named Abbé Bataille of Roubaix called on Joseph Wibaux, now nominally head of the Consortium, to make Ley alter the tone of his circulars. If he failed to do so, Bataille warned,

---

[65] Glorieux, "Répartition," p. 107.
[66] Quoted in Talmy, *Syndicalisme chrétien*, p. 185. Eugène Duthoit, born into the Roubaix bourgeoisie, was professor of constitutional law and later of political economy at the University of Lille, the organizer of the yearly social Catholic conferences, the Semaines Sociales, and one of the most influential public figures in the Nord. On Duthoit, see Pierre Pierrard, *Gens du Nord* (Paris: Arthaud, 1985), pp. 219–23; André Caudron, "Eugène Duthoit et la première génération de Catholiques sociaux," *Revue du Nord*, 73: nos. 290–1 (Apr.–Sept. 1991), pp. 315–20.
[67] "Le conflit du textile du Nord," CFTC, *Circulaire*, 72 (Aug.–Oct. 1928), p. 520.
[68] Ley, quoted in Talmy, *Syndicalisme chrétien*, p. 187.

the church itself would be compelled to pronounce on the true social doctrine.

The growing discomfort of Catholic leaders with Consortium policy crystallized into opposition in 1928–9, when the Consortium fought a seven-month general strike involving some twenty thousand workers in and around the town of Halluin. Halluin was strongly communist, and the strike had been called by the communist unions on the heels of an earlier conflict. Catholic workers, who opposed it, tried to go back to work but were deterred by both the degree of popular solidarity and fears of violence. The Catholic unions offered to mediate the strike; the Consortium, however, preferred to see them as in league with the communists, and refused all contact. The strike thus quickly moved from the plane of wages to that of trade union rights: as the Prefect perceptively noted, the strike was undertaken less for the "dix sous" but "to force respect for trade union rights, which the employer today declares he no longer wants to recognize."[69]

As the strike dragged on, government ministers grew increasingly short-tempered with Ley, who assured employers that he had no intention of ever talking to the agitators (*les meneurs*). Raymond Poincaré and Louis Loucheur, now minister of labor, both urged Mathon and Ley to negotiate with the CGT. In the end, however, the strike was brought to a close only through the intervention of the Catholic hierarchy, which sided openly with the workers – and, more remarkably, with the liberal state.[70] Achille Liénart, the archbishop of Lille, commended the Catholic trade unionists for appealing for arbitration, stating:

> Arbitration is a means of resolving conflict, morally superior to merciless struggle. Those who propose and accept it, without knowing at all whom the arbitrator will decide in favor of, make a gesture of which the Church and conscience approve.[71]

---

[69] AN F7 13917, prefect to the minister of the interior, 29 Sept. 1929. Excellent coverage of the strike is given by the prefect's reports to both the Ministry of the Interior (AN F7 13917) and the Ministry of Labor (AN F22 190 and 191); also by the CFTC, *Circulaire*, 70 (Apr. 1928); 72 (Aug.–Oct. 1928); 73 (Nov.–Dec. 1928); and 76 (Apr.–May 1929). Michel Hastings provides an account of this very famous strike in *Halluin la rouge, 1919–1939: Aspects d'un communisme identitaire* (Lille: Presses Universitaires de Lille, 1991), pp. 335–45; see also his "Identité culturelle locale et politique festive communiste: Halluin la rouge, 1920–1934," *Le Mouvement Social*, 139 (Apr.–June 1987), pp. 7–25.

[70] AN F22 191: Ley, Circular no. 286bis, 24 Sept. 1928; idem, "Note Confidentielle," 7 Sept. 1928, in a report from the prefect to the minister of labor, 19 Sept. 1928; idem, Circular no. 288, 28 Sept. 1928; Letter from M. Bilger, Deputy, to the Ministry of Labor, 4 Oct. 1928.

[71] "Communication de Mgr. l'Evêque de Lille," *Croix du Nord*, 2 Mar. 1929, copy in AN

Liénart's defense of the rights of trade unions was confirmed soon after by the Vatican itself, which rejected the substance of Mathon's protests, defended the doctrinal soundness of the Catholic unions, and urged the employers to meet with them on a common confessional basis. The Vatican's letter paid tribute to the Consortium's "magnificent works of employer benevolence" – especially family allowances – but warned that true social peace could only be based on the complete acceptance of the social doctrines of the church.[72] The Holy See was unable to make the Consortium change its policies, but it could deprive the employers of their ideological justifications and their claim to the support of the church.

Despite this loss of Catholic support, during the 1920s the Consortium had managed to construct a set of policies that effectively undermined workers' mobility and attacked their right to strike. Inevitably, however, this strategy pitted the textile employers not only against Catholics and trade unionists, but also against less authoritarian employers and ministers like Loucheur committed to a modernizing vision of industrial regulation through collective bargaining. Maurice Olivier, head of the local engineering employers' syndicate and a supporter of social insurance proposals, castigated Ley for using employers' contributions to fund not only social work but also "a strange and secret fund serving a range of schemes and sidelines that have nothing to do with the family!!!"[73] The development of state intervention will be discussed in Chapter 7, but it is worth noting here that Louis Loucheur's activism as minister of labor in the sphere of family policy was due in part to his frustration with the Consortium's intransigence and its rejection of both collective bargaining and government arbitration. Declaring his intention to introduce legislation extending the system of family allowances to all workers, and with the Consortium clearly in mind, he explained the reasons for state intervention:

> What motivates me above all is a concern for social justice and the desire to extend a system that, one can say, has been approved by the whole country. But we have another concern, perhaps less pressing, but which, for me, is nevertheless important.

F22 190, prefect to the minister of labor, 6 Mar. 1929. On Liénart, see Pierrard, *Gens du Nord*, pp. 214–19; Catherine Masson-Gadenne, "Le Cardinal Liénart, évêque social: Action et pensée sociale dans les années trente," *Revue du Nord*, 73: nos. 290–1 (Apr.–Sept. 1991), pp. 401–10.

[72] Sbaretti to Liénart, 5 June 1929, in CFTC, *Circulaire*, 78 (Aug.–Sept. 1929), pp. 570–4.

[73] "Comment à Roubaix-Tourcoing patrons métallurgistes et Consortium textile s'opposent à propos de l'application des assurances sociales," *Le peuple*, 20 Aug. 1928.

Under the cloak of family allowances, arrangements have been made that we cannot allow. There are certain family allowance funds, happily not many, which only give allowances under unacceptable conditions which we will henceforth prohibit.

We do not want payment of family allowances to be conditional, for example, on presence at work during all 25 days of the month. This sometimes acts as a barrier to the right to stop work which the worker holds by law.[74]

A clearer signal could not have been given: the government would not tolerate benefit systems that impinged on liberal doctrines of free labor.

In 1930, then, the Consortium was threatened by the reform of its family allowance and social insurance systems through state supervision. Ley viewed the movement toward state intervention with disgust: at all times, he had argued that all worker needs should be met by employers' voluntary action, uncomplicated by either state interference or collective bargaining. In 1926, seeing social insurance legislation on the horizon, the Consortium had instituted sickness benefits. Behind this willingness unilaterally to assume the burden of all welfare programs was, of course, the fear that state supervision would prevent the Consortium from using its benefits system as a tool against collective bargaining and the trade unions. In December 1929, Ley sent Loucheur a proposal that the Consortium pay for and administer its own sickness, accident, and old-age benefits, thus circuiting the secular mutualist funds projected to administer the social insurance law. Despite much national coverage – including a public debate with Olivier – the Consortium's offer was not accepted.[75] In June 1930, the Consortium faced not merely the prospect of a 4% employer contribution to social security and the fear of coming state control of their allowance system, but also the threat of strikes from the trade unions, who declared that wages must be raised in order for workers to be able to afford their new 4% social insurance contributions.

The solution that Désiré Ley devised to meet this dilemma amounted to a last-ditch effort to save the labor-control aspects of the family allowance system. On 30 June 1930, the Consortium stated that it would henceforth pay a *prime de fidelité* (loyalty bonus) precisely equal to the 4% worker's contribution to the social insurance

---

[74] *JO Débats (Chambre)*, 22 Jan 1929, p. 185.
[75] See Comité National d'Etudes, *Les assurances sociales* (Paris, 1930); Hatzfeld, *Du paupérisme*, pp. 168–70; Dominique Simon, "Le patronat face aux assurances sociales," *Le Mouvement Social*, 137 (Oct.–Dec. 1986), pp. 7–27.

system. This bonus, Ley announced, would be paid at the end of each year, on condition of the worker's uninterrupted presence in the factory for that entire year. Any unexcused absence, whether for personal reasons or because of strikes, would result in the suppression of the full year's benefit. The bonus thus openly declared itself as a measure against labor mobility and the right to strike. Unlike family allowances, the bonus did not masquerade as benevolence, nor would anyone have believed such claims, had the employers chosen to put them forward.[76]

To no one's great surprise, the workers did not welcome the new bonus. The CGTU called it the "slavery bonus," and the name stuck. It was aimed, CGT posters announced to the populace, "to wrap you in a circle of tyranny." It was openly condemned by Eugène Duthoit and the Christian unions, and even the prefect, reporting to the ministry of labor, speculated that the new bonus was only a "new means of exercising authority over the workers."[77] Furthermore, for the first time, the Consortium faced defection within its own ranks. On 12 July 1930, with a strike imminent, the firms of François Roussel and Les Fils d'Alfred Motte, the owners of which were prominent within Catholic circles, pulled out of the Consortium and declared they were prepared to pay 70% of their workers' social insurance contributions.[78] Throughout the ensuing conflict, Ley castigated these employers for having "betrayed their cause, treading underfoot their reputation, their past and their name." The remaining employers must hold firm: "It will not be said that the *patronat* of Roubaix-Tourcoing is incapable of resistance."[79]

The trade unions, however, were equally adamant in their opposition to the yearly bonus, knowing that it would render trade union action almost impossible. Operating under the restrictions of the family allowance system was hard enough; perhaps the most telling evidence for the success of Ley's policies was that the unions waited until 1 August to declare a general strike so that workers would not lose their July family allowances.[80] In a letter to Pierre Laval, now minister of labor, L. Decostère of the CGT drew a direct link between the Consortium's proposed bonus and past labor policy:

---

[76] AN F22 212, Consortium, "Les assurances sociales" (30 June 1930).
[77] Posters of various trade unions are in AN F22 212; see also AN F22 212, prefect to minister of labor, 10 and 27 July 1930.
[78] AN F22 212, prefect to the minister of labor, 12 July 1930. The two firms together employed about eight thousand workers.
[79] AN F22 212, Ley, Circular no. 344, 26 Aug. 1930.
[80] *Journal de Roubaix*, 1 Aug. 1930, copy in AN F22 212.

Family allowances, which seem a work of benevolence, were introduced by the Textile Consortium without consultation with the workers' organizations. Only the beneficiaries would be able to tell of the
moral torments they sometimes endure in order to satisfy the conditions imposed by the Consortium for receipt of this money – which
is nonetheless indispensable to their children's lives.

And it's because the Consortium knows about the different legislative proposals on this subject, and sees its prey escaping, that it
wants to recover its domination by taking advantage of the hardship
created by insufficient wages in workers' households.[81]

With stakes this high, the unions could not afford to lose. As the
prefect remarked, the conflict was ostensibly about wages but it had
another end: "to divide the Consortium and to wreck its future
power."[82]

The regional strike affected over 100,000 workers and lasted from
4 August to mid-September. Although publicly condemned by the
employers, the strike was privately welcomed, since industrialists had
built up enough stocks to meet their orders for some time. Ley himself
insisted to Laval that the strike was "purely political" and attempted
to close ranks by deluging Consortium employers with increasingly
hysterical denunciations not only of the strikers but also of the jour-
nalists covering the strike and those government ministers attempting
to mediate it. The trade unions, by comparison, appeared moderate,
and Ley himself was forced to admit that public opinion was hard-
ening against the Consortium. Pressure for arbitration mounted both
in the Chamber and in the press and after several failed efforts at
conciliation, Laval did succeed in negotiating a settlement. The Consortium agreed to change the *prime de fidelité* into a *prime de présence*,
which, like the former, would only be paid after a solid year of work,
but which would be paid pro rata for the amount of time worked
rather than simply suppressed in the case of absences. If the unions
were unable to force the Consortium to bargain and won no wage
increases, they were able to prevent the imposition of a benefits policy
that essentially made a portion of wages dependent upon nonparti-
cipation in strikes.[83]

And by 1930, Ley was losing his hold. The Roubaix-Tourcoing

---

[81] AN F7 13935, Decostère to Laval, 25 Aug. 1930.
[82] AN F22 212, prefect to minister of labor, 8 Aug. 1930.
[83] AN F22 212: prefect to minister of labor, 21 July 1930, and minister of labor to prefect,
2 Aug. 1930; Ley, Circular no. 342, 12 Aug. 1930, and no. 351, 17 Sept. 1930, and
"Note confidentielle," no. 210, 23 Aug. 1930; Ley, Letter, 29 Aug. 1930; Ley to Laval,
28 Aug. 1930.

unions fought a further general strike in 1931 as the textile industry slid into depression. This time, however, the strike was straightforwardly over wage cuts, and union cohesion outlasted that of the employers. Continuous labor unrest, the incessant criticisms of the Consortium by such prominent Catholic leaders as Duthoit and Liénart, and the intervention of the government convinced a significant portion of employers to declare themselves independent: on 2 September 1931 the Christian unions and those affiliated to the CGT signed a contract with firms employing over 25,000 workers – including the 1930 breakaway employers Motte and Roussel and the social Catholic employer Philippe Leclercq, who had been one of the few to remain independent throughout the 1920s. The independent firms grouped less than a third of the textile workers in Roubaix-Tourcoing, and the Consortium itself weathered the strike without concessions. Nevertheless, both Ley and the unions saw the 1931 agreement, the first collective contract signed in the textile industry there since the ill-fated accord of 1919, as a Consortium defeat.[84]

Ley's attempts to tie wages to continuous presence through the *prime de fidelité* foundered under the combined opposition of the unions and government intervention; nor was he able to manipulate family allowances at will after the introduction of state control. Although the Consortium, like other employers' organizations, continued to administer allowances after the Ministry of Labor began formal supervision in 1933, it was no longer allowed either to enforce a qualification period for allowances or to cut them off for absences. Allowances were made payable to parents alone, and the Consortium was forbidden to deduct a portion of them if all adult family members did not work for the Consortium. These new restrictions made allowances worthless as a labor-control and strikebreaking tool. Indeed, probably the best evidence that the Consortium had subjected its social policy to these aims is that it unilaterally reduced its rates by about one-half after the introduction of state control. Not until 1938 and 1939, when the government raised rates by administrative decree, did the Consortium's payments for family allowances approach their pre-1932 level. For families, however, state control made allowances a far more reliable source of income. Although the Consortium paid out *less* in allowances in 1938 than in 1930, the amount received per family and per child about *doubled*, with families receiving nearly the amount that

---

[84] On the 1931 strike, see Michel Launay, "Le syndicalisme chrétien dans un grand conflit du travail," *Le Mouvement Social*, 73 (Oct.–Dec. 1970), pp. 39–78.

would have been granted if allowances had been paid in full without any consideration of attendance at work (see Table 5.5).

Although the unions never won their battle with the Consortium, Désiré Ley lost as well. His hierarchical centralization of the Consortium, his paranoid attempt to brand even Catholic trade unionists as cryptocommunists, and the transparency of his strategy of using family allowances as a means of labor control drove Catholics – potential allies – into opposition, while the attack on the basic guarantees of the liberal state forced the hand of ministers who would unquestionably have preferred to remain uninvolved. Throughout the 1930s, Ley continued to administer the Consortium and responded to ministerial directives with aggrieved and evasive letters, foot-dragging, and finally reluctant compliance.[85] Since all employers were required to enroll in an approved fund, the Consortium grew moderately during the mid-thirties, but internal dissension and economic crisis limited its capacity for strikebreaking and labor control. Eugène Mathon devoted his time to trying to save the failing wool industry and to refining his corporatist ideas, which had to wait until 1940 to find a new audience among the Vichy leaders.

When we look at the Consortium's strategy in the period before state supervision, we find both successes and failures. It is understandable that employers in the textile industry, with its high labor costs and little scope for further mechanization and technical improvement, would have looked primarily to labor-control measures to increase productivity. Ironically, though, the Consortium had less success in curtailing union power than in restraining wages, although the two were certainly related. The Consortium's real achievement, laid out in Table 5.6, was in forcing real wages steadily downward throughout the twenties. Family allowances, by providing for children much more cheaply than would overall wage increases, unquestionably contributed to this outcome. Insofar as workers maintained their standard of living, they did so by working more hours or by bringing more family members into Consortium firms. Total hours worked in Consortium firms increased throughout the twenties out of proportion to the increase in the number of workers, suggesting that individual

[85] As late as 1938, the Ministère du Travail was writing to Ley to tell him the *caisse* could not pay daily rates equivalent to ¹⁄₂₅ of a month's rate, since the law on the forty-hour week meant that no worker should be working twenty-five days per month; and therefore the textile *caisse* was denying full allowances to workers who were simply complying with the forty-hour law. See AN F22 1553 for correspondence between the Ministry of Labor and Ley.

Table 5.6. *Consortium wages and cost-of-living indices, 1921 = 100*

Year	Total wage bill (thousand francs)	Total hours worked (thousands)	Average hourly wage	Hourly wage index	Cost-of-living index	Real wage index
1921	145,658	62,204	2.34	100	100	100
1922	271,623	127,648	2.13	91	–	–
1923	295,847	137,248	2.16	92	121	76
1924	334,803	142,124	2.36	101	139	72
1925	375,256	148,896	2.52	108	150	72
1926	488,549	167,636	2.91	124	182	68
1927	516,323	162,312	3.18	136	205	66
1928	574,825	175,156	3.28	140	210	67
1929	595,764	181,568	3.28	140	213	66
1930	559,991	170,332	3.29	141	209	67

Source: See Table 5.2. Cost-of-living indices from the official commission established at the end of the war are given in Robert Bruyneel, *L'industrie textile de Roubaix-Tourcoing devant la crise économique et la législation sociale* (Paris: Bossuet, 1932), p. 57.

workers were growing accustomed to working longer and more regular hours. Insofar as the family allowance system motivated this discipline, it served employers well.

The Consortium's strategy had a further unintended consequence. Like other *caisses*, the Consortium used profamily rhetoric and claimed it was restoring the unity of the patriarchal family. In fact, however, the Consortium's policy of low wages and recruitment of all ages and sexes tore apart the family economy more thoroughly than any policies – theoretical or applied – we have examined thus far. Wages were lower in textiles than in other industrial work, but women as well as men routinely worked. The Consortium said that some 60% of the mothers in households with children under age 13 did not work, but most likely they simply did not work for the Consortium, since in 1938 fewer than one-third of mothers in such households were able to meet the "no waged employment" qualification for the new *allocation pour la mère au foyer* (housewife's allowance). But if wages were lower and waged work more evenly distributed between the sexes, family allowances were far higher in Roubaix-Tourcoing than in other industries. In principle, then, adult members of the family earned their own living; dependent children were supported through allowances. Although ringed with coercive regulations, the Consortium's system untied the bonds of dependence and maintenance between young and old, women and men. High female employment combined with family allowances disaggregated the family as an economic unit, redistributing income from childless adults of both sexes to those with children. Within the region of Roubaix-Tourcoing, then, the Consortium created a miniature "welfare state" on the parental model described in the Introduction. Catholic doctrine notwithstanding, the Consortium's policy was the diametric opposite of the British ideal of separate spheres and the family wage.

During the twenties, the Consortium developed a comprehensive and extreme strategy for using family policy to restrain and disaggregate wages. In the long term, however, employers sacrificed this highly flexible tool to an impossible vision of a return to the total employer hegemony of the prewar period. Yet family allowances could serve other ends as well. The failure of the Roubaix-Tourcoing model did not doom more modest efforts. In Paris, Pierre Richemond and the leaders of the French engineering industry attempted, with greater success, to present family allowances as relatively uncontroversial measures of maternal and infant welfare while safeguarding their wage restraint functions. It is to their initiatives that we must now turn.

Family allowances in the service of economic reconstruction: The Caisse de Compensation de la Région Parisienne

The years of industrial peace in Roubaix-Tourcoing during the twenties lent the Consortium prestige among employers. The Consortium's policy of combining social work with centralized labor control was seen as a successful strategy for both wage restraint and political hegemony. In 1927, when the Parisian metalworking employers' federation, the Groupe des Industries Métallurgiques, Mécaniques et Connexes de la Région Parisienne (GIMM, here called the Metals Group), considered setting up camping and leisure-time activities for its younger workers, they noted that the Consortium's work offered a valuable example of how "to defend employers' interests by the gradual improvement of working-class living standards."[86] Four years later, however, the Metals Group was far less certain of the success of the Consortium's model and particularly of the value of collective decisions on wages. They blamed the centralized wage policy of the Consortium for the debilitating strikes of 1930 and 1931. The Metals

---

[86] AN 39 AS 850, Groupe des Industrie, Métallurgiques, Mécaniques et Connexes de la Région Parisienne [GIMM], Conseil d'Administration, Ordre du Jour, 7 Dec. 1927, p. 13.

Group, by contrast, had managed to keep wage rates largely stable since 1921 precisely by avoiding – or seeming to avoid – collective decisions on wages.[87]

The experiences of the Consortium confirmed the faith of the Metals Group in their own industrial policy. Like the textile employers of Roubaix-Tourcoing, the Parisian engineering employers placed family allowances in the center of their wage strategy; however, their approach to family policy differed in two key respects from that of the Consortium. First, although the engineering employers shared the Consortium's goal of ensuring a regular supply of labor at stable wages, their strategy was dictated by the very different needs of an industry undergoing expansion and rationalization. The Metals Group's wage policies thus aimed less at making a proportion of the wage dependent on noneconomic factors such as regularity, docility, or nonmembership in unions, than at removing "noneconomic" factors entirely from wage discussions. Above all they sought to undermine wage claims based on family needs. Employers pressing for increased productivity through Fordist methods hoped to base wages entirely on output and meet dependency needs through family allowances: they therefore resisted trying to use the family allowance system explicitly as a strikebreaking tool or, indeed, for any ends but wage restraint.

Second, although the engineering employers were, if anything, even more highly organized than their compatriots in textiles, they chose to veil their control over Parisian family policy. The links between the Metals Group and the huge Caisse de Compensation de la Région Parisienne (CCRP) were hidden from most recipients of family allowances. The wage strategy of the Metals Group, since it operated largely through the ostensibly independent CCRP, was thus extremely opaque. Only by looking inside the administrative councils of the Group and the CCRP can we uncover the links of interest and decision making and assess the success of employer strategies.

The French engineering industry, heavily concentrated in the Paris region, emerged after the First World War as the most dynamic sector of the French economy. As we saw in Chapter 2, the pressures of the war economy, and the concomitant government intervention, significantly altered the size, structure, and organization of the metals sector. In 1906, the total active population in the metals sector (iron, steel, engineering, and fine metals) was 857,000; by 1921, after the wartime boom had settled out, it reached 1,369,000. More than

[87] AN 39 AS 851, GIMM Conseil d'Administration, Ordre du Jour, 3 Nov. 1931.

400,000 of these workers were concentrated in the Paris region. Firms also grew in size: in 1906, only 228 of the Paris region firms employed more than 100 workers; by 1921, 530 firms had more than 100 workers, and 24 more than 1,000. The highly concentrated automobile industry, in particular, exploded: Renault, for example, grew from 4,000–6,000 in 1914 to 22,000 in 1918.[88] The war intensified use of piece-rate payment systems and job rationalization: by 1922, the major automobile manufacturers had all introduced assembly-line production. And some 15% of the postwar Parisian engineering labor force was female, a proportion that rose to 25% at highly rationalized Renault, 35% at Peugeot.[89]

The iron and steel industry had already boasted the strongest employers' organizations before 1914 in the Comité des Forges and the Union des Industries Métallurgiques et Minières (UIMM), but the war further expanded their powers and gave rise to new organizations. During the war, engineering employers' organizations had grown accustomed to apportioning supplies and coordinating labor strategies. In the postwar period, vertical integration of the metals sector was strengthened when Pierre Richemond, Louis Renault, and Baron Petiet set up the monopsonistic Union des Consommateurs de Produits Minières et Industriels, effectively controlling many of their suppliers. The precursor to the Metals Group, the Groupe des Industriels de la Région Parisienne (GIRP), also owed its birth to wartime pressures. It was formed by Louis Renault in January 1917 at the urging of Minister of Munitions Louis Loucheur, who found the disorganized munitions contractors far more frustrating to deal with than the organized trade unions. By 1923, its successor, the Metals Group, comprised more than a thousand affiliated companies employing some 163,000 workers.[90]

In a sense, Louis Loucheur was also the father of the Metals Group's wage policy, for it was his wartime experiments in flexible wage scales

---

[88] The Paris region included Paris (Ville), Seine (Banlieue), Seine-et-Oise, Seine-et-Marne, and Oise. These figures were compiled from *Annuaire statistique* (1909), p. 190, and (1927), p. 192; Statistique Générale de la France, *Résultats statistiques du recensement général de la population effectué le 6 mars 1921*, 2 (Paris, 1925), secs. 1–5. On the automobile industry, see esp. Patrick Fridenson, *Histoire des usines Renault* (Paris: Seuil, 1972).

[89] Aimée Moutet, "Patrons de progrès ou patrons de combat?" in *Recherches*, 32–3, "Le soldat du travail" (Sept. 1978), p. 463; Fridenson, *Histoire des usines Renault*, pp. 94–5. For accounts of women workers at Renault and Panhard during the interwar period, see Annie Fourcaut, *Femmes à l'usine: Ouvrières et surintendantes dans les entreprises françaises de l'entre-deux-guerres* (Paris: François Maspero, 1982), pp. 93–103, 123–5.

[90] AN 39 AS 873, GIMM, *Annuaire*, 2 (1923), pp. 11–12.

that taught the engineering employers the value of increasingly complex and differentiated payment systems. As the war progressed and inflation became more serious, the government began intervening systematically in wage setting. From January 1917, as we have seen in Chapter 2, the Ministry of Munitions set wages by statute and experimented with compulsory arbitration. Galloping inflation was the government's main headache in wage negotiations, and the new wage scales established for Parisian engineering by Loucheur in November 1917 included significant cost-of-living bonuses. Loucheur hoped such bonuses would allow the ministry some flexibility in adjusting earnings to inflation without having to revise actual wage scales.[91] The cost-of-living bonuses were unpopular with the unions, who saw them – rightly – as a means of avoiding all-round wage rises in line with inflation, but they suggested to employers a means of restraining costs and avoiding a wage spiral.

In April of 1918, when faced with demands from the Metalworkers' Federation (Fédération des Métaux) that the various bonuses be incorporated into basic wages, the wartime Paris metals syndicate began to formulate a wage policy for the immediate postwar period. Increased taxes and national debt necessitated a restriction of future costs – especially wages – or the cost of living would grow indefinitely, claimed the GIRP. Nevertheless, while the aim was a wage scale based strictly on productivity, variable cost-of-living bonuses were unavoidable under the "passing influences of the present moment." If cost-of-living bonuses were to be continued, however, they "should be based on family responsibilities." The GIRP essentially proposed to avoid a wage spiral by pegging wages to the cost of living only for workers with dependent children.[92]

The Parisian engineering employers were not alone in trying to integrate family benefits into their wage policies. In the immediate postwar period, spokesmen for their national affiliate, the Union des Industries Métallurgiques et Minières (UIMM), felt that business must preempt the state in the field of family policy, and that the *caisse* system was a workable way to do so. In March 1919, Lambert-Ribot, general secretary of the UIMM, sent a circular to all affiliated regional chambers drawing attention to the "happy initiative" of the *caisse* cre-

[91] Judith Vichniac, "Industrial Relations in Historical Perspective: A Case Study of the French Iron and Steel Industry (1830–1921)," Ph.D. diss. Harvard University, 1981, pp. 279–80; Stephen Douglas Carls, "Louis Loucheur: A French Technocrat in Government, 1916–1920," Ph.D. diss. University of Minnesota, 1982, pp. 181–3.

[92] AN 39 AS 914, File: "Revendication de la Fédération des Métaux, 26 avril, 1918," Document: "Rapport sur les revendications ouvrières concernant les salaires."

ated by Romanet and the Grenoble metal syndicate, recommending that other regional employers' associations study similar measures designed to lighten the burdens of large families and implying that the government might itself introduce legislation in this area.[93] Regional metal syndicates were quick to respond: of fifty-five regional employers' associations in the UIMM, forty-three took an active part in founding *caisses de compensation*, either on an industrial or a regional basis. By 1923, metalworking and engineering employers paid in family allowances Fr 37 million of the total Fr 96 million distributed by the *caisses* and a further Fr 45 million on their own. By 1929, 90% of engineering firms with over five hundred workers paid allowances.[94] The dominance of the metal syndicates in the family allowance movement was reflected in the early organization of the Comité Central: although it was presided over by the textile magnate Eugène Mathon, for the first few years of its existence it owed its office space, financing, and chief administrator, Georges Bonvoisin, to the benevolence of the UIMM. Figure 5.1 illustrates the ties between the family allowance funds and employers' syndicates in the Paris engineering sector and nationally.

The June 1919 general strike for the eight-hour day and for increased wages in the Paris engineering sector convinced employers in different branches of the trade of the need for a collective strategy on wages and social policy.[95] The following year, they officially inaugurated the Groupe des Industries Métallurgiques, Mécaniques et Connexes de la Région Parisienne and gave it three tasks: to maintain a precise documentation on wages, to defend employers' interests during strikes, and to organize social work.[96] Employers considered the first extremely important: since the Metals Group refused to condone collective bargaining, they stressed that all wage changes must be based on accepted statistics.[97] Wage statistics – as well as lists of

[93] Union des Industries Métallurgiques et Minières [UIMM], Circular, 25 Mar. 1919, Copy furnished by the UIMM.

[94] Robert Pinot, *Les oeuvres sociales des industries métallurgiques* (Paris: Armand Colin, 1924), p. 160; Jean Duporcq, *Les oeuvres sociales dans la métallurgie française* (Paris: Librairie Générale de Droit et de Jurisprudence, 1936), p. 39; A. Sayour, *Les oeuvres sociales du patronat* (Paris: Réveil Economique [1929?]), p. 9.

[95] AN 39 AS 914, File: "Enquête sur les concessions possibles," Document: Chambre Syndicale de la Mécanique à Groupe des Industriels de la Région Parisienne [GIRP], 2 June 1919; File: "Liaison avec les syndicats patronaux," Document: Chambre syndicale de la soudure autogène, *Circulaire* (3 June [*sic* – should be July] 1919), p. 5; AN 39 AS 856, GIMM, Assemblée Générale, 31 Mar. 1921, "Rapport."

[96] AN 39 AS 850, GIMM Conseil d'Administration, Ordre du jour, 7 Dec. 1927.

[97] Ibid., 10 Mar. 1921.

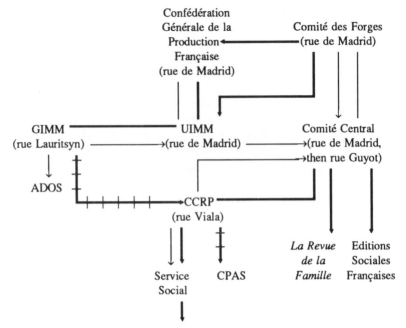

Key:

⟶ Financial subsidy

⟶ Tied through staff or offices

⟶ Affiliation

⟶ Created and officially linked

⟶ Officially autonomous, but created and dependent

Figure 5.1. Ties between employers' organizations and the family allowance funds. ADOS denotes Association pour le Développement des Oeuvres Sociales dans les Industries Métallurgiques et Mécaniques de la Région Parisienne, a GIMM group running camping, sports, and leisure activities. CPAS denotes Comité Parisien des Assurances Sociales, an employers' organization coordinating strategies concerning social insurance in the Paris area.

known "agitators" (*meneurs*) – were then put at the disposal of individual firms faced with wage claims, and in the event of a strike, other firms in the Metals Group would institute a hiring freeze.[98] Finally, the Metals Group, and most particularly its president, Pierre Riche-

---

[98] See, for example, the GIMM response to the 1921 strike in AN 39 AS 856, GIMM

mond, insisted that employers' interests could be effectively safeguarded only through the development of a positive social strategy.
They must align themselves, he argued, with "that section of the
patronat that thinks that it has a social role to play, that it cannot remain
inactive in the face of an ongoing evolution of events, and that this
evolution will take place *with it, or against it*."[99]

The Metals Group did eventually become involved in a variety of
social work, but its first and most significant achievement was the
establishment of a comprehensive program of family allowances for
its employees. The general meeting that officially established the Metals Group on 1 March 1920 also approved the creation of the Caisse
de Compensation de la Région Parisienne (CCRP). In 1919, the Metals
Group's wartime predecessor organization had discovered that fully
61% of the 99,650 male workers it surveyed had no dependent children, while over three-quarters of the remaining 39% had only one
or two. The average burden of dependency was thus quite low, at
0.67 children per worker.[100] Possibly for this reason, the Metals Group
went beyond the UIMM's recommendation of family allowances only
for children in excess of two, drawing up a plan for allowances for
all children of its employees.[101] The industrialist Pierre Richemond,
president of the *caisse* from its inception until its transformation in
1947, also felt strongly that the *caisses* should be regionally rather than
industrially organized, since the cost of children varied by region
rather than between, say, the textile and metal industries.[102] Nevertheless, although the CCRP welcomed enrollment from firms in a
variety of sectors, the engineering firms, following Louis Renault's
personal lead, dominated the *caisse*. At its inception, then, the CCRP
included 490 firms and some 150,000 workers and grew steadily (see
Table 5.7).[103]

Assemblée Générale, 31 Mar. 1921 and Assemblée Extraordinaire, 10 May 1921; for
the work of the strike service, see 39 AS 915, "Revendications depuis nov. 1923."

[99] AN 39 AS 856, GIMM Assemblée Générale, 31 Mar. 1921, "Rapport," p. 17.

[100] Pierre Richemond, "Allocations pour charges de famille et caisses de compensation,"
Revue d'Economie Politique, 34: 5 (Sept.–Oct. 1920), pp. 590–1.

[101] AN 39 AS 837, Villey to Lambert-Ribot, 7 Oct. 1919; Villey to Bonvoisin, 26 Nov.
1919; Villey to Lambert-Ribot, 23 Dec. 1919.

[102] Richemond, "Allocations," p. 597.

[103] The most thorough history of the CCRP is Jean Lygrisse, "Monographie de la Caisse
de Compensation de la Région Parisienne, 1920–1946" (typescript, Paris, 1978). I am
indebted to M. Lygrisse for lending me a copy of his work as well as other valuable
documents on the early history of the CCRP. See also Gustave Maignan, *Les allocations
familiales dans l'industrie et le commerce* (Paris: R. Delaye, Oct. 1942), appendix; idem,

Table 5.7. *Growth of the Caisse de Compensation de la Région Parisienne*

Year	Firms affiliated	Workers covered	Children benefiting	Allowances paid (thousand francs)
1920	480	193,776	62,176	4,115
1921	626	152,626	64,112	
1923				20,000
1926				48,000
1927	1,893	308,310	125,475	
1928	2,079	354,510		
1929	2,313	415,000		72,700
1930	2,350	390,000		76,260
1931	2,300	330,000		74,694
1932	2,266	320,000		69,955
— Law of 11 March 1932 made affiliation obligatory —				
1933	10,000	500,000		93,525
1934	17,176	701,540	291,804	129,804
1935	20,342	742,831	325,063	141,781
1936	25,255	807,717	354,450	167,349
1937	32,758	838,200	398,300	325,929
1938	33,508	863,365	401,928	407,732
1939	25,000	690,000	326,870	625,538

Sources: Jean Lygrisse, "Monographie de la Caisse de Compensation de la Région Parisienne, 1920–1946" (Typescript, Paris, 1986); Gustave Maignan, "La Caisse de Compensation de la Région Parisienne," CNAF, *Compte rendu*, 13 (1933), p. 17; *Rapports de la Commission de Gestion*, in AN F22 1536. Complete statistics for 1934–9 (which differ slightly from those given in the *Rapports*) are in AN F22 1512–13.

Although the Paris *caisse* did pay uniform rates, employers soon insisted on separate accounting for each industrial sector. In 1924, the CCRP was divided into a number of separate sections, each with a distinct scale of employer contributions. By 1932, there were fourteen such sections, and the metals section, which contained fully 198,500 of the CCRP's total 330,700 workers, was further subdivided into ten subsections.[104] The sectioning of the CCRP reproduced almost exactly the structure of employers' organizations; essentially, the heads of major employer syndicates represented their industry on the

"La Caisse de Compensation de la Région Parisienne," CNAF, *Compte rendu*, 13 (1933), p. 16–19.

[104] Maignan, "La Caisse de Compensation," p. 17; AN F22 1536, 1, File: "Agrément 28 juillet 1933 pour la Seine," Document: "Sections professionnelles de la Caisse de Compensation de la Région Parisienne [1932]."

CCRP's board of directors. In addition to Richemond (simultaneously president of the UIMM, the Metals Group, and the *caisse*) and René Duchemin (president of the Confédération Générale de la Production Française and of the Union des Industries Chimiques, and vice-president of the *caisse*), the CCRP's board during the interwar years included such prominent industrialists as Renault, André Citroën, Paul Panhard, Etienne Partiot, Ernest Dalbouze, and Auguste Detoeuf.

The CCRP was, quite simply, the creature of the employers' organizations; nevertheless, these links were not always clear. The *caisse* management, although it took orders from a board of businessmen, was never identified with policies of individual firms. Gustave Maignan, who was the director of the CCRP for most of the interwar period, steered it through Vichy and emerged after 1945 at the head of the new, state-run, amalgamated Caisse d'Allocations Familiales de la Région Parisienne, scarcely concerned himself with industrial policy. Unlike Désiré Ley, he was a model of probity, an unflappable bureaucrat: I found no record of any attack directed against Maignan from either employers, workers, or beneficiaries during the entire history of the *caisse*.

Furthermore, in its early years, the CCRP seemed to operate only as an accounting office. The payment of allowances was left up to the individual firms, who sent them by mail to the mother or the individual having care of the children. The *caisse* merely figured out the percentage of the wage bill needed to cover the cost of allowances for all affiliated firms and charged or reimbursed firms to the extent that their payments fell short of or exceeded their contribution. Employees qualified for benefits after one month of work and, while the allowance would be reduced proportionately for missed days (except in cases of sickness or injury), it was not cut off entirely as a penalty for absence.

The *caisse* thus appeared as a rather anodyne organization; why did employers join? When the leaders of the *caisse* publicly tried to recruit new adherents, they used a combination of pronatalist, economic, and antistatist arguments. How could France, plagued by *dénatalité* and economic crisis, meet the challenge of foreign – and especially German – competition? Industrial prosperity was inextricably linked to population increase, argued the CCRP, for industry would need both more consumers and more workers in the interwar period. The propaganda of the Comité Central, circulated to employers, issued a more blatant threat: "You who still hesitate, DON'T WAIT for the LAW to FORCE you to do what you could have done voluntarily at less cost."[105]

Yet if we look behind the rhetoric produced by the *caisse* for public

---

[105] Quoted in Lygrisse, "Monographie," p. 53.

Table 5.8. *Monthly rates for CCRP family allowances (francs)*

Children under 13	1920	Sept. 1923	Mar. 1926	Oct. 1936	Nov. 1937	Apr. 1939
1	10	10	30	30	60	75
2	30	40	70	80	160	225
3	60	90	120	200	310	450
4	90	170	200	400	510	675
5	120	250	280	600	710	900
Each addnl.	30	80	80	200	200	225
Birth bonus						
First	250	250	250	—	—	—
Each addnl.	150	150	150	—	—	—

Source: See Table 5.7.

consumption to the frank discussions of the directors of the CCRP and the Metals Group, we find that pronatalist and political interests increasingly took second place to the construction of a comprehensive wage strategy. Developments in the payment of benefits confirm this interpretation. Although monthly children's allowances were initially only one of the *caisse*'s family benefits and in fact compared rather unfavorably to the sizable birth bonuses, the latter were held stable while the monthly rates were increased a number of times during the 1920s (see Table 5.8). Monthly children's allowances thus gradually became a significant portion of the income of working families. If we look briefly at the wage crises of 1923 and 1926, we can see how the CCRP, taking its cue from the Metals Group, effectively used family allowances to undercut wage demands.

After falling steadily throughout 1921, the cost of living in the Paris area stabilized in 1922 and, in the last trimester, began to rise. In December 1922, the board of directors of the Metals Group met to discuss the best strategy for meeting the growing claims for wage increases. Agreeing that the best idea would be to raise family allowances "to a level which allows us to set aside consideration of family burdens," the board unanimously voted to call upon the CCRP to raise rates.[106] As the board told the general assembly of the Metals Group:

> Allowances allow us to compare prewar and current wages on a juster and better-defined basis. Thanks to them, one can, when talking of "wages," only compare those portions which are actually comparable:

[106] AN 39 AS 850, GIMM Conseil d'Administration, Procès-verbal, 18 Dec. 1922, p. 7.

that is, the payment for actual work. The worker's family situation
is *another question*, treated on *another basis*.[107]

Unfortunately, they admitted, the current level of allowances was not
high enough to separate out entirely the question of support for the
family. By raising the employers' contribution by 0.5% of the wage
bill to about 1.8%, however, the CCRP would be able to raise rates
significantly. The assembly agreed to raise allowances for the second
child and beyond, but to refuse any general wage increases.

Allowances were thus explicitly granted in lieu of wages and to
deter wage claims. They should be seen, then, as an alternative form
of wage distribution, one based on workers' dependency needs. Allowances "cost" childless workers their deferred wage increases, but
they significantly increased basic wages for families of more than one
child dependent on a single earner. Furthermore, because allowances
were paid as a flat rate, they were a far more substantial addition to
unskilled than to skilled wages. In 1923, the allowance for four children amounted to only 27% of the wage of a skilled turner in full
work, but 42% of the wage of an unskilled laborer.[108]

The employers' decision on allowances allowed them to meet union
demands for increased wages on a strong footing. Pierre Richemond,
meeting with representatives of the communist-affiliated Seine Metalworkers' Union, pointed out that wages had remained stable but
employers had nevertheless set up family allowances to aid their workers. Union leaders objected to the principle of allowances, arguing
that "the worker ought to be able to support his family without giving
information on its situation and needs,"[109] but found themselves out-
maneuvered. The Metals Group easily broke a May 1923 strike by
adopting a collective hiring freeze and countered early-1924 wage
demands by pointing out that their 1923 increase in allowances meant
that family needs were better met.[110] Although the cost of living rose
by some 25% between 1923 and 1926, firms in the Metals Group
avoided across-the-board wage increases, meeting claims on a case-
by-case basis.

In 1926, a number of the Metals Group's firms, "convinced of the

---

[107] AN 39 AS 856, GIMM Assemblée Générale, 22 Mar. 1923, ordre du jour, p. 4.
[108] The hourly wage was 3.18 francs for a turner, and 2 francs for a laborer in GIMM
firms (rates cited in AN 39 AS 850, GIMM Conseil d'Administration, 19 Mar. 1923).
[109] AN 39 AS 915, File: "Revendications et grèves, 1923," Document: "Procès verbal de
la réunion du 12 avril 1923," p. 5.
[110] AN 39 AS 850, GIMM Conseil d'Administration, 23 May 1923; 39 AS 856, Assemblées
Générales, 25 Feb. and 28 Mar. 1924.

Table 5.9. *CCRP family allowances as a percentage of a full-time monthly wage at the average hourly rate for Metals Group firms*

Year and trimester	Number of children in family								Avg. wage (francs)
	1	2	3	4	5	6	7	8	
1921 (4)	2.0	6	12	18	23	29	35	41	512
1924 (1)	1.5	6	14	26	39	51	63	76	647
1927 (1)	3.3	8	13	22	31	40	49	58	903
1930 (3)	2.6	6	10	17	24	31	37	44	1,172
1933 (3)	2.6	6	10	17	24	31	38	45	1,151
1936 (4)	2.5	7	16	33	49	68	82	98	1,218
1938 (3)	1.7	9	17	28	40	51	62	73	1,793

Source: See Table 5.7. Wage figures are from the *Bulletin de la Statistique Générale de la France.*

usefulness of the family allowance system as a means of moderating excessive wage demands"[111] (in their own words), launched another preemptive strike. In a move that increased their cost to employers by about 65%, the Metals Group and the CCRP raised allowances substantially for the first and second child.[112] A series of spring strikes at Renault and other firms only strengthened employers' resolve, and the Metals Group's board of directors recommended adopting long-service bonuses in preference to across-the-board wage increases.[113] By 1927, children's allowances would raise a laborer's wage by about 4% for one child, 10% for two, and 40% for five, although they were less significant for better-paid skilled workers.

This was the last increase in rates until 1936, and allowances did not keep up with wages. By 1930, the family allowance as a percentage of a laborer's wage had slipped to 3.45% for one child, 8% for two, 23% for five, 60% for eight, and so forth.[114] Nevertheless, throughout the interwar period, and as we can see from Table 5.9, these allowances significantly altered the wage system, especially for large families dependent on a single earner. Engineering employers used allowances to redistribute income from childless workers to those with children, thus creating in their factories – as in Roubaix-Tourcoing – a pre-

---

[111] AN 39 AS 850, GIMM Conseil d'Administration, 17 Mar. 1926, ordre du jour, p. 1.

[112] AN 39 AS 856, GIMM Assemblée Générale, 17 Mar. 1926; Conseil d'Administration, 19 Mar. 1926.

[113] AN 39 AS 850, GIMM Conseil d'Administration, 19 May and 30 July 1926.

[114] Wage figures, from which these calculations are derived, are from Lygrisse, "Monographie," p. 72, and François Villey, *Le complément familial du salaire: Etude des allocations familiales dans leur rapports avec le salaire* (Paris: Ed. Sociales Françaises, 1946), p. 200.

cursor to the parental welfare state. Furthermore, they were able to do this at a relatively low cost: employers' contribution rates fluctuated at around 2% of the wage bill in the period before state control. The family policy of the CCRP thus successfully tore apart the family wage, redistributing income in favor of dependent children.

In contrast to Consortium policy, however, which was essentially gender-blind – paying all adult workers for all dependent children – the CCRP's policy also redistributed income between women and men. The Paris *caisse* paid the allowance by statute to the mother, whether or not she was herself gainfully employed. This was in part a pragmatic decision: employers had little faith that allowances paid to men would be spent on children.[115] But by paying directly to women, employers to some extent pitted the interests of the unwaged (especially unwaged wives) against those of the waged. Furthermore, other policies set up by the *caisse* administrators could fragment family loyalties as well as income. The CCRP appealed to women as wives and mothers through the development of home-based social services that bore little obvious relation to employer interests.

The Social Service of the CCRP became famous as the model for home-based maternal and infant social work. However, a genuine concern among CCRP social workers for both public health and domestic morality dovetailed neatly with employers' desires for access to their employees' families. The Social Service was a key pillar of the employers' strategy not only because effective wage restraint was seen to be dependent on the domestic education of women, but also because social workers, not explicitly connected with specific firms, could be used to investigate particular problems and to "police" families. Employers worried about the disruptive and potentially revolutionary influence of the heavily male, heavily communist Parisian unions thus attempted to remake the Parisian working class through a direct appeal to women. Through the twin pillars of economic support and social services, the CCRP tried to create an alliance of interests between capital and women, against the workplace-centered politics of organized men.

The social strategy of the CCRP operated through two main programs: a home visiting service and home economics teaching. Soon after the founding of the CCRP, employers expressed concern that mothers might not be using allowances wisely. In response, the *caisse* founded its Social Service, hiring five women as "home visitors." Direction of the service was entrusted to the redoubtable Mlle Hardouin,

---

[115] Richemond, "Allocations," p. 598.

who also served on the board of a school for training women as factory welfare supervisors set up in 1924 by Cécile Brunschvicg and other social reforming women. Hardouin, Brunschvicg, and other bourgeois women social workers sought to build up a cadre of trained women welfare workers, along the lines of that developed by the Ministry of Munitions in Britain during the First World War, and were eager to cooperate with employers.[116] By 1933, the *caisse* employed 115 visitors, who made more than 200,000 visits per year in the Paris area.[117] Visitors made prenatal visits to all expectant mothers, distributed layettes, and returned to check up on young babies. As a result, Pierre Richemond claimed, infant mortality among CCRP families was only half that of the Paris population generally.[118] Visitors also kept an eye on the health of other household members, and the *caisse* sent sick children on cures and placed others in summer camps.

The home visitors hired by the CCRP were trained nurses, but they saw their role as primarily that of counselors and moral exemplars. CCRP home visitors acted much like the English women who volunteered for the Soldiers' and Sailors' Families Association and shared their vision of cross-class harmony and their moralizing mission. They attempted to create relationships of trust between themselves and the mothers they visited, and in fact ties between families and visitors did multiply. While visitors were initially sent to particular families at the request of employers, by 1932 only 2,000 of the 45,120 households visited were called on at the request of the employer.[119] Yet the employers valued their ability to call on the visitors to look into the domestic life of their employees, and some employers used the visitors as factory supervisors.[120]

Home visiting was the first and most important type of social intervention directed at women, but it was complemented by a growing attempt to shape the CCRP's female work force within the factory

[116] For the early history of the "surintendantes," see Mlle Hardouin, "Les surintendantes d'usine et de service sociaux," in "L'hygiène sociale," *Les Cahiers du Redressement Français*, no. 17 (Paris: Editions de la S.A.P.E. [1927]), pp. 119–35.

[117] On the origins of the Social Service, see Caisse d'Allocations Familiales de la Région Parisienne, *Cinquantenaire d'un service d'action sociale: L'économie familiale de 1927 à 1977* (Paris, 1977); Maignan in CNAF, *Compte rendu*, 13 (1933), pp. 18–19.

[118] AN F22 1536, 2, File: "Correspondence," Document: *Bulletin du GIMMCRP*, 15 (July 1933), p. 2.

[119] Ibid., p. 3.

[120] Records of the CCRP Social Service can be found in AN F22 1536, 2, File: "Etats et bilans." See also Mlle Hardouin, "L'action 'des visiteuses' dans la famille ouvrière," CNAF, *Compte rendu*, 4 (1924), pp. 89–96; Yvonne Knibiehler, *Nous les assistantes sociales* (Paris: Aubier, 1980), esp. pp. 195–7, for an account by a social worker for the CCRP.

into rationalized and thrifty housewives. In 1927, the *caisse* began experimenting with various types of home economics courses. In July 1925, the government had passed a finance law setting up an apprenticeship tax but exempted employers who contributed to training their personnel. Home economics was included in such training, so the CCRP was able to recoup almost all of its costs. Initially, the *caisse* had difficulty in attracting students: parents objected to girls returning home late in the evening, and the workers themselves refused to give up their Saturday half-day to the course. The *caisse* therefore began holding early evening classes inside the factory itself, with the employer paying the worker for a portion of the class time – a strategy that ensured "perfect attendance."

Courses met once or twice a week and were rigorously practical: in addition to lessons in sewing, mending, and childcare, much attention was paid to economical cooking. Students went shopping together and were taught, essentially, how to rationalize housework – to pay attention to seasonality and price, to use leftovers, and to waste nothing.[121] A woman factory superintendent who underwent a training period at Peugeot wrote in 1933 that the factory's home economics courses raised the moral character of the students, arousing in them "a concern to avoid the vulgar pleasures, to live better both materially and morally, and a desire better to fulfill [their] social duties at home."[122] By the eve of the Second World War, the CCRP was running over 450 home economics courses per year for more than six thousand students.[123]

The CCRP's home economics teaching complemented both their home visiting and their wage restraint strategy. By applying the lessons of labor rationalization to the home, employers sought to minimize the time, effort, and cost of the reproduction of the work force.[124] Yet such interventionist social work also gave them a timely defense against Catholics and pronatalists who campaigned fiercely in the thirties against married women's work. Social Catholic campaigns, which will be discussed fully in Chapter 7, were especially threatening to firms dependent on cheap female labor. Social services for women

---

[121] Mlle Hardouin, "L'enseignement ménager," CNAF, *Compte rendu*, 8 (1928), pp. 87–95.
[122] Fourcaut, *Femmes à l'usine*, p. 203.
[123] Figures on home economics courses are from the CCRP's "Rapports de la Commission de Gestion," AN F22 1536, 2, File: "Etats et Bilans."
[124] For an account of some of the debates over housework and its rationalization, see Martine Martin, "Ménagère: Une profession? Les dilemmes de l'entre-deux-guerres," *Le Mouvement Social*, 140 (July–Sept. 1987), pp. 89–106.

workers allowed employers to continue to employ women without forfeiting the moral high ground – largely ceded by the Consortium – of profamily rhetoric. Waged work for women had become a necessity since the war, Mlle Hardouin claimed, but while the factory could become the enemy of home life, the social programs introduced by industrialists allowed women to reconcile their dual roles as mothers and workers. The training provided by the *caisse* could even revitalize the home, since an attractive *foyer* was, she argued, the best weapon for combating alcoholism and the cabaret.[125]

The social strategy of the Parisian employers, combining wage restraint with direct intervention in family life, proved virtually impervious to trade union attack. A 1932 Metals Group report stated that while the CCRP was not so closely identified with the Metals Group in public as to lead to campaigns against it, it was nevertheless "hard to imagine better management of employer policy than that currently followed by the Directorate of the Family Allowance Fund."[126] In Roubaix-Tourcoing the textile unions lost almost every battle, but they had no trouble identifying their opponent and deciphering Consortium strategy. In Paris, by contrast, the links between the Metals Group and the CCRP were opaque, and it was not until the mid-twenties that the largely communist Parisian metal unions began to perceive rationalization, wage restraint, and family policy as parallel and interlocking strategies.

When the Parisian employers first considered setting up a family allowance scheme, union opinion was mixed. Gustave Maignan claimed that the CCRP was created only after a favorable interview with Alphonse Merrheim, secretary of the Metalworkers' Federation, but admitted that the majority of the CGT was hostile.[127] The Federation's own National Committee resolved in no uncertain terms that the family allowance "aggravates the humiliation of the exploited worker by destroying his belief that his work alone supports his household"; it is, they concluded, "in opposition to the fundamental principles of trade unionism."[128] In 1920, however, the Parisian metal unions were far too absorbed in the problems of rationalization and wage fragmentation on the one hand and the split between com-

---

[125] Hardouin, "L'enseignement ménager."

[126] AN 39 AS 851, GIMM Conseil d'Administration, 14 Dec. 1932, "Rapport sur le Projet . . . " (5 Dec. 1932), p. 14.

[127] Maignan, *Les allocations familiales dans l'industrie, le commerce et les professions libérales* (Paris: UNCAF, 1954), p. 10.

[128] Quoted in Louis Deschamps, Congrès National de la Natalité, *Compte rendu*, 2 (1920), p. 193.

munists and socialists on the other to devote more than cursory attention to the operation of family allowances. When the CGT split in December 1921, the Metalworkers' Federation did so as well, with the Parisian unions siding overwhelmingly with the communist wing, the CGTU. The CGTU paid little attention in the early twenties to the extension of the *caisses*, and the CCRP's policy of payment to the mother to some extent masked the relationship between allowances and wages. Just as with the British TUC, family allowances were first discussed by the CGTU's Women's Conference, presumably on the assumption that family policy was a "women's issue" not requiring the time of busy male trade unionists.

In the mid-twenties, however, the CGTU, and most particularly the Parisian unions, woke up to the centrality of family allowances to employer strategies and to the link between allowances and rationalization. During the labor unrest of 1926, *L'Humanité* identified family allowances as part of a wider strategy to make wages increasingly dependent on an entire range of both economic (output, ability) and noneconomic (loyalty, regularity) factors.[129] Rationalization and the *sursalaire* were parallel strategies aimed at dividing and stabilizing the work force and at disaggregating and reducing wages, the CGTU claimed in a 1927 report.[130] In November 1928, the National Committee of the Metalworkers' Federation resolved "that the wage should first of all recover its unified form, and not be fragmented in a distribution which has no other purpose than to mask its inadequacy."[131] In discussion, however, one union militant admitted that while it might be possible to reintegrate cost-of-living bonuses into base rates, the same strategy would not work with family allowances. "Events have passed us by," he reiterated four years later: family allowances were here to stay.[132] Communist official policy on family allowances, hammered out in the late twenties, thus called for the constitution of an autonomous national *caisse*, under the administrative control of workers, which would pay family allowances for all children without regard to unemployment, strikes, or other actions.[133]

---

[129] "Pour la préparation du congrès des usines de la métallurgie," *L'Humanité*, 10 Nov. 1926; "Pour le Congrès de la métallurgie," *L'Humanité*, 4 Nov. 1926.

[130] "Les caisses de compensation patronales," *La Vie Syndicale*, 27 (June–July 1927), pp. 588–96.

[131] Fédération des Ouvriers en Métaux, Congrès Fédéral, *Compte rendu,* 9 (1929), p. 15.

[132] Ibid., pp. 99–100; Fédération des Ouvriers en Métaux, Congrès Fédéral, *Compte rendu,* 11 (1933), p. 230.

[133] *La Vie Syndicale*, 29 (Oct.–Dec. 1927), p. 754; CGTU, Congrès, *Compte rendu,* 4 (1927), pp. 513–14.

If the communist CGTU had some trouble unraveling the complex links between rationalization and family allowances, it had just as much trouble responding to the CCRP's increasingly interventionist social work. The success of employer policy toward women stemmed from the fact that the unions themselves had real difficulty – not to mention ambivalence about – organizing women. Before 1936, trade unionism was weak among women in Paris metal trades, and wages were routinely lower than those of men even on the same work. Seine metalworkers, threatened with the entrance of low-paid women into deskilled jobs, were tempted to oppose women's work altogether as incompatible with home and family. They could therefore be sympathetic to the rhetoric of domesticity expounded by the Social Service as well as to policies aimed at keeping women in the home. In fact, like the social Catholics in Roubaix-Tourcoing, they could criticize the *caisse* for not being patriarchal enough: the policy of payment to the mother could be seen as an infringement of the rights of the *père de famille*. In language reminiscent of that employed across the channel, one speaker at the 1925 congress of the Metalworkers' Federation asked whether trade unionists could allow the *caisses* "to inflict this gratuitous insult on workers by sending the family allowance payment to the wife, rather than giving it directly to the worker (*producteur*)."[134]

Yet the positions of left-wing workers' organizations were rarely so overtly patriarchal. Both communists and socialists made real efforts in the twenties to integrate women – as workers and housewives – into organized working-class politics; both officially supported some degree of "socialization" of the work of reproduction, even calling on occasion for the direct state support of mothers. And a kind of proletarian and egalitarian feminism flourished within some communist circles at least, with some activists insisting that women's independence must stem from participation in wage earning and not maternity alone, even if the latter were eased by allowances. It was the CGTU that defended women's work rights most forthrightly in the twenties, not only on the grounds that such work was a tragic necessity ever since industrialization brought about the primeval fall from domestic grace – the dominant opinion in the CGT – but also because "the woman has the right to live by her labor and not be subordinate to anyone, not even a man."[135] It was the communist teacher Marthe Bigot who as early as 1922 undertook to study the family allowance system and who warned readers of the communist *L'Ouvrière* that

---

[134] Fédération des Ouvriers en Métaux, Congrès Fédéral, *Compte rendu*, 7 (1925), p. 287.
[135] CGTU, Congrès, *Compte rendu*, 3 (1925) p. 537.

such benefits would not only hold down wages but also, if paid to men, would "further accentuate the economic inferiority of the wife and place her absolutely under her husband's domination."[136] Less willing to accept familist ideology itself as a good thing, albeit in the wrong hands, communists were also among the first to recognize that the rhetoric of separate spheres, of the *mère au foyer*, could divide working-class families along sex lines. In a perceptive study of the uses of allowances by the *patronat*, one communist warned that the home visitors were

> veritable agents of the employer, insinuating themselves in the family, spying, and, when necessary, not hesitating to try to set the mother – in the name of the children's immediate interests – against the father engaged in the struggle for better wages, which would support the family better than the employer's alms.[137]

The CGTU combated such strategies in the twenties not by arguing that women should go back to their kitchens and that any aid be given to the *père de famille*, but rather by opposing employers' stranglehold over administration of the welfare funds. Its own family allowance proposals provided for payment to the person having effective care of the children – a formula that would give payment in most cases to the mother, but without assuming an unbreakable link between sex and social role.

The CGTU's growing understanding of the multivalent strategy of the CCRP did not win it state support, since, in their relations with public authorities, the Metals Group and CCRP proved far more politic than the Roubaix-Tourcoing Consortium. The government was largely indifferent to employer strategies, provided they did not interfere with the formal rights of free labor, and they found the social work of the CCRP commendable. Furthermore, while the CCRP had initially opposed state intervention in the *caisse* system, when intervention looked likely they adopted a far more conciliatory position and sought to safeguard the central elements of their system: big business dominance, social work, and the parallel organization of industrial chambers and *caisse* sections.

The CCRP carefully refined its structure to ensure big business control as soon as state intervention seemed likely. In 1929 its statutes were altered so that firms voted in proportion to the number of work-

---

[136] Marthe Bigot, "Charges familiales," *L'Ouvrière*, 1: 22 (5 Aug. 1922).
[137] "Les allocations familiales, armes patronales," *Cahiers du Bolchevisme*, 3: 4 (June 1928), p. 500.

ers employed, a formula that would prevent the small businesses from controlling policy, should they be required to affiliate to a fund.[138] When the state did make affiliation mandatory for all such firms in 1932, the Metals Group pressed the Ministry of Labor for early application, with no special consideration given to small businesses.[139] The CCRP, as the largest Parisian *caisse* and the first granted ministerial approval, was thus able to absorb most of the less-organized small businesses without substantially modifying its operation. On the eve of the law, 2,524 firms with 330,700 workers (or 131 workers per firm) were affiliated to the CCRP; in the automobiles subsection, 26 affiliated firms alone employed 70,000 workers. By 1934, an additional 14,652 firms employing 400,840 workers (a mere 23 workers per firm) had enrolled, but the latter were too divided to exercise any real control over CCRP policy.[140]

One of the major complaints of the new affiliates was that CCRP costs were too high. They strenuously objected to paying for programs not required by law, especially for the Social Service. Yet while home visiting held little appeal for small businessmen who dealt directly with their employees, it was the principal means by which the large firms kept in touch with the families of their workers. Fortunately for the CCRP, the government had no intention of undermining what it viewed as useful public health work carried out at no cost to the state. Thus, when small businesses tried both to set up funds of their own with lower employer contribution rates and to convince the CCRP to exempt them from social work expenses, the Ministry of Labor and the CCRP collaborated to defeat these maneuvers and compel affiliation to preexisting funds.[141] The progress of social work continued: whereas 62 *caisses* had such services before 1932, 124 *caisses* operated social services in 1936, which were staffed altogether by 400 visiting

---

[138] CCRP Archives, Commission de Gestion, Procès verbal, 12 Nov. 1929.

[139] AN 39 AS 830, Villey to Ministry of Labor, 6 Apr. 1933, Villey to Commission Supérieure des Allocations Familiales, 5 July 1933.

[140] Figures for 1932 are derived from a document, "Sections professionnelles de la caisse de compensation," now in AN F22 1536, 1, File: "Agrément 28 juillet 1933." Figures for 1934 were included among materials sent by Maignan to the ministry on 25 July 1935, now in AN F22 1536, 2, File: "Etats et bilans."

[141] See, for example, the correspondence between Maignan, ministry officials, and the president of the Shoemakers' Syndicate in October and November of 1933, in AN F22 1536, File: "Correspondance." Ministerial and CCRP negotiations are discussed in the "Rapport de la Commission de Gestion" for 1932 and 1933, in AN F22 1536, 2, File: "Etats et bilans"; also CCRP Archives, Commission de Gestion, Procès verbal, 1 Dec. 1932.

nurses. Fully 158 of the nurses worked for the CCRP, which jealously guarded control over its social programs against the Popular Front government. Employers feared that any extension of state control would deprive them of "their main opportunities of entering into [workers'] families."[142]

Having ensured the continuation of big-business dominance and of its social strategy, the CCRP set about winning government approval for its sectoral organization. For employers, organization by industrial sector facilitated the use of allowances to manage wage demands. The Ministry of Labor, however, had expressed a clear preference for funds established across industry ("interprofessionally"), ruling that it would allow industrial sections within a *caisse* only if they included more than 50% of the workers in that industry. The CCRP had no trouble meeting this condition for its engineering section, which was approved in the summer of 1933. The *caisse* had temporarily suppressed its other industrial sections following the passage of the law but planned to reconstitute them as soon as possible. In early 1934, Maignan warned the ministry that if the CCRP was not allowed to reestablish its industrial sections, these firms would break away and form dissident industrially based *caisses*; the regional clothing employers' syndicate, waiting for ministerial approval to set up a CCRP section, issued a similar threat. Such breakaways would have dissipated the coordinated social work of the fund, welcomed by the ministry; thus, by the middle of 1934 the CCRP's largest industrial sections – metals, printing, clothing, food, leather, and head offices – had all been approved.[143] Unlike the Consortium, the CCRP had used state intervention if anything to consolidate its position. It had absorbed the small businesses brought in by the 1932 law without granting them a significant voice in policy; its Social Service remained intact; and it retained close links between employers' organizations and the *caisse*. These achievements survived even the 1936 strikes and the Popular Front.

The massive strikes of May and June 1936 in the Paris engineering industry, and the resulting collective bargaining agreement, are often viewed as the main stimuli to collective organization by a lethargic

---

[142] CCRP Archives, File: "Commission Sociale," Sous-Commission de Service Social et d'Enseignement Ménager, "Procès verbal de la réunion du 2 octobre 1936," p. 3; see also M. Colcomb, "Les services sociaux des caisses de compensation," CNAF, *Compte rendu*, 16 (1936), pp. 69–74.

[143] CCRP Archives, Commission de Gestion, Procès verbal, 7 June 1933; AN F22 1536, 1, File "Arrêté du 27 jan. 1934."

and divided business class.[144] Yet these strikes came as a shock less because employers were disorganized and caught off guard by the newly reunited union movement, than because they were complacent. Employers thought their strategy of rationalization, wage restraint, and family policy had been entirely successful since they had not signed collective contracts in the metals industry since the ill-fated accord on the eight-hour day extracted in the social turmoil of 1919. Yet while family allowances had successfully limited wage claims and increases, employers were too complacent in the late twenties, and too hard-pressed during the depression, to see that they kept pace with wage increases or the cost of living. In the beginning of 1935, the CCRP's management had even considered reducing rates.[145]

The June strikes, with their factory occupations and festive air, shattered this complacency.[146] In the wake of the Matignon accords, employers looked once again to family policy as a tool of industrial defense. Three of the four signatories to the accords for the employers – Richemond, Dalbouze, and Duchemin – were on the board of the CCRP, and they quickly turned to the *caisse* to limit the damage. The June 1936 contract in the engineering industry had granted substantial wage increases,[147] but employers felt that higher allowances could fend off further demands. Family allowances had not been taken into consideration in the June discussions, Richemond admitted to the CCRP board, but perhaps that was because they were simply not high enough.[148] An increase in rates not only would show workers that gains could be won without strikes, Maignan argued, but also would allow employers to remove the question of the *famille nombreuse* entirely from wage negotiations, since the rate for children beyond the third would actually be enough to keep the child.[149] Recalling its

[144] The argument that the employers were in disarray on the eve of the 1936 strikes is given in Ehrmann, *Organized Business*, pp. 6–7.

[145] CCRP Archives, Commission de Gestion, Procès verbal, 9 Jan. 1935.

[146] On the June strikes, see especially Julian Jackson's excellent synthetic account, *The Popular Front in France: Defending Democracy, 1934–38* (Cambridge University Press, 1988), pp. 85–112.

[147] The 13 June 1936 contract was signed between the GIMM and Citroën on the one hand and the Fédération des Métaux on the other. It recognized trade union rights and collective bargaining and granted substantial wage increases (especially in view of the parallel reduction in hours from forty-eight to forty). As of 1936, the GIMM counted 3,120 firms, representing about 80% of the Parisian metal industry; the Fédération des Métaux represented 290,000 workers, or 87% of the Parisian metalworkers. The original agreement and supporting documentation are in AN F22 1633, 1.

[148] CCRP Archives, Commission de Gestion, Procès verbal, 22 July 1936.

[149] Ibid., 15 Sept. 1936.

earlier claim that social policy was the first line of employers' defense, the board of the CCRP called together its adherents and urged a substantial increase in rates:

> Some employers, understandably disappointed by the attitude of their workers, may have been tempted to do nothing more than meet their minimum legal responsibilities, and to abandon all social work. This would be, we think, the *most serious mistake* that could be made. It would be a capitulation that would pave the way to total surrender.[150]

The assembly agreed, winning the congratulations of pronatalists and government administrators.[151] Once again, the CCRP had anticipated and preempted government policy: ministerial directives merely confirmed their decisions.

In the late thirties, the French state did begin to play a leading – if sporadic – role in family policy, as government arbitrators and administrators with pronatalist leanings raised family allowance rates through contracts and decrees.[152] For almost two decades, however, the decisions of the CCRP – in effect, the decisions of the Paris engineering sector – set the standard for the extension and uses of family policy. The firms enrolled in the CCRP hoped to extend rationalization and piecework payment while protecting themselves from claims that "men have families to keep." Family allowances, they decided, were their best hope, by far the cheapest way to meet dependency needs in an industry that was, by and large, prosperous and expanding.

How successful was their policy? Hourly wages outstripped the cost of living in the period before the Matignon accords, but by no means approached the rate of increase of productivity. Although wages in firms affiliated to the Metals Group rose by 68% between 1920 and 1929 while the cost of living rose by only 48%, productivity in the automobile industry quadrupled in the same period. Unlike the Con-

---

[150] Ibid., Transcript of the report of the Commission de Gestion; and Lygrisse, p. 115.

[151] *Revue*, no. 290 (Oct. 1936), pp. 263–5.

[152] In February 1937, William Oualid raised family allowance rates substantially in an arbitration decision in Paris metallurgy. Much praised by pronatalists, the decision caused havoc within the CCRP, which found itself compelled to apply a number of different scales. In October 1937, some 40% of the CCRP's beneficiaries, scattered among various sections, were still receiving old rates. The *caisses* together put pressure on the government to regularize the rates, which were raised to conform to the Oualid decision for the entire Seine region. Boverat, "De magnifiques succès," *Revue*, 38: 295 (Mar. 1937), pp. 65–70; CCRP Archives, Commission de Gestion, Procès verbal, 24 May and 11 Oct. 1937.

Table 5.10. *Index of real wages*[a] *in Metals Group firms and national production indices*

Year and trimester [b]	Hourly average wage (francs)	Paris cost-of-living index (1920=100)	Real-wage index (1920=100)	National production indices	
				Engineering (1920=100)	Automobile (1921=100)
1920 (4)	3.01	100	100	100	
1921 (4)	2.54	80	105	95	100
1922 (1)	2.68	79	113	125	107
1923 (1)	2.90	88	109	143	130
1924 (1)	3.21	99	108	195	177
1925 (1)	3.43	104	110	183	194
1926 (1)	3.86	122	105	210	228
1927 (1)	4.48	142	105	181	220
1928 (1)	4.57	137	111	219	256
1929 (1)	5.06	148	114	249	276
1930 (3)	5.82	160	121	244	268
1931 (3)	5.76	153	125	167	229
1932 (3)	5.47	140	130	154	179
1933 (3)	5.71	139	137	174	196
1934 (3)	5.65	138	136	163	190
1935 (3)	5.60	127	146	163	168
1936 (4)	7.25	146	165 (138)[c]	177	195
1937 (3)	9.60	170	188 (157)[c]	199	199
1938 (3)	10.68	186	191 (160)[c]	172	224

[a] Wages include bonuses but exclude family allowances.
[b] Trimester is for wage and cost-of-living figures.
[c] Figures in parentheses are corrected for the diminution of earnings resulting from the reduction of the work week.
Sources: Wage figures and cost-of-living statistics are found in the *Bulletin de la Statistique Générale de la France* and in the 1936 GIMM *Annuaire*, AN 39 AS 873, p. 196. Production statistics are taken from Alfred Sauvy, *Histoire économique de la France entre les deux guerres* (Paris: Economica, 1984), vol. 2, pp. 316–17.

sortium, the Metals Group could not hold wages below the cost-of-living increases, but this degree of wage restraint in a period of real industrial advance was a respectable achievement – especially since partisans of scientific management like Citroën and Renault supported the Fordist doctrine of high wages linked to increased productivity.[153] Family allowances were obviously only one facet of the

[153] On the attempt of the automobile manufacturers to reconcile their social conservatism

Metals Group's strategy, yet the group itself believed that the allowance did serve to limit both wage demands and discontent. Table 5.10 compares real-wage indices with national production indices for engineering and for the automobile industry, heavily concentrated in the Paris region.

Results in the thirties were more mixed, when employers simultaneously confronted economic slump, a newly reunited and powerful union movement, and after 1936, increasing state intervention. Nevertheless, the identification between family and economic policy could not be unraveled, and the close relationship between wages and allowances insisted upon by the Metals Group and the CCRP held. Family allowances continued to be seen as a legitimate way to pay some portion of the wage bill, not as a welfare benefit dependent on financing by redistributive taxes. Later state activism was predicated on the agreement that family policy was a question of economic prosperity as well as national defense, and that industry, not the government, would foot the bill. The innovation of big business in the interwar period permanently altered the wage structure in France, with lasting effects less on demography than on industrial relations and the structure of the French welfare state.

Conclusion

Family allowances occupied a central place in the business strategies of both the Consortium and the engineering employers who created the CCRP. Both institutions were the conscious creation of the most highly organized industrial sectors. In the words of one communist writer, the Consortium was "the best organized and possibly the most combative *patronat* in the whole of France."[154] This extraordinary level of cohesion among employers made it possible for the Consortium to create some of the most ambitious and illiberal social policies in France. The Consortium's family allowances scheme was intended to disaggregate and restrain wages, of course; but it also had other purposes. Through regulations that made uninterrupted presence at work a condition of benefit, the Consortium sought to inculcate habits

with their attempt to rationalize and modernize production techniques, see Patrick Fridenson, "L'idéologie des grands constructeurs dans l'entre-deux-guerres," *Le Mouvement Social*, 81 (Oct.–Dec. 1972), pp. 51–68; Moutet, "Patrons de progrès," p. 476; Pierre Delune, "Rendez-vous avec M. André Citroën," *Revue de la Famille*, 23 (Nov. 1929), pp. 4–6.

[154] J. Berlioz, "La grève du textile du Nord," *Cahiers du Bolchevisme*, 3: 8 (Oct. 1928), p. 971.

of regularity and docility in their workforce, to create a severe financial disincentive to strike, and to undermine both the popular appeal and room to maneuver of the trade unions. Both the wage and labor control strategies were, for a time, successful; in the end, however, the illiberalism of the Consortium's labor policies and the arrogance of its leadership proved more than either government ministers or the local Catholic hierarchy could tolerate, and they joined trade unionists in opposition.

The strategy of the engineering employers, while equally self-conscious, was much more subtle, uniting wage restraint and interventionist social work behind a veil of legally autonomous philanthropic organizations. Gradually, trade unionists came to realize the multivalent character of the Metals Group's policy:

> Their strategy rests above all on the collective organization of wage cuts, organization of lock-outs, and limitation of hiring, but also on the application of an adroit social policy encompassing family allowances, various forms of apprenticeship, the introduction of factory cooperatives, home visitors, youth circles, factory sports clubs, camping, etc.[155]

For the Metals Group, family allowances were part of a total strategy aimed at increasing the productivity of a rationalized labor force. The health of the engineering industry in the interwar years gave the Metals Group far more leeway than the Consortium in its labor policy: whereas wool and cotton textiles production scarcely reached its pre-war level throughout the interwar period, the output of the automobile industry multiplied sixfold between 1913 and 1929.[156] Throughout the twenties and early thirties, the Metals Group did restrain wages without embroiling itself in such serious labor conflict as afflicted textile employers. Furthermore, the opacity of CCRP administration and the support of the government for the *caisse's* highly successful social work rendered the CCRP virtually impervious to attack and made it the model for family policy.

The CCRP's strategy of indirect wage restraint and multivalent intervention came increasingly to dominate the Comité Central. In the late twenties, Jacques Lebel, one of the members of the CCRP's board of directors, replaced the Consortium's Mathon as its president, and for a time the Consortium even stopped attending the national

---

[155] AN F7 13771, Union Syndicale des Travailleurs de la Métallurgie, Voiture-Aviation, et Similaires de la Région Parisienne, X⁰ Congrès, ordre du jour (1931), p. 10.

[156] Alfred Sauvy, *Histoire économique de la France entre les deux guerres*, 2 (Paris: Economica, 1984), p. 317.

congresses of the *caisses*. Other *caisses* followed the CCRP's lead in social work, and the Comité Central began publishing a *Revue de la Famille*, which many sent to all benefiting families. The *Revue* epitomized business strategy in the arena of family policy: it was not published under the Comité Central's name, and its contents seem far from didactic, including children's games, household tips, and information about benefits and services. However, as the editor Paul Leclercq explained to the tenth congress of the *caisses*, the *Revue* could also ensure, "through the mediation of the family, the economic and social education of the worker himself."

> It can explain to its readers the laws of the modern economy, and if it doesn't close its eyes to the causes of economic crises, it is careful not to push its readers into despair, anger, or anticipation of the benevolence of the Welfare State. On the contrary, it seeks in the facts themselves reasons for hope, and doesn't cease reminding its readers that whatever the laws of the State, they can always only save themselves, by their honesty, by their work and their energy.[157]

In particular, the *Revue* devoted much space to explaining the benefits of rationalization and scientific management, arguing that increased output was the only permanent solution to the inflationary spiral. In 1929, Leclercq urged all workers to participate in "the more rational organization of labor, the struggle against waste, the race against loss of time and toward higher productivity":

> The worker who commits himself to this in good faith gains doubly: as a wage earner by seeing his earnings secured, and as a consumer in benefiting from a final cessation to price increases.[158]

Like the CCRP's home visitor, the *Revue* brought a highly nuanced social strategy into working-class families without revealing the links between these social aims and employers' interests.

Historians have commonly stressed the weakness of French employers' organizations before 1936. Henry Ehrmann has argued that the June strikes found the metal employers without even reliable wage statistics; more recently, Ingo Kolboom has claimed that it was only the "capitulation" of 1936 that drove small business in particular to search for coherent industrial and social strategies.[159] This chapter

---

[157] Paul Leclercq, "L'éducation économique et sociale de la famille," in CNAF, *Compte rendu*, 10 (1930), p. 113.

[158] Paul Leclercq, "Tout augmente," *Revue de la Famille*, 18 (June 1929), p. 3.

[159] Ehrmann, *Organized Business*, pp. 15–32; Ingo Kolboom, *La revanche des patrons* (Paris: Flammarion, 1986).

has told a rather different story. Within certain industries, and even across industries, employers adopted careful, centralized, and well-documented strategies in the twenties and thirties aimed at containing wages. These strategies have largely escaped the detection and scrutiny of historians because they operated through the legally autonomous, ostensibly benevolent, and apolitical family allowance funds. Nevertheless, as we have seen, the funds were entirely controlled by employers who effectively used them to undercut wage claims and combat union organization.

Although employers seized on family allowances largely for their economic usefulness, the broader cultural and discursive context in which they acted did contribute to their success. Paternalistic intervention fit comfortably within Catholic and corporatist intellectual traditions, both of which viewed the family rather than the individual as the fundamental social unit.[160] Pronatalist concerns also weaned republican politicians away from individualist rhetoric, convincing them of the worthiness of policies that, in Britain, would have been seen as antithetical to liberal economic principles and intolerably intrusive in the "private" sphere. French trade unionists, unlike their British counterparts, were too powerless to block developments deeply inimical to their industrial position.

In comparison with feminists and socialists who supported family allowances in Britain, French businessmen are remarkable not only for their ability to garner support from "the great and the good," but also for their own resources and capacities. Employers did not *influence* the state, they replaced it; their *caisses* could extract voluntary contributions from businessmen that the Ministry of Finance could only dream of. Operating "independently," they forced the logic of family-based redistribution outside the restricted sphere of industries sheltered by state control. By doing so, however, they created a financial system that made a comprehensive national policy – and their own ultimate supersession – possible. The centrality of family policy to the French welfare state is the consequence of their work.

---

[160] Gérard Noiriel places this turn to interventionist social work in the interwar period within the context of paternalistic ideas and strategies across two centuries in "Du 'patronage' au 'paternalisme': La réstructuration des formes de domination de la main-d'oeuvre ouvrière dans l'industrie métallurgique française," *Le Mouvement Social*, 144 (July–Sept. 1988), pp. 17–35.

Part III

THE POLITICS OF STATE INTERVENTION IN THE THIRTIES

The institution of family allowances marks a great and noble stage in social progress. This evolution tends essentially towards the attenuation of the inequalities that our social order requires. Amid these inequalities, there is one that has long been lost to view, but that nevertheless is perhaps the most serious: the inequality that results from the diversity of familial situations within the same social class.

> Adolphe Landry, minister of labor, speaking in the Senate in support of the state extension of family allowances (21 Jan. 1932)

Family Allowances will tend to dig at the roots of a virile Trade Unionism.

> H. L. Bullock, National Union of General and Municipal Workers, "Family or Children's Allowances" (25 Feb. 1941)

By the midtwenties, family allowances had become a recognized feature of the system of industrial relations in France. Even trade unionists accepted the futility of opposition. Although he would have hesitated to voice such opinions to his members, the secretary of the CGT wrote to the Family Endowment Council in 1924 that while allowances may have reacted on single men's wages, "in actual practice an organism which aims at equity and solidarity justifies certain sacrifices. . . . We in France regard the allowances as purely and simply a redistribution on sounder and more humane lines of the wage bill."[1]

British trade unionists did not share his opinion. When Eleanor Rathbone brought out a new edition of *The Disinherited Family* in May

---

[1] Quoted in Eleanor Rathbone, *The Disinherited Family*, 3d ed. (London: Allen & Unwin, 1927), p. 331.

289

1927, she was forced to admit that her cause had progressed only in the realm of public opinion, and that this debate had also given voice to "a few people irreconcilably opposed to our proposed reform, and a large number who vaguely dislike it."[2] Public control of the distributive system, however appealing to theoretically inclined feminists like Rathbone, also aroused the suspicion of many working-class men and women, who were quite as outraged as their wealthier compatriots would have been by the prospect of official meddling in their private affairs or the suggestion that they could not amicably resolve their own disputes.

Politicians in both countries may have shared their sentiments: indeed, one of the advantages of the French system was that public figures could approve its development without themselves becoming vulnerable to the charge of overenthusiastic meddling by the state in citizens' private lives. With the worldwide economic and financial crisis of the early thirties, however, politicians could no longer avoid state intervention. Unemployment figures climbed rapidly in Britain in the period of the early thirties, forcing more and more families to turn to public assistance; French workers, while spared the worst ravages of unemployment, watched employers drive down wage rates as trade and investment declined. Depression-era governments, whatever their political stripe, were forced to make some effort to maintain at least minimal working-class living standards as the economy contracted.

Two very different social welfare systems emerged from their interventions, and the two chapters that comprise Part III will treat British and French developments in turn. In Britain, the problem of working-class family poverty was quickly collapsed into the problem of the unemployed. The maintenance of the unemployed, through the insurance system if possible, and through public assistance ("the dole") when necessary, became the principal social concern of both Conservative and Labour governments. And though developments were uneven and piecemeal, British innovations did deepen a gender-based logic of social welfare. French politicians, by contrast, left the relief of unemployed workers to the localities, concentrating instead on social supports for vulnerable children. While accepting wage cuts with equanimity, they sought to safeguard, control, and even extend the family allowance systems inaugurated by private industrialists.

The 1930s thus appear as the key decade in which the future shape of national family policies was determined. Yet state action took place

---

[2] Ibid., pp. 317, 320.

within – and was constrained by – the rhetorical and institutional frameworks that had influenced prior developments. French policy-makers certainly profited from pronatalists' long elaboration of the selfishness of the childless worker and the national imperative to increase births, but they were also careful to win the support of big business before requiring that all firms adhere to a *caisse*. Not until 1945 did the state finally take over direct control of the *caisses*, and even then the principles of administration remained virtually unchanged. And while the National Government in Britain took advantage of the depression to introduce social polices that struck at both the economic and domestic status of working men, the wartime government accepted the legitimacy of trade unionists' concern to protect the family wage, refusing to act upon all-party enthusiasm for family allowances until the General Council of the Trades Union Congress (TUC) gave its "whole-hearted support."[3] Patterns of consultation, like patterns of policy, proved lasting.

[3] The words are Kingsley Wood's, in response to a deputation by Rathbone and others. See PRO, PIN 8/163, Treasury, "Notes of a Deputation . . . 16 June 1941."

6

ENGENDERING THE BRITISH WELFARE STATE

By 1930, with the second Labour government bewildered and buffeted by a financial and economic crisis of unprecedented proportions, the prospect for bold initiatives in the field of family policy must have seemed remote indeed. The hope of an early introduction of child allowances, always rather utopian, died with the failure of the "living wage" inquiry, and in any case, the 1929 government was too weak and divided to bring about comprehensive social reform. The Labour ministers spent their unhappy two years in office scrambling from one stopgap measure to another in their attempt to cope with worsening budget deficits.

Yet the failure to introduce explicit programs aimed at distributing the cost of children among the population as a whole should not be taken to mean that the policies developed during the depression were innocent of any wider implications for the relationship between the state and the family. Prime ministers, chancellors, and ministers of labor (and their civil servant advisers) may have had little interest in comprehensive endowment schemes, but as they developed measures – however piecemeal – to relieve the growing numbers of the unemployed, they were necessarily driven to grapple with the problem of familial dependence. The solutions they devised provided a basis for Beveridge's more generous wartime proposals.

In Chapter 1, I argued that prewar policymakers oscillated between two alternative visions of social welfare policy. The first, epitomized in the 1908 legislation on school meals, favored granting entitlements to deserving nonearners (especially children and their mothers) outside the realm of men's wages. It was this ideal that fueled the campaigns to endow motherhood and introduce a living wage. Both Rathbone's Family Endowment Society (FES) and the Independent Labour Party (ILP) supported children's allowances not only from a concern for children's health and well-being, but also to redistribute

292

income to women and the poorest sections of the working class. Yet it was this vision of a "separate but equal" welfare state that was the casualty of the depression. As we saw in Chapters 3 and 4, family allowances were defeated because they were associated with transformative socialist and feminist political agendas that found little favor with economic and political groups exercising a significant influence over the formation of social policy.

Many of the policymakers who had opposed endowment and family allowances clung to an older ideal of labor and social policy. Their conception drew on a widely accepted vision of self-supporting male breadwinner families with dependent wives and children, relying on state aid only when men's earnings failed. In this vision, a sex-segregated labor market, distributing wages disproportionately to men, remained the chief means by which families were to be supported. The welfare state would concentrate primarily on protecting men's labor-market position, supporting them and their families only when wages failed.

It was this vision of the parallel operation of a sex-segregated labor market and social supports directed at male heads of household that was both challenged and reinforced by the unemployment and poverty policies of the thirties and that reached its apogee in the Beveridge Plan. As we shall see, the "economizing" measures of both the Labour government of 1929–31 and the Conservative-dominated National Government contributed to its construction, albeit in quite different ways. The Labour Government responded to growing all-party pressure for unemployment insurance reform by introducing legislation that prevented many married women from receiving insurance benefits (but not from paying contributions), thus deepening the system's gender bias. The National Government, by contrast, concentrated on subjecting *all* workers who had exhausted their benefit to humiliating tests of family resources. Both policies reinforced the familial dependence of particular groups, whether of married women in the former case or of the long-term unemployed (disproportionately men) in the latter. Yet it was the new dependence of men that evoked the most sustained opposition, providing a basis of popular support for later wartime demands for full employment and comprehensive social insurance reform.

Ironically, however, while the thirties silenced some of the more utopian initiatives of the twenties, they also opened up political "space" for a new consensus around aid to children. Evidence of child poverty and the realization that reasonable support for children of the unemployed was unlikely unless such allowances were extended to low-wage workers as well sparked interest in a national scheme of family allowances among a broad coalition of interests aloof from feminist issues. The Beveridge Plan built on both of these responses, envisaging the coexistence of a labor market and a welfare state organized to preserve men's breadwinner status with family allowances designed to prevent child poverty. Yet family allowances always remained the poor relative in the British welfare state – present at the table, but never given a fair share of the meal. As the comparison with France bears out, the "male-breadwinner" characteristics of the resulting British welfare state far outweighed its "parental," child-support aspects.

Unemployment policies and the enforcement of dependence

Since no interwar government undertook to provide much work, debates over unemployment policy were largely debates over how, and for how long, unemployed workers should be maintained. Here, policymakers confronted the unhappy legacy of decisions hastily arrived at after the First World War. We have seen how the war contributed to the replacement of a small, actuarially precise unemployment insurance scheme aimed at helping a restricted group of workers over short periods of unemployment by a far more substantial scheme covering almost 12 million workers and all the major trades except agriculture, domestic service, and the public sector. The very limited payments of 1911 had given way to subsistence-level benefits that, from 1921, included payments for dependents.

In the course of this transformation, the strict relationship between contributions and entitlement, insisted on in the 1911 act, had been repeatedly breached. Not only had the postwar Coalition government granted immediate entitlement to many workers who had not yet paid into the fund, but governments of the twenties had also repeatedly passed stopgap legislation allowing workers who had exhausted the "covenanted" benefit to which they were entitled by virtue of their contributions to continue to draw "transitional" or "extended" or "uncovenanted" benefit. By 1929, although in theory only workers who had paid at least thirty insurance contributions over two years were entitled to the full twenty-six weeks of unemployment benefit without tests of need, in practice workers no longer entitled continued to claim under much the same conditions. Indeed, both those on covenanted and uncovenanted benefit were required to prove that they were "genuinely seeking work," a requirement increasingly stringently enforced as officials sought to reduce reliance on the fund. Claimants cordially detested the "genuinely seeking work" clause, and the Labour Party was pledged to repeal it.[1]

These extensions of the insurance system may have been politically expedient and even humane, but they were disastrous for the Unemployment Fund, which was deeply in deficit when the Labour government took office in 1929. The new government's decision to go ahead with the abolition of the "genuinely seeking work" clause, over the objections of Margaret Bondfield, now minister of labor, unfortunately coincided with a worsening of the industrial depression and thus with the Unemployment Fund's increased dependence on Treasury loans. The number of persons on the unemployment registers increased from 1.5 to 2.5 million in 1930 alone, and numbers on both covenanted and transitional payments continued to rise rapidly. Problems of this order were beyond the capacity of a hard-pressed minority government to solve, and Labour attempted to spread the burden by appointing first an all-party advisory committee to discuss the problem and later a Royal Commission charged with reviewing administration of the unemployment insurance system. Yet "official opinion," as represented by these bodies, hardened as the slump worsened. Conservatives and Liberals represented on the all-party committee insisted that the fund must be placed on a sound actuarial footing, with the Conservatives in particular urging that the number of workers supported through insurance be drastically reduced.[2] The majority of the Royal Commission on Unemployment Insurance agreed, and in their *First Report* issued on 1 June 1931 recommended a reduction in the rate of benefit, increased contributions, the introduction of a means test for selected categories of workers on transitional benefit, and immediate legislation against "abuses" of the insurance system.[3] These recommendations were endorsed and stiffened in the report of the Committee on National Expenditure ("the May Committee"), issued on 24 July, which among other things called for an immediate 20% reduction of the rates of benefit and the introduction of a means

---

[1] The preceding two paragraphs draw on two excellent summaries of the course of unemployment policy in the twenties: W. R. Garside, *British Unemployment, 1919–1939: A Study in Public Policy* (Cambridge University Press, 1990); Alan Deacon, *In Search of the Scrounger: The Administration of Unemployment Insurance in Britain, 1920–1931* (London: G. Bell & Sons, 1976).

[2] The recommendations of the three-party advisory committee on unemployment insurance are discussed in PRO, Cab. 24/215, C.P. 318 (30), "Unemployment Insurance: Legislation in the Immediate Future" (10 Oct. 1930).

[3] Royal Commission on Unemployment Insurance, *First Report*, *PP* 1930–1, XVII, Cmd. 3872.

test for all who had exhausted their covenanted benefit.[4] By the summer of 1931, many outside the ranks of Labour were convinced that any satisfactory reform of the insurance system must involve not only lower rates and higher contributions, but also action against claimants who were "abusing" the fund and the establishment of a separate and means-tested scheme for workers who had exhausted their right to insurance benefit.

As we know, the Labour government in the end proved unwilling to endorse most of this agenda, viewing unemployment as a consequence of a broader economic failure and not the fault of the individual worker. As the TUC witnesses told the Royal Commission, "There is no real difference in principle between workers who are equally available for and capable of work, and we protest against any attempt to make an artificial difference."[5] The Labour government did continue to extend the eligibility of those on transitional payment, and in the end the Cabinet preferred to resign rather than cut benefits.[6] Yet this government did not refuse to take any action whatsoever to reduce the deficit of the fund: they did pass one piece of legislation, the Unemployment Insurance (No. 3) Act of 1931 (more commonly known as the Anomalies Act), which restricted access to benefit for particular classes of workers, especially married women.[7] In view of the reluctance of the trade unions to consider independent entitlements for working-class mothers, it is perhaps unsurprising that the Labour government's sole contribution to the solution of the insurance crisis was legislation that made it extremely difficult for any married woman worker with a co-residing husband to take advantage of the insurance system to which she had contributed. The anomalies legislation may not have affected anything like the numbers of workers hit by the National Government's policies of cutting benefit and introducing a means test, but the two deserve to be studied side by side. Both helped make explicit the gender bias of the social insurance

[4] Committee on National Expenditure, *Report*, PP 1930–1, XVI, Cmd. 3920.
[5] Royal Commission on Unemployment Insurance, *Minutes of Evidence . . . 4 May 1931* (London: HMSO, 1931), p. 967.
[6] For the Labour government's agony over unemployment benefit, see Robert Skidelsky, *Politicians and the Slump* (London: Macmillan, 1967); Bentley B. Gilbert, *British Social Policy, 1914–1939* (London: B. T. Batsford, 1970), pp. 162–75.
[7] The most complete discussions of the married women's anomalies regulations are: J. D. Tomlinson, "Women as 'Anomalies': The Anomalies Regulations of 1931, Their Background and Implications," *Public Administration*, 62 (Winter 1984), pp. 423–37, and Polly Hill, *The Unemployment Services* (London: Routledge, 1940), pp. 126–37.

system, a bias that ultimately found expression in the Beveridgian welfare state.

The anomalies regulations

The legislation against the so-called abuse of insurance was the Cabinet's sop to Margaret Bondfield, who had been left with the thankless task of convincing an increasingly restive House that the government was indeed doing something about the worsening deficit of the fund. In October 1930, Bondfield tried to convince her colleagues on the Cabinet's Panel of Ministers on Unemployment to consider legislation to correct abuses, which she defined as the payment of benefit to a range of workers whom the fund had never intended to cover: seasonal workers, short-time workers, and married women. Bondfield suggested that the first group be required to prove their intent to try to find work in the off season, but both short-time workers and married women were a greater problem. Almost 600,000 "short-time" workers receiving benefit had not actually lost their jobs; rather, they had been "temporarily stopped" by employers who were using the insurance system as a means of supporting their workers during a slack period. Many of these workers were unionized, however, and Bondfield could only suggest that the government consult both the unions and the employers about ways to lessen their reliance on the fund.[8]

Equally troubling but easier to "reform" was the situation of married women. As early as July 1930, Bondfield had noted with dismay not only that claims by women in general were increasing, but also that the increase was concentrated largely among married women. Although only 25% of insured women workers were married, fully 50% of women claiming benefit were married.[9] Some of these women, Bondfield felt, must be claiming without any real desire for further employment. She therefore suggested in October that married women be granted benefit only in regions in which the employment of married women was customary, and that claimants be required to prove that they had a reasonable expectation of obtaining employment.[10]

---

[8] PRO, Cab. 24/215, C.P. 318 (30), "Unemployment Insurance – Legislation in the Immediate Future: Memorandum by the Minister of Labour" (10 Oct. 1930).

[9] PRO, Cab. 24/213, C.P. 240 (30), "Married Women in Receipt of Unemployment Benefit: Memorandum by the Minister of Labour" (14 July 1930).

[10] PRO, Cab. 24/215, C.P. 318 (30).

The Cabinet's Panel of Ministers on Unemployment and, in turn, the Cabinet decided to appoint a Royal Commission to review the entire operation and financing of the unemployment insurance system but agreed to consider legislating on particular cases if the Ministry of Labour could provide evidence of abuse.[11]

Bondfield thus submitted a memorandum in November detailing numerous cases of abuse. Yet while Bondfield and MacDonald had argued that married women had no intention of seeking work, many of the cases told another story. The problem stemmed not from the lack of desire of the women for work but rather from the prevailing reluctance of many employers to hire married women and their propensity to fire them at the first sign of industrial downturn. Evidence from a wide range of areas concurred that the married women on their registers had "no prospect whatever of ... obtaining employment" since local employers often operated a marriage bar, only occasionally hiring back former workers during rush periods. Examples from the pottery trade in Hanley and some Birmingham metalworks showed that employers simply preferred to hire women under 21 at juvenile rates, while in the printing trade in Cardiff a marriage bar was insisted on by the trade unions.[12] When the Royal Commission on Unemployment Insurance issued its *First Report* on 1 June 1931, it confirmed that it was "a common, and perhaps a growing, practice among employers to refuse to engage married women and to dismiss women from employment on marriage."[13]

But did the fact that these women could not find work mean that they should also be denied the benefits for which, as compulsorily insured workers, they had been required to contribute? Bondfield and all the members of the Royal Commission save Clara Rackham of the Standing Joint Committee of Industrial Women's Organizations believed that they should lose their entitlement. Since industrial employment "cannot be regarded as the normal condition" of married women, the commission's majority wrote, such women could well be claiming benefit when they had no intention of working. They therefore recommended that a married woman be entitled to benefit only if she could prove not only that she had not abandoned

---

[11] PRO, Cab. 27/438, Cabinet Panel of Ministers on Unemployment, 11th meeting (20 Oct. 1930); Cab. 24/216, C.P. 354 (30), "Interim Report by the Panel of Ministers on Unemployment" (21 Oct. 1930); Cab. 23/65, Cabinet 62, 22 Oct. 1930, pp. 8–9.

[12] PRO, Cab. 24/216, C.P. 381 (30), "Unemployment Insurance: Memorandum by the Minister of Labour" (14 Nov. 1930).

[13] Royal Commission on Unemployment Insurance, *First Report*, p. 42.

insurable employment, but also that "having regard to her industrial experience and to the industrial circumstances of the district she can reasonably expect to obtain insurable employment in the district in which she is residing."[14] Essentially, the woman would have to prove not only that she wanted work but that she had a good chance of finding it.

Married women were thus to be placed in a bizarre type of double jeopardy. Not only did they confront discrimination when seeking work, but the fact that such discrimination existed was made grounds for denying them benefit as well. The justification for such a policy was, of course, that the government was not in the business of telling employers what to do, and that the insurance system must mirror rather than attempt to correct labor market realities. Yet while it is certainly true that both employers and trade unionists tended to agree that women should be restricted to designated "women's" jobs and discouraged from continuing to work after marriage, they were not alone in these views.[15] Government action had itself materially contributed to the creation of married women's disadvantaged labor market position.[16]

True, in the aftermath of the suffrage struggle in 1919, Parliament had passed the Sex Disqualification (Removal) Act, which stated straightforwardly that "a person shall not be disqualified by sex or marriage from the exercise of any public function or from being

---

[14] Ibid., p. 43.

[15] The importance of employer–union collusion in creating women's disadvantaged labor market position in the interwar period is stressed by Sylvia Walby, *Patriarchy at Work* (Cambridge: Polity Press, 1986). But the "minor orthodoxy" of the importance of patriarchal unions in excluding women has been questioned by Mike Savage, who has pointed out that employers often willingly excluded women without significant union pressure. In capital-intensive industry where labor costs were less significant, they often preferred what they saw as more reliable male workers, while even in labor-intensive industries women could be undercut by cheaper juvenile labor. See Savage, "Trade Unionism, Sex Segregation, and the State: Women's Employment in 'New Industries' in Inter-War Britain," *Social History* 13: 2 (May 1988), pp. 209–29. Miriam Glucksmann also argues that the highly stratified nature of the labor market meant that women rarely threatened men's jobs, but that trade unionists *nevertheless* typically blamed married women for the shortage of work and low pay; Glucksmann, *Women Assemble: Women Workers and the New Industries in Inter-War Britain* (London: Routledge, 1990), esp. pp. 216–25.

[16] Jane Lewis has provided a valuable summary of the role of state policy in the construction of female dependence in her article "Dealing with Dependency: State Practices and Social Realities, 1870–1945," in Jane Lewis, ed., *Women's Welfare, Women's Rights* (London: Croom Helm, 1983), pp. 17–37.

appointed to or holding any civil or judicial office or post or from entering or assuming or carrying on any civil profession or vocation."[17] Yet the act was interpreted to mean that although marriage did not actually *disqualify* women from employment, employers were not constrained to keep on married women if they did not so choose.[18] The intent of the act was thus almost completely ignored not only by private employers but also by national and local government itself. Local authorities did not wait until 1929 to move against married women workers but reacted to the economic downturn of the early twenties and an oversupply of teachers by selectively firing married women teachers.[19] Government policy in the civil service was even more avowedly discriminatory. Not only was resignation mandatory for women upon marriage and the employment of women hedged in by separate pay scales and promotion ladders, but the Treasury also followed a deliberate policy of firing women after the war in order to hire former servicemen, even when the qualifications of the latter were far inferior.[20] Although a small all-party coalition of M.P.s – including, ironically, Margaret Bondfield – sponsored a bill in 1927 designed to uphold married women's right to work, the bill was opposed not only by backbenchers who warned that "any attempt to place women exactly on an equality with men has accelerated the downfall of States and of Empires," but also by the Conservative government, which easily defeated it.[21]

When the unemployment crisis reached unprecedented proportions in 1929 and 1930, then, married women had already been defined as marginal and secondary workers. Systematic and government-supported discrimination in the labor market confronted them at every turn. Public opinion seems to have been no more tolerant; indeed, as Winifred Holtby recalled, employed women were viewed during the slump as a particularly disagreeable form of

[17] Quoted in Alison Oram, "Serving Two Masters? The Introduction of a Marriage Bar in Teaching in the 1920s," in London Feminist History Group, ed., *The Sexual Dynamics of History* (London: Pluto Press, 1983), p. 136.

[18] Harold L. Smith, "British Feminism in the 1920s," in Harold Smith, ed., *British Feminism in the Twentieth Century* (Amherst: University of Massachusetts Press, 1990), pp. 52–3.

[19] On the marriage bar in teaching, see Oram, "Serving Two Masters"; Dina M. Copelman, " 'A New Comradeship between Men and Women': Family, Marriage and London's Women Teachers, 1870–1914," in Jane Lewis, ed., *Labour and Love* (Oxford: Basil Blackwell, 1986), pp. 175–93.

[20] Meta Zimmeck, "Strategies and Stratagems for the Employment of Women in the British Civil Service, 1919–1939," *Historical Journal*, 27: 4 (1984), pp. 901–24.

[21] The quotation is of Sir Gerald Strickland, 205 *H.C. Deb.*, 5th ser., 29 Apr. 1927, col. 1210.

prcfiteer, willing to pursue their desire for silk stockings and nights at the cinema even at the expense of the employment of fathers of families.[22] Many who felt that women had no right to be working anyway were particularly hostile to the payment of unemployment benefits subsidized by the Treasury (and therefore by taxes) to married women whose husbands were able to support them. The fact that these women were paid-up contributors still entitled to benefit did not mitigate their identification as scroungers living off the public purse.[23]

Nor was this the first attack on women's insurance rights. As we have seen in the case of the demobilization following the First World War, women had always had to combat anger and prejudice when claiming unemployment benefits of any kind. Insured women had always paid lower contributions and drew out benefits at lower rates; throughout the twenties, as Alan Deacon has shown, they were also more frequently disqualified from benefit under the "genuinely seeking work" clause, often simply because a husband's ability to maintain was taken as evidence that the wife could not be seeking work with sufficient assiduity.[24] Women trade unionists routinely protested that officials were denying benefit to trained women industrial workers who had refused to take positions as domestic servants, even though no one "would suggest that a [male] house painter or stonemason should change his trade."[25] Yet the Anomalies Act took this process one step further, identifying married women by name as a group for whom waged work was, by definition, "anomalous."

It was the fact that a portion of the labor movement shared this opinion that left married women particularly vulnerable. Although the two Labour members on the Royal Commission on Unemployment Insurance objected to all of the majority's other recommendations, in the case of the proposal to apply special regulations to married women, the Labour man agreed with the majority.[26] Only Clara Rackham of the Standing Joint Committee of Industrial Women's Organisations argued that the disproportionate number of married women

[22] Winifred Holtby, *Women and a Changing Civilization* (1934; rpt. Chicago: Academy Press, 1978), pp. 111–16.

[23] This debate is extensively covered by Skidelsky. For the Conservatives' point of view, see Stuart Ball, *Baldwin and the Conservative Party: The Crisis of 1929–1931* (New Haven, Conn.: Yale University Press, 1988), esp. pp. 154–9.

[24] Alan Deacon provides a careful analysis of the different effects of the "genuinely seeking work" clause on male and female claimants in *In Search*, pp. 54–68, 98–101.

[25] Trades Union Congress [TUC], *Report*, 56 (1924), p. 365.

[26] Royal Commission on Unemployment Insurance, *First Report*, p. 61.

claiming benefit was easily explicable in view of the depression in the pottery and textile trades, and that it was absurd to judge a married woman's "intention to work by her ability to obtain work, especially in a time of depression."[27] Her solitary opposition was ignored. When the Cabinet Committee on Unemployment Insurance met on 9 June 1931 to discuss the Royal Commission's *First Report*, they agreed that there was abuse arising from receipt of benefit by married women workers and recommended adopting the restrictions foreseen by the majority.[28]

Furthermore, although Bondfield had initially charged that short-time workers were also abusing the fund, Cabinet attention focused overwhelmingly on the case of married women. This was in large part because the TUC made known its hostility to the proposed restrictions on benefits for casual and short-time workers. John Beard, Ernest Bevin, Walter Citrine, and other members of the TUC General Council met with the Cabinet Committee on Unemployment Insurance three times on 15 and 16 June 1931 and insisted on safeguards that in the end made the regulations ineffective for casual or intermittent workers.[29] After learning that the General Council did not however object to restrictions on married women and seasonal workers, the committee recommended that the government introduce legislation giving the minister of labor power to set up such restrictions after consulting with representatives of the National Confederation of Employers' Organizations and the TUC.[30]

The resulting unemployment insurance (no. 3) bill was introduced on 18 July and passed through the Commons in record time, receiving the Royal Assent less than two weeks later. The ILP and the Mosley group objected to the bill as an attempt to make the poorest workers bear the cost of industrial mismanagement, and a small group of feminists led by Eleanor Rathbone and Ellen Wilkinson attempted to remove the special references to married women.[31] The bill passed easily, however, and by late July Bondfield had established an advisory committee charged with drafting the regulations. The committee

[27] Ibid., p. 63.
[28] PRO, Cab. 24/221, C.P. 149 (31), "Unemployment Insurance: Report of the Cabinet Committee" (9 June 1931); and Cab. 23/67, Cabinet 32, 10 June 1931, pp. 11–13.
[29] PRO, Cab. 27/452, Cabinet Unemployment Insurance Committee, 4th, 6th, and 7th meetings, 15 and 16 June 1931.
[30] PRO, Cab. 24/222, C.P. 153 (31), Unemployment Insurance Committee, "Second Report" (16 June 1931). For the Cabinet's grudging approval, see Cab. 23/67, Cabinet 34, 17 June 1931, pp. 6–10.
[31] Bill papers dealing with objections by M.P.s are in PRO, PIN 3/30.

Table 6.1. *Operation of the anomalies regulations, 3 October 1931 to 29 April 1933*

Class of worker	Cases considered	Cases disallowed	Decisions appealed	Decisions reversed
Highly paid part-time	—	1	1	1
Seasonal	59,650	44,186	5,359	2,762
Short-time	6,976	4,820	629	337
Married women	262,539	205,920	5,778	2,493

Source: *Report on the Operation of the Anomalies Regulations, PP*, 1932–3, IV, Cmd. 4346.

grouped equal numbers of representatives of the employers, the unions, and the government but expressly excluded any representative of its main target – married women. The government representatives must be impartial, one civil servant minuted Bondfield, and should not be identified with any "sectional interest – and I should call the 'married woman' such an interest – which has not secured direct representation otherwise."[32] By the time the committee reported, the Labour government had been replaced by the National Government, but this did prevent the anomalies regulations from taking effect on 21 October 1931, virtually in the form recommended by the Royal Commission.[33]

The anomalies regulations were largely ineffective in denying benefit to the part-time or short-time workers protected by the unions, but they did successfully strip the more vulnerable seasonal workers and married women workers of their insurance benefits. Married women were unquestionably the major victims. As Table 6.1 shows, fully 78% of the claims made by married women, or over 200,000 workers, were disallowed in the nineteen months following the introduction of the regulations. Although the regulations had ostensibly been designed to disallow only married women who were not intending to work, they were used quite indiscriminately. Even in the Northwest Division, an area with a long tradition of married women's work, 58,128 of 76,668 married women considered for benefit under the regulations were disallowed.[34]

Yet when the Royal Commission on Unemployment Insurance reviewed the operation of the regulations in their *Final Report* of

---

[32] PRO, PIN 3/30, Minute to Bondfield, 22 July 1931.
[33] Advisory Committee on Draft Regulations, *Report, PP* 1930–1, XVII.
[34] *Report on the Operation of the Anomalies Regulations, PP* 1932–3, XV, Cmd. 4346, p. 8.

November 1932, they reiterated that the disallowance of women's claims was legitimate in view of the fact that wage earning by married women was "exceptional."[35] Only Clara Rackham (again) pointed out that while the regulations had indeed removed "the few who were claiming benefit without any particular intention of wage-earning," they had done so "at the price of disallowing thousands of women, fully paid-up contributors, genuinely seeking work, and in many cases in financial need of it."[36] Such scapegoating of women was particularly unjust, Rackham argued, as the insurance fund profited hugely from women's participation. Most women were insured workers when young and unlikely to be unemployed. They often gave up work on marriage, thus relinquishing any claim on the fund to which they had contributed. Between 1929 and 1931, men contributed more than three times as much as women did to the fund, but they drew out just under *six times* as much in benefits.[37] As she pointed out, and as Table 6.2 demonstrates, although married women claimed at a higher rate than did single women, women as a group claimed at a *lower* rate than did men as a group. The anomalies regulations were introduced as soon as the men's and women's rates began to converge and, by disallowing most married women's claims, once again made working men twice as likely as working women to benefit from the fund. Women workers, a poor and vulnerable group in the labor force, were thus required to contribute to a scheme from which they had little hope of benefiting; in short, they were subsidizing men. Through the anomalies regulations, the unemployment insurance scheme became a device for redistributing income not only from the employed to the unemployed, but also, ridiculously, from women to men.

The married women's regulation worked well – so well, in fact, that it made even civil servants at the Ministry of Labour uneasy. The regulation was intended to exclude only women who were unemployed because of marriage, argued one memorandum in early 1933, but it had been used to disallow married women in trades – like cotton weaving – where, were it not for the trade depression, they would normally be employed.[38] On the recommendation of the Unemployment Insurance Anomalies Advisory Committee headed by Sir Wil-

---

[35] Royal Commission on Unemployment Insurance, *Final Report*, PP 1931–2, XIII, Cmd. 4185, pp. 242–3.

[36] Ibid., p. 473.

[37] Ibid., p. 479.

[38] PRO, PIN 7/134, "Anomalies Acts and Regulations: Note for Consideration of Amendments" [draft, 11 Jan. 1933]; and "Anomalies Act and Regulations: Consideration of Amendments" (2 Feb. 1933).

Table 6.2. *Percentage of insured workers drawing unemployment benefit*

Date	Men	Women
January 1929	13.8	8.5
July 1929	11.0	7.1
January 1930	13.4	10.4
July 1930	17.4	16.5
January 1931	22.1	19.9
July 1931	23.8	19.5
— Anomalies regulations came into effect 21 October 1931 —		
December 1931	23.2	15.0
January 1932	25.1	15.4
February 1932	25.0	14.2
March 1932	24.1	12.5
April 1932	24.7	12.7
May 1932	25.3	13.9
June 1932	25.7	13.5
July 1932	26.3	14.1
August 1932	26.5	14.2
September 1932	26.5	13.6

Source: Royal Commission on Unemployment Insurance, *Final Report,* *PP,* 1931–2, XIII, Cmd. 4185, p. 478, and NCLW, *Report,* 13 (1932), p. 17.

liam Beveridge, the regulation was reworded so that the woman had to prove not that she was likely to find work (a difficult task in a depression), but rather that her chance of finding work was not lower than it would be if she were single.[39] This new wording was intended to make it easier for married women to establish claims in areas where such women were commonly employed; once again, however, it left the woman in the absurd position of having to prove that there was no discrimination against married women in her trade – a difficult case even for women textile workers to make, since married women were often the first fired. Despite this amendment, married women continued to be disallowed at the rate of three to four thousand per month in 1934 and 1935 – and indeed in 1940.[40]

What can we conclude from the case of the anomalies regulations? Certainly, they demonstrate, once again, how labor and social policies

[39] Advisory Committee on Draft Regulations, *Second Report, PP* 1932–3, XV, Cmd. 4407.
[40] PRO, PIN 7/158, "Deputation from the Standing Joint Committee... Note for the Minister's Use" (typescript, 1935); Polly Hill, *The Unemployment Services,* p. 130.

cannot be considered in isolation. The government clearly insisted that social policy should mirror rather than correct labor market realities, even if these "realities" had been created by other social policies. They thus refused to support married women workers as a group in any regions or trades in which private employers – or even the government itself – denied them jobs. Whether married women wanted to work was considered irrelevant. As one civil servant noted, it was always intended "that the Regulation should operate against women who lose employment as a result of employers' practice of discharging married women."[41] The very act of getting married in a district where employers often discharged married women was interpreted as a statement that the woman had relinquished her insurance rights.

Yet this bland tolerance of the marriage bar was possible only because of the assumption, so pervasive as to be almost unspoken, that married women did not – and should not – normally earn wages. The relevant fact considered in determining whether the woman was "genuinely seeking work" and deserving of benefit became not whether she was looking for work, had worked, and had paid her contributions, but whether there was a man in the house. One civil servant's minute admitted frankly in 1933 that the anomalies regulations were introduced because a married woman "can be presumed to have a husband to support her and therefore not to have necessarily the same incentive to seek work."[42] The state did have to support the unemployed citizen, the governments of the thirties decided, but a married woman was a wife, not a citizen: her claim was on her husband, not the state. By making explicit the gender assumptions that had long structured social policy, the anomalies regulations of the thirties stand as the strongest state endorsement of the male breadwinner norm in the interwar period.

Yet the anomalies regulations evoked surprisingly little response. Henry Betterton, the new minister of labor under the National Government, was able to report in January 1932 that no unified press campaign had opposed the regulations, and the occasional complaints of unions need not be taken seriously.[43] Although the TUC did recommend repealing or reviewing the regulations in the mid-thirties, in 1932 only Labour's women's organizations systematically defended married women's rights to unemployment benefit on the same terms

[41] PRO, PIN 7/158, "Deputation from the Standing Joint Committee . . . Note for the Minister's Use."
[42] PRO, PIN 6/63, two-page note [probably Jan. 1933].
[43] PRO, Cab. 24/227, C.P. 16 (32), "Unemployment Benefit – Anomalies Regulations. Memorandum by the Minister of Labour" (11 Jan. 1932).

as men.[44] In theory, Labour women could have allied with those equalitarian feminists unenamored of Rathbone's maternalist focus who had formed organizations like the Six Point Group and the Open Door Council aimed at protecting women's work rights. Yet these feminist organizations were deeply distrusted by the Labour movement, and Labour women's organizations sometimes felt called on to demonstrate their loyalty by denouncing equalitarian feminists as extremists eager to return women to the mines.[45] Furthermore, by the early thirties, Labour women had found other, more popular causes. While the household means test introduced by the National Government also forced particular groups into dependence, it aroused more emotion and more hostility, even among women, than did the anomalies regulations. To understand why the defense of men's familial status came to form the heart of "progressive" social policy, we must look at the introduction and operation of the household means test.

The household means test

The National Government formed in August 1931 quickly put through a version of the "economy" measures resisted by the Labour Cabinet, including a 10% cut in the rate of standard benefit. In November 1931, after the government was confirmed in power by the electoral landslide of October, a more significant change was introduced. From 12 November 1931, all those who had exhausted their covenanted benefit would receive their "transitional benefit" through the local Public Assistance Committees (PACs) and after a means test of the resources of the household.[46] Thus was born the infamous means-tested "dole," the most evocative and hated memory of the thirties.

[44] TUC, *Report*, 66 (1934), pp. 117–18; 67 (1935), p. 119; National Conference of Labor Women [NCLW], *Report*, 13 (1932), pp. 17–21; Dorothy Elliot, "Married Women Defrauded," *Labour Woman*, 20: 4 (Apr. 1932), pp. 56–7.
[45] The Labour women's organizations expressed their hostility to the feminist call for egalitarian labor laws in a series of articles in *Labour Woman* in 1924 and 1925; after the formation of the Open Door Council, they began attacking the council directly. See "Pet Bogey of Extreme Feminism: Protective Legislation for Women Workers," *Labour Woman*, 17: 3 (1 Mar. 1929), p. 39; [Standing Joint Committee of Industrial Women's Organisations], *The Open Door Movement and the Protection of Women Workers* (London: Labour Party, 1930). In 1931, the TUC opposed any alteration in the prohibition of night work for women; see TUC, *Report*, 63 (1931), pp. 227–8.
[46] *Report of the Ministry of Labour for the Year 1931*, PP 1931–2, XI, Cmd. 4044, pp. 87–91.

The introduction of the household means test was intended to save the government money, but it also reestablished the lapsed distinction between insurance benefit, to which workers were entitled by virtue of their contributions, and assistance, which was based straightforwardly on need. Large numbers of workers who had exhausted their benefit were transferred to this new scheme of means-tested transitional payments in the first few weeks, and by the end of January of 1932, 804,759 workers registered on the employment exchange were receiving such benefits.[47] Yet the introduction of the means test did lower both numbers of recipients and amounts received. Between late January and early September 1932, the PACs received 936,757 initial applications for transitional benefit: 50.8% of the applicants were granted benefit at the old insurance rate, 30.9% were given a lower level of support, and 18.3% were rejected entirely.[48]

There were, however, great regional variations: Birmingham, for example, disallowed fully 34.8% of all applications, while Methyr disallowed a mere 0.5%.[49] When the Royal Commission on Unemployment Insurance issued their *Final Report* in November 1932, the majority thus recommended the creation of a new national board to take over the support and administration of those who had exhausted their benefit; two years later, the Unemployment Assistance Board (UAB) was set up to standardize relief for the still sizable body of those supported by the PACs. The public outcry that resulted from the publication of the board's projected scales of relief forced the government to delay their implementation; between 1936 and 1938, however, workers on transitional benefit were gradually taken over by the UAB.

The story of unemployment assistance in the thirties has been told many times; here we will look only at how the massive extension of means-tested benefit altered treatment of familial dependence and influenced the long-term development of family policy.[50] Two points are key. First, unemployment assistance, like unemployment insurance, was very largely a men's benefit. Although women did initially apply in substantial numbers, they were less likely to be granted benefit at their old rate, more likely to be disallowed entirely, and perhaps

---

[47] *Report of the Ministry of Labour for the Year 1932*, PP 1932–3, XIII, Cmd. 4281, p. 65.
[48] Royal Commission on Unemployment Insurance, *Final Report*, p. 62.
[49] Ibid.
[50] On the establishment and operation of the Unemployment Assistance Board, see especially Garside, *British Unemployment*, pp. 66–87; Gilbert, *British Social Policy*, pp. 182–92. Violet Markham, who served on the board for many years, sheds much light on its operation in her autobiography, *Return Passage* (Oxford University Press, 1953).

as a consequence, less likely to renew their applications. Between 12 November 1931 and 23 January 1932, the PACs granted 53% of men's claims at the old rate and 35% at the reduced rate; by contrast, only 32% of women's claims were granted at the full rate and 31% at the reduced rate. Just 12% of men's claims but fully 37% of women's claims were turned down altogether.[51] By 25 January 1932, 732,809 men were receiving payments, in comparison with 71,950 women. By the end of the year, the number of men receiving had risen to 983,198 but that of women had fallen to 56,176.[52] These ratios did not change much through the thirties. The proportion of women among UAB recipients hovered between 5 and 8% from 1936 to 1938.[53]

Yet if transitional payments and unemployment assistance were very largely paid to men, they were paid with a difference. Men's claims may have been disallowed at lower rates, but while women had always been subject to special conditions or arbitrary refusals, most men had grown accustomed to receiving unemployment benefit as a matter of right. Applicants for transitional benefit after 1931 were, by and large, men who had exhausted their insurance but felt they had a right to support: the fact that almost 50% of these men saw their claims either disallowed or paid at a lower rate came as something of a shock. Very significant numbers of working men – around 400,000 at any point in 1932 – were thus driven to rely in whole or in part on other household resources, usually the earnings of other family members. As Violet Markham, member and later vice-chairman of the UAB, pointed out in her autobiography, such "family resources" were "not wholly negligible" and reduced relief costs considerably. In 1935, for example, the state paid out over £42 million in unemployment assistance to almost 700,000 persons; but that same group was found to have more than £24 million in other resources.[54] In 1936, 54.3% of the applicants in a sample analyzed by the UAB had no resources at all, and 17.3% had resources that the board did not take into account, but 28.4% were still having their payments reduced because of other resources.[55]

It was this enforcement of dependence on ordinary working men

[51] *Report of the Ministry of Labour for the Year 1932*, p. 64.

[52] Ibid., p. 65.

[53] Figures are from the Unemployment Assistance Board [UAB], *Reports: For the Year Ending 31 December 1936*, PP 1936–7, XII, Cmd. 5526, p. 198; *For the Year Ending 31 December 1937*, PP 1937–8, XIII, Cmd. 5752, p. 192; *For the Year Ending 31 December 1938*, PP 1938–9, XII, Cmd. 6021, p. 182.

[54] See Garside, *British Unemployment*, p. 84; Markham, *Return Passage*, p. 197.

[55] UAB, *Report for the Year Ending 31 December 1936*, p. 201.

that constitutes the second and most significant aspect of the National Government's unemployment policy. While the government accepted that workers who had paid their contributions were owed "honorable" benefit for themselves and their families for a short period of time, they did not accept that such men should be supported indefinitely. They thus concentrated on creating an indelible distinction between the legitimate unemployed, who would continue to draw benefit, and the long-term unemployed, who were treated quite differently. It is of crucial importance that this "difference" took the form of the household means test, an invasive measure that undermined men's familial status. Having failed to earn a family wage, always the critical test of respectable masculinity, the long-term unemployed were to be treated, essentially, as women, forced to live on the earnings of their spouses and children.

The imposition of the household means test converted what had been a rights-based benefit into a humiliating dole, and independent breadwinners into, in some cases, dependents. Loss of economic status and loss of familial status became inextricable – hence the common observation that men experienced unemployment as an assault on their manhood. E. W. Bakke, who lived in working-class Greenwich in 1931, remarked that "practically every man who had a family showed evidences of the blow his self-confidence had suffered from the fact that the traditional head of the family was not able to perform his formal function." "It's hell when a man can't even support his own family," one boiler-maker told him.[56] The experience of living on the dole, J. B. Priestley agreed in his *English Journey* of 1934, stripped men of their self-respect: "Their very manhood was going."[57] The Pilgrim Trust's study of 1938 similarly stressed the psychological burden felt by the long-term unemployed. Men who lost their benefit because of co-resident earners nevertheless "feel the loss of an independent income ... very acutely, and in many such cases the home appears to represent two standards, the earning children being often smartly dressed and happy, while the fathers were shabby and suffering from a sense of their dependence." Although most recipients of assistance were not bitter about the UAB, the trust reported, among men forced to live off their children, bitterness "was the rule rather than the exception."[58]

Opponents of the means test dwelt on its pernicious effects on

[56] E. Wight Bakke, *The Unemployed Man: A Social Study* (New York: Dutton, 1934), p. 70.

[57] J. B. Priestley, *English Journey* (New York: Harper & Brothers, 1934), p. 324.

[58] Pilgrim Trust, *Men without Work* (Cambridge University Press, 1938), p. 148.

family life. As the General Council of the TUC wrote, the means test "destroys the unity of family life, breaks the bonds of natural affection, introduces dissension and conflict between members of the family."[59] What is striking, however, is the extent to which families did not disintegrate under its intrusive impact. Ross McKibbin, John Stevenson, and Chris Cook all make the point that unemployment did not lead to widespread demoralization and unrest precisely because the unemployed continued to share the broader community and familial norms of the working class.[60] Bakke, Priestley, Orwell, and other observers all remarked on this in the thirties, of course; as Orwell wrote, "Families are impoverished, but the family-system has not broken up." Rather, the unemployed were living "a reduced version of their former lives," settling down "to make the best of things on a fish-and-chip standard." And while the means test may have diminished the authority of parents, relations between the sexes remained largely unchanged. As Orwell noted, "Unemployment – the man being out of work while the woman's work continues – has not altered the relative standing of the sexes"; the man was still the "master" and "practically never" did any housework. This situation, however seemingly unfair, was accepted by the wives since "they, as well as the men, feel that a man would lose his manhood if, merely because he was out of work, he developed into a 'Mary Ann.' "[61]

Orwell was, of course, a highly partial and unreliable witness, given his own opinion that such male "mastery" was both the sign of a "sane and comely" home life and the touchstone of a "decent" and "English" socialism.[62] Yet other observers' reports and quantitative studies confirmed that the gendered division of labor remained largely intact. Very few wives reacted to their husbands' unemployment by going out to work: in the thirty-four families surveyed by Bakke in Greenwich in 1931, only two wives had done so.[63] In most regions, most families aided by the UAB *were* partially supported by wages, the economist Percy Ford found when he analyzed samples of UAB data in the late thirties, but when the husband or father was unemployed

---

[59] TUC, *Report*, 68 (1936), p. 71.
[60] Ross McKibbin, "The Social Psychology of Unemployment in Inter-War Britain," in idem, *The Ideologies of Class: Social Relations in Britain, 1880–1950* (Oxford University Press, 1990), pp. 228–58; John Stevenson and Chris Cook, *The Slump: Society and Politics during the Depression* (1977; rpt. London: Quartet, 1979), esp. chaps. 4 and 5.
[61] George Orwell, *The Road to Wigan Pier* (1937; rpt. New York: Harcourt, Brace, Jovanovich, 1957), pp. 88, 90, 81.
[62] Ibid., p. 117.
[63] Bakke, *The Unemployed Man*, p. 164.

it was children rather than wives who were first relied upon. No doubt this was partly because very little work was available to married women in many areas; thus, in Consett only 4% of households containing husbands assisted by the UAB also contained wives who earned, whether by employment or by taking in lodgers. In Bolton, by contrast, where married women's work was accepted and more widely available – one survey in 1924 had found that 12% of households were partially supported by wives – fully one-third of households with husbands assisted by the board also relied on contributions from wives (the highest rate of wives' earning in any area studied by Ford).[64] The UAB's own regulations may have discouraged wives from earning, since if the man had exhausted his insurance benefits and was now on means-tested payments, most of the wife's income would count against his benefit. The Pilgrim Trust thus found that some wives refused to work because the family would be "no better off" for it; it was, they concluded, "more usual for a wife to give up work when her husband came on the Means Test than it was for her to try to obtain work."[65]

Yet some women also refused to work out of a wish to avoid family conflict, or because they perceptively realized that the economic support they could provide by working was less important to their husbands than the psychological support they would provide by loyally upholding their husbands' breadwinner status. Sometimes when wives did return to work, the Pilgrim Trust reported, "there was evident unhappiness as a result." They cited a case in Leicester, "where the woman had left her work because she could not bear to be the breadwinner while her husband, young and fit, did nothing," and another in Blackburn, "where a young married woman, working, with an unemployed husband, said that 'it made him wild' to be about with no money in his pocket."[66] Demoralization among older male workers forced to live off their families was a serious enough problem for the UAB to take to distributing token discretionary payments, revealingly called "dignity" money, to some who found it impossible to ask their previously dependent children or other relatives for pocket money.[67]

The reaction elicited in working-class families and communities by

[64] P. Ford, *Income, Means Tests and Personal Responsibility* (London: P. S. King & Son, 1939), pp. 39, 45–7, 59.

[65] Pilgrim Trust, *Men without Work*, pp. 169–70.

[66] Ibid., p. 147.

[67] British Library of Political and Economic Science (BLPES), Markham Papers 6/13, Board Memo no. 272, " 'Dignity' Money," (28 July 1938). "Dignity" money was paid in relatively few cases, some four thousand in 1938.

the imposition of the household means test helps us understand why the defense of working-class living standards often brought with it a defense of the gendered division of labor and the male-breadwinner norm. That this family form privileged men is unquestionably true, yet it is also true that women rallied to its defense. The means test may have merely applied to men the tests of dependency that had been used to restrict women's access to benefits all along, but many women as well as men seem to have seen the targeting of men as an assault on the very fundamentals of working-class family life. Even the Labour Party's Women's Sections, who had in the twenties pursued the causes of endowment of motherhood and of birth control over the opposition of the party and, at times, of their own leadership, in the thirties abjured such "individualist" or feminist causes to concentrate on the defense of the family. In 1932, 1933, and 1934, branches sent more resolutions to the National Conference of Labour Women protesting the evils of the means test they they did on any other issue; not until 1936 were the old concerns about maternal welfare services and the party's treatment of women's issues back at the top of the agenda.[68]

Hatred of the means test was similarly expressed at the TUC and Labour Party conferences and fueled the marches and protests of the National Unemployed Workers' Movement. No policy since the New Poor Law aroused the same level of resentment and rhetoric. Defenders of the means test, the General Council stated in 1936,

> have no conception of the passionate resentment and embitterment of feeling it has produced among the working people; and that resentment and bitterness are not lessened by the knowledge that the means test is insisted upon ... by representatives of the wealthier classes who have never known a moment's anxiety, or suffered an hour's real hardship, and have never done a hand's turn for themselves in their lives.... No argument used to justify the means test can reconcile us to it. We hate it with the same intensity that we hate the thought of the workhouse.[69]

The unemployed were being made to bear the burden of economic mismanagement, the General Council protested to the minister of labor in 1932, and that same year the TUC reiterated that "unless the community so organises its resources as to provide work for every willing worker," the unemployed were entitled to maintenance as a

---

[68] NCLW, *First Agenda*, for the conferences of 1932, 1933, 1934, and 1936, Labour Party Archives, Harvester Microfilms, Series 2, Items 32/15, 33/33, 34/31, and 36/29.

[69] TUC, *Report*, 68 (1936), p. 71.

matter of right.[70] If a man was willing to work, trade unionists claimed, the energies of the government would be better spent in providing employment than in penalizing those who were unable to find it.

This point of view would be accepted after the Second World War, but the governments of the thirties found such positive policies beyond them and concentrated on identifying particular "undeserving" groups to bear the brunt of the cuts. Both the household means test and the anomalies regulations forced workers to depend on their families rather than the state for support. From a purely individualist point of view, the anomalies regulations may appear the greater injustice; after all, the means test was applied only to those who had exhausted insurance benefits, whereas the women barred from benefit under the anomalies regulations were paid-up contributors to the fund. Yet it is undoubtedly true that the anomalies regulations never evoked the tremendous public hostility aroused by the means test; this pointed attack on women's independence was far less unpopular than the National Government's challenge to men's familial status. Indeed, a resolution at the TUC of 1933 calling for the abolition of both the means test and the anomalies regulations aroused opposition from speakers who objected to linking the two issues, claiming that the anomalies regulations were necessary to prevent abuse of the insurance system.[71] The male-breadwinner norm, itself in part the creation of social policy, was by the thirties pervasive enough to make the regulations seem reasonable and only the household means test an "injustice."

Once again, then, labor market inequalities, gendered social policies, and the normative ideal of the male breadwinner proved mutually reinforcing, turning sexually inegalitarian policies into "common sense." It is important to recognize the extent to which sharp gender differences in work, pay, and opportunities underwrote these responses. In 1937, when the UAB gathered the information on wages presented in Table 6.3, they found that men's and women's wages were not only unequal but indeed scarcely overlapped at all: almost all women workers were paid less than almost all men. Many women also worked in sectors in which marriage led automatically to dismissal. Inequalities like these structured not only choices but desires and help us understand why even Labour women often viewed the role of housewife and mother as more rewarding (and as a source of greater domestic power) than that of wage earner and sought work

[70] TUC, *Report*, 64 (1932), pp. 115–17, 268.
[71] TUC, *Report*, 65 (1933), pp. 284–8.

Table 6.3. *Normal wages of workers receiving benefits from the Unemployment Assistance Board, 1937*

Weekly wages (shillings)	Men (%)	Women (%)
Under 20	1.2	21.4
20–30	2.7	51.6
30–40	9.7	20.5
40–50	39.3	4.6
50–60	31.4	1.1
Over 60	15.7	0.8

Source: Unemployment Assistance Board, *Report for the Year Ending 31 Dec. 1937, PP,* 1937–8, XIII, Cmd. 5752, p. 81.

after marriage only as a last resort. Indeed, given the deep hostility to married women's work, what is surprising is that some groups of employed women, notably some textile and professional workers, were able to maintain their pride in their identity both as workers and as wives in a period in which the two roles were held to be incompatible and, in concert, deviant.[72]

Not even the renewed employment of women during the Second World War could do more than temporarily strain these structures and preferences. True, the employment of women, and especially of married women, grew very substantially during the war, and the government made some effort to provide day-care facilities for these workers' children. Yet, once again, this expansion (and these services) were explicitly deemed temporary and extraordinary, and wage differentials between men and women did not significantly narrow. Although the wartime experience did spark new demands by women for equal pay and improved services, both the wartime coalition and the postwar Labour government resisted these demands, usually viewing women as a useful pool of cheap labor, to be mobilized when the nation required but left to meet domestic responsibilities largely un-

---

[72] Diana Gittins found that couples in which both spouses worked, and textile workers in particular, had far more egalitarian relationships, but such life choices were nevertheless relatively rare; Elizabeth Roberts confirms that most working-class women shared the opinion that wives should not work after marriage. Gittins, *Fair Sex: Family Size and Structure in Britain, 1900–1939* (New York: St. Martin's, 1982); Roberts, *A Woman's Place: An Oral History of Working Class Women, 1890–1940* (London: Basil Blackwell, 1984), esp. pp. 135–48.

aided.[73] Faced with heavy burdens and few supports, small wonder that substantial numbers of women workers surveyed in 1943 stated that they hoped to give up waged work after the war, and that almost as many women felt that men should be preferentially hired for any given job as felt that the job should go to the best person.[74] "Separate spheres" may indeed have seemed preferable to, and even more egalitarian than, the proffered alternative of a double day at half pay.

It was, then, not the virtual exclusion of married women from both work and insurance, but a household means test reducing breadwinners to dependency that became the symbol of the past to be rejected in a reconstructed welfare state. Whereas Beveridge's plan made full employment an "assumption" in the hopes of avoiding any repetition of such widespread reliance on a means-tested dole, he dealt with the problem of the anomalies regulations simply by allowing married women to contract out of unemployment insurance entirely. Both responses brought the insurance system closer to the ideal of the male breadwinner norm. Yet at the same time, Beveridge insisted that a system of family allowances was a necessary precondition to any developed scheme of social security. To understand how a gender-biased welfare state came to incorporate children's benefits, we must trace the developing awareness of child poverty in the thirties.

A new case for children's allowances

Early in 1931, Marjorie Green, the secretary of the FES, published a short article in the *Labour Woman*. "Family Endowment is coming," she asserted. "Perhaps not this year or next, but sometime soon."[75] Given that the TUC had just rejected state-funded allowances and that the Labour Government was plagued with a budgetary deficit to which there seemed no solution, her optimism seemed misplaced. Yet within ten years political consensus around the need for a scheme of

---

[73] This interpretation is upheld by Penny Summerfield, *Women Workers in the Second World War: Production and Patriarchy in Conflict* (London: Croom Helm, 1984); Harold L. Smith, "The Womanpower Problem in Britain during the Second World War," *Historical Journal*, 27: 4 (1984), pp. 925–45. The "preference" of many women to return home in the immediate postwar period is placed in its political and cultural context by Janice Winship, "Nation before Family: *Woman*, The National Home Weekly, 1945–1953," in *Formations of Nation and People* (London: Routledge, 1984).

[74] These results are discussed by Harold L. Smith, "The Effect of the War on the Status of Women," in *War and Social Change: British Society in the Second World War* (Manchester: Manchester University Press, 1986), pp. 217–18.

[75] Marjorie Green, "Shall We Endow Our Children?" *Labour Woman*, 19: 2 (Feb. 1931), p. 19.

children's allowances had grown to such an extent that even the TUC began to reconsider its policy. With the final defeat of the feminist and socialist vision of family policy as a path to women's economic independence or "socialism in our time," a new political consensus could develop around more modest goals. Family allowances came to be accepted as a way to aid children, not women, and to relieve poverty rather than to achieve some more expansive vision of distributive justice.

This shift in focus was a consequence not only of the renewed awareness of poverty, but also of the decline of feminism as a political force. After the divisions and defeats of the twenties, many feminist organizations could scarcely sustain themselves. The equalitarians were beset by continued attacks on women's work rights and ambivalent about maternalist campaigns; the old National Union of Societies for Equal Citizenship, far from acting as an umbrella organization, had dwindled to little more than a pressure group. In 1932, NUSEC became the National Council for Equal Citizenship, and from the mid-thirties overlapped almost completely in policies and staff with Rathbone's maternalist lobbies, the Family Endowment Society and the Children's Minimum Council. All of these organizations operated on a shoestring, however. Whereas before the war the two largest suffrage bodies had had annual budgets of tens of thousands of pounds, by 1938 expenses for the National Council had dwindled to 433 pounds per year, less even than the 759 pounds needed to keep the Children's Minimum Council in envelopes and postage stamps.[76]

Yet the thirties, ironically, put family policy back on the agenda. The individuals and organizations Arthur Marwick has defined as the spokesmen for "middle opinion" – the planning advocates who formed the pressure group Political and Economic Planning, the advanced businessmen who formed the Management Research Groups, and backbench M.P.s disgusted with the social policies of the National Government – became the new converts to children's allowances.[77]

---

[76] Budget figures are derived from the National Council for Equal Citizenship *Reports*, held at the Fawcett Library; the Children's Minimum Council income and expense account for 1938–9 is in University of Liverpool, Eleanor Rathbone Papers, Item XIV.2.7 (16).

[77] Arthur Marwick, "Middle Opinion in the Thirties: Planning, Progress and Political 'Agreement,' " *English Historical Review*, 79: 311 (Apr. 1964), pp. 285–98. For the dogged perseverance of the Family Endowment Society in the thirties, see especially their publication *The Family Endowment Chronicle* and the two excellent studies of the development of family allowances: John Macnicol, *The Movement for Family Allowances, 1918–1945* (London: Heinemann, 1980); Hilary Land, "The Introduction of Family Allowances:

Children's allowances interested moderates and social reformers for very different reasons from those that made them appealing to feminists, and Rathbone and other advocates shifted their arguments when confronted by the different political and economic constraints of the thirties. Rathbone and her indomitable co-campaigner Eva Hubback scarcely mentioned their earlier claim for endowment of motherhood, instead developing more conservative demographic or administrative justifications for allowances.

When advocates of allowances had discussed population concerns in the twenties, their arguments were cast within the eugenic terms that so pervaded (and disfigured) interwar public discourse. Many social reformers, including Rathbone and Hubback, accepted the argument made by the Eugenics Society – still a dominant voice on population questions – that success in the competitive struggle (or, more bluntly, social class) was the best available measure of eugenic worth. When Eleanor Rathbone read a paper entitled "Family Endowment in its Bearing on the Question of Population" to the Eugenics Society in 1924, she thus concentrated on refuting the fears of its members that allowances would disproportionately encourage the reproduction of the "less fit." In fact, the birthrate of the very poor would probably fall if their economic situation were improved, she contended; and in any case professional groups could establish occupational schemes to ensure higher benefits for their members.[78] Sir William Beveridge appeared to find this type of argument convincing enough to establish a very generous scheme of allowances for the administrative and teaching staff of the London School of Economics in 1925,[79] and the Eugenics Society as a whole seemed worried enough about the prospect of universal flat-rate allowances to resolve that any scheme should be proportional to earnings in order to promote births among "superior types" – whom, they continued to assume, were identifiable by social class.[80]

An Act of Historic Justice?" in Phoebe Hall et al., eds., *Change, Choice and Conflict in Social Policy* (London: Heinemann, 1975), pp. 157–230.

[78] Eleanor Rathbone, "Family Endowment in Its Bearing on the Question of Population," *Eugenics Review*, 16: 4 (Jan. 1925). John Macnicol provides a careful summary of the demographic case made for allowances; Macnicol, *Movement*, pp. 75–101.

[79] In 1939, benefits were paid at the rate of thirty pounds per year for children under age 13 and sixty pounds per year for children over 13 but under 23 who were in school or university full-time; L. J. Cadbury, "Family Allowances," in [British Medical Association], *Nutrition and Public Health . . . Proceedings of a National Conference on the Wider Aspects of Nutrition, April 27–9, 1939* (London: BMA, 1939), pp. 1–2.

[80] "An Outline of a Practical Eugenic Policy," *Eugenics Review*, 18: 2 (July 1926), pp. 95–9.

Rathbone and to an even greater extent Hubback continued to court the Eugenics Society in the thirties,[81] but as the birthrate fell below replacement level and massive unemployment put child poverty back on the agenda, the elitism of the old obsession with *differential* fertility came under fire. In 1934, the left-wing statistician Enid Charles projected a drastic decline in the population should current fertility trends continue and stated bluntly that the much-canvassed issue of differential fertility between classes was a red herring. There was no evidence that differences in intelligence were independent of environment, she argued:

> The peril of the low fertility of the professional classes as a purely qualitative aspect of the population problem has been chiefly proclaimed by persons who themselves belong to the professional class, often by those who are themselves conspicuously infertile. In the course of human history we may doubt whether any privileged class in process of extinction has refrained from lamenting its disappearance as an irreparable loss to civilization.[82]

Charles was skeptical of the value of economic inducements to childbearing, but both Rathbone and Marjorie Green, the secretary of the FES, seized on her statistics to argue that family allowances could at least help reduce the economic incentive to limit births.[83]

Supporters of family endowment thus tried to use the new alarmism about population trends to strengthen their case, and certainly Conservatives like Leo Amery, concerned about Britain's capacity to maintain its imperial and world role as prospects for international peace deteriorated, found it compelling. Yet pronatalist concerns never really occupied center stage; it was the growing evidence of current ill health, not the prospect of future decline, that preoccupied most advocates. "It is primarily in justice to the growing children of the existing generation that I would appeal for immediate consideration

---

[81] Eva Hubback and M. E. Green, "Family Endowment. II. A Proposal for Constructive Eugenics in England," *Eugenics Review*, 25: 1 (April 1933), pp. 33–6. On Hubback, see Diana Hopkinson, *Family Inheritance: A Life of Eva Hubback* (London: Staples Press, 1954).

[82] Enid Charles, *The Twilight of Parenthood* (London: Watts & Co., 1934), p. 134.

[83] Marjorie Green, "Poverty and the Birth-Rate," *Manchester Guardian*, 28 Sept. 1935; "Towards National Extinction," *Manchester Guardian*, 10 Oct. 1935. Advocates often pointed to Continental schemes of allowances, and several researchers examined these in the thirties, even though they usually concluded pessimistically that at best these had reduced the rate of population decline: David V. Glass, *The Struggle for Population* (Oxford University Press, 1936), p. 84; A. M. Carr Saunders, *World Population: Past Growth and Present Trends* (Oxford University Press, 1936), p. 241.

of this overdue reform," Amery wrote to the *Times* in June of 1938.[84] The most convincing and widely supported case for family allowances was an antipoverty case, born of the controversies over the health and welfare of working-class families during a period of chronic unemployment.

Much ink has been spilled on the subject of working-class health during the depression, both by contemporaries and by historians.[85] For our purposes, however, whether the thirties were indeed "healthy or hungry" is less important than the fact that many contemporary social investigators and reformers believed that the depression and unemployment were damaging the health of the populace, especially children. The government asserted that infant mortality rates and other indicators of public health showed no evidence of declining standards, but this neither convinced nor quieted the doctors and social investigators who made the "condition of England" once again a subject for public scrutiny and worry. The depression thus resulted in a frenzy of measurement – of the amount of food needed to keep an unemployed man in a fit condition, of the income needed to support families of different sizes, even of the amount of cleaning agents consumed by the average family – all in an effort to establish a scientific "poverty line," a reliable figure of the amount needed to keep a family going on what Ernest Bevin contemptuously called "the fodder basis." The British Medical Association published their estimates of the content and minimum cost of a healthy diet in 1933;[86] Seebohm Rowntree, John Boyd Orr, Herbert Tout, R. F. George, and other social scientists went on to survey how well household incomes in York, Liverpool, Bristol, London, and elsewhere met subsistence needs. All of these investigations reiterated one fact: that the proportion of children in poverty was far higher than the proportion of adults. Just as advocates of family allowances had always stressed, since wages did not vary with family needs, larger families – and thus a disproportionate number of children – often lived in poverty. In November 1938, when Leo Amery made a much-publicized speech in favor of family allowances in the Commons, he pointed out that there were now reliable surveys estimating the proportion of children below a poverty line capable of maintaining health to be 25% in the Merseyside area, 27% in Sheffield, 30% in Southampton, 39% in the

[84] L. S. Amery, "The Worker and His Family," *Times*, 24 June 1938.
[85] See especially Stevenson and Cook, *The Slump*, pp. 8–53; Charles Webster, "Healthy or Hungry Thirties?" *History Workshop Journal*, 13 (Spring 1982), pp. 110–29.
[86] British Medical Association, *Report of the Committee on Nutrition* (London: BMA, 1933).

poorer areas of Lancashire, and 75% in the rural areas of West Sussex.[87]

The growing evidence of the extent of child poverty did not feed directly into a demand for cash allowances, but it did reunite activists who had been divided over the endowment of motherhood or the "living wage" campaign. Faced with such dismaying evidence, whether aid was given in cash or in kind suddenly became less important, and worried social reformers began to support virtually any measure that would aid children. In early 1934, Eleanor Rathbone formed the Children's Minimum Committee, aimed at ensuring that no child be denied a minimum standard of living because of the parents' poverty, and shifted much of the resources of the FES and the National Council for Equal Citizenship into the new campaign. The Fabian Barbara Drake, who had left the FES because of its paramount emphasis on women's independence, and Gertrude Tuckwell, who had advised Milne-Bailey of the TUC that social services were far preferable to cash allowances, both joined Rathbone's committee to fight for better services *and* benefits.[88] Labour women's organizations, the Women's Cooperative Guild, and the Maternal Mortality Committee also made maternal and child welfare their primary focus during the thirties. All argued that the government must guarantee a minimum standard of care for all children by increasing unemployment benefits, extending social services, and making compulsory the local provision of school meals and public health services.[89] Services for children could unite people divided over the question of the family wage.

[87] Amery's speech is reprinted in his autobiography; Leo S. Amery, *My Political Life*, vol. 3, *The Unforgiving Years, 1929–1940* (London: Hutchinson, 1955), pp. 433–9.

[88] University of Liverpool Library, Eleanor Rathbone Papers, Item XIV.2.7(5), Children's Minimum Council, "Report for the Year Ending June 30, 1938."

[89] "Notes," *Family Endowment Chronicle*, 3: 2 (Aug. 1934), pp. 9–11; Women's Cooperative Guild, *Report* (1934), pp. 6–7; Maternal Mortality Committee, *Maternal Mortality Report* (London: Caledonian Press, Oct. 1934). Labour women's organizations paid close attention to developing evidence on nutrition and child health; see especially their reports "Nutrition and Food Supplies" (NCLW, *Report*, 17 [1936], pp. 49–82), and "A Children's Charter" (NCLW, *Report*, 18 [1937], pp. 38–77). There is some evidence, however, that mothers and not children bore the brunt of unemployment and poverty. Stevenson and Cook point out that maternal mortality trends were far worse than infant mortality trends; see Stevenson and Cook, *The Slump*, pp. 41–3. Labour women's organizations in particular tried to draw attention to the ill health of mothers, but many thought this an intractable problem, given the presumably "natural" propensity of mothers to sacrifice their health for their husbands and children. See especially E. Sylvia Pankhurst, *Save the Mothers* (London: Knopf, 1930); Margery Spring-Rice, *Working Class Wives* (Harmondsworth: Penguin, 1939). The best summary of campaigns and devel-

Extensive research into child poverty created a strong case for better social services. Yet the establishment of a broad consensus among many social reformers that the state must take better care of its children by no means meant that such assistance would be forthcoming, still less that it would take the form of cash allowances. Family allowances became thinkable because they came to be seen as compatible with – indeed a necessary part of – existing social policies and wage practices. The problem of unemployment during the thirties created not only a new political consensus, but also a set of practical administrative problems that many felt could be solved only by children's allowances.

To begin with, by the thirties cash allowances for children had become an accepted part of many social programs. Children's allowances had been included in unemployment insurance in 1921 and in widows' pensions in 1925, although health insurance continued to cover the worker alone. Ostensibly, such benefits were granted in recognition of the fact that men's wages supported women and children; hence, many who believed that the state had no business either setting wages or interfering with a man's responsibility to support his family nevertheless admitted that the state must maintain the unemployed worker *and his family* at a decent level. But what if such family maintenance outstripped the level of wages, creating, as with the Speenhamland system during the Napoleonic Wars, a "demoralizing" disincentive to work? Family benefits may have been intended to compensate for the family wage, but social surveys during the thirties revealed that male wages were often nowhere near a "family" level. Children, in other words, could be better off with a father out of work than with one employed.

This problem, which became known as the "wage–benefit overlap," bedeviled social policymakers, placing them in the unpalatable position either of abandoning any concern to maintain work incentives or of setting rates at levels they knew to be inadequate for subsistence needs.[90] The majority of the Royal Commission on Unemployment

---

opments in the sphere of maternal and infant health is Jane Lewis, *The Politics of Motherhood* (London: Croom Helm, 1980).

[90] John Macnicol has argued persuasively for the importance of fears of the wage–benefit overlap in winning governmental attention for allowances. This is certainly true, but I would dissent from his conclusion that family allowances became attractive principally as a way of avoiding a more costly wage rise: "Family allowances would alter the wages of the married man just enough to shore up the principle of 'less eligibility' and the real issue of wages vis-à-vis profits would be neatly avoided." Certainly some civil servants and ministers would have preferred allowances to higher wages, but it is hard to claim

Insurance came down firmly on the side of work incentives, laying down as "a rule of cardinal importance ... that the amount of assistance in respect of unemployment, however provided, should be less than the wages of employment."[91] Yet could politicians and administrators adhere to this cardinal rule even to the point of driving assistance below the level of subsistence family needs? This dilemma plagued the UAB after it took over responsibility for maintaining the long-term unemployed. When the board first met to set its scales in the summer of 1934, they found that even rates that were "not in general excessive" would leave a large number of families with benefits in excess of wages. "A further slight deduction is therefore desirable," they concluded.[92]

The establishment of unemployment assistance at a level both below the rates of transitional benefit in many areas and below the level of any respectable poverty line unquestionably caused serious hardship in many families and made the government an easy target for Labour leaders, social reformers, and "poverty experts." In 1935, the Children's Minimum Committee used the government's own figures to estimate the costs of family maintenance and discovered that both insurance benefit and unemployment assistance for families with more than three children were seriously below the level required to meet subsistence needs. The table they submitted to the Unemployment Insurance Statutory Committee, reproduced as Table 6.4, showed that the larger the family, the greater the shortfall and the greater the number of children left in poverty.

Yet what was the government to do? The real achievement of Rathbone and her allies was in convincing a wide range of "respectable" opinion that there could be no real solution to the problem of the wage–benefit overlap until the government introduced a scheme of family allowances for wage earners.[93] This was not in fact strictly true.

(as Macnicol does) that these were the "two alternative solutions to the problem of the benefit/wages overlap," since few believed there could be a rise in wages substantial enough to lift all poor children out of poverty. We can however take Macnicol's claim that the "real issue" concerning poverty was the distribution of the product of industry between labor and capital and not the lack of "fit" between wages and family needs as evidence of the dominance of wage-centered analyses in British scholarship: see Macnicol, "Family Allowances and Less Eligibility," in Pat Thane, ed., *The Origins of British Social Policy* (London: Croom Helm, 1978), esp. pp. 192–3, 197.

[91] Royal Commission on Unemployment Insurance, *Final Report*, p. 124.

[92] BLPES, Markham Papers, 6/6, board memorandum no. 13 (30 Aug. 1934).

[93] See Rathbone's early articles: "Unemployment and the Family," *New Statesman and Nation*, 2: 20 (11 July 1931), pp. 38–9; "The Dependency Factor in Unemployment," *Family Endowment Chronicle*, 1: 2 (July 1931), p. 2.

Table 6.4. *Family needs compared with unemployment benefits, 1935 (shillings/pence per week)*

	Couple	And 1 child	And 3 children	And 5 children
Food	12/1	14/10	22/4	30/8
Clothing, etc.	5/3	6/4	8/6	10/9
Rent	7/6	7/6	8/7	10/1
Total needs	24/10	28/8	39/5	51/6
Unemployment insurance	26/-	28/-	32/-	36/-
Unemployment assistance	24/-	28/-	34/6-	40/6

Note: The food needs were based on the BMA scales, clothing needs on the Merseyside survey, and rent on the Unemployment Assistance Board's estimates. The children's ages in the three-child family were taken as 1–2, 6–8, and 8–10; those in the five-child family as 1–2, 4–5, 6–8, 11, 12–14.
Sources: "The Children's Minimum Campaign," *Family Endowment Chronicle*, 3:3 (Apr. 1935), p. 21; Markham Papers, Part 1, Item 7/9, Children's Minimum Committee, "Precis of Evidence to the Unemployment Insurance Statutory Committee," 4 Feb. 1935.

The government could have extended in-kind provision of milk and meals to needy children without counting this assistance as part of the cash benefit, as Rathbone urged the board to do in 1934.[94] This alternative could have safeguarded child health while maintaining the incentive to wage earning, since unpopular in-kind assistance would hardly have been preferred to wages.

Such a solution would have required a far more extensive and coordinated network of social services, however, and was not in the power of the Unemployment Assistance Board to establish. The board thus contented itself with pointing out in 1936 that even their low rate of benefit left some family men with virtually as much money as they would have earned at low-wage jobs, "with the result that they show little disposition to take work or to hold it when it is given to them."[95] In 1938, they essentially washed their hands of the problem, stating that the task of maintaining "a reasonable relationship" between allowances and wages was not really compatible with the board's

---

[94] BLPES, Markham Papers, 7/9, E. F. Rathbone [for the Children's Minimum Committee], "Memorandum on the Scale of Needs Suitable for Adoption by the Unemployment Assistance Board..." (July 1934).

[95] UAB, *Report for the Year Ending 31 Dec. 1935*, PP 1935–6, XIII, Cmd. 5177, p. 12.

"primary duty of meeting need," and that the problem was beyond their ability to solve.[96]

The Pilgrim Trust's survey of the long-term unemployed confirmed the existence of an overlap between wages and levels of benefit for men with large families but nevertheless found serious poverty among large families on assistance. These facts, they concluded, "point irresistibly to the necessity of some system of family allowances to those who are working."[97] Or as the FES argued to the Unemployment Insurance Statutory Committee in 1938:

> The only practical method of maintaining an adjustment between wages and relief without sacrificing the health and physique of the children of the unemployed is to approximate the wage to the family through a system of family allowances. The family wage would then exceed a reasonable and adequate family insurance benefit or relief allowance, just as now a single man's wage exceeds the single man's benefit.[98]

No government, however, was going to introduce a family allowance scheme for all wage earners simply to justify improved benefits for unemployed families. But the discovery that wages could be below the benefit levels of family men led to a more chilling realization: that children of these men in full work could be just as badly off (and hence just as in need of state support) as children of the unemployed. Havelock Ellis's stepchild François Lafitte, who acted as the researcher for the Population Policies Committee formed by the Eugenics Society and Political and Economic Planning, put the case most cogently:

> [The wage–benefit overlap] is serious not primarily because it means that some of the unemployed may grow into workshies and loafers, but rather because of the light which it throws on the standard of living of that considerable body of men with large families who are actually at work and earning no more than the U.A.B. would give them. It means that the poverty which we found to be so widespread among the unemployed is probably shared by many of the large families whose breadwinners are employed in unskilled and low-paid occupations.

He concluded that the "poverty of the large family on a wage system which ignores family needs is the basic problem to be tackled."[99]

---

[96] UAB, *Report for the Year Ending 31 Dec. 1937*, p. 6.
[97] Pilgrim Trust, *Men without Work*, p. 209.
[98] BLPES, Markham Papers, 9/1, Family Endowment Society [FES], "Statement to the Unemployment Insurance Statutory Committee" (Jan. 1938).
[99] BLPES, Political and Economic Planning [PEP] papers, Population Policies Committee,

The depression and the widespread evidence of child poverty allowed family allowances advocates to make a new case, but it was a case aimed largely at a restricted circle of policymakers and experts. In the twenties, family allowances had been a progressive demand, supported by a large section of the labor movement; when interest grew among those responsible for administering some of the National Government's most detested social policies, these earlier supporters became suspicious. The argument that allowances would make the means-tested dole operate more efficiently scarcely aroused enthusiasm among those who felt that the government should be concerned with relieving need and not maintaining work incentives; the point that they would help low-paid families in particular evoked the retort that the wages themselves should be raised. In 1937, the National Conference of Labour Women, hitherto a staunch supporter of family allowances, felt that bargaining power in some sectors had been so disastrously weakened by the depression that allowances would simply drive wages down further and agreed that their introduction should be postponed until the labor movement was in a stronger position.[100]

Furthermore, arguments based on child poverty or administrative rationality by no means led new converts to the conclusion that the nation needed a universal state-funded scheme. Since the alleviation of poverty in large families and not a general transfer of income from the childless to those with children was the goal, even sympathetic social reformers and administrators willing to consider cash allowances were prone to favor very limited schemes. In 1938, when the UAB finally considered the case for family allowances, they concluded that huge universal systems were irrelevant since most wages were sufficient for the needs of a five-person family but that a smaller system could be established to meet the needs of the 6.7% of men over age 20 who had more than three dependent children.[101] When a few private firms, including Cadbury's, introduced allowance schemes for their workers in 1938 and 1939, they paid benefits only for the third or fourth child and beyond.[102] Right up until the Second

PWS 1/1, 2973/38/Population, "Unemployment Pay – Relation to Wages and Family Needs" (28 June 1938), pp. 26–7, 36; see also "The Economics of Having Children," *Planning*, no. 134 (15 Nov. 1938), pp. 2–12.

[100] NCLW, *Annual Conference Report*, 18 (1937), pp. 39–40, 65–7.

[101] BLPES, Markham Papers, 6/13, Board memo no. 280, "Family Allowances" (19 Oct. 1938).

[102] These developments received some press coverage and were discussed in a pamphlet by the National Industrial Alliance; see *Daily Telegraph*, 5 Jan. and 17 Nov. 1938;

World War, moderate social reformers like Seebohm Rowntree continued to support statutory minimum wages capable of maintaining a family of five as the main cure to poverty, with allowances for all dependent children beyond the third to meet the special needs of large families.[103] Family allowances came to be seen as a useful device for mitigating the irrationality of the wage system in the case of large families, but they were by no means accepted as an appropriate way to support all children – much less to improve the position of wives, as Rathbone had originally intended.

It was only the Second World War that made a more extensive scheme possible and that converted many in policy-making circles to a national, universal, and state-financed scheme. In January 1940, when Eleanor Rathbone published a pamphlet entitled *The Case for the Immediate Introduction of a System of Family Allowances*, she was able to marshal several arguments based on wartime conditions.[104] To begin with, the war gave new purchase to prewar evidence of the declining birthrate and hence to proposals for social services aimed at arresting this decline. Wartime pronatalism was often couched in egalitarian terms – as a report by the survey organization Mass Observation put it, "Let's get ahead with numbers, and to hell with eugenics"[105] – but there is much evidence that working-class women strongly resented the implication "that a woman is prepared to bear children for a few pieces of silver."[106] Many of the women interviewed by Mass Observation during the war were suspicious of official interest in the birthrate and said that children were wanted only as cannon fodder.[107] It was, once again, policy-making elites – even ostensible

---

Manchester Guardian, 6 Apr. 1938; National Industrial Alliance, *The Case for and against Family Allowances* (London, [1939]).

[103] Asa Briggs, *Social Thought and Social Action: A Study of the Work of Seebohm Rowntree, 1871–1954* (London: Longmans, Green, 1961), pp. 274–5.

[104] Eleanor Rathbone, *The Case for the Immediate Introduction of a System of Family Allowances* (London: FES, Jan. 1940). For the relationship between children's allowances under various social programs and on separation allowances, see Land, "The Introduction of Family Allowances," pp. 202–4.

[105] Mass Observation, *Britain and Her Birth Rate* (London: John Murray, 1945), p. 206.

[106] NCLW, *Report*, 20 (1940), p. 55; see also "Population Problems: Readers' Views," *Labour Woman*, 32: 1 (Jan. 1944), p. 9.

[107] Mass Observation, *Britain and Her Birth Rate*, esp. pp. 30–6, 188–9. Mass Observation concluded that the problem was not that people were unable to have more children for economic reasons, but rather that they did not *want* large families. Fears of a return to unemployment, skepticism of promises of reconstruction, memories of their own mothers' hard lives, and a desire for a fuller life and some leisure of their own underlay many women's preference for smaller families.

Table 6.5. *Children's allowances in social programs, 1942 (shillings/pence)*

Program	Position of child in family		
	First	Second	Third onward
Unemployment insurance	4/-	4/-	3/-
Health insurance	None	None	None
Widows' pensions	5/-	3/-	3/-
Orphans' pensions	7/6	7/6	7/6
Separation allowance	9/6	7/-	5/6
Workers' compensation	4/-	4/-	3/-
Unemployment assistance [a]	—	—	—
Poor relief [b]	—	—	—

[a] Varies from 7/9 to 4/9 for ages 0–16.
[b] Varies by local authority.
Source: Social Insurance and Allied Services: A Report by Sir William Beveridge, PP, 1942–3, IV, Cmd. 6404, pp. 203–33.

progressives like Richard and Kathleen Titmuss – who found the prospect of a decline in Britain's world position alarming and pro-natalist arguments convincing.[108]

Rathbone also pointed to the large numbers of servicemen's families and evacuees already receiving allowances and the increasingly complicated proliferation of schemes and rates.[109] By 1942, as Table 6.5 shows, dependents' benefits had been incorporated into so many social programs and benefited so many children that children of wage earners seemed unfairly excluded. The principal new argument, however, and the one to which both Rathbone and Beveridge gave pride of place, was that allowances could enable the government to safeguard public health while avoiding an inflationary upward spiral of wages and prices. Political and Economic Planning likewise concluded that one could only restrict civilian consumption while at the same time delivering scarce goods and services to children by introducing a system of family allowances.[110]

---

[108] Liberals, when constructing arguments about the need to preserve Britain's population, often fell into paternalistic arguments about the "duty" of those who had "evolved a higher way of life . . . to help and guide the teeming millions of India and Africa to a more abundant life." Richard Titmuss and Kathleen Titmuss, *Parents Revolt* (London: Secker & Warburg, 1942), p. 104.

[109] Eleanor Rathbone, *The Case for the Immediate Introduction of a System of Family Allowances*, pp. 3–4.

[110] BLPES, PEP Papers, Document Book M5, Executive Committee Minutes, 16 June 1942; also "Family Allowance Schemes," *Planning*, no. 162 (27 Feb. 1940), pp. 3–14.

The most influential wartime convert to universalism was Seebohm Rowntree, who early in 1941 published a much-noted article in the *Times* arguing for the introduction of a system of allowances for *all* children as an interim wartime measure. In this article, and again in *Poverty and Progress*, his updated survey of York published in 1941, Rowntree argued for universal allowances as a pressing public health measure. More than 50% of children with *employed* fathers were born in poverty in 1936; worse, 47% of all children would be undernourished for five years, and fully 31.5% for ten years. An attempt to improve child health through substantial wage increases in wartime would hardly be effective – since 58% of male workers had no dependent children, while 9% had fully 42% of the children – and would undoubtedly set off an inflationary wage spiral. By contrast, the establishment of a lower minimum wage combined with allowances of five shillings per week for all children would abolish 89% of all poverty.[111] With Rowntree's support, the Liberal Assembly endorsed family allowances at the rate of five shillings per week in July 1941.[112]

The conversion of Rowntree and pressure from Beveridge and Amery gave the campaign new credibility, but its success was made possible primarily because the war once again altered the institutional balance of power and thus the constraints over and scope for reforms. As Richard Titmuss, Samuel Beer, and Paul Addison have all argued, "total war" did inaugurate a new contract both among the political parties and between the government and the people.[113] Comprehensive social services quickly became an accepted goal, and politicians and social reformers no longer tolerated Treasury pleas of financial constraints as an excuse for inaction. A projected cost of £125 million for family allowances was not prohibitive, the *New Statesman* argued, since the figure paled in comparison to war costs.[114] Parliamentary backbenchers agreed, and Rathbone and Amery were able quickly to forge a parliamentary alliance in support of family allowances.

On 15 February 1940, Amery and Rathbone convened a meeting of sympathetic M.P.s at the House of Commons, at which Amery presented the case for the immediate introduction of children's allowances. Family allowances, he argued,

---

[111] B. Seebohm Rowntree, "Wages in Wartime," *Times*, 4 Jan. 1941; idem, *Poverty and Progress: A Second Social Survey of York* (London: Longmans, Green, 1941), esp. p. 459.
[112] "Family Allowances: Civil Defence," *Manchester Guardian*, 21 July 1941.
[113] Samuel H. Beer, *Modern British Politics* (London: Faber, 1969); Richard Titmuss, *Problems of Social Policy* (London: HMSO, 1950), esp. pp. 506–7; Paul Addison, *The Road to 1945* (1975; rpt. London: Quartet, 1977).
[114] "Family Allowances," *New Statesman and Nation*, 23: 587 (23 May 1942), pp. 332–3.

should be an All-Party reform. They are a Conservative measure, in so far as Conservatism believes in healthy family life as the foundation of the State. They are a Socialist measure, in so far as they are based on the principle of giving to each according to his needs. They are a Liberal measure, in so far as they aim at securing the maximum of equality of opportunity for every child born in this country. They are a national measure, in so far as they can make an immediate contribution to winning the war without injury to the future health of the nation.[115]

Although some anxiety was expressed at the meeting about the possible opposition of the TUC, members agreed to form an all-party committee.[116] On 23 April 1941, Cecil Wright, Rathbone, and the young Labour M.P. Edith Summerskill tabled a motion supported by 114 M.P.s stating that the House "would welcome the introduction of a national State-paid scheme of allowances for dependent children, payable to their mothers or acting guardians, as a means of safeguarding the health and well-being of the rising generation."[117] By May, the Family Allowances Group had the support of 160 M.P.s, and its size was growing steadily.[118]

The parliamentary enthusiasm for allowances was not entirely welcome to the government, which took refuge from its critics by pointing to the past veto of the TUC. When the Commons Family Allowances Group brought their first deputation to the Chancellor of the Exchequer, Sir Kingsley Wood, on 16 June 1941, Eleanor Rathbone "challenged" the Chancellor

> to produce a single expert in economics, in industrial welfare, in sociology, who has really studied it who has not come down in favour of family allowances....
>
> Who are you afraid of? Is not the plain fact this, that a small but vocal number of Trade Union leaders are jealous that the wage-earning classes should obtain anything except through their means of collective bargaining...?

In his response, Sir Kingsley Wood refused to "rise to the suggestions and incitements that have been made to me by Miss Rathbone" and reiterated that the government would not accept a policy on which

---

[115] TUC File 118.2, "Family Allowances: Summary of Mr. Amery's Address to the Preliminary Meeting Held on Feb. 15th [1940]."

[116] "The Case for Family Allowances," *Times*, 16 Feb. 1940.

[117] TUC File 118.2, All Party Family Allowances Group, Circular (July 1941); "Family Allowances: Commons Motion Backed by 114 M. P.s," *Times*, 30 Apr. 1941.

[118] "Family Allowances: Chancellor to Receive Deputation of M.P.s," *Times*, 23 May 1941.

trade unions were so sharply divided. "It would be very unwise," he stated, "at a time when we are endeavouring to maintain national unity...to go forward without their wholehearted support."[119] In early 1942, however, the General Council of the TUC suddenly changed its position and agreed to support children's allowances.

It would be hard to argue that theirs was a wholehearted conversion. The council for several years resisted pressure from the Labour Party to reconsider their position, while individual trade unionists tended to express their opposition in such unfortunate but revealing phrases as that employed by H. L. Bullock of the National Union of General and Municipal Workers: "Family Allowances will tend to dig at the roots of a virile Trade Unionism."[120] In time, however, a few leaders (Citrine among them) began to find the position of the TUC a liability, particularly in light of the widening political consensus around allowances. When the TUC had rejected children's allowances in 1930, they were the ideological property of feminist and socialist groups with whom the General Council had little sympathy; by 1939, with such prominent and diverse political figures as Leo Amery and Seebohm Rowntree as their foremost advocates, the TUC's continued opposition seemed less centrist than self-interested.

Amery and Rowntree did not hesitate to cajole, harangue, pressure, and virtually blackmail the TUC. When a representative from the TUC reiterated the congress's preference for social services at a conference on nutrition convened by the British Medical Association shortly before the outbreak of the war, Leo Amery said angrily if inaccurately: "A question of this sort had to be discussed on its merits. It did not matter 'tuppence' what was said by the TUC. No sort of papal encyclical on the subject could really influence any thinking person."[121] Seebohm Rowntree, while no less direct, was more conciliatory. When he heard that the congress planned to discuss allowances at its 1941 conference, he asked Citrine for a delegate list so he could try to influence the conference directly. "The Chancellor of the Exchequer recently stated that he could not recommend the adoption of a State scheme of family allowances if the Trade Union movement was not in favor of it," Rowntree wrote to Citrine. "By this state-

---

[119] PRO, PIN 8/163, Treasury, "Notes of a Deputation Received by the Chancellor of the Exchequer...16 June 1941," pp. 9–10.

[120] TUC File 118.2, H. L. Bullock, "Family or Children's Allowances" [typescript, four pages, 25 Feb. 1941].

[121] [British Medical Association], *Nutrition and the Public Health*, p. 121. Amery nevertheless lobbied Citrine directly on the subject of family allowances; see the exchange of letters in February and March 1940 in TUC File 118.2.

ment the Chancellor has placed upon the Trade Union movement the responsibility of withholding a reform of supreme importance to the welfare of the poorest section of our workers."[122] By 1941, many supporters of allowances shared Rowntree's opinion that the opposition of the General Council was the main barrier to the introduction of a national scheme.

The General Council found this position embarrassing, as did the Labour Party. In February 1940, the council had told the party that it was to make no decision about allowances until they had become the policy of the General Council, and while the party faithfully adhered to that stricture, its leaders badgered the General Council continuously.[123] Individual Labour M.P.s supported Rathbone and Amery's initiatives, and a Labour Family Allowances Group, operating from the same address as the FES, propagandized within the party.[124] In June 1940, and over the objections of its trade unionist members, the Labour Executive even authorized its own Policy Sub-Committee to reexamine the question.[125] Citrine admitted that he was unhappy with the party's decision to proceed on its own but was convinced they would "make no separate declarations."[126] When the Policy Sub-Committee reported in favor of a universal tax-funded scheme, the Executive thus asked the TUC to reopen the question.[127] The TUC's Economic Committee did therefore meet with the Labour Party's Policy Sub-Committee and in turn reported to the General Council in favor of the principle of allowances.[128] When the General Council met to discuss the Economic Committee's recommendation in April, however, Charles Dukes and H. L. Bullock of the General and Municipal Workers and Arthur Deakin, Ernest Bevin's successor as general secretary of the Transport and General Workers' Union, all expressed strong opposition, and the council decided to adjourn the matter sine die.[129]

This time, the Labour Party was unwilling to drop the issue. Al-

[122] TUC File 118.2, Rowntree to Citrine, 14 Aug. 1941; and "Memorandum by B. Seebohm Rowntree" (9 Apr. 1941).

[123] TUC File 118.2, GC Minutes, 28 Feb. 1940.

[124] For FES-style propaganda within the party, see the two very similar pamphlets issued by the FES and the Family Allowances Labour Group, *Family Allowances Today*, and *Family Allowances and the Labour Movement*, both dated July 1941.

[125] TUC File 118.2, GC Minutes, 28 Feb. 1940; and Dukes to Citrine, 28 June 1940.

[126] Ibid., Citrine to Dukes, 1 July 1940.

[127] Ibid., GC Minutes, 23 Oct. 1940.

[128] TUC File 118.2, Assistant secretary of the TUC to Middleton, 17 Feb. 1941.

[129] TUC File 118.2, GC Minutes, 23 Apr. 1941.

though the Executive did not recommend any scheme to the 1941 conference, they did publish the Policy Sub-Committee's favorable report and allow for a heated discussion, during which Charles Dukes's claim that the only solution to poverty lay in collective bargaining came under fire from Edith Summerskill.[130] The General Council also found itself facing a resolution in favor of children's allowances at the 1941 congress of the TUC, although the unions supporting the measure agreed to remit the question to the council for consideration.[131] Sir William Beveridge also treated representatives from the TUC to a long disquisition on the importance of family allowances in the war against poverty when they came to give evidence to his committee on social insurance in January 1942.[132] By February, then, when J. S. Middleton, the secretary of the Labour Party, wrote to Citrine asking the General Council to reconsider its position jointly with the Labour Executive, the trade union movement was under considerable pressure to change its mind.[133]

On 18 March 1942, the General Council thus held a special meeting to discuss the question of allowances. Opponents expressed the same reservations they had in 1930: they distrusted the advocates of allowances, including those within the party, and feared that state benefits would weaken wage claims and the appeal of trade unionism. Support had broadened, however, coming not only from those who argued that wages could never be brought high enough to meet all children's needs, but also from pragmatists who felt that family allowances were probably inevitable and that the TUC should therefore work to ensure an agreeable scheme. The most surprising convert to the latter school of thought was Walter Citrine himself, who wondered "whether perhaps they were not too much influenced by the fact that the idea had not come from the movement in the first instance." Perhaps they would have been more sympathetic, he thought, if the idea had not come from the ILP; in any case, they ought now "to divest themselves from prejudice" and consider the question again. With Citrine's support, the pragmatists and the advocates won the day, passing a resolution by a majority of seventeen to eight in favor of children's allowances "paid directly by the State, on a non-contributory basis, unaccompanied by any Means Test." Significantly, however, the res-

---

[130] Labour Party, *Report*, 40 (1941), pp. 32, 189–93, 166–9.
[131] TUC, *Report*, 73 (1941), pp. 183–4, 372–6.
[132] PRO, Cab. 87/77, Social Insurance Committee, 1st meeting, 14 Jan. 1942, pp. 36–40.
[133] TUC File 118.2, Middleton to Citrine, 12 Feb. 1942; and Citrine to Middleton, 16 Feb. 1942.

olution did not include the suggestion made by Anne Loughlin of the Tailors and Garment Workers that allowances be paid to the mother.[134] Economic benefits for women – as opposed to for children – remained controversial for trade unionists.

The acquiescence of the General Council enabled the Labour Party to include support for a scheme of family allowances in a composite resolution on social insurance discussed at the 1942 party conference. The resolution passed handily, but the clause on family allowances was still controversial. An amendment to omit any mention of allowances received more than a quarter of the conference votes and was supported by Arthur Deakin, who also voiced reservations about the new policy at the TUC a few weeks later.[135] Nevertheless, the incorporation of Labour as "full partners" during the war and the presence of Ernest Bevin at the Ministry of Labour allowed the movement as a whole to contemplate state action with less trepidation.[136] The endorsement of the TUC also removed the last refuge of Conservatives within the government unenthusiastic about a national scheme.

Since only a state-funded scheme was seriously under consideration by 1941, one would perhaps expect the employers' organizations to have marshaled opposition, but once again, they scarcely considered the question until it was almost decided. While Rowntree's and a few other firms introduced allowance schemes for large families early in the war, only the forward-looking members of the Management Research Groups collectively considered the question.[137] In August 1941, when Sir Horace Wilson, the head of the civil service and former permanent secretary of the Ministry of Labour, wrote to Sir John Forbes Watson of the British Employers' Confederation to ask if they had written anything on family allowances, Forbes Watson was forced to admit that his organization had not considered the question.[138] Wilson told Forbes Watson that allowances were one of the most important current political issues, but the employers seem to have ignored his implicit warning. When Beveridge asked them for their

---

[134] TUC File 118.2, General Council, "Report of a Special Meeting held on March 18, 1942, to Discuss the Question of Family Allowances" [typescript, eleven pages].

[135] Labour Party, *Report*, 41 (1942), pp. 132–7; TUC, *Report*, 74 (1942), pp. 301–2.

[136] Land, "The Introduction of Family Allowances," p. 179.

[137] On Management Research Groups' discussion of the issue, see BLPES, Henry Ward Papers, Management Research Groups, Circular nos. 727, 738, 746, 751; also Briggs, *Social Thought*, pp. 272–7.

[138] Modern Records Centre, University of Warwick Library, C.B.I. Predecessor Archive, MSS 200 B/3/2/C262, Sir Horace Wilson to John Forbes Watson, 11 Aug. 1941; and reply of 12 Aug. 1941 with penciled notations of 21 Aug. 1941.

opinion in May 1942, Forbes Watson said that the confederation had not considered the question of allowances because the TUC had been opposed, and "as a rule we wait until they have given us their orders."[139] Surely one could find no more telling acknowledgment of the influence of the TUC – or of the supine incapacity of employers – in the realm of social policy.

Once the TUC had approved, parliamentary pressure increased. Even in 1941, Treasury officials accepted that the degree of parliamentary support made it virtually impossible for them to avoid beginning inquiries into the question.[140] They resisted favoring any particular scheme, however, and when the government's *White Paper on Family Allowances* was finally published in May 1942, it merely provided estimates of the cost of various schemes, whether funded through insurance contributions or by the state alone, and including either all children or only children in excess of the first or the first two.[141] The unenthusiastic tone of the white paper did not prevent the Commons from resolving in favor of a national scheme of family allowances two months later.[142] In this area, Parliament decided to give the lead, convinced that allowances were, as the *Times* put it, "an agreed principle."[143]

The period of the thirties and the Second World War saw the elaboration of two rather different approaches to the problem of familial dependence. On the one hand, the depression and the crisis of unemployment resulted in policies that by defining married women's dependence as normative and penalizing men who failed to find work, incorporated the breadwinner paradigm explicitly into social policy. The welfare state, as epitomized by the social insurance system, was thus structurally inegalitarian but also coercive. While men held a privileged position in the insurance system, being granted maintenance for their families as well as themselves without the special and rigorous conditions that limited women's claims, their claim was not absolute. Should they fail to find work, they would lose their status not only as workers but also as heads of households, and be forced to turn to assistance programs that ultimately left them dependent on the families they had hitherto maintained.

---

[139] PRO, Cab. 87/77, Social Insurance Committee, 11th meeting (20 May 1942), p. 18.
[140] PRO, ACT 1/644, Maddox, "Miss Rathbone's Question on Family Allowances" (17 May 1941).
[141] *Family Allowances: Memorandum by the Chancellor of the Exchequer*, PP 1941–2, IX, Cmd. 6354.
[142] 380 *H.C. Deb.* 5th ser., 23 June 1942, esp. cols. 1853–8.
[143] "An Agreed Principle," *Times*, 11 June 1942.

On the other hand, the depression also committed the state to the difficult task of maintaining large numbers of unemployed workers – *and their children* – at a decent level. It was the difficulties of doing this without causing an overlap between relief and wages and the resulting discovery that wages were often well below a family level, that created a new political consensus around the usefulness of direct allowances for workers' children. Their previous commitment to a family wage notwithstanding, social reformers like Rowntree discovered that the problem of child poverty could require state aid to *all* dependent children.

But did the movement for family allowances result in a decisive shift toward an explicit family policy, toward a parental welfare state redistributing income between childless families and those with children? If one were to look at family allowances in isolation, one might answer the question in the affirmative. But in fact allowances were merely one part of the general unification and rationalization of the social welfare system that grew out of the war. In order to evaluate the resulting character of the British welfare state as a whole, we must look briefly at the simultaneous formulation and enactment of family allowances and of the unified social insurance scheme foreshadowed by the Beveridge Plan.

The place of family policy in the Beveridgian welfare state

The Interdepartmental Committee on Social Insurance and Allied Services that gave rise to the famous Beveridge Report was appointed in June 1941 by Arthur Greenwood, then minister without portfolio in the wartime Coalition government and the chairman of the Cabinet's Committee on Reconstruction Problems. Initially comprised of officials from various government departments under the chairmanship of Sir William Beveridge, the committee was asked to survey "existing schemes of social insurance and allied services...and to make recommendations."[144] By January 1942, however, as it became clear to the Cabinet that Beveridge was planning to recommend a more comprehensive reform than anyone had imagined, the government decided that the departmental representatives should serve only as advisers and the report be Beveridge's alone. This decision was resented by Beveridge, but in the end suited his abilities and ambitions admirably. On 20 November 1942, he submitted his report to Sir

---

[144] PRO, Cab. 87/1, R.P. (41) 16, "Social Insurance and Allied Services: Memorandum by the Minister without Portfolio" (23 June 1941).

William Jowitt, the paymaster general, now charged with recon-struction.

Beveridge presented his plan for comprehensive social insurance in the postwar period as a sui generis vision of an ideal welfare state, developed with joint regard to humanitarian interests and adminis-trative logic. Yet as José Harris has shown, Beveridge was a better synthesizer and propagandist than an innovator. Indeed, the popu-larity of the report stemmed largely from the fact that the recom-mendations reflected a progressive consensus on social policy: programs were to be improved and rationalized, but the basic frame-work was not changed.[145] A comprehensive account of the Beveridge Plan is beyond the scope of this book, but we do need to ask how Beveridge's proposals and, in particular, his incorporation of family allowances built on and transformed the precedents of the thirties. Three questions are key. First, what did Beveridge see as the main purpose of social insurance, and what was the place of family allow-ances within that scheme? Second, how did the implementers – min-isters and civil servants – alter both the logic of the scheme and the place of family allowances? Finally, what was lost in the translation of ideals into policies, and how were these particular policy outcomes possible?

The Beveridge Plan was, according to its author, "a scheme of social insurance against interruption and destruction of earning power and for special expenditure arising at birth, marriage or death."[146] The primary role of welfare state, then, should continue to be that of compensating for the loss of wages. But who, in fact, should be com-pensated and for what? Should married women, for example, be compensated directly when their work was "interrupted" by years of child rearing? Beveridge, like any policymaker, confronted immedi-ately the dilemma of how to accommodate the insurance system to varying patterns of dependence and maintenance within families.

Beveridge solved this problem by dividing the population into six classes, classes that were defined in part by their labor market position

---

[145] On the Beveridge Report, see especially José Harris, "Social Planning in War-time: Some Aspects of the Beveridge Report," in J. M. Winter, ed., *War and Economic De-velopment* (Cambridge University Press, 1975), pp. 239–56; also idem, *William Beveridge: A Biography* (Oxford University Press, 1977); and, for his own account, William Bev-eridge, *Power and Influence* (London: Hodder & Stoughton, 1953). The significance of the Beveridge Report for the introduction of allowances is discussed thoroughly by Macnicol, *The Movement for Family Allowances*, esp. pp. 182–91.

[146] *Social Insurance and Allied Services. A Report by Sir William Beveridge* [hereafter *Beveridge Report*], PP 1942–3, VI, Cmd. 6404, p. 9.

but also in part by age or marital status. By far the largest category was that of employed persons (18.4 million of 46.5 million), a category covering all male and female wage earners but excluding all married women. Most women did not work after marriage, he noted, and in any case such work was anomalous and scarcely desirable. "In the next thirty years," he wrote, "housewives as mothers will have vital work to do in ensuring the adequate continuance of the British race and of British ideals in the world."[147] In approaching families, then, the insurance system should take the married couple as the basic unit needing insurance and treat the husband and wife as a "team."[148] Interruption of the man's earnings was considered the main risk confronting this team; in such cases, benefits for the wife would be included automatically in the man's benefit.

In its identification of risks and its assumptions about dependence, the Beveridge Plan built on the precedents of the interwar period. Working men remained the principal focus of the insurance system; the tasks of finding work and supporting wives were placed squarely on their shoulders, and those who refused employment were again relegated to means-tested assistance. Where Beveridge differed radically from interwar governments was in his conviction – indistinguishable from that voiced by Hobhouse and other "new liberals" before 1914 – that the state must create the conditions in which this meritorious conduct was possible. Beveridge thus made full employment – along with a national health service and family allowances – one of his three cardinal "assumptions"; comprehensive social insurance, he claimed, could work only if the government accepted the responsibility (resisted by the governments of the thirties) for maintaining the level of employment. This was the case not only because the cost of comprehensive social security could only be met if the level of employment remained high, but also because the only adequate "test" of one's right to benefit was whether or not one would take work – a test that it was impossible to apply under conditions of mass unemployment. Full employment would allow the state to avoid the expedients of the thirties, whereby men genuinely eager for work were subjected to means testing simply because there was no work to be had; rather, the availability of work would enable the state accurately to distinguish the deserving from the work-shy.[149] With a policy

[147] Ibid., p. 53.
[148] Ibid., p. 49.
[149] Ibid., p. 163.

of full employment, postwar governments made the fulfillment of the ideal of the male breadwinner possible.

Beveridge realized that the policy of assuming a male-breadwinner family "team" left some 1.4 million married women wage earners in an "anomalous" position, in 1942 as in 1931. Yet they were housewives before they were workers, he decided. Wage earning was not the normal state for a married woman, Beveridge told the representatives of the National Council of Women when they came to give evidence, nor were her needs when sick or unemployed as great as a single woman, so long as her husband was still earning. She had other, more important risks: for example, "She has the liability to have pregnancy, and ought to have it; that is what she is in a sense there for."[150] Rather than treating married women workers like other workers in the new insurance system, he proposed that they be normally exempt from the work-related provisions. Married women could choose to contract into the system of sickness, unemployment, and disability insurance covering men and single women – in which case they would have to reestablish their right to benefit by building up their contributions all over again – but they would be granted benefits at a lower rate, and their husband's benefit during interruption of earnings would also be lower. Normally, however, married women, whether unwaged or earning, would form a distinct insurance class of "housewives," with benefits tailored to their particular needs.[151]

Beveridge's proposal to label housewives as a special insurance class gave his report an egalitarian tint; as Janet Beveridge said, the plan was infused with an "unconscious fairness to women."[152] Much of this "fairness" was merely rhetorical flourishes – such as Beveridge's fulsome tributes to the housewife's work as "vital though unpaid" – but he did also attempt to identify and plan for the special "needs" and "risks" of the unwaged wife.[153] Many features of the report that strike us as curious today – Beveridge's support for a "marriage bounty" refunding a woman's insurance contributions upon renunciation of paid work, his proposals that the divorced wife be compensated by the state for loss of maintenance if she were divorced without her consent and that incapacitated married women be provided with home

---

[150] PRO, Cab. 87/77, Social Insurance Committee, 5th meeting, 11 Mar. 1942.
[151] *Beveridge Report*, pp. 48–53.
[152] Janet Beveridge, *Beveridge and His Plan* (London: Hodder & Stoughton, 1954), pp. 182–3.
[153] *Beveridge Report*, p. 49.

helps to take over their "job" – were logical extensions of the assumption that upon marriage a woman became a household worker, unpaid but supported, and that she therefore needed insurance against loss of both her capacity for housework and her maintenance by her husband.[154]

The Beveridge Plan thus claimed to be a blueprint for a welfare state with "separate but equal" provisions for men and women. Yet the fundamental imbalance remained: a married woman's entitlements, being based on the assumption that her work was unremunerated, could scarcely be equal to her husband's. Indeed, although Beveridge initially considered providing a grant to incapacitated housewives, he set this benefit at the derisory level of five shillings per week – at best enough to pay for a few hours' help – and later abandoned it entirely, deciding it was "not an essential feature."[155] While married men's benefits when unemployed or ill included maintenance for women and children, married women's waged work was often uninsured, and their unwaged work remained private. Their relationship to the state (unlike that of their husbands) was indirect: whereas the man contracted directly with the state, the woman contracted with her husband and had recourse to the public purse only when this first contract broke down. So long as a man was alive and co-resident, her welfare, whether derived from wages or benefits, was in his hands.

Beveridge's decision to presume that male maintenance and female dependence was the normal condition of the married couple did not solve the problem of the relationship between family needs and income, since dependent children were scattered unevenly among wage earners. Freedom from want, Beveridge claimed, thus required the "adjustment of incomes, in periods of earning as well as interruption of earning, to family needs, that is to say, in one form or another it requires allowances for children."[156] Beveridge was also convinced that he could not achieve his goal of setting social insurance benefits at an adequate level unless a family allowance scheme were introduced that would raise the income of low-waged families and hence prevent any overlap between wages and benefits. In Beveridge's Plan, then, children's allowances figured as another underlying "assumption." But if children's allowances were actually to adjust income to needs,

[154] Ibid., pp. 131–4.
[155] PRO, Cab. 87/76, S.I.C. (41) 20, Beveridge, "Basic Problems of Social Security with Heads of a Scheme" (11 Dec. 1941), p. 25.
[156] *Beveridge Report*, pp. 7–8.

they had to be adequate to maintain the child – a principle admitted by Beveridge, who set them in 1942 at eight shillings per week.[157] Initially, Beveridge proposed such allowances for *all* children,[158] but when pressed to limit the cost of the scheme, he omitted the first child on the grounds that wages were – or should be – normally able to support a man, wife, and one child.[159]

Beveridge's solution to the problem of children's dependence fell somewhere between the principle that wage earners' children should be supported by their parents and the principle that they should be entirely supported by the state. The assumption was preserved that men should in normal circumstances maintain their wives (and one child), but additional children were to be supported entirely by adequate state-funded allowances. This compromise went some way to meeting Eleanor Rathbone's case – and indeed was preferred by the FES to the alternative economy of paying for all children at very low rates[160] – but it was highly illogical. The omission of the first child from the allowance scheme was essentially a stopgap measure motivated by the need for economy, but it meant that the old argument that family allowances would allow for equal pay between men and women no longer applied. All men, whatever their family situation, were still expected to earn family wages higher than those earned by women.

The Beveridge Report was released to the Commons on 1 December 1942; by early January of 1943, Rowntree, Rathbone, and other members of the FES were back in the offices of Kingsley Wood, then chancellor of the exchequer, arguing that the further endorsement of the TUC gave the government a clear signal to proceed with a national scheme of children's allowances.[161] Action on the report was slow, however, both because of the degree of official scrutiny a proposal this comprehensive would entail and, in time, because of sharp divisions within the Cabinet.[162] After an initial review in December

---

[157] Ibid., p. 90.

[158] PRO, Cab. 87/76, S.I.C. (41) 20, pp. 2, 20.

[159] PRO, Cab. 87/81, S.I.C. (42) 100 (Revised) 6, "Draft Report by Sir William Beveridge" (30 Sept. 1942), pp. 1–6.

[160] PRO, Cab. 87/77, Social Insurance Committee, 12th meeting, 2 June 1942, p. 9.

[161] PRO, PIN 8/16, Treasury, "Notes of a Deputation . . . 14 January 1943."

[162] The Beveridge Report became a bone of contention almost immediately. The first concern of the Conservative ministers was to keep Beveridge himself from propagandizing in its favor, but this was soon given up as a hopeless task and the government decided, as Churchill put it, that "once it is out, he can bark to his heart's content." See PRO, T172/2093, Jowitt to P.M., 23 Nov. 1942; Cab. 65/28, Cabinet 153, 16 Nov. 1942.

1942 by a committee of senior officials from relevant departments under the chairmanship of Thomas Phillips of the Ministry of Labour,[163] consideration of the report devolved on the one hand to a "central staff" of officials from relevant departments, coordinated by Thomas Sheepshanks of the Ministry of Home Security and reporting to William Jowitt,[164] and on the other hand to the Cabinet Committee on Reconstruction Priorities, appointed in January 1943 under the chairmanship of John Anderson (then lord president of council),[165] and subsumed into the new Reconstruction Committee under Lord Woolton in 1944.[166]

In theory, officials were to deal with administrative questions and ministers with questions of policy, but the boundaries between the two were unclear, and most questions were canvassed in both arenas. The Conservative and Labour ministers on the various reconstruction committees found themselves at loggerheads over the government's ability to fund the proposed measures and the ethics of introducing domestic social reforms in wartime, and these disagreements soon spilled over into the Cabinet.[167] In the face of parliamentary pressure, the Cabinet did announce its acceptance of the principles of a National Health Service and of children's allowances at the reduced rate of five shillings per week for each child beyond the first in February 1943, but the government was still too divided to make any definite commitment to the plan itself.[168] The process of review continued, how-

---

[163] For the remit to the Officials' Committee, see Cab. 87/2, Committee on Reconstruction Problems, 14th meeting, 3 Dec. 1942. Minutes and papers of the Official Committee on the Beveridge Report [Phillips Committee] are in PRO, PIN 8/115 and 116.

[164] The extensive papers of the "central staff" are in PRO, PIN 8.

[165] For the appointment of the Committee on Reconstruction Priorities, see Cab. 65/33, Cabinet 8, 14 Jan. 1943. The committee's minutes and memoranda are in Cab. 87/12–13.

[166] Minutes and memoranda of the Cabinet Committee on Reconstruction, which also absorbed the earlier Committee on Reconstruction Problems, are in Cab. 87/5–9.

[167] Kingsley Wood, then chancellor of the exchequer, presented very pessimistic estimates of the government's capacity to fund the Beveridge proposals and pointed out that any commitments must be weighed against future military spending: PRO, Cab. 87/3, R.P. (43) 5, "The Financial Aspects of the Social Security Plan: Memorandum by the Chancellor of the Exchequer" (11 Jan. 1943). Herbert Morrison disputed these figures, claiming that "finance is within very wide limits a handmaid of policy": PRO, Cab. 87/13, P.R. (43) 2, "The Social Security Plan: Memorandum by the Home Secretary" (20 Jan. 1943).

[168] PRO, Cab. 87/13, Committee on Reconstruction Priorities, "The Beveridge Plan: Interim Report" (11 Feb. 1943); Cab. 66/34, W.P. (43) 65, "Beveridge Report: Note by the Prime Minister," (15 Feb. 1943); Cab. 65/33, Cabinet 28, 12 Feb. 1943, and Cabinet 29, 15 Feb. 1943. For Sir John Anderson's announcement of the government's

ever, and by 1944 the government had worked out detailed proposals on most aspects of the Beveridge Plan.[169] It revised the original proposals a good deal, however, changing both the content of the "housewife's policy" and the weight of children's allowances within the whole system.

Although ministers and civil servants questioned many of Beveridge's specific proposals and rates, they overwhelmingly endorsed his intent to rationalize and unify the insurance system, as well as his argument that such insurance must be based on the paradigm of the male breadwinner and dependent wife. The Cabinet Committee on Reconstruction Priorities accepted that housewives should be a distinct class, and agreed that married women workers could be exempt from contributions, and that those earning particularly low wages should be compulsorily exempt. They agreed that the social insurance system should be gender-specific, identifying classes also by sex and marital status, rather than by labor market position alone. Yet they recognized much of the "housewife's policy" for the window dressing it was: the marriage bounty was rejected, and little was heard of either government compensation for divorced women or a comprehensive home helps service.[170]

When it came to the question of family allowances, however, ministers and civil servants disagreed with some of Beveridge's proposals. First, they rejected the idea that the family wage ideal should be done away with for children beyond the first and, therefore, were unwilling to make the benefits for these children adequate to subsistence needs. By proposing subsistence rates, Beveridge had implicitly accepted that the state had a responsibility not only to prevent serious poverty in

acceptance of the principle of children's allowances, see 386 *H.C. Deb.*, 5th ser., 16 Feb. 1943, col. 1667.

[169] In June and July 1943, there was an open argument between Attlee, Bevin, and Morrison on the one hand and Churchill and Kingsley Wood on the other over whether the government could in fact commit itself to some postwar measures. See Cab. 66/38, W.P. (43) 255, Clement Attlee, Ernest Bevin and Herbert Morrison, "The Need for Decisions" (26 June 1943); Cab. 66/39, W.P. (43) 308, "Note by the Prime Minister on 'The Need for Decisions' " (14 July 1943); Cab. 66/39, W.P. (43) 324, Attlee, Bevin, and Morrison, "The Need for Decisions" (20 July 1943). These memos were discussed in Cabinet in October, and it was decided that the government would enact measures designed to ease the postwar transition but not long-term reforms. See Cab. 65/36, Cabinet 140, 14 Oct. 1943, and Cabinet 144, 21 Oct. 1943. Similar arguments continued throughout 1944.

[170] PRO, Cab. 87/12, Committee on Reconstruction Priorities, 25th meeting, 21 Oct. 1943; Cab. 87/13, P.R. (43) 83, Committee on Reconstruction Priorities, "Position of Married Women: Housewife's Policy" (22 Oct. 1943).

families with many children, but also to provide a minimum standard of living for every child, whatever the family's class or "neediness." This was a much-expanded vision of the responsibility of the state for the welfare of children, and was unpalatable to both ministers and civil servants. When considering the report in December 1942, the Phillips committee was skeptical of the usefulness of allowances altogether and soon whittled the rate down to five shillings per child, which, they said, "had the virtue of *not* pretending to be a subsistence rate."[171] The Treasury found even this reduced rate excessive. Because allowances were genuinely intended to prevent want in some large families on low wages, "it does not follow that... allowances to all families, irrespective of wages, is a necessary and appropriate remedy."[172] In February 1943, the chancellor was willing to consider only a restricted scheme for low-income families with more than two dependent children.[173] The Ministry of Labour, now under Ernest Bevin, an old opponent of allowances, also argued that the French and Belgian experiences showed that allowances would tend to keep down wages and would be opposed by many unions.[174] The Cabinet's Committee on Reconstruction Priorities did ultimately accept the principle of universal allowances for all children beyond the first, but at the five-shilling rate, a rate three shillings lower than that proposed by Beveridge and declining steadily in value as wages and prices rose.[175] Some members of the Cabinet also continued to prefer social services to allowances, on the grounds that these had less likelihood of depressing wage levels.[176]

The government's affection for the five-shilling rate led to the usual protests and deputations, but these had no effect. When the family allowances bill reached its second reading in March 1945, the rate was still five shillings, now far below subsistence. Indeed, when Mass Observation asked young wives late in the war how much they thought the family allowance should be, their suggested rates averaged be-

[171] PRO, PIN 8/115, Official Committee on the Beveridge Report, 5th Meeting, 29 Dec. 1942, p. 4; Official Committee on the Beveridge Report, "Report," [Jan. 1942], pp. 20–2.

[172] PRO, PIN 8/115, "Appendix C. – Family Allowances: Memorandum by the Treasury" [24 Dec. 1942].

[173] PRO, Cab. 87/13, P.R. (43) 9, "Draft Memo by the Chancellor of the Exchequer" (7 Feb. 1943).

[174] PRO, PIN 8/116, Ministry of Labour, "The Effect of Children's Allowances on Wages" (18 Dec. 1942).

[175] PRO, Cab. 66/34, W.P. (43) 58, "The Beveridge Plan: Interim Report of the Committee on Reconstruction Priorities" (11 Feb. 1943).

[176] PRO, Cab. 65/33, Cabinet 28, 12 Feb. 1943.

tween fourteen and eighteen shillings per child – double the amount suggested by Beveridge and three times that proposed by the government.[177] One Labour member complained in the House that this low rate violated the Beveridge Plan's "cardinal principle" of tying benefits to the cost of living,[178] but the government retorted that the allowance – unlike insurance benefits – was intended to help the parents support children, not to meet entirely these financial responsibilities.[179] In 1945, when French family allowances could almost double the income of a family with four children, the equivalent British family would receive a mere 15 shillings per week – at a time when the average weekly wage for men was 121 shillings. Benefits at this rate identified allowances as a means of combating poverty in large families, not of socializing the cost of children among the population as a whole or of disaggregating the family wage.

Second, ministers and civil servants rejected the claim that allowances should serve another redistributive function, shifting income from men to women in the family itself. Children's allowances had always appealed to feminists partly because they were a means of mitigating the economic dependence of wives, although during the thirties the FES had scarcely mentioned this unpopular point of view. Yet payment to the mother continued to be taken as axiomatic; virtually all resolutions calling for allowances in the early years of the war endorsed this plan. In the summer of 1944, then, family allowance advocates were shocked to learn that the government might well propose payment to the father.[180] When the government's *White Paper on Social Insurance* was published in September 1944, it did in fact designate the allowance as the property of the father, although it stipulated that it would be "natural and appropriate" for him to deputize his wife to draw the money.[181] This would be entirely his choice, however, as its legal owner. With this recommendation, the government finalized the divorce of family policy and women's emancipation, destroying feminists' hopes of using state policy to redistribute income and power within the family itself. How was such a recommendation possible?

---

[177] Mass Observation, *Britain and Her Birth Rate*, pp. 129–30.

[178] 408 *H.C. Deb.* 5th series, 8 Mar. 1945, col. 2340.

[179] The *White Paper on Social Insurance* insisted that the allowance was not intended to provide full maintenance but was "a general contribution to the needs of families with children." *White Paper on Social Insurance*, PP 1943–4, VIII, Cmd. 6550, p. 14.

[180] Fawcett Library, Pamphlet Box 331.226, Family Endowment Society, "A Call to Women's Societies – Children's Allowances: Payment to the Mother" (14 July 1944).

[181] *White Paper on Social Insurance*, p. 15.

It is important to realize that the recommendation was far from unanimous. For the three years that the government considered family allowances, no question was more divisive and controversial than that of who was to receive the allowance. When Edward Hale of the Treasury began studying the issue of allowances in May 1941 in order to draft the *White Paper on Family Allowances*, he was already chafing at the thought of payment to the mother. "To create an impression that the father has no responsibility and that the maintenance of the children is a matter between the mother and the State might have unfortunate consequences, both social and financial," he wrote.[182] When the FES argued forcefully in evidence to the Beveridge committee in favor of payment to the mother, one of the official members accused them of having "a very low opinion of fathers," and Beveridge himself avoided the issue in his report.[183] The responsible officials thought that the government might be forced by political pressure to pay to the mother but recorded that the Ministry of Labour opposed this course, although it is not clear whether Bevin himself was behind this opinion.[184] The Cabinet's Committee on Reconstruction Priorities, when asked by Jowitt in July 1943 to decide the issue, could only record its inability to come to agreement.[185] Jowitt then solicited the opinion of the TUC, which, after reflection, decided that allowances should be paid to the mother, but even this generous decision did not end the controversy.[186] When the government began to prepare its *White Paper on Social Insurance*, the Cabinet subcommittee appointed to resolve issues still outstanding found itself almost evenly divided on the question.[187] Although the white paper finally named the father as the legal recipient, even in the drafting stage some versions of the bill proposed to pay to the father while others provided for payment to the mother.[188]

The fact that civil servants were so divided over payment to the

---

[182] PRO, ACT 1/664, E. Hale, "Family Allowances" (9 May 1941).

[183] PRO, Cab. 87/77, Social Insurance Committee, 12th meeting, 2 June 1942, pp. 19–20; Cab. 87/79, S.I.C. (42) 42, "Evidence by Mrs. Hubback on Behalf of the Family Endowment Society" (Apr. 1942), p. 14.

[184] PRO, PIN 8/2, Central Staff, "Draft" [Children's Allowances], eleven pages, n.d., p. 5.

[185] PRO, Cab. 87/12, Committee on Reconstruction Priorities, 14th meeting, 26 July 1943, p. 3.

[186] PRO, PIN 8/7, TUC, "Deputation to Sir William Jowitt on the Beveridge Report" (12 Aug. 1943).

[187] PRO, Cab. 87/7, R (44) 36, Reconstruction Committee, "Report of the Subcommittee on Social Insurance" (3 Mar. 1944), p. 2.

[188] See the draft bill papers in PRO, PIN 3/65.

Table 6.6. *Payment of family allowances to the mother: public support and opposition by sex and class, 1943*

Persons polled	Percentage preferring payment to		
	The father	The mother	Either
Total	16	59	25
By sex			
Men	24	50	26
Women	8	68	24
By age			
21–29	15	68	17
30–49	15	60	25
50+	17	57	26
By economic group			
Higher	32	44	24
Middle	18	60	22
Lower	15	59	26

Note: Ministry of Information Opinion Survey 104b, 19 Dec. 1943. Question 1: "If the Government agree to pay allowances for children, should the money be paid over to the Father or to the Mother?"
Source: PRO, PIN 17/4, Stephen Taylor, Ministry of Information, to M. A. Hamilton, Reconstruction Secretariat, 28 Dec. 1943.

mother is striking since there was no real public sentiment against it. In fact, when the Ministry of Information polled the public on the question in December 1943, they found a strong preference for payment to the mother among *both* sexes and *all* social classes. Their results, reproduced in Table 6.6, show that only among the highest economic group was there any significant amount of support for payment to the father. Given the overwhelming opposition of women of all classes to payment to the father, this would imply that only among upper-class men – exactly the group represented in the upper reaches of the civil service – was there any significant feeling in favor of payment to the father.[189]

Ministers and civil servants supporting payment to the mother made three now-familiar arguments: that such a policy would help distinguish the allowance from the wage; that it would elevate the status of the housewife; and that it would lessen the chance that the money would be (as it was delicately termed) "misapplied." Those supporting payment to the father on the other hand resorted in the first instance

[189] PRO, PIN 17/4, Stephen Taylor, Ministry of Information, to M. A. Hamilton, Reconstruction Secretariat, 28 Dec. 1943.

to legal arguments, stating firmly (if inaccurately) that the father was the legal as well as economic head and was the person both liable for tax and eligible for relief.[190] William Jowitt, however, grew rather tired of such legalistic hairsplitting and in March 1944 wrote to Lord Woolton, now minister of reconstruction, urging that any decision be based on practical considerations, "and not on subtle legalistic arguments as to the superior right of the father in law." Such arguments were unconvincing, since Parliament had itself overturned the absolute right of the father in order to treat the welfare of the child as paramount in the Equal Guardianship of Infants Act almost twenty years earlier.[191]

Deprived of legal arguments, opponents of payment to the mother fell back on a defense of the character of working men and a rhetoric of the sanctity of family life. Woolton, when confronted with Jowitt's argument that the question should simply be decided on the grounds of child welfare, seemed to feel that to pay to the mother was to imply that most marriages were not "reasonably happy" and that the division of labor by which – as he characterized it – men dealt with the government and women with the shopping was somehow not the "sensible" one.[192] It seemed "natural" to designate the father as head of the family, one civil servant minuted Jowitt, and such a designation was unproblematic, since "happily, most husbands and wives live together in perfect amity, and the White Paper proposal seems to fit this normal position perfectly."[193] R. A. Butler at the Ministry of Health also questioned the assumption that the money would be safer in women's hands. "If fathers like beer, mothers may also like port and lemon or gin," he wrote; "Nor can Government presume to intervene in unhappy family life by suggesting payment should be made to [the] mother."[194] If motherhood should be more highly valued, one civil servant wrote, "it seems curious to rely on the payment of a few shillings a week to achieve this desirable end."[195] Yet these "few shillings" were not so trivial as to prevent some ministers from considering them the thin end of the wedge. "It would be destructive of

---

[190] Edward Hale, who drafted the *White Paper on Family Allowances* for the Treasury, particularly stressed this point of view. See PRO, ACT 1/664, Hale, Draft memo for the chancellor (8 July 1941).
[191] PRO, PIN 17/4, Jowitt to Woolton, 2 Mar. 1944.
[192] PRO, PIN 17/4, Woolton to Jowitt, 7 Mar. 1944.
[193] PRO, PIN 8/68, "Deputation on Family Allowances, 10 Oct. 1944" (note for Jowitt), pp. 1–2.
[194] PRO, PIN 8/78, Butler to Sheepshanks, 20 Oct. 1944, p. 12.
[195] PRO, PIN 8/68, "Deputation on Family Allowances, 10 Oct. 1944," p. 2.

the whole conception of the family to provide a separate income for the wife in this way," one ministerial subcommittee reported, and might give rise to feminist demands for greater state support.[196] Paying the mother was thus interpreted as dangerous to gender norms for both sexes: as an incitement both to paternal irresponsibility and to feminist claims for economic independence for wives.

Only a determined campaign by supporters of allowances in Parliament and the press prevented ministers and civil servants from paying the money to the father. From the summer of 1944 until the passage of the bill almost one year later, prominent women sent the newspapers and the government a barrage of letters endorsing payment to the mother on the grounds of both child welfare and women's rights. The FES also organized a deputation by women's societies on the question to Jowitt in October 1944.[197] When the bill was presented to Parliament, it still provided for payment to the father (who could then "deputize" his wife), but amendments were also proposed – including one backed by the Labour Party – in favor of payment to the mother.

On 6 March 1945, the Cabinet discussed payment to the mother for the last time and decided that since it seemed likely that the proposal to pay to the mother would receive wide support in the Commons, it would leave the question to a free vote.[198] During the second reading on 8 March, Eleanor Rathbone made an impassioned plea for payment to the mother, and stated:

> If the Bill goes through in its present form I cannot vote for the Third Reading, although I have worked for this thing for over 25 years. It would be one of the bitterest disappointments of my political life if the Bill did not go through. But I foresee too well the consequences if it goes through in a form which practically throws an insult in the faces of those to whom the country owes most, the actual or potential mothers.[199]

---

[196] PRO, Cab. 87/7, R (44) 36, Reconstruction Committee, "Report of the Sub-Committee on Social Insurance" (3 Mar. 1944), p. 2.

[197] On this subject, see especially Rathbone's letter to the *Times*, 26 June 1944, and to the *Manchester Guardian*, 21 Feb. 1945; Violet Bonham Carter to the *Times*, 29 June 1944; Megan Lloyd George and Thelma Cazalet Keir to *The Times*, 22 Feb. 1943; and Hubback to the *New Statesman and Nation*, 29: 733 (10 Mar. 1945). Payment to the mother was endorsed by the *Manchester Guardian*, 21 Feb. 1945, and by the *Times*, 8 Mar. 1945. For an account of the women's societies' deputation, and civil servants' hostile response, see PRO, PIN 8/68.

[198] PRO, Cab. 65/49, Cabinet 26, 6 Mar. 1945.

[199] 408 *H.C. Deb.*, 5th ser., 8 Mar. 1945, col. 2283.

Her amendment was accepted, and family allowances, payable to the mother, at last became law.

But was this a decisive victory for women? In retrospect, the size of the achievement seems out of keeping with the magnitude of the struggle, especially if one accepts that payment to the mother was possible in part because discriminatory labor and insurance policies had so restricted women's independent access to work, wages, and benefits as to indelibly identify married women with the home. Five shillings a week can in no way be seen as the "endowment of motherhood," and it was small compensation for the virtual barring of women from adequately waged work and the normal benefits of the insured worker.

In France, those funds that paid to the mother did so for pragmatic reasons; nevertheless, because allowances were large and funded directly through the wage bill, such a practice could redistribute a substantial portion of household income from men to women. In Britain, ironically, where feminists consciously advocated payment to the mother as a means of increasing women's power, benefits were held down to a derisory, anti-poverty level. In the translation from program to policy, family allowances lost their ability either to disaggregate the family wage or to transfer income to a significant degree from men to women. The identification of what was lost leads to our final question: how was such an outcome possible?

In his insightful study of the movement for family allowances, John Macnicol posed a similar question. On what terms, he asked, did family allowances become acceptable to the government? They were acceptable, he concluded, only when they were compatible with conservative economic ends – when they came to be seen as useful ways of meeting dependency needs outside the wage system and thus of avoiding an inflationary wage spiral.[200] This study points to a rather different conclusion. Universal allowances distributing the cost of children among the population as a whole *never* really became acceptable to the government. Their possible usefulness as a means of restraining wages was only one slight sweetener to an otherwise bitter pill. In fact, the response of the government, prominent civil servants, and trade unionists to the idea of family allowances was remarkably similar: all saw them as a policy largely irreconcilable with a welfare system aimed at compensating men *and their families* for loss of wages and with a wage system by agreement left relatively free of state interference.

Thus in April 1941, when R. V. N. Hopkins and Horace Wilson

[200] Macnicol, *The Movement for Family Allowances*, pp. 216–19.

wrote a memorandum on family allowances for the Treasury, these senior civil servants opposed allowances in almost the same terms their trade unionist counterparts Charles Dukes and Rhys Davies had employed ten and fifteen years earlier. The argument made by Eleanor Rathbone in the Commons and Lord Wolmer in the Lords that it was wasteful to pay "family wages" to single men, so Hopkins and Wilson wrote, overlooked the fact that single men got married and used their savings to set up house.

> If *Miss* [*sic*] Rathbone and Lord Wolmer had their way, apparently, wages of single men would be paid at bare subsistence level. I don't believe this would be either popular or sensible, nor would it be socially desirable.
>
> Another point that is ignored is the natural dislike of workpeople to have to parade their domestic circumstances: would Lord Wolmer have liked to go to his employer (or some public authority) on each of the six occasions when he had another child – and again on each occasion when one or other of the children reached the age when a child's allowance was no longer claimable?[201]

Trade unionists and civil servants alike vastly preferred to leave the responsibility of maintaining families to men and their unions. Family allowances were acceptable not as an alternative to wages, but only when they were so whittled down – by the omission of the first child and their reduction to below-subsistence levels – to be assured of having no impact on wage levels at all. In such a form, they would relieve the most extreme manifestations of child poverty without undermining men's claims to the family wage or the paradigm of the male breadwinner and dependent wife.

The development of social policy, I have argued, cannot be studied only as a history of particular ideas and campaigns, not only because the choices of policymakers in one area were often constrained by prior choices made in other areas, but also because such a focus would tend to obscure how powerful economic and institutional forces could influence outcomes less by direct opposition than by protecting such related areas from any interference. On issues of social policy during the Second World War, trade unionists found it easier than employers to catch the ear of the government, and civil servants exhibited some sensitivity toward TUC preferences.[202] The fact that organized labor

---

[201] PRO, T172/1956, R. V. N. Hopkins and H. J. W. [Horace Wilson], "Note" (3 Apr. 1941).

[202] On this point, note, for example, Sir Kingsley Wood's refusal to meet with the British Employers' Confederation on the subject of workmen's compensation, in PRO, T172/1924.

never became enthusiastic about family allowances made it easier to keep allowances at the margins of postwar reconstruction. When the Treasury estimated the total cost of the government's own welfare commitments for 1945, it came up with a total bill of £673 million, within which the family allowances bill of £57 million appears relatively modest.[203]

The elaboration of policy in consultation with interests and through bureaucratic channels not entirely subject to democratic and parliamentary control will always exclude certain groups. Women were never constructed as an "interest group" or incorporated into the policy-making structure. They were, to begin with, deeply divided; thus, some groups were subsumed under other identities as collectivist tendencies increased, while others lost their earlier limited influence in moral or charitable arenas. The Labour Party's Women's Sections, which had always argued that housewives were workers and citizens deserving of political incorporation and social supports – and indeed sometimes called themselves "the Housewife's Trade Union" – were probably best satisfied with the wartime social insurance plans. Labour women welcomed the Beveridge Plan's insistence that the full-time housewife was indeed "occupied" on work of value to both the family "team" and the nation. While they welcomed the introduction of family allowances (if objecting to their "niggardly" size), they were even more insistent on the need for a unification and extension of social services, especially in the areas of maternal and child welfare.[204] The housing and health policies of the postwar Labour government, on which Labour women had some influence, went some distance toward satisfying their demand "for proper conditions in the sphere where the role of men and women is different."[205]

The weakened nonparty successors to the huge Edwardian charitable and suffrage women's organizations fared less well. Even feminists like Rathbone and Hubback, who had subordinated their egalitarian impulses to endorse maternalist and child welfare policies, were barely tolerated by civil servants and were, in any case, derided for their claims to expertise.[206] On the other hand, the equalitarian

[203] Estimates from PRO, Cab. 66/52, W.P. (44) 353, "Post-War Financial Commitments: Memorandum by the Chancellor of the Exchequer" (28 June 1944).
[204] NCLW, *Report*, 23 (1945), pp. 42–3.
[205] "The Work of Housewife and Mother," *Labour Woman*, 32: 2 (Feb. 1944), p. 17.
[206] Civil servants felt it impossible to refuse when Rathbone and Hubback asked to meet with officials concerned with the family allowances legislation, but Sir Thomas Sheepshanks of the "central staff" concluded after the meeting that the two "had not really

feminists who had broken with Rathbone over family allowances and fought the discriminatory insurance and labor legislation of the thirties scarcely received a hearing at all. There is no better evidence of the entire irrelevance of equalitarian claims by 1944 than the response to the National Council of Women's request to meet with the minister of reconstruction on the Beveridge Report. The National Council of Women was the heir to the Edwardian National Union of Women Workers, a moderate, scarcely feminist umbrella organization for a wide range of women's philanthropic and professional associations. The council's request to have its point of view heard was met with extreme irritation by the civil servants coordinating work on the Beveridge Report.[207] "If these bodies were reasonable people," one responded, "the sensible course would be to suggest that they should defer their deputation until after the Government White Paper has been published, because in that event there could obviously be a freer, more profitable and more informed discussion.... Unfortunately, however, they are not reasonable." They may as well come now, he concluded; perhaps they would think some of the changes already agreed to but not yet made public had been due to their intervention.[208] At no time did he or any other political figure – including Beveridge – think that their opinions should be taken into account.

Yet these women were deeply concerned about the direction of social policy in the postwar period, and since their views were so resolutely disregarded by ministers and civil servants alike, perhaps it is appropriate to let them have the last word here. In 1942, the National Council of Women had urged William Beveridge to adopt equal contribution and benefit rates for men and women and to treat married and unmarried women equally. "It is in our opinion wrong and wholly irrelevant to use marriage or non-marriage as a factor governing insurance rights," they wrote.[209] When the Beveridge Report created a distinct class of housewives, insured these women not against loss of earnings but against loss of their men, and collapsed most of their benefits into those of their husbands, the council was understandably upset. Their deputation protested to Sir William Jowitt that "although the Report acknowledged the married couple as a

applied their minds to all the difficulties and had only the most nebulous ideas." PRO, PIN 8/16, Rathbone to Jowitt, 4 June 1943; Sheepshanks to Daish, 5 and 8 June 1943.
[207] PRO, PIN 8/48, Tate to Woolton, 7 Feb. 1944.
[208] PRO, PIN 8/48, Sheepshanks to Daish, 19 Feb. 1944.
[209] PRO, Cab. 87/79, S.I.C. (43) 46, E. Wilhelmina Ness, National Council of Women, to Beveridge, circulated 9 May 1942.

'team,' the woman was in fact treated as a dependant."[210] They felt, by contrast, that married women, whether waged or unwaged, should be independently insured against sickness or incapacity and that the appropriate benefits should be paid directly to them. Widows should receive not a permanent pension but a grant to cover job training or, if raising children single-handedly, a guardianship benefit.

Their strongest criticism, however, was reserved for Beveridge's decision to exempt married women from compulsory insurance. Elizabeth Abbott of the Open Door International objected that such a policy would tempt precisely those most in need of insurance to do without it and would create "a new pool of intermittent cheap labour."[211] The National Council of Women wanted welfare provisions organized around the assumption of women's economic equality and independence. By 1944, however, with such egalitarianism diluted by the campaigns of the separate-spheres feminists, with the male-breadwinner norm well established in the insurance system, and with the Beveridge Plan moving into place, this had become an "unreasonable" demand.

Conclusion

The postwar implementation of a modified Beveridge Plan was the culmination of a process – which we have traced from the separation allowances of the Great War through the discriminatory insurance of the thirties – of the construction of a male-breadwinner welfare state. In this model, full employment and social insurance programs enabled married men to maintain themselves and their families both in work and out of it. Single women were treated as single men, but married women were insured not primarily against loss of wages but rather against loss of men.

Family allowances fit uncomfortably within this system. The state redistribution of income from the childless to those with children would challenge the assumption that male wages should be adequate to family needs, just as payment to the mother would threaten the unspoken rule against state benefits for women whenever a man was

---

[210] PRO, PIN 8/48, "National Council of Women and Other Women's Societies: Deputation to Sir William Jowitt on the Beveridge Report, 25 Feb. 1944" (transcript), p. 1. The point of view articulated by the deputation was laid out in an expanded form in Elizabeth Abbott and Katherine Bompas, *The Woman Citizen and Social Security* (London: Women's Freedom League, 1943); see also PRO, PIN 8/48, "Points Agreed by the NCW Executive, Dec., 1943."

[211] PRO, PIN 8/48, "National Council of Women . . . Deputation" (transcript), p. 2.

present. Allowances were made palatable in the thirties only because advocates stressed that they could mitigate child poverty and not that they could potentially disaggregate the male family wage or increase the independence of wives. In 1942, unenthusiastic civil servants and a reluctant TUC agreed to the introduction of allowances on the condition that they would have little effect on wages. Had they been substantial in size, family allowances could have undermined the wage-centered character of the British welfare state, but they were small on introduction and deteriorated further in value over the next twenty years. Only the rediscovery of child poverty in the sixties and the rising unemployment of the seventies revived interest in benefits for children as an integral part of the welfare state.

The success of this male-breadwinner model of welfare policy raises an implicit question about the possible alternatives forsworn. Certainly the scope of policy-making during the depression was restricted. The political constraints faced by minority and coalition governments, their limited imagination, and economic problems beyond their understanding made comprehensive state-funded policies such as the child allowances advocated by the ILP unlikely, if not unthinkable. Even more unthinkable in the early thirties were programs like the endowment of motherhood, which would have uncoupled family maintenance from the male wage. Insofar as the state would maintain family income, it was clear it would do so only by providing benefits to the deserving unemployed. By 1931, the choice faced by the beset Labour Cabinet was not which alternative program to implement, but which program would be cut first, and how severely.

Yet even within such a restricted sphere, the decisions of governments were crucial and were by no means dictated simply by financial considerations or difficult economic conditions. The coherent pattern of preferences revealed by politicians, administrators, and economic organizations when confronted by a series of unappealing choices strengthened a particular "logic" of welfare, even when this "logic" dictated costlier programs than alternative visions. Thus, when the second Labour government was forced to consider cuts in the unemployment insurance system, it turned to anomalies regulations targeting married women in particular rather than the universal reductions in rates and duration of benefit also advocated by the May Committee on National Expenditure, even though the former would have saved a mere £3 million while the latter was projected to save almost £29 million.[212] They did so because they wished to preserve

[212] Gilbert, *British Social Policy*, p. 166.

what they viewed as the heart of the unemployment insurance system, but it was precisely in distinguishing the "anomalous" from the "normal" that their deeply held preferences were revealed. Their decisions were predictable and rational only if one recognizes the extent to which a model of appropriate family structure, and not of individual entitlement, underlay social policy formation.

Nor can one claim that the governments of the thirties were simply hostage to financial and economic constraints, for such constraints made only some options impossible. The counterexample of France, to which we shall now turn, demonstrates how policymakers equally concerned to avoid costly public expenditures were nevertheless able to extend the system of family allowances during the thirties. They were able to do so, certainly, because the business experiments of the twenties had provided them with a means of financing allowances at no direct cost to the taxpayer or the state. Such options were unavailable to the British not because they were costly, but because most advocates of allowances accepted a priori that, unlike social insurance, they could not be funded in part out of a redistribution of the wage bill. British policy-making was hostage not only to financial considerations but to the illogical insistence that allowances could not affect precisely what they were intended to break down: the male family wage.

7

DISTRIBUTIVE JUSTICE AND THE FAMILY
Toward a parental welfare state

French family policy in the twenties was largely the creature of organized business. Simply by following economic interest, the French *grand patronat* created the particular logic of welfare, which I have termed "parental," by which income was redistributed not between the waged and unwaged, employed and unemployed, or men and women, but simply between wage earners with children and those without. French businessmen did not assume male wages were adequate to support families or that all men had dependents; they simply paid for children when and where they found them. In targeting children rather than (presumably male) workers or (presumably female) homemakers, French family policy also made no consistent attempt to transform family structures and gender relations. Allowances partially disaggregated wages by providing for children directly but were not made conditional on particular family roles for women and men.

This industrial system of family allowances did have its limits. As Chapter 5 demonstrated, family allowances were overwhelmingly a strategy of advanced or, in the case of textiles, highly organized industrial sectors. By the late twenties, some 4 million workers were covered for family allowances: over 1.5 million were covered through the *caisses*, another 1.3 million through the railroad and mining funds, and a further million civil servants directly by the state. But the system, while huge, was lopsided. While virtually all large-scale employers, public or private, had enrolled in this system, allowances were unknown outside this sphere. Even by 1928, only 20,000 of France's 1.5 million employers were affiliated to a *caisse*.[1] Left in private hands, the family allowance system would have remained a wage-restraint

---

[1] Figures in this paragraph are taken from two legislative proposals on family allowances: *Journal Officiel* [*JO*] *Documents (Chambre)*, 1929, ann. 1135, p. 98; ann. 1159, p. 120.

357

strategy used by organized business and could not become a universal *welfare* measure covering small employers, the self-employed, and the still-enormous peasant class.

Yet allowances did become a universal benefit. Between 1929 and 1939, politicians and civil servants gradually extended public control, transforming the *caisse* system into a national family policy. In 1932, after several years of study and planning, the Chamber of Deputies passed a law requiring that all employers in business and commerce affiliate to a *caisse*. This law was applied to various industries throughout the early thirties, and by 1935 plans were underway to bring in the self-employed. In 1938 and 1939, with a comprehensive system in place, the government raised rates substantially. By the time the war broke out in 1939, France had established the outlines of a family policy that remained in place during Vichy and after the war.

What was the impetus behind this extension of state control? The logic of business interests alone cannot explain this outcome. During the twenties, businessmen had forced the pace of policy-making, but their enthusiasm for family policy was strictly dependent on their ability to subordinate it to their own economic ends. The benefits of a national system were less clear, and we do not find businessmen leading the movement for state control. Nor were ministers and civil servants primarily concerned to restrain wages during the depression or to extend industrial stability to other sectors. We must look beyond economic interests to explain why politicians – even those doctrinally opposed to "statist" controls – agreed that a comprehensive and state-supervised family policy was in the national interest.

We must return, then, to the realm of political debate and ask which groups and agendas were able to move family policy forward. During the thirties in France, a wide variety of social groups – pronatalists, social Catholics, civil servants, feminists, and businessmen – all sought to harness the family allowance system to their particular social and political agendas. Of this group, only pronatalists were particularly successful, dominating public discussion and convincing a majority of legislators of the need for some reform. The emerging consensus over pronatalism pushed the logic of family-based redistribution far past the level supported by businessmen: a system redistributing income in particular industries between childless wage earners and those with children grew into one at least partly equalizing the burden of children among the entire population. Yet not all pronatalist interventions were so successful. Pronatalists hoped to do two things: to share the economic burden of childbearing among the entire population and to limit married women's participation in the labor force.

Only the first campaign was unambiguously successful. This chapter will examine the two campaigns and explore the reasons for their different outcomes after first surveying the ideology and institutional supports of pronatalists in the interwar years.

"Il faut faire naître": The creation of a pronatalist consensus

French pronatalists hold a special place in this study, for they were the only group of political actors in either France or Britain united primarily by conviction rather than by economic interest to have a significant influence on family policy. True, after the failure of feminist and socialist campaigns in Britain, social reformers were able to construct a new, more moderate coalition concerned to safeguard child health. The demands of this coalition were limited in the thirties, however, and even its later achievements were due in part to the larger consensus that formed around the Beveridge Report. Only pronatalists in France were able significantly to influence policy in the thirties.

What did pronatalists believe? Interwar pronatalists, like their predecessors, started from a position of staunch nationalism. They were concerned about the birthrate largely because they feared it would lead to the military and national decline of France. The Alliance Nationale pour l'Accroissement de la Population Française, which grew in strength and power in the interwar years, made constant reference to the dangers of the discrepancy in population between France and other countries, especially Germany, whose population passed 65 million in the midthirties, while France's stagnated at around 41 million.[2] The Alliance Nationale worried incessantly about the belligerent intentions of France's more populous neighbor, especially after the Nazis inaugurated comprehensive pronatalist policies of their own. To critics who charged them with a desire for more cannon fodder, pronatalists retorted that a strong population was the best guarantee of peace: the First World War would not have happened (they claimed) if France had dominated Europe as it had in the eighteenth century. An increased population was the first con-

---

[2] On interwar pronatalism, see especially Françoise Thébaud, "Le mouvement nataliste dans la France de l'entre-deux-guerres," *Revue d'Histoire Moderne et Contemporaine*, 32 (April–June 1985), pp. 276–301. Alliance Nationale membership grew from 4,000 before the First World War to 12,000 in 1922, 25,000 in 1924, and 35,000 on the eve of the March 1928 elections. Figures on the size of the Alliance Nationale are taken from *Revue de l'Alliance Nationale* (hereafter *Revue*), no. 126 (Jan. 1923); no. 145 (Aug. 1924), p. 246; no. 188 (Mar. 1928), pp. 66–7.

dition of French revival. Reproduction, far from being a private concern, became a foreign policy consideration, an element of high politics.[3]

The identification of population increase with the national interest was the doctrinal foundation of the pronatalist faith. Sheer numbers were their only concern, and pronatalists distanced themselves from both the eugenic concerns of birth-controllers and racists and the public health concerns of doctors and social workers. Quality would not replace quantity, pronatalists insisted, and they were hostile to public health advocates, leftist politicians, and feminists who all tended to see caring for existing children as more important than encouraging new ones. On the contrary, births must be increased at all costs. But how, exactly, was this to be done? During the interwar period, pronatalists developed a comprehensive policy platform based on a unique theory of citizenship and social organization. The main architect of this doctrine was Fernand Boverat, veteran, father of four, and the dominant influence in both the Alliance Nationale and the Conseil Supérieur de la Natalité (CSN), established in 1920 by the Bloc National government.[4]

Pronatalists – unlike social Catholics – frankly accepted the fact that it was impossible to return to the days of unplanned parenthood, and that even religious revival would not induce people to accept unlimited childbirth. The Alliance Nationale, by studying the statistics, had come to the correct conclusion that voluntary restriction of births had become the norm, although it incorrectly believed that "Malthusian" devices – condoms, sponges, and so on – were almost universally in use. "I am convinced," wrote Boverat,

> that the spread, in all social classes, of knowledge of ways to control women's fertility has played a much larger role in the decline of the birthrate than the diminution of religious belief. . . . The couple that wants to control its fertility is now practically able to do so, and this

---

[3] The account of pronatalist beliefs given in this section is based largely on articles in the Alliance Nationale's *Revue*, on their propaganda leaflets put out in the late thirties under the title of "Natalité," and on the reports and minutes of the Conseil Supérieur de la Natalité, copies of which can be found at the Institut National des Etudes Démographiques, Paris. The Archives of the Ministry of Labor, SAN series, contain many specimens of Alliance Nationale propaganda from the interwar and Vichy periods. This material is repetitive, and individual citations will only be provided for direct quotations.

[4] On Boverat, see "Fernand Boverat, président de l'Alliance Nationale," *Revue*, no. 304 (Dec. 1937), pp. 359–60; Robert Talmy, *Histoire du mouvement familiale en France, 1896–1939*, 2 (Paris: UNCAF, 1962), pp. 222–3.

is almost as true for the poor and ignorant classes as it is for the better-off.[5]

With procreation a voluntary act, the production of children could no longer be left to chance. Rather, one must make people have babies: "Il faut faire naître."

Pronatalist theory of how this could be done turned on two major tenets. First, the nation must generate a new definition of citizenship, one in which procreation, rather than laboring or fighting, was seen as the task of each healthy (male) citizen. Second, however, the rights and privileges of the family, not the *individual* citizen, must be extended and protected. If pronatalists thought it impossible to turn back the clock to more traditional reproductive behavior, they were also unwilling to endorse a futurist vision of babies bought and raised by the state, along the lines of that imagined by H. G. Wells in England. Both the Alliance Nationale and the CSN agreed that the birthrate could only be decisively increased by stabilizing and privileging the legitimate family, and whatever their desire for increased births, they were unsympathetic to any attempt to give equal aid to unmarried mothers.

All of the pressure groups discussed hitherto based their claim for increased rights and privileges less on abstract theories of individual entitlement than on the belief that the performance of a particular functional role – working, soldiering, or mothering – entitled the performer to the recognition and recompense of the state. Pronatalists also had a doctrine of citizenship, on which they based their claim to family-based rights and benefits. "What are the duties of the citizen?" Paul Haury, editor of the Alliance Nationale's *Revue*, asked in the early thirties.

> One commonly includes among these duties that of ensuring the proper functioning of government through taxes, and its defense against aggression through military service. To these we must today add – since what used to seem natural has ceased to be so – the duty of ensuring the life and future of the national community by a sufficient number of children.[6]

If procreation was a form of national service, the refusal to marry was, for the Alliance Nationale, the equivalent of treason, and throughout the interwar period the group called for a campaign of public censure against childless men. In 1923, Boverat wrote:

[5] Fernand Boverat, "Il faut faire naître," *Revue*, no. 143 (June 1924), p. 165.
[6] Paul Haury, "Votre bonheur, jeunes filles," *Revue*, no. 266 (Sept. 1934), pp. 270–1.

The voluntarily childless [man] ought not to be able to pass before the tomb of a soldier without blushing, or see without blushing a mother surrounded by her children. His throat should constrict with shame when he wants to cry "Vive la France," this France he is letting die. He must know that all the accomplishments of his work, courage and genius will be inadequate to honor his name if, at the time when the fate of the land is tied to a recovery of the birthrate, he fails in the duty of transmitting life.[7]

If citizenship was consonant with procreation, small wonder the pronatalists were eager to paint a picture of the especially prolific as civic-minded, self-sacrificing, and patriotic. In doing so, however, they confronted a particular problem. The pronatalists condemned single men as egoistic, pleasure-seeking sensualists, but evidence – at least the production of children – seemed to indicate that it was the self-sacrificing *père de famille* who was engaging in unrestrained sexual activity, not the childless *célibataire*. Pronatalists extracted themselves from this dilemma not by expounding the virtues of sexual activity itself, but by asserting that while the childless were preventing conception through birth control, fathers of families were having children as an act of deliberate choice.[8] The claim that fathers of large families were refraining from (rather than ignorant of) birth control allowed pronatalists to argue that they were neither sexual libertines nor improvident, but, rather, were abstaining from the immoral practices by which others were able to avoid the consequences of their appetites.

It is interesting to note that British and French population experts, largely because of the difference between eugenic and pronatalist concerns, thus operated on precisely opposite moral assumptions. The British tended to see restriction of births as a sign of education, planning, even ability; the French, by contrast, saw the conception of children as an act of deliberate choice and hence as a decision undertaken out of patriotism, duty, and a sense of responsibility. Fathers of large families, precisely the group identified in England as improvident and abusive, were thus described in France as model citizens, "men attached to the uplift of public morality."[9]

If the remorseless and repeated impregnation of one's wife without

---

[7] Fernard Boverat, "Femmes de France, secondez-nous," *Revue*, no. 134 (Sept. 1923), p. 284.

[8] See, e.g., "Résumé du rapport de M. Paul Haury sur l'adaption des salaires à la révolution démographique," Congrès National de la Natalité, *Compte rendu*, 18 (1936), p. 68, in which Haury claimed that large families resulted from parents' deliberate choice.

[9] The words are those of Georges Risler at the Congrès National de la Natalité, *Compte rendu*, 9 (1927), p. 216.

consideration for her wishes or for the future support of these off-spring seems a bizarre definition of civic morality, it was one that proved remarkably resilient, even in the face of contradictory evidence from social investigations. In 1929, the noted social worker Céline Lhotte published a study of working-class life based on four years of daily contact with some five hundred poor families in Le Havre. In direct contrast to pronatalist assumptions, she found that all families had their children utterly by accident, and that birth control was unheard of except among communists. Fathers of large families, far from being a working-class elite, formed a disproportionate percentage of the unskilled class, and their children were more likely to be illiterate.[10] "Honors" accorded to fathers of large families – like the infamous Cognacq-Jay prizes, which each year showered Fr 25,000 on 90 fathers of ten living children and Fr 10,000 on 203 fathers of five – could backfire: one miner with fourteen children happily pocketed the cash and ran off with a 16-year-old girl.[11] Revelations like this had no effect, however, on pronatalist propaganda, which continued to assert that these men were a moral and social elite, voluntarily accepting family burdens in the interest of public morality.

How did women fit into this rather astonishing social vision? Pronatalist attitudes to women appear rather schizophrenic, since they were torn between their wish to rain blessings on the deserving *mère de famille* and the hope of preventing women from having any real alternatives to childbearing. Women, denied the right to vote by the Third Republic, could scarcely be considered citizens, but still less could the production of future citizens be carried on without them. Pronatalists had essentially two choices of how to address women directly. They could adopt a positive policy of increasing women's direct claim on the state as mothers (the endowment of motherhood option) or a negative one of so restricting their personal and economic freedoms that they had no alternatives but marriage and no way of preventing repeated childbirth once married (essentially, the Vichy ideal).

Although pronatalists at times supported both of these options, they in fact tried to avoid this choice. Pronatalist propaganda seems to have been overwhelmingly addressed to either "the family," "la France," or a citizenry conceived of as male. Insofar as pronatalists addressed

---

[10] Discussed in Paul Haury, "Pour les heureux du monde," *Revue*, no. 205 (Aug. 1929), pp. 249–56.
[11] Dr. L. Bouchacourt, "La lutte pour l'augmentation de la natalité française," *Le Problème Sexuel*, 6 (June 1935), pp. 16–18.

women directly, they contented themselves with ringing endorsements of the joys of motherhood, relying on dubious medical evidence to argue that repeated childbearing improved women's health.[12] Only children, furthermore, could develop women's unique moral and social gifts. The single woman, Boverat claimed, was without moral value and the childless spouse a virtual danger:

> The wife who hopes to benefit from the respectability and freedom which marriage brings, but who refuses to have children, is in no way worthy; she lives parasitically off society, since she wants to have only the pleasures of conjugal life without taking on its normal burdens: what does she have in common with the mother who raises her children? What influence can she exercise on those around her if not a pernicious one, by her laziness, her idleness and her frivolity?[13]

Pronatalists were eager to grant moral recognition to mothers through medals and prizes, but they were ambivalent about backing these honors with any rights that could be construed as an attack on the authority of the *père de famille*. Although pronatalists sometimes verged on a definition of women's citizenship as reproducers similar to that put forward by some British feminists, their interest in women's rights was at all times subordinate to their concern for military needs.

The attempt to cull a consistent attitude toward either men or women out of pronatalist propaganda may, however, be a misguided task, since unlike social Catholics or feminists, they were interested in neither men nor women per se, but rather in couples and families. Having decided that the systematic production of children could not take place except within stable marriages, their first concern was to limit the liberties of women or men as individuals and to strengthen their claims as family members both on other family members and on the state. Whereas in Britain family policy advocates based welfare claims on the citizenship functions of particular individuals – so that trade unionists claimed rights in recognition of their role as breadwinners, and feminists called for endowment of motherhood in recognition of the work of child rearing – French pronatalists rejected

---

[12] See, e.g., Dr. O. Pasteau, "Ce que la famille peut attendre du médecin," *Congrès National de la Natalité, Compte rendu*, 6 (1924), pp. 231–9.

[13] Fernand Boverat, "Un peu de mépris, s'il vous plaît," *Revue*, no. 246 (Jan. 1933), p. 9. Interwar pronatalism in relation to women is discussed in Françoise Thébaud, "Maternité et famille entre les deux guerres: Idéologies et politique familiale," in Rita Thalmann, ed., *Femmes et fascismes* (France: Editions Tierce, 1986), pp. 85–97.

these formulas as far too individualistic. Paul Haury, editor of the Alliance Nationale's paper, when looking back to the war, thought that it was "clear that *each nation was saved*, not by its men nor by its women taken individually, but by its families."[14] "The citizen," for the pronatalists, was less either the man or the woman – or even the father or the mother – than the family itself.

"Famille d'abord," in politics and economics, was, then, the second and most crucial tenet of French pronatalism. Having first defined the legitimate and fruitful family as the archetype of the virtuous citizen, pronatalist campaigns concentrated on the one hand on encouraging the constitution of such families and discouraging their dissolution and on the other on reworking the political and economic order to discriminate between such virtuous families and the immoral, selfish, parasitic *célibataire*. The pronatalist campaigns of the twenties and thirties, which taken individually can appear as a hodgepodge of right-wing fanaticism and crank antimodernism, gain coherence when viewed in the light of the mind set just discussed.

First, then, pronatalists hoped to reconstruct the family as an indisseverable social unit through cultural and legal means and to "protect" it from immorality and counterexample. They therefore supported state-financed marriage loans to encourage young people to marry, with a portion of the loans written off at the birth of each child. Once the family was constituted, however, they opposed any increase in the liberties of individual members. They opposed any liberalization of divorce laws, supported the continued and vigorous repression of birth control and abortion, and opposed ending married women's civil incapacity, although the latter reform was finally achieved in 1938.[15]

Believing that immodesty led to birth control and birth control to *dénatalité*, the Alliance Nationale and the CSN also lent their support to a number of traditionalist points of view, combating everything from sex education to prostitution. Occasionally the concern of the pronatalists to protect the modesty of the French family bordered on

---

[14] Haury, "Votre bonheur, jeunes filles," p. 273, emphasis in the original.
[15] The CSN's position on divorce was based on their concern for family stability rather than for men's rights. Rather than increasing married women's individual freedoms, the CSN argued that wives should be given the same veto power over their husbands' decisions that men had over their wives'. For the CSN's position on divorce, see Boverat's report in Conseil Supérieur de la Natalité [CSN], *Rapports*, 1924: no. 1, 4ᵉ sess. (29 Jan. 1924), pp. 12–22. For CSN opposition to liberalization of the civil code, see CSN, *Rapports*, 1933: no. 1, 22ᵉ sess. (Jan. 1933), pp. 25–33; CSN, *Rapports*, 1937: no. 4, 31ᵉ sess. (28 June 1937), pp. 3–8.

the ridiculous, as when Boverat personally took a court case against a nude dancer or when the CSN, noting sagely that the incidence of fertility decline was greatest in countries where nudism was widespread, earnestly condemned the practice of nudism even within private homes.[16]

Once families were protected through such moral and legal measures, pronatalists argued for a second series of political and economic reforms aimed at actively discriminating between fruitful families and childless individuals. They thus campaigned to reform the franchise to take into account men and women not as individual citizens, but as fathers and mothers. The interwar period saw a variety of proposals by pronatalists and Catholics to grant additional votes to the *chef de famille* – usually the father – for his dependent children. Faced with feminist demands for women's suffrage, some advocates supported compromise proposals dividing these additional votes between mothers and fathers, provided, of course, that fathers were given the first additional vote and male electoral dominance was preserved.[17] Most crucially for our story, pronatalists also called for a wide range of policies aimed at redistributing resources from the childless to those with children. Distribution, like representation, was to take into account the greater needs and moral value of the dependent family.

Pronatalist economics were deceptively simple. They could be summed up in a single phrase. "For equal work (in quantity and quality), an equal standard of living, whether one has children or not."[18] Children, as a national resource, should not make people poorer. The pronatalists' position in some ways resembled that put forward by advocates of children's allowances in England: like Eleanor Rathbone, pronatalists felt that *whatever* the distribution of income between classes, that between the childless and those with children must be equalized. Unlike their British counterparts, however, pronatalists were entirely uninterested in income redistribution across classes or sexes and never identified their goals with other "progressive" causes. As a result, pronatalists espoused the most elementary vision of the parental welfare state that we have encountered thus

---

[16] *Revue*, no. 272 (Mar. 1935); Fernand Boverat, "Rapport sur un nouveau péril social: Le nudisme," CSN, *Rapports*, 1932: no. 1, 20ᵉ sess. (Jan. 1932), pp. 4–7.

[17] On the proposals for family suffrage, see Talmy, *Histoire du mouvement familial*, 2, pp. 99–119, 213–217.

[18] Archives of the Ministry of Labor, SAN 7733, File: "Le danger de la dénatalité," Document: Alliance Nationale, "Aux grands maux, les grands remèdes," *Natalité*, no. 23 (Feb. 1939).

far: an ideal of family-based redistribution relatively unencumbered by other political aims. Pronatalists backed their claim for family-based distributive justice by arguing that the greatest social injustice was not class inequality but rather inequality between families and single people of the same social class.[19] Social reformers, they contended, and particularly those on the left, had hitherto inexplicably ignored this central injustice. Boverat wrote that a single worker

> who finds it scandalous that his boss, the head of his department, or an engineer in his factory earns four times as much as he does, finds it entirely natural that one of his comrades with six children doesn't have a wage greater than his; any proposal to reduce the pay of those who don't have dependent children in order to increase that of fathers of families seems to him reactionary, unjust and dishonest, contrary to a principle of would-be equality that he is quick to cite: "equal pay for equal work."[20]

In fact, claimed the pronatalists, this formula was quite *in*egalitarian, since it condemned large families to live at a level many times below that of single workers. True social justice, they argued, would consist of equalizing living standards regardless of family size. This, they claimed, was the aim of family policy.

A family policy able to spread the entire cost of children among the whole population was an ideal espoused by pronatalists from the twenties. In 1924, in his landmark article, "Il faut faire naître," Boverat argued that the population crisis required the creation of a new social order based on "the equalization of financial burdens . . . among all Frenchmen in proportion to the number of their children."[21] Pronatalists argued that material aid to the family must expand beyond the relatively minute category of large families to embrace all families and must be regular, substantial, and national. The erratic prizes and baby contests sponsored by some enthusiasts did nothing to improve the population, one medical member of the CSN argued, since parents, spurred by the prospect of prize money for the healthiest-looking baby, forcefed their infants like geese, causing intestinal and liver problems.[22] The Alliance Nationale's 1928 electoral program, by con-

---

[19] Fernand Boverat, "Les théoriciens de la justice sociale et le mépris de la famille," *Revue*, no. 270 (Jan. 1935), pp. 9–11; see also, idem, "La grande injustice," *Revue*, no. 275 (June 1935), pp. 161–6.
[20] Boverat, "Les théoriciens," p. 11.
[21] Boverat, "Il faut faire naître," p. 164.
[22] CSN, *Communication*, 1927: no. 2, 10ᵉ sess. (Jan. 1927), p. 5.

trast, called for universal birth bonuses, higher allowances for large families, pensions for widows with dependent children, extensive tax relief for children, and lower inheritance taxes.[23] But where would the money for such allowances and bonuses come from?

Pronatalists looked to the *caisses* to solve this problem. By simply requiring all employers to adhere to a *caisse*, the state could bring about a massive redistribution of the wage bill from childless families to those with children, *at no cost to itself*. This plan was too attractive for pronatalists to pass up, and the Alliance Nationale made it the main plank in its 1928 platform.[24] These efforts helped to transform an industrial wage policy into a national family policy.

Before we turn to their campaign for state extension of allowances, we should briefly assess the sources of pronatalists' power. Pronatalist strength in France was in part rhetorical. Sarcastic critics might laugh at the more fervent "lapiniers," but during the thirties it became virtually impossible for politicians of any stripe – even communists – to contest the new definition of procreation as a public function deserving state support, much less to assert that individuals' rights outweighed the claims of collective entities. Perhaps the best measure of their success in changing the terms of political debate is the fact that even feminists – and, more astonishingly, communists – adopted pronatalist rhetoric, to their cost. French feminists had always claimed that women had no intention of abandoning their familial duties if granted a larger public role, and in 1929 the Etats Généraux du Féminisme endorsed the legal extension of family allowances not only because the measure would protect mothers but also because "it tends to encourage the birthrate, and that's already a reason for us to applaud it."[25] Cécile Brunschvicg, president of the Union Française pour le Suffrage des Femmes, challenged those pronatalists who charged that women's suffrage would further compromise France's demographic security to find any feminists preaching against childbearing; to the contrary, she argued, feminists were everywhere in the forefront of campaigns to combat infant mortality and were well aware of their maternal duties.[26] Even more surprising, left-wing politicians

---

[23] "L'Alliance Nationale et les élections," *Revue*, no. 188 (Mar. 1928), pp. 65–6.

[24] "La généralisation des allocations familiales," *Revue*, no. 187 (Feb. 1928), pp. 38–9.

[25] Etats Généraux du Féminisme, *Compte rendu* (Paris, 1929), p. 124.

[26] C. Brunschvicg, "Féminisme et natalité," *La Française*, 25: 961 (10 Jan. 1931); see also Anne Cova, "Cécile Brunschvicg (1877–1946) et la protection de la maternité," *Actes du 113ᵉ Congrès National des Sociétés Savantes: Colloque sur l'histoire de la sécurité sociale (1988)* (Paris: Association pour l'Etude de l'Histoire de la Sécurité Sociale, 1989), pp. 90–2.

and publicists, who had spent the twenties damning the pronatalists for their macabre lust for more "cannon fodder," made an about-face during the period of the Popular Front. Was it desirable to take power in a country weakened by population decline? asked Doctor Raymond in the *Cahiers du Bolchevisme*.[27] The communists continued to try to distinguish themselves from reactionary repopulators by emphasizing the material rather than moral causes of population decline, but in fact their position was quite close to that of the Alliance Nationale, as Boverat delightedly discovered when he called on Maurice Thorez in 1936.[28] The Communist Party explicitly called for a pronatalist policy at its 1937 congress, and by 1939 articles heavily laced with Alliance Nationale propaganda were appearing in the communist press.[29]

If vulnerable groups like feminists and communists felt obliged to adopt pronatalist rhetoric, within the political center it held unquestioned sway. Pronatalism had always enjoyed a high degree of official patronage. In 1926, the annual conference on the birthrate was presided over by the president of the republic – "very well chosen considering he's a confirmed bachelor," the communist *L'Ouvrière* remarked sourly[30] – and in the thirties the Alliance Nationale's propaganda was subsidized by the Ministry of Public Health.[31] As the depression worsened, the chorus of official endorsement became a deafening roar. In 1934, the Alliance Nationale convinced twenty national leaders – including Millerand, Poincaré, Herriot, industrialists André Michelin and Robert Peugeot, familist leaders Auguste Isaac and Georges Pernot, and Cardinal Verdier of Paris – to sign an

---

[27] Dr. Raymond, "La dépopulation et la misère de l'enfance," *Cahiers du Bolchevisme* 13: 1–2 (15 Jan. 1936), pp. 101–9. Raymond argued that communists should support measures aimed at effectively combating *dénatalité*, regardless of what quarter they came from – a real about-face from earlier rhetoric deploring pronatalism as an effort to reduce working-class living standards. François Delpha traces the gradual adoption of natalist rhetoric by the communist press in "Les communistes français et la sexualité, 1932–1938," *Le Mouvement Social*, 91 (1975), pp. 121–52.

[28] Fernand Boverat, "Une conversation avec Maurice Thorez," *Revue*, no. 287 (June 1936), pp. 173–4.

[29] A resolution at the 1937 Communist Party Congress supported "the adoption of a national policy for the protection of childhood, maternity, and the family, capable of ending – by an endlessly increasing well-being – the scourge of *dénatalité*, and of contributing to realizing the dream of all good Frenchmen, that of making our country FREE, STRONG, and HAPPY." "Sauver la famille!" *Cahiers du Bolchevisme*, 14: 2 (20 Feb. 1937), p. 243; see also G. Lévy, "Pour une politique de protection de la famille et de l'enfance," *Cahiers du Bolchevisme*, 16: 3 (Mar. 1939), pp. 362–73.

[30] "Le Congrès de la Natalité," *L'Ouvrière*, 5: 212 (30 Sept. 1926).

[31] On subsidies, see *Revue*, no. 230 (Sept. 1931), pp. 615–16, and no. 305 (Jan. 1938), pp. 20–1.

"Appeal to the Nation" calling for increased births. "Under pain of death," France must follow the example of Italy and Germany and inaugurate strong pronatalist policies. The appeal endorsed the Alliance's Nationale's definition of reproduction as a duty of citizenship, claiming that "it is now a duty for all Frenchmen to raise at least three children: whoever doesn't want to or can't fulfill this duty should contribute in proportion to his means to raising the children of others."[32] Some six months later the Chambers of Commerce came out in support of family-based suffrage, the restriction of divorce, repression of abortion, and the return of mothers to the home.[33] The social Catholics were natural allies, with the French cardinals issuing an appeal in favor of increased births in 1939.[34]

This chorus turned pronatalism into "common sense." In political debates, pronatalism evoked a degree of allegiance in France similar to that generated in Britain by the male-breadwinner norm. As we have seen in Britain, however, common sense could only become policy when it found an institutional voice. Pronatalist ideology worked its way into policy through the medium of the CSN and with the growth of all-party pronatalist lobbies in the Chamber and Senate. The CSN possessed impeccably pronatalist credentials: virtually all its members were prominent leaders of the Alliance Nationale or other profamily groups; the left was virtually unrepresented; and the group included only one woman. Along with the Alliance Nationale, the CSN was able to arrogate authority as the official voice of "the family." The Chamber's Social Insurance Commission consulted directly with the CSN when drafting social legislation, and the group was given statutory representation on the new Commission Supérieure des Allocations Familiales in 1932. The official authority of pronatalists grew steadily in the thirties, so that by 1939, when the government appointed a committee to draft a unified family code, they simply appointed Boverat and four other pronatalists.

Pronatalists also exercised considerable authority within the legislature. The Alliance Nationale had canvassed all candidates before the 1928 elections: those from the center and right supported strong pronatalist policies, although left-wing candidates continued to stress the importance of the struggle against infant mortality rather than

---

[32] "Appel à la nation," *Revue*, no. 264 (July 1934), pp. 193–5.
[33] "Les chambres de commerce et la dénatalité," *Revue*, no. 269 (Dec. 1934), p. 380.
[34] Archives of the Ministry of Labor, SAN 7545, File: "Lutte contre la dénatalité," Document: Alliance Nationale, "Appel de LL EEm. les cardinaux . . . " (Paris, 1939).

for increased births.[35] The 1928–32 legislature thus took a more explicit pronatalist stance, not only passing the family allowances bill but also calling on prefects and communal assemblies to propagandize forcefully in favor of increased births.[36] Individual deputies found it politic to adhere to the pronatalist group, which grew from 130 members in 1923 to 367 in 1929, or well over half of the 606 deputies then in the Chamber.[37]

What exactly did these politicians agree on? Léon Blum, one of the least likely spokesmen for pronatalism, answered this question in 1936, during his first premiership:

> We all agree that the birth of a child in a family of small or modest means should not be a kind of misfortune that one should have been able to avoid....
>
> We also all agree,... I imagine, that work should be an option but not a necessity for the mother, and that the wage of the head of the household should be adequate to support the needs of the entire family in a comfortable condition.[38]

This statement shows us the lowest common denominator of party-political consensus. Family policy, politicians agreed, should do two things. It should aim at lightening the burden of raising children, whether through increased state aid or through family-based redistribution; and it should work to enable married women to stay home. Politicians, in other words, hoped to extend the redistribution of income from families without children to those with children, begun by businessmen, but they also hoped to rework allowances to favor families with unwaged mothers. If we look at the family policy bills that swamped the Chamber in the thirties, we can see that most did fall within these two aims. Many aimed at extending family allowances to new groups and raising rates, others at granting higher allowances to families with a *mère au foyer*. The first of these aims was consistent with the logic of the parental welfare state, but the second brought a new element, that of gender relations within the family itself, into the

---

[35] "L'Alliance Nationale et les élections," *Revue*, no. 188 (Mar. 1928), pp. 65–6; "Les partis politiques et la natalité," *Revue*, no. 187 (Feb. 1928), pp. 33–4.
[36] "Une circulaire ministérielle...," *Revue*, no. 224 (Mar. 1931), pp. 431–2.
[37] Figures for the size of the Groupe de Défense des Familles Nombreuses, later renamed Groupe de la Famille et de la Natalité, are given in *Revue*, no. 130 (May 1923), pp. 165–6; and no. 199 (Feb. 1929). p. 51. For the influence of pronatalism on politics more widely, see Richard Peter Tomlinson, "The Politics of Dénatalité during the Third French Republic, 1890–1940," Diss., Cambridge University, 1983.
[38] *JO Débats (Chambre)*, 6 Aug. 1936, p. 2481.

equation. The next two sections will explore the success of state initiatives in these two areas and describe the resulting character of family policy on the eve of the Second World War.

The progress of state intervention

In the immediate postwar period, the creators of the caisses seemed to view the possibility of state intervention as an insidious form of communism and had successfully fought off state control. By 1929, however, with pressure to extend allowances coming even from business's usual allies on the right and with an administration increasingly unhappy to leave workers' access to substantial benefits at the mercy of employers' whims, such intervention became inevitable. Between 1929 and 1932 the government piloted legislation through the Chamber and Senate requiring all employers to join a *caisse*. With the possible exception of the social insurance legislation of 1930,[39] the family allowances law of 11 March 1932 was the single most important piece of social legislation passed in interwar France. In comparison with the bitter, ten-year wrangle over social insurance, however, the three-year gestation of the family allowances law seems like record time, and the degree of political consensus almost miraculous. The 1932 law established the basis on which allowances would be extended in the thirties, reconciling business interests with pronatalist demands for a national family policy. Its passage was a triumph of contractual bargaining, but it was a peculiarly French type of contract, with the legislature, the Ministry of Labor, and the employers – the same partners in the wartime economic mobilization – each receiving a significant share of institutional power, to the exclusion of the CGT.

In the making of family policy, the legislature acted almost entirely as the mouthpiece of pronatalist interests. By 1928, not only the Alliance Nationale but also the large family associations and all the political parties had come out in favor of the legal extension of family

---

[39] The insurance scheme introduced in 1928 and passed in 1930 insured all employed persons of either sex below particular wage levels against the risks of sickness, disability, maternity, death, and old age. Significantly, unemployment insurance was not included in the scheme; the unemployed during the depression were – to the disgust of the CGT – supported by relief payments from local unemployment funds, which were in turn subsidized and overseen by central government grants. Wesley Sharp provides a cogent summary of the workings of the social insurance system in the thirties in *The Government of the French Republic* (New York: Van Nostrand, 1938), pp. 267–72.

allowances.[40] As soon as the new legislature was constituted, two private bills on allowances were submitted to the Chamber, one authored by a group of social Catholics led by Jean Lerolle, the other signed by 223 members of the Chamber's pronatalist group led by Adolphe Landry.[41] Although the Lerolle proposition paid special tribute to the Catholic concept of the dignity of labor and the just wage, both gave pride of place to pronatalist interests. Adolphe Landry stated frankly that his bill would tend to increase the birthrate, and "far from wanting to conceal this argument, we want to emphasize it."[42] It was clear to the newly formed government of Raymond Poincaré that Parliament would welcome legislation aimed at extending the allowance system, and Louis Loucheur, the new minister of labor, had in fact already pledged the government to work out an acceptable proposal.[43]

The government was faced, however, with the problem of winning business acceptance. The creators of the *caisses* in the twenties had not disguised their hostility toward what Bonvoisin in 1929 still called "the octopus state" (*la pieuvre étatiste*) – an expanding and enveloping bureaucracy squeezing the life and blood out of private initiatives.[44] Weaned on the antirepublican and organicist thought characteristic of the French right, business leaders feared that the state would seize and denature their carefully wrought system. Their language revealed their fears. At the 1923 congress of the *caisses*, Eugène Mathon, president of the Comité Central des Allocations Familiales, told the minister of health, Paul Strauss, that he had identified a deadly virus that had eluded the government's scientists and laboratories:

> This terrible virus, once it's moved in somewhere, grows with an extraordinary speed, to the detriment of the organism it has invaded. It seizes on its victim with an energy that saps the strongest wills. Chased from one place, it reappears in another. It threatens us within our organizations, although it takes a latent and insidious form, but we have located and diagnosed it: it's the virus of Statism.[45]

---

[40] CSN, *Rapport et voeux*, 1927: no. 1, 10ᵉ sess., (Jan. 1927), pp. 9–13; Etienne Partiot, "Rapport sur un projet de loi tendant à rendre obligatoire . . . " CSN, *Rapports et voeux*, 1930: no. 4, 17ᵉ sess. (June 1930), pp. 7–12.

[41] *JO Documents (Chambre)*, 1929, ann. 1135, p. 97; ann. 1159, p. 119.

[42] Ibid., ann. 1159, p. 120.

[43] *JO Débats (Chambre)*, 22 Jan. 1929, p. 185; see also Loucheur's statement that the government was willing to go "jusqu'au bout" in the matter of family policy, 17 Jan. 1929, p. 131.

[44] Congrès National des Allocations Familiales [CNAF], *Compte rendu*, 9 (1929), p. 129.

[45] Ibid., 3 (1923), p. 67.

Why consider the French as "a castrated people" (*un peuple d'eunuques*), he asked, incapable of acts of will, organization, and self-government outside the bounds of the state?[46]

How implacable was business–state hostility? Business leaders continued to use this type of language in public in the late twenties, but in private they prepared for a greater degree of state intervention. The egregious Eugène Mathon was replaced as president of the Comité Central by the more conciliatory Jacques Lebel, vice-president of the CCRP, and the Comité Central began working with pronatalist and business allies as well as civil servants to prepare for the new state system. The Comité Central became more flexible on the issue of state intervention partly at the urging of Redressement Français, Ernest Mercier's lobby of forward-looking businessmen, administrators and social reformers. Some of the *caisses* had close ties to Redressement Français, whose emphasis on the need for a unified program of economic rationalization and social reform dovetailed nicely with their own work.[47]

The ambitions (and connections) of Redressement Français were displayed at the organization's first national conference, held in April 1927 to formalize its aims and legislative agenda. Pierre Richemond and René Duchemin, those representatives of the *grand patronat* (and of the Paris *caisse*), served along with a constellation of religious and political luminaries on the Comité de Patronage of the conference, as did Eugène Duthoit from the University of Lille (although not, significantly, Eugène Mathon). Many of the individuals we have encountered in the context of the wartime mobilization, the development of the *caisses*, and the articulation of pronatalist concerns were also present. Jacques Lebel, Auguste Detoeuf, and Mlle Hardouin, all important in the Paris *caisse*, were there discussing industrial organization and factory welfare work. William Oualid, the versatile law professor who had helped negotiate some of the wartime wage contracts, presented a report on immigrant workers. The pronatalists were represented, with Boverat himself authoring the reports and resolutions on the birthrate. Even Mme Brunschvicg was there, not in her role as the president of the Union Français pour le Suffrage des Femmes, but rather as one of the founders of a school for factory social workers and an expert on social policies to combat alcoholism.

---

[46] Ibid., p. 70.
[47] On Redressement Français, see, Richard Kuisel, *Capitalism and the State in Modern France* (Cambridge University Press, 1981), pp. 88–90.

Engineers and bureaucrats, the core constituency of the group, were there in force.[48]

It was in this environment that Bonvoisin addressed directly the problem of the legal extension of allowances. Thus far, the industrialists who had led the movement had expressed strong opposition to state interference in a matter touching on their own relations with their work force. Nevertheless, he admitted, many of his colleagues on the committee of Redressement Français charged with studying the question felt equally strongly that only legal obligation could force the system farther, and that such intervention need not threaten employers' control of the funds. Bonvoisin himself thus offered a compromise resolution, which stipulated that legal intervention might indeed be useful provided administration were left in private hands, and urged the Comité Central to collaborate with Redressement Français in drafting such a law.[49]

Bonvoisin's flexible stance within the sympathetic circles of Redressement Français did not prevent him, a year later, from fulminating against "the policeman and his handcuffs, the Administration and its red tape, the State and its inspectors" when addressing the Paris Chamber of Commerce on the subject of social insurance and family allowance legislation.[50] Yet such seemingly extreme language had become part of an elaborate and strategic dance, aimed on the one hand at warning the Ministry of Labor that businessmen would tolerate no interference with the internal administration of the funds and on the other at reassuring employers fearful that the Comité Central might sacrifice business interests in their concern to extend the system of allowances. But if *caisse* administrators proved far more conciliatory than their rhetoric implies, government leaders were also less interested in wresting administration out of their hands. Just as

[48] The proceedings and resolutions of the conference were published as "Le Premier Congrès National de l'Organisation Métropolitaine et Coloniale. I. Compte rendu des séances," *Les Cahiers du Redressement Français*, no. 34 (Paris: Editions de la S.A.P.E., 1927); "II. Voeux et solutions," *Les Cahiers du Redressement Français*, no. 35 (Paris: Editions de la S.A.P.E., 1927).

[49] Bonvoisin's speech to the conference was reprinted as "L'aide matérielle à la famille," in "Pour Restaurer la Famille," *Les Cahier du Redressement Français*, no. 19 (Paris: Editions de la S.A.P.E., 1927), pp. 69–86; a typescript copy dated 15 March 1927 is in Archives of the Ministry of Labor, SAN 7547. The speech was summarized in "Le Premier Congrès National," pp. 104–5, and the resolution is in "Voeux et solutions," pp. 78–9.

[50] G. Bonvoisin, *La loi sur les assurances sociales et les allocations familiales: Conférence faite à la Chambre de Commerce de Paris, 1er mars 1928* (Paris, 1928), p. 11.

Loucheur had been committed to corporatist control of wartime armaments production, so too he promised to bring all interested parties together to work out a government bill on family allowances.[51] "Interested parties" turned out, unsurprisingly, to be representatives of the government, Parliament, and the *caisses*, who were organized into the Commission Supérieure des Allocations Familiales.[52] The *caisses* were thus centrally involved in shaping legislation: it was not forced on them against their will. The only real point of controversy between the Ministry of Labor and the *caisses* in the twenties had been the propensity of some funds to make benefits conditional on uninterrupted presence at work. With Mathon excluded from the new commission, this practice was unanimously condemned, and collaboration between business, the administration, and Parliament proceeded amicably.

The government project was ready for submission to the Chamber by July 1929 and, after only minor amendments by the Chamber's Social Insurance and Labor commissions, was passed unanimously and without discussion in March 1931.[53] It was made clear in the deliberations that the law would be applied gradually and that the complicated case of agriculture would be dealt with separately; in consequence, the law passed through the Senate smoothly, meeting only mild criticism for increasing the financial burdens of employers during a depression.[54] Businessmen could, however, take comfort from the statement of the Senate spokesman on the bill, Charles François-Saint-Maur, that pronatalists had no objections to wage cuts provided allowances were safeguarded. He proclaimed:

> Tomorrow, perhaps, we are going to be obliged, because of the circumstances that prevail upon us, to ask certain sacrifices of the working class. But it is not necessary that these sacrifices apply directly to that which is the very future of the family, that is to say, to

---

[51] *JO Débats (Chambre)*, 22 Jan. 1929, p. 185.

[52] The composition and work of the Commission Supérieure des Allocations Familiales is discussed in *JO Documents (Chambre)*, 1929, ann. 2171, p. 1235, and ann. 4294, p. 339.

[53] The Loucheur *projet* is in *JO Documents (Chambre)*, 1929, p. 1235. The main report by Jean Lerolle for the Social Insurance Commission is in ibid., 1930, ann. 3827, p. 1391; that by Louis Duval-Arnould for the Labor Commission is in ibid., ann. 4294, p. 337. Additional reports are in ibid., 1931, ann. 4682, p. 390, and ann. 4692, p. 395. For the passage of the law, see *JO Débats (Chambre)*, 30 Mar. 1931, pp. 2416–7.

[54] The most important Senate reports on the law were those by François-Saint-Maur for the Health and Social Insurance Commission (*JO Documents [Sénat]*, 1931, ann. 545, p. 1035) and by Darteyre for the Agriculture Commission (ibid., ann. 886, p. 1241). For the debate on the passage, see *JO Débats (Sénat)*, 21 Jan. 1932, pp. 35–43.

the family allowance. Wage cuts: so be it; but at least the allowance should be maintained and the *caisses* able to continue their work.[55]

Nevertheless, in perusing the debates over the passage of the 1932 law, one is left with the strong impression that politicians endorsed the existing form of allowances for quite different reasons from those of the textile or metal employers who had built them up. Like these businessmen, they supported continued control of administration and finance because they were ideologically opposed to the extension of state power; they also felt that it would be impossible to wrest comparable amounts of money from the state. Their main concern remained, however, to equalize standards of living across family lines. Jean Lerolle, who presented the report of the Chamber's Social Insurance Commission, thus dwelt at length on the injustice (and the danger to national strength) of a wage system that turned the most natural of human acts – founding a family – into a hardship. It would be a mistake to address this problem through the social insurance system, however, for the arrival of a child was "a normal event . . . the very purpose of the family," not an "insurable risk."

> It is by his labor that the worker ought to be able to support his family; the question is not one of social insurance but a question of remuneration, of the wage. The *caisses de compensation* have resolved this question. They've proven themselves: today, it's only a question of making them compulsory.[56]

Allowances, by attenuating the hardship borne by families with dependent children, were both prudent and just.

The depth of pronatalist sentiment was crucial to the passage of the 1932 law, but the government did not overlook business interests or decisively alter the character of family policy. Rejecting the urging of communists and socialists to finance and control the *caisses* directly, the government proved very sensitive to businessmen's desire to retain administrative control. The law merely required that every employer affiliate with a fund approved by the Ministry of Labor, and that the funds pay allowances at least at minimum rates for every legitimate, adopted, or recognized child of an affiliated worker. Large concerns that had paid allowances for years – especially railroads and mines – could ask to be exempted from the obligation to affiliate and continue to pay allowances on their own as a *service particulier*. The job of granting approvals or exemptions rested with the ministry, but rec-

[55] *JO Débats (Sénat)*, 21 Jan. 1932, p. 38.
[56] *JO Documents (Chambre)*, 1930, ann. 3827, p. 1394.

ommendations were given by the reorganized Commission Supérieure des Allocations familiales, which again largely grouped representatives of industry, state administration, the legislative bodies, and the *caisses* themselves.[57]

In further deference to economic interests, the government planned to apply the law gradually and after consultation with the industrial chambers. Administrative regulations laying out the conditions of application for industry and commerce only appeared in March 1933, and whereas the mining, chemical, metals, and textile industries were required to comply by October 1933, commerce and agriculture were brought in much more slowly.[58] By 1 June 1934, the law had been applied to some 596,572 firms employing 5.9 million workers, including 97% of those in industry and transport, 37% of those in commerce, and 12% of those in the liberal professions. Two years later, 7.4 million workers were covered, including 75% of those in commerce and banking. The gradual extension of the law did not, however, mean all workers entitled to allowances received them. Of the 5.9 million workers subject to the law in 1934, only 4.2 million, or 71%, were working for firms in compliance. Even more startling, by 1936 more than 50% of employers required to affiliate to a *caisse* had still failed to do so.[59] Put differently, in 1936 there were just over 10 million French children under age 14, but only 3.5 million of these (excluding children of civil servants) were benefiting from family allowances. Table 7.1 gives figures for the expansion of the *caisse* system.

The government's problems with compliance were only one aspect of a broader difficulty in giving a largely industrial policy national scope. Family allowances had always been a strategy of big business: they allowed large, corporate organizations to equalize and restrain their wage costs and to bind workers to the firm. They made little sense, however, in small business, where management was still per-

---

[57] Laws and decrees concerning family allowances were published in the *Bulletin de l'Inspection du Travail*, 40 (1932). For the 1932 law, see pp. 3–7; for the decrees reestablishing the Commission Supérieure des Allocations Familiales, see pp. 76–7 and 97–9. The circular of 25 June 1932 urging prefects to encourage affiliation to the *caisses* is in ibid., pp. 107–117.

[58] All laws in France must be followed by a *règlement d'administration publique* (RAP) outlining the conditions of their application. The RAP for the 1932 law was issued on 14 Mar. 1933; see *Bulletin de l'Inspection du Travail*, 41 (1933), pp. 30–8.

[59] Comprehensive statistics on the application of the 1932 law were published in the *Bulletin du Ministère du Travail* see especially 41: 4–6 (Apr.–June 1934), pp. 121–7; 43: 4–6 (Apr.–June 1936), pp. 196–8. Charles Picquenard reported on the progress of state control in CNAF, *Compte Rendu*, 14 (1934), pp. 107–10.

Table 7.1. *Expansion of the caisses, 1934–9*

Year	Companies enrolled	Workers covered (thousands)	Children benefiting (thousands)	Allowances paid (million francs)
1934	152,269	4,081	2,437	808
1935	210,968	4,857	3,163	1,470
1936	275,322	5,519	3,501	1,613
1937	409,486	6,227	3,814	2,340
1938	454,632	6,508	3,904	3,077
1939	416,234	5,618	3,434	3,939

Note: Figures include *caisses* organized on industrial and regional lines, as well as the independent funds run by the railroads, mines, and a few large firms.
Source: Compiled from the statistics kept by the Ministry of Labor, AN F22 1513.

sonal, wages individually set, and the distinction between "employer" and "worker" ambiguous. A greengrocer with four children, for example, would see little reason to pay into a *caisse* in order to provide theoretical coverage for one or two probably childless workers while receiving no benefits himself. The family allowance law extended the system as it was developed by big business, with little consideration for the problems of small businessmen, who often reacted by ignoring the law. The *caisses* themselves grew increasingly critical of the government in the late thirties for its lethargic enforcement of the family allowances law, but the Ministry of Labor was equally reluctant to force small employers to pay during the depression.[60] Only continued pressure from pronatalists would push the government to extend allowances beyond industry and commerce, and transform them into a truly national program. The detailed plan for family allowances developed by pronatalists in the midthirties became the blueprint for the nationwide family legislation of the late thirties.

The key figure in developing this plan was, once again, Boverat. In 1934, he presented the CSN with the first of several key reports on economic aid to the family. He began by drawing up a hypothetical table of family needs: if a single man's needs could be taken to equal 100, a couple's should be about 150, and each additional child would increase needs by another 50. The needs of a family with three children would thus be three times that of a single man, but even the

[60] Complaints and resolutions about reluctant enforcement can be found in CNAF, *Compte rendu*, 13 (1933), pp. 53–64; and 16 (1936), pp. 34–7, 117–18. See also Alfred Sauvy, *Histoire économique de la France entre les deux guerres* (Paris: Economica, 1984), 1, p. 254.

best system of allowances – that paid by the state to civil servants – would raise this father's income by only 35%. Obviously, Boverat argued, such aid was entirely insufficient, but by a reworking of allowances, housing subsidies, and other aid, a real redistribution was possible.[61] The CSN, impressed with Boverat's report, passed a resolution denouncing the privileged position of the *célibataire* and calling for the systematic study of a means of equalizing resources between the childless and heads of households.[62]

Boverat continued to study the problem and by early 1936 was ready with a plan for the partial redistribution of resources on the basis of family needs. A complete equalization of costs was, he decided, impossible, but the country could make a serious step in the right direction by raising all allowances to the level of those given civil servants and by instituting an additional bonus for unwaged mothers caring for children. The cost of this system would be about Fr 9.6 billion, 7.5 billion more than the amount currently distributed by the state and the *caisses* combined. This seemed a huge amount, Boverat admitted, but with gross domestic income around Fr 180 billion – one-half of which was paid out in wages – it was far from impossible.[63]

Fortunately for Boverat, the CSN discussed the plan on 28 June, three weeks after the Matignon agreements. Business leaders had been slow to raise family allowance rates in the early thirties, but the May strikes and the sizable increases won by the newly powerful trade unions made them sympathetic to pronatalist demands. Georges Pernot, president of the Fédération Nationale des Associations des Familles Nombreuses had denounced the Matignon accords in the Senate for failing to take account of family needs, and businessmen and pronatalists were agreed in 1936 that further wage increases must be strenuously opposed and allowances raised substantially.[64] As we have seen, the Paris engineering firms in which the May strikes had begun raised allowances without state pressure immediately following the Matignon agreements. The administrators of the *caisses* nevertheless

[61] Fernand Boverat, "Rapport sur les encouragements matériels à la natalité," CSN, *Rapports*, 1934: no. 4, 25ᵉ sess. (June 1934), pp. 1–16.

[62] CSN, *Procès verbaux*, 1934: no. 5, 25ᵉ sess. (26 June 1934), pp. 2–3.

[63] Fernand Boverat, "Un plan d'ensemble de péréquation partielle des resources aux charges de famille," typescript inserted in CSN, *Communications*, 1936: no. 3. The plan was discussed at the 3 Feb. 1936 session of the Section Permanente, and a revised version was printed in CSN, *Rapports*, 1936: no. 4, 29ᵉ sess. (June 1936), pp. 3–24.

[64] See the discussion of the reaction of the Caisse de Compensation de la Région Parisienne to the Matignon accords in Chapter 5. Also, see Fernand Boverat, "Allocations familiales, salaires et prix de la vie," *Revue*, no. 289 (Aug.–Sept. 1936), pp. 239–43.

were reluctant to support so comprehensive a plan as Boverat's, although they were willing to consider funding allowances at civil service levels by suppressing the allowance for the first child.[65] In spite of this muted opposition, Boverat's plan was adopted by the CSN, and its influence was soon'apparent in bills proposed to the Chamber.[66]

The main conduit for Boverat's ideas in the Chamber was Adolphe Landry, himself a former minister and a noted demographer, who in his own person strategically linked the CSN (of which he was a vice-president) with the Chamber's Social Insurance Commission. During the early thirties, individual deputies introduced a series of resolutions and bills aimed at speeding up the application of the 1932 law, but the most comprehensive proposal was made in the form of a resolution by Landry himself in late 1936. Essentially presenting the doctrine of the CSN to the Chamber, Landry argued that "no one will deny that the most sublime statement of distributive justice is: to each according to his needs." His own proposal – to increase all family allowance rates to those given civil servants – would be merely "a small step toward that other equalization, the ideal equalization." Landry proposed to fund this Fr 9.1 billion plan – some 6 billion of which would be new expenditure – primarily through the *caisses* and the mutualist funds, thus obviating the need for new taxation.[67]

The Chamber's Social Insurance Commission agreed that the government should unify and improve the allowance system,[68] but decided that the best way to do so was not by raising rates to the civil servants' level, but rather by fixing them in proportion to a notional wage in each department. They suggested paying families 5% of that wage for the first child, 10% for the second, 15% for the third, and 20% for each subsequent child – a proposal Boverat had submitted to Léon Blum in May 1937. Finance, once again, would be left to the *caisses*, since, as Landry bluntly admitted, "to hope that such a cost would be supported through public finance, either entirely or even to however minor an extent would, to be frank, render this reform impossible."[69] The state would, however, take on the job of organizing a subsidized fund for the self-employed and would pay allowances at civil servant rates to those who still fell outside the scope of the proposal. Once again, pronatalists sought to push the logic of family-

[65] See Partiot's comments in CSN, *Rapports*, 1936: no. 4, 29ᵉ sess. (June 1936), pp. 39–44.

[66] CSN, *Procès Verbaux*, 1936: no. 5, 29ᵉ sess. (28 June 1936), pp. 3–8.

[67] *JO Documents (Chambre)*, 1936, ann. 1578, pp. 1229, 1230.

[68] Ibid., 1937, ann. 2079, p. 367.

[69] Ibid., 1937, ann. 2756, p. 553.

based redistribution beyond the level advocated by the *caisses* themselves, but they did not propose to alter the essential character of the system. They continued to look to business for financial support and tied allowances explicitly to wages. Only the case of agriculture forced them to modify even slightly the industrial system in the interest of universality.

Agriculture posed particular problems for the extension of allowances, since a rural proletariat was scarcely developed, and the aforementioned distinction between "employer" and "worker" was particularly unclear. The majority of French farms in the thirties were small family concerns, and farmers often employed one or two workers – usually young – of the same social class. In 1938, 87% of all farms were under 20 hectares, and unwaged peasant-owners made up 86% of the active agricultural population – versus a mere 14% for waged workers. Family allowances had been virtually undeveloped in agriculture before the 1932 law, and the obvious difficulties of application induced the government to foresee a separate and gradual application after consultation with the Agricultural Chambers. The separate decree for agriculture was slow in appearing, however, and by 1935 a mere four thousand children of agricultural workers were receiving allowances.[70]

Both the embattled agrarian *caisses* and politicians worried about the effects of rural emigration on *dénatalité* pressed the governments of the thirties to extend allowances to agriculture. When agricultural workers were finally brought into the system by the Popular Front government, however, the system proved unworkable. Bringing in agricultural wage earners while excluding unwaged small farmers created chaos. The two groups belonged to the same social class, and the attempt to make peasants pay contributions while restricting benefits to landless workers aroused resentment. Small farmers in the late thirties reacted to the obligation to pay into the *caisses* much the way their ancestors had met the eighteenth-century tax collector: with

---

[70] Despite the proliferation of smallholdings, some 60% of *land* consisted of large farms, usually rented out. Large farms, unlike peasant holdings, were modern and mechanized. The agrarian crisis of the thirties squeezed smallholding peasants, leading to some degree of concentration. See Philippe Bernard and Henri Dubief, *The Decline of the Third Republic, 1914–1938* (Cambridge University Press, 1985), pp. 236–41. The reservations of the Chamber's Social Insurance Commission about application to agriculture come out clearly in their deliberations; see Archives of the Assemblée Nationale (Versailles), 14ᵉ legisl, Box A10. The figure for agricultural workers covered is from G. Bonvoisin, "Rapport Moral," in Fédération Nationale des Caisses Agricoles d'Allocations Familiales, *Compte Rendu de la Journée Agricole du CNAF*, 16 (1936), p. 42.

stubborn noncompliance and occasional riot. If allowances were to function in agriculture, small farmers had to receive benefits as well as pay contributions. Finance was the main stumbling block, however: both the governments of the thirties and the parliamentary right resisted state funding, and peasants were too poor to bear the entire burden themselves.[71]

Dilemmas like this do not, politically speaking, require solutions: they can drag on forever. There was no compelling administrative or economic reason requiring the extension of allowances to agriculture and the transformation of family allowances into a national system. Agriculture fit uncomfortably into the allowance system, and agricultural interests themselves were ambivalent since peasants, while happy to collect allowances, resisted paying into the *caisses*. Yet literally dozens of bills and resolutions proposing the extension of the system to agriculture were submitted to the Chamber in the mid-thirties. These can be attributed in part to the strength of the ubiquitous agrarian lobby, but they were also another manifestation of pronatalist influence within the legislature. Peasant families were the most vigilant guardians of the domestic virtues and France's best hope for demographic revival, conservative senators told the Chautemps government during extensive debates over family policy in February 1938, and measures that discriminated against small proprietors to give benefits to urban workers or landless laborers could only arouse their resentment.[72] Bowing to such pressure, the Blum and Daladier governments issued decrees subsidizing the rural *caisses* and extending allowances to small farmers – although the decrees weren't actually applied until 1940.[73]

The pronatalists' attempt to rework the distributive system gathered

[71] For the opinions of the *caisses* concerning the application in agriculture, see the yearly reports of the Fédération Nationale des Caisses Agricoles d'Allocations Familiales, *Compte Rendu de la Journée Agricole du CNAF*, 1932–8. The *caisses* had strongly supported extension to agriculture but recommended beginning with areas of large-scale farming where there was a rural proletariat. The confusion caused by the Popular Front's 5 August 1936 decree extending allowances to all rural wage earners, as well as parliamentary pressure, led the second Blum government to study extension to small farmers as well; estimates of numbers involved and cost are in AN F10 2754. The same file contains clippings of newspaper reports covering peasant resistance to *caisse* attempts to collect allowance contributions.

[72] See especially the speeches by François-Saint-Maur, *JO Débats (Sénat)*, 8 Feb. 1938, pp. 100–2, and by Veyssière, ibid., 10 Feb. 1938, pp. 113–16.

[73] On the gradual application of allowances to agriculture, see Dominique Ceccaldi, *Histoire des prestations familiales en France* (Paris: UNCAF, 1957), pp. 52–3, 71–2; Talmy, *Histoire du mouvement familial*, 2, pp. 227–8.

momentum in the late thirties by activity on a number of fronts. The Alliance Nationale continued to distribute tracts pointing out the danger of *dénatalité* for national security, propaganda that grew more strident – and also more believable – as Germany and Italy grew more belligerent. Worse, in the late thirties the annual number of deaths actually surpassed the number of births, partly because the proportionally fewer children born during the war years could not produce as many children of their own as could the cohorts that preceded them.[74] The Alliance Nationale was able to exploit these new figures because they had, over the years, built up a reputation as reliable demographic experts. Possibly their most effective propaganda tool was their reliance on statistical projections. The two most famous of these were the studies done for the Alliance Nationale by the government statistician Alfred Sauvy, predicting the future size of the French population if current trends continued. In 1932, Sauvy had calculated the size of France in fifty years according to two hypotheses, the first holding mortality and fecundity rates constant, and the second assuming they would reach the levels prevailing in the Seine department. If the first hypothesis proved true, the population would remain relatively constant although its age structure would shift, but in the second case it would fall from some 40.5 million to 29 million by 1980.[75]

In 1936, Sauvy repeated his study, using the same first hypothesis, but assuming in the second case that the fecundity and mortality rates would continue falling at the rate of recent years. The results of this second hypothesis were virtually identical – again the population would fall to 29.6 million by 1984 – but the results of the first hypothesis were far more frightening. Even if fecundity and mortality remained constant at 1935 rates, the population would fall to 34 million by 1984.[76] The Alliance Nationale publicized both studies widely, and the second in particular was referred to in parliamentary debates. Sauvy's seemingly irrefutable statistics served in France the same legitimizing function for pronatalist policies that Rowntree's household studies served for the male-breadwinner norm in England

---

[74] For figures on births and deaths, see Talmy, *Histoire du mouvement familial*, 2 p. 219.
[75] Alfred Sauvy, "Calculs démographiques sur la population française jusqu'en 1980," *Revue*, no. 239 (June 1932), pp. 164–74.
[76] "Une étude sensationnelle. Les perspectives démographiques de la France calculées scientifiquement," *Revue*, no. 291 (Nov. 1936), pp. 289–97. See also "Rapport sur les nouvelles perspectives démographiques," CSN, *Rapports*, 1937: no. 1, 30ᵉ sess. (1 Feb. 1937), pp. 19–24.

in the twenties. Statistics elevated mere prophecy into a scientifically verifiable future.

As the demographic situation worsened, the Alliance Nationale counseled deputies against endorsing high wages, since these would deplete the funds available for allowances, and resolved over and over that any future increases in the remuneration of labor be granted in family allowances alone.[77] They justified this wage policy by arguing that childless men were already receiving family wages, and were simply failing in their duty to produce the children their income allowed for.[78] They also attempted to affect wage negotiations themselves by appealing to government arbitrators to include increased allowances in settlements and were particularly pleased by the arbitration conducted by William Oualid – Picquenard's wartime collaborator at the Ministry of Labor and a strong supporter of allowances – which raised allowances in the Parisian metal industry above the level granted to civil servants.[79]

The governments of Léon Blum and Camille Chautemps did not put through the systematic reorganization of family allowance rates called for by the pronatalists. While the left was willing to support public health measures, they resisted the argument that benefits like family allowances were more important than (and could in part replace) wages. When the Senate spent three days debating the demographic situation in February 1938, Marc Rucart, minister of public health in the Chautemps government, insisted that while the government was entirely disposed to increase its pronatalist effort, it also felt that

> in our developed countries, the best means of increasing the birthrate is to create prosperity. Our peoples are too advanced to agree happily to bring children into the world whose lives may be threatened by unemployment, poverty, sickness or war.[80]

This view was anathema to the pronatalists, who countered that any prosperity that fell on the just *chef de famille* and unjust *célibataire* alike could never encourage increased births.

---

[77] Archives of the Ministry of Labor, SAN 7733, File: "Le danger de la dénatalité," Document: Alliance Nationale, "Monsieur le Deputé . . ." [1936 or 1937]; see also CSN, *Procès verbaux*, 1938: no. 5, 33ᶜ sess. (27 June 1938), pp. 4–8; Congrès National de la Natalité, *Compte rendu*, 20 (1938), p. 52.

[78] Fernand Boverat, "Pourquoi verse-t-on un salaire familial aux travailleurs sans charges de famille?" *Revue*, no. 309 (May 1938), pp. 129–35.

[79] Fernand Boverat, "De magnifiques succès," *Revue*, no. 295 (Mar. 1937), pp. 65–70.

[80] *JO Débats (Sénat)*, 15 Feb. 1938, p. 105.

The pronatalists' *revanche* came with the Daladier government of April 1938, which increased military expenditures, abrogated the forty-hour week for defense industries, and instituted a strong family policy. The Daladier government not only found the money to solve the vexing problem of the rural *caisses*; they also granted many of the changes urged by Boverat and Landry. Their decrees of 11 and 12 November, which took effect in April 1939, went a significant distance toward family-based distributive justice by pegging allowances explicitly to wages. Family allowances were henceforth to vary with mean departmental wage figures established by the Ministry of Labor: 5% for the first child, 10% for the second, and 15% for each additional. Furthermore, an allowance was foreseen for the *mère au foyer*, set in March 1939 at 10% (provisionally 5%) of the wage.[81] The *Revue de l'Alliance Nationale* heralded the decrees as "a great success," but in fact the hold of the pronatalists on the government – as opposed to the legislature – was still tenuous. Even though the financial burden would fall on business and not the government, the Ministry of Finance opposed the extension of allowances, and attempted to block the publication of the decrees. In the end, the November decrees went through only because their author, the Alliance Nationale's most valuable administrative ally, Alfred Sauvy, threatened to resign if they were not put through.[82]

In early 1939, however, both Daladier and Minister of Finance Paul Reynaud agreed to work with the pronatalists to oversee the expansion and reorganization of family policy. Both Georges Pernot and Boverat suggested that the government appoint a small committee of "specialists" – read, "pronatalists" – to draft a coherent policy for increasing the population.[83] On 23 February 1939, the High Committee on Population was created, consisting of the Prime Minister, representatives of the Interior, Finance, Labor, Agriculture, and Public Health ministries, and five experts – including Boverat, Pernot, and Landry. The constitution of the High Committee was the final step in the incorporation of the pronatalists into government decision making. The committee was largely guided by Boverat, who drafted most of its proposals, but the government members ensured that the results

---

[81] The decree of 12 Nov. 1938 is in *JO Lois et Décrets*, 15 Nov. 1938; the decree of 31 Mar. 1939 that governed its application is in ibid., 2 Apr. 1939.
[82] "Un grand succès," *Revue*, no. 316 (Dec. 1938), pp. 368–71; Sauvy, *Histoire économique*, 1, p. 350.
[83] See Pernot in *JO Débats (Sénat)*, 8 Feb. 1938; Fernand Boverat, "Lenteur, incohérence, inertie: Cela ne peut pas continuer," *Revue*, no. 319 (Mar. 1939), pp. 71–6.

were financially acceptable, since they could outvote the pronatalists and occasionally did so. The result of the committee's deliberations, the Family Code (Code de la Famille), appeared on 29 July 1939, and was applied in piecemeal installments after the outbreak of the war.[84]

The Family Code suppressed the first child's allowance – against Boverat's wishes – and instituted a hefty one-time bonus for a first child born within two years of marriage. It maintained the principle of linking allowances to wages and raised rates, but set up different rates for urban and rural areas within each department and restricted the mother's allowance to urban families with dependent children living on a single wage. Civil servants would be brought into the new national system; groups unable to finance allowances on their own – independent workers, some agricultural workers, and so forth – would be organized into *caisses* subsidized by the state; and a national equalization of costs between industries would be established. The Family Code, which occupied twenty pages of fine print in the *Journal Officiel*, also put through many reforms dear to the pronatalist heart: loans for young rural couples, stricter penalties for abortion, the repression of pornography, and the compulsory teaching of demography in the schools. By far the most important aspect of the code, however, was its continued extension of the principle that the distributive system should be reworked through allowances so that family income would vary with family needs. The practical results of this principle were striking, as can be seen in Table 7.2. If the government did index allowances to a realistic "base wage," allowances could effectively double the income of a family with six dependent children living on a single wage.

The Family Code was to take effect on 1 January 1940. While some of its provisions were put off by the war, others were faithfully applied and lasted throughout the Vichy regime. The Vichy government completed the process of ceding official power to the pro-family lobby, with the creation of both the Commissariat Général à la Famille and the Conseil Supérieur de la Famille, whose members included many prominent pronatalists and familists – including Bonvoisin, Paul Haury, and Georges Pernot. Whatever its other innovations, the regime left the family allowance system largely untouched. Rates were raised in 1941 by administrative decree, but less dramatically than the

---

[84] On the constitution and deliberations of the High Committee, see Fernand Boverat, "Le décret-loi sur la famille et la natalité," *Revue*, no. 324 (Aug. 1939), pp. 243–63. The text of the Family Code is in *JO Lois et Décrets*, 30 July 1939.

Table 7.2. *Family allowances as a percentage of the base wage, 1938 and 1939 laws*

Children in family	Law of 12 Nov. 1938[a] FA	MA	Total	Family Code, 29 July 1939[a] FA	MA	Total
1 (under five)	5	5	10	0	10	10
1 (over five)	0	5	5	0	0	0
2	15	5	20	10	10	20
3	30	5	35	30	10	40
4	45	5	50	50	10	60
5	60	5	65	70	10	80
6	75	5	80	90	10	100
Each addnl.	15			20		

[a] FA, Family allowance; MA, unwaged mother's allowance.

percentages in Table 7.3 imply, since the notional base wage on which they were based was not raised to keep up with inflation. More important, finance and administration were left in the hands of the employers. The *caisses* themselves were reorganized only in 1945–6, when a single family-allowance *caisse* was established for each department, and administration was turned over to a council elected by the beneficiaries.[85]

If we look at developments across the thirties as a whole, we can see how a demographic panic and the consistent pressure of the Alliance Nationale and pronatalist deputies forced the government to extend and amplify the family allowance system. Pronatalists replaced businessmen as the main innovators in the field of family policy and, by doing so, at times incurred the hostility of the leaders of the *caisses*, who objected to increased costs and argued that pronatalists were trying to force allowances beyond their legitimate scope. Even if simply paying for children were sufficient to raise the birthrate, Bonvoisin told the 1939 congress of the *caisses*, "the fact remains that . . . it is not

---

[85] The Vichy regime also converted the mother's allowance – to be discussed in detail later – into an "allocation de salaire unique." On Vichy family policy, see Paul Durand, "Allocations familiales et allocation de salaire unique," *Collection droit social*, 11 "Le nouveau régime du travail" (1941–2), p. 25; Alfred Sauvy, *La vie économique des français de 1939 à 1945* (Paris: Flammarion, 1978), pp. 201–7; Michele Bordeaux, "Femmes hors d'état français, 1940–1944," in Thalmann, ed., *Femmes et fascismes*, pp. 135–55.

Table 7.3. *Family allowances as a percentage of the base wage,*
Vichy laws of 15 February and 29 March 1941

Children in family	Family allowance	Single wage allowance	Total
1 (under 5)	0	20	20
1 (over 5)	0	10	10
2	10	25	35
3	30	30	60
4	60	30	90
5	90	30	120
6	120	30	150
Each addnl.	30		

Source: Paul Durand, "Allocations familiales et allocation de salaire unique," *Collection droit social*, 11, "Le nouveau régime du travail" (1941–2).

the responsibility of industry to make people have babies."[86] Business leaders had set up the *caisses* to meet the needs of specific industries and objected strenuously to any attempt to equalize costs across industries.[87] Yet the claim that family allowances could be the tool of demographic renewal – an argument that businessmen had themselves done much to disseminate and promote – had by 1939 convinced many across political lines that such allowances could not be left to the rather arbitrary benevolence of businessmen alone. By playing the pronatalist card, modernizing businessmen made a case for the national importance, but also the national control, of their ostensibly philanthropic effort.

At the outset of this chapter I stated that pronatalists, unlike other pressure groups, were uniquely successful in influencing the development of welfare policy. Yet did their intervention significantly alter the fundamental nature of the family allowance system? From the preceding account, it is clear that pronatalists were successful in forcing policy forward, but only in a direction already heavily determined by business interests. Businessmen had introduced allowances, as Bonvoisin had explained in the early twenties, in the hopes of establishing a system of "a wage corresponding to the needs of a single person,

[86] G. Bonvoisin, "Le nouveau régime des allocations familiales," CNAF, *Compte rendu*, 19 (1939), p. 83.
[87] Ibid., pp. 76–91.

but adjusted by allowances for fathers of families."[88] This goal of wage restraint shared by virtually all *caisses* was in the end more palatable to politicians and administrators than the Consortium's effort to restrict workers' mobility, and it was the former aspect that continued into the national system. Family allowances continued to be financed essentially through the redistribution of wages, and as rates increased businessmen grew more insistent that these costs be passed on to workers. Indeed, the legislation of the late thirties, by pegging allowances to mean departmental wages, made the disaggregation of the family wage more explicit. As employers, the self-employed, and agricultural workers were included, the system lost its industrial character to become simply a reapportionment of national income from the childless to those with children.[89]

What is striking – especially in comparison with Britain – is just how substantial this redistribution was. Some 2% of the national wage bill was paid out in allowances in 1938; by 1949, this proportion had risen to 9%, and was double that in industry and commerce. Family allowances amounted to less than 1% of GNP in 1938; after the consolidation and improvements of the late forties, and as the figures compiled by Jacques Hochard and reproduced in Table 7.4 show, family allowances paid through the national *caisse* alone accounted for more than 2% of GNP and all family allowances for almost 4%. By the late forties, as Table 7.5 shows, almost as much money was paid out in family allowances was paid out in old-age pensions.[90]

Critics charged, truthfully enough, that the system was almost entirely nonredistributive across class lines; it did, however, significantly raise the living standard of families with dependent children – al-

---

[88] G. Bonvoisin, "Rapport moral," CNAF, *Compte rendu*, 2 (1922), p. 71.

[89] Beginning in the late thirties, both the *caisses* and the administration began to study the possibility of equalizing costs between industries and among *caisses*. Resolutions and appeals for a system of national "surcompensation," particularly by small towns forced to pay allowances out of meager funds, are found in AN F2 2023. The question of national cost sharing was controversial among businessmen, who felt that allowance systems should be geared to meet the needs of particular industries. The Ministry of Labor did bring up the question of a national cost sharing, but when it became clear that relatively impoverished trades with a low burden of dependency – say, grocers – would end up subsidizing wealthy industries with high dependency rates, like engineering, these negotiations ground to a halt (Caisse de Compensation de Région Parisienne [CCRP], Commission de Gestion, 1 June 1939; CNAF, *Compte rendu*, 19 [1939], pp. 28–40).

[90] Figures in this paragraph are taken from Jacques Hochard, *Aspects économiques des prestations familiales* (Paris: UNCAF, 1961), pp. 22, 174–6; also Pierre Laroque, *Social Welfare in France* (Paris: La Documentation Française, 1966), p. 484.

Table 7.4. *Development of family allowances, 1938–58*

Date	Wages as % of GNP	Social benefits as % of GNP	Family allowances All systems As % of benefits	Family allowances All systems As % of GNP	Family allowances General system As % of benefits	Family allowances General system As % of GNP
1938	32.5	5.3	12.9	0.8	—	—
1949	32.8	9.6	38.7	3.6	22.1	2.1
1950	31.6	10.2	38.7	3.6	20.0	2.0
1951	32.6	10.6	36.0	3.8	20.6	2.2
1952	32.8	10.5	36.6	3.9	21.8	2.3
1953	32.8	11.0	36.0	4.0	21.8	2.4
1954	33.2	11.5	34.2	3.9	18.8	2.2
1955	34.4	11.7	34.9	4.1	20.0	2.3
1956	35.1	12.0	33.8	4.1	19.3	2.3
1957	35.4	12.2	31.7	3.9	18.4	2.3
1958	35.5	11.7	32.3	3.8	18.9	2.2

Sources: See Table 7.1 and Jacques Hochard, *Aspects économiques des prestations familiales* (Paris: UNCAF, 1961), pp. 22, 175.

though not to the pronatalists' ideal level of absolute equality between single wage earners and families. Pierre Laroque has estimated that allowances raised the income of the man with four dependent children by about one-third by 1939; ten years later, after the reforms and improvements introduced after the Second World War, allowances would double family income. In other words, and as Table 7.6 below shows, four children essentially entitled the wage earner to a second full wage.

In comparison with England, French family policy reads like a success story. Businessmen had not sought to create a national system of family-based redistribution, but the logic of their interests and the campaigns of nationalists concerned about French decline coincided. The result was a system that was very different from the British male breadwinner model. First, as we have seen, the French model of family policy was purely parental, with little attention paid to claims for distributive justice across class lines. Allowances effected a redistribution of income from the childless to those with children, while circumventing the controversial issue of state finance. Second, while British campaigns, at least in the twenties, had been predicated on particular fixed assumptions about gender roles and family structures, French policy was more fluid. Businessmen were often fairly agnostic about the actual structure of the families they aided. Their interest

Table 7.5. *Breakdown of social benefits (percentages), 1938–58*

Program	1938[a]	1949[a]	1958
Pensions	80	39	40
Family allowances	13	38	32
Social insurance	7	23	23
Workers' compensation	—	—	5

[a] Workers' compensation is not included in the breakdown for these years.
Source: Jacques Hochard, *Aspects économiques des prestations familiales* (Paris: UNCAF, 1961), pp. 38, 175.

Table 7.6. *Income differentials between unmarried workers and workers with families at the base wage level, 1939 and 1949*

Family situation	1939	1949
Unmarried	100	100
2 children	109	142
3 children	120	174
4 children	130	198
5 children	141	223

Source: Pierre Laroque, comp., *Social Welfare in France* (Paris: La Documentation Française, 1966), p. 485.

was to alter the wage system and not to promote any particular vision of family life.

Pronatalists agreed with businessmen's wage strategy, but they also had other plans. With many social Catholics, they hoped to see family allowances not merely extended but reworked to favor disproportionally families with male breadwinners and dependent wives. Since many industries relied on women workers, there was much less business support for such a venture, and in fact only during the depression were businessmen and civil servants at all sympathetic. The attempt to rework the family allowance system in order to engineer particular gender roles was the second aspect of pronatalist policy, and it is to the more ambiguous results of this campaign that we now turn.

What manner of family? Gender and dependence in the parental welfare state

We have seen throughout this study that family policy often affects gender relations within both the labor market and the family. By distributing money to particular persons in recognition of their parental roles, policies can create new relationships of dependence and authority. Yet while the implications of family allowances for the wage system were explicit in France, the effects of allowances on domestic relations remained rather opaque. The business leaders, government administrators, and pronatalists who had the most to do with their introduction certainly shared the gender anxieties of their class – including a tendency to view wage earning (and especially factory work) by women as an agent of demoralization and *dénatalité* – but they did not make the roles and relations of husbands and wives the central focus of their work. It was the self-proclaimed feminist and Catholic organizations who, albeit from very different perspectives, were concerned above all with the relations between women and men within the family itself. Both attempted to influence the development of family policy but had little ability to do so on their own. It was not until the thirties – when the depression and continued *dénatalité* made married women's waged work newly problematic – that Catholics were able to interest more influential actors in their plan to rework allowances to favor families with unwaged wives and thus encourage married women to "return" home.

The campaign to "return the mother to the home" began in earnest in 1931 and was led by a social Catholic women's organization, the Union Féminine Civique et Sociale. The UFCS had been founded in 1925 by Andrée Butillard, who had already made a name for herself as an organizer of working women, and the new organization soon grew to embrace a "cadre" of over ten thousand women. The group situated itself on the social Catholic wing of the church, and had close ties to prominent confessional politicians, trade unionists, and reformers – including the ubiquitous Eugène Duthoit, the old opponent of the Consortium Textile de Roubaix-Tourcoing. Although the UFCS was active on a number of issues during this period, it sought above all to bring about reforms that would induce married women workers to "return" to their homes.[91]

Why was this their major goal? The campaigns of the UFCS are comprehensible only in terms of the evolution of French Catholicism, and especially of its continued engagement with the problem of

[91] The most detailed account of Butillard's life and work with the UFCS is Henri Rollet, *Andrée Butillard et le féminisme chrétien* (Paris: Spes, 1960); see also Martine Martin, "Les femmes et le travail ménager en France entre les deux guerres," Thesis, University of Paris VII, 1984; Naomi Black, *Social Feminism* (Ithaca, N.Y.: Cornell University Press, 1989).

"woman." Social Catholicism flourished in the interwar period, influenced not only by the older teachings of Leo XIII, Count Albert de Mun, Léon Harmel, and others, but also by a new generation of politicians, labor leaders, and "worker priests," and profiting from the Vatican's condemnation of the protofascist Action Française in 1926. Social Catholics, believing that the problems of poverty and class conflict were inextricable from the spread of irreligion and "demoralization" at all levels of society, placed social reform at the heart of a wider mission of rechristianization. They defined themselves in opposition equally to liberal individualism and market capitalism – which, they argued, had torn apart the ties of corporation, family, and faith and had replaced the concept of mutuality and duty with that of contract and right – and to socialism, which had merely extended the economistic logic of liberalism to its logical conclusion of class struggle. Only a revival of corporate institutions, associations that would bring together individuals of unequal status on the basis of shared faith, could wean the people from false and individualist values and reknit the social fabric of the nation.

No institution was more important in Catholic thought than the family, which taught how authority could be tempered by love and collective good furthered by the sacrifice of self. In discussing women – or, as they invariably put it, "woman" – Catholic thought invariably began with the family; the family was, Duthoit argued, "the essential context for the woman question." If one began with the understanding that the rights of the family to protection and self-perpetuation took precedence over any individual right, the relative duties and claims of the sexes and generations would fall into place. But if "woman's" maternal role and her subordination to her husband were both defined by doctrine and underscored in the unequal physical and intellectual capacities with which (Duthoit said) Providence had endowed the sexes, such inequality did not preclude a true complementarity, nor did it render the sexes spiritually unequal.[92] Andrée Butillard adopted and elaborated this doctrine of equal honor within separate spheres, arguing that "woman's" special intuitions and capacity for self-sacrifice made her better suited to exercise influence over her family than to be its head (*chef*). Indeed, it was precisely in such roles – and not in the public world of work urged on them by secular feminists – that women would find true fulfillment. "Legiti-

---

[92] Eugène Duthoit, "La famille. Donnée essentielle du problème de la femme," *Semaine Sociale* 19 (1927), p. 49.

mate feminism," she argued, "consists in taking hold of [women's] marvelous natural gifts and using them to advantage (*les mettre en valeur*)."[93]

The UFCS's social campaigns attempted to do just that. Catholics intended not to extend equal rights to women in men's sphere, but to create a society that would allow women to fulfill the roles that God and nature had ordained for them. The UFCS perceived its task as twofold: on the one hand, to revalorize motherhood through public education and, on the other, to construct economic and social policies that would enable women to stay in their homes. Toward the first aim, the UFCS published booklets, held meetings, organized home economics courses, and in 1935, founded a housewives' league – the *Ligue de la Mère au Foyer*. It viewed the family allowance system as the most hopeful tool with which to achieve the second. Having found through a 1929–30 inquiry that most employed married women claimed they worked because of economic need,[94] the UFCS accepted that only some mitigation of that need could lure women back home. Economic causes required economic remedies, it argued, and in 1931 the group appealed to industrialists to pay higher family allowances to men whose wives were unwaged and to organize part-time work and homework for women.[95] The UFCS was encouraged by Vatican support for its campaign and by the conversion of a few important businessmen, including the Catholic textile manufacturer

---

[93] Andrée Butillard, "Bon et mauvais féminisme," *La Femme dans la Vie Sociale*, no. 19 (Mar. 1929).

[94] The Union Féminine Civique et Sociale (UFCS) made much of its inquiry, but it was conducted among only 506 working mothers. Certainly the vast majority of these said they were working out of economic need (one wonders what their husbands would have answered), which the UFCS interpreted as meaning that they would have preferred to stay home. The results of the inquiry are discussed in Union Féminine Civique et Sociale, *Le travail industriel de la mère et le foyer ouvrier – Documents d'études: Extraits du congrès international de juin 1933* (Paris: UFCS, 1933), p. 250.

[95] "Aux industriels," *La Femme dans la Vie Sociale*, no. 42 (June 1931). Major statements published by UFCS militants include Marie de Tailhandier, "Le travail industriel de la mère de famille," *La Femme dans la Vie Sociale*, no. 42 (June 1931); Eve Baudouin, *La mère au travail et le retour au foyer* (Paris: Bloud et Gay, 1931); Eve Baudouin, *Comment envisager le retour de la mère au foyer* (Paris: Spes, 1933). The UFCS held two international congresses on the problems of waged work and the desirability of returning women to the home, and published the proceedings; see Union Féminine Civique et Sociale, *Le travail industriel de la mère* (1933); idem, *La mère au foyer, ouvrière de progrès humain – Documents d'études: Extraits du congrès international de juin 1937* (Paris: UFCS, 1937). The UFCS's monthly paper, *La Femme dans la Vie Sociale*, gave continuous coverage of their campaigns.

Philippe Leclercq, who established a special *caisse* in the Roubaix-Tourcoing area to pay higher family allowances to households with unwaged wives.[96]

Pleas for differential family allowances may remind us of early British arguments for the endowment of motherhood: in both cases, advocates hoped to allow – rather than to force – hard-pressed mothers to devote themselves to their children. Yet as in Britain, maternalist arguments could be marshaled to serve more coercive ends. If the welfare system was to be altered to reward unwaged wives, surely the labor market should also be reworked to discriminate against recalcitrant married women wage earners. The UFCS in fact never endorsed legal restrictions on married women's work, believing that such measures would merely encourage couples to restrict births or live together without marriage.[97] It did, however, insist that such work was "against nature"[98] and employed a discourse that made its legal suppression imaginable.[99] In books, pamphlets, and talks, UFCS activists laid the responsibility for virtually every social ill from juvenile delinquency to *dénatalité* at the feet of married women's work. Nor did they refrain from condemning women who found in their work a noneconomic reward. Butillard reserved her harshest criticism for married women who, given a choice, nevertheless resisted "returning home." At a 1937 conference, she stated, "If, married and a mother, [the woman] has freely preferred the exercise of a profession to the accomplishment of her providential mission, she will simply have run away from the duties of her station."[100]

In fact, the image of infants torn from their mothers' arms by the

---

[96] A letter from Cardinal Pacelli approving the UFCS's campaigns is in a file entitled "Préparation du congrès 1933," held by the UFCS, rue Béranger, Paris. The Leclercq initiative is described in UFCS, *La mère au foyer* (1937), pp. 143–8.

[97] The UFCS made clear its opposition to legal prohibition in Andrée Butillard, "Désagrégation de la famille par le travail de la mère au dehors," *La Femme dans la Vie Sociale*, no. 35 (November 1930).

[98] Quoted in F. Van Goethem, "Enquête internationale sur le travail salarié de la femme mariée," *Chronique Sociale de France*, Jan. 1933, p. 21.

[99] It is significant that the UFCS's position on the waged work of mothers and on family allowances became standard argumentation in law theses on these subjects. See, notably: Mathilde Decouvelaere, *Le travail industriel des femmes mariées*, Thesis, University of Lille, Faculty of Law (Paris: Rousseau, 1934); Magdeleine Caunes, *Des mésures juridique propres à faciliter la présence de la mère au foyer ouvrier*, Thesis, University of Paris, Faculty of Law (Paris: A. Pedone, 1938); Jeanne Cann, *Les allocations familiales, l'allocation de la mère au foyer et l'allocation de salaire unique dans le commerce et l'industrie*, Thesis, University of Rennes, Faculty of Law (Loudeac: Imprimerie Traonouil-Anger, 1944).

[100] UFCS, *La mère au foyer* (1937), p. 18.

inhumane force of industrial capitalism scarcely described the reality of women's work in France. In 1931, one-half of working women in France were single, widowed, or divorced, and of the 3.9 million married women in the labor force, the overwhelming majority worked with their husbands in farms or shops.[101] Yet France still remained a country in which rates of married women's work were quite high – especially in comparison with Britain, where only about 10% of married women were formally "employed" – and a rhetoric stigmatizing women's work was music to many ears during the depression. Despite the fact that unemployment in France was a good deal less serious than in most other European countries – officially running around 300,000 throughout 1933 – the backlash against women's work was severe. The controversy reached its height in 1931, when Charles Richet wrote to the Parisian daily *Le Matin* calling for a legal prohibition on all married women's work, and the matter continued to be much debated throughout the thirties and into the Vichy period.[102] Some Catholics, already opposed to married women's work on moral grounds, were quick to see the depression as, in the words of Joseph Danel, professor at the Catholic University of Lille, "an opportunity that one shouldn't let pass by." Perhaps, he thought, one could begin to bar women from work that was "incompatible with their sex, their strength, their special abilities, their dignity."[103]

No legal prohibition of married women's work was passed before the Vichy regime, but nothing brought out the core values of republican feminists and Catholic women more clearly than this implied threat. On paper, the positions of Cécile Brunschvicg's Union Française pour le Suffrage des Femmes and the UFCS often seemed quite close: both groups were opposed to legal restrictions on married women's work, but both often professed themselves favorable to measures that would "allow" women to return home.[104] In the face of deepening hostility to married women's work, however, republican feminists quickly rallied to the cause of individual liberty. The feminist weekly

[101] Evelyne Sullerot, "Condition de la femme," in Alfred Sauvy, ed., *Histoire économique*, 3, p. 203.
[102] For the controversy over married women's work in the thirties, see ibid. and the coverage in *La Française*.
[103] Joseph Danel, "Le travail des mères hors du foyer," in Butillard et al., eds., *Le travail de la mère hors de son foyer et sa répercussion sur la natalité: Commission catholique du 14ᵉ congrès de la natalité ... Sept. 1932* (Paris: Editions Mariage et Famille, 1933), p. 53.
[104] For feminist support for family allowances and other means of aiding the *mère au foyer* see C. Brunschvicg, "Les allocations familiales obligatoires," *La Française*, 25: 1009 (13 Feb. 1932); "Le Congrès National de l'UFSF," *La Française*, 26: 1069 (10 June 1933).

La Française made the defense of married women's work rights their main focus from 1931, and as this campaign absorbed more of their time, they grew a bit short-tempered with the UFCS. The redoubtable Cécile Brunschvicg warned feminists that the international conference organized by the UFCS in 1933 had merely allowed that it was "neither possible nor opportune *in the current circumstances*" to call for a general legal prohibition on married women's work and noted that such views could easily lead to wider restrictions.[105] By late 1935, when the UFCS published a declaration demanding a male wage adequate to support a family and financial incentives to return women to the home, *La Française* curtly remarked:

> Let us hope that the leaders of the movement created to "return woman to the home" finally understand their duty to end a public opinion campaign which, badly understood, currently only serves to support the battle against women's freedom to work.[106]

Having learned that separate-spheres rhetoric could be a double-edged sword, in the years immediately before the Second World War feminists talked less of women's work as an unhappy necessity and more of it as an inalienable right. They moved into alliance with the socialist Confédération Générale du Travail, to whose staunch opposition to legal restrictions they owed – as they recognized – the defense of married women's work rights.[107]

If the depression served to remind republican feminists of their attachment to individualist values, the UFCS responded quite differently. Not only did they seek to exploit the depression to deepen public disapprobation of married women's work, they also looked for allies beyond Catholic circles. They turned especially to the pronatalists, long sympathetic to Catholic initiatives and equally distressed by France's high rates of women's employment. The Alliance Nationale began covering the UFCS's campaign in February 1932; in September of the same year a speech by Butillard at the 14th National Birthrate Congress arguing that the waged work of wives caused *dénatalité* caught the interest of the CSN.[108] The CSN asked one of its

---

[105] [Cécile Brunschvicg], "Le travail industriel de la mère et le foyer ouvrier," *La Française*, 26: 1071 (24 June 1933).

[106] "Le droit de la femme au travail," *La Française*, 28: 1172 (14 Dec. 1935). The text of the UFCS declaration is in Bibliothèque Nationale, Dossier 4 Wz 5743.

[107] Both the CGT and the CGTU passed resolutions defending married women's right to work in the thirties. See Brunschvicg's tribute to the CGT in S.C., "Le Congrès National de l'UFSF. Deuxième Journée," *La Française*, 28: 1144 (23 Mar. 1935).

[108] Paul Haury, "Comment ramener la femme au foyer," *Revue*, 33: 235 (Feb. 1932), pp. 54–7.

members – Mme Raymonde Grégoire, mother of ten – to study the question and soon joined the UFCS in calling on the *caisses* to increase family allowances for unwaged wives and so induce mothers to stay home.[109] By 1933, leaders of both the Alliance Nationale and the CSN were on the UFCS's national campaign committee, and both organizations came to take as axiomatic the pronatalist desirability of offering mothers financial incentives to return home.[110]

An unwaged mothers' allowance thus appeared by the midthirties as the felicitous solution to two problems: the depression-era shortage of work and *dénatalité*. Legislative proposals along these lines soon followed: in late 1934, one socialist deputy presented a resolution calling on the government to give married women's jobs to unemployed men and the men's unemployment allowance to married women; a few months later the UFCS took a deputation to the Ministry of Labor asking for a special allowance for the mother of a young child who withdrew from the labor market to make room for an unemployed person.[111] The UFCS also drafted a law with Catholic deputies that would have authorized the *caisses* to suppress the first child's allowance for the waged mother and use the money to pay higher allowances to households with unwaged mothers, on the grounds that "when so many men search in vain for work, it is abnormal for women to be employed."[112] Similar proposals were submitted in 1936 and 1937,[113] and when the government proved slow to act, the Alliance Nationale canvassed government wage negotiators directly, urging them to increase allowances by arbitration and to set up a special benefit for unwaged mothers.[114]

The campaign to return married women to the home recalls the strategies adopted by British employers, trade unionists, and government policymakers alike in the thirties. In both France and Britain,

---

[109] See the minutes of the Permanent Section of the CSN for 7 Nov. and 19 Dec. 1932, and 16 Jan. 1933, all in CSN, *Communications*, 1934: no. 3.

[110] For the list of UFCS committee members, see *La Femme dans la Vie Sociale*, no. 65 (Dec. 1933); for the place of the housewife's allowance within the CSN's program, see CSN, *Procès verbal*, 1936: no. 5, 29ᵉ sess. (28 June 1936), pp. 3–8.

[111] Maria Vérone, "Femmes, défendez-vous!" *L'Oeuvre*, 14 Dec. 1934; "Une double démarche au Ministère du Travail," *La Femme dans la Vie Sociale*, 8: 79 (Apr. 1935).

[112] *JO Documents (Chambre)*, 1935, ann. 5193, p. 777.

[113] Ibid., 1936, ann. 176, p. 822; ann. 801, p. 1443; 1937, ann. 2356, p. 567.

[114] Marie de Tailhandier, "L'action pour la mère au foyer," *La Femme dans la Vie Sociale*, 10: 101 (June 1937). Both the international congress organized by the UFCS in 1937 and the 19th Congrès National de la Natalité supported arbitration decisions to provide for an unwaged mother's allowance: UFCS, *La mère au foyer* (1937), p. 273; "La question de la mère au foyer," *Revue de la Plus Grande Famille*, Sept. 1937.

rising unemployment led to proposals aimed at forcing married women out of work. Yet the means considered in France (financial incentives) were actually less draconian, reflecting both French women's stronger position in the labor market and the less entrenched nature of the male-breadwinner norm. Unlike in Britain, French campaigners did not assume that if women were forced out of work men could simply support them; the British solution of denying both work and welfare benefits to married women would have been seen as the equivalent of consigning women to prostitution or starvation.[115] Rather, both the Alliance Nationale and the UFCS accepted that married women's work was essential to their families, and that any campaign to limit such wage earning must begin by compensating those families for lost wages. Yet the *caisses* proved reluctant to adopt the new role of supporting housewives. Meddling by enthusiastic government arbitrators inspired by pronatalist propaganda had created so many administrative problems for the *caisses* that the Ministry of Labor forbade arbitrators from making any decisions about allowances after 1938; employers also feared that the Catholics' campaign would jeopardize their access to cheaper female labor. Paul Leclercq, editor of the Comité Central's *Revue de la Famille* spoke for many businessmen when he said the UFCS's campaign was morally valuable but impractical: "Better to look reality in the face," he wrote, "and adjust to it by allowing women workers to adapt their work to their family life as harmoniously as possible" – as the *caisses* tried to do through their home economics courses.[116] The 1938 national conference of the *caisses* was willing to resolve only that the state not block initiatives taken by the funds themselves – a policy that would have restricted innovations to those industries able to do without women's work.[117] By late 1938, the UFCS announced that some 300,000 families were

---

[115] Catholics did not always accept this argument. For example, two social workers active in the Catholic girls' organization, Jeunesse Ouvrière Chrétienne Féminine, compiled budgets "proving" that married women's waged work actually *reduced* family income, since with careful economizing, a little paid sewing, and all that time now available for mending, knitting, and cooking, the far-sighted housewife could reduce household expenditures substantially. See Céline Lhotte and Elisabeth Dupéyrat, "Une enquête de la J.O.C.F.: La préparation du futur foyer de la jeune travailleuse. Deuxième partie: I. Le travail de la femme mariée hors du foyer," *Les Dossiers de l'Action Populaire*, 391 (15 Sept. 1937), pp. 1745–70.

[116] Paul Leclercq, "A notre point de vue: Le père et la mère au foyer," *Revue de la Famille*, 67 (July 1933), p. 3.

[117] Gustave Maignan, "Nature et portée des mésures prises en faveur du maintien de la mère au foyer," in CNAF, *Compte rendu*, 18 (1938), pp. 39–49; see also the congress resolution, ibid., p. 105.

receiving allowances for nonwaged mothers, not an insignificant number but substantially less than the 1.6 million receiving family allowances as a whole.[118]

In November 1938, however, when the Daladier government bowed to pronatalist pressure and its own fears and introduced the package of reforms later extended in the Family Code, they included an unwaged mother's allowance (*allocation pour la mère au foyer*) in their plans. The allowance was small – being set at a mere 10% (provisionally 5%) of a notional "base wage" – and the *caisses* continued to think its introduction misguided, predicting that it would prove inadequate to induce women to leave employment in cases of real need and unnecessary in other cases. It seemed something of an anomaly, and the *caisses* recommended it be replaced – as it was during Vichy – by an allowance to any household living on a single wage.[119]

The introduction of the unwaged mother's allowance was important, however, for it signaled a critical – if temporary – shift in policy. French family policy had hitherto developed on parental lines, compensating parents for dependent children but not husbands for wives or wives for their unwaged labor. With the introduction of the unwaged mothers' allowance, however, the state signaled its acceptance of the responsibility not merely to equalize the cost of children across the population, but also to favor a particular family form. What is particularly striking about the French campaign for the mother's allowance, however, especially in comparison with the British campaigns for endowment of motherhood or family allowances, is the marginality of feminist concerns to its introduction. In Britain, feminists supported benefits for mothers as a means of granting some measure of economic independence to women whose hope of earning wages was effectively nil; in France, by contrast, such measures were proposed as a means of inducing women to abjure the "individualistic" role of wage earning to devote themselves to their families. And far from seeking to lessen the authority of husbands over wives – always a central concern of Rathbone and the "new feminists" – French Catholics and pronatalists usually refused to consider the possibility that men and women within families could have different interests and

---

[118] "La préparation des décret-lois et l'action de l'UFCS," *La Femme dans la Vie Sociale*, 11: 115 (Dec. 1938); statistics on total allowances are compiled from Archives Nationales (AN) F22 1513.

[119] "Majoration 'mère au foyer'. Principales conclusions des travaux du congrès des allocations familiales" (19 May 1939), in AN 40 AS 57. A good summary of the workings of the unwaged mother's allowance and the single-wage allowance is give by Cann, *Les allocations familiales.*

thus exhibited little concern for the distribution of income within the family itself. Mothers' allowances were thus introduced in France bereft of any emancipatory rhetoric of women's rights and were greeted by French feminists with ambivalence.

Probably the best evidence of the very different cast given to issues of gender in France was the fact that the most effective advocates of payment of allowances to the mother – considered a core feminist demand in Britain – were pronatalists entirely unconcerned with women's freedom. The proposal to pay allowances directly to mothers was made in the first instance for practical reasons: women, after all, took care of children and would, many thought, be less likely to spend the money on drink. This was the same logic that had driven the Chamber's Social Insurance Commission to propose (unsuccessfully) to pay the allowances given to large families to the mother; it was also the reason that some of the *caisses*, including the huge Caisse de Compensation de la Région Parisienne, paid all benefits to the mother and convinced the government to allow them to continue to do so after 1932. Some Catholics objected to payment to the mother as an insult to the *père de famille*, but Boverat, who was concerned about births and not men's rights, retorted that "any *chef de famille* worthy of that name would support such a measure... and fathers of large families more willingly than all the others."[120] Boverat was able to convince the Conseil supérieur in 1936 to support the payment of both family allowances and unemployed workers' children's benefits to the mother.[121] The UFCS, by contrast, reluctant to question the legitimacy of family hierarchy, avoided the issue of payment until 1939, when it agreed that the benefits introduced by the 1938 decree should be paid to the mother.[122]

Republican feminists, by contrast, did consider the question of payment to be more than a matter of mere convenience and were quick to object to the suggestion that if one improved the wages or benefits of men, the status of mothers would take care of itself. As one of the correspondents for *La Française* wrote forthrightly:

> We repudiate *absolutely* this view that would, in order to combat unemployment, offer the man a family wage supplement, while reducing the woman to her domestic and maternal functions alone; what we *ask for, insist upon*, is that the woman's biological and familial

---

[120] Boverat, "Le décret-loi," p. 253.
[121] CSN, *Procès verbaux*, 1936: no 5, 29ᵉ sess. (28 June 1936), pp. 8, 15.
[122] "Action pour la mère au foyer," *La Femme dans la Vie Sociale*, 12: 117 (Feb. 1939).

functions be *publicly acknowledged* as *social functions* and rewarded as such.[123]

Maternal love should not be exploited to keep a mother in the "disguised slavery" of economic dependence on her husband, this writer contended; rather, family benefits should be paid to her directly in compensation for her social role.[124] Such arguments were anathema to Catholic women, however, who countered that family life involved sacrifice for both husband and wife; attempting to weigh the respective rights and remuneration of each would only lead to conflict and bitterness. Just as men worked to support the entire family, the mother's work benefited not the husband but the family as a whole. The interests of individuals were inextricable.[125]

The battle of words between the feminists and the Catholics gets to the heart of their respective concerns and brings us back to their most fundamental differences. While many moderates within the feminist movement, including Brunschvicg, were uncomfortable with the concept of endowment and thought children should be considered in the first instance a parental rather than a "social" responsibility,[126] and many others viewed payment to the mother largely as a question of practicality,[127] the pages of *La Française* were always open to those whose support for payment to the mother turned on their belief that the economic dependence of women upon men within the family was at the root of women's oppression. In 1938, Lydie Morel put this claim most uncompromisingly when she said:

> Far from favoring a sound and peaceable family life, where the man and the woman are equally called upon to make efforts and concessions to get along, the economic dependence of the married woman encourages male tyranny and vices, and creates households where the spouses are tied not because they wish it but because the one who holds economic power enslaves the other.[128]

---

[123] M. C., "Les droits de la femme," *La Française*, 28: 1199 (11 July 1936).
[124] M. C., "Les ménagères et les lois nouvelles – La maternité: Fonction sociale," *La Française*, 30: 1240 (9 Oct. 1937).
[125] Anne-Marie Louis Couvreur, "Valeur économique du travail ménager," *La Femme dans la Vie Sociale*, 12: 121 (June 1939).
[126] On Brunschvicg, see Cova, "Cécile Brunschvicg," pp. 87–90.
[127] [Mme Pichon-Landry], "Allocations familiales et travail féminine," *La Française*, 31: 1275 (3–10 Dec. 1938).
[128] Lydie Morel, *Le droit au travail de la femme mariée* (Geneva: Labor, 1937), p. 30; see also Marie Lenoël, "Le droit au travail de la femme mariée: Une visite à Mme Lydia Morel," *La Française*, 31: 1255 (5 Mar. 1938).

Catholic women, by contrast, subscribed to an organicist vision of functional differentiation and complementarity that eschewed virtually any idea of conflict, particularly within the family. In an article entitled "Two Philosophies," Butillard condemned "individualist" thought generally – and Kant, Rousseau, the Renaissance, the Reformation, eighteenth-century philosophes, and the secular feminists in particular – for their mistaken idea that the individual was an end in himself or herself. On the contrary, she said, the individual was incomplete; a social being, "he only finds in the association the possibility of being fully himself: family first,... then various associations."[129] The family, the providential union of complementary beings for human perpetuation, was more than the sum of its parts, its collective right greater than the individual right of each member. The UFCS's social theory in the end made its alliance with the pronatalists more logical than with the feminists, since the former shared its conviction that if justice to families were secured, individual rights would become largely irrelevant.

Arguments for payment to the mother were feminist attempts to reconcile the rhetoric of separate spheres with women's economic independence, yet even within the feminist movement they had their critics. A few isolated voices spoke up to say that the ideology of separate spheres was itself problematic. Maria Vérone of the Ligue Française pour les Droits des Femmes, Marie Lenoël of the Catholic but egalitarian Saint Joan's Social and Political Alliance, socialist Suzanne Buisson, communist Jeanne Rougé and others defended women's work outside the home as an essential condition of their personal growth as well as of economic freedom. Lenoël intervened at the UFCS's 1933 International Congress to say that married women's waged work was not only a fundamental right; it was also a necessary condition of intellectual, social, and moral development.[130] Rougé went further. Explicitly denouncing the UFCS's campaign, she said:

> The return of woman to the home, to the kitchen, that means wanting to shut the woman up in the narrow circle of the family, in the landscape of the stewpot of the husband and the chamberpot of the children. It means keeping her in domestic slavery. Eliminating the woman from production leaves her with one means of livelihood,

---

[129] Andrée Butillard, "Deux philosophies: Pour la mère au foyer," *La Femme dans la Vie Sociale*, 6: 64 (Nov. 1933).

[130] UFCS, *Le travail industriel de la mère* (1933), pp. 182–3. See also Maria Vérone, "Le travail de la femme mariée," *L'Oeuvre* (24 Oct. 1931).

the sale of her body: to one man by marriage or to many by prostitution.[131]

And while the conventional socialist call for "payment for motherhood" would solve the problem of women's economic dependence on a particular man, Suzanne Buisson worried that it too would define her as "a slave to nature," limiting her intellectual horizons and her participation in "the human struggle for progress."[132]

Lenoël, Buisson, and Rougé suggested that the problem of women's oppression was, in fact, only partly economic; a far deeper problem lay in considering women only as reproducers, thus excluding them from wider questions of public life. Yet the scope for feminist demands that both public and private life be equally shared between the sexes actually narrowed in the thirties. In the twenties, feminists demanding strict equality for men and women could find a haven in the Communist Party, but in its Popular Front phase the party exhibited a new tolerance for family policy, pronatalism, and separate spheres. The brave communist women who put out a tract in 1923 calling for the equal division of housework among all adult members of the family, or who in 1926 supported waged work as a means of making women conscious of the "masculine yoke" that oppressed them, had few successors a decade later.[133] In the atmosphere of the

---

[131] Jeanne Rougé, "Le retour de la femme au foyer," *Cahiers du Bolchevisme*, 10: 5 (1 Mar. 1933), pp. 296–8.

[132] Buisson questioned the call for endowment of motherhood issued by the 1st National Conference of Socialist Women in 1933, in *Les répercussions du travail féminin* (Paris: Librairie Populaire, 1934), pp. 21–4.

[133] Confédération Générale du Travail Unitaire [CGTU], Congrès, *Compte rendu*, 2 (1923), "Conférence féminine," pp. 615–6. The second reference is to a 1926 article by Marie Roncière, who opposed the ideal of the "femme au foyer" by writing: "So long as the woman stayed 'at home' she had no consciousness of the injustice of her lot, of the masculine yoke that oppressed her, of her state as unpaid servant, wetnurse and sicknurse. The day she left that home, she understood that she was oppressed as a worker like men themselves, but also as a wife (*femme*) by her husband. Bit by bit, she took an active part in social life, and wanted to throw off the two yokes that oppressed her: the yoke of the husband, the yoke of the boss (*patron*)" (Roncière, "La femme et son rôle social," *L'Ouvrière*, 5: 195 [27 May 1926]. By 1936, by contrast, one prominent woman publicist was arguing that while the Communist Party must reach out to women, it must remember that they had family duties and leave them enough time to fulfill their wifely obligations. The Communist Party must remember that communist women were also, in the end, *women*, "with the charm and physical weakness of their sex," and develop a politics suited to their abilities and special interests. Cilly Vassart, "Il nous faut gagner les femmes," *Cahiers du Bolchevisme*, 13: 16–17 (1 Oct. 1936), pp. 1103–14; idem, "Les femmes dans le Parti Communiste," *Cahiers du Bolchevisme*, 14: 1 (15 Jan. 1937), pp. 118–21.

thirties, the most women could hope for was to be allowed to work their double day in peace. Not even the ultraegalitarian Open Door International would resolve in favor of men doing the housework.[134]

If we want to capture the character of the debate over French family policy by 1939, it may be useful to ask not which policies were proposed but rather which had become impossible and almost unthinkable. The argument that became taboo in the France of the thirties was not that women should be paid for motherhood – the taboo argument in Britain – but rather that motherhood might be a matter of choice. Pronatalists who viewed women only as so many walking wombs were willing to pay them for increased production; Boverat was even able to convince the 1939 High Committee to propose the payment of all family benefits to the mother.[135] Although subject to sex-specific legislation and lower pay, married women in France retained a greater role in the labor market than did their British counterparts, and family benefits were often paid to the mother.[136] Yet was this admittedly circumscribed degree of economic independence in any way liberating for women? How meaningful were such payments in the absence of the most basic political rights or of an articulated theory of women's personhood outside of family roles?

Feminist historians have tended to see financial independence as the sine qua non of women's emancipation, but the history of French family policy leads us to question that assumption. Certainly French women had greater access both to wages and to cash social benefits than their British counterparts, but this access was a consequence of the structure of the French labor force and of pronatalist strategies

---

[134] In 1933, the third conference of the Open Door International passed a resolution defending married women's right to work. In the original version, the resolution said that married couples should share equally the work of cooking, cleaning, and child care; this resolution was amended to read simply that the additional work brought on by marriage was the "joint responsibility of husband and wife." Open Door International, *Report of the Third Conference* (1933), pp. 26–7. For a very unusual argument in favor of splitting the housework, see, Jacques Debu-Bridel, "Le foyer moderne: Vers une juste collaboration des époux à la maison comme au dehors," *Les Cahiers Féministes*, 3: 23 [Dec. 1934?], pp. 77–84.

[135] Despite this decision, when the decree was published some half of these provisions on payment to the mother had unaccountably vanished. In its final form, the Family Code provided for the payment of the bonus for the first birth to the mother, but the allowances for the children were payable to either the mother or the father. *JO Lois et Décrets*, 30 July 1939, p. 9610; Boverat, "Le Décret-loi," pp. 253–4.

[136] Allowances for children could be paid to either parent, but the mother's allowance was – like the birth bonus – payable by statute to the mother. See Andrée Jack, "la mise en application de l'allocation de 'la mère au foyer,' " *La Française*, 32: 1284 (15–22 Apr. 1939).

and not of a desire to extend women's individual rights, as mothers or as citizens. The pronatalist rhetoric of childbearing as a patriotic duty and Catholic doctrines of the unity of the family were so powerful, so verbose, as to limit the liberating potential of any family policy. Politically marginal, still voteless, French women found themselves facing pronatalists willing to pay for babies but not willing to take no for an answer. If pronatalists had their way, women would be endowed but unfree.

Furthermore, these economic benefits for women came under attack during Vichy, when the more coercive alternative to the proposal to "endow mothers" – blatant discrimination in the law and the labor market – gained a new lease on life. Vichy broke with the liberalism of the Third Republic with the passage of the law of 11 October 1940, which barred state services from hiring married women whose husbands were able to support them and envisaged methods with which to retire those currently employed. To this attempt to forcibly return mothers to the *foyer*, Vichy added the harsh repression of birth control and abortion, as well as a powerful campaign of propaganda aimed at increasing births.[137]

Vichy pronatalist propaganda was unsubtle and rather unpleasantly commercial, combining a blunt tabulation of the financial benefits available to the fertile with cloying descriptions of the happiness and healthiness of the well-stocked home.[138] Yet Vichy family policy as a whole, both in material and ideological terms, brought to fruition rather than repudiated the pronatalist agenda of the thirties. The attempted exclusion of married women from the labor market, if never actually enforced by the regime, had been an ideal of many interwar pronatalists, while the egregious propaganda disseminated by the state often echoed (or was published by) the Alliance Nationale. Even the harsh repression of abortion, often viewed as typically expressive of Vichy ideas, was prefigured in Boverat's programs in the thirties. As early as 1935, Boverat called for mobile police units to catch abortionists and a mitigation of the medical rules of professional secrecy in the case of abortion prosecutions. In 1939, when Boverat

---

[137] On Vichy policy toward women and the family, see Bordeaux, "Femmes hors d'état," and Sarah Fishman, *We Will Wait: Wives of French Prisoners of War, 1940–1945* (New Haven, Conn.: Yale University Press, 1991), pp. 42–5.

[138] There is a good collection of Vichy propaganda toward women in SAN 7545 and 7548 at the Ministry of Labor, Paris. This includes a rather astonishing Alliance Nationale leaflet reviving the eighteenth-century idea that sperm is necessary to women's health. See "Les dangers des pratiques anticonceptionnelles" (Alliance Nationale, 1944), in SAN 7545.

claimed that France was losing 400,000 births per year to abortion, the Catholic church joined with the Alliance Nationale to begin a major offensive against abortion.[139]

If Vichy policy built on the legacy of the thirties, it also left its mark on the character of the postwar system. The one area in which Vichy was truly innovative was in replacing the unwaged mother's allowance by a larger allowance paid to all families with dependent children living on a single wage. Vichy policymakers were influenced in this action by the hope of aiding the displaced families and large numbers of wives of prisoners left economically vulnerable during the war.[140] But the single-wage allowance retained its important place after 1945, when the De Gaulle government forced the *caisses* in each *département* to amalgamate and took administration out of employers' hands. With the act of 22 August 1946, the government then extended family benefits, increasing the rates of both children's allowances and the single-wage allowance.

Insofar as French family policy came to affect gender roles, it was through the strengthening of this allowance for families with dependent children living on a single wage. Yet this allowance was not necessarily paid to families with a male wage earner and dependent wife. Since the only requirement for its receipt was that only one substantial wage enter the household, it could also have benefited divorced or single parents; furthermore, the presence of an additional wage earner did not disqualify a family from receipt, provided the second wage amounted to less than one-third (or, in some cases, one-half) the primary wage. The single-wage allowance, although substantial in size, far from made up for the loss of a full wage, and social security administrators argued it had no measurable effect on married women's labor force participation as a whole. Nevertheless, it probably encouraged married women with small children to give up or curtail earning, since in the early sixties some 90% of families receiving benefits for two or more dependent children were also benefiting from the single-wage allowance; by 1970, that figure had fallen only to

---

[139] See Fernand Boverat, "L'avortement est assimilable à l'assassinat," CSN, *Rapports*, 1935: no. 4, 27ᵉ sess. (June 1935) and 1935: no. 1, 26ᵉ sess. (Jan 1935), pp. 31–9; idem, *Le massacre des innocents* (Alliance Nationale [1939]), in Ministry of Labor Archives, SAN 7733, File: "Danger de la dépopulation."

[140] Sauvy, *La vie économique*, p. 202. On the hardships faced by prisoner-of-war wives during Vichy, see Fishman, *We Will Wait*, and idem, "Waiting for the Captive Sons of France: Prisoner of War Wives, 1940–1945," in Margaret Higonnet et al., eds., *Behind the Lines: Gender and the Two World Wars* (New Haven, Conn.: Yale University Press, 1987), pp. 182–93.

slightly below 80%. The single-wage allowance thus operated de facto if not de jure to favor a particular type of family structure. In 1955–6, this "favoring" was made explicit, when the government introduced an unwaged mother's allowance for the self-employed in agriculture and other sectors who had been ineligible for the single-wage allowance.[141]

During the first three decades after the war, then, French family policy came to some extent to serve a "gendering" function, privileging families with a male wage earner and dependent wife or a wife employed part-time. Yet policymakers always seemed uncomfortable with the single-wage and unwaged mother's allowances, particularly when women's labor force participation rates began climbing in the sixties and seventies: despite the large number of families benefiting, they were allowed to decline in real value, and in 1972 eligibility was limited through the introduction of a means test.[142] Finally, in 1978, the government once again broke with the principle of constructing benefits around women's labor market status rather than children's needs, replacing the unwaged mother's allowance, the single-wage allowance, and an allowance previously available to defray child care costs with a special bonus (the *complément familial*) for families below a moderate income ceiling with at least three children *or* with a child under age 3, which these families could use to finance day care or to compensate for lost wages, as they chose.[143] By 1987, when an aston-

---

[141] The preceding account is drawn from Pierre Laroque, *Social Welfare in France* (Paris: La Documentation Française, 1966), pp. 455–7, and Nicole Questiaux and Jacques Fournier, "France," in Sheila Kamerman and Alfred J. Kahn, eds., *Family Policy: Government and Families in Fourteen Countries* (New York: Columbia University Press, 1978), p. 139.

[142] The single-wage allowance appeared at first glance to be more substantial than it really was, since it was set at 40% of a basic wage for a family with two children in 1963, while the children's allowances were only 22% of the basic wage. These percentages are extremely misleading, however, for the "basic wage" was set at a smaller figure when calculating the single-wage allowance; thus, a Parisian family with two children received about Fr 71 in children's allowances and Fr 78 in the single-wage allowance, while one with four children received Fr 283 in children's allowances and Fr 97 in the single-wage allowance (Laroque, *Social Welfare in France*, p. 456). And the relative importance of the single-wage allowance steadily declined. By 1970, the mean children's allowance for a family with four children had reached Fr 5,560, but the single-wage allowance was less than a fifth of that amount, at Fr 1,071 (Questiaux and Fournier, "France," p. 139).

[143] Questiaux and Fournier, "France," p. 140; Colin Birks, "Social Welfare Provision in France," in Roslyn Ford and Mono Chakrabarti, eds., *Welfare Abroad: An Introduction to Welfare Provision in Seven Countries* (Edinburgh: Scottish Academic Press, 1987), pp. 74–5.

ishing 70.6% of women between the ages of 25 and 54 were in the labor force (up from 44.5% in 1968), any economic incentive for women to stay home had disappeared.[144] French family policy returned to its most fundamental principles, redistributing income from families without children to those with children, with little regard to gender relations within the families they aided.[145]

Conclusion

In tracing the development of family policies on both sides of the Channel, we have found that economic interest groups often played a major role in determining outcomes. This was perhaps to be expected, since policies like family allowances directly affected wages. More surprising, perhaps, is the extraordinary influence of pronatalists – a group not identifiable with any clear political wing or economic interest group – in pushing forward the redistributive logic of French policy in the thirties. Pronatalists, drawing in part on a rich French tradition of organicist and illiberal thought, were able to identify themselves as the spokesmen for a legitimate corporate interest: "the family." Pronatalism thus became common sense in France much the way the male right to maintain did in Britain, but pronatalists were far more successful than any group in Britain at identifying their goals with the national good, and were largely delegated authority over the formation of policies for the "interest" they represented.

In the end, pronatalist consensus had a major effect on French family policy but did not utterly transform it. Business strategies in the twenties had left French family policy with a particular imprint: allowances were strongly tied to wages and were financed by direct levies on employers. These aspects were encoded in the 1932 law and were never contested. State control and the incorporation of pronatalists into political decision making pushed the logic of family-based

[144] Labor force participation rates by age and sex are given by Jean-Claude Chesnais, "Les hommes et l'économie: La croissance et les changements structurels," in Jacques Dupâquier, ed., *Histoire de la population française*, vol. 4, *De 1914 à nos jours* (Paris: Presses Universitaires de France, 1988), p. 356.

[145] Jean-Claude Chesnais argues that French family policy does seem to have been successful in moderating French demographic decline. Whereas French population growth lagged behind that of many of its Continental neighbors in the interwar period, France experienced a more sustained "baby boom" after 1945 and a less precipitous population decline in the seventies and eighties than did Europe as a whole. See Chesnais, "La politique de population française depuis 1914," in Dupâquier, ed., *Histoire de la Population Française*, vol. 4, p. 214.

redistribution forward, extending allowances to groups unreachable by industry, but such growth did not change the system's essential character. Furthermore, the main challenge to the character of this parental welfare state – the Catholic attempt to use family policy to revive a traditional family structure – had mixed results. Policies addressing sexual relations within the family fit uncomfortably within the broader French framework of wage-based policy, and Catholics, being largely irrelevant within policy-making circles, could only achieve their goals by delivering over their campaign to the pronatalists. The campaign to strengthen the gender-based character of policy came to only dubious (and temporary) fruition during Vichy.

CONCLUSION

[Professor Gray] seems to regard the Equality of Wage System as an ultimate and a dispensation of nature. It is neither. What the French have achieved is much better worth study by the Professor and the leaders of the movement in England than the theoretical issues that are raised so gratuitously.

John Murray, "Review of Alexander Gray's *Family Endowment*," *Eugenics Review* (Oct. 1927)

Family policy is often wage policy in another guise. What the French achieved with their system of family allowances that John Murray thought so worthy of study was not the pure addition to wages that British socialists hoped for, nor ultimately the wage restraint French employers intended, but rather a simple redistribution of the wage bill in accordance with family needs. Employers, and later the state, sequestered a portion of the general wage bill and paid it out only to workers with dependent children, thus effectively distributing the cost of children among the population. One could perhaps fault this system for not remedying wider inequalities of income distribution across class lines, but it is arguable that this worthy goal is not best achieved through family policy.

The British, faced with the same problem of the lack of fit between wages and family needs, chose a different solution. By holding to the ideal of the male family wage, they protected the integrity and superiority of male wages as a whole, but at the cost of any more precise pegging of wages to family needs. French policies reflected what I have termed a "parental" logic of welfare while British choices exhibited a "male breadwinner" logic, since in the former some portion of the earnings of all adults was forcibly expended in the support of all children, while in the latter both wage and benefit income was

413

Table C.1. *Breakdown of social insurance and family allowance benefits, 1960–85*

	France			United Kingdom		
	Family		Other	Family		Other
Date	allowances	Pensions	insurance[a]	allowances	Pensions	insurance[a]
1960	35.0	30.8	34.2	11.5	66.6	21.9
1965	28.0	32.4	40.7	8.9	69.2	21.9
1970	20.7[b]	35.5	43.8	12.2	63.3	23.5
1975	15.1[b]	42.1	42.8	7.3	75.8	16.9
1980	14.1[b]	41.3	44.3	10.4	42.8	46.8
1985	14.6[b]	43.9	41.5	10.7	45.4	43.8

Note: Figures are percentages.
[a] Including sickness, accident, and unemployment insurance.
[b] Includes only family allowances paid under the general system. Payments by the exempted autonomous funds (for miners, railway workers, and so on) are included under "Pensions." In the 1950s slightly less than 60% of all family allowances were paid through the general system. These figures thus underestimate the importance of family allowances by at least one-third.
Sources: International Labour Office, *The Cost of Social Security: Eighth International Enquiry* (Geneva, ILO, 1976); ILO, *The Cost of Social Security: Thirteenth International Enquiry* (Geneva, ILO, 1992).

directed disproportionately to men in the expectation that some would use it to support dependent wives and children.

Once chosen, these two lines of development became self-reinforcing. While both countries did, in time, develop both comprehensive insurance against loss of earnings and universal child benefit policies, the preferences established by 1945 proved lasting. Although the French did systematize and reform their social security system in 1945, unemployment insurance was not introduced until 1958, and family benefits remained a central feature of the French welfare state. As Table C.1 shows, such benefits accounted for a far larger proportion of total spending on pensions, insurance, and allowances in France than in Britain in 1960, and while the proportion of spending on family benefits has certainly declined in France over the past twenty-five years,[1]

---

[1] Yet while the French have come to target some family benefits, they have identified deserving families more by number of children or family type than by parental occupation or income. The unwillingness of French policymakers to use family policies to redistribute income across class lines has drawn criticism; see especially Jean-Pierre Jallade, "Redistribution in the Welfare State: An Assessment of the French Performance," in

the current practice of including only payments made by the national family allowances fund under the rubric of allowances in the French statistics has meant that this decline has often been overstated. If payments through the semiprivate funds amounted to no more than one-third of all family benefits in the eighties (a conservative estimate), family benefits would still absorb more than 20% of all spending on pensions, insurance, and allowances, compared with 15.3% in Sweden, 10.7% in the United Kingdom, and 4% in the Federal Republic of Germany. Comparative research by Michael O'Higgins confirms the *relative* decline but continued *absolute* superiority of French family benefits. Between 1960 and 1985, the percentage of Gross Domestic Product going to family benefits fell from 3.8% to 2.8% in France, while in Britain it grew from 0.6% to 1.9%; by comparison, Swedish benefits hovered between 1.2% and 1.6%, and German benefits fluctuated between 0.3% (in 1960), 1.4% (in 1975), and 0.8% (in 1984).[2]

Family policies remain central to the French welfare state partly because the logic on which they operate is supported across the political spectrum and is popular within society as a whole. In Britain, by contrast, family allowances remain a subordinate and contested part of a welfare system organized largely around the wage. Postwar Labour governments often found it difficult to transfer money "from wallet to purse," while Conservative governments preferred means-tested family benefits targeted at the poorest families alone. The extent of poverty among low-wage and single-parent families has meant that spending on such policies has continued to rise (as O'Higgins's figures show), yet entitlements for children have never won the British public's affection to the extent that the National Health Service has done – the long campaigns of the Child Poverty Action Group notwithstanding. Rather, and precisely because such benefits are identified as "antipoverty" measures, they have been resented as less acceptable than – or even barriers to – decent wages. The principle that living standards should be equalized between the childless and

Jallade, ed., *The Crisis of Redistribution in European Welfare States* (Stoke-on-Trent: Trentham, 1988), pp. 221–53. More typical, however, is the response of Jean-Claude Chesnais, whose strenous objections to the targeting of family benefits and the tendency to prefer spending on pensions to spending on children are detailed in "La politique de population française depuis 1914," in Jacques Dupâquier, ed., *Histoire de la population française*, vol. 4 (Paris: Presses Universitaires de France, 1988), pp. 181–231.

2   Michael O'Higgins, "The Allocation of Public Resources to Children and the Elderly in OECD Countries," in John L. Palmer, Timothy Smeeding, and Barbara Boyle Torrey, eds., *The Vulnerable* (Washington, D.C.: Urban Institute Press, 1988), pp. 214–15.

Table C.2. *Spending on social security schemes as a percentage of GDP, selected European countries, 1960–85*

Date	France	Germany (FRG)	Sweden	United Kingdom
1960ᵃ	13.2	15.5	11.0	10.8
1965ᵃ	15.6	16.5	13.8	11.8
1970	15.1	17.1	18.6	13.7
1975	23.9	23.7	25.0	17.1
1980	26.3	24.0	31.9	18.1
1985	28.7	23.8	30.7	20.3

Note: Includes pensions and other forms of insurance, family allowances, medical care, and income maintenance programs.
ᵃ Figures for the U.K. are from 1959–60 and 1964–5.
Sources: See Table C.1.

those with children even within any given social class – a principle at the very heart of French family policy – is neither well understood nor widely supported.[3]

Family policies thus continue to hold a very different place in the two countries, a fact that has had a profound impact on the health and well-being of both the dependent children whose life chances they are designed to enhance and indeed the two welfare states themselves. In the last decades, French welfare provisions have come to rival or surpass those offered by states conventionally considered more advanced. As Table C.2 shows, the rates of French spending on social welfare have grown steadily over the last twenty-five years; by 1986, such spending amounted to $3,829 per head of population, compared with $4,908 in Sweden, $3,705 in Germany, and a mere $1,885 in the United Kingdom. Historians and social scientists have begun to recognize that the complex and confusing institutions developed between the wars served as the foundation for this success;[4] certainly the administrative and distributional choices established by the family allowance funds have contributed to this growth and stability. The jealousy with which interwar employers clung to their creations and

[3] For the very different reception of family policy by public opinion in two countries, see especially, John Baker, "Comparing National Priorities: Family and Population Policy in Britain and France," *Journal of Social Policy*, 15: 4 (Oct. 1986), pp. 421–42.

[4] This revisionist literature is discussed in the Introduction, but for a particularly coherent view, see Douglas E. Ashford, "Advantages of Complexity: Social Insurance in France," in John S. Ambler, ed., *The French Welfare State: Surviving Social and Ideological Change* (New York: New York University Press, 1991), pp. 32–57.

Table C.3. *Breakdown of contributions for social insurance and family allowances, 1960–85*

	France			United Kingdom		
Date	Employers	Employees	State	Employers	Employees	State
1960	68.9	18.9	6.9	34.4	34.2	28.6
1965	67.8	20.5	6.6	37.5	36.1	22.9
1970	n.a.	n.a.	n.a.	39.2	34.4	23.8
1975	66.2	22.3	6.3	46.5	30.4	20.6
1980	60.2	26.2	9.2	25.9	17.9	53.6
1985	55.0	27.1	11.1	25.6	24.9	47.7

Note: Figures are percentages for major sources of funding only. Small amounts from special taxes, other authorities, or capital income are excluded.
Sources: See Table C.1.

the agility with which they schemed to retain administrative and financial control find their legacy today in the state's continued tolerance of semiautonomous and industrially based funds. In keeping with such interwar preferences, France also continues to fund its welfare state largely out of employers' contributions: as Table C.3 shows, in 1985 fully 55% of the cost of the social security and family allowance systems was still met in this way. In Britain, by contrast, the proportion of these costs met directly by the state rose to more than 50% by 1980 and has remained quite high, a pattern of funding that has deepened the vulnerability of such programs to political attacks.

For the men, women, and children who live within these structures, the impact of such divergent development has been equally profound. From the standpoint of families with dependent children alone, considered apart from the troubling questions of the individual claims of mothers and fathers, there is no question but that the French system of family allowances has proven far more effective at safeguarding a decent standard of living than has the British pursuit of the elusive family wage. The fact that family allowances in France have been kept relatively independent of parental occupations and roles has meant that families with dependent children do quite well in France across a wide variety of family types. By contrast, and as empirical studies have shown, the relative underdevelopment of redistributive family policies in Britain has left British families with dependent children poorer than comparable French families not only absolutely but also in relation to childless families within the same social class. And while family policies in the early eighties did succeed in lifting substantial numbers of children out of poverty in both countries, poverty rates remained worryingly high in Britain for children in one-parent families.[5]

The question of outcomes is not so simple, however, especially when we break down the family and consider the impact of such policies on gender relations, a subject the French often hoped to avoid but that was always at the heart of the British policy debate. Social policy is often seen as a reflection of persistent social realities and, as we have seen, is heavily marked by the structure of the labor market and the patterns of maintenance and dependence prevalent in society at the point of its articulation. But policies can also react back on relations of authority and dependence in public and private, challenging or upholding particular social behaviors or choices. Reformers and policymakers were not blind to these possibilities, but they did not always predict accurately how men and women would respond. The effects of family policies on gender relations were profound but also somewhat unexpected.

Conceptions of appropriate male roles and entitlements lay at the core of the British social insurance system as it developed in the 1930s. For men, the primary distinction between the unemployment *insurance* scheme and the *assistance* system to which they were relegated

---

[5] Empirical studies underscore the real differences in living standards of comparable families in the two countries. For an analysis based on 1971 figures, see P. E. Dawson, "Family Benefits and Income Redistribution in France and the United Kingdom, 1891–1971," Ph.D. diss., University of York, 1979. An eight-country study directed by A. J. Kahn and Sheila Kamerman in the early eighties also found French policy to be the most generous except for Sweden (which equalizes incomes in large part through heavy taxes on the better-off). Moreover, they add, France's "generosity is the most consistent among all the countries we have explored." Britain ranked fourth in this study, behind Sweden, France, and Germany, but ahead of Canada, Australia, Israel, and the United States. Large families and unemployed workers not on training schemes did relatively poorly in Britain. See Alfred J. Kahn and Sheila B. Kamerman, *Income Transfers for Families with Children: An Eight-Country Study* (Philadelphia: Temple University Press, 1983). Kamerman and Kahn's essay in the recent comparative volume on policies toward children and the elderly underscores the effectiveness of French family policy: in 1984, they note, family benefits succeeded in reducing potential poverty rates from 18% to 5% in two-parent families and from 37% to 14% in single-parent families; Kamerman and Kahn, "Social Policy and Children in the United States and Europe," in Palmer et al., eds., *The Vulnerable*, p. 357. By contrast, Timothy Smeeding, Barbara Boyle Torrey, and Martin Rein's study of data published between 1979 and 1982 found that 38.6% of children in one-parent families and 9.5% of children in two-parent families in the United Kingdom remained in poverty even after taxes and transfers; Smeeding, Torrey, and Rein, "Patterns of Income and Poverty: The Economic Status of Children and the Elderly in Eight Countries," in ibid., p. 102.

when their insurance period expired was that the former presumed they were the breadwinners of their families, while the latter stripped them of that status by requiring that the earnings of other family members be used to support them. It was precisely this state enforcement of familial interdependence, without regard for the hierarchies of sex and generation, that Beveridge and other liberals found intolerable and pledged to eradicate, not only by perfecting the insurance system but also by introducing policies to guarantee full employment.

From the point of view of women – and especially married women – the trajectory was quite different. Women had trouble throughout the interwar period claiming the identity of worker, since the marriage bar, protective legislation, union restrictions and indeed cultural norms all turned on the assumption that marriage was for them, under normal circumstances, incompatible with waged work. Social insurance mirrored this assumption. Married women did not confront the same disheartening loss of status when moving from unemployment insurance to assistance in the thirties because they never held the same status in the first place. After the passage of the anomalies regulations, even married women with long records of employment and years of paid-up contributions had to go to extraordinary lengths to prove that they were regular wage earners and hence entitled to benefits. Through these dual processes – restricting women's access to work and denying equal treatment in insurance – the British welfare state institutionalized the very relations of dependence it took as normative.

Yet once a system was established premised on the principle of male maintenance of families, the very condition that made it credible – low rates of married women's employment – collapsed. The proportion of married women in the "official" labor market hovered around 10% in the interwar period; by 1961, this proportion had risen to 35% and by 1989 to fully 57%.[6] For married women, the social policies adopted by postwar governments proved doubly dysfunctional. Although family allowances were paid by statute to women, these remained very small, and housewives' status within insurance was long determined by their husbands' position. Furthermore, married

---

[6] In the spring of 1989, 76% of men and 53% of women over age 16 were in the labor force. Married women were actually more likely to be employed than were the unmarried (57% of married women were employed versus 46% of unmarried women), but this may be due to high unemployment rates and the continuation in school of many younger women. Married women were, however, far more likely to work part-time: 52% of all married working women worked part-time, as compared with 25% of unmarried working women and only 5% of working men. See Office of Population Censuses and Surveys, *Labour Force Survey, 1988 and 1989* (London: HMSO, 1991), p. 15.

women (especially those working part-time) often retained that dependent welfare status even when employed, being usually exempt from the normal insurance scheme compulsory for men and single women. Such policies enshrined women's disadvantaged status in the labor market. When married women reentered (or even remained in) the labor force in Britain, they did so explicitly as secondary workers, working in segregated jobs at low pay.

In France, by contrast, the employers who created the *caisses* exhibited little concern for the impact of their policies on gender relations within the family. In cases where the *caisses* chose to pay directly to the mother, allowances substantially redistributed income within the household, yet without being considered a measure of "women's rights." Nor did family allowances push women out of the work force, and in fact labor force participation rates for women between the ages of 25 and 54 expanded from 43% in 1954 to 71% in 1987.[7] The expanded single-wage allowance after the Second World War enabled married women with small children to stay home but did not force them to do so and could just as adequately have supplemented the income of divorced or single parents. As the doyen of the French social security system, Pierre Laroque, explained, the liberalism of French family policy was a deliberate policy choice:

> The terms and conditions of benefits show the *absence of an overall plan for families.* There was undoubtedly a strong temptation to impose on beneficiaries conditions inspired by the ideological basis of demographic and family policy. Generally speaking, the authorities have rejected the idea of using this kind of pressure in this way.[8]

By targeting children, rather than the particular functional activities of breadwinning or full-time child rearing, French policymakers left negotiations over gender roles to individual women and men.

Policies with such profound implications force us to search for the causes underlying dissimilar outcomes. We cannot explain them by reference to the campaigns of public-spirited reformers alone. As we have seen, a wide variety of groups put forward competing visions of the appropriate place of the family within the distributive system and of the allowable degree of state intervention, but not all were successful. This study has argued that an examination of the articulation

---

[7] Jean–Claude Chesnais, "Les hommes et l'économie: La croissance et les changements structurels," Dupâquier, ed., *Histoire de la population française*, vol. 4, p. 356.

[8] Pierre Laroque, comp., *Social Welfare in France* (Paris: La Documentation Française, 1966), p. 447.

and reception of claims on behalf of dependent children or based on normative ideals of family life within the realms both of public debate and of political and economic negotiation can help us understand the final shape of policies.

The articulation of policy agendas and the range of groups with the capacity to influence debate were quite different in Britain and France. Debate in Britain was noticeably more open, and far more attuned to the individual claims of specific family members, apart from their corporate identity. A generation of public activism gave British women a powerful voice in questions relating to the family; similarly, a concern to mitigate social inequality, shared by Liberal and Labour supporters alike, made class an inescapable part of all discussions. The merits of a redistribution across class and gender lines – as well as between the childless and those with children – were thus from the outset part of the family policy debate. Yet complexity of debate did not necessarily lead to success; campaigns for family allowances in Britain derailed when encumbered by transformative ideals they were unable to bear. Nevertheless, the degree to which feminists and socialists dominated the debate (if not the enactment) of family policy in Britain is striking, particularly when compared with the French case.

In France, family policy was, from the outset, a conservative crusade – its articulation, for the most part, confined to a landscape dominated by nationalists, pronatalists, and social Catholics. The vision of distributive justice held by these groups was at once simpler and less controversial than that held by British campaigners. Rather than link entitlements to the performance of particular gender roles, they isolated the family as a social unit, and put forward a vision of social equality in which the injustices suffered by individuals dwindled into insignificance when contrasted with the hardships inflicted on those "patriotic" couples producing children for *la patrie*. Children's dependence was thus isolated as an urgent social problem apart from the quite different issues of wage levels or women's inequality.

Yet to say French policy conceived of the family as a legitimate social unit – rather than as the private property of an individual man or as a tense partnership between two individuals with limited common interests – is not to say that most policymakers did not have a deeply conventional view of appropriate relations between the sexes and in the home. Frenchmen were quite as attached as Britons to the ideal of the *mère au foyer*; they by no means created a more egalitarian system out of concern for women's rights. To the contrary – and counterintuitively – it was precisely because this domestic ideal was directly challenged in France only by forces on the margins of the bourgeois polity that the redistribution of income to children, and even in some cases to wives, seemed unproblematic for domestic relations. It was because gender relations were so deeply contested in Britain that proposals to aid children almost inevitably degenerated into rather unseemly battles between those representing the rival interests of mothers and fathers. If feminist campaigns succeeded in identifying family policy with women's emancipation, they did so at the cost of reminding politicians, civil servants, trade unionists, and social scientists of exactly why they found such policies objectionable and of deepening these groups' attachment to the defense of men's breadwinner status.

Different redistributive agendas, and the degree to which such agendas became encumbered with more controversial questions of women's emancipation or containment, thus go some way toward explaining different policy outcomes. Yet we cannot construct an explanation out of rhetoric and representation alone. The relative ease of French policy development was the result not of right-wing dominance of the debate, but rather of the affinity between the framework offered by those who shaped public debate and the interests of those with the capacity to introduce comprehensive measures. Similarly, British policy developments were uneven and sometimes contradictory because of the real incompatibility between the rhetorical presentation of redistributive family policies and the interests of those (often less vocal) groups capable of blocking their introduction. The translation of proposals into concrete programs depended, in the end, on the conjuncture – often fortuitous and unplanned – between the rhetorical formulations of activists and the interests of groups with the ability to force the hand of the state – or, alternatively, to circumvent the state entirely.

An understanding of the institutional structure of policy-making, and of the interests and capacities of groups active within it, has thus been the second key to our explanation. Discussion of political capacity has usually meant, in the literature on policy-making, a discussion of the state,[9] but, as was shown in France, this need not be the case.

---

[9] Theda Skocpol being, of course, the notable proponent of the trend toward "bringing the state back in." Yet it should be noted that Skocpol has herself warned against replacing unsatisfying society-centered explanations with equally inadequate state-determinist models. A complete explanation, she argues, must "examine states *in relation to* particular kinds of socioeconomic and political environments populated by actors with given interests and resources." See Skocpol, "Bringing the State Back In: Strategies of Analysis

While widespread public hostility to state intervention and a limited ability to tax did curtail the scope of French legislative action, social programs could be (and were) developed by business associations hoping to control their work force and to undermine pressures to pay a male family wage. The capacity and vigor of these organizations in the absence of comparable state initiatives has been overlooked largely because employers successfully operated comprehensive and often coercive labor and wage policies through the medium of seemingly benevolent, family-centered social programs. This discovery confirms and extends recent revisionist claims concerning the vitality of French business in the interwar period.[10]

The British trade union movement – or, more precisely, the General Council of the Trades Union Congress – did not have the same opportunities and capacities as French employers, but it was not so weak as scholars have often supposed. Both Hugh Heclo and Mary Ruggie, in careful comparative accounts of the development of social policies in Britain and Sweden, note that the TUC has rarely played an active role in the development of social policy. Ruggie in particular takes this as a sign of labor's weakness; the British polity, she argues, is far less "corporatist" than that of Sweden, and labor has remained an unequal, junior partner.[11] Margaret Weir and Theda Skocpol similarly argue that the paucity of welfare innovation in interwar Britain demonstrates the inability of labor organizations to make their interests felt.[12]

in Current Research," in Peter Evans, Dietrich Rueschemeyer, and Theda Skocpol, eds., *Bringing the State Back In* (Cambridge University Press, 1985), p. 19.

[10] For a survey of literature upholding the revisionist argument, see Robert Aldrich, "Late-Comer or Early-Starter? New Views on French Economic History," *Journal of European Economic History*, 16: 1 (Spring 1987), pp. 89–100. Also see Patrick Fridenson and André Straus, *Le capitalisme français, XIXᵉ–XXᵉ siècle: Blocages et dynamismes d'une croissance* (Paris: Fayard, 1987).

[11] Hugh Heclo, *Modern Social Politics in Britain and Sweden* (New Haven, Conn.: Yale University Press, 1974), esp. p. 300; Mary Ruggie, *The State and Working Women: A Comparative Study of Britain and Sweden* (Princeton, N.J.: Princeton University Press, 1984), pp. 18, 298–9.

[12] Margaret Weir and Theda Skocpol, noting the presence of a large industrial working class, powerful trade unions, and a Labour government at the onset of the depression, claim that the "the first full-employment welfare state should have been launched in Britain, if these models [attributing social policy outcomes to the degree of working-class strength] adequately explain public policy development." See Weir and Skocpol, "State Structures and the Possibilities for 'Keynesian' Responses to the Great Depression in Sweden, Britain, and the United States," in Peter Evans, Dietrich Rueschemeyer, and Theda Skocpol, eds., *Bringing the State Back In* (Cambridge University Press, 1985), p. 114.

Yet can the failure of British unions to achieve policies lessening the dependence of workers' families on wages be taken as a sign of labor's weakness when, as we have seen, unions exhibited little interest in such goals? I would argue, on the contrary, that the continued "liberalism" of the system of industrial relations in interwar Britain and the protection of the wage from "political" intervention should be seen as achievements of the British union movement, and were in many respects directly in its interest. Family allowances were often introduced on the Continent by employers eager to restrain wages and control workers; inasmuch as they were financed out of wages and paid to wives, they redistributed income decisively against the interests of organized men. The fact that such policies did not develop in Britain at a time when they garnered a good deal of political support on the Continent was a sign both of the limits to British employers' capacity to rework wage and welfare policies independently, and of politicians' acceptance of the legitimacy of the TUC's interest in matters relating to wages. The TUC may not have been able to force the introduction of policies it favored, but its presence did prevent employers from contemplating, and the state from sanctioning, social policies so antithetical to the old ideal of the man's responsibility to maintain.

In demonstrating the crucial importance of economic interest groups in the shaping of social policy, this study by no means seeks to rehabilitate arguments that attribute the emergence of welfare states to the relative strength of various "class interests."[13] Rather, I hope to have demonstrated that while economic organizations often do exercise a significant and sometimes dominant influence over policy formation, their interests cannot be reduced to those of "class" alone. Before we conclude that economic organizations are relatively powerless and that the primary locus of social policy formation is the hallways of government office buildings, we must explain not only

---

[13] Theda Skocpol has been a sharp critic of arguments that see the degree of "working-class strength" as *the* key determinant of welfare policies, pointing out that the strength of labor movements does not correlate in any simple way with social policy; see, e.g., Ann Shola Orloff and Theda Skocpol, "Why Not Equal Protection? Explaining the Politics of Public Social Spending in Britain, 1900–1911, and the United States, 1880s–1920," *American Sociological Review*, 49: 6 (Dec. 1984), pp. 726–50. While I am indebted to this work, I feel that such a finding should lead us not only to pay more attention to the political and institutional context within which labor movements operate, but also to question whether labor movements do in fact necessarily reflect "class interest." Mike Savage is, I believe, on the right track in attempting to specify the conditions under which labor organizations prefer economistic strategies to universalistic social policies; see, Savage, *The Dynamics of Working-Class Politics: The Labour Movement in Preston, 1880–1940* (Cambridge University Press, 1987).

why organizations do not bring about the policies historians think they "should" have brought about, but also why they often exhibit little interest in such policies. To assess accurately the role of such organizations in the formation of social policy, we must cease to treat aggregate class defense as the sole or even primary "interest" underlying the actions of economic interest groups; we must look instead at their position, composition, and the real pattern of preferences revealed by their actions. Such an examination often uncovers deep and crosscutting commitments to particular sectional or gender interests, to the maintenance of the organization's influence and stability, or to a vision of respectable family life.

The cases of British trade unions and French employers' associations again underscore these points. During the First World War, the claims of craft overrode those of class unity within the trade unions, while in the case of family policy, unions represented the specific occupational and gender interests of their members – male, better-paid, disproportionately skilled workers – far better than the "interests" of the working class as a whole.[14] Similarly, the willingness of French employers to introduce comprehensive welfare programs was rooted in the capacity of such programs to restrain wages during a period of inflation and within specific industrial sectors, but employers also sought to exploit conflicts between husbands and wives and to promote ideals of domestic harmony in order to restrain the radicalism of working men. In both cases, then, their strategic choices revealed intersecting and sometimes contradictory interests of organization, gender, culture, and class.

In seeking to defend or disaggregate the family wage, both employers and trade unionists – and indeed pronatalists and feminists – constantly evoked the interests of the child; as we have seen, however, none did so disinterestedly. Children, like Marx's peasants, could not represent themselves and had to be represented, and their well-being was shamelessly linked to efforts to increase the population, stabilize the labor force, restore paternal authority, or emancipate

---

[14] Violet Markham of the Unemployment Assistance Board recognized the distance between an expansive rhetoric of class solidarity and the narrow construction of union interest when faced by the Building Workers' Union's implacable resistance to the hiring of any unemployed workers for public works, since such schemes would – at least in theory – reduce the possibility that union members would be hired for such work. "In the interests of accuracy," she complained in her autobiography, "I am moved to point out that the protection of privilege can take place as fully within the ranks of the workers as in other, more exalted spheres." Markham, *Return Passage* (Oxford University Press, 1953), p. 210.

wives. Such linkages profoundly affected the fate and character of policies, and while some of these linkages have been broken, others remain. The propensity in many states to base social benefits on normative definitions of gender roles has too often left us with welfare systems that define us only in functional terms and minimize our choices. To argue that welfare states should be liberalized in many areas is not to argue, however, that the state should pay no attention to the problem of family welfare or poverty. The support and care of children is too weighty a burden for many parents to meet alone; comprehensive family policies distribute that burden not only toward the better-off and the childless but also, like old-age pensions, across the working life. One need not subscribe to the unpalatable theories of interwar French pronatalists to conclude that children should be seen in part as a collective charge, their welfare not made hostage to the concern either to promote particular domestic relations or to recruit and manage particular groups of workers. Unless one intends to visit the sins – or, in the case of poverty, the misfortunes – of the parents upon the children, a greater recognition of the claims of children forms a necessary pillar to any modern welfare state.

BIBLIOGRAPHY

This study was based very largely on official records and on the archives and published records of key organizations. Since specific documents are identified fully in the notes, Sections 1 and 2 of this bibliography list only the principal classes of official and organizational records consulted; Section 3 lists archives of individuals. Section 4 lists key periodicals and Section 5 important contemporary articles and essays; in both cases, less essential or ephemeral materials do not appear but are cited (when necessary) in the notes. Section 6 provides a bibliography of the key scholarly works consulted. Only this last section lists works on Britain and France together; in other sections materials for the two countries are listed separately.

1. Official records and publications

Britain

Government Actuary's Office (ACT 1), Cabinet (CAB 23, 24, 27, 37, 65, 66, 75, 87), Home Office (HO 158, 185), Pensions and Insurance (PIN 3, 4, 6, 7, 8, 15, 17), Ministry of Reconstruction (RECO 1), Treasury (T 1, 172) and War Office (WO 32, 33) papers, Public Record Office, London.
Man Power Distribution Board Papers, Imperial War Museum.
War Cabinet Committee on Women in Industry. Minutes of Evidence, Imperial War Museum.
Women's Employment Committee of the Ministry of Reconstruction Papers, BLPES.

House of Commons Debates
Parliamentary Papers (*PP*) (individual documents cited in notes)

France

Administration Départementale (F2), Ministère de l'Intérieur (F7), Ministère de l'Agriculture (F10), Ministère des Travaux Publics (F14), and Ministère du Travail (F22) Archives, Archives Nationales, Paris.

Chambre des Deputés, Commission d'Assurance et de Prévoyance Sociales. Minutes, held at the Assemblée Nationale Archives, Versailles.

Conseil Supérieur de la Natalité. Reports, minutes, and correspondence, Institut National d'Etudes Démographiques.

Ministère du Travail. Interwar Files on Public Health (SAN series), Archives of the Ministère du Travail, Paris.

Annuaire Statistique
Bulletin de l'Inspection du Travail
Bulletin du Ministère du Travail
Bulletin de la Statistique Générale de la France
Journal Officiel (individual documents cited in notes)

2. Archives and records of organizations

Britain

Family Endowment Society. Papers, pamphlets, and *Annual Reports*, BLPES.

Federation of British Industry. Correspondence, Confederation of British Industry Predecessor Archive, Modern Records Centre, University of Warwick Library.

Independent Labour Party. National Administrative Council minutes and Pamphlets (Harvester Microfilm); *Annual Conference Reports*.

Labour Party. Pamphlets, National Executive Committee minutes, National Conference of Labour Women agendas, Standing Joint Committee of Industrial Women's Organizations publications (Harvester Microfilm and Microfiche); *Annual Conference Reports*.

Management Research Groups. Henry Ward Papers, BLPES.

National Conference of Labour Women. *Annual Reports*.

National Council of Women of Great Britain. *Handbooks*, Fawcett Library.

National Union of Societies for Equal Citizenship (later, National Council for Equal Citizenship). Papers, *Annual Reports*, Fawcett Library.

National Union of Women Workers. *Conference Reports*.

Open Door International. *Conference Reports*.

Political and Economic Planning. Papers, BLPES.

Soldiers' and Sailors' Families Association. *Proceedings of the Annual Meeting and Annual Report*.

Trades Union Congress. General Council minutes, pamphlets, and publications (Harvester Microfilm); Records of the Joint Committee on the Living Wage (Congress House, London); *Report of Proceedings*. Congress reports and journals of various trade unions consulted at the Labor Collection, Harvard University, and Congress House.

War Emergency: Workers' National Committee. Executive Committee minutes, BLPES.

Women's Cooperative Guild. Papers, *Annual Reports*, BLPES.
Women's Freedom League. *Annual Conference Reports*, Fawcett Library.
Women's Trade Union Conference, and Unions Catering for Women Workers. *Annual Conference Reports*, Congress House.
Women's Trade Union League. *Annual Reports*.

France

Caisse de Compensation de la Région Parisienne. Archives, held by Caisse d'Allocations Familiales de la Région Parisienne, Paris; additional material furnished by M. Jean Lygrisse.
Comité Central des Allocations Familiales. *Annuaires, Manuels pratiques*, and various pamphlets.
Compagnie du Chemin de Fer du Nord. Archives, Archives Nationales (series 48 AQ).
Confédération Générale du Travail. Congrès. *Comptes rendus*.
Confédération Générale du Travail Unitaire. Congrès. *Comptes rendus*.
Congrès National des Allocations Familiales. *Comptes rendus*.
Congrès National de la Natalité. *Comptes rendus*.
Fédération des Ouvriers en Métaux. Congrès. *Rapports moraux,Comptes rendus*.
Fédération Nationale des Caisses Agricoles d'Allocations Familiales. *Comptes rendus de la Journée Agricole de la Congrès National des Allocations Familiales*.
Groupe des Industries Métallurgiques, Mécaniques et Connexes de la Région Parisienne. Archives, Archives Nationales (series 39 AS).
Semaines Sociales de France. *Compte rendus*.
Union Féminine Civique et Sociale. Archives, UFCS, Paris.

3. Papers of individuals

Walter Citrine Papers, BLPES
Louis Loucheur Papers, Stanford
Violet Markham Papers, BLPES
Eleanor Rathbone Papers, Sidney Jones Library, University of Liverpool
B. Seebohm Rowntree Papers, University of York

4. Selected newspapers and journals

Britain

Common Cause
Eugenics Review
Family Endowment Chronicle
Family Endowment Society Monthly Notes
Freewoman
Labour Woman

Manchester Guardian
Nation
New Dawn
New Leader
New Statesman (later, *New Statesman and Nation*)
Nineteenth Century and After
Planning
Socialist Review
Sociological Review
Times
Vote
Woman Clerk
Woman's Leader

France

Bulletin des Allocations Familiales et des Assurances Sociales
Les Cahiers du Bolchevisme
Les Cahiers du Redressement Français
CFTC Circulaire
Chronique Sociale de France
Dossiers de l'Action Populaire
La Femme dans la Vie Sociale
La Française
L'Humanité
L'Ouvrière
Le Peuple
Le Populaire
Revue de l'Alliance Nationale pour l'Accroissement de la Population Française (cited as *Revue*)
La Revue de la Famille
La Revue de la Plus Grande Famille
Le Syndicalisme Chrétien (CFTC)
La Vie Ouvrière
La Vie Syndicale (CGTU)
La Voix du Peuple (CGT)
La Voix Sociale

5. Books, articles, and essays

Britain

Abbott, Elizabeth, and Katherine Bompas. *The Woman Citizen and Social Security*. London: Women's Freedom League, 1943.

Amery, Leo S. *My Political Life.* Vol. 3, *The Unforgiving Years, 1929–1940.* London: Hutchinson, 1955.

Anderson, A. M. *Women in the Factory.* London: John Murray, 1922.

Andrews, Irene Osgood, and Margarett A. Hobbs. *Economic Effects of the World War upon Women and Children in Great Britain.* Rev. ed. New York: Oxford University Press, 1921.

[Atkinson, Mabel]. *The Economic Foundations of the Women's Movement.* Fabian Tract no. 175. London: Fabian Society, June 1914.

Bakke, E. Wight. *The Unemployed Man: A Social Study.* New York: Dutton, 1934.

Bell, Lady Florence. *At the Works: A Study of a Manufacturing Town.* 1907; rpt. London: Virago, 1985.

Beveridge, Sir William. *Power and Influence.* London: Hodder & Stoughton, 1953.

"Unemployment Insurance in the War and After." In *War and Insurance.* By Norman Hill et al. London: Humphrey Milford, 1927, pp. 229–50.

Black, Clementina, ed. *Married Women's Work.* London: G. Bell & Sons, 1915.

Bondfield, Margaret. *A Life's Work.* London: Hutchinson, [1948].

Bosanquet, Helen. *The Family.* London: Macmillan, 1906.

Bowley, Arthur L. *Prices and Wages in the United Kingdom, 1914–1920.* Oxford University Press, 1921.

Brailsford, H. N., John A. Hobson, A. Creech Jones, and E. F. Wise. *The Living Wage.* London: ILP, 1926.

British Association for the Advancement of Science. *British Labour: Replacement and Conciliation, 1914–21.* Comp. L. Grier, A. Ashley, and A. W. Kirkaldy. London: Pitman & Son, 1921.

British Medical Association. *Nutrition and the Public Health . . . Proceedings of a National Conference on the Wider Aspects of Nutrition, April 27–9, 1939.* London: BMA, 1939.

Report of the Committee on Nutrition. London: BMA, 1933.

Brittain, Vera. *Testament of Youth.* 1933; rpt. New York: Seaview, 1980.

Women's Work in Modern England. London: Noel Douglas, 1928.

Brockway, Fenner. *Inside the Left.* London: Allen & Unwin, 1942.

Burns, Eveline M. "The Economics of Family Endowment." *Economica,* 5: 14 (June 1925), pp. 155–64.

Cadbury, Edward, M. Cécile Matheson, and George Shann. *Women's Work and Wages: A Phase of Life in an Industrial City.* London: T. Fisher Unwin, 1909.

Caird, Mona. *The Morality of Marriage.* London: G. Redway, 1897.

Carr Saunders, A. M. *World Population: Past Growth and Present Trends.* Oxford University Press, 1936.

Charles, Enid. *The Twilight of Parenthood.* London: Watts & Co., 1934.

Cohen, Joseph L. *Family Income Insurance: A Scheme of Family Endowment by the Method of Insurance.* London: P. S. King & Son, 1926.

Cole, G. D. H. *Trade Unionism and Munitions.* Oxford University Press, 1923.

Dalton, Hugh. *Call Back Yesterday: Memoirs, 1887–1931.* London: Frederick Muller, 1953.

Davies, Margaret Llewelyn, ed. *Maternity: Letters from Working Women.* 1915; rpt. New York: Norton, 1978.

Drake, Barbara. *Women in the Engineering Trades.* London: Allen & Unwin, 1917.

Women in Trade Unions. London: Labour Research Dept., 1920.

Eder, Dr. M. D. *The Endowment of Motherhood.* London: New Age Press, 1908.

Family Endowment Committee. *Equal Pay and the Family.* London: Headley Brothers, 1918.

Ford, Percy. *Income, Means Tests and Personal Responsibility.* London: P. S. King & Sons, 1939.

Gallacher, William. *Revolt on the Clyde.* New York: International Publishers, 1937.

George, R. F. "A New Calculation of the Poverty Line." *Journal of the Royal Statistical Society,* 100: 1 (1937), pp. 74–95.

Glasier, Katherine Bruce. *Socialism and the Home.* London: ILP, [1910].

Glass, David V. *The Struggle for Population.* Oxford University Press, 1936.

Gollancz, Victor, ed. *The Making of Women. Oxford Essays in Feminism.* London: Allen & Unwin, 1917.

Gray, Alexander. *Family Endowment: A Critical Analysis.* London: Ernest Benn, 1927.

Green, Marjorie E. *Family Allowances.* London: FES, 1938.

Hamilton, Cicely. *Marriage as a Trade.* 1909; rpt. London: Women's Press, 1981.

Hamilton, Mary Agnes. *Mary Macarthur.* New York: Thomas Seltzer, 1926.

Harben, Henry D. *The Endowment of Motherhood.* Fabian Tract no. 149. London: Fabian Society, 1910.

Hill, Polly. *The Unemployment Services.* London: Routledge, 1940.

Hobhouse, L. T. *Liberalism.* 1911; rpt. Westport, Conn.: Greenwood, 1980.

Hogg, Margaret H. "Dependants on Women Wage-earners." *Economica,* 1: 1 (Jan. 1921), pp. 69–86.

Holtby, Winifred. *Women and a Changing Civilization.* 1934; rpt. Chicago: Academy Press, 1978.

Hubback, Eva M. "Family Allowances in Relation to Population Problems." *Sociological Review,* 29: 3 (July 1937), pp. 272–38.

A New Plea for Family Allowances. London: FES, 1943.

Hunter, Ernest E. *Wages and Families: Why Trade Unionists Should Support Children's Allowances.* London: ILP, [1928].

Hutchins, B. L. *Conflicting Ideals: Two Sides of the Woman's Question.* London: T. Murby, 1913.

Women in Industry after the War. London: Athenaeum, 1917.

International Association for Social Progress, British Section. *Report on "Family Endowment."* London: Cooperative Printing Society, 1927.

Report on Family Provision through Social Insurance and Other Services. London: Cooperative Printing Society, 1928.

International Labour Office. *Family Allowances: The Remuneration of Labour According to Need.* Studies and Reports, Series D (Wages and Hours), no. 13. Geneva: ILO, 1924.

Kenney, Rowland. "Soldiers' Dependents." *English Review* (Dec. 1914), pp. 112–18.

Keynes, J. M., and H. D. Henderson. *Can Lloyd George Do It?* London: Nation & Athenaeum, 1929.

Labour Party and Trades Union Congress, Advisory Committee of the Joint Research and Information Department. *Motherhood and Child Endowment: First Interim Report.* London: TUC & Labour Party [1922].

Liberal Industrial Inquiry. *Britain's Industrial Future.* London: E. Benn, Ltd., [1928].

Lloyd George, David. *War Memoirs, 1914–1915.* Boston: Little, Brown, 1933. *War Memoirs, 1917.* Boston: Little, Brown, 1934.

MacGregor, D. H. "Family Allowances." *Economic Journal*, 36: 141 (Mar. 1926), pp. 1–10.

Macnamara, T. J. "Physical Condition of Working Class Children." *Nineteenth Century and After*, 56: 330 (Aug. 1904), pp. 307–11.

Mahler, Emma. "The Social Effects of Separation Allowances: An Experiment in the Endowment of Motherhood." *Englishwoman*, 36: 108 (Dec. 1917), pp. 191–9.

Mahler, Emma, and E. F. Rathbone. *Payment of Seamen: The Present System.* Liverpool: C. Tinling, 1911.

Markham, Violet. *Return Passage.* Oxford University Press, 1953.

Marshall, H. J. "The Case for Family Allowances." *Charity Organisation Quarterly* (Oct. 1938), pp. 202–10.

Martin, Anna. "The Irresponsibility of the Father." *Nineteenth Century and After*, pt. 1, 84: 502 (Dec. 1918), pp. 1091–1103; pt. 2, 85: 505 (Mar. 1919), pp. 548–62; pt. 3, 85: 507 (May 1919), pp. 956–70.

"The Married Working Woman: A Study." *Nineteenth Century and After*, pt. 1, 68: 406 (Dec. 1910), pp. 1102–18; 2, 69: 407 (Jan. 1911), pp. 108–22.

"The Mother and Social Reform." *Nineteenth Century and After*, pt. 1, 73: 435 (May 1913), 1060–79; pt. 2, 73: 436 (June 1913), 1235–55.

Mass Observation. *Britain and Her Birth Rate.* London: John Murray, 1945.

Maternal Mortality Committee. *Report.* London: Caledonian Press, 1934.

McLaren, Laura. *The Woman's Charter of Rights and Liberties.* London: John Sewell, 1909.

Meikle, Wilma. *Towards a Sane Feminism.* London: Grant Richards, 1916.

Mess, Henry A. *Factory Legislation and Its Administration, 1891–1924.* London: P.S. King & Sons, 1926.

Mill, John Stuart, and Harriet Taylor Mill. *Essays on Sex Equality.* Ed. Alice S. Rossi. Chicago: University of Chicago Press, 1970.

Principles of Political Economy. 1848; rpt. Harmondsworth: Penguin, 1985.

Milne-Bailey, W. *Trade Unions and the State.* London: Allen & Unwin, 1934.

National Council of Public Morals, National Birth Rate Commisssion. *Problems of Population and Parenthood.* London: Chapman & Hall, 1920.

National Industrial Alliance. *The Case for and against Family Allowances.* London, [1939].

Neville, Edith. *Family Life, Considered in Connection with the Proposals for the National Endowment of Motherhood.* London: Charity Organisation Society, Mar. 1919.

Orwell, George. *The Road to Wigan Pier.* 1937; rpt. New York: Harcourt, Brace, Jovanovich, 1957.

Pankhurst, E. Sylvia. *The Home Front.* London: Hutchinson, 1932.

Save the Mothers. London: Knopf, 1930.

Pember Reeves, Maud. *Round About a Pound a Week.* 1913; rpt. London: Virago, 1979.

Phillips, Marion, ed. *Women and the Labour Party.* London: Headley Brothers, 1918.

Pilgrim Trust. *Men Without Work.* Cambridge University Press, 1938.

Purcell, A. A. *The Demand for "Family Allowances."* Manchester and Salford Trades Council, 1930.

Priestley, J. B. *English Journey.* New York: Harper & Brothers, 1934.

Rathbone, Eleanor. "Changes in Public Life." In *Our Freedom and Its Results.* Ed. Ray Strachey. London: Hogarth Press, 1936, pp. 13–76.

The Condition of Widows under the Poor Law in Liverpool. Liverpool: Lee & Nightingale, 1913.

The Disinherited Family. London: Edward Arnold, 1924; 3d ed. London: Allen & Unwin, 1927; new ed. London: Falling Wall, 1986.

The Ethics and Economics of Family Endowment. London: Epworth Press, 1927.

How the Casual Labourer Lives: Report of the Liverpool Joint Research Committee on the Domestic Condition and Expenditure of the Families of Certain Liverpool Labourers. Liverpool: Northern Publishing Co., 1909.

The Problem of Women's Wages. Liverpool: Northern Publishing Co., 1912.

"The Remuneration of Women's Services." *Economic Journal,* 27: 105 (Mar. 1917), pp. 55–68.

Richardson, J. H. "The Family Allowance System." *Economic Journal,* 34: 135 (Sept. 1924), pp. 373–86.

Roberts, Robert. *The Classic Slum.* Harmondsworth: Penguin, 1973.

Robertson, Dennis H. "Family Endowment." In *Economic Fragments.* London: P. S. King & Son, 1931, pp. 145–54.

Rowntree, B. Seebohm. *The Human Needs of Labour.* London: T. Nelson & Sons, Ltd., [1918].

Poverty: A Study of Town Life. London: Macmillan, 1901.

Poverty and Progress: A Second Social Survey of York. London: Longmans, Green, 1941.

Rowntree, B. Seebohm, and Frank Stuart. *The Responsibility of Woman Workers for Dependants.* Oxford University Press, 1921.

Royden, A. Maude. *National Endowment of Motherhood.* London: Women's International League, 1919.

Russell, Dora. *The Tamarisk Tree.* Vol. 1, *My Quest for Liberty and Love.* 1975; rpt. London: Virago, 1977.

Schreiner, Olive. *Woman and Labour.* 1911; rpt. London: Virago, 1978.

Smith, Ellen. *Wage-Earning Women and Their Dependants.* London: Fabian Society, 1915.

Snowden, Ethel. *The Feminist Movement.* London: Collins [1913].

Socialist Party of Great Britain. *Family Allowances: A Socialist Analysis.* London: Socialist Party of Great Britain, [1943?].

Spring-Rice, Margery. *Working Class Wives.* Harmondsworth: Penguin, 1939.

Stocks, Mary Danvers. *The Case for Family Endowment.* London: Labour Publishing Co., 1927.

The Meaning of Family Endowment. London: Labour Publishing Co., 1921.

My Commonplace Book. London: Peter Davies, 1970.

Strachey, Ray. *Millicent Garrett Fawcett.* London: J. Murray, 1931.

Strachey, Ray, ed. *Our Freedom and Its Results.* London: Hogarth Press, 1936.

Swanwick, Helena. *The Future of the Women's Movement.* London: G. Bell & Sons, 1913.

Summerskill, Dr. Edith. *A Woman's World.* London: Heinemann, 1967.

Titmuss, Richard. *Problems of Social Policy.* London: HMSO, 1950.

Titmuss, Richard, and Kathleen Titmuss. *Parents Revolt.* London: Secker & Warburg, 1942.

Trades Union Congress. *Family Allowances – Text of the Minority and Majority Reports Issued by the TUC and Labour Party Joint Committee. Verbatim Report of the Debate at the Nottingham Congress.* London: TUC, 1930.

Trades Union Congress and Labour Party, Joint Committee on the Living Wage. *Interim Report on Family Allowances and Child Welfare.* London: TUC & Labour Party, 1928.

Tuckwell, Gertrude. "The Story of the Trade Boards Act." *Contemporary Review,* 120 (Nov. 1921), pp. 600–6.

Vibart, Hugh H. R. *Family Allowances in Practice.* London: P. S. King & Son, 1926.

Vlasto, Oleg. "Family Allowances and the Skilled Worker." *Economic Journal,* 36: 144 (Dec. 1926), pp. 577–85.

Foreign and Colonial Experiments in Family Allowances. Rev. ed. London: FES, 1926.

Webb, Beatrice. *The Wages of Men and Women: Should They Be Equal?* London: Fabian Society, 1919.

Webb, Sidney. *The Decline of the Birth Rate.* Fabian Tract no. 131. London: Fabian Society, Mar. 1907.

Wells, H. G. *Ann Veronica.* 1909; rpt. London: Dent, 1971.

Marriage. 1912; rpt. London: Hogarth Press, 1986.

The New Machiavelli. London: John Lane, 1911.

New Worlds for Old. 1908; rpt. New York: Macmillan, 1919.

Socialism and the Family. London: A. C. Fifield, 1906.

West, Rebecca. *The Young Rebecca: Writings of Rebecca West, 1911–1917.* Ed. Jane Marcus. New York: Viking, 1982.

Western, Paul. *Family Allowances: A Policy for Liberals.* Liverpool: Lee & Nightingale, 1929.

Whetham, W. C. D., and Catherine Whetham. "The Extinction of the Upper Classes." *Nineteenth Century,* 66: 389 (July 1909), 97–108.

The Family and the Nation. London: Longmans, Green, 1909.

Wolfe, Humbert. *Labour Supply and Regulation.* Oxford University Press, 1923.

Women's National Liberal Federation. *Children's Allowances: Final Report of the Family Endowment Enquiry Committee of the Women's National Liberal Federation.* London: WNLF, 1927.

Yates, L. K. *The Women's Part: A Record of Munitions Work.* New York: George H. Doran, 1918.

Yates, M. L. *Wages and Labour Conditions in British Engineering.* London: MacDonald & Evans, 1937.

France

Aftalion, Albert. *L'industrie textile en France pendant la guerre.* Paris: Presses Universitaires de France, [1924?].

Angot, E. *Féminisme et natalité.* Paris: Emile-Paul Frères, [1923].

Audouin, Louis. *Les caisses de compensation et les allocations familiales dans l'industrie française.* Poitiers: Librairie H. Mansuy, 1928.

Baudouin, Eve. *Comment envisager le retour de la mère au foyer?* Paris: Spes, 1933.

La mère au travail et le retour au foyer. Paris: Bloud et Gay, 1931.

Blanchard, Marie [Berthe Dangennes]. *Mariée ou non, la femme doit être indépendante.* Paris: Nilsson, 1923.

Blanqui, Jérôme-Adolphe. *History of Political Economy in Europe.* 4th ed. Trans. Emily J. Leonard. New York: G. P. Putnam's Sons, 1880.

Bonvoisin, Georges. "L'action sociale du patronat moderne." In *Famille, travail, épargne.* Paris: Spes, 1935.

La dénatalité. Ses causes, ses remèdes. Paris: Ed. Sociales Françaises, 1937.

The French Institution of Family Allowances. Paris: Centre d'Informations Documentaires, n.d.

La loi sur les assurances sociales et les allocations familiales. Conférence faite à la Chambre de Commerce de Paris, 1er mars 1928. Paris, 1928.

"La politique des allocations exerce-t-elle une influence sur le taux de la natalité?" *Revue Médico-Sociale,* 6: 6 (1938), pp. 502–7.

Bonvoisin, Georges, and Gustave Maignan. *Allocations familiales et caisses de compensation.* Paris: Sirey, 1930.

Boyer, François. *Des essais d'application du sursalaire familial et des caisses de compensation.* Paris: Société Moderne d'Impression et d'Edition, 1925.

Bruyneel, Robert. *L'industrie textile de Roubaix-Tourcoing devant la crise éconimique et la législation sociale.* Thesis, University of Paris, Faculty of Law. Paris: P. Bossuet, 1932.

Buisson, Georges. *Les compléments de salaire.* Paris: CGT, 1926.

"La participation aux bénéfices – les allocations familales." In *Pour l'éducation ouvrière.* N.p., 1924.

Buisson, Suzanne. *Les répercussions du travail féminin.* Paris: Librairie Populaire du Parti Socialiste, 1934.

[Butillard, Andrée]. *La femme au service du pays.* Paris: UFCS, 1942.

Butillard, Andrée, Joseph Danel et al. *Le travail de la mère hors de son foyer et sa répercussion sur la natalité.* Paris: Ed. Mariage & Famille, 1933.

Cann, Jeanne. *Les allocations familiales, l'allocation de la mère au foyer et l'allocation de salaire unique dans le commerce et l'industrie.* Thesis, University of Rennes, Faculty of Law. Loudéac: Imprimerie Traonouil-Anger, 1944.

Carlen, Claudia, ed. *The Papal Encyclicals.* Vol. 2, *1878–1903.* Wilmington, N.C.: McGrath, 1981.

Cattier, Dr. *Des bébés, s'il vous plait.* Paris: Plon, 1923.

Caunes, Magdeleine. *Des mesures juridiques propres à faciliter la présence de la mère au foyer ouvrier.* Thesis, University of Paris, Faculty of Law. Paris: A. Pedone, 1938.

Clark, M. R. "Organized Labour and the Family Allowance System in France." *Journal of Political Economy,* 39: 4 (Aug. 1931), pp. 526–37.

Comité National d'Etudes. *Les assurances sociales: Un point de vue patronal spécial (celui du Consortium Textile de Roubaix-Tourcoing).* Paris, 1930.

Debu-Bridel, Jacques. "Le foyer moderne: Vers une juste collaboration des époux à la maison comme au dehors." *Les Cahiers Féministes,* 3: 23 (Dec. 1934), pp. 77–84.

Decouvelaere, Mathilde. *Le travail industriel des femmes mariées.* Thesis, University of Lille, Faculty of Law. Paris: Rousseau, 1934.

Delvoye, J. *Patrons et Ouvriers: Les meneurs et la question des salaires dans l'industrie textile.* Paris: Dunod, 1928.

Depret, Paul. *Etude sur l'oeuvre sociale de la Compagnie des Chemins de Fer de l'Est.* Verdun: H. Frémont et Fils, 1936.

Dequidt, Dr. G., and Dr. G. Forestier. "Une expérience de natalité. L'efficacité des allocations familiales sur la natalité est-elle démontrée?" *Le Mouvement Sanitaire* (31 July 1926), pp. 485–503.

Doléris, J. A., and Jean Bouscatel. *Néo-malthusianisme, maternité et féminisme, éducation sexuelle.* Paris: Masson, 1918.

Duporcq, Jean. *Les oeuvres sociales dans la métallurgie française.* Paris: Librairie Générale de Droit et de Jurisprudence, 1936.

Durand, Paul. "Allocations familiales et allocation de salaire unique." *Collection*

Droit Social. Special issue, "Le nouveau régime du travail," 11 (1941–2), pp. 19–27.

Durkheim, Emile. *The Division of Labor in Society.* 1893; rpt. New York: Free Press, 1984.

Etats Généraux du Féminisme. *Compte rendu.* Paris, 1929.

Fontaine, Arthur. *French Industry during the War.* New Haven, Conn.: Yale University Press, 1926.

Frois, Marcel. *La santé et le travail des femmes pendant la guerre.* Paris: Presses Universitaires de France, 1926.

Grenier, Fernand. *Les assurances sociales: Les manoeuvres du Consortium Textile.* Paris: La Maison des Syndicats, 1929.

A bas le Consortium! A bas Désiré Ley! Lille: Société Lilloise d'Editions et d'Impressions, n.d.

Helleu, Yves. *Les caisses de compensation d'allocations familiales depuis la loi du 11 mars 1932.* Paris: Librairie Technique et Economique, 1937.

Herriot, Edouard. *Créer.* 1919; rpt. Paris: Payot, 1925.

Lapuyade, Henri. *Le sursalaire familial.* Toulouse: J. Fournier, 1921.

Laroque, Pierre. *Les rapports entre patrons et ouvriers.* Paris: Fernand Aubier, 1938.

Lebreton, André. *La famille et les lois sur les allocations de guerre: Les pensions militaires et le pécule.* Saint-Brieuc: Imprimerie de René Prud'homme, 1921.

Lebrun, Marguerite ["Vérine"]. *La femme et l'amour dans la société de demain.* Paris: Spés, 1930.

Leconte, Sébastien-Charles. *L'assistance nationale aux mères.* Paris: Marchal et Billard, 1910.

Leidecker-Schaeffer, Marguerite. *La mère au foyer: Nécessité de majorer et de réorganiser les allocations familiales.* N.p., 1933.

Lemonnier, Claire. "Le deuxième congrès international de la mère au foyer." *Le Devoir des Femmes,* 3: 7–8 (July–Aug. 1937), pp. 10-11.

Leroy-Beaulieu, Paul. *Collectivism.* Trans. Sir Arthur Clay. London: John Murray, 1908.

Lhotte, Céline, and Elisabeth Dupéyrat. *Préparation du futur foyer. I. Comment assurer le pain quotidien; II. Comment assurer le bonheur.* Courbevoie: Ed. JOCF, [1936, 1937].

"Une enquête de la J.O.C.F.: La préparation du future foyer de la jeune travailleuse. Deuxième Partie: I. Le travail de la femme mariée hors du foyer." *Les Dossiers de l'Action Populaire,* 391 (15 Sept. 1937), pp. 1745–70.

[Ligue de la Mère au Foyer]. *La mère au foyer dans la vie sociale.* Paris: J. Guyot, [1944].

La mère au foyer. Ouvrière de progrès humain. Paris: Ligue de la Mère au Foyer, [1941].

Louis-Lévy, Marthe. *L'émancipation politique des femmes.* Paris: Librairie Populaire du Parti Socialiste, 1934.

Maignan, Gustave. *Les allocations familiales dans l'industrie et le commerce.* Paris: R. Delaye, 1942.

Les allocations familiales dans l'industrie, le commerce et les professions libérales. Paris: UNCAF, 1954.

Mathon, Eugène. *Crise économique et crise morale.* Paris: André Tournon, 1934.

L'effort du patronat française. Paris: La Journée Industrielle, 1922.

Le producteur, la corporation, l'état. Paris: Andre Tournon, 1935.

Mazas, Pierre. *Le fondement de l'obligation aux allocations familiales.* Paris: Sirey, 1936.

Michelin, André. *Une expérience concluante: La natalité dans les usines Michelin.* Paris: Alliance Nationale, [1926].

Michelin et Cie. *Une expérience de natalité.* Clermont-Ferrand: Michelin, 1926.

"Une expérience de natalité." *Prospérité,* 1: 4 (Jan.–Mar. 1929).

Moreau, Armand. *L'oeuvre sociale du P.L.M.* Paris: Imprimerie du Montparnasse et de Persan-Beaumont, 1927.

Morel, Lydie. *Le droit au travail de la femme mariée.* Geneva: Labor, 1937.

Netter, Yvonne. *Le travail de la femme mariée, son activité professionnelle.* Paris: Presses Universitaires de France, 1923.

Nicolitch, Suzanne D. *Le socialisme et les femmes.* Paris: Librairie Populaire du Parti Socialiste, 1934.

Oualid, William, and Charles Picquenard. *Salaires et tarifs, conventions collectives et grèves: La politique du Ministère du Travail.* Paris: Presses Universitaires de France, 1928.

Picard, Roger. *Le mouvement syndical durant la guerre.* Paris: Presses Universitaires de France, 1927.

Pinot, Robert. *Les oeuvres sociales des industries métallurgiques.* Paris: Colin, 1924.

Pinte, Jean. *Les allocations familiales.* Paris: Sirey, 1935.

Richemond, Pierre. "Allocations pour charges de famille et caisses de compensation." *Revue d'Economie Politique,* 34: 5 (Sept.-Oct. 1920), pp. 590–606.

Romanet, Emile. *L'organisation des entreprises au point de vue social.* Mulhouse: Bader, 1921.

La répartition équitable des bénéfices. Grenoble: Les Alpes Industrielles, 1920.

Le salaire familial. Grenoble: Aubert, 1918.

Roussel, Nelly. *Dernier combats.* Paris: L'Emancipatrice, 1932.

Sayour, A. *Les oeuvres sociales du patronat.* Paris: Réveil Economique, [1929?].

Sertillanges, A.-D. *La vie civique et religieuse du foyer.* Paris: Spes, 1934.

Simon, Jules. *L'ouvrière.* Paris: Hachette, 1862.

Touzet, Maria-Louise. *Ma vision.* Dole (Jura): Librairie Veuve Karrer, 1907.

Trylnik, Benoit. *Le Consortium de l'Industrie Textile de Roubaix-Tourcoing.* Thesis, University of Lille. Lille: Marquant, 1926.

Union Féminine Civique et Sociale. *La famille dans la vie sociale.* Paris: Spes [1937].

La mère au foyer: Ouvrière de progrès humain. Documents d'études. Extraits du Congrès International de Juin 1937. Paris: UFCS, 1937.

Le travail industriel de la mère et le foyer ouvrier. Documents d'études, Extraits du congrès international du juin 1933. Paris: UFCS, 1933.

Villey, François. *Le complément familial du salaire: Etude des allocations familiales dans leurs rapports avec le salaire.* Paris: Ed. Sociales Françaises, 1946.

Zola, Emile. *Fécondité.* Paris: Charpentier, 1899. Trans. as *Fruitfulness* by Ernest Alfred Vizetelly. London: Chatto & Windus, 1900.

6. Selected secondary works

Dissertations and Theses

Carls, Stephen Douglas. "Louis Loucheur: A French Technocrat in Government, 1916–1920." Ph.D. diss. University of Minnesota, 1982.

Dawson, P. E. "Family Benefits and Income Redistribution in France and the United Kingdom, 1891–1971." Diss. University of York, 1979.

Downs, Laura Lee. "Women in Industry, 1914–1939 – The Employers' Perspective: A Comparative Study of the French and British Metals Industry." Ph.D. diss. Columbia University, 1987.

Fine, Martin. "Toward Corporatism: The Movement for Capital–Labor Collaboration in France, 1914–1936." Ph.D. diss. University of Wisconsin, 1971.

Kanipe, Esther. "The Family, Private Property and the State in France, 1870–1914." Ph.D. diss., University of Wisconsin, 1976.

Kozak, Marion. "Women Munition Workers during the First World War with Special Reference to Engineering." Diss. Hull University, 1976.

Lygrisse, Jean. "Monographie de la Caisse de Compensation la Région Parisienne, 1920–1946." Typescript, Caisse d'Allocations Familiales de la Région Parisienne, Paris, 1978.

Martin, Martine. "Les femmes et le travail ménager en France entre les deux guerres." Thesis, University of Paris VII, 1984.

Pedersen, Susan. "Explaining the Persistence of Gender Hierarchy at Work: The Dilution of Labor in British Munitions Industries, 1914–1918." B.A. thesis, Harvard-Radcliffe, 1982.

"Social Policy and the Reconstruction of the Family in Britain and France, 1900–1945." Ph.D. diss. Harvard University, 1989.

Peiter, Henry Donald. "Men of Good Will: French Businessmen and the First World War." Ph.D. diss. University of Michigan, 1973.

Rossiter, Adrian Martin. "Experiments with Corporatist Politics in Republican France, 1916–1939." D.Phil. Oxford University, 1986.

Rust, Michael Jared. "Business and Politics in the Third Republic: The Comité des Forges and the French Steel Industry, 1896–1914." Ph.D. diss., Princeton University, 1973.

Simon, Dominique. "Les origines des assurances sociales au début des années 1930." Thesis, University of Paris I, 1983.

Thom, Deborah. "Women Munition Workers at Woolwich Arsenal in the 1914–1918 War." M.A. thesis, University of Warwick, 1974.

Tomlinson, Richard Peter. "The Politics of Dénatalité during the Third French Republic, 1890–1940." Diss., Cambridge University, 1983.

Vichniac, Judith. "Industrial Relations in Historical Perspective: A Case Study of the French Iron and Steel Industry (1830–1921)." Ph.D. diss., Harvard University, 1981.

Published Books and Articles

Abrams, Mark Alexander. *Social Surveys and Social Action*. London: Heinemann, 1951.

Acker, Joan. "Class, Gender and the Relations of Distribution." *Signs*, 13: 3 (Spring 1988), pp. 473–97.

Adams, R. J. Q., and Philip P. Poirier. *The Conscription Controversy in Great Britain, 1900–18*. London: Macmillan, 1987.

Addison, Paul. *The Road to 1945*. 1975; rpt. London: Quartet, 1977.

Alberti, Johanna. *Beyond Suffrage: Feminists in War and Peace, 1914–1928*. London: Macmillan, 1989.

Aldrich, Robert. "Late-Comer or Early-Starter? New Views on French Economic History." *Journal of European Economic History*, 16: 1 (Spring 1987), pp. 89–100.

Ambler, John S. "Ideas, Interests and the French Welfare State." In *The French Welfare State: Surviving Social and Ideological Change*. Ed. John S. Ambler. New York: New York University Press, 1991, pp. 1–31.

Ashford, Douglas. *The Emergence of the Welfare States*. Oxford: Basil Blackwell, 1986.

    "Advantages of Complexity: Social Insurance in France." In *The French Welfare State: Surviving Social and Ideological Change*. Ed. John S. Ambler. New York: New York University Press, 1991, pp. 32–57.

Badie, Bertrand. "Les grèves du Front Populaire aux usines Renault." *Mouvement Social*, 81 (Oct.–Dec. 1972), pp. 69–109.

Baguley, David. *Fécondité d'Emile Zola*. Toronto: University of Toronto Press, 1973.

Baker, John. "Comparing National Priorities: Family and Population Policy in Britain and France." *Journal of Social Policy*, 15: 4 (Oct. 1986), pp. 421–42.

Baldwin, Peter. *The Politics of Social Solidarity: Class Bases of the European Welfare State, 1875–1975*. Cambridge University Press, 1990.

Ball, Stuart. *Baldwin and the Conservative Party: The Crisis of 1929–1931*. New Haven, Conn.: Yale University Press, 1988.

Barrett, Michèle. *Women's Oppression Today*. London: New Left Books, 1980.

Barrett, Michèle, and Mary McIntosh. *The Anti-social Family*. London: Verso, 1982.

"The 'Family Wage': Some Problems for Socialists and Feminists." *Capital and Class*, 11 (Summer 1980), pp. 51–72.

Becchia, Alain. "Les milieux parlementaires et la dépopulation de 1900 à 1914." *Communications*, 44 (1986), pp. 201–46.

Becker, Jean-Jacques. *The Great War and the French People*. New York: St. Martin's, 1986.

Beer, Samuel H. *Modern British Politics*. London: Faber, 1969.

Behlmer, George K. *Child Abuse and Moral Reform in England, 1870–1908*. Stanford, Calif.: Stanford University Press, 1982.

Berg, Maxine. "Women's Work, Mechanisation and the Early Phases of Industrialisation in England." In *The Historical Meanings of Work*. Ed. Patrick Joyce. Cambridge University Press, 1987, pp. 64–98.

Bernard, Philippe, and Henri Dubief. *The Decline of the Third Republic, 1914–1938*. Cambridge University Press, 1985.

Berstein, Serge. *Edouard Herriot ou la république en personne*. Paris: Presses de la Fondation Nationale des Sciences Politiques, 1985.

Histoire du Parti Radical. 2 vols. Paris: Presses de la Fondation Nationale des Sciences Politiques, 1980–2.

Beveridge, Janet. *Beveridge and His Plan*. London: Hodder & Stoughton, 1954.

Birks, Colin. "Social Welfare Provision in France." In *Welfare Abroad: An Introduction to Welfare Provision in Seven Countries*. Ed. Roslyn Ford and Mono Chakrabarti. Edinburgh: Scottish Academic Press, 1987, pp. 66–98.

Black, Naomi. *Social Feminism*. Ithaca, N.Y.: Cornell University Press, 1989.

Bland, Lucy. "Marriage Laid Bare: Middle-Class Women and Marital Sex, 1880s–1914." In *Labour and Love: Women's Experience of Home and Family, 1850–1940*. Ed. Jane Lewis. Oxford: Basil Blackwell, 1986, pp. 122–46.

Blum, Françoise, Colette Chambelland, and Michel Dreyfus. "Les mouvements de femmes, 1919–1940. Guide des sources documentaires." *La Vie Sociale*, 11–12 (1984).

Blythell, Duncan. *The Sweated Trades: Outwork in Nineteenth Century Britain*. New York: St. Martin's, 1978.

Booth, Alan, and Melvyn Pack. *Employment, Capital and Economic Policy: Great Britain, 1918–1939*. Oxford: Basil Blackwell, 1985.

Bordeaux, Michele. "Femmes hors d'état français – 1940–1944." In *Femmes et fascismes*. Ed. Rita Thalmann. Tierce, 1986, pp. 135–55.

Boxer, Marilyn. "Protective Legislation and Home Industry: The Marginalization of Women Workers in Late Nineteenth-Century- Early Twentieth-Century France." *Journal of Social History*, 20: 1 (Fall 1986), 45–65.

"Socialism Faces Feminism: The Failure of Synthesis in France, 1879–1914." In *Socialist Women: European Socialist Feminism in the Nineteenth and Early Twentieth Centuries*. Ed. Marilyn J. Boxer and Jean H. Quartaert. New York: Elsevier, 1978, pp. 75–111.

"When Radical and Socialist Feminism were Joined: The Extraordinary

Failure of Madeleine Pelletier." In *European Women on the Left: Socialism, Feminism, and the Problems Faced by Political Women, 1880 to the Present.* Ed. Jane Slaughter and Robert Kern. Westport, Conn.: Greenwood, 1981, pp. 51–73.

Braybon, Gail. *Women Workers and the First World War.* London: Croom Helm, 1981.

Briggs, Asa. *Social Thought and Social Action: A Study of the Work of Seebohm Rowntree, 1871–1954.* London: Longmans, Green, 1961.

Brockway, Fenner. *Socialism over Sixty Years: The Life of Jowett of Bradford, 1864–1944.* London: Allen & Unwin, 1946.

Bruce, Maurice. *The Coming of the Welfare State.* 4th ed. London: B. T. Batsford, 1968.

Bullock, Alan. *The Life and Times of Ernest Bevin.* Vol. 1. *Trade Union Leader, 1881–1940.* London: Heinemann, 1960.

Burdy, Jean-Paul, Mathilde Dubesset, and Michelle Zancarini-Fournel. "Rôles, travaux et métiers de femmes dans une ville industrielle: Saint-Etienne, 1900–1950." *Mouvement Social,* 140 (July–Sept. 1987), pp. 27–53.

Burk, Kathleen, ed. *War and the State: The Transformation of British Government, 1914–1919.* London: Allen & Unwin, 1982.

Burman, Sandra, ed. *Fit Work for Women.* London: Croom Helm, 1979.

Burnett, John, ed. *The Annals of Labor.* Bloomington: Indiana University Press, 1974.

Buthman, William. *The Rise of Integral Nationalism in France.* New York: Columbia University Press, 1939.

Bythell, Duncan. *The Sweated Trades: Outwork in Nineteenth-Century Britain.* New York: St. Martin's, 1978.

Caisse d'Allocations Familiales de la Région Parisienne. *Cinquantenaire d'un service d'action sociale: L'économie familiale de 1927 à 1977.* Paris, 1977.

Cameron, David R. "Continuity and Change in French Social Policy: The Welfare State under Gaullism, Liberalism and Socialism." In *The French Welfare State: Surviving Social and Ideological Change.* Ed. John L Ambler. New York: New York University Press, 1991, pp. 58–93.

Camp, Wesley D. *Marriage and the Family in France since the Revolution.* New York: Bookman Associates, 1961.

Campbell, Beatrix. *Wigan Pier Revisited: Poverty and Politics in the Eighties.* London: Virago, 1984.

Cartter, Allan M. "Income-tax Allowances and the Family in Great Britain." *Population Studies,* 6: 3 (Mar. 1953), pp. 218–232.

Ceccaldi, Dominique. *Histoire des prestations familiales en France.* Paris: UNCAF, 1957.

Cent ans de catholicisme social dans la région du Nord. Special issue, *Revue du Nord,* 73: 290–1 (Apr.–Sept. 1991).

Challener, Richard. *The French Theory of the Nation in Arms, 1866–1939.* New York: Columbia University Press, 1955.

Charbit, Yves. *Du Malthusianism au populationnisme: Les économistes français et la population, 1840–1870.* Paris: Presses Universitaires de France, 1981.

Charbit, Yves, and André Béjin. "La pensée démographique." In *Histoire de la population française.* Vol. 3. Paris: Presses Universitaires de France, 1988, pp. 465–501.

Chesnais, Jean-Claude. "Les hommes et l'économie: La croissance et les changements structurels." In *Histoire de la population française.* Vol. 4. Paris: Presses Universitaires de France, 1988, pp. 345–86.

"La politique de population française depuis 1914." In *Histoire de la population française.* Vol. 4. Paris: Presses Universitaires de France, 1988, pp. 181–231.

Clark, Linda L. *Schooling the Daughters of Marianne: Textbooks and the Socialization of Girls in Modern French Primary Schools.* Albany: State University of New York Press, 1984.

Cook, Chris. *A Short History of the Liberal Party, 1900–1976.* New York: St. Martin's, 1976.

Copelman, Dina M. " 'A New Comradeship between Men and Women': Family, Marriage and London's Women Teachers, 1870–1914." In *Labour and Love: Women's Experience of Home and Family, 1850–1940.* Ed Jane Lewis. Oxford: Basil Blackwell, 1986, pp. 175–93.

Cottereau, Alain. "The Distinctiveness of Working-Class Cultures in France, 1848–1900." In *Working-Class Formation: Nineteenth-Century Patterns in Western Europe and the United States.* Ed. Ira Katznelson and Aristide R. Zolberg. Princeton, N.J.: Princeton University Press, 1986, pp. 111–54.

Cova, Anne. "Cécile Brunschvicg (1877–1946) et la protection de la maternité." In *Actes du 113 Congrès National des Sociétés Savantes: Colloque sur l'histoire de la sécurité sociale (1988).* Paris: Association pour l'Etude de l'Histoire de la Sécurité Sociale, 1989, pp. 75–104.

"French Feminism and Maternity: Theories and Policies, 1890–1918." In *Maternity and Gender Policies: Women and the Rise of the European Welfare States, 1880s–1950s.* Ed. Gisela Bock and Pat Thane. London: Routledge, 1991, pp. 119–37.

Cowan, Ruth Schwartz. *More Work for Mother: The Ironies of Household Technology from the Open Hearth to the Microwave.* New York: Basic, 1982.

Cronin, James E. "The British State and the Structure of Political Opportunity." *Journal of British Studies,* 27 (July 1988), pp. 199–231.

The Politics of State Expansion: War, State and Society in Twentieth-Century Britain. London: Routledge, 1991.

Cross, Gary. *A Quest for Time: The Reduction of Work in Britain and France, 1840–1940.* Berkeley and Los Angeles: University of California Press, 1989.

Crowther, M. A. "Family Responsibility and State Responsibility in Britain before the Welfare State." *Historical Journal,* 25: 1 (1982), pp. 131–45.

Dale, Jennifer, and Peggy Foster. *Feminists and State Welfare.* London: Routledge & Kegan Paul, 1986.

Davidoff, Leonore. "Mastered for Life: Servant and Wife in Victorian and Edwardian England." *Journal of Social History*, 8: 4 (Summer 1974), pp. 406–28.

"The Separation of Home and Work? Landladies and Lodgers in Nineteenth- and Twentieth-Century England." In *Fit Work for Women*. Ed. Sandra Burman. London: Croom Helm, 1979, pp. 64–97.

Davidoff, Leonore, and Catherine Hall. *Family Fortunes: Men and Women of the English Middle Class, 1780–1950*. Chicago: University of Chicago Press, 1987.

Davin, Anna. "Imperialism and Motherhood." *History Workshop Journal*, 5 (Spring 1978), pp. 9–65.

Deacon, Alan. *In Search of the Scrounger: The Administration of Unemployment Insurance in Britain, 1920–1931*. London: G. Bell & Sons, 1976.

Delbreil, Jean-Claude. *Centrisme et Démocratie-Chrétienne en France: Le Parti Démocrate Populaire des origines au M.R.P., 1919–1944*. Paris: Publications de la Sorbonne, 1990.

Deldycke, T., H. Gelders, and J.-M. Limbor. *La population active et sa structure*. Brussels: Editions de l'Institut de Sociologie de l'Université Libre de Bruxelles, 1968.

Delpha, François. "Les communistes français et la sexualité (1932–1938)." *Mouvement Social*, 91 (1975), pp. 121–52.

Delphy, Christine. *Close to Home: A Materialist Analysis of Women's Oppression*. London: Hutchinson, 1984.

De Swaan, Abram. *In Care of the State: Health Care, Education and Welfare in Europe in the Modern Era*. New York: Oxford University Press, 1988.

Donzelot, Jacques. *The Policing of Families*. New York: Pantheon, 1979.

Dowse, Robert E. *Left in the Centre: The Independent Labour Party, 1893–1940*. London: Longmans, Green, 1966.

Dreyfus, Paul. *Emile Romanet, père des allocations familiales*. Paris: Arthaud, 1965.

Dubly, Henri-Louis. *Vers un ordre économique et social: Eugène Mathon, 1860–1935*. Paris, 1946.

Dupâquier, Jacques, ed. *Histoire de la population française*. Vol. 3, *De 1789 à 1914*; Vol 4, *De 1914 à nos jours*. Paris: Presses Universitaires de France, 1988.

Duriez, Bruno, and Didier Cornuel. "La naissance de la politique urbaine: Le cas de Roubaix." *Annales de la Recherche Urbaine*, 4 (1979), pp. 22–84.

Dwork, Deborah. *War Is Good for Babies and Other Young Children*. London: Tavistock, 1987.

Dyer, Colin. *Population and Society in Twentieth-Century France*. New York: Holmes & Meier, 1978.

Ehrmann, Henry. *Organized Business in France*. Princeton, N.J.: Princeton University Press, 1957.

Elbow, Matthew. *French Corporative Theory, 1789–1948*. New York: Columbia University Press, 1953.

Elwitt, Sanford. *The Third Republic Defended: Bourgeois Reform in France, 1880–1914*. Baton Rouge: Louisiana State University Press, 1986.

Esping-Andersen, Gøsta. "The Comparison of Policy Regimes: An Introduction." In *The Rise and Fall of Policy Regimes*. Ed. Martin Rein, Gøsta Esping-Andersen, and Lee Rainwater. Armonk, N.Y.: Sharpe, 1987, pp. 3–12.

The Three Worlds of Welfare Capitalism. Princeton, N.J.: Princeton University Press, 1990.

Ewald, François. *L'état providence*. Paris: Grasset, 1986.

Fayet-Scribe, Sylvie. *Associations féminines et Catholicisme: De la charité à l'action sociale, XIXᵉ–XXᵉ siècle*. Paris: Editions Ouvrières, 1990.

Ferguson, Sheila. "Labour Women and the Social Services." In *Women in the Labour Movement: The British Experience*. Ed. Lucy Middleton. London: Croom Helm, 1977, pp. 38–56.

Field, Frank. *Poverty and Politics*. London: Heinemann, 1982.

Finer, Morris, and O. R. MacGregor. "The History of the Obligation to Maintain." Appendix 5 of the *Report of the Commission on One-Parent Families, PP* 1974, XVI, pp. 85–149.

Fishman, Sarah. *We Will Wait: Wives of French Prisoners of War, 1940–1945*. New Haven, Conn.: Yale University Press, 1991.

Fleming, Suzie. "Eleanor Rathbone: Spokeswoman for a Movement." New introduction to Eleanor Rathbone, *The Disinherited Family*. 1924; new ed. London: Falling Wall Press, 1986, pp. 9–120.

Fletcher, Sheila. *Maude Royden: A Life*. Oxford: Basil Blackwell, 1989.

Flora, Peter, and Jens Alber. "Modernization, Democratization and the Development of Welfare States in Western Europe." In *The Development of Welfare States in Europe and America*. Ed. Peter Flora and Arnold J. Heidenheimer. New Brunswick, N.J.: Transaction Books, 1981, pp. 37–80.

Flora, Peter, and Arnold J. Heidenheimer. "The Historical Core and Changing Boundaries of the Welfare State." In *The Development of Welfare States in Europe and America*. Ed. Peter Flora and Arnold J. Heidenheimer. New Brunswick, N.J.: Transaction Books, 1981, pp. 17–34.

Ford, Jill. "Social Welfare Provision in the United Kingdom." In *Welfare Abroad: An Introduction to Welfare Provision in Seven Countries*. Ed. Roslyn Ford and Mono Chakrabarti. Edinburgh, Scottish Academic Press, 1987, pp. 1–28.

Fourcaut, Annie. *Femmes à l'usine: Ouvrières et surintendants dans les entreprises françaises de l'entre-deux-guerres*. Paris: François Maspero, 1982.

Fraser, Derek. *Evolution of the British Welfare State*. 2d ed. London: Macmillan, 1984.

Freeden, Michael. "Eugenics and Progressive Thought: A Study in Ideological Affinity." *Historical Journal*, 22: 3 (Sept. 1979), pp. 645–71.

The New Liberalism: An Ideology of Social Reform. Oxford University Press, 1978.

Fridenson, Patrick. *Histoire des Usines Renault*. Paris: Seuil, 1972.

"L'idéologie des grands constructeurs dans l'entre-deux-guerres." *Mouvement Social*, 81 (Oct.–Dec. 1972), pp. 51–68.

Fridenson, Patrick, ed. *1914–1918: L'autre front.* Paris: Editions Ouvrières, 1977.

Fridenson, Patrick, and André Straus. *Le capitalisme français, XIXe–XXe siècle: Blocages et dynamismes d'une croissance.* Paris: Fayard, 1987.

Fuchs, Rachel. *Abandoned Children: Foundlings and Child Welfare in Nineteenth-Century France.* Albany: State University of New York Press, 1984.

"Morality and Poverty: Public Welfare for Mothers in Paris, 1870–1900." *French History*, 2: 3 (Sept. 1988), pp. 288–311.

Gaffin, Jean, and David Thoms. *Caring and Sharing: The Centenary History of the Cooperative Women's Guild.* Manchester: Cooperative Union, Ltd., 1983.

Gani, Léon. "Jules Guesde, Paul Lafargue et les problèmes de population." *Population*, 34 (1979), pp. 1023–43.

Garden, Maurice. "L'évolution de la population active." In *Histoire de la population française.* Vol. 3, *De 1789 à 1914.* Paris: Presses Universitaires de France, 1988, pp. 243–68.

Garside, W. R. *British Unemployment, 1919–1939: A Study in Public Policy.* Cambridge University Press, 1990.

Gide, Charles, ed. *Effects of the War upon French Economic Life.* Oxford University Press, 1923.

Gide, Charles, and William Oualid. *Le bilan de la guerre pour la France.* Paris: Presses Universitaires de France, 1931.

Gilbert, Bentley B. *British Social Policy, 1914–1939.* London: B. T. Batsford, 1970.

The Evolution of National Insurance in Great Britain. London: Michael Joseph, 1966.

Gilbert, Sandra. "Soldier's Heart: Literary Men, Literary Women, and the Great War." In *Behind the Lines: Gender and the Two World Wars.* Ed. Margaret Higonnet et. al. New Haven, Conn.: Yale University Press, 1987, 197–226.

Gittins, Diana. *Fair Sex: Family Size and Structure in Britain, 1900–1939.* New York: St. Martin's, 1982.

"Marital Status, Work and Kinship, 1850–1930." In *Labour and Love: Women's Experience of Home and Family, 1850–1940.* Ed. Jane Lewis. Oxford: Basil Blackwell, 1986, pp. 223–48.

Glucksmann, Miriam. *Women Assemble: Women Workers and the New Industries in Inter-War Britain.* London: Routledge, 1990.

Godfrey, John F. *Capitalism at War: Industrial Policy and Bureaucracy in France, 1914–1918.* Leamington Spa: Berg, 1987.

Godwin, Dame Anne. "Early Years in the Trade Unions." In *Women in the Labour Movement.* London: Croom Helm, 1977, 94–112.

Goguel, François. *La Politique des Partis Sous la IIIe République.* Paris: Seuil, 1946.

Gordon, David. "Liberalism and Socialism in the Nord: Eugène Motte and Republican Politics in Roubaix." *French History*, 3: 3 (1989), pp. 312–43.

Gordon, Linda. "The New Feminist Scholarship on the Welfare State." In *Women, the State and Welfare*. Ed. Linda Gordon. Madison: University of Wisconsin Press, 1990, pp. 9–35.

Gray, Robert. "The Languages of Factory Reform in Britain, c. 1830–1860." In *The Historical Meanings of Work*. Ed. Patrick Joyce. Cambridge University Press, 1987, pp. 143–79.

Grieves, Keith. *The Politics of Manpower, 1914–18*. Manchester: Manchester University Press, 1988.

Sir Eric Geddes: Business and Government in War and Peace. Manchester: Manchester University Press, 1989.

Guilbert, Madeleine. *Les femmes et l'organisation syndicale avant 1914*. Paris: CNRS, 1966.

Hakim, Catherine. "Census Reports as Documentary Evidence: The Census Commentaries, 1801–1951." *Sociological Review* 28: 3 (Aug. 1980), pp. 551–580.

Hall, Catherine. "The Early Formation of Victorian Domestic Ideology." In *Fit Work for Women*. Ed. Sandra Burman. London: Croom Helm, 1979, pp. 15–32.

"The Tale of Samuel and Jemima: Gender and Working-Class Culture in Early Nineteenth-Century England." In *Popular Culture and Social Relations*. Ed. Tony Bennett et al. Milton Keynes: Open University Press, 1986, pp. 73–92.

Hardach, Gerd. *The First World War, 1914–1918*. Berkeley and Los Angeles: University of California Press, 1977.

"La mobilisation industrielle en 1914–1918: Production, planification et idéologie." In *1914–1918: L'autre front*. Ed. Patrick Fridenson. Paris: Editions Ouvrières, 1977, pp. 81–109.

Harris, José. "Social Planning in Wartime: Some Aspects of the Beveridge Report." In *War and Economic Development*. Ed. J. M. Winter. Cambridge University Press, 1975, pp. 239–56.

"Society and the State in Twentieth-Century Britain." In *The Cambridge Social History of Britain, 1750–1950*. Ed. F. M. L. Thompson. Vol. 3. Cambridge University Press, 1990, pp. 63–117.

"The Transition to High Politics in English Social Policy, 1880–1914." In *High and Low Politics in Modern Britain*. Ed. Michael Bentley and John Stevenson. Oxford University Press, 1983, pp. 58–79.

Unemployment and Politics: A Study in English Social Policy, 1886–1914. Oxford University Press, 1972.

William Beveridge: A Biography. Oxford University Press, 1977.

Harrison, Brian. *Prudent Revolutionaries: Portraits of British Feminists between the Wars*. Oxford University Press, 1987.

Separate Spheres: The Opposition to Women's Suffrage in Britain. London: Croom Helm, 1978.

Harrison, Royden. "The War Emergency Workers' National Committee, 1914–1920." In *Essays in Labour History, 1886–1923*. Ed. Asa Briggs and John Saville. Vol. 2. London: Macmillan, 1971, pp. 211–59.

Hartmann, Heidi. "Capitalism, Patriarchy and Job Segregation by Sex." In *Capitalist Patriarchy and the Case for Socialist Feminism*. Ed. Zillah R. Eisenstein. New York: Monthly Review Press, 1979, pp. 1–42.

Hastings, Michel. *Halluin la rouge, 1919–1939: Aspects d'un communisme identitaire*. Lille: Presses Universitaires de Lille, 1991.

"Identité culturelle locale et politique festive communiste: Halluin la rouge 1920–1934." *Mouvement Social*, 139 (Apr.–June 1987), pp. 7–25.

Hatzfeld, Henri. *Du paupérisme à la sécurité sociale, 1850–1940*. Paris: Armand Colin, 1971.

Hause, Steven C., with Anne R. Kenney. *Women's Suffrage and Social Politics in the French Third Republic*. Princeton, N.J.: Princeton University Press, 1984.

Hay, J. R. *The Origins of the Liberal Welfare Reforms, 1906–1914*. London: Macmillan, 1975.

Hay, Roy. "Employers and Social Policy in Britain: The Evolution of Welfare Legislation." *Social History*, 4 (Jan. 1977), pp. 435–55.

Hayward, J. E. S. "The Official Social Philosophy of the French Third Republic: Léon Bourgeois and Solidarism."*International Review of Social History*, 6 (1961), pp. 19–48.

"Solidarity: The Social History of an Idea in Nineteenth-Century France." *International Review of Social History*, 4: 2 (1959), pp. 261–84.

Heclo, Hugh. *Modern Social Politics in Britain and Sweden: From Relief to Income Maintenance*. New Haven, Conn.: Yale University Press, 1974.

"Generational Politics." In *The Vulnerable*. Ed. John L. Palmer, Timothy Smeeding, and Barbara Boyle Torrey. Washington D.C.: Urban Institute Press, 1988, pp. 381–411.

Heidenheimer, Arnold J., Hugh Heclo, and Carolyn Teich Adams. *Comparative Public Policy: The Politics of Social Choice in America, Europe and Japan*. 3d ed. New York: St. Martin's, 1990.

Henriques, U. R. Q. *Before the Welfare State: Social Administration in Early Industrial Britain*. London: Longman, 1979.

Hewitt, Margaret. *Wives and Mothers in Victorian Industry*. 1958; rpt. Westport, Conn.: Greenwood, 1975.

Heywood, Colin. *Childhood in Nineteenth-Century France: Work, Health and Education among the 'Classes Populaires'*. Cambridge University Press, 1988.

Higonnet, Margaret, et al. *Behind the Lines: Gender and the Two World Wars*. New Haven, Conn.: Yale University Press, 1987.

Hilaire, Yves-Marie. "Les ouvriers de la région du Nord devant l'église catholique." *Le Mouvement Social*, 57 (Oct.–Dec. 1966), pp. 181–201.

Hilden, Patricia. *Working Women and Socialist Politics in France, 1880–1914: A Regional Study*. Oxford University Press, 1986.

Hinton, James. *The First Shop Stewards' Movement.* London: Allen & Unwin, 1973.

Hirshfield, Claire. "Fractured Faith: Liberal Party Women and the Suffrage Issue in Britain, 1892–1914." *Gender & History,* 2: 2 (Summer 1990), pp. 172–97.

Hochard, Jacques. *Aspects économiques des prestations familiales.* Paris: UNCAF, 1961.

"Les origines françaises des allocations familiales avant 1920." In *Actes du 108e Congrès National des Sociétés Savantes (1983), Colloque sur l'histoire de la sécurité sociale.* Paris: Association pour l'Etude de l'Histoire de la Sécurité Sociale, 1984, pp. 101–13.

Hopkinson, Diana. *Family Inheritance: A Life of Eva Hubback.* London: Staples Press, 1954.

Horne, John N. *Labour At War: France and Britain, 1914–1918.* Oxford University Press, 1991.

Humphries, Jane. "Class Struggle and the Persistence of the Working-Class Family." *Cambridge Journal of Economics,* 1: 3 (Sept. 1977), pp. 241–58.

"Protective Legislation, the Capitalist State, and Working Class Men: The Case of the 1842 Mines Regulation Act." *Feminist Review,* 7 (Spring 1981), pp. 1–33.

Hunter, John C. "The Problem of the French Birth Rate on the Eve of World War I." *French Historical Studies,* 2: 4 (Fall 1962), pp. 490–503.

Huston, Nancy. "The Matrix of War: Mothers and Heroes." In *The Female Body in Western Culture.* Ed. Susan Rubin Suleiman. Cambridge, Mass.: Harvard University Press, 1986, pp. 119–36.

Hyman, Richard. *The Workers' Union.* Oxford University Press, 1971.

International Labour Office. *The Cost of Social Security: Eighth International Inquiry.* Geneva: ILO, 1976.

The Cost of Social Security: Thirteenth International Inquiry. Geneva: ILO, 1992.

Jackson, Julian. *The Popular Front in France: Defending Democracy, 1934–1938.* Cambridge University Press, 1988.

Jallade, Jean-Pierre. "Redistribution in the Welfare State: An Assessment of the French Performance." In *The Crisis of Redistribution in European Welfare States.* Ed. Jean-Pierre Jallade. Stoke-on-Trent: Trentham Books, 1988, pp. 221–53.

"The Redistributive Efficiency of European Welfare States: Basic Issues." In *The Crisis of Redistribution in European Welfare States.* Ed. Jean-Pierre Jallade. Stoke-on-Trent: Trentham Books, 1988, pp. 1–23.

Jamieson, Lynn. "Limited Resources and Limiting Conventions: Working-Class Mothers and Daughters in Urban Scotland, c. 1890–1925." In *Labour and Love.* Ed. Jane Lewis. Oxford: Basil Blackwell, 1986, pp. 49–69.

Jefferys, James. *The Story of the Engineers, 1800–1945.* London: Lawrence & Wishart, 1945.

Jenson, Jane. "Gender and Reproduction: Or, Babies and the State." *Studies in Political Economy,* 20 (Summer 1986), pp. 9–46.

John, Angela V., ed. *Unequal Opportunities: Women's Employment in England, 1800–1918*. Oxford: Basil Blackwell, 1986.

Johnson, Paul. *Land Fit for Heroes: The Planning of British Reconstruction, 1916–1919*. Chicago: University of Chicago Press, 1968.

Jones, Gareth Stedman. *Outcast London*. 2d ed. New York: Pantheon, 1984.

Jones, Greta. "Eugenics and Social Policy between the Wars." *Historical Journal*, 25: 3 (1982), pp. 717–28.

Kahn, Alfred J., and Sheila B. Kamerman. *Income Transfers for Families with Children: An Eight-Country Study*. Philadelphia: Temple University Press, 1983.

Kamerman, Sheila B., and Alfred J. Kahn, eds. *Family Policy: Government and Families in Fourteen Countries*. New York: Columbia University Press, 1978.

"Social Policy and Children in the United States and Europe." In *The Vulnerable*. Ed. John L. Palmer, Timothy Smeeding, and Barbara Boyle Torrey. Washington D.C.: Urban Institute Press, 1988, pp. 351–80.

Kent, Susan Kingsley. "The Politics of Sexual Difference: World War I and the Demise of British Feminism." *Journal of British Studies*, 27: 3 (July 1988), pp. 232–53.

Sex and Suffrage in Britain, 1860–1914. Princeton, N.J.: Princeton University Press, 1987.

Kevles, Daniel J. *In the Name of Eugenics: Genetics and the Uses of Human Heredity*. New York: Knopf, 1985.

Klejman, Laurence, and Florence Rochefort. *L'égalité en marche: Le féminisme sous la Troisième République*. Paris: Presses de la Fondation Nationale des Sciences Politiques, 1989.

Knibiehler, Yvonne, ed. *Nous, les assistantes sociales*. Paris: Aubier Montaigne, 1980.

Knibiehler, Yvonne, and Catherine Fouquet. *L'histoire des mères du moyen-âge à nos jours*. Paris: Montalba, 1977.

Kolboom, Ingo. *La revanche des patrons: Le patronat français face au front populaire*. Paris: Flammarion, 1986.

Kuisel, Richard F. *Capitalism and the State in Modern France*. Cambridge University Press, 1981.

Lamoot, Jules. *Eugène Duthoit*. Paris: Spés, 1955.

Land, Hilary. "The Family Wage." *Feminist Review*, 6 (1980), 55–78.

"The Introduction of Family Allowances: An Act of Historic Justice?" In *Change, Choice and Conflict in Social Policy*. Ed. Phoebe Hall et al. London: Heinemann, 1975, pp. 157–230.

"Who Cares for the Family?" *Journal of Social Policy*, 7: 3 (July 1978), pp. 257–84.

Landes, Joan. *Women and the Public Sphere in the Age of the French Revolution*. Ithaca, N.Y.: Cornell University Press, 1988.

Langan, Mary, and Ilona Ostner. "Gender and Welfare." In *Towards a European Welfare State?* Ed. Graham Room. Bristol: School for Advanced Urban Studies, 1991, pp. 127–50.

Laroque, Pierre, comp. *Social Welfare in France*. Paris: La Documentation Française, 1966.

Launay, Michel. *La C.F.T.C.: Origines et développement, 1919–1940*. Paris: Publications de la Sorbonne, 1986.

"Le syndicalisme chrétien dans un grand conflit du travail." *Le Mouvement Social*, 73 (Oct.–Dec. 1970), pp. 39–78.

Lebrun, François. *Histoire des catholiques en France du XVe siècle à nos jours*. Toulouse: Privat, 1980.

Lefranc, Georges. *Les organisations patronales en France: Du passé au présent*. Paris: Payot, 1976.

Lenoir, Rémi. "Family Policy in France since 1938." In *The French Welfare State: Surviving Social and Ideological Change*. Ed. John S. Ambler. New York: New State University Press, 1991, pp. 144–86.

Leventhal, F. M. *The Last Dissenter: H. N. Brailsford and His World*. Oxford University Press, 1985.

Levine, David. "Punctuated Equilibrium: The Modernization of the Proletarian Family in the Age of Ascendant Capitalism." *International Labor and Working-Class History*, 39 (Spring 1991), pp. 3–20.

Reproducing Families: The Political Economy of English Population History. Cambridge University Press, 1987.

Lévy-Leboyer, Maurice. "Innovation and Business Strategies in Nineteenth- and Twentieth-Century France." In *Enterprise and Entrepreneurs in Nineteenth- and Twentieth-Century France*. Ed. Edward C. Carter II, et al. Baltimore, Md.: Johns Hopkins University Press, 1976, pp. 87–135.

"Le patronat français, 1912–1973." In *Le patronat de la seconde industrialisation*. Ed. M. Lévy-Leboyer. Paris: Editions Ouvrières, 1979, pp. 137–88.

Lewis, Jane. "Beyond Suffrage: English Feminism in the 1920s." *Maryland Historian*, 6: 1 (Spring 1975), pp. 1–17.

"Dealing with Dependency: State Practices and Social Realities, 1875–1945." In *Women's Welfare, Women's Rights*. Ed. Jane Lewis. London: Croom Helm, 1983, pp. 17–37.

"Models of Equality for Women: The Case of State Support for Children in Twentieth-Century Britain." *Maternity and Gender Policies: Women and the Rise of the European Welfare States, 1880s–1950s*. Ed. Gisela Bock and Pat Thane. London: Routledge, 1991, pp. 73–92.

The Politics of Motherhood: Child and Maternal Welfare in England, 1900–1939. London: Croom Helm, 1980.

"The Working Class Wife and Mother and State Intervention, 1870–1918." In *Labour and Love: Women's Experience of Home and Family, 1850–1940*. Ed. Jane Lewis. Oxford: Basil Blackwell, 1986, pp. 99–120.

Linklater, Andro. *An Unhusbanded Life – Charlotte Despard: Suffragette, Socialist and Sinn Feiner*. London: Hutchinson, 1980.

Lister, Ruth. "Women, Economic Dependency and Citizenship." *Journal of Social Policy*, 19: 4 (Oct. 1990), pp. 445–67.

Lowe, Rodney. *Adjusting to Democracy: The Role of the Ministry of Labour in British Politics, 1916–1939.* Oxford University Press, 1986.

Lynch, Katherine A. *Family, Class and Ideology in Early Industrial France: Social Policy and the Working-Class Family, 1825–1848.* Madison: University of Wisconsin Press, 1988.

Macnicol, John. *The Movement for Family Allowances, 1918–1945: A Study in Social Policy Development.* London: Heinemann, 1980.

"Family Allowances and Less Eligibility." In *The Origins of British Social Policy.* Ed. Pat Thane. London: Croom Helm, 1978, pp. 173–202.

Maier, Charles S. "Between Taylorism and Technocracy: European Ideologies and the Vision of Industrial Productivity in the 1920s." *Journal of Contemporary History,* 5: 2 (1970), pp. 27–61.

Recasting Bourgeois Europe. Princeton, N.J.: Princeton University Press, 1975.

Mappen, Ellen F. "Strategies for Change: Social Feminist Approaches to the Problem of Women's Work." In *Unequal Opportunities: Women's Employment in England, 1800–1918.* Ed. Angela John. Oxford: Basil Blackwell, 1986, pp. 235–59.

Mark-Lawson, Jane, and Anne Witz. "From 'Family Labour' to 'Family Wage'? The Case of Women's Labour in Nineteenth-Century Coalmining." *Social History,* 13: 2 (May 1988), pp. 151–174.

Mark-Lawson, Jane, Mike Savage and Alan Warde. "Gender and Local Politics: Struggles over Welfare Policies, 1918–1939." In *Localities, Class and Gender.* Ed. Linda Murgatroyd et al. London: Pion, 1985, pp. 195–215.

Marquand, David. *Ramsay MacDonald.* London: Jonathan Cape, 1977.

Marshall, T. H. *Class, Citizenship and Social Development.* Garden City, N.Y.: Doubleday, 1964.

Martin, Martine. "Ménagère: Une profession? Les dilemmes de l'entre-deux-guerres." *Mouvement Social,* 140 (July–Sept. 1987), pp. 89–106.

Martin, Ross M. *TUC: The Growth of a Pressure Group, 1868–1976.* Oxford University Press, 1980.

Marwick, Arthur. *The Deluge.* London: Bodley Head, 1965.

"Middle Opinion in the Thirties: Planning, Progress and 'Political Agreement.'" *English Historical Review,* 79: 311 (Apr. 1964), pp. 285–98.

May, Martha. "The Historical Problem of the Family Wage: The Ford Motor Company and the Five Dollar Day." *Feminist Studies,* 8: 2 (Summer 1982), pp. 399–424.

Mayeur, Jean-Marie. "Le Catholicisme social en France." *Le Mouvement Social,* 77 (Oct.–Dec. 1971), pp. 113–21.

Mayeur, Jean-Marie, and Madeleine Rebérioux. *The Third Republic from Its Origins to the Great War, 1871–1914.* Cambridge University Press, 1984.

McCarthy, Michael. *Campaigning for the Poor: C.P.A.G. and the Politics of Welfare.* London: Croom Helm, 1986.

McClelland, J. S., ed. *The French Right: From De Maistre to Maurras.* London: Jonathan Cape, 1970.

McClelland, Keith. "Time to Work, Time to Live: Some Aspects of Work and the Re-formation of Class in Britain, 1850–1880." In *The Historical Meanings of Work*. Ed. Patrick Joyce. Cambridge University Press, 1987, pp. 180–209.

McDougall, Mary Lynn. "Protecting Infants: The French Campaign for Maternity Leaves, 1890s–1913." *French Historical Studies*, 13: 1 (Spring 1983), pp. 79–105.

McIntosh, Mary. "The State and the Oppression of Women." In *Feminism and Materialism*. Ed. Annette Kuhn and Ann Marie Wolpe. London: Routledge, 1978, pp. 254–89.

"The Welfare State and the Needs of the Dependent Family." In *Fit Work for Women*. Ed. Sandra Burman. London: Croom Helm, 1979, pp. 153–72.

McKendrick, Neil. "Home Demand and Economic Growth: A New View of the Role of Women and Children in the Industrial Revolution." In *Historical Perspectives: Studies in English Thought and Society*. Ed. Neil McKendrick. Europa, 1974, pp. 152–210.

McKibbin, Ross. *The Ideologies of Class: Social Relations in Britain, 1880–1950*. Oxford University Press, 1990.

McLaren, Angus. *Sexuality and Social Order*. New York: Holmes & Meier, 1983.

McMillan, James F. *Housewife or Harlot: The Place of Women in French Society, 1870–1940*. New York: St. Martin's, 1981.

Meyer, Philippe. *L'enfant et la raison d'état*. Paris: Seuil, 1977.

Michel, Sonya, and Seth Koven. "Womanly Duties: Maternalist Politics and the Origins of Welfare States in France, Germany, Great Britain and the United States, 1880–1920." *American Historical Review*, 95: 4 (Oct. 1990), pp. 1076–1108.

Middlemas, Keith. *Politics in Industrial Society: The Experience of the British System since 1911*. London: André Deutsch, 1979.

Middleton, Lucy, ed. *Women and the Labour Movement*. London: Croom Helm, 1977.

Miller, Michael. *The Bon Marché: Bourgeois Culture and the Department Store, 1869–1920*. Princeton, N.J.: Princeton University Press, 1981.

Minor, Iris. "Working-Class Women and Matrimonial Law Reform, 1890–1914." In *Ideology and the Labour Movement*. Ed. David E. Martin and David Rubinstein. London: Croom Helm, 1979, pp. 103–24.

Mitchell, B. R. *European Historical Statistics*. 1975; 2d rev. ed., New York: Facts on File, 1981.

Moch, Leslie Page, and Louise Tilly. "Joining the Urban World: Occupation, Family, and Migration in Three French Cities." *Comparative Studies in Society and History*, 27: 1 (Jan. 1985), pp. 33–56.

Moon, Parker Thomas. *The Labor Problem and the Social Catholic Movement in France*. New York: Macmillan, 1921.

Moutet, Aimée. "Patrons de progrès ou patrons de combat?" *Recherches*, 32–3 (Sept. 1978).

Mowat, Charles Loch. *Britain between the Wars, 1918–1940*. Boston: Beacon, 1971.

The Charity Organisation Society, 1869–1913. London: Methuen, 1961.

Nada, Nadine. *Bibliographie sur les prestations familiales*. Paris: UNCAF, 1966.

Noiriel, Gérard. "Du 'patronage' au 'paternalisme': La restructuration des formes de domination de la main-d'oeuvre ouvrière dans l'industrie métallurgique française." *Le Mouvement Social*, 144 (July–Sept. 1988), pp. 17–35.

Workers in French Society in the 19th and 20th Centuries. 1986; trans. New York: Berg, 1990.

Offen, Karen. "Body Politics: Women, Work and the Politics of Motherhood in France, 1920–1950." In *Maternity and Gender Policies: Women and the Rise of the European Welfare States, 1880s–1950s*. Ed. Gisela Bock and Pat Thane. London: Routledge, 1991, pp. 138–59.

"Depopulation, Nationalism and Feminism in Fin-de-siècle France." *American Historical Review*, 89: 3 (June 1984), pp. 648–76.

Ogden, Philip E., and Marie-Monique Huss. "Demography and pronatalism in France in the Nineteenth and Twentieth Centuries." *Journal of Historical Geography*, 8: 3 (1982), pp. 283–98.

O'Higgins, Michael. "Inequality, Social Policy and Income Distribution in the United Kingdom." In *The Crisis of Redistribution in European Welfare States*. Ed. Jean-Pierre Jallade. Stoke-on-Trent: Trentham Books, 1988, pp. 25–72.

"The Allocation of Public Resources to Children and the Elderly in OECD Countries." In *The Vulnerable*. Ed. John L. Palmer, Timothy Smeeding, and Barbara Boyle Torrey. Washington D.C.: Urban Institute Press, 1988, pp. 201–28.

Oram, Alison. "Serving Two Masters? The Introduction of a Marriage Bar in Teaching in the 1920s." In *The Sexual Dynamics of History*. Ed. London Feminist History Group. London: Pluto Press, 1983, pp. 134–48.

Oren, Laura. "The Welfare of Women in Laboring Families: England, 1860–1950." In *Clio's Consciousness Raised*. Ed. Mary Hartman and Lois W. Banner. New York: Harper & Row, 1974, pp. 226–44.

Orloff, Ann Shola, and Theda Skocpol. "Why Not Equal Protection? Explaining the Politics of Public Social Spending in Britain, 1900–1911, and the United States, 1880s–1920." *American Sociological Review*, 49: 6 (Dec. 1984), pp. 726–50.

Owen, David. *English Philanthropy, 1660–1960*. Cambridge, Mass.: Harvard University Press, 1964.

Palmer, John L., Timothy Smeeding, and Barbara Boyle Torrey, eds. *The Vulnerable*. Washington D.C.: Urban Institute Press, 1988.

Panitch, Leo. "The Development of Corporatism in Liberal Democracies." In *Trends towards Corporatist Intermediation*. Ed. Philippe C. Schmitter and Gerhard Lehmbruch. London: Sage, 1979, pp. 119–46.

Parker, Olive. *For the Family's Sake: A History of the Mothers' Union, 1876–1976.* Folkestone: Bailey Brothers & Swinfen, 1975.

Pascall, Gillian. *Social Policy: A Feminist Analysis.* London: Tavistock, 1986.

Pateman, Carole. "The Patriarchal Welfare State." In *Democracy and the Welfare State.* Ed. Amy Gutman. Princeton, N.J.: Princeton University Press, 1988, pp. 231–60.

The Sexual Contract. Stanford, Calif.: Stanford University Press, 1988.

Paul, Harry W. *The Second Ralliement: The Rapprochement between Church and State in France in the Twentieth Century.* Washington, D.C.: Catholic University of America Press, 1967.

Pedersen, Susan. "The Failure of Feminism in the Making of the British Welfare State." *Radical History Review,* 43 (1989), pp. 86–110.

"Gender, Welfare, and Citizenship in Britain during the Great War." *American Historical Review,* 95: 4 (Oct. 1990), pp. 983–1006.

Pelling, Henry. *A History of British Trade Unionism.* London: Macmillan, 1963.

"The Working Class and the Origins of the Welfare State." In *Popular Politics and Society in Late Victorian Britain.* 1968; 2d. ed. London: Macmillan, 1979, pp. 1–18.

Perrot, Michèle. "On the Formation of the French Working Class." In *Working-Class Formation: Nineteenth-Century Patterns in Western Europe and the United States.* Ed. Ira Katznelson and Aristide R. Zolberg. Princeton, N.J.: Princeton University Press, 1986, pp. 71–110.

"The Three Ages of Industrial Discipline in Nineteenth-Century France." In *Consciousness and Class Experience in Nineteenth-Century Europe.* Ed. John M. Merriman. New York: Holmes & Meier, 1980, pp. 149–168.

Phillips, Anne, and Barbara Taylor. "Sex and Skill: Notes towards a Feminist Economics." *Feminist Review,* 6 (1980), 79–88.

Pierrard, Pierre. *L'église et les Ouvriers en France (1840–1940).* Paris: Hachette, 1984.

Gens du Nord. Paris: Arthaud, 1985.

Pimlott, Ben. *Labour and the Left in the 1930s.* Cambridge University Press, 1977.

Prochaska, F. K. "Philanthropy." In *The Cambridge Social History of Britain, 1750–1950.* Ed. F. M. L. Thompson. Vol. 3. Cambridge University Press, 1990, pp. 357–93.

Women and Philanthropy in 19th Century England. Oxford University Press, 1980.

Prost, Antoine. "Catholic Conservatives, Population, and the Family in Twentieth Century France." In *Population and Resources in Western Intellectual Traditions.* Ed. Michael S. Teitelbaum and Jay M. Winter. Cambridge University Press, 1988, pp. 147–64.

"L'évolution de la politique familiale en France de 1938 à 1981." *Le Mouvement Social,* no. 129 (Oct.–Dec. 1984), pp. 7–28.

Pugh, Martin. *The Making of Modern British Politics, 1867–1939.* Oxford: Basil Blackwell, 1982.

Quadagno, Jill. "Theories of the Welfare State." *Annual Review of Sociology*, 13 (1987), 109–28.

Questiaux, Nicole, and Jacques Fournier. "France." In *Family Policy: Government and Families in Fourteen Countries*. Ed. Sheila B. Kamerman and Alfred J Kahn. New York: Columbia University Press, 1978, pp. 118–82.

Reddy, William. *The Rise of Market Culture*. Cambridge University Press, 1984.

Register, Cheri. "Motherhood at Center: Ellen Key's Social Vision." *Women's Studies International Forum*, 5: 6 (1982), pp. 599–610.

Rein, Martin, and Lee Rainwater. "From Welfare State to Welfare Society." In *The Rise and Fall of Policy Regimes*. Ed. Martin Rein, Gøsta Esping-Andersen, and Lee Rainwater. Armonk, N.Y.: Sharpe, 1987, pp. 143–59.

Rémond, René. *The Right Wing in France from 1815 to De Gaulle*. Philadelphia: University of Pennsylvania Press, 1966.

Rémond, René, and Janine Bourdin, eds. *Edouard Daladier: Chef de gouvernement*. Paris: Presses de la Fondation Nationale des Sciences Politiques, 1977.

Rémond, René, with Aline Coutrot. *Les Catholiques dans la France des années 30*. 2d ed. Paris: Cana, 1979.

Riley, Denise. "The Free Mothers: Pronatalism and Working Mothers in Industry at the End of the Last War in Britain." *History Workshop Journal*, 11 (Spring 1981), pp. 59–118.

War in the Nursery: Theories of the Child and Mother. London: Virago, 1983.

Robert, Jean-Louis. "La C.G.T. et la famille ouvrière, 1914–1918: Première approche." *Le Mouvement Social*, 116 (July–Sept. 1981), pp. 47–66.

La Scission Syndicale de 1921. Paris: Publications de la Sorbonne. 1980.

"Women and Work in France during the First World War." In *The Upheaval of War: Family, Work and Welfare in Europe, 1914–1918*. Ed. Richard Wall and Jay Winter. Cambridge University Press, 1988, pp. 251–66.

Roberts, Elizabeth. *A Woman's Place: An Oral History of Working-Classs Women, 1890–1940*. London: Basil Blackwell, 1984.

Rodgers, Terence. "Employers' Organizations, Unemployment and Social Politics in Britain during the Interwar Period." *Social History*, 13: 3 (Oct. 1988), pp. 315–41.

Rollet, Henri. *L'action sociale des catholiques en France*. Vol. 1: Paris: Boivin, 1947; Vol. 2: Paris: Desclée de Brouwer, 1958.

Albert De Mun et le parti catholique. Paris: Boivin, 1949.

Andrée Butillard et le féminisme chrétien. Paris: Spes, 1960.

Rollet-Echalier, Catherine. *La politique à l'égard de la petite enfance sous la IIIᵉ République*. Paris: Presses Universitaires de France, 1990.

Ronsin, Francis. *La grève des ventres: Propagande néo-Malthusienne et baisse de la natalité française (19ᵉ–20ᵉ siècles)*. Paris: Aubier Montaigne, 1980.

Rose, Hilary. "Rereading Titmuss: The Sexual Division of Welfare." *Journal of Social Policy*, 10: 4 (Oct. 1981), pp. 477–502.

Rose, Michael E. *The Relief of Poverty, 1834–1914*. London: Macmillan, 1972.

Rose, Sonya O. "Gender Antagonism and Class Conflict: Exclusionary Strategies of Male Trade Unionists in Nineteenth-Century Britain." *Social History*, 13: 2 (May 1988), pp. 191–208.

Limited Livelihoods: Gender and Class in Nineteenth-Century England. Berkeley and Los Angeles: University of California Press, 1992.

Ross, Ellen. " 'Fierce Questions and Taunts': Married Life in Working-Class London." *Feminist Studies*, 8: 3 (Fall 1982), pp. 575–602.

"Hungry Children: Housewives and London Charity, 1870–1918." In *The Uses of Charity.* Ed. Peter Mandler. Philadelphia: University of Pennsylvania Press, 1990, pp. 161–96.

"Labour and Love: Rediscovering London's Working-Class Mothers, 1870–1918." In *Labour and Love: Women's Experience of Home and Family, 1850–1940.* Ed. Jane Lewis. Oxford: Basil Blackwell, 1986, pp. 73–96.

Routh, Guy. *Occupation and Pay in Great Britain, 1906–1960.* Cambridge University Press, 1965.

Rowan, Caroline. " 'Mothers, Vote Labour!' The State, the Labour Movement and Working-Class Mothers, 1900–1918." In *Feminism, Culture and Politics.* Ed. Rosalind Brunt and Caroline Rowan. London: Lawrence & Wishart, 1982, pp. 59–84.

"Women in the Labour Party, 1906–1920." *Feminist Review*, 12 (1982), pp. 74–91.

Rubin, Gerry R. *War, Law and Labour: The Munitions Acts, State Regulation and the Unions, 1915–1921.* Oxford University Press, 1987.

Rubinstein, David. *Before the Suffragettes: Women's Emancipation in the 1890s.* Sussex: Harvester Press, 1986.

Ruggie, Mary. *The State and Working Women: A Comparative Study of Britain and Sweden.* Princeton, N.J.: Princeton University Press, 1984.

Sauvy, Alfred. *Histoire économique de la France entre les deux guerres.* 3 vols. Paris: Economica, 1984.

La vie économique des Français de 1939 à 1945. Paris: Flammarion, 1978.

Savage, Mike. *The Dynamics of Working-Class Politics: The Labour Movement in Preston, 1880–1940.* Cambridge University Press, 1987.

"Trade Unionism, Sex Segregation and the State: Women's Employment in 'New Industries' in Inter-war Britain." *Social History*, 13: 2 (May 1988), pp. 209–30.

Schneider, William. "Towards the Improvement of the Human Race: The History of Eugenics in France." *Journal of Modern History*, 54 (June 1982), pp. 268–91.

Scott, Joan. " 'L'ouvrière! Mot impie, sordide...': Women Workers in the Discourse of French Political Economy, 1840–1860." In *The Historical Meanings of Work.* Ed. Patrick Joyce. Cambridge University Press, 1987, pp. 119–42.

Searle, Geoffrey. *The Quest for National Efficiency, 1899–1914.* Oxford: Basil Blackwell, 1971.

Seccombe, Wally. "Patriarchy Stabilized: The Construction of the Male Breadwinner Wage Norm in Nineteenth-Century Britain." *Social History*, 11: 1 (Jan. 1986), pp. 53–76.

Semmel, Bernard. *Imperialism and Social Reform: English Social-Imperial Thought, 1895–1914*. Cambridge, Mass.: Harvard University Press, 1960.

Sewell, William H., Jr. *Work and Revolution in France: The Language of Labor from the Old Regime to 1848*. Cambridge University Press, 1980.

Sharp, Walter Rice. *The French Civil Service: Bureaucracy in Transition*. New York: Macmillan, 1931.

——. *The Government of the French Republic*. New York: Van Nostrand, 1938.

Shorter, Edward, and Charles Tilly. *Strikes in France, 1830–1968*. Cambridge University Press, 1974.

Silver, Catherine Bodard, ed. *Frédéric Le Play: On Family, Work, and Social Change*. Chicago: University of Chicago Press, 1982.

Simey, Margaret. *Eleanor Rathbone: A Centenary Tribute*. Liverpool: University of Liverpool Press, 1974.

Simon, Dominique. "Le patronat face aux assurances sociales." *Le Mouvement Social*, no. 137 (Oct.–Dec. 1986), pp. 7–27.

Skidelsky, Robert. *Politicians and the Slump: The Labour Government of 1929–1931*. London: Macmillan, 1967.

Skocpol, Theda. "Bringing the State Back In: Strategies of Analysis in Current Research." In *Bringing the State Back In*. Ed. Peter Evans, Dietrich Rueschemeyer, and Theda Skocpol. Cambridge University Press, 1985, pp. 3–37.

——. *Protecting Soldiers and Mothers: Political Origins of Social Policy in the United States*. Cambridge, Mass.: Harvard University Press, 1992.

Smeeding, Timothy M., Michael O'Higgins, and Lee Rainwater, eds. *Poverty, Inequality and Income Distribution in Comparative Perspective: The Luxembourg Income Study (LIS)*. New York: Harvester Wheatsheaf, 1990.

Smeeding, Timothy, Barbara Boyle Torrey, and Martin Rein. "Patterns of Income and Poverty: The Economic Status of Children and the Elderly in Eight Countries." In *The Vulnerable*. Ed. John L. Palmer, Timothy Smeeding, and Barbara Boyle Torrey. Washington D.C.: Urban Institute Press, 1988, pp. 89–119.

Smith, Bonnie G. *Ladies of the Leisure Class: The Bourgeoises of Northern France in the Nineteenth Century*. Princeton, N.J.: Princeton University Press, 1981.

Smith, Harold L. "The Womanpower Problem in Britain during the Second World War." *Historical Journal*, 27: 4 (1984), pp. 925–45.

Smith, Harold L., ed. *British Feminism in the Twentieth Century*. Amherst: University of Massachusetts Press, 1990.

——. *War and Social Change: British Society in the Second World War*. Manchester: Manchester University Press, 1986.

Smith, Ruth L., and Deborah M. Valenze. "Mutuality and Marginality: Liberal Moral Theory and Working-Class Women in Nineteenth-Century England." *Signs*, 13: 2 (1988), pp. 277–98.

Snell, Keith. *Annals of the Labouring Poor: Social Change and Agrarian England, 1660–1900.* Cambridge University Press, 1985.

Sohn, Anne-Marie. "Catholic Women and Political Affairs: The Case of the Patriotic League of French Women." In *Women in Culture and Politics: A Century of Change.* Ed. Judith Friedlander et. al. Bloomington: Indiana University Press, 1986, pp. 237–55.

Soloway, Richard Allen. "Feminism, Fertility and Eugenics in Victorian and Edwardian England." In *Political Symbolism in Modern Europe.* Ed. Seymour Drescher, David Sabean, and Allan Sharlin. London: Transaction, 1982, pp. 121–45.

Soucy, Robert. *French Fascism: The First Wave, 1924–1933.* New Haven, Conn.: Yale University Press, 1986.

Sowerwine, Charles. *Sisters or Citizens? Women and Socialism in France since 1876.* Cambridge University Press, 1982.

"Workers and Women in France before 1914: The Debate over the Couriau Affair." *Journal of Modern History,* 55: 3 (Sept. 1983), pp. 411–41.

Spengler, Joseph J. *France Faces Depopulation.* Durham, N.C.: Duke University Press, 1938.

Stanley, Liz, ed. *The Diaries of Hannah Cullwick, Victorian Maidservant.* New Brunswick, N.J.: Rutgers University Press, 1974.

Stearns, Peter. "Working-Class Women in Britain, 1890–1914." In *Suffer and Be Still.* Ed. Martha Vicinus. Bloomington: Indiana University Press, 1972, pp. 100–120.

Sternhell, Zeev. *Ni droite, ni gauche: L'idéologie fasciste en France.* Paris: Seuil, 1983.

Stevenson, John. "The Making of Unemployment Policy, 1931–35." In *High and Low Politics in Modern Britain.* Ed. Michael Bentley and John Stevenson. Oxford University Press, 1983, pp. 182–213.

Stevenson, John, and Chris Cook. *The Slump: Society and Politics during the Depression.* 1977; rpt. London: Quartet, 1979.

Stewart, Mary Lynn. *Women, Work and the French State: Labour Protection and Social Patriarchy, 1879–1919.* Kingston: McGill-Queen's University Press, 1989.

Stocks, Mary Danvers. *Eleanor Rathbone: A Biography.* London: Gollancz, 1949.

Stone, Judith F. "The Radicals and the Interventionist State: Attitudes, Ambiguities and Transformations, 1880–1910." *French History,* 2: 2 (June 1988), pp. 173–86.

The Search for Social Peace. Albany: State University of New York Press, 1985.

Sullerot, Evelyne. "Condition de la femme." In *Histoire économique de la France entre les deux guerres.* Vol. 3. Paris: Economica, 1984, pp. 194–209.

Summerfield, Penny. *Women Workers in the Second World War: Production and Patriarchy in Conflict.* London: Croom Helm, 1984.

Sussman, George D. *Selling Mothers' Milk: The Wet-Nursing Business in France, 1715–1914.* Urbana: University of Illinois Press, 1982.

Swaan, Abram de. *In Care of the State: Health Care, Education and Welfare in*

Europe and the USA in the Modern Era. New York: Oxford University Press, 1988.

Talmy, Robert. *Histoire du mouvement familial en France, 1896–1939.* 2 vols. Paris: UNCAF, 1962.

Le syndicalisme chrétien en France, 1871–1930. Paris: Bloud & Gay, 1965.

Tanner, Duncan. *Political Change and the Labour Party, 1900–1918.* Cambridge University Press, 1990.

Tawney, R. H. "Abolition of Economic Controls, 1918–1921." *Economic History Review,* 13 (1943), pp. 1–30.

Taylor, Barbara. *Eve and the New Jerusalem.* New York: Pantheon, 1983.

Tebbutt, Melanie. *Making Ends Meet: Pawnbroking and Working-Class Credit.* Leicester: Leicester University Press, 1983.

Teitelbaum, Michael S., and Jay M. Winter. *The Fear of Population Decline.* New York: Academic Press, 1985.

Thane, Pat. *The Foundations of the Welfare State.* London: Longman, 1982.

"Government and Society in England and Wales, 1750–1914." In *The Cambridge Social History of Britain, 1750–1950.* Ed. F. M. L. Thompson. Vol. 3. Cambridge University Press, 1990, pp. 1–61.

"Visions of Gender in the Making of the British Welfare State: The Case of Women in the British Labour Party and Social Policy, 1906–1945." In *Maternity and Gender Policies: Women and the Rise of the European Welfare States, 1880s–1950s.* Ed. Gisela Bock and Pat Thane. London: Routledge, 1991, pp. 92–118.

"Women and the Poor Law in Victorian and Edwardian England." *History Workshop Journal,* 6 (Autumn 1978), pp. 29–51.

"The Working Class and State 'Welfare' in Britain, 1880–1914." *Historical Journal,* 27: 4 (1984), pp. 877–900.

Thébaud, Françoise. *La femme au temps de la guerre de 14.* Paris: Stock, 1986.

"Maternité et famille entre les deux guerres: Idéologies et politique familiale." In *Femmes et Fascismes.* Ed. Rita Thalmann. France: Tierce, 1986, pp. 85–97.

"Le mouvement nataliste dans la France de l'entre-deux-guerres." *Revue d'Histoire Moderne et Contemporaine,* 32 (Apr.–June 1985), pp. 276–301.

Quand nos grand-mères donnaient la vie: La maternité en France dans l'entre-deux-guerres. Lyon: Presses Universitaires de Lyon, 1986.

Thompson, Dorothy. "Women in Nineteenth Century Radical Politics: A Lost Dimension." In *The Rights and Wrongs of Women.* Ed. Juliet Mitchell and Ann Oakley. Harmondsworth: Penguin, 1976, pp. 112–38.

Titmuss, Richard. *Social Policy: An Introduction.* London: George Allen & Unwin, 1974.

Tomlinson, J. D. "Women as 'Anomalies': The Anomalies Regulations of 1931, Their Background and Implications." *Public Administration,* 62 (Winter 1984), pp. 423–37.

Trustram, Myna. *Women of the Regiment: Marriage and the Victorian Army.* Cambridge University Press, 1984.

Turner, John. "The Politics of 'Organised Business' in the First World War."

In *Businessmen in Politics: Studies of Business Activity in British Politics, 1900–1945*. Ed. John Turner. London: Heinemann, 1984, pp. 33–49.

Vicinus, Martha. *Independent Women: Work and Community for Single Women, 1850–1920*. London: Virago, 1985.

Waites, Bernard. *A Class Society at War: England 1914–18*. Leamington Spa: Berg, 1987.

Walby, Sylvia. *Patriarchy at Work: Patriarchal and Capitalist Relations in Employment*. Cambridge: Polity Press, 1986.

Walkowitz, Judith. "Male Vice and Feminist Virtue: Feminism and the Politics of Prostitution in Nineteenth Century Britain." *History Workshop Journal*, 13 (Spring 1982), pp. 79–93.

"Science, Feminism and Romance: The Men and Women's Club 1885–1889." *History Workshop Journal*, 21 (Spring 1986), pp. 37–59.

Wall, Richard, and Jay Winter, eds. *The Upheaval of War: Family, Work and Welfare in Europe, 1914–1918*. Cambridge University Press, 1988.

Weber, Eugen. *The Nationalist Revival in France, 1905–1914*. Berkeley and Los Angeles: University of California Press, 1959.

Webster, Charles. "Healthy or Hungry Thirties?" *History Workshop Journal*, 13 (Spring 1982), pp. 110–29.

Weeks, Jeffrey. *Sex, Politics and Society*. London: Longman, 1981.

Weir, Margaret, and Theda Skocpol. "State Structures and the Possibilities for 'Keynesian' Responses to the Great Depression in Sweden, Britain, and the United States." In *Bringing the State Back In*. Ed. Peter Evans, Dietrich Rueschemeyer, and Theda Skocpol. Cambridge University Press, 1985, pp. 107–163.

Weiss, John H. "Origins of the French Welfare State: Poor Relief in the Third Republic, 1871–1914." *French Historical Studies*, 13: 1 (Spring 1983), pp. 47–78.

Weissbach, Lee Shai. *Child Labor Reform in Nineteenth-Century France: Assuring the Future Harvest*. Baton Rouge: Louisiana State University Press, 1989.

Wheaton, Robert, and Tamara K. Hareven, eds. *Family and Sexuality in French History*. Philadelphia: University of Pennsylvania Press, 1980.

Whiteside, Noelle. "Welfare Insurance and Casual Labour: A Study of Administrative Intervention in Industrial Employment, 1906–1926." *Economic History Review*, 2d ser., 32: 4 (Nov. 1979), pp. 507–22.

"Welfare Legislation and the Unions during the First World War." *Historical Journal*, 23: 4 (1980), pp. 857–74.

Williamson, Philip. *National Crisis and National Government: British Politics, the Economy and Empire, 1926–1932*. Cambridge University Press, 1992.

Wilson, Elizabeth. *Women and the Welfare State*. London: Tavistock, 1977.

Winship, Janice. "Nation before Family: *Woman, The National Home Weekly*, 1945–1953." In *Formations of Nation and People*. London: Routledge, 1984.

Winter, J. M. "The Impact of the First World War on Civilian Health in Britain." *Economic History Review*, 2d ser., 30: 3 (Aug. 1977), pp. 487–503.

The Great War and the British People. Cambridge, Mass.: Harvard University Press, 1986.

Wootton, Graham. *The Politics of Influence: British Ex-servicemen, Cabinet Decisions and Cultural Change (1917–57)*. Cambridge, Mass.: Harvard University Press, 1963.

Wynn, Margaret. *Family Policy*. London: Michael Joseph, 1971.

Zerner, Sylvie. "De la couture aux presses: L'emploi féminin entre les deux guerres." *Mouvement Social*, 140 (July–Sept. 1987), pp. 9–25.

Zimmeck, Meta. "The 'New Woman' in the Machinery of Government: A Spanner in the Works?" In *Government and Expertise: Specialists, Administrators and Professionals, 1860–1914*. Ed. Roy MacLeod. Cambridge University Press, 1988, pp. 185–202.

"Strategies and Stratagems for the Employment of Women in the British Civil Service, 1919–1939." *Historical Journal*, 27: 4 (1984), pp. 901–24.

INDEX

Abbott, Elizabeth, 354
abortion, 132, 365, 387, 407–8
Action Française, 394
acts of Parliament (Britain); *see also*
  House of Commons
  Children's Act (1908), 52
  Education (Provision of Meals) Act
    (1906), 53–4
  Equal Guardianship of Infants Act
    (1925), 348
  Family Allowances Act (1945), 344–5,
    349–50
  Labour Exchanges Act (1909), 49, 58
  Maternal and Infant Welfare Act
    (1918), 150
  Military Service Acts (1916), 82
  Munitions Acts (1915, 1916), 83–4
  National Insurance Act (1911), 49–50,
    58, 294
  National Insurance (Munition
    Workers) Act (1916), 125
  Restoration of Prewar Practices Act
    (1919), 122
  Sex Disqualification (Removal) Act
    (1919), 299–300
  Trade Boards Act (1909), 50, 58–9,
    122
  Unemployed Workers' Dependents
    (Temporary Provisions) Act (1921),
    127
  Unemployment Insurance Act (1920),
    127, 294
  Unemployment Insurance (No. 3) Act
    (the Anomalies Act) (1931), 296,
    302–3
  Widows', Orphans', and Old Age
  (Contributory Pensions) Act (1925),
    168, 171–2
Adamson, Jennie, 197 n. 54, 205 n. 83
Addison, Christopher, 84, 169–71
agriculture, 37, 70–1, 376, 382–3
Allen, Clifford, 189–90
Allen, Grant, 42
Alliance Nationale pour l'Accroissement
  de la Population Française, 26, 60–
  8, 73, 76–7, 131, 233–5, 359–72
  passim, 384–6, 398–400, 407–8; *see
  also* birthrate, annual conference
  on; birthrate, decline of;
  pronatalism
allowances, *see* endowment of
  motherhood (Britain); family
  allowances (Britain); family
  allowances (France); maternity
  benefit; separation allowances;
  unemployment assistance (Britain);
  unemployment insurance (Britain);
  unwaged mother's allowance
  (France)
Amery, Leo, 319–20, 329, 331
Anderson, Adelaide, 122–3
Anderson, Sir John, 172, 342
Anomalies Act, *see* acts of Parliament
anomalies regulations, *see*
  unemployment insurance (Britain)
Ashby, Margery Corbett, 183
Asquith, H. H., 81–2, 109
Assistance Publique, 69
Association Catholique des Patrons du
  Nord, 241
Astor, Nancy, 169 n. 87
Atkin, Sir James Richard, 155

465

Atkinson, Mabel, 42–3
Attlee, Clement, 343 n. 169
automobile industry (France), 263, 280, 284, 286

Bakke, E. W., 310–11
Baldwin, Peter, 7
Baldwin, Stanley, 170, 172
Balfour of Burleigh, Lord (Alexander Hugh Bruce), 186
Bamber, Mary, 213–14
Barnes, George, 111
Barnett, Henrietta, 151
Barton, Eleanor, 201–2, 210
Bataille, Abbé, 252
Beard, John, 197 n. 54, 205 n. 83, 216, 302
Beck, Cecil, 57
Bell, Florence, 39
Bell, Mrs. Harrison, 166
Bell-Richards, Mrs., 212–13
Bentham, Ethel, 204 n. 80, 205 n. 83
Bertillon, Jacques, 60
Betterton, Henry, 306
Beveridge, Janet, 339
Beveridge, Sir William, 6, 49, 125, 181, 184, 186, 293, 305, 316, 318, 328–9, 333–46 passim, 353–4
Beveridge Committee, *see* committees and commissions, official (Britain)
Beveridge Plan, 13, 293, 294, 337–43
  family allowances within, 338, 340–1, 343, 345
  government response to, 342–5
  married women within, 337–40, 352–4
Bevin, Ernest, 167, 194–5, 206, 208, 215, 217, 302, 320, 334, 343 n. 169, 344, 346
Bigot, Marthe, 278–9
birth control, 65–7, 131–2, 360–2, 365, 387, 396, 407
birthrate, annual conference on, 131, 228–9, 234, 369, 398
birthrate, decline of; *see also* Alliance Nationale pour l'Accroissement de la Population Française; pronatalism
  Britain, 53, 150, 318–20, 327–8
  France, 59–69, 76–7, 359–72 passim, 384–5, 388–9, 410 n. 145
Black, Clementina, 43

Bloc National, 131, 135, 360
Blum, Léon, 371,
  governments of, 381, 383, 385
Boer War, 47, 53, 110
Bokanowski, Maurice, 229–30
Bon Marché, 75
Bonar Law, Andrew, 170
Bondfield, Margaret, 135, 150 n. 28, 195, 197 n. 54, 198, 204 n. 80, 295, 297–8, 300, 302–3
Bonvoisin, Georges, 234–6, 265, 373, 375, 387–90
Booth, Charles, 47
Booth, Frederick, 57
Bosanquet, Helen, 48
Boverat, Fernand, 3, 359–68 passim, 370, 374, 379–81, 386, 402, 406–8
Bowley, Arthur, 153
Brailsford, Henry Noel, 145, 189–91, 194
Britain's Industrial Future, see Liberal Industrial Inquiry
British Medical Association, 320, 331
Brittain, Vera, 91
Bromley, John, 216
Brunschvicg, Cécile, 274, 368, 374, 397–8, 403
Buisson, Georges, 241, 249
Buisson, Suzanne, 404–5
Bullock, H. L., 289, 331–2
Bureau, Paul, 128
Burns, Elinor, 145
Burns, Emile, 145
Butillard, Andrée, 393–6, 398, 404
Butler, R. A., 348

Cadbury (firm), 326
Caisse de Compensation de la Région Parisienne, 226–7, 261–85 passim; *see also* Groupe des Industries Métallurgiques, Mécaniques et Connexes de la Région Parisienne
  and family allowances, 267–73
  and links to the employers' organizations, 262–71
  payment of benefits to the mother, 273, 276–9, 402
  response to state intervention, 279–81, 283 n. 152
  social work of, 273–6, 280–1, 286–7, 288 n. 160, 400

caisses de compensation, see Caisse de Compensation de la Région Parisienne; Consortium Textile de Roubaix-Tourcoing; family allowance funds (France)

Campbell, Janet, 155

Catholics (France)
and the birthrate, 63, 398–9
and the Consortium Textile de Roubaix-Tourcoing, 248–9, 251–4
and employer paternalism, 75, 227, 238 n. 37
and family allowances, 225 n. 2, 227–8, 231–3, 251, 373
and feminism, 393–4, 401–4
and women's work, 275, 393–8

census evidence, 36–9, 61, 71, 124–5, 171 n. 95

Chamber of Deputies; *see also* committees and commission, official (France)
Labor Commission, 376
Social Insurance Commission, 129–30, 230–1, 370, 376–7, 381, 402
and family allowances, 229–31, 358, 376–7, 381–3
pronatalist lobby within, 65, 67, 233, 371, 373, 383
and the unwaged mother's allowance, 399

Chamberlain, Neville, 168, 172, 175–6

Chambers of Commerce, 228–9, 370, 375

Charity Organisation Society, 47–8, 53 n. 66, 58, 147 n. 19

Charles, Enid, 319

Chautemps government, 383, 385

Chew, Ada Nield, 41, 46, 148

Cheysson, Emile, 60

child labor legislation, 35, 68–69, 72

child poverty, *see* poverty

Child Poverty Action Group, 415

child welfare legislation, 51–4, 68–9, 150, 222

children's allowances, *see* family allowances (Britain); family allowances (France)

Children's Minimum Council, 317, 321, 323

Churchill, Winston, 49, 81, 341 n. 162, 343 n. 169

citizenship and social rights, 5–8, 55, 56, 111–12, 127–8, 144–7, 167–8, 175–7, 306, 361–5, 406–7

Citrine, Walter, 195, 197, 200, 203, 205–7, 214–15, 221–2, 302, 331–3

Citroën, André, 123, 269, 284

Citroën (firm), 104

Civil Code (France), 61, 72, 116, 118, 365

civil service, 74, 116–17, 120–1, 169–75 passim, 300, 357, 380

Clay, Mary, 166 n. 80

Clémentel, Etienne, 87

coal industry, *see* mining industry

coalition governments (Britain)
(1915–18), 125–6, 169–70
(1918–22), 126–7, 135, 170–2, 294, 299
(1940–5), 315–16, 330–1, 335, 341–54 passim

Cognacq-Jay prizes, 363

Cohen, Joseph, 200

Cole, G. D. H., 206

collective bargaining, *see* wages

Comité d'Action, 83

Comité Central des Allocations Familiales, 224 n. 1, 226, 229, 232, 234–6, 265–6, 286–7, 373–6

Comité des Forges, 87, 103, 263, 266

Commission Intersyndicale de l'Industrie Textile de Roubaix-Tourcoing, 242

committees and commissions, official (Britain)
Committee on Insurance and Other Social Services (Anderson Committee), 172–3
Committee on National Debt and Taxation, 214
Committee on National Expenditure (May Committee), 295–6, 355
Committee on Recruitment to the Civil Service, 120–1
Health of Munitions Workers Committee, 97–8
Interdepartmental Committee on Social Insurance and Allied Services (Beveridge Committee), 333, 336–7
Ministry of Reconstruction Committee on the Machinery of Government, 120–1

Official Committee on the Beveridge Report (Phillips Committee), 342, 344

Royal Commission on the Coal Industry, 186–8

Royal Commission on Unemployment Insurance, 295, 298–9, 301–2, 303–4, 308, 322–3

Unemployment Insurance Anomalies Advisory Committee, 304–5

Unemployment Insurance Statutory Committee, 323–5

War Cabinet Committee on Women in Industry, 95–6, 100–1, 120–1, 151–2, 154–6, 159

Women's Employment Committee of the Ministry of Reconstruction, 120–1, 159

committees and commissions, official (France)

Commissariat Général à la Famille, 387

Commission Supérieure des Allocations Familiales, 370, 376, 378

Conseil Supérieur de la Famille, 387

Conseil Supérieur de la Natalité, 131, 233, 360–1, 365–6, 370, 379–81, 398–9, 402

Conseil Supérieur de Travail, 230

Extra-Parliamentary Commissions on Depopulation, 67–8

High Committee on Population, 386–7, 406

Women's Work Committee, 102, 105–6

communism (France), 131, 253, 277–9, 369, 405; *see also* Confédération Générale du Travail Unitaire

Compagnie du Chemin de Fer du Nord, 75–6

compulsory arbitration, *see* wages

Confédération Française des Travailleurs Chrétiens, 251–4, 256

Confédération Générale de la Production Française, 88, 266, 269

Confédération Générale du Travail, 82, 92, 103, 239, 249–51, 253, 256, 277, 239, 398

congresses: (1923), 241–2, 249; (1929), 249

Confédération Générale du Travail Unitaire, 250–1, 253, 256, 277–9, 405 n. 133

congresses: (1925), 278; (1927), 277

Congrès National des Allocations Familiales, *see* family allowance funds (France)

conscription and enlistment, *see* World War I

Conseil Supérieur de la Natalité, *see* committees and commissions (France)

Conseil Supérieur de Travail, *see* committees and commissions (France)

Conservative governments (Britain); *see also* National governments

(1902–5), 52

(1922–4), 172

(1925–9), 169–72, 175–7

Consortium Textile de Roubaix-Tourcoing, 226, 236–61, 285–6

and conflicts with trade unions, 249–58

and conflicts with the Catholic hierarchy, 252–4

and conflicts with government ministers, 254–5, 259

and family allowances legislation, 258–9

family policies of, 236–7, 241–8, 259–61

labor policies of, 240–8, 255–8, 262

and social insurance legislation, 255–7

corporatism (France), 62–5, 239–40, 376, 394

Courtney, Kathleen, 143, 145, 183

Craik, Henry, 54 n. 71

Cramp, C. T., 218–9

Daladier government, 386, 401

Dalbouze, Ernest, 269, 282

Dalton, Hugh, 163, 181, 199, 207

Danel, Joseph, 397

Davies, Margaret Llewelyn, 161

Davies, Rhys, 167–8, 209–10, 213, 351

De Mun, Count Albert, 75, 240, 394

Deakin, Arthur, 332, 335

Decostère, L., 256–7

Deschamps, Louis, 228, 230, 232–3

Detoeuf, Auguste, 269, 374
diet, 110 n. 81, 159–60, 320–1
dilution of labor, *see* World War I
Disinherited Family, The, 2–3, 179–85,
    289–90; *see also* Rathbone, Eleanor
division of labor, *see* labor force,
    structure of (Britain); labor force,
    structure of (France)
Doig, Peter, 214
Dollan, P. J., 216
domestic service, 36–7, 43 n. 38, 91,
    123, 126
Dooley, Mrs., 210–11
Drake, Barbara, 154–5, 163, 181 n. 3,
    321
Duchemin, René, 269, 282, 374
Dukes, Charles, 167, 332–3, 351
Durkheim, Emile, 64 n. 96
Duthoit, Eugène, 23, 131, 252 n. 66,
    256, 258, 374, 393–4

Elvin, H. H., 167, 197 n. 54, 200–1, 203,
    205 n. 84
employers (Britain), 185–6, 334; *see also*
    engineering industry; mining
    industry; National Confederation of
    Employers' Organisations
employers (France); *see also* Caisse de
    Compensation de la Région
    Parisienne; Consortium Textile de
    Roubaix-Tourcoing; engineering
    industry; family allowance funds;
    Groupe des Industries
    Métallurgiques, Mécaniques et
    Connexes de la Région Parisienne;
    mining industry; textile industry;
    rationalization
  and Catholicism, 227–33, 395–6
  and family allowances: nationally,
    224–36, 373–9, 416–7, 422–3; in
    the textile industry in Roubaix-
    Tourcoing, 236–61; in the
    engineering industry in the Paris
    region, 261–85
  historiography of, 287–8
  and married women's work, 395–6
  and paternalism before 1914, 75–6
  and pronatalism, 233–5, 388–9
  and the unwaged mother's allowance,
    395

and wartime negotiations over
    production, 86–8
employment, *see* wage-earning women
    (Britain); wage-earning women
    (France)
endowment of motherhood (Britain); *see
    also* unwaged mother's allowance
    (France)
  compared with French campaigns,
    396
  debates before 1914, 30–1, 44–7, 55–8
  debates in the twenties: among civil
    servants, 169–75; among feminists,
    136–52; among social investigators,
    152–60; within the Labour Party,
    160–8
  separation allowances as a model for,
    107, 114, 139, 143
engineering industry
  Britain, 82–5, 93–9
  France, 86, 101–5, 123, 226–8, 262–9,
    280–5, 378
equal pay, *see* wages
Equal Pay and the Family (pamphlet), 145
Esping-Andersen, Gøsta, 8–9
Etats Généraux du Féminisme, 368
eugenics, 42–3, 46–7, 174 n. 107, 318–
    19, 327, 360
Eugenics Society, 318–19, 325
evangelicalism, 33
Evans, Dorothy, 212, 220

Fabian Society, 26, 43
Fabian Women's Group, 44–5, 55, 153–
    4, 156, 159–60, 177
factory legislation, 35, 69, 72
Familia, 241
family allowance funds (France); *see also*
    Caisse de Compensation de la
    Région Parisienne; Consortium
    Textile de Roubaix-Tourcoing
  development of, 224–33, 357–8, 378–
    9
  in the engineering industry in the
    Paris region, 261–85, 385
  and pronatalism, 225 n. 2, 233–5,
    269, 380–1, 388–9
  and social Catholicism, 225 n. 2, 227,
    231–3, 248–9, 251–4
  state regulation of, 229–31, 254–6,

258–9, 280–3, 290–1, 358, 372–9,
388, 390 n. 89, 408
in the textile industry in the Nord,
236–261
conferences of: (1921), 231–2; (1922),
235–6; (1923), 236, 246, 373;
(1925), 232–3; (1929), 373; (1930),
287; (1933), 379 n. 60; (1934), 378
n. 59; (1936), 379 n. 60; (1938),
400; (1939), 388–9, 401
family allowances (Britain); *see also*
endowment of motherhood
(Britain); Family Endowment
Society; separation allowances
campaign for: in the twenties, 185–96;
in the thirties, 293–4, 316–27;
during World War II, 327–36
and the Beveridge Plan, 340–54
and employers' organizations, 185–8,
334–5
and the Independent Labour Party,
178–9, 189–96
introduction of: in the private sector,
318, 326; nationally, 343–52
and the Labour Party, 193–4, 197–
223 passim, 332–5
and the Liberal Party, 188–9, 329
payment to the mother, 196, 334,
345–50
and the Trades Union Congress, 194–
5, 197–223 passim, 331–5
trade union attitudes toward, 208–23,
291, 331–5
and the welfare state, 13–14, 413–18
family allowances (France); *see also*
separation allowances; unwaged
mother's allowance (France)
for agricultural workers, 382–3, 387
for employees of government
contractors, 231
for government employees, 74–5,
116–17, 119, 357, 381, 387
for large families, 61, 73–4, 128
for miners, 117, 357, 377
in private industry, *see* family
allowance funds (France)
payment to the mother, 119, 129–30,
273, 279, 402–6, 406 n. 135–6
for railway workers, 75–6, 117, 119,
357, 377

single-wage allowance, 401, 408–10
state regulation of, 386–92
and the welfare state, 17, 413–20
Family Code, 386–8, 401; *see also* laws
and decrees (France)
family endowment, *see* endowment of
motherhood (Britain); family
allowances (Britain); family
allowances (France)
Family Endowment Committee, 145–7,
150–2, 183
Family Endowment Society, 135, 181 n.
3, 183–8, 199–201, 204, 208–9,
217–18, 292, 316–19, 321, 325, 332,
341, 345–6, 349
family wage, *see* male-breadwinner wage
norm (Britain); male-breadwinner
wage norm (France)
fascism (France), 239 n. 39
Fawcett, Millicent Garrett, 141, 147–9
Fécondité (Zola), 26–32
femininity, *see* identities
feminism (Britain)
before 1914, 41–7
and the Beveridge Plan, 352–4
divisions within and decline of, 133,
307, 317, 352–3
and World War I, 88, 114, 133, 138–9
"new feminism," 138–52
feminism (France)
and the birthrate, 65–8, 129, 131, 368
and communism, 278–9, 404–5
and economic dependence, 402–6
and married women's work, 397–8
and support for the war, 88 n. 19
Fête des Mères, 130
Florence, Philip Sargant, 206
Forbes Watson, Sir John, 185, 334–5
Fordism, *see* rationalization
François Roussel (firm), 256, 258
Fraser, Helen, 148
Freewoman (journal), 23, 31, 41–2, 45–6

Geddes, Sir Auckland, 170
gender, *see* identities
General Council, *see* Trades Union
Congress
George, R. F., 320
Germany, 8 n. 14, 9 n. 16, 15, 60, 81,
128 n. 122, 269, 370, 384, 415–16

Glyn-Jones, William, 56
Gollancz, Victor, 145
Gould, Barbara Ayrton, 163, 183, 204 n.
    80, 205 n. 83
government (Britain), *see* coalition
    governments; Conservative
    governments; House of Commons;
    Labour governments; Liberal
    governments; National
    governments; ministries (Britain)
government (France), *see* Bloc National;
    Blum, Léon; Chamber of Deputies;
    Chautemps government; Daladier
    government; ministries (France);
    Popular Front; Senate (France);
    Vichy government
Gray, Alexander, 3, 181–3, 199, 413
Green, Marjorie, 316, 319
Greenwood, Arthur, 169
Grégoire, Mme Raymonde, 399
Griffiths, John, 219
Groupe des Industriels de la Région
    Parisienne, 263–4
Groupe des Industries Métallurgiques,
    Mécaniques et Connexes de la
    Région Parisienne, 261–88 passim;
    see also Caisse de Compensation de
    la Région Parisienne
  family policies of, 262, 267–76, 283–5
  labor policies of, 262
  links to the Caisse de Compensation
    de la Région Parisienne, 262, 266–9
  organization of, 263–7
  relations with trade unions, 271, 276–
    9, 281–2
guardianship of children, 69, 348
Guesde, Jules, 67, 238

Haldane, Richard Burdon, 120
Hamilton, Cicely, 41, 148
Hardouin, Mlle, 273–6, 374
Harmel, Jacques, 75
Harmel, Léon, 75, 227, 240, 394
Haury, Paul, 361, 365, 387
Hayday, Arthur, 167, 219
health insurance, 50, 56–7, 328
Henderson, Arthur, 82, 197, 198, 203,
    204 n. 80, 207
Herriot, Edouard, 129, 369
Hill, John, 197 n. 54, 205 n. 83, 211

Hobhouse, L.T., 49, 338
Hobson, John A., 190, 191
Holtby, Winifred, 300–1
homework, 50, 70, 72–3
Honnorat, Auguste, 60
Hopkins, R. V. N., 350, 351
House of Commons; *see also* committees
    and commissions, official (Britain)
  Select Committee on Naval and
    Military Services (Pensions and
    Grants), 110–1
  debates: anomalies regulations, 302;
    family allowances and social
    security, 342 n. 168, 345, 349–50;
    married women's work, 300;
    maternity benefit, 56–8; school
    meals, 54; separation allowances,
    108, 110–12, 114
  Family Allowance Group within, 329–
    31
household means test, *see*
    unemployment assistance (Britain)
housewives, 38 n. 22, 39, 160–2, 166,
    219–20, 236, 273–6, 314–15, 338–
    40, 352–4, 395
housework, 39, 41, 274–5, 339–40, 400
    n. 115, 405–6, 406 n. 134
Hubback, Eva, 318, 319, 352
Hunter, Ernest, 196 n. 52, 210
Hutchins, B. L., 43–4
Hutchinson, W. H., 204 n. 80, 205
identities
  working men's, 36, 78, 310–13
  working-class women's, 34 n. 13, 39,
    44, 92, 100, 312–15
Independent Labour Party, 26, 45–6,
    302, 333; and the "living wage"
    campaign, 178–9, 189–96, 198–9,
    204, 216–19, 221, 292; *see also*
    Living Wage, The
infant mortality and welfare, 69, 72–3,
    150–1, 274, 320, 321 n. 89, 368,
    370
insurance, *see* health insurance;
    unemployment insurance (Britain)
interests, defined, 20–1, 424–5
Isaac, Auguste, 229, 369

Jaurès, Jean, 81
Javal, Emile, 60

Jean, Victor, 230
Jeunesse Ouvrière Chrétienne, 248
Jewson, Dorothy, 196 n. 52, 210
Joint Committee on the Living Wage, *see*
    Labour Party
Jones, Arthur Creech, 190, 194
Jones, Joseph, Mrs., 204 n. 80, 205 n.
    83
Jones, R. T., 197 n. 54, 205 n. 83
Jouhaux, Léon, 103
Jowett, Fred, 204 n. 80, 205 n. 83
Jowitt, Sir William, 337, 342, 346, 348–
    9, 353

Kean, Charles, 217
Kelly, W. T., 154
Keynes, John Maynard, 206
Kitchener, Earl, 81

labor exchanges, 49, 58
labor force, structure of (Britain); *see
    also* married women workers; wage-
    earning women (Britain)
    pre–1914, 36–9
    World War I, 89–91
    after demobilization, 123–5
labor force, structure of (France); *see
    also* married women workers; wage-
    earning women (France)
    pre–1914, 37–8, 70–1
    World War I, 89–91
    after demobilization, 123–5
    in the engineering industry, 104–5,
        262–3
    in the textile industry, 238, 245 n. 30
labor movement, *see* Labour Party; Parti
    Socialiste; trade unions (Britain);
    trade unions (France)
Labour governments (Britain)
    (1924), 168–9, 172
    (1929–31), 204 n. 80, 293, 295–9,
        302–3, 316, 355
    (1945–51), 315–16
Labour Party; *see also* House of
    Commons; Labour governments;
    National Conference of Labour
    Women
    Advisory Committee on Motherhood
        and Child Endowment, 163–6

Joint Committee on the Living Wage,
    195–208, 210–1
    and children's allowances, 179, 184,
        193, 197–8, 202–8, 222–3, 331–3
    concerns before 1914, 50–1, 54, 58
    relations with the Trades Union
        Congress, 194–5, 203–4, 206–7,
        220–3, 331–4
    and widowed mothers' pensions, 162–
        4, 167–9
    women's organizations, 55–6, 133,
        161–7, 201–2, 219, 298, 301, 306–7,
        313, 321 n. 89, 326, 352
    conferences: (1921), 162, 165; (1922),
        162; (1926), 194; (1927), 219–20;
        (1928), 203; (1929), 209, 215–17,
        220; (1930), 207, 210, 219; (1941),
        333; (1942), 334
Lafargue, Paul, 67
Lafitte, François, 325
Lambert-Ribot, A., 264
Landry, Adophe, 289, 373, 381, 386
Lansbury, George, 197, 204 n. 80
Laroque, Pierre, 391, 420
Lathan, George, 197 n. 54
Laval, Pierre, 256, 257
Lawrence, Susan, 163
laws and decrees (France); *see also*
    Chamber of Deputies
    assistance to large families (1913), 73–
        74
    encouragement of large families
        (1923), 128–30
    family allowances: in public works
        (1922), 231; nationally (1932), 231,
        376–7; increases (1938), 386, 388;
        increases (1941), 387, 389; unified
        (1945), 388
    Family Code (1939), 387–8
    restriction of married women's work
        (1940), 407
    social insurance (1930), 372 n. 39
    unwaged mother's allowance (1938),
        401
laws and legislation (Britain), *see* acts of
    Parliament; House of Commons
Layton, Dorothea, 183
Le Play, Frédéric, 62–3, 68, 131
Lebel, Jacques, 286, 374
Leclercq, Paul, 287, 400

Leclercq, Philippe (firm), 258, 396
Lefebvre, Henri, 242
Lenoël, Marie, 404–5
Leo XIII, 23, 63, 75, 226, 251, 394
Lerolle, Jean, 373, 377
Les Fils d'Alfred Motte (firm), 256, 258
Ley, Désiré, 241–4, 249, 252–9, 269
Lhotte, Céline, 363
Liberal governments (Britain), 49–59
  passim, 81–9, 109
Liberal Industrial Inquiry, 188, 190–1
Liberal Party, 184, 188, 329
liberalism, 34 n. 13, 35–6, 50–1, 61–2,
  147–8, 254–5, 394
Liénart, Achille, 253, 258
Living Wage, The, 190–9, 220; *see also*
  Independent Labour Party
Lloyd, C. M., 206
Lloyd George, David, 83, 84, 122, 188
London School of Economics, 318
Loucheur, Louis, 87, 123, 253–5, 263–4,
  373 n. 43, 376
Loughlin, Anne, 204 n. 80, 209, 210,
  334

Macadam, Elizabeth, 141
Macarthur, Mary, 100
Macassey, Lynden, 155
MacDonald, Margaret, 50
MacDonald, Ramsay, 50, 193–4, 219,
  222, 298
MacGregor, D. H., 199
Macnamara, T. J., 53
Maignan, Gustave, 269, 281, 282,
maintenance, legal responsibility for and
  rights to, 32, 35 and n. 34, 44, 45 n.
  43, 52, 54, 116, 143
male-breadwinner wage norm (Britain);
  see also trade unions (Britain)
  criticisms of, 142–5, 153–5, 179–85
  development of and defense of, 35–9,
    48–9, 50–1, 97–8, 100–1, 155–9,
    164, 213–14, 354–6
  state recognition of, 80, 97–8, 113–14,
    120–8, 306
male-breadwinner wage norm (France)
  criticisms of, 403–6
  deviation from, 71, 260–1, 270–1,
    390–1
  support for, 63, 103, 278–9, 398

Management Research Groups, 317, 334
Markham, Violet, 309, 425 n. 14
Marriage (Wells), 26–32
marriage bar, *see* married women
  workers
married women workers
  campaigns against (France), 275–6,
    278, 393–407
  discrimination against (Britain), 121–
    2, 298–301, 314–15
  position within labor force: Britain,
    36, 38–9, 91–2, 98, 124–5, 311–12,
    419–20; France, 71–2, 105, 124–5,
    260–1, 395 n. 94, 396–7, 409–10,
    420
  restrictions on insurance rights of
    (Britain), 50, 297–9, 301–7, 419–20
Marshall, T. H., 5–6
Martin, Anna, 44–5
masculinity, *see* identities
Mass Observation, 327, 344–5
Masterman, Charles, 56
Maternal Mortality Committee, 321
maternity benefit, 45 n. 45, 50, 56–8,
  201–2
maternity leaves, 73, 105
Mathon, Eugène, 63, 226, 229, 239–40,
  244, 251–3, 259, 265, 286, 373–4
Matignon accords, 281–2, 380
means test, *see* unemployment assistance
  (Britain); unemployment insurance
  (Britain)
Meikle, Wilma, 42
Mercier, Ernest, 374
Merrheim, Alphonse, 103, 276
Metalworkers' Federation, *see* trade
  unions (France)
Michelin, André, 369
Michelin (firm), 233–5
Middleton, J. S., 333
military allowances, *see* separation
  allowances
Mill, John Stuart, 1–2, 40
Millerand, Alexandre, 369
Milne-Bailey, Walter, 135, 197–203, 217,
  220
Miners' Federation of Great Britain, *see*
  trade unions (Britain)
mining industry
  Britain, 180, 186–8

France, 117, 377–8
ministries (Britain); *see also* committes
    and commissions, official (Britain)
Admiralty, 85
Home Office, 97
Information, 347
Labour, 122, 135, 295, 298, 304, 306,
    334, 342, 344, 346
Local Government Board, 40 n. 27,
    55, 151
Munitions, 84–6, 98, 135
Pensions, 111–12
Reconstruction, 135, 151, 169, 170,
    173–4, 177
Treasury, 58, 109, 111, 115, 121, 136,
    139, 170–2, 178, 186, 300–1, 329,
    335, 342 n. 167, 344
War Office, 85, 111
ministries (France); *see also* committees
    and commissions, official (France)
Agriculture, 386
Finance, 74, 132, 231, 386
Interior, 386
Labor, 87, 89, 102, 104–6, 117, 230,
    244, 253–9, 280–1, 372, 375–9, 386,
    390 n. 89, 399, 400
Munitions, 86–7, 102–4, 117, 123, 264
Navy, 74
Public Health, 386
Public Works, 119
Morant, Robert, 120
Morel, Lydie, 403
Morrison, Herbert, 197, 204 n. 80, 342
    n. 167, 343 n. 169
Morten, Honnor, 53
Mosley, Oswald, 197, 204 n. 80, 302
mothers' pensions, *see* endowment of
    motherhood (Britain); unwaged
    mother's allowance (France);
    widows, pensions for
Mothers' Union, 166 n. 80
Muir, Ramsay, 184
munitions industries, 83–4, 89–91, 93–6,
    99–100, 120
Murray, Gilbert, 184
Murray, John, 184, 413

Nash, Mrs. Vaughan, 169
Nathan, Matthew, 155, 170

National Birth Rate Commission, 151,
    159, 177
National Confederation of Employers'
    Organizations, 185, 302, 334, 351 n.
    202
National Conference of Labour Women:
    (1921), 161; (1922), 163–4, 166;
    (1923), 164; (1927), 201, 208, 219;
    (1932), 313; (1933), 313; (1934),
    313; (1935), 313; (1937), 326
National Council for Equal Citizenship,
    317, 321
National Council of Women, 339, 353–4
National Federation of Women
    Workers, *see* trade unions (Britain)
National Government, 48, 293, 303, 307
National Joint Council of Labour, 221
National Unemployed Workers'
    Movement, 313
National Union of Societies for Equal
    Citizenship, 141, 147, 149, 152, 317
National Union of Women's Suffrage
    Societies, 46, 88, 138, 141
National Union of Women Workers, 53,
    353
Naylor, T. E., 215
Neil, Judge Henry, 151
new feminism, *see* feminism (Britain)
new liberalism, 48–51, 338

old-age pensions, 51
Olivier, Maurice, 254–5
Open Door Council/International, 307,
    354, 406
Orr, John Boyd, 320
Orwell, George, 311
Oualid, William, 283 n. 152, 374, 385
out-of-work donation, 122, 126–7

Panhard, Paul, 269
Panhard (firm), 104
Parti Socialiste, 82
Partiot, Etienne, 269
paternalism, *see* employers (France)
Pernot, Georges, 369, 380, 386–7
Petiet, Baron, 263
Peugeot, Robert, 369
Peugeot (firm), 263, 275
philanthropy, 40, 52, 66
Phillips, Marion, 163–5, 201–2

Phillips, Sir Thomas, 342
Picquenard, Charles, 117, 230
Pilgrim Trust, 312
Poincaré, Raymond, 253, 369, 373
Political and Economic Planning, 317,
    325, 328
political economy, 34–6, 61–2, 63 n. 92
poor relief and the Poor Law, 35, 40,
    52, 69, 73–4, 127, 141–2, 147, 151
Popular Front, 382, 405
Population Policies Committee, 325
population trends, 60, 410 n. 145; *see
    also* birthrate, decline of;
    pronatalism
poverty
    familial cycle of, 4, 47, 159–60,
    of children, 293, 320–7, 329, 418 n. 5
Priestley, J. B., 310–1
Principles of Political Economy (Mill), 1–2,
    40
pronatalism; *see also* Alliance Nationale
    pour l'Accroisement de la
    Population Française; birthrate,
    decline of
    Britain, 318–20, 327–8
    France, 59–77 passim, 130–2, 228–9,
    233–6, 269–70, 358–73, 383–92,
    402, 406–8, 410–11
protective legislation, 35, 69, 72, 307
Pugh, Arthur, 195, 206, 217
Purcell, A. A., 214

Rackham, Clara, 298, 301, 304
Radical Party, 64, 129, 131
railroad companies (France), 75–6, 117,
    119, 357, 377–8
Rathbone, Eleanor, 2–3, 43 n. 39, 52,
    110, 114, 132–3, 135–53 passim,
    160, 174 n. 107, 175, 178, 185–7,
    192, 195, 199, 200, 209, 211, 217,
    289–90, 292, 302, 307, 318, 319,
    321, 323, 327–30, 332, 341, 349,
    351, 352, 366, 401
    on the endowment of motherhood,
    143–5, 152–3
    life, 140–1
    on widows, 141–2
    on women's wages, 142–5
    writings: *The Problem of Women's
    Wages*, 142–3; "The Remuneration

of Women's Services," 144–5, 156;
    The Disinherited Family, 179–85;
    Wages Plus Family Allowances, 185;
    *The Case for the Immediate Introduction
    of Family Allowances*, 327–8
rationalization, 123, 225, 263, 273–9,
    283–7, 288 n. 160
Raymond, Dr., 369
Redressement Français, 374–5
Reeves, Maude Pember, 160, 177
Réforme Sociale, 63, 65
Régis Joya, 227–8
Renault, Louis, 263, 267, 269
Renault (firm), 104, 263, 272, 284
Rerum Novarum (papal encyclical), 63, 75
Revue de la Famille (journal), 287
Reynaud, Paul, 386
Richemond, Pierre, 226, 235, 263, 266–
    7, 271, 282, 374
Richet, Charles, 60, 397
Roberts, George, 56–7
Roberts, F. O., 197 n. 54, 204 n. 80
Robertson, Dennis, 182
Robin, Paul, 67
Romanet, Emile, 227–8, 235
Rougé, Jeanne, 404–5
Roussel, Nelly, 66
Rowntree, B. Seebohm, 47, 98, 152,
    156–8, 164, 186, 320, 327, 329,
    331–2, 336, 341
Rowntree (firm), 334
Royal Commissions, *see* committees and
    commissions (Britain)
Royden, Maude, 143–6, 150–1, 177 n.
    112
Rucart, Marc, 385
Russell, Dora, 165

Sauvy, Alfred, 384, 386
school meals, 52–4
Schreiner, Olive, 42
scientific management, *see* rationalization
Semaines Sociales, 65, 248, 394
Senate (France), 376, 385
separation allowances, 80, 107–16, 119,
    126, 143, 151, 202, 328
Sheepshanks, Sir Thomas, 342, 352 n.
    206
Simon, E. D., 184
Simon, Jules, 72

single-wage allowance, *see* family
    allowances (France)
Six Point Group, 307
skill
    and masculinity, 33 n. 11, 36
    and the wartime dilution of labor, 80,
        91 n. 23, 93–6, 104
Snell, Harry, 204 n. 80
Snowden, Philip, 57, 168–9, 172, 179,
    207, 222
social insurance (Britain), 336–54, 414–
    16; *see also* Beveridge Plan; health
    insurance; unemployment insurance
    (Britain); welfare state; widows,
    pensions for
social insurance (France), 128, 230–1,
    255, 372 n. 39, 414–16
socialism (France); *see also* Confédération
    Générale du Travail
    and the birthrate, 66–8
    and World War I, 82
    and women's work, 70–2, 371
Soldiers' and Sailors' Families'
    Association, 110–14, 140, 274
solidarism, 64
Speenhamland system of poor relief,
    147, 214, 322
Standing Joint Committee of Industrial
    Women's Organizations, *see* Labour
    Party, women's organizations
State Children's Association, 151
Stocks, Mary, 145, 163, 166, 183, 192,
    196 n. 52, 199, 200, 209
Strauss, Paul, 373
Stuart, Frank, 156–8
suffrage
    family, 366
    men's, 36, 68, 130
    women's, 59, 132, 363
Summerskill, Edith, 330, 333
Sweden, 8 n. 14, 9 n. 16, 11, 15 n. 30,
    415–16

Tawney, R. H., 206
tax allowance, children's, 54–5, 73, 368
Taylor, Harriet, 1–2
teaching profession, 43 n. 38, 74, 180,
    300
textile industry
    Britain, 43 n. 38, 305, 315

France, 71, 226–8, 237–9, 378
Thomas, Albert, 82, 87, 103–4
Titmuss, Kathleen, 328
Titmuss, Richard, 8–9, 328
Tout, Herbert, 320
trade boards, 50, 122
trade unions (Britain); *see also* Trades
    Union Congress
    Amalgamated Society of Engineers/
        Amalgamated Engineering Union,
        83, 93–6, 99, 208
    Association of Women Clerks and
        Secretaries, 212
    Engineering and Shipbuilding
        Draughtsmen, 214
    Iron and Steel Trades Confederation,
        214
    Miners' Federation of Great Britain,
        186–8, 218–19
    National Federation of Women
        Workers, 99–100, 133
    National Union of Boot and Shoe
        Operatives, 208, 212–13, 215
    National Union of Distributive and
        Allied Workers, 208, 213–14, 216
    National Union of Enginemen,
        Firemen, Mechanics and Electrical
        Workers, 217
    Transport and General Workers'
        Union, 208
    Wall Paper Workers' Union, 217, 332,
        334
    Workers' Union, 95, 99, 154
    and family allowances, 203–4, 208–23
    and the family wage, 36, 58, 103, 424
    and World War I, 82–6, 92–7
    and women workers, 88, 92, 133, 301
trade unions (France); *see also*
        Confédération Française des
        Travailleurs Chrétiens; Conféd-
        ération Générale du Travail;
        Confédération Générale du Travail
        Unitaire
    Metalworkers' Federation, 103–4, 264,
        276–8, 282 n. 147
    Seine Metalworkers' Union, 271
    and family allowances, 230, 237, 242,
        249–59 passim, 271, 276–9, 289–90
    and World War I, 82, 102–4
    in the Paris region, 271, 276–9, 282

in Roubaix-Tourcoing, 249–59
Trades Union Congress, 51, 82, 108, 351, 424; see also Labour Party; trade unions (Britain)
  General Council of, 133, 179, 194–5, 203, 205–8, 218–19, 221–2, 291, 302, 311, 313, 331–4, 351
  and family allowances, 179, 193–208 passim, 316–17, 330–4, 346
  relations with the Labour Party, 194–5, 203–4, 206–7, 219–23, 331–4
  and unemployment assistance, 311, 313–14
  and unemployment insurance, 213, 296, 302, 306
  and widows' pensions, 162–4, 167–8
  annual conferences: (1915–24), 162; (1930), 209, 211, 218–20; (1932), 313–14; (1933), 314; (1941), 333; (1942), 334
Treasury (Britain), see ministries
Treasury Agreement, 83, 92–3, 100
Tuckwell, Gertrude, 321
Turner, Ben, 197 n. 54, 204 n. 80, 211, 218

unemployment, 51, 123, 125–8, 290, 294–5, 297–8, 397
unemployment assistance (Britain), 290–1, 307–16, 418–19; see also "out-of-work" donation
  dependents' benefits within, 323–5, 328
Unemployment Assistance Board, 308–16, 323–5
unemployment insurance (Britain), 49–51, 125–8, 290–1, 294–307, 418–19; see also social insurance (Britain)
  "abuses" of, 295–8, 302
  anomalies regulations, 297–307
  Cabinet committees on, 302
  dependents' benefits within, 126–8, 322–4, 328
  genuinely seeking work clause, 294–5, 301
  and means tests, 295–6
  trade union criticisms of, 213, 296, 302
  and the "wage–benefit overlap," 322–5

Union des Consommateurs de Produits Minières et Industriels, 263
Union Féminine Civique et Sociale, 392–410 passim; see also Catholics (France)
Union Française pour le Suffrage des Femmes, 368, 374, 397
Union des Industries Chimiques, 269
Union des Industries Métallurgiques et Minières, 263–6
Union des Intérêts Economiques, 229
unwaged mother's allowance (France), 380, 395–6, 399–402, 406 n. 136, 407–9

Vatican, 251–2, 254, 394–5
Verdier, Cardinal, 369
Vérone, Maria, 404
Vichy government, 387–9, 407–8

wage-earning women (Britain); see also labor force, structure of (Britain); married women workers
  and family responsibilities, 152–9
  and the marriage bar, 121, 212, 298–300
  after 1945, 419–20
  before 1914, 32–9, 50
  between the wars, 299 n. 15, 299–301, 314–15
  during demobilization, 120–5, 301
  during World War I, 89–101
  during World War II, 315–16
wage-earning women (France); see also labor force, structure of (France); married women workers
  after 1945, 409–10, 420
  before 1914, 70–3
  between the wars, 396–7
  during demobilization, 123–5
  during World War I, 101–6
  in the engineering industry, 123, 263 n. 89, 274–5
  in the textile industry, 71, 260–1
wages; see also male-breadwinner wage norm (Britain); male-breadwinner wage norm (France)
  and arbitration, 84, 87, 92–3, 102, 239, 283 n. 152, 253–4, 385, 399

Catholic doctrines of, 63, 228–9, 231–3

and collective bargaining, 104, 216, 239, 241, 258, 281–2

and cost-of-living bonuses, 117 n. 100, 241, 263–4

effects of family allowances on, 75–6, 235–6, 203–8, 214–15, 244–9, 259–61, 270–3, 283–5

and employers' strategies, 262, 265–7, 270–3, 277, 281–3, 285–8

equal pay, 97, 100, 154–6, 212, 341, 367

familial distribution of, 159–60, 181, 401–3

government regulation of, 50, 87, 92, 102, 117, 122, 263–4, 283

and inflation, 116–18, 264, 350

inquiries into, 143–4, 152–9, 179–80, 190–3, 227–8, 320–1, 329

and labor disputes, 242–3, 253, 255–8, 281–3, 186–8

sex differentials in, 91, 93–7, 104, 122, 126, 278, 314–15

skill differentials in, 91, 271

and the wage–benefit overlap, 322–5

War Emergency Workers' National Committee, 82–3, 108–9

Ward, John, 57

Watson, Sir Alfred, 169–75

Webb, Beatrice, 49, 95, 101, 155

Webb, Sidney, 49, 53, 120

Weber, Max, 20

welfare state

British, characterized, 12–14, 15 n. 30, 18–19, 413–18

cross-national comparisons, 15 n. 29 and 30, 415–16

effects of World War I on, 79–80

French, characterized, 14–19, 413–18

scholarship on, 5–12

typology of, 17–18, 413–14

Wells, H. G., 23, 26–32, 45–6, 140, 148

West, Rebecca, 31

wet-nursing, 69

White Paper on Family Allowances, 335, 346

White Paper on Social Insurance, 345–6

Wibaux, Joseph, 252

widows

and poor relief, 52, 141–2

pensions for, 139, 141–2, 152, 158–9, 167–77, 328, 368

Wilkinson, Ellen, 163, 176, 197, 202, 204 n. 80, 209–10, 302

Williams, Ted, 211

Wilson, Horace, 334, 350–1

Wilson, Mona, 169

Wilson, W. T., 54

Wise, E. F., 190, 198

Wolstencroft, F., 204 n. 80, 205 n. 84

women workers, *see* wage-earning women (Britain); wage-earning women (France); married women workers

Women's Cooperative Guild, 44, 46, 55, 56, 58, 150, 159, 161, 177, 201–2, 210, 321

Women's Freedom League, 149

Women's Industrial Council, 43, 58, 113, 154

Women's International League for Peace and Freedom, 138, 143

Women's Labour League, 55, 133

Women's Social and Political Union, 138

Women's Trade Union League, 133

women's work, *see* housework; wage-earning women (Britain); wage-earning women (France)

Wood, Sir Kingsley, 330–1, 341, 342 n. 167, 343 n. 169, 351 n. 202

Woolton, Lord (Frederick James Marquis), 342, 348

workers' compensation, 328

Workers' Union, *see* trade unions (Britain)

working women, *see* wage-earning women (Britain); wage-earning women (France)

World War I, 79–133 passim

and conscription, 81–86

and demobilization, 120–30

military losses, 128

military participation rates, 79

and the organization of labor, 83–107, 239

and social policy innovations, 107–19

World War II, 315–16, 327–9, 351

Wright, Cecil, 330

Zola, Emile, 26–32